D1789253

THE OTHER SIDE OF THE WIRE VOLUME 2

The Battle of the Somme.
With the German XIV Reserve Corps, 1 July 1916

Ralph J. Whitehead

Hardback edition produced in a strictly
limited printing of 750 individually
numbered and signed copies

This is copy number **653** of 750

THE OTHER SIDE OF THE WIRE VOLUME 2

The Battle of the Somme. With the German XIV Reserve Corps, 1 July 1916

Ralph J. Whitehead

Helion & Company Ltd

Dedication

From the men who went off to the wars from the Whitehead family, including four who I recently discovered had served in the Great War in the British Army, all of whom survived to come home again but one, Private Bert Whitehead, Co. B, 4th Engineers, died on 21 February 1918 of bronchitis following an attack of measles. Of the men who went off to war in my wife's family, many did not return. This book is dedicated to their memory: Corporal Charles F. Webber, Coy A, 14th Brooklyn (84th New York Volunteers), fatally wounded 1 July 1863, Gettysburg, Pa.; Corporal Otto E.F. Ernst, Co. I, 165th U.S. Infantry, killed in action 28 July 1918 near the Ourq River, France; Technical Sergeant Joseph Grubel, Coy F, 16th U.S. Infantry, killed in action near Mayenne France 12 August 1944. I would also like to mention that the latest family member to serve his country, Andrew J. Whitehead, has safely returned from his tour of duty in Iraq.

Helion & Company Limited
26 Willow Road
Solihull
West Midlands
B91 1UE
England
Tel. 0121 705 3393
Fax 0121 711 4075
Email: info@helion.co.uk
Website: www.helion.co.uk

Published by Helion & Company 2013

Designed and typeset by Farr out Publications, Wokingham, Berkshire
Cover designed by Farr out Publications, Wokingham, Berkshire
Printed by Gutenberg Press Limited, Tarxien, Malta

© Ralph J. Whitehead 2012

ISBN 978-1-907677-12-0

British Library Cataloguing-in-Publication Data.
A catalogue record for this book is available from the British Library.

All rights reserved. No part of this publication may be reproduced, stored in a retrieval system,or transmitted, in any form, or by any means, electronic, mechanical, photocopying, recording or otherwise, without the express written consent of Helion & Company Limited.

For details of other military history titles published by Helion & Company Limited contact the above address, or visit our website: http://www.helion.co.uk.

We always welcome receiving book proposals from prospective authors.

Contents

*   The author's *Verlustlisten* are so extensive that we were unable to include them as appendices in the book. However, they appear in full as PDF documents on a disc attached to the inside rear cover of this book.

List of Illustrations

List of Maps

Preface

One of the goals I had for publishing my book *The Other Side of the Wire Volume 1 – With the German XIV Reserve Corps on the Somme, September 1914–June 1916'* was to provide a different perspective on the war and to restore a sense of humanity to the men who were often referred to as 'the enemy' in most written works.

From many of the comments I received since the first volume appeared it would seem that I was successful in some small degree. There was one particular incident, not even considered when I was preparing the book that nevertheless shows just how relevant the study of the war is to the events of today.

On pages 412 and 413 of Volume 1 there appeared two photographs of British prisoners of war and their captors. The photographs were taken following a raid by the men from RIR 99 on 7 May 1916 by Thiepval Wood. The majority of the prisoners belong to the 1st Dorset Regiment while one other was a sergeant from the 17th Northumberland Fusiliers and several men who were members of the Machine Gun Corps.

One person who had purchased Volume 1 did so with a particular interest in the events taking place near Thiepval in 1916. After obtaining the book and reading through the appropriate section the gentleman, Dr. David Davin from Northern Ireland, was surprised to find not only an account of the raid in which his father had been captured but also recognized his father from among the many men in the two photographs. He confirmed his remarkable discovery with his sister who resides nearby.

I was contacted by Dr. Davin, who was gracious enough to share some of the details surrounding his father's service. Private Arthur James Davin had enlisted in the 10th Battalion Royal Inniskilling Fusiliers (The Derry Boys) in September 1914 at age 18. At some point in his military career private Davin volunteered to join the new formation known as the Machine Gun Corps. Many years later, Dr. Davin found out that his father had joined the machine Gun Corps as the men were paid an additional one shilling and sixpence per week to the normal army pay.

Arthur Davin did not talk about his time in the war or the events that led up to his capture until many years had passed. Dr. Davin was able to piece together the details of his father's service and the information provided in Volume 1 filled in the remaining holes in the story.

Private Davin can be seen on the photograph on page 412 as the third man from the left. He is bareheaded with his hands crossed. He can be seen on the photograph on page 413 in the second row standing, second man from the left with his hands still crossed. On 6/7 May 1916 Arthur Davin was with his machine gun located in a forward position near Hammerhead Sap on the edge of Thiepval Wood. On this night there were two raids, one by the men from RIR 99, the other by the Ulster Division against the German trenches. The sounds of fighting were going on all around Private Davin and his gun team until all of a sudden it grew very quiet.

Arthur Davin was sent to the rear by his gun commander in order to see what was going on. After making his way back to the main trench he was surprised to see that the Germans had overrun the position. All around him were British soldiers with their hands in the air while well armed German soldiers stood nearby. Private Davin realized that he did not have any chance at escape and reluctantly joined his companions. The full cooperation of the numerous British prisoners was assured after a large, stubborn Ulsterman from Coleraine made it quite clear he was not going to cooperate with the Germans nor was he going to take their orders. This attitude was not to be tolerated by the men from RIR 99 who promptly shot the man. The remaining prisoners had to walk over the body as they were taken back to the German lines.

The same fate was met by at least two members of the machine Gun Corps, probably men from Davin's gun crew, who also offered resistance when being taken prisoner. They too were killed on the spot as the raiding party did not have the luxury of trying to control unruly prisoners.

The prisoners were taken across no man's land and locked up in what Davin called 'a small town hall' for the night. Early on the next morning some French nuns passed bread to the men through the barred windows. Later the prisoners were assembled before General von Soden, commander of the 26th Reserve Division, and it was at this time that the photographs were taken. Private Davin was eventually sent back to Giessen in the Ruhr Valley where he remained for the next 30 months. During the time at Giessen Davin was put to work in a steel mill where the work was apparently very physical and demanding. Arthur Davin was eventually returned home where he later married and had two children. He died in 1982, rarely ever discussing his wartime experiences before his death.

This last point is something that I have seen often. I have attempted to discuss wartime experiences with veterans of both the Great War and the Second World War. In most cases the men were either very reluctant to provide any information at all or in some cases only a fraction of the details that they experienced. I found this reluctance by veterans of the Great War to discuss past events to be the strongest with the men who had experienced the worst of the fighting. My father was no different and I have only small bits and pieces of his experiences fighting in the Pacific during World War II when he was a member of VMF 124, a Marine Fighter Squadron stationed on Guadalcanal that was the first to be equipped with the F4U Corsair. Since his death many years ago I have made every effort to write down every story I could recall, no matter how small. If I did not, then his experiences in the war could be lost forever.

This reluctance to talk about their experiences in a war could be one of the major factors why so few firsthand accounts of the fighting on the Somme exist today despite the tens of thousands of men who participated in the battle. As it appears that every veteran of the Great War has now died there will never be an opportunity to expand on our pool of knowledge from the very men who experienced the fighting firsthand. Every attempt should be made to preserve what details we have of this conflict, from personal letters to diaries and memoirs. Whether you believe in the old saying 'those who forget their history are doomed to repeat it' or not I believe it is important to identify and discuss the reasons and causes for this conflict and all others that occurred before and after 1914-1918. We need to see what can be done to prevent any of them from being repeated in the future.

My opinion has not diminished over time, especially as my son just completed the last two months of his service in Iraq as I am finishing this book. I am happy to say that he has since returned home safe and sound. Many of the events that are taking place in the world today can be traced back to the Great War. We need to understand these issues and hopefully make better choices in the future.

In writing this volume it was my intention to provide an account of the events of 1 July as experienced by the German soldier. The source for much of this information has come from firsthand accounts, post-war regimental histories and similar publications produced during the war. I am hopeful that in some small way I have been able to provide the reader with a better understanding of the experiences of the men in Field Grey who fought on the Somme some 95 years ago, the men from the other side of the wire.

Acknowledgments

Shortly after completing the finished manuscript for Volume 1 of *The Other Side of the Wire* I noticed a few errors and omissions in reference to the people who had helped me with the final product. I was and still am very absent minded when it comes to keeping accurate records and my wife often chides me when she accurately states that I am terribly disorganized. I must agree with her assessment as I have folders, papers and books scattered about in numerous locations. I often lose track of vital materials and generally rediscover them by accident when looking for another missing folder of critical importance to my current research. I have only myself to blame, as it appears I have been disorganized for over 50 years.

As such, I wanted to make amends for these oversights and as I mentioned in my previous volume, if I did not mention a particular name it was not an attempt to minimize or disregard that person's efforts and assistance. In this regard I would like to make mention of David Neale, who resides in Hong Kong, for supplying key materials used in Volume 1. I would like to extend my thanks to Lawrence Brown who currently resides in France, who graciously provided critical opinions on both volumes 1 and 2 and who opened his superb collection of photographs and maps and allowed me to utilize these in both volumes. Lawrence was very helpful in helping to provide illustrations that were directly related to the very men mentioned in the two books.

I would like to extend a special thanks to Jack Sheldon for his kind comments, support for the project and for providing key information and sources that proved very helpful in my work. Jack has been a prolific writer on the German side of the Great War, as can be seen by his numerous books on the subject, all of which I heartily recommend to anyone with an interest in experiencing a well-rounded view of the war that looks at the events and accounts from both sides of the fighting. The study of the German experience in the Great War is a relatively new field despite the passing of 92 years since the end of the fighting. I am very happy to call Jack a friend and to wish him all the best on his future books as I will be looking forward to each one as they come into print.

I want to make a correction and to recognize a key figure in the presentation of the war in a personal manner, Martin Middlebrook. Mr. Middlebrook has been gracious enough to allow me to utilize quotations taken from his book *The First Day on the Somme* and to integrate them into my narrative. Given the momentous events of 1 July 1916 one might expect there to be an almost endless amount of firsthand accounts from all of the participants of the fighting. The fact is that few accounts exist from the German side in particular. Many familiar ones have been used in many of the different books and television documentaries over the last decades. Mr. Middlebrook was able to locate and interview some of the men who fought on 1 July and who managed to survive the war and the decades that followed. Now, that every known Great War veteran has passed away these accounts are a lasting legacy to the men who took part in this battle.

It is our loss that efforts made by Mr. Middlebrook were not attempted by others in the decades following the war. I suspect that the social upheaval of the post-war years, the worldwide economic disaster of the Great Depression and the events of the 1930s and

1940s with the political situation that existed and the subsequent World War would have made this effort almost impossible. While the ever dwindling numbers of veterans of the Great War occasionally met at a reunion and swapped war stories over a meal the average person in that tumultuous time had far more to worry about with the many social and political changes people were experiencing than what happened years earlier.

The correction I referenced above relates to Volume 1 where I made a mistake in the reference to Mr. Middlebrook's book on the Somme. I apparently overlooked it after a dozen or so reviews and it goes to show that it can be helpful to have another set of eyes look over your work. I referenced the book *The First Day on the Somme* as *First Day on the Somme*, an abbreviation I used when preparing the book. For that error I would like to extend my heartfelt apologies to Mr. Middlebrook. This error apparently came about by my glancing at the dustcover of my edition purchased shortly after the book came into print; it simply reads *First Day on the Somme*.

I would like to extend my gratitude to Chris Jordan, who resides in Virginia. Without his help I would not have been able to provide the level of detail that appears in many of the *Verlustlisten* charts that appear on the disc enclosed with this book. I would also like to thank Desmond Blackadder, from Ballymena, Northern Ireland, for his friendship and years of discussions on the events surrounding the men of the 36th (Ulster Division). His efforts were very helpful in trying to piece together the events that occurred on both sides of the Ancre on 1 July 1916; Felix Fregin of the Netherlands, for his invaluable assistance in translating the Karl Losch letters and for the use of illustrations from his extensive photographic collection; Frank Grosse, who was instrumental in planning the entire series of books and for making his extensive collection available to me. I would like to extend my thanks to Brett Butterworth from Melbourne, Australia for sharing photos from his superb collection of German army images.

The following publishers and organizations have graciously allowed me to quote from their works – John Montgomery and Adrian Johnston from the Royal United Services Institute for Defence and Security Studies (RUSI) in allowing me to quote from the 'Report on the Defence of Gommecourt on July 1st, 1916', *Journal of the Royal United Service Institution*, August 1917; Richard Baumgartner of Blue Acorn Press for allowing me to quote from his book '*This Carnival of Hell*'; Michelle Griffin of Blackstaff Press for allowing me to quote from the book by Philip Orr, *The Road to the Somme*, (Blackstaff Press, 2008), reproduced by permission of Blackstaff Press on behalf of the author; Jon Cooksey, for his kind permission to allow me to utilize portions of his superb book, *The Barnsley Pals* and for his good advice and friendship these past years; to Pen & Sword Books, for allowing me to use quotes from Montauban from the *Battleground Europe* series on the Somme.

I would also like to thank Dave Stowe for his expertise on items relating to the chapter on Fricourt; Graham Stewart for his kind assistance in tracking down period battalion reports and newspaper articles relating to the Somme battle; John Sheen, for his help in obtaining a photograph of a grave site.

I would also like to especially thank my wife Elizabeth for all of her help in preparing this volume for publication. While she does not have the same level of interest that I apparently have in the subject her good advice and suggestions were very helpful in creating the final outline of the book.

Once again, I wish to thank everyone who provided materials or opinions and suggestions for the completion of Volume 2 and whose names I may have left out. I did try to be more efficient and organized while working on this volume but I am sure I will come across a folder or paper with the names of people who should be mentioned here long after the book goes into print.

A Note to the Reader

Acumulative index for all three volumes will be printed in Volume 3. The third and final volume will also include corrections and supplementary material for the previous two volumes.

Please note that all of the casualty lists for Volume 2 are included as PDF files on a disc in a sleeve inside the rear cover.

German Army Organization and Rank Comparison

In order for the reader to better understand the military terms and ranks mentioned in this book I have prepared a basic breakdown of the formation of the German army and the comparison of ranks between the German Army and the British Army.

The German Army consisted of several parts including Active regiments, Reserve regiments, *Landwehr* regiments and *Landsturm* units. All qualified German males would be required to serve 2 years in the Active Army starting at age 20. 4-5 years in the Reserve, 11 years in the Landwehr and 7 years in the Landsturm 2nd Ban followed this.

The basic infantry regiment consisted of three battalions of infantry, designated I, II and III. Each battalion consisted of four companies (1-4, 5-8 and 9-12 respectively) that were further broken down into three platoons (*Zug*) and then into sections or *Gruppe* that consisted of 1 Non-Commissioned Officer and 8 men. Each soldier in a reserve regiment would have been armed with the M98 Mauser rifle or the M88 rifle. Each regiment would normally contain one Machine Gun Company armed with six MG08 heavy machine guns and one spare gun. The average strength of the regiment would have been 83 officers and 3,204 men.

The XIV Reserve Corps that is presented in Volume 2 has been expanded to include four additional divisions; 2nd Guard Reserve, 52nd, 12th and 10th Bavarian. The men who fought on 1 July 1916 would come from nearly every corner of Germany as well as men who had been born in the United States, South America, the Middle East and many other locations. The different divisions contained men from active regiments as well as reserve regiments. The men who fought on the German side could range in age from their late teens to a few in their 50s and 60s.

The field artillery was normally established into three sections or *Abteilung*. The I and II *Abteilung* consisted of 3 batteries each of M96 7.7cm field guns while the III *Abteilung* consisted of 3 batteries of M98.09 10.5cm light field howitzers.

As in most cases there were always exceptions to the rules. RIR 99 was one of the regiments in the army that had 4 battalions (I, II, III, IV) instead of the normal 3 and therefore had 16 companies of infantry at the start of the war.

The 27th RFAR assigned to the 28th Reserve Division consisted of two *Abteilung* (I and II) and was not equipped with the light field howitzers, something not uncommon in reserve units.

Abbreviations used to designate the different military units found in this book.

RIR 99	Reserve Infantry Regiment Nr. 99
IR 180	Infantry Regiment Nr. 180
II/RFAR 26	II *Abteilung* Reserve Field Artillery Regiment Nr. 26
4/R109	4th Company Reserve Infantry Regiment Nr. 109
III/R111	III Battalion Reserve Infantry Regiment Nr. 111
9/180	9th Company Infantry Regiment Nr. 180

III(F)/FAR 12   III *Abteilung*, (howitzers), Field Artillery Regiment Nr. 12
1R/*Pionier* Bn 13   1st Reserve Company 13th *Pionier* Battalion
Rank Comparison
Grenadier }   Ranks equivalent to a Private Soldier. The different terms were
Musketier }   due to the type of unit the soldier belonged to, the military
Füsilier }   class of the soldier or from tradition.
Jäger }
Wehrmann }
Landsturmmann }
Landsturmpflichtiger }
Reservist}
Infanterist }
Soldat }
Ersatz-Reservist}
Schütze}   (Normally associated with Machine Gun troops)
Einjährig Freiwilliger   One Year Volunteer
Kriegsfreiwilliger   War Volunteer
Kanonier   Gunner
Radfahrer   Cyclist
Pionier   Sapper
Fahrer   Driver
Hornist   Trumpeter
Tambour   Drummer
Krankenträger   Stretcher-bearer
Gefreiter   Lance Corporal
Oberjäger   Corporal (*Jäger* units)
Unteroffizier   Corporal
Sergeant   Sergeant
Vizefeldwebel   Staff Sergeant
Vizewachtmeister   Staff Sergeant (Cavalry, artillery, train)
Feldwebel   Sergeant Major
Wachtmeister   Sergeant Major (Cavalry, artillery)
Fähnrich   Officer Cadet
Offizier Stellvertreter   Acting officer
Feldwebelleutnant   Sergeant Major Lieutenant
Leutnant   Second Lieutenant
Oberleutnant   Lieutenant
Rittmeister   Captain (Mounted unit, Transport)
Hauptmann   Captain
Major   Major
Oberstleutnant   Lieutenant Colonel
Oberst   Colonel
Generalmajor   Major General
Generalleutnant   Lieutenant General
General der Artillerie   General of Artillery
General der Infanterie   General of Infantry

General der Kavallerie	General of Cavalry
Medical Staff	
Sanitäter	Medical Assistant
Assistenzarzt	Second Lieutenant
Oberarzt	Lieutenant
Stabsarzt	Captain
Oberstabsarzt	Major or higher
Chaplains	
Pfarrer	Padre

One final point regarding terminology used in the Great War. The reader will note the use of terms such as shrapnel and shellfire. These represent two different types of ammunition used during the war. High explosive shells formed fragments or splinters when exploding and were set off by impact fuzes. Shrapnel shells were basically large shotgun shells. Each shrapnel shell was filled with numerous lead balls that were expelled by an explosive charge inside the shell casing. This was accomplished with the use of a time fuze so that the shell would burst at an appropriate height above enemy troops scattering the lead balls over a wide area. The term shrapnel only applies to the latter type of shell and should not be confused with the modern version of this term.

Introduction

1 July 1916 promised to be a warm, sunny day for the men of the XIV Reserve Corps. However, most of the men were unable to enjoy the prospect of a pleasant day as they were deep underground in their mined dugouts or standing on sentry duty amidst exploding shells. It was the start of the eighth day of an unprecedented artillery bombardment.

The German army had long anticipated that an attack would take place on the Somme. Every event for the past six months or more had reinforced this opinion. Even British newspapers gave clues that a major offensive was about to take place when munition workers were asked to postpone a scheduled Bank Holiday in the summer. The only unknown was the exact date the British would attack.

Enemy prisoners captured in the week-long bombardment had provided different dates for the attack. Intercepted messages also provided clues but the men still did not know when their ordeal would end. While effective in some ways, the bombardment had failed to destroy many of the German dugouts and the men remained in relative safety for the most part. However the strain on their nerves was growing larger with each passing day. For many it had reached the point where their only thought was when they would have the chance at getting even with their tormentors.

The Germans along the Somme front were kept busy maintaining the exits to their dugouts that in many cases had become damaged or partially filled in from the debris of exploding shells. All attempts at repairing the wire entanglements had been abandoned due to the level of enemy fire; it was almost certain death to expose the men with such duties. Every man would be needed to repel the attack. Trench blocks and knife rests had been prepared in advance and were set up wherever it was felt they were needed.

All weapons had been kept oiled and cleaned. Equipment was positioned nearby or worn in order to allow the men to take their posts as quickly as possible. Food was not a major issue as the bombardment had caused many men to lose their appetite but the lack or shortage of water was becoming a major problem. The heat, the strain of the bombardment and the dust filled air resulted in the men being far thirstier than had been expected. In many places the water supply was critically low. With each passing day it became harder and harder for supplies to reach the front lines and the men were forced to make do with what was at hand.

Messages intercepted by the listening post 'Moritz 28' received early on 1 July all indicated that an attack was to take place within a few hours. Every command was notified; the officers placed their men on alert and awaited the attack. The men stood upon the dugout stairs, rifles and hand grenades at the ready. Many of the men wore their soft *Feldmütze* instead of their *Pickelhaube* simply out of convenience and comfort. Some would eventually fight in their shirtsleeves as wearing a uniform tunic in the heat was too much to bear. In some instances the men also felt the tunic restricted their movement when throwing hand grenades at the enemy.

The machine gun crews had moved their heavy machine guns to a spot where they could quickly carry them up into the trenches and prepare them to fire. Boxes of machine gun ammunition were stacked nearby, ready to supply the needs of each gun. Most machine guns in the XIV Reserve Corps had at least 4,500 rounds of ammunition in belts for instant use and a large supply of spare ammunition that could be quickly placed in empty belts as needed.

On the other side of the wire the British soldiers had a fairly easy time of it compared to their German counterpart. While the British lines were still being shelled it was not at the same level of intensity that the Germans were receiving. Many British soldiers could watch the bombardment with impunity when just a few days earlier they would have most likely become victims of a German marksman. Food and water was not an issue as supplies could be carried to the front with relative ease.

The level of preparedness was almost overwhelming to the average British soldier; from the complexity of the attack orders to the instructions that seemed to take into account every smallest detail. The level of the bombardment surely meant that the German defenses were being destroyed, the wire entanglements swept away and the dreaded German machine guns crushed beyond recognition. The feeling was that there would be few Germans alive once the attack took place. If any were found they would not be in any condition to offer resistance, which was a welcome expectation.

Morale was very high. With the numbers of men, guns and equipment at hand surely they must be successful when the battle started; how could the attack fail?

The British gunners worked feverishly in the last hours before 7.30 a.m., the time set for the attack. The bombardment had died down considerably in the early hours of 1 July as the gunners made preparations for the final burst of fire that would strain the guns and the men who served them to their limits.

Many of the guns were becoming worn out from the volume of shells being fired. Most of the gunners were exhausted from the seemingly non-stop activity and the hard work needed to replenish the mountains of ammunition they required. Toward the end of the bombardment the level of fire increased even more as trench mortars joined in to provide the maximum level of destruction possible to the German lines. Surely nothing could survive the weight of shells being fired at the Germans.

One man was watching the time very carefully. He was given the task of detonating the first mine to be set off that effectively signaled the start of the attack. As the minutes passed until the scheduled time to press the plunger it probably seemed that the hands on the watch would never reach the required moment.

Then, at 7.20 a.m. a member of the 252nd Mining Coy RE, depressed his plunger and almost instantaneously a 40,000 pound charge of Ammonal positioned under a projecting point of the German front lines near Beaumont-Hamel was set off. The explosion was captured on a relatively new invention, moving pictures. Goeffrey Malins, an official British War Photographer, was able to capture the moment of the explosion on film. The size of the explosion was massive and even more impressive than the film portrays when you realize that Malins was positioned nearly a mile from the blast. As the earth rose up into the air and then slowly collapsed back to earth it left a massive hole where the men of the 9/R119 had been awaiting the attack. The time had come; the Battle of the Somme was underway.

1

Beaumont-Hamel

The mine that had been detonated underneath the German lines on Hawthorn Ridge on 1 July had been under construction in secret for many months prior to this day. Everything depended upon the location of the mine remaining undiscovered by the Germans and in this the 252nd Mining Coy had been successful.

The men in RIR 119 and the *pioniers* attached to the regiment had been aware of the presence of the British mine but despite all of their efforts they were unable to determine its location under the German lines and therefore could not take any effective counter measures. The big questions were, where exactly the mine was and what date and time would it explode? There was no way to predict what portion of the line was vulnerable.

The seven-day bombardment by the English did not cause us many losses. Our battalion occupied a three-line trench system and had built very strong and deep shelters. Our dugouts were eight to 10 meters deep and had been strengthened with heavy wooden beams and railroad ties. Lucky for us this provided quite adequate shelter. But several days before 1 July we had heard underground digging and knew a mine was being dug and prepared.

The explosion of the mine at 7.20 a.m. near Beaumont-Hamel heralded the start of the Somme battle in the section we occupied. The terrific explosion under our first-

The village of Beaumont-Hamel. (Felix Fregin)

The mine crater on Hawthorn Ridge. (*Die 26. Reserve Division 1914-1918*)

line trench blew a hole 80 meters wide. I was only 60 to 70 meters away when it went up, and then was occupied by English infantry. *Grenadier* Walter Peeck, 12/R119[1]

Reserve *Infanterie* Regiment 119 occupied the trenches in the Beaumont-Hamel sector when the battle began. Two battalions occupied the front line while one, the II/R119 was positioned in the rear in reserve. The sector was divided into two parts; *Beaumont-Nord* and *Beaumont-Süd*. Each of these parts was further divided into seven sub-sectors, B1 located in the village of Beaumont through B7 located at the northern bank of the Ancre River. *Beaumont-Nord* was occupied by the III/R119, *Beaumont-Süd* was occupied by the I/R119.

The Beaumont Sector offered many advantages to the defending troops. The area between the opposing lines was very wide in places that would expose any attacking force to strong defensive fire for the extended length of time needed to cross the terrain. No man's land consisted mostly of open ground, devoid of cover that also contained a ravine near the Ancre that had steep sides, in some cases 20 feet high that would act as an obstacle to any organized enemy attack.

The regiment contained two machine gun companies in July 1916. The guns of the 2MG/R119 were in positions that could effectively cover the entire regimental front. There were numerous machine gun posts that were sited in a manner that would provide interlocking fields of fire across the entire front.

The 1MG/R119 was located on the southern bank of the Ancre on 1 July where it would become involved in the fighting around St. Pierre-Divion and Thiepval. Due to the nature of the terrain along the Ancre the 1MG/R119 could still provide some support from their positions on the southern bank of the Ancre. They could enfilade any attack against a

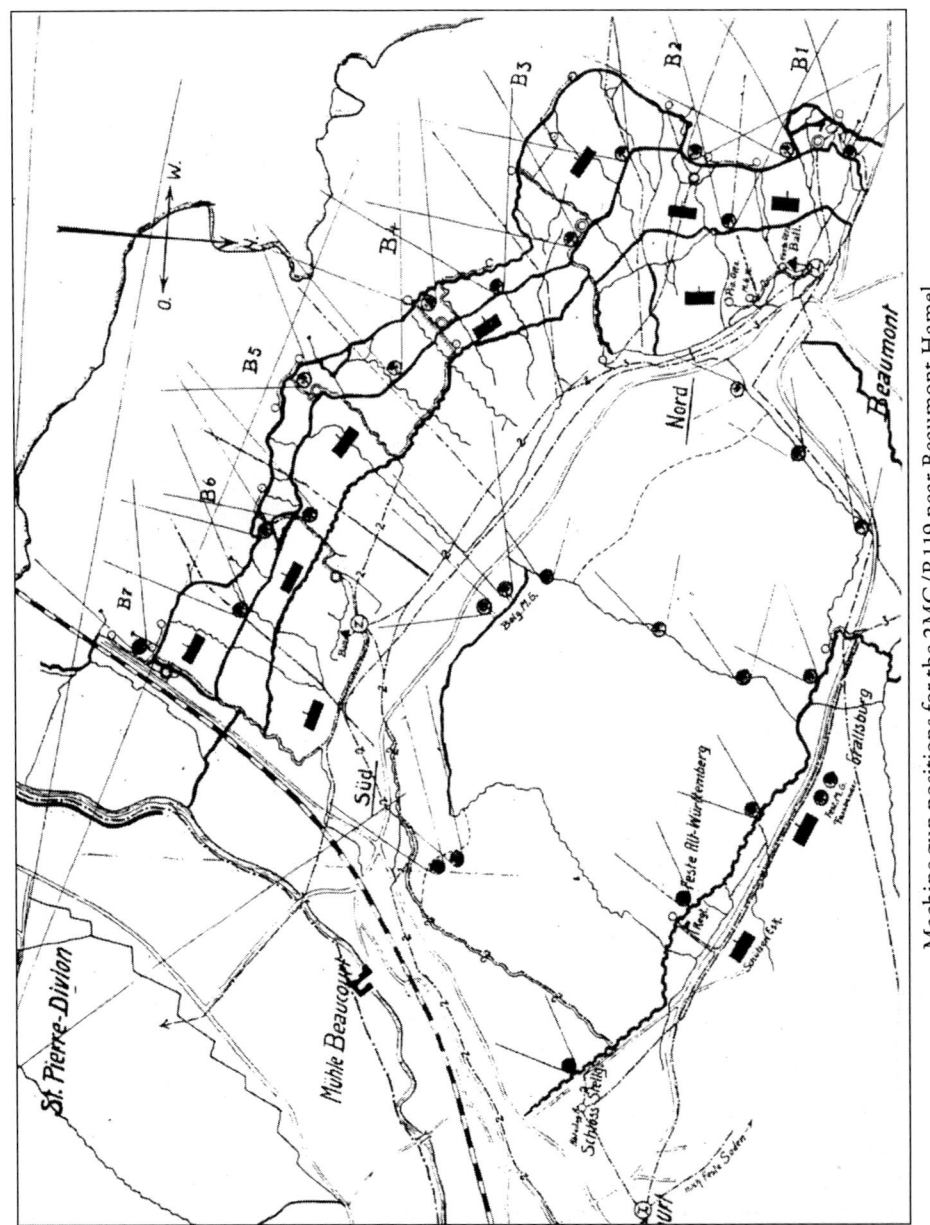

Machine gun positions for the 2MG/R119 near Beaumont-Hamel.

large portion of the Beaumont sector.

All of the defensive measures were in direct response to the increased level of activity the sector had experienced since 1914. The lessons the men had learned from their time spent in the trenches, from raids and patrols were all integrated into the extensive defensive system.

The German positions by Beaumont-Hamel had been under construction for almost 2 years when the attack occurred on 1 July. There were several successive defensive lines that had numerous interconnecting communication trenches, support trenches and switch lines, all of which were protected by dense belts of barbed wire entanglements. The switch lines were created to allow the trench garrison to contain any penetration of the German defenses. The German positions were also constructed on high ground that overlooked and dominated the British trenches and no man's land.

Holding the high ground gave the German observers an advantage over their opponents. They could see far into the rear of the British lines while their opposite numbers had a limited view due to the numerous ridges and ravines found on this part of the battlefield. The arrangement of the German trenches allowed the men at many locations in the second and third lines to fire over the heads of the men located in the front line trench. This added much needed fire support at critical locations whenever it was needed.

Due to the nature of the ground the Germans had created numerous mined dugouts and tunnels that provided ample protection against the heaviest bombardment that could be brought to bear on them. Many of these tunnels were driven directly into the hillsides and they contained numerous exit points. The convex shape of the slope facing the enemy was a factor that prevented the British heavy guns from targeting the German lines effectively. As a result much of the German trench system had received relatively little fire during the preliminary bombardment and as such was mostly intact when the attack came.

Facing the men of RIR 119 was the 29th Division, part of the VIII Corps. A veteran division from the Gallipoli Campaign, the men knew the Beaumont-Hamel sector well having been covering this portion of the line for some months prior to 1 July. The main attack would take place 10 minutes following the mine explosion on Hawthorn Ridge.

The plan called for the 86th and 87th Brigades to attack in the first wave while the 88th Brigade would act as support at first and then become involved in a follow up attack. Accompanying the 29th Division in the advance would be two battalions of the 108th Brigade from the neighboring 36th (Ulster) Division located on the right flank. The 9th Royal Irish Fusiliers and 12th Royal Irish Rifles were to attack *Beaumont-Süd* along the

View of the terrain the British faced attacking north of the Ancre, probably taken from the area of the Leiling Schlucht (Y Ravine). (*Der Weltkrieg 1914-1918*)

Ancre. The remainder of the 36th Division would attack the German lines between St. Pierre-Divion and Thiepval on the south side of the river. Due to the nature of the ground around the Ancre the units found on each side of the river were unable to provide any mutual support.

The overall plan of attack at Beaumont-Hamel was very detailed. Months of planning had gone into virtually every aspect of the attack and every contingency expected had been covered. The artillery that had been firing on the German lines for the last week had a comprehensive plan to follow that would assist the infantry in attaining their objectives. The entire VIII Corps artillery would be following the same plan of action for the light and medium guns. The Corps front extended from Serre in the north to the Ancre in the south.

The VIII Corps orders laid down six lifts for the artillery: off the front trench at zero; off the 'first objective', at 15 or 20 minutes after zero, varying with its distance from the front line; off the second objective at 40 or 45 minutes after zero (but at 1 hour 20 minutes for the flank near Beaucourt); and at 3 hours 30 minutes after zero off the third objective, Puisieux Trench....with intermediate lifts at 1 hour 35 minutes and 2 hours 40 minutes. These times applied to the field artillery.[2]

The heavy artillery plan was slightly different, calling for lifts 5 minutes earlier and straight on to the objective. There was an attempt to create a rudimentary creeping barrage in order to assist the overall attack and to bring the full weight of the artillery on each objective as it was reached.

> At the commencement of each infantry attack the divisional artillery will lift 100 yards and continue lifting at the rate of 50 yards a minute to the objective, firing three rounds per gun at each step.
>
> The rate of advance of the infantry has been calculated at 50 yards a minute.
>
> Infantry must not arrive before the times shown on the map [the times given above], as the artillery will still be firing on these points. It is the intention of divisional artillery to assist the infantry forward by lifting very slowly 50 yards each minute, i.e. at the same rate as it is calculated the infantry will advance.
>
> The times once settled cannot be altered. The infantry therefore must make their pace conform to the rate of the artillery lifts. If the infantry find themselves checked by our own barrage, they must halt and wait till the barrage moves forward.
>
> The success or otherwise of the assault largely depends on the infantry thoroughly understanding the 'creeping' method of the artillery.[3]

There was also a provision that the 4.5-inch howitzers would concentrate their fire on the German machine gun posts and front line dugouts. Two 18-pdr batteries were made ready to follow the infantry and provide additional close range support. Three tunnels were constructed before the attack. Two came to within 30 yards of the German lines. These were to be opened at 2 a.m. on 1 July and become utilized as emplacements for batteries of Stokes mortars. The third would be opened up and become a communication trench to the sunken lane, the same location where so many patrol actions were fought in the months before the battle.

When the mine under Hawthorn Ridge was detonated at 7.20 a.m. all of the heavy artillery of the VIII Corps would lift from the front line trenches as well and proceed to direct their fire on the reserve trenches followed by the howitzers joining them at 7.25 a.m.

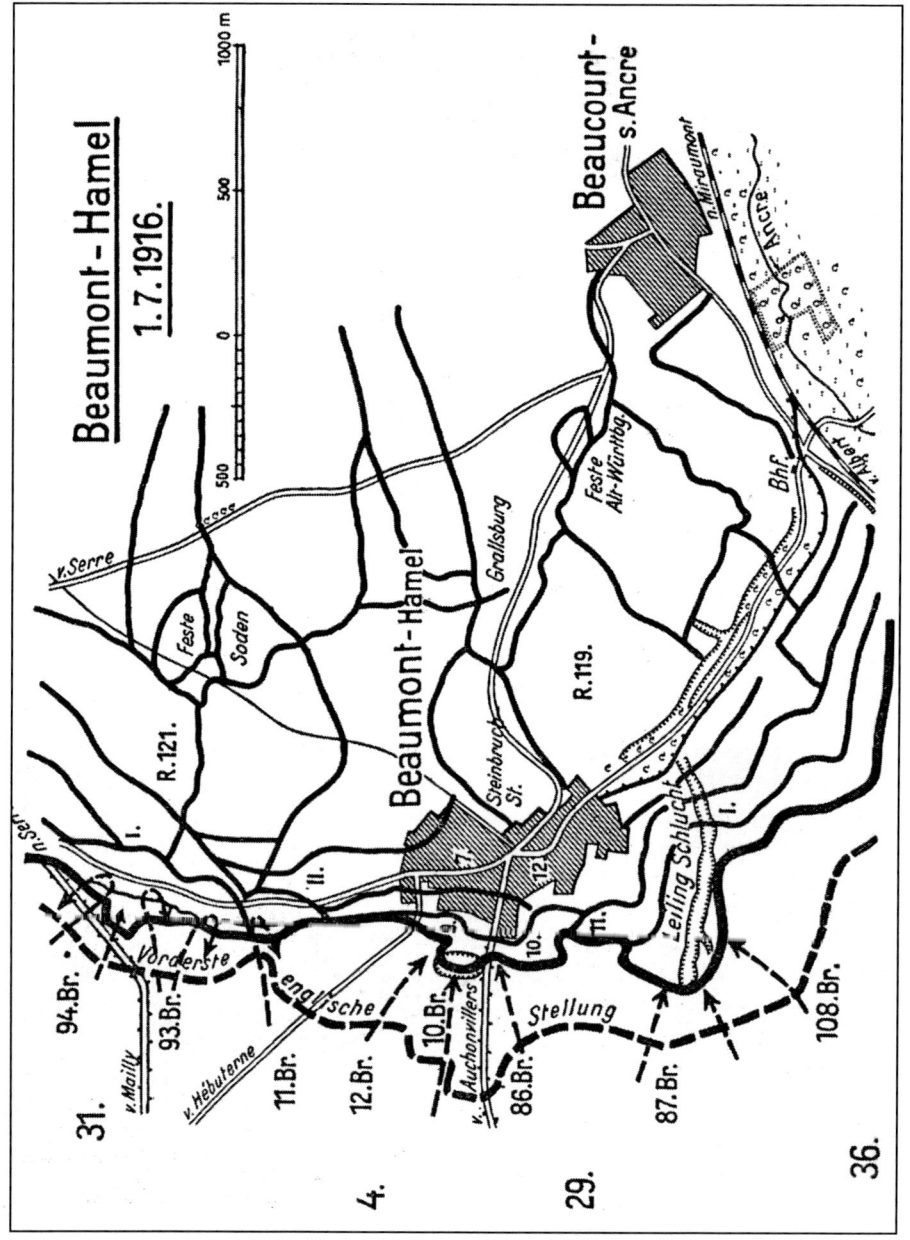

Overall map of British attack against Beaumont-Hamel, 1 July 1916.

In addition to this aspect of the artillery plan, half of the field guns firing on the 29th Division front would lift from the front line at 3 minutes before zero with the other half lifting at zero. This meant that the German trenches facing the 29th Division and the two battalions of the 36th Division would have no heavy artillery fire coming down on them for the last ten minutes and only half of a weak field gun barrage for the last three minutes before the infantry attacked. It was a fortunate opportunity that would not be squandered by the men of RIR 119.

In order for the infantry to conform to the artillery plan and reach their ultimate objective – the German second position some 4,000 yards inside the German lines – the men would have to cover this distance in three and one half hours. Once the objective was reached small parties with Lewis Guns would be sent forward to a sunken road and the position would be consolidated for defense.

During the planning phase there were numerous disagreements among the officers who were given the responsibility of preparing for the biggest attack ever attempted by the British army so far in the war. Perhaps the greatest controversy that arose involved the time the Hawthorn Ridge mine would be set off. Originally the plan had called for the mine to be detonated at 3.30 a.m. Any advance to occupy the crater could be completed well before the main attack and there would be enough time between the explosion and the attack where the Germans would be lulled into thinking it was simply a raid.

This idea was dismissed as it was felt that the Germans were far superior in mine warfare and there was a good chance that German troops would occupy and fortify the crater, thereby creating an additional barrier to the attack that followed.

The next suggestion was to detonate the mine in conjunction with the mines located further south, just a few minutes before the main attack. Any idea of setting the mine off at zero was dismissed as well as there could be losses from the falling debris. After some

Infantrymen – RIR 119. (Author's collection)

Infantryman – RIR 119. (Author's collection)

additional discussion it was decided to detonate the Hawthorn Ridge mine 10 minutes before the infantry attack would begin.

The British Headquarters knew full well that the ten minutes between the explosion and the assault could give the Germans ample warning about the attack but it could also help direct the German attention away from the events taking place further south where the attack was deemed to be more critical. As the other mines were scheduled to explode closer to zero there would be no real advantage of setting off the Hawthorn Ridge mine early. The difference in timing between the mine explosions was so small that even if the Germans had decided to respond to the earlier detonation by moving reserves they could not have set anything in motion in such a short period of time.

It appeared that nothing had been left to chance in order to ensure success, nothing except the presence of the German soldiers and the German artillery. The plan could be considered overly optimistic in that a rigid time table had been prepared that did not allow for any alteration in the execution of the attack other than if the men were ahead of schedule. The terrain that needed to be covered by the men even without opposing infantry shooting at them would be a major obstacle in maintaining the rapid pace laid down in orders.

Still, as the men in the British lines watched the final moments of the bombardment they must have felt that nothing could survive the intensive shelling and victory was inevitable. Surely such an army as the British had assembled on the Somme, supported by hundreds of artillery pieces would be able to overwhelm the German army on the Somme!

Well before the start of the attack the men of RIR 119 were ready for action. They had been alerted and awaited the signal from the trench sentries when to exit their dugouts once the enemy barrage had lifted from the front line. Just before the time of the attack the men were already wearing their equipment. Everyone carried a full load of ammunition; some

Men from the 9/R119 shortly before the attack. The man on the far right (marked with an X) was killed on 1 July 1916. (Author's collection)

even more as extra chargers of cartridges were stuffed into their ammunition pouches, hand grenades had been prepared for use and were hung from their belts. Rifles were at the ready and the machine guns were oiled and ready to be carried up the steep steps and put into position within minutes of the final alarm being sounded, just as they had been practicing the weeks and months before 1 July.

The men along the front line had received a warning earlier in the morning following the interception of a British message from Moritz Station 28 located at the tip of La Boisselle. Each division, brigade, regiment and company was warned that the long awaited attack was to begin at 4.30 that morning. When the time came and went and no attack took place the level of tension did not subside. The increased level of the bombardment that followed surely indicated something was going to happen shortly.

Then, at 7.20 a.m. there was the massive explosion followed by a giant fountain of earth and debris from the area where moments before the men from the 9/R119 had been waiting inside their dugouts.

At 8.15 a.m. [sic], a mine with an extraordinarily large charge was blown under the projecting 'nose' in the middle of B1. Almost all of 1st Platoon (*Leutnant* Renz) and elements on the left of the 2nd Platoon (*Leutnant* Böhm) were crushed and buried in their dugouts by the explosion. All the entrances to the 3rd Platoon dugouts (*Leutnant* Breitmeyer) and some of those belonging to the dugouts of the 2nd Platoon (*Leutnant*

Memorial card to Johannes Ruggaber, Cabinetmaker and Sexton, 9/R119. Killed
in action 1 July 1916 two days before his 38th birthday. (Author's collection)

Böhm) were buried by falling rock. Only very few men of the 9th Company, those on
the left flank and the right flank where the machine guns were located, succeeded in
getting straight out into the open and occupying their battle positions. The enormous
crater was about 50 meters long and 15 meters deep. Within a few moments further
men managed to dig themselves out, so that the 9th Company had about two sections
ready to do battle.[4]

More than three *Gruppen* from the 1st Platoon of the 9/R119 had been killed outright
when the mine exploded. Many of the exits of the nearby dugouts were covered over by
tons of debris making it impossible for the men to get out. For many death was almost
instantaneous as their dugouts were crushed or the men were caught up in the blast from the
high explosives. For some it would prove to be an agonizing death as they slowly suffocated
inside their dugouts, unable to dig themselves free before all of their oxygen ran out.

After the debris settled from the explosion the terrain all around the crater was covered
in pieces of white chalk that gave the impression to any observer that the ground was
covered with snow. Everyone instinctively knew that the mine was the signal for the attack.
Almost immediately numerous red flares climbed high into the air calling for the artillery
defensive barrage fire.

All across the Beaumont-Hamel Sector men poured out of their dugouts as fast as they
could rush up the steps. Some men were delayed slightly if their dugout exits were partially
blocked by debris but even this did not stop the majority of the German defenders from
reaching their assigned positions in time to repel the British attack.

The heavy machine guns were carried up to the surface. Some were placed on makeshift wooden bases instead of the heavy steel sledges. This allowed for rapid deployment of the gun. The trade off was a decrease in accuracy but in this instance speed was considered more important than accuracy. Other machine guns were still mounted on their *Schlitten* that allowed for a stable firing platform and increased accuracy, especially at long distance targets.

The lack of heavy shells and the overall reduction of the field gun bombardment for much of the last ten minutes before the main attack on the German front line allowed the men to set up their firing positions, organize their ammunition supplies and stocks of hand grenades. The officers had an opportunity to look over the terrain and assess the situation and give last minute orders to their men in relative safety.

The British plan, once the mine had detonated, called for two companies of the 2nd Royal Fusiliers along with four machine guns and four Stokes mortars to rush forward and occupy the mine crater. Following the mine explosion the men started their advance toward the crater. They immediately came under heavy rifle and machine gun fire from the German trenches on both flanks as well as from the far lip of the mine crater.

The response by the men from RIR 119 must have come as a surprise to the men of the 2nd Royal Fusiliers as no Germans were considered capable of offering opposition. However many of the men in the 10th and 11/R119 had already exited their dugouts before the mine was even set off and were able to fire at the approaching enemy column as it appeared in front of them. In addition some men from the 9/R119 that had survived the explosion also joined in the defensive fire.

The 2nd Royal Fusiliers suffered many losses before reaching the far edge of the crater. However, with the majority of the 9/R119 being placed out of action there was a gap in the German front line and this was exploited by the surviving members of the Fusilier

Machine gun crew – RIR 119. (Author's collection)

companies.

After entering the crater the survivors of the Royal Fusiliers made their way into the adjoining German front line trench to the left of the crater where a portion of the 3rd Platoon of the 9/R119 was trapped inside their dugout. Three of the four exits of a large dugout had been completely covered over from the debris of the mine explosion and the fourth exit consisted of a small opening that a sentry was attempting to widen just as the British infantry arrived. Among the men awaiting rescue from their underground prison was the platoon commander *Leutnant* Breitmeyer as well as the company commander *Oberleutnant* Anton Mühlbayer who were standing behind the sentry with their men lined up behind them on the steps.

Suddenly the sentry fell back dead onto the dugout steps, killed by a bayonet thrust from a man in the 2nd Royal Fusiliers. *Vizefeldwebel* Davidsohn, who was also standing nearby, fired several flares through the narrow opening, aiming at the heads of the British troops standing inside the trench. There was immediate retaliation by the 2nd Royal Fusiliers when several Mills bombs and smoke grenades were thrown through the opening, forcing the dugout garrison back down the steps into the depths below.

The British soldiers up above inside the trench shouted down into the dugout and demanded that Mühlbayer and his men surrender. The men trapped below refused to answer, there was still hope that their comrades would come by shortly and be able to free them.

A machine gun in the 2MG/R119 under the command of *Unteroffizier* Aicheler had been in a sap just south of where the mine went off. When the mine exploded the gun had been knocked over, Aicheler and his men quickly set it right once more. As soon as the gun

View of British trenches from the German lines near Beaumont-Hamel. (Lawrence Brown)

was back into position Aicheler saw approximately 20 British soldiers already inside the German wire, about 25 paces from his machine gun.

Aicheler opened fire but the gun jammed after only 10 rounds. He quickly cleared the jam and resumed firing only to have it jam again after another 10 rounds. The cause of these jams was most likely from dirt caught up in the belt being fed through the gun. With his location known, the British, most likely men from Z Company, 2nd Royal Fusiliers, now began to throw hand grenades at Aicheler and his men.

The gun crew picked up the heavy weapon and carried it back to the next traverse where they were able to clear the jam once again and place the gun back into action. When they set up the gun on the parapet they noted only a few enemy soldiers inside the trench. Just at that moment they were startled to see another wave of British soldiers approaching the German barbed wire, probably the remaining companies of the 2nd Royal Fusiliers that had attacked at 7.30 a.m. with the rest of the 29th Division.

While this drama was taking place around the newly formed crater the other men in the 29th Division had formed up for the attack that started at 7.30 a.m. As the men exited their trenches and took up position by the British wire they immediately came under heavy rifle and machine gun fire from the German trenches, something they had also not anticipated.

The men from RIR 119 could be seen taking up firing positions, some even taking to standing on their parapet, others taking up positions in nearby shell craters. The ten-minute delay between the mine and the attack had proven to be a disaster from the start. The highly detailed and rigid plan of attack had already unraveled in the opening minutes of the offensive.

The 86th Brigade, 29th Division, advanced on the left of the division front facing the village of Beaumont. The first two battalions, the 2nd Royal Fusiliers on the left (less two companies that had been assigned to occupy the crater) and the 1st Lancashire Fusiliers on the right, were in the first wave. The Lancashire Fusiliers was also accompanied by a large bombing party that consisted of 100 men with an additional 2 machine guns and 4 Stokes mortars.

The Lancashire Fusiliers had utilized the sap that led into the sunken lane half way across no man's land. It was hoped that this would increase the odds of the men reaching and penetrating the German front line.

As soon as the 2nd Royal Fusiliers advanced they came under intense machine gun fire and suffered heavy losses at the onset of the attack. About 30-40 men were seen to veer off to the left and enter the Hawthorn Mine crater where they continued their fight against the German garrison with the other members of the regiment.

The 1st Bn Lancashire Fusiliers were literally destroyed within yards of the sunken lane. Most of the men were hit by machine gun fire as they came into view above the depression where the lane was located. Only about 50 men managed to reach the low bank beyond the sunken lane.

The German artillery had been waiting for the signal to open fire in the final minutes before the attack started. Some guns had already been in action during the morning hours. However once the red flares were observed by the batteries in the rear in conjunction with having received messages to open fire that had successfully reached the battery telephone exchange through the few intact phone lines, all of the guns went into action in accordance with the defensive artillery plan. Within minutes of the opening attack at 7.30 a.m. all of the German batteries protecting the Beaumont-Hamel Sector opened fire.

Light field guns and light field howitzers placed a wall of fire across the entire British front line. This should effectively prevent the enemy infantry from crossing no man's land by creating a fire barrier that could not be crossed without suffering large losses. Heavier howitzers including 21cm heavy field howitzers dropped shell after shell into the British front line and assembly trenches. The batteries had every point on the map targeted and they systematically obliterated each section of trench before moving on to the next.

The artillery fire combined with the utter confusion inside the trenches that were now filled with dead and wounded men made it extremely difficult for the following waves to move forward through the communication trenches. Walking wounded and men on stretchers clogged the routes and it took far longer than planned to assemble the second wave for the attack.

The German defensive artillery barrage was very effective at the onset of the attack when the batteries were directing their fire across no man's land and at the British trenches facing the men of RIR 119. However, in a short time many of the guns were given orders to re-direct their fire in support of the neighboring sector along the left flank of the sector where they were needed most in the fighting around *Feste Schwaben*. This left the bulk of the defensive fire in the Beaumont-Hamel Sector to the infantrymen and the machine guns of the 2MG/R119.

Finally, shortly before 8 a.m., the 16th Middlesex and 1st Royal Dublin Fusiliers crossed the British parapet and began their attack. They immediately found there were far too few gaps in the wire and these were already filled with dead and wounded from the first wave of men.

With the approach of new British forces the German position on the right hand side of the crater was vulnerable as most of the garrison had been placed out of action. Fortunately for the dazed survivors of the 9/R119 additional support was quickly approaching the threatened sector. One platoon from the 7/R119 located in the second trench and one platoon from the 12/R119 along with two *Musketen* located in the third trench had received orders to help eject the British troops from the German front line on the right of the crater.

> Several comrades and I immediately ran forward. Enemy mortar fire fell in front of us and hot iron splinters seared the air. But none of us was hit. We were able to reach our front line, now only a devastated trench with shell holes, in order to put up a defense against the enemy. My 12th Company was able to throw back the enemy and hold on to the forward section of the line. We even took a few prisoners. *Grenadier* Walter Peeck, 12/R119[5]

Both platoons left the safety of their trenches and advanced in the open toward the trenches occupied by the 2nd Royal Fusiliers. The Germans took up positions in the shell craters between the first and second trenches and opened fire on the Fusiliers. Some of the men from the 12/R119 occupied the edge of the crater near Machine Gun No. 2 and opened fire.

Heavy and accurate machine gun fire poured onto the ranks of the second British wave, including machine gun fire from the *Bergwerk* located on Beaucourt Ridge behind the northern edge of Beaumont-Hamel. The attack against the right side of the crater was quickly destroyed in the combined fire from the trench garrison and supporting fire

Machine gun crew – RIR 119. (Author's collection)

from RIR 121 on the right flank. The men of the second wave that had survived the heavy German fire had taken cover in the numerous shell craters and directed their fire toward the positions held by RIR 121 but they were too few to be any real threat.

Once the attack had been stopped the men of RIR 119 could now direct much of their attention to the exposed right flank of the British waves advancing against the positions of RIR 121 and help to stop them before being able to penetrate the German lines further to the north. Mutual support such as this example was a key factor at many places along the German front in stopping the bulk of the British infantry in front of the German wire.

The men of the 86th Brigade had very little chance of successfully reaching or penetrating the German lines on their front. The terrain between the lines was open and devoid of cover. The men in RIR 119 knew every inch of ground. The machine gun posts were sited to give the guns the best field of fire and the staggered positions of the guns allowed for a deadly crossfire to be brought down on any attacking force.

Other than approximately 120 men from the 2nd Royal Fusiliers no other men in the 86th Brigade managed to reach the German lines. The attack along this portion of the front was a failure. The level of heavy fire coming from the 2MG/R119 as well as the 10th and 11/R119 was devastating as the defenders fired as rapidly as possible. The lines of British troops offered a target that simply could not be missed. Since the British artillery fire had long lifted off the German trenches there was no threat to the men as they stood inside their trenches.

One of the machine guns facing the attack of the 86th Brigade was Machine Gun No. 1 under the command of *Unteroffizier* Braungart.[6] His crew of six men included *Gefreiter*

Eisenmann who was operating the machine gun. The gun position was located north of what the British called the Hawthorn Redoubt and slightly back from the front line. The gun had an excellent field of fire along the southern slope of the valley as well as overlooking the valley between the opposing trenches and the north-facing slope.

The machine gun was in place and ready to fire within minutes of observing the start of the attack. The gun crew could see enemy troops emerging from Sectors 40 and 41, the right wing of the 4th Division attack against the *Heidenkopf* Sector and the 1st Lancashire Fusiliers in the 29th Division. Eisenmann operated his gun with deadly accuracy.

> The first wave had advanced so far that two officers who were going in front of the wave with swords drawn, had already arrived in front of our entanglement. The well-aimed fire finished off the two leaders together with the first wave of men before the first belt was emptied.[7]

When the leading waves had been eliminated Eisenmann turned his attention to the subsequent waves of men following behind. According to the gun crew there was little German artillery fire falling on the advancing waves, so it appeared that the machine gun crews were responsible for stopping the attack. Accordingly their deadly fire was concentrated into the dense masses in front of them.

As the waves of enemy infantry were broken up the individual British soldiers took cover in the numerous shell craters that dotted the landscape. Given the excellent field of fire enjoyed by the machine gun crew and their elevated position they were able to easily pick off many of the British troops whenever they observed any movement. It was not possible in most cases to distinguish between wounded enemy soldiers and the potential threat from an intact infantryman. Any movement that was observed called for immediate fire.

Later in the morning, when there was little to fire at close range, Eisenmann turned his machine gun against targets that were at considerable distances, some 950 meters or more from the gun position. Eisenmann fired whenever a target became visible. Even with the long range fire the crew only expended 2,600 rounds on 1 July, slightly less than twelve belts of ammunition.

Many of the losses suffered by the 2nd Royal Fusiliers that followed in the wake of the mine explosion were probably caused by the fire from Machine Gun No. 3 under *Unteroffizier* Boehme.[8] Boehme and his gun crew were located in the second trench north of the *Leiling Schlucht* [Y Ravine]. From his position his gun could fire across Hawthorn ridge and the enemy lines south of the *Leiling Schlucht*.

One member of the 2nd Royal Fusiliers, Lance Corporal Robert Stannard, apparently could see the machine gun firing at him. This was very likely Boehme's gun that was being operated by *Gefreiter* Drobele. Stannard recalled seeing the German machine gunner operating his gun in a calm manner while it was sitting on top of the parapet. Stannard did a quick calculation in his head regarding the rate of traverse of the machine gun and determined he would not be in any danger though at one point the gun was pointed directly at him.

If it was Drobele firing at the 2nd Royal Fusiliers there was a point when firing the third belt of ammunition that the gun became jammed due to a defective cartridge. This type of jam was quickly cleared and the gun was back in action once more. Some British troops managed to get close enough to Drobele to toss hand grenades at the gun position.

Captured machine gun and crew, RIR 119. (Author's collection)

Several exploded nearby causing the gun and crew to be thrown backwards. Other than an ammunition box being set on fire the machine gun was intact and the crew was uninjured and soon back in action once more.

Drobele was also probably responsible for many of the losses suffered by the 16th Middlesex and 1st Royal Dublin Fusiliers in the second wave. Once targets became scarce in front of their original gun position, Machine Gun No. 3 was moved to a second position where it could fire against targets further in the British rear. Like all German regiments, the machine gun crews had every location within range of their guns marked in their target books. This included any target that could be reached from each of the different machine gun posts they could use during the fighting.

The men of the 86th Brigade also came under the fire of Belgian Machine Gun B1 under the command of *Gefreiter* Bürk.[9] Bürk engaged targets on the 4th Division front along the right flank of the regiment in support of the neighboring RIR 121.

Directly in front of the neighboring 87th Brigade was the *Leiling Schlucht*. Due to the nature of the ground much of the German wire could not be directly observed and much had been uncut in this portion of the front line. The terrain allowed the Germans to easily create a deadly crossfire with their machine guns while the British troops out in the open terrain could do little to fight back.

The first wave of the 87th Brigade included two battalions, the 1st Royal Inniskilling Fusiliers on the right with the 2nd South Wales Borderers on the left. The right wing of the brigade formed on Mary Redan, the left wing directly facing the *Leiling Schlucht*.

There was no cover as the men crossed no man's land. The Inniskillings moved out at 7.30 a.m. in excellent order as they advanced toward the German lines. From the start of the attack the men came under strong machine gun and rifle fire and men fell at every step, including the commanding officer Colonel R.C. Pierce.

The survivors that managed to reach the German lines were held up when the wire was found to be intact. The few gaps the Inniskilling Fusiliers found only allowed small groups to make it into the German front line and in some cases down into the valley beyond. The small number of men never had a chance as they came up against the defenders of the second German trench.

Stiff German resistance on their front combined with attacks from both flanks and rear resulted in every man who made it into the German trenches either being killed or captured. It was suspected that the Germans who appeared in the rear of the men who made it inside the German lines had come up from their dugouts in the front line after the Inniskillings had passed over them. The failure to mop up the dugouts they encountered had apparently proved to be a major factor in the destruction of the 1st Royal Inniskilling Fusiliers. There was little the Inniskillings could do about this problem as no one could be spared to check each dugout given the number of men at their disposal. Many of the dugouts along this portion of the German line were interconnected and had numerous exits. It would have taken a considerable number of men to clear each one carefully.

The 2nd South Wales Borderers on the left of the attack opposite the *Leiling Schlucht* encountered such heavy fire they were unable to reach the German lines except for small groups in the left company who were then destroyed at the German wire. The battalion was cut to ribbons by the crossfire from at least three German machine guns that were operated with relative impunity once the British barrage had lifted off of the front line. By 7.35 a.m. almost nothing remained of the Borderers with the exception of scattered men all taking cover a short distance from the German wire. It had taken 5 minutes to completely stop the attack on this portion of the front line.

On the right flank of the 29th Division, in the area between Mary Redan and the Ancre, were two lone battalions from the 108th Brigade, 36th (Ulster) Division. Separated from the rest of their division by the Ancre these battalions were supposed to advance in conjunction with the 29th Division and take Beaucourt Railway Station and the area just to the north of it.

The two battalions, the 12th Royal Irish Rifles (Central Antrim) and 9th Royal Irish Fusiliers (Armagh, Cavan and Monaghans) were essentially on their own during the attack. They could rely only upon support from the neighboring 87th Brigade on their left flank. Their right flank was exposed and lacked any support as a result of the marshy ground along the River Ancre.

To make matters worse the companies of the 12th Royal Irish Rifles would be separated during the attack. Three companies of the 12th Royal Irish Rifles, A, C and D would attack alongside the 87th Brigade, 29th Division. The 9th Royal Irish Fusiliers would be on the right of the 12th. Two platoons from B Coy, 12th Royal Irish Rifles were to attack alongside the Ancre as the far right flank of the attack north of the river. The remaining platoons of B Coy were to provide support for the 9th Royal Irish Fusiliers during the attack.

The men of the 12th Royal Irish Rifles on the right flank of the attack north of the Ancre left the safety of their trenches approximately ten minutes before zero and formed up in front of the British wire. The men were lying down on the grass waiting for the signal for the attack. In accordance with the plans a smoke screen was created by a battery of Stokes mortars that should have effectively hidden their advance across the wide expanse of no man's land. When the attack began at 7.30 a.m. the far right hand platoon (8th) of B Coy split into three sections, one heading left, one heading right along the swampy Ancre ground and one heading up the center.

Infantrymen – 2/R119. (Author's collection)

The smoke screen did help at first but the lack of German defensive fire was more likely the time needed by the German artillery to prepare the guns for firing on pre-determined coordinates than the cover provided by the smoke. The long time spent on the Somme had allowed the batteries of the 26th Reserve Division and all supporting batteries to have every target area covered down to the meter, as in many places along the Somme front the German defenders who were unable to see the British lines due to smoke and fog simply opened fire into the opaque mass. The volume of fire made it inevitable that many of the attackers would be hit by the numerous shrapnel and high explosive shells combined with the steady stream of rifle and machine gun fire.

Some defenders from the I/R119 were guilty of poor judgment when many of the men left the safety of their trench and stood up upon the parapet to fire at the enemy. This phenomenon was to be repeated on many other sectors of the German front line on 1 July 1916. The tension from the bombardment combined with the desire to get even with their tormentors had caused many men in the XIV Reserve Corps to ignore common sense and military discipline as they left the safety of their trenches and took up positions on top of the parapet. While it was true that the men could aim better at the approaching enemy soldiers or throw their hand grenades further they also stood out against the sky and made excellent targets. In this aspect the bombardment could be considered successful in that many of the men from the XIV Reserve Corps became casualties by needlessly exposing their person to British fire.

Shortly after the attack began against *Beaumont-Süd Vizefeldwebel* Karl Losch was among those killed in action. The promising military career and all hopes for promotion to the officer class were dashed for Karl on the morning of 1 July 1916. He was one of many men who abandoned all caution and common sense when the attack finally came. He had jumped up out of his trench and stood upon the parapet as the attack started, regardless of the personal danger involved.

While the leading wave of British troops missed the opening of the German artillery barrage fire and machine gun fire the men in following waves were caught in the heavy fire and suffered immense losses. The smoke screen proved to be completely ineffectual as the men quickly came under shellfire and, in particular, especially heavy and accurate machine gun fire from guns located on their left and right. The 8th Platoon of B Coy also most likely came under the sights of German machine guns located on the southern bank of the Ancre that had a clear field of fire across the river. This allowed them to effectively enfilade any British attack near the Ancre.

There was no shortage of bravery on the part of the men of the 12th Royal Irish Rifles. The left hand party of the 8th Platoon had suffered horrendous losses mainly from machine gun fire, only Sergeant Hamilton and three to four men managed to reach a German advanced sap after crossing nearly 600 yards of no man's land, the rest of the platoon lay dead or wounded, scattered along the wide expanse of terrain. Some were possibly pinned down by the heavy fire and unable to move forward or back. The men under Sergeant Hamilton could not stay in their exposed position under such heavy fire and were forced to abandon the sap.

The right hand section of No. 8 Platoon faired even worse. Coming under heavy and accurate machine gun fire the section commander, Sergeant Benson was killed along with many of his men. The advance was stopped dead in its tracks. A surviving NCO, Sergeant Hoare, sent back a runner who was directed to advise the battalion commander that they could not advance any further under the level of fire they were receiving. The runner returned with new orders for the section to retire to the British line. The few survivors worked their way back to the relative safety of the trenches they had left only a short time earlier.

The 6th Platoon, B Coy under Lieutenant Lemon, was positioned on the right of the 9th Royal Irish Fusiliers. This platoon was given the assignment to take the Railway Sap, the *Tal Stellung* portion that extended out toward the Ancre. Like the 8th Platoon the men under Lieutenant Lemon left their trenches shortly before zero hour and lay down until it was time to attack. At 7.30 the men rose up and started to advance. Before the 6th Platoon could reach the ravine in the middle of no man's land the entire platoon with the exception of Lieutenant Lemon and 12 men had become casualties, primarily by German machine gun fire. The Lewis Gun team accompanying the platoon had all become casualties before reaching the ravine and the gun was placed out of action due to a German shell splinter.

Unperturbed, Lemon continued his advance and after leaving the ravine he advanced toward the sap. Finding it unoccupied Lemon and now only 9 men entered the German lines along the railway bank by the Ancre. Sergeant Miller and three men started to bomb their way down the sap but soon all had become casualties.

The defenders of this portion of the German line, the men of the I/R119, quickly put their training into practice as bombing parties engaged the enemy. It was an uneven fight as Sergeant Miller had so few men and in a short time the men of RIR 119 had completely eliminated this threat.

Lemon and the remaining men advanced into the main sap where they came across bundles of thick cables running along the wall into a large tunnel. The men quickly cut the

Bombing party, RIR 119. (*Die 26. Reserve Division 1914-1918*)

cables and continued their advance.

There was a machine gun firing across the sap from the mouth of a small tunnel, quite possibly Machine Gun No. 7 under *Unteroffizier* Kaeser. Kaeser and his gun crew were in the German 1st Line between Mary Redan and William Redan. There was little cover in front of the gun other than a ravine and the gunner, *Gefreiter* Leuze could see almost the entire area where the British had to cross in order to reach the first German trench.

Lemon then climbed above a small tunnel with some bombs in order to catch any Germans who might come out of the tunnel, in the meantime he sent his remaining men on through the main sap. Shortly afterward Lemon was shot by two German officers who fire their rifles at him from the top of a dugout that apparently led into the tunnel Lemon was watching. It was reported afterward that the two officers were killed when a hand grenade exploded at their feet. There is no mention of this incident in the regimental history for RIR 119. However, two officers in the 3/R119 were reported as killed in action during the fighting on 1 July, it is possible these are the same officers who shot at Lemon.

The rest of the party Lemon sent into the German trenches was intercepted by bombing parties from RIR 119 as they tried to advance deeper into the German lines. The small numbers of men from the 12th Royal Irish Rifles became trapped between the 1st and 2nd German trenches and were quickly overwhelmed by the defenders. Only two men from the original party from the 6th Platoon managed to make it out of the German lines safely, Corporal Burgess and Rifleman McNeilly. During the trip back to the British lines the two men became separated and only McNeilly managed to report to several non-commissioned officers of the 9th Royal Irish Fusiliers. No one knew what had become of Burgess.

Captured machine gun and crew, RIR 119. (Author's collection)

The crew of Machine Gun No. 7 had been observing the British lines with the use of a mirror that allowed the men to watch for the moment of the attack in relative safety from the shells bursting all around. Still, from time-to-time one man would go out to the edge of the machine gun position and look out across no man's land. On one of these occasions *Schütze* Vogt was killed when a shell exploded near the gun. The training of the gun crew quickly took over and Vogt's position was immediately taken over by another member of the crew without any interruption in the operation of the gun.

The start of the British advance was observed in the mirror and the machine gun was quickly brought into action against the 9th Royal Irish Fusiliers as they formed for the attack. The last moments of the British bombardment were still falling on the German front line and after the gun had fired 280 rounds a shell exploded in front of the position. The gun was buried and *Gefreiter* Leuze was slightly wounded. It proved to be a superficial wound that allowed Leuze to remain with his gun crew after receiving basic first aid.

The gun was quickly restored to an upright position and opened fire once more as the men of the 9th Royal Irish Fusiliers reached the near side of the valley. Machine Gun No. 7 continued to fire until the attack was considered finished. The total ammunition expenditure was a mere ten belts, 2,500 rounds.

The day had started poorly for the 9th Royal Irish Fusiliers, long before the attack began. During the early morning hours a large German shell had caused almost 50 casualties in the battalion. Apparently the German guns had not been silenced as had been expected after the week-long bombardment.

The 9th was well equipped for the attack. The men along with their rifles and hand grenades carried Lewis guns, Stokes mortars, Vickers machine guns and Bangalore torpedoes. The battalion objectives were the German 1st, 2nd and 3rd line trenches from Railway Sap to A25 in the 1st Line, Beaucourt Railway station and the trench north of it with some local houses found nearby. In order to reach the first objective the men had to cross over 400 yards of open ground. There was one obstacle in no man's land that could also provide some protection from the German fire, a ravine approximately 70 yards in length with steep sides, 15 to 20 feet in places.

In order for the men to successfully cross the wide expanse of no man's land it was decided to begin the attack approximately 150 yards from the German trenches. This meant that the 9th Royal Irish Fusiliers needed to be well out beyond their own wire at 7.30 a.m. In order to achieve this, the first wave needed to cross the British parapet at 7.10 a.m., the second wave at 7.15 a.m., the third wave at 7.20 a.m. and the fourth wave at 7.30 a.m.

The 1st wave made it through the gaps in the British wire with few losses. As the men made their way across no man's land they came under increasingly heavy machine gun fire as more and more German guns spotted their advance and opened fire. The first wave reported particularly heavy fire coming from their left flank.

The 2nd wave had more difficulty getting through the British wire. By now the German machine guns had determined that an attack had started and were able to direct their fire at the 9th Royal Irish Fusiliers as they left the British trenches and tried to get through the gaps in the wire. Before the 2nd wave could reach the ravine most of the officers in the two left companies, C and D, had become casualties.

The 3rd and 4th waves, A and B Coy, suffered the most. By now the German machine gunners had trained their sights to cover the narrow gaps in the British wire that funneled the enemy into a small target area. Given the level of training the machine gunners had received during their service it was not very difficult to concentrate their fire on such a large target at such close range. In addition, the last two waves had to contend with the German artillery defensive fire that had started in earnest. The last two companies were virtually annihilated in this fire.

Despite the heavy fire the few surviving men continued to advance. Once the much reduced battalion came to within 150 yards of the German trenches they came under even more devastating infantry fire. The Germans manning the front line were firing over the parapet as fast as they could load and fire their rifles. Like *Vizefeldwebel* Losch, many of the men were so eager to get back at their tormentors that they too left the safety of their trenches and fired upright while standing on their parapet. This would also prove to be fatal to many of the men as they came under return fire from the advancing British troops.

Despite the intense rifle fire and the supporting machine guns that were firing at targets at what might be considered point blank range some of the men from the right wing, A Coy, as well as the two left companies, C and D, managed to reach the German wire. At some places it was reported that the men from RIR 119 held up their hands to surrender but upon seeing the small numbers of men opposite them and the lack of any following support troops they quickly resumed firing at the ever-shrinking numbers of the 9th Royal Irish Fusiliers they faced.

There were reports that the right center company, B, had suffered the least casualties

German trench near Beaumont-Hamel. (Felix Fregin)

and small parties from this company supposedly penetrated at least three German trench lines and managed to reach Beaucourt Railway station. This sounds like a magnificent achievement given the circumstances the men faced but it is not supported by the records of RIR 119.

Once the men of the I/R119 realized that British troops had managed to enter their first line trench the months of training quickly took over. The men of RIR 119 had been taught to take control of the situation facing them without having to consult senior commanders, in each company sector the company leader and his non-commissioned officers were all capable of assessing the situation and taking the appropriate action as the situation required.

According to the reports made by the I/R119 the British were only able to penetrate the German front line at individual places in Sector B5, near the *Cirkus Graben*. The opposing lines were at their closest at this point and much of the German wire had been badly damaged during the preliminary bombardment.

All access routes to the threatened area were blocked off by bombing parties supported by riflemen. The garrison of the second trench that ran parallel to the first trench quickly sized up the situation and attacked frontally. The surviving British were quickly forced out of the position and into the wire. In the process the Germans also captured two Lewis Guns. These were highly prized and could quickly become used against their former owners.

The situation of the 9th Royal Irish Fusiliers was desperate and support was needed or the attack would fail. Several runners were sent back from the German front line, one managed to make his way to the British front line. He had come from the commander of the left center company, C, who was located some 30 yards from the ravine. His message simply stated, 'Cannot advance without support'.

The only available supports at hand were the few men from No. 7 Platoon, B Coy. The men advanced as ordered but the heavy fire stopped them before they were able to go much beyond the British wire. The platoon was effectively destroyed within a few minutes of starting the attack.

Small groups of the Irish Rifles and probably men from the right hand company of the 9th Royal Irish Fusiliers took up positions in the numerous craters that covered the terrain. From here the men opened fire on the German lines. The Germans quickly brought down accurate machine gun fire from guns positioned near the *Grallsburg* and *Feste Alt-Württemberg* located north of Station road. In addition several of the supporting artillery pieces directed their fire into the sector being occupied by the British and their losses began to mount even further.

Close range support weapons also joined in the fighting. The area by the Ancre was covered by several *Erdmörser* that lobbed over large shells filled with high explosives and as much scrap metal as the Germans could fit into the shells. While not overly accurate the destructive force of the blast was devastating and the intense fire eventually forced the few survivors to withdraw back toward the British lines. The I/R119 reported that the attack against their sector was over by 9 o'clock.

The attack by the 9th Royal Irish Fusiliers was effectively finished. The few surviving men trapped in no man's land were forced to remain out of sight as any movement quickly brought down German fire from rifles and machine guns. Once darkness fell the men would be able to make their way to the rear.

Other than the small success achieved by the men of the 2nd Royal Fusiliers at the Hawthorn mine crater, the initial attack by six battalions of infantry was a complete disaster. In many cases the attacking troops were stopped within minutes of starting their

View of mine crater on Hawthorn Ridge. (*Das Württembergische Reserve-Infanterie-Regiment Nr. 119 im Weltkrieg 1914-1918*)

advance so intense was the defensive machine gun fire.

Once the main attack had been destroyed there still was the situation facing the men of the 9/R119 and the neighboring units located near the mine crater. The breach in their lines caused by the mine explosion needed to be contained. *Unteroffizier* Aicheler was still occupied with defending the threatened position where a large part of the garrison from the 9th Coy had been destroyed in the mine explosion.

When the second wave of attackers appeared in front of the German wire approximately 40 men from the 2nd Royal Fusiliers managed to get inside the crater. While the British Official History indicates that these men were able to hold out in the crater the records of RIR 119 provide a different fate. These men were apparently all reported killed or wounded in the almost point blank fire from Aicheler's machine gun; they never stood a chance out in the open, without any form of cover.

While Aicheler was holding the German trench near the crater almost single-handedly, help was nearby. About 20 men from the 9th Coy slowly assembled behind Aicheler's gun position. At first the men were not in any fit state to join in the defense of the position. Most were still dazed and concussed from the mine blast.

A *Vizefeldwebel* from RIR 119 took control of the situation and after repeated orders given to the dazed men a number of them reacted and were convinced to join an advance against the 2nd Royal Fusiliers still inside the German trenches. A hand grenade fight broke out between the opposing sides as the Germans and British both tried to gain the upper hand. The German bombing parties were being supported by Aicheler who fired at any British soldier that showed himself. The fire was so intense at such close range that six British soldiers were later found almost cut in two as a result, four others surrendered when it became obvious that any further resistance was futile.

The situation facing the men of RIR 119 on the left side of the crater was far more serious. The British troops had established a foothold inside the German front line and

Trenches near Beaumont-Hamel. (Felix Fregin)

Infantryman – RIR 119. (Author's collection)

there were enough men and machine guns in support to allow them to attempt to expand their gains.

At first the resistance was down to a few audacious individuals who tried to stop the British from rolling up more of the first trench, men like *Vizefeldwebel* Mögle. Mögle used his supply of hand grenades to bomb the British and drive them back. He was having little luck in accomplishing this but he was preventing them from advancing any further.

The British advance was being supported by a machine gun that was located at the edge of the crater and from its elevated position had a wide field of fire. The entire area still held by the men of RIR 119 was under an almost constant spray of bullets and many of the defenders had been killed or wounded by head shots. Finally, *Unteroffiziers* Hess and Rapp managed to shoot down the gun crew.

At the same time *Leutnant der Landwehr* Blessing, 10th Coy had quickly assessed the situation from his vantage point in the second trench. He assembled a bombing party from men of the 10th Coy; *Unteroffizier der Landwehr* Emil Brose, *Reservist* Karl Fauser, Hermann Lutz, and Kappelmann and advanced against the English located in the German lines.[10]

Mögle also applied pressure against the nest of enemy troops with a small group he had assembled consisting of men from the 7th and 12/R119 and 'it developed into a fierce battle'. The British were destroyed in the fighting and their leader, described as a brave Lieutenant, was wounded and taken prisoner.

With this threat ended for the time being the men trapped inside the nearby dugout could be freed. The dugout entrance was widened and Mühlbayer, Breitmeyer and their men exited the dugout and joined in with the defense of the front line.

At this time a new threat appeared, a British machine gun was being made ready to fire barely 15 meters in front of the German trench. *Schütze* Hermann from Machine Gun No. 2 could clearly see the enemy gun and quickly took action. He was able to place the gun crew out of action with 4-5 pistol shots. He then ran forward, grabbed the machine gun and brought it back. The gun could not be used as it was missing the lock and Hermann had been unable to locate it.

The newly freed platoon from the 9/R119 was hardly in position when new waves of enemy infantry accompanied by machine guns were seen to advance against the German lines. The enemy was very well armed. It was estimated that in an area barely 100 meters wide there were approximately 10 Maxim and Lewis Guns and one mine thrower.

This last advance by the enemy was also completely broken in the heavy defensive fire of the 7th, 9th, 10th and 12/R119. The survivors took cover behind the chalk spill on the far lip of the crater. Although protected from the fire of the men around the crater edge the British behind the lip of the mine were completely exposed to the fire from the neighboring RIR 121 from the *Bergwerk*. The machine gun located with the 5/R121 positioned further north fired directly into the mass of enemy soldiers. The cone of fire covered the entire enemy position.

The attack faltered and the surviving British soldiers dropped to the ground and returned fire against the flanking machine gun. The heavy fire hitting the British left flank soon forced the survivors to retreat back across no man's land, all the while under rifle and machine gun fire. Most of the men did not make it. It was about 10.30 a.m. and the attack was over.

While the latest enemy attack was over there was still the situation of having British troops lodged inside the German trenches near the crater edge. Reinforcements from the 7th and 12th Coy arrived at the front line with the added firepower of the two *Musketen*

British dead surrounding the edge of the crater. (*Das Württembergische Reserve-Infanterie-Regiment Nr. 119 im Weltkrieg 1914-1918*)

a firefight broke out between the opposing sides at point blank range. *Oberleutnant der Reserve* Mühlbayer ordered Aicheler to move his gun closer to the edge of the crater. Once in position *Gefreiter* Eisenmann opened fire on a Lewis Gun located on the far edge of the crater. After firing 500 rounds the Lewis Gun went silent.

Aicheler's gun then jammed, probably as a result of a defective cartridge. While attempting to clear the jam *Schütze* Pfuhler was shot in the head and severely wounded.[11] He was quickly removed to a safe location and his place on the gun team was immediately taken up by *Schütze* Kohnle.

During the fight for the crater the men of the 12/R119 came under attack by a lone British aircraft that dropped several bombs on their position that resulted in minimal damage. The threat from enemy aircraft was considered to be insignificant along this portion of the front line and the fighting continued unabated.

Now a full-fledged battle had started for possession of the German front line trench and crater that was still occupied by British troops. The men of the 10th and 11/R119 as well as the survivors of the 9/R119 could see the enemy inside the trenches adjacent to the crater. They were determined to eject them once and for all as quickly as possible.

Bombing parties took up position and all access routes were blocked off to prevent the enemy from extending their gains. The bombers then advanced against the small group of British soldiers from all sides. The enemy held out as long as possible but soon those not killed or wounded made their way back toward the British lines as best they could.

A new attack that was forming in the British lines against the *Leiling Schlucht* quickly

German trenches west of Beaumont after being cleared. While damaged, the trenches were still adequate to provide protection to the defenders. (*Die 26. Reserve Division 1914-1918*)

came under fire from the 2nd and 11/R119. The men fired their rifles so rapidly that the barrels appeared to glow and they burned the hands of the men. The men in the 11/R119 located in the elevated second trench were able to fire over the heads of the front line trench against this new threat.

Further attacks also came under intense infantry and machine gun fire. At this point in the fighting near Beaumont there was still only sporadic German artillery fire falling on the battlefield. Most of the guns were directed to fire at the trenches near Thiepval and *Feste Schwaben* in support of the counter attacks taking place in the neighboring sector. There continued to be a great deal of reliance placed on the machine guns positioned across the regimental sector as well as the supporting fire coming from machine guns located with RIR 121 just to the north of the regiment. The crossfire created by these guns effectively destroyed every British attempt to reach the German lines. Finally, the defensive fire had proved to be too much for the British troops and the survivors could be seen flooding back to their trenches. It was 12 noon and the attack was over.

The scene facing the men from RIR 119 was terrible. The chlorine gas released over the last week had bleached and corroded the long grass. 'Khaki-brown' dead and wounded lay in the hundreds among the obstacles and across no man's land. The battlefield surrounding the crater was probably the worst of all.

The 'Englishmen' lay in dense piles around the lip and inside the crater. A wreath of dead from the 7th, 9th and 12/R119 also lined the area around the crater. It had the appearance of a charnel house. Most of the trenches near the crater had been completely destroyed or filled in with the upcast from the mine. The remains of tunnels that had been destroyed in the explosion could be seen along the walls of the crater.

The leader of the 1st Platoon, 9th Coy was missing along with many of his men. No traces of the former dugout entrances used by his platoon could be found and in all likelihood the men still remain where they fell on 1 July some 96 years later. In other locations the outline of dugout entrances could be made out and every attempt was made to dig out the debris and open them up in case there were any survivors. Chalk debris lay everywhere in piles a meter high or more.

Some time between 12 and 1 p.m. *Leutnant der Reserve* Renz and several other men suddenly emerged from a small opening in the ground at the edge of the crater. The explosion had buried every exit to their dugout and had left only a small portion of the shelter intact.

During the heavy fighting Renz and his companions were struggling to dig their way out of their predicament, scraping earth and chalk with whatever tool was available. Almost at the moment when their limited air supply was to run out the men managed to reach the surface and break free of their prison. Their appearance and almost miraculous escape from death was greeted by their comrades with great joy.

While these events took place *Landwehrmann* Schneider was in the German front line and observing how some of the enemy 'dead' appeared to be lifting their heads. Schneider spoke and understood perfect English so he shouted at them loudly and told them to come into the German trench. After some hesitancy several wounded men came in together and brought their severely wounded First Lieutenant with them.

When other wounded men still lying on the ground saw that their comrades were being rescued and treated well they also raised their hands and asked and shouted for help. Despite being under sporadic fire several men from the 9th Coy ventured out and retrieved several men including some who were unwounded who had pretended to be dead. The number of

Husband and wife, RIR 119. (Author's collection)

prisoners collected now rose to a total of 36; 31 other ranks and 5 officers. Among the items confiscated from the prisoners were important documents that were found on a captured regimental adjutant.

Once the attack was considered finally over the men of RIR 119 had time to clear away the dead and transport them to a central burial location. All of the wounded were assembled and sent to nearby dressing stations. When the entire casualty reports had been sent in to the regimental headquarters it was discovered that RIR 119 had lost 8 officers, 93 other ranks killed and 191 men wounded.

There was a great deal of damage to the trenches that required immediate attention and there was the never-ending need to bring up fresh supplies of ammunition, equipment as well as food and water for the men. The regiment now had time to review the losses it had suffered by each company and to properly record the identities and fate of the men killed, wounded or injured on 1 July 1916.

As was customary the families of the men who were killed were notified through official channels. Within a few days of 1 July the families of the unfortunate men began receiving letters advising them that their loved one had been killed. Their names would eventually be listed among the *Verlustlisten* but this would not occur for some weeks or months in some cases.

The family of *Vizefeldwebel* Karl Losch was representative of the hundreds of families throughout Germany who received such letters. One of the biggest questions that consumed many of the surviving family members was how their loved one had died and most importantly of all, where he was buried.

Beaumont-Hamel sector on 2 July 1916. (*Die 26. Reserve Division 1914-1918*)

When looking through hundreds of letters sent home by front line troops to their families in Germany there was one common theme that stood out. Both the men in the trenches and their families safe at home were concerned over the proper burial of the dead. The sons, brothers, husbands and fathers of those left behind had been killed and their families and friends would never see them again.

If the deceased soldier was lucky he received a marked burial in one of the many cemeteries that appeared in the villages behind the front or in some cases in small cemeteries very close to the front line. In either case it was common to send home a photograph showing the final resting place of a loved one.

In cases such as *Landwehrmann* Jakob Hönes, RIR 121, killed in June 1915 and who was buried behind the trench in which he had fallen, there was no grave to photograph and send home. However Hönes and his comrades were remembered with a memorial wreath placed inside the trench near the spot where they were killed. The wreath was photographed and sent home to the families whose loved ones were buried in the unmarked graves. The photograph provided a sense of closure and tangible evidence of the death of their loved one to each family. Possibly most importantly, the memento also meant that the men were still remembered by their comrades.

The matter involving *Vizefeldwebel* Losch was no different. Shortly after the Losch family had received the official notice of the death of their son they also received letters of condolence from Karl's friends who was serving in another regiment in the division.

Leutnant der Reserve Richard Seeger XIV Army Corps 26th Reserve Division Reserve Infantry Regiment 121, 8th Company, 6 July 1916.

Dear Family Losch!

I extend my heartfelt sympathy to you all about the heavy loss that concerns you. I have lost a true friend in Karl and you will already so surely know from his letters how much we've been together and how well we understood one another. Now I'm the only *Treubündler* in the 26th Reserve Division who is still alive, and I want to know how I deserve this. But the war is not over, and you do not know if you will see home again. I will never forget your dear Karl for the rest of my life, in addition I've loved him very much, and while we will not see him again in this life, I hope to in eternity. You are cordially greeted by your devoted Richard Seeger.[12]

The correspondence between the Losch family and the friends of their son Karl continued into the summer in an attempt to learn more about his last hours on earth and his final resting place.

Leutnant der Reserve Richard Seeger XIV Army Corps 26th Reserve Division Reserve Infantry Regiment 121, 8th Company. 2 August 1916

Dear Mr. Losch!

Unfortunately I've only now come to answer your dear letter from the 14th of July. I have waited further to see if it would not be possible for me to look after Karl's grave, but even this has not been possible for me given the tense situation we are still faced with. As much as the *Vizefeldwebel* of the 3/R119 wrote to me, I sent in a letter to H. Sütterlin, Karl is in the _____ that is behind the ___ trench in a protected valley, buried with even more friends. I am so very sad to be separated from my friend. Also until now I could learn very little about the last hours of dear Karl. This much is certain, that he also fell in the attack on the morning of 1st July in the victorious battle. The day before I was together with Karl a great deal, and his constant concern was, "will we be able to hold out?" Probably neither had any idea that they would both seal their loyalty with their lives. I have lost so very much with Karl, perhaps because we had adjusted our contrasts together so well and have spent many, many pleasant times together and I will be eternally grateful to dear Karl. Such a loyal friend I have lost with his death, I will probably not find anyone like him. As soon as it is somehow possible for me to make inquiries about Karl I'll do it, and I will instantly write. Hopefully, the Englishmen will soon be exhausted due to their many unsuccessful attacks that they may have to give up the offensive ... Then it is our ardent desire that the war may have an early end. Now to you and your good wife the warmest greetings, from your humble Richard Seeger.[13]

At the same time the letter from Richard Seeger arrived the Losch family finally received further news from a man who was in the same company and platoon that Karl served in. Finally, the family had some idea of what had happened to their son on the morning of 1 July 1916.

Reservist Gottlob Mauss 3/R119 XIV Reserve Corps, 26th Reserve Division. *Beaumont Süd* 1st August 1916

Dear Family Losch!

I have received your esteemed letter with thanks; I also see from your words that you have learned more details about the death of your very dear son. I'm really sorry I have not been able to tell much until now. For the 24th of July [Sic] was the beginning of the offensive, for 8 days we were located under the heaviest deadly fire, where *Vizefeldwebel* Losch often came twice a day to see *Leutnant* Sütterlin [and] they often said to each other ... 'we hope we make it through the offensive'. On the same morning, at approximately 6:30 a.m., *Leutnant* Sütterlin and *Vizefeldwebel* Losch said goodbye to each other until they saw each other again, at 7:30 a.m. the Englishmen climbed out of their trench, after which they were received with fire from us. No one could keep to the trenches and they jumped out and fired standing up. Even your dear son was also there. They were all full of anger; he was struck by three shots according to the man fighting next to him. With the first *Vizefeldwebel* Losch picked himself up once more, then all at once *Vizefeldwebel* Losch fell down and after a few seconds he was hit by another shot. What happened there was simply dreadful. After midday during a lull in the fighting the dead were carried away by the *Sanitäts* Other Ranks and were all placed in one grave where 60-70 men lie next to each other, where in any case, *Herr* Losch, your dear son is also there. Even the company does not yet know the list of the men buried there accurately. I know definitely that *Leutnant* Sütterlin has been removed and had been carried back to Miraumont. One knows nothing at all about the grave for every day we are very much under deadly fire from British counter-attacks. Until now we have lost 86 men in the company, 25-30 killed, we lose more men each day. I will conclude now, I think that I will soon be able to provide very specific answers, and I will do everything I can possibly about it. Finally I want to mention my heartfelt sympathy about the loss of your dear Son, and especially also the sympathy from the 2nd and 3rd Platoons who *Vizefeldwebel* Losch was with. Best regards, *Reservist* Gottlob Mauss 3/R119[14]

Für die wohltuenden Beweise herzlicher Teilnahme bei dem schweren Verluste unseres im Kampfe für das Vaterland gefallenen lieben Sohnes und Bruders

Karl Losch, Kaufmann

sagen wir unsern innigsten Dank.

Karl Losch, Kanzleirat
und Familie.

Stuttgart, den 11. Juli 1916.

Memorial notice for Karl Losch. (Felix Fregin)

With this latest letter the Losch family finally knew what had happened to their oldest son. It was still the hope of the family to have a photograph of his resting place as it apparently meant a great deal to the family.

Beaumont Süd 24th August 1916

Dear Family Losch!

Please accept many thanks for your very dear gift that I have just received, but, dear family Losch, it was not necessary, because I am willing to give information at any time. On this day I have also encountered a friend of your dear son Karl, Mr. Kiesener from Stuttgart, who also immediately asked after your dear son, Karl. I gave Mr. Kiesener directions about the exact resting place of your dear son Karl. As soon as the situation is in a better position it will allow Mr. Kiesener to photograph it and send you a picture of the resting place of your dear son ... Of course it is slow, fixing up the resting place of our dear comrades. Every day there is deadly activity and it is really heavy again. Yesterday, a shell killed 10 men 100 meters away from the resting place of your son, Karl. The resting place of your dear son Karl shall soon number over 100 men. Again I [want to] mention to family Losch my heartfelt thanks for your gift and best wishes for your kindness, Gottlob Mauss.[15]

By the number of letters and personal visits made to the 26th Reserve Division by friends of the late *Vizefeldwebel* Losch it was evident he was a popular young man and if fate had been kinder it appears he could have made a success of his life. One moment of poor judgment had made all of the difference. Letters continued to arrive at the Losch household with additional information about Karl

Krankenträger Wilhelm Schaibb 3/R119. Posted 5 August 1916

Dear Mr. Losch!

Allow me to write you a few lines that I was always together with your beloved son Karl, however Karl was unfortunately called away from us too soon. At 9 o'clock in the morning on 1 July Karl received a fatal bullet in the head, where after 10 minutes Karl died from it without regaining consciousness again and is buried with about 80 of his comrades. Dear Mr. Losch, I want to ask you if you could send a photograph of Karl, as I will never forget our experiences. I would be very grateful. I send my best greetings to you. Wilhelm Schaibb.[16]

The final letter between Herr Losch and the members of RIR 119 that is known to exist was written on 25 August 1916 when *Krankenträger* Wilhelm Schaibb 3/R119 wrote to the Losch family thanking them for their kind gift package. Schaibb provided the last piece of information the family had been searching for, the exact directions to the location of their son's grave. Armed with the step-by-step instructions we will never know if Karl Losch's family ever made the journey to visit his final resting place.

Schaibb was going to provide one last item to the family, a photograph and the grave site. He expected to be able to take the photograph a few days after writing the letter and once it was developed he promised to send them a copy. While the hundreds of *Feldpost* letters written by Karl Losch and his friends were kept by the family it is unfortunate that no known photographs exist of Karl Losch for the sake of historic posterity. It is very likely that hundreds of similar letters were exchanged between the families of the men killed fighting on the Somme and their comrades still at the front.

Notes

1.   R. Baumgartner, *This Carnival of Hell*, p. 65.
2.   J. Edmonds, *History of the Great War. Military Operations France and Belgium 1916. Sir Douglas Haig's Command to the 1st July: Battle of the Somme*, pp. 427-428
3.   J. Edmonds, *History of the Great War. Military Operations France and Belgium 1916. Sir Douglas Haig's Command to the 1st July: Battle of the Somme*, p. 428.
4.   J. Sheldon, *The Germans on the Somme*, p. 138.
5.   Baumgartner, op. cit., pp. 65-66.
6.   Machine Gun No. 1 was the standard Maxim MG 08. The gun crew consisted of: *Unteroffizier* Braungart, *Gefreiter* Eisenmann (Gun Layer), *Schützen* Gottlieb Müller, Arndt, Danner, Morlok and Wilhelm Stengele. Stengele had been transferred from Machine Gun Marksman Detachment 98.
7.   Report of 2nd MG Coy, RIR 119, translation provided by Jack Sheldon.
8.   Machine Gun No. 3 was a standard Maxim MG 08. The gun crew consisted of *Unteroffizier* Boehme, *Gefreiter* Drobele (Gun Layer), *Schützen* Adolf Mayer, Fetzer, Palmer and Knoelle.
9.   Belgian Machine Gun B1 was a captured weapon put into use by the German army. The gun had a smaller crew than the standard MG 08 and in addition to *Gefreiter* Buerk it also included *Schützen* Rothacker, Scheerer and Stuhler.
10.   *Unteroffizier der Landwehr* Emil Brose and *Reservist* Karl Fauser were killed during the fighting on 1 July.
11.   *Landstpfl.* Otto Pfuhler from Ringingen was transferred from the 12th Coy to the 2nd MG Coy on 26 June 1916 to fill in several vacancies in the company. He was assigned to MG No. 2 commanded by *Unteroffizier* Aicheler.
12.   R. Seeger, *Leutnant der Reserve* 8/R121, *Feldpost* letter dated 6 July 1916. A *Treubündler* was a member of a conservative Prussian organization.
13.   Seeger op. cit. Feldpost dated 2 August 1916.
14.   G. Mauss, *Reservist* 3/R119, *Feldpost* letter dated 1 August 1916. Most of the men killed in RIR 119 on or near 1 July 1916 do not have a known grave including *Leutnant der Reserve* Sütterlin, who had been removed from the original mass grave and later buried in Miraumont. It is probable that the remains of the enlisted men were later removed and buried in one of the German cemeteries located on the Somme Battlefield and subsequently lost or that these men still rest in the mass grave as unknown soldiers.
15.   Mauss op. cit. *Feldpost* letter dated 24 August 1916.
16.   W. Schaibb, *Krankenträger* 3/R119, Feldpost letter dated 5 August 1916. The letters regarding the final resting place of Karl Losch have been edited to remove certain details that might provide clues to the location of the mass grave containing the men from RIR 119 that were killed in July 1916. There is a remote possibility that these bodies could still be at the same location and in an attempt to avoid any possible disturbance by unauthorized individuals the burial details have been omitted. The author has been involved at a Great War archaeological dig where local individuals came by at night and looted the site. They took numerous items, most that will remain unknown to the archaeologists as they were still in the ground when the

site was left for the day. The looters did leave behind several live pieces of ordnance including a Stokes mortar shell. It is hoped that if the grave containing Karl Losch does still exist that it will be excavated under the guidance of the French authorities and handled in a professional and respectful manner, as were the mass graves located near Pheasant Wood by Fromelles.

2

The *Heidenkopf*

The 4th Division (VIII Corps) under Major-General Hon. W. Lambton was given the task of attacking the German lines between Beaumont and Serre. This portion of the German front line contained a distinctive feature known as the *Heidenkopf*, named after the German officer who had overseen its creation. It was part of the German line that extended far out into no man's land, a remnant of the heavy fighting against the French in June 1915. The British had named this location the Quadrilateral Redoubt as a result of its shape.

The men of 4th Division were given 3½ hours to advance 4,000 yards to the German Second Position. In order to achieve the goals set for the division the infantry was expected to advance at 50 yards per minute. The bombardment lasting seven days should have prepared the way by destroying the German trenches, wire entanglements, machine gun posts and either killing or incapacitating the garrison.

The British artillery plan on the day of the attack was the same as for the attack against Beaumont-Hamel. There would be six lifts of artillery fire in total. It also called for the entire VIII Corps heavy artillery to lift its fire from the German front lines at 7.20 a.m. to coincide with the mine explosion at Hawthorn Ridge. The heavy guns would then fire on the reserve trenches and at 7.25 a.m. they would be joined by the howitzers that had been firing on the support trenches. This left only a thin barrage of 18-pdr shrapnel fire along the front line trenches for the last 10 minutes before the infantry attack.

The bombardment had been considered a success. Numerous reports indicated that the wire entanglements and trenches were badly damaged and in some areas completely destroyed. Dugouts were crushed in and the occupants killed or seriously wounded. However, without any independent verification the latter claims were apparently based upon supposition alone.

Firsthand experiences by the front line troops provided a contradictory point of view. These experiences seemed to show that some of the reports were overly optimistic and were in direct contrast to the failure of the trench raids that took place during the course of the preliminary bombardment. In nearly every case the raiding parties sent out during the bombardment had come up against alert sentries, intact wire entanglements and extremely heavy and effective German resistance.

The apparent contradiction between the official reports and personal experiences led to confusion and anxiety in the minds of some British troops. On one hand they had been assured that the preparation fire would virtually eliminate German resistance. On the other hand if the bombardment had indeed successfully destroyed the enemy defenses and killed or incapacitated the garrison then the Germans would have been incapable of such active resistance against the raiding parties.

In one instance patrols sent out in the two nights before the attack from the 1st East Lancashire Regiment could find no appreciable gaps in the German wire. Both patrols reported the wire was insufficiently cut at the portion of the line they examined.

Infantrymen – RIR 121. (Author's collection)

The officers qualified their reports stating that they were unable to check or verify wire conditions along the entire battalion front. What they did not know was that the German wire was apparently intact for the most part in front of C and A Coy, the center and left hand portion of the battalion front in the upcoming attack.

A closer look at the German trenches would have revealed that while effective, the bombardment had not performed as had been expected. It was true that the German trenches were badly damaged but considering their depth and the extensive network of fire trenches, communication trenches and support lines even in a damaged condition they created a serious obstacle to any attack and provided ample cover for the defenders.

It was true that some of the wire entanglements were cut on the division front but in many cases it was only damaged and in some locations almost completely intact. Part of the problem in cutting the wire was the inability of the observers actually being able to see the entanglements in many locations due to the lay of the land. High grass also hid belts of wire from aerial observation quite effectively.

The 4th Division consisted of three brigades of infantry – the 10th, 11th and 12th. The 11th Brigade, commanded by Brigadier-General C.B. Prowse, would lead the attack. The plan called for the 11th Brigade to capture the 1st and 2nd objectives after which the 10th and 12th Brigades would pass through their ranks and assault the 3rd objective.

Three battalions would be in the front line and three more in support. The 1st Battalion East Lancashire Regiment was on the right, the 1st Rifle Brigade in the center and the 1/8th Royal Warwickshire on the left. The second line would consist of the 1st Hampshires, 1st Somerset Light Infantry and 1/6th Royal Warwickshire. Both the 1/6th and 1/8th Royal Warwickshire were on loan from the 48th Division.

Two communication tunnels; 'Cat' and 'Rat', had been constructed on the 4th Division front prior to the attack. The exits to these tunnels were positioned about ten yards from the German line and in accordance with the attack plan the exits were opened at 11 p.m. on 30 June. At 7.25 a.m. on the morning of 1 July a Lewis gun would be mounted at the exit of each tunnel that would provide fire support for the attacking troops.

The portion of the German front line being attacked by the 4th Division corresponded

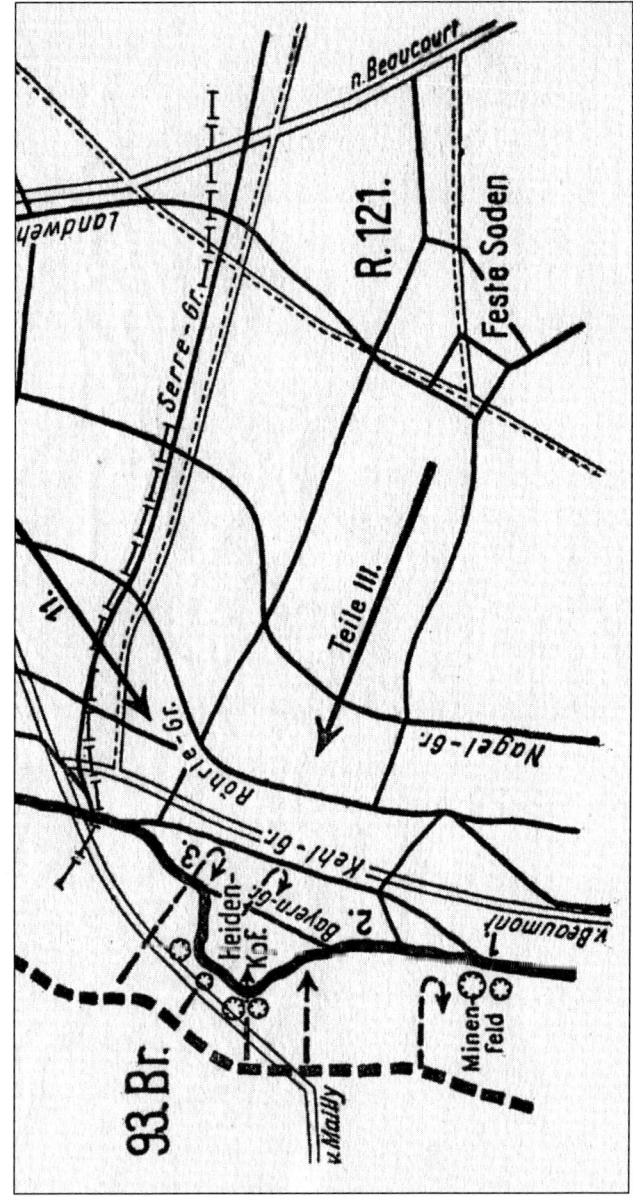

Map of the sector that included the *Heidenkopf* and RIR 121. While fairly accurate in regard to the German positions the placement of the attacking British units was often slightly off.

almost exactly to the sector being defended by (Württemberg) *Reserve Infanterie Regiment* 121. Two battalions of the regiment occupied the front line; on the left the II Battalion had three companies in the front line and one company in support. The right of the line, including the *Heidenkopf* was occupied by the I Battalion commanded by *Hauptmann* Winter following the death of *Hauptmann* Frhr. von Ziegesar several days earlier. The 3/ R121 was on the far right adjacent to the 52nd Division followed by the 2nd and 1/R121 with the 4th Coy in support. The sectors being held by the regiment were designated as H1 through H6. Each of the six sectors was held by an individual company. The four companies of the III/R121 were positioned in the rear support trenches, ready for action in the event they were needed.

Two machine gun companies had positioned their guns in strategic locations throughout the line in order to provide the greatest possible fire support during any attack against the regiment. The machine gun crews were very familiar with the sector and had range cards with full details for every possible target their weapons could reach. Multiple gun emplacements had been created to ensure that each weapon could be used to its maximum effectiveness. If an emplacement was damaged or destroyed the gun could quickly be moved and back in action within a short time.

Additional close support weapons available to the regiment included 2 heavy, 1 medium and 1 light *Minenwerfer* from *Minenwerfer* Coy 226 as well as *Erdmörsers, Priesterwerfer* and *Albrecht mörsers*. The latter were operated by men from RIR 121 and positioned at several locations in the regimental sector.

While the heavier *Minenwerfer* was slow to load the destructive effect of their large shells was devastating. The heavy shells could destroy anything within 10 meters of impact. The medium gun, 17cm caliber, was only slightly less destructive. The light, 7.6cm Minenwerfer shell was easier to load and had the highest rate of fire of all three weapons.

In times of great need the light *Minenwerfer* could achieve a rate of fire up to 48 rounds per minute. Setting the firing pin to the fired position and dropping the shells down into the tube as rapidly as possible after each one had fired accomplished this high rate of fire. This bypassed the normal method of operating the weapon by loading individual shells and using a lanyard to fire them. This rate of fire could only be kept up for a short period of time as the recoil mechanism of the gun could fail and place the gun out of action or the tube could crack or explode from the excessive use.

The projecting *Heidenkopf* was far too exposed to enemy fire and considered too vulnerable to attack. It had been evacuated during the week-long bombardment except for a *pionier* detachment, one machine gun and a small trench garrison from RIR 121.

Prior to the start of the British offensive four large mines had been created by the 4/13th *Pionier* Battalion, commanded by *Leutnant der Reserve* Eitel that had been spread across the face of the *Heidenkopf*. The mines were loaded with explosives during the week-long bombardment and made ready to detonate so they could be set off as the British infantry advanced. If timed properly, the mines would cause heavy losses among the attacking troops.

Four 7.7cm field gun batteries, one 10.5cm light field howitzer battery, one 15cm heavy field howitzer battery and one 21cm heavy mortar protected the sector held by RIR 121. These batteries would provide fire protection in accordance with the artillery plan set in place by the XIV Reserve Corps.

The British artillery fire reached unheard of strength in the final hours before the attack. Everything was ready to go; apparently nothing had been left to chance. As the

Infantrymen – 12/R121. (Author's collection)

shells fell along the German front lines it seemed that nothing could stop the 4th Division from reaching their objectives.

On the German side the men of RIR 121 spent the last few hours before the attack deep inside their mined dugouts. It was imperative that the trench sentries keep a close watch on the British lines so that the moment that the enemy artillery fire lifted from the German front line the trench garrison could be alerted and given time to exit their dugouts in order to meet the attack.

At 7.20 a.m. the mine under the nearby Hawthorn Redoubt was detonated. There would be a ten-minute delay before the infantry would begin their attack. This ten-minute delay would prove to be a fatal mistake on the part of the British planners along this portion of the front line as it had by Beaumont-Hamel.

The mine explosion was felt by many of the German defenders inside of their dugouts and it provided ample evidence that this was the day the attack was going to take place. However, the mine explosion was missed by many of the men because of the level of noise generated by the heavy bombardment. Still, when the heavy artillery lifted from the front line at the time of the explosion it only confirmed the opinion of many that the attack was imminent. Many of the trench sentries alerted the men inside the deep dugouts who then came up and manned their positions well before the British attack began.

While these events were taking place there was an ominous noise that could be heard between the shell detonations on the morning of 1 July. It was a sound that could be clearly heard even before the mine explosion at 7.20 a.m. It was the staccato bursts of fire from German machine guns firing intermittently on the British lines during the height of the final bombardment.

It was quite apparent that the machine guns had not been destroyed as expected by many. As the British infantry left the safety of their trenches and began to form up for the attack the German machine gun fire grew in intensity until it was continuous across the British front. The men began to suffer losses from this harassment fire but it was nothing close to what they would experience in the next few minutes.

> 07.25. Enemy machine guns opened up all along line. Three minutes later our troops are lined up lying on the parapet ready to advance.[1]

The tunnels 'Cat' and 'Rat' were manned at 7.25 a.m. according to plan and the Lewis guns were set up. These positions were quickly spotted by the men of RIR 121 and were covered in a hail of rifle and machine gun bullets. Within ten minutes both guns were out of action and the crews either dead or wounded. Bombing parties from RIR 121 then occupied the positions and proceeded to block off the tunnels leading back toward the British lines.

Just before the infantry attack on the morning of 1 July the men of the 4th Division sat on the parapet of their trench, cheering like mad 'just as though they were watching a firework display in a London park.'[2] Despite some earlier misgivings about the level of destruction of the German defenses it would seem that as in many similar instances, it is far easier to believe the good news than to accept potentially bad news. To one observer inside the German trenches there was no doubt that the attack was about to begin.

> The morning of 1 July arrived. Everything was enveloped in fumes and smoke. The bombardment, which had slackened to some extent, was mostly coming down on our batteries. As the visibility improved, I could see that the British trenches were overflowing with masses of troops. They stood there laughing and joking, some groups were having a quiet smoke, sitting on the parapet with all their equipment on. The enemy fire increased in intensity, reaching hurricane proportions toward 8.00 a.m. Suddenly it lifted onto our rear positions and we felt the earth shake violently – this was caused by a mine going off near Beaumont. In no time flat the slope opposite resembled an ant heap. Wave after wave of assaulting British troops hurled themselves forward through the dust and smoke towards our position. I was just able to report the start of the attack to Battalion Headquarters then my rearward communications, my underground cable, was cut. *Leutnant der Reserve* Beck[3]

The transfer of the last of the British artillery fire from the front line to the rear happened suddenly and without warning to the trench garrison. Due to the proximity of the opposing trenches the men of RIR 121 that were still sitting inside their deep dugouts had only a few moments to react before the British infantry would be upon them. Speed was critical at this juncture. The weeks and months of alarm training had all been worth the effort. As the men poured out of their dugouts the British columns were already from 30-50 meters in front of the German line. In a very few moments the noise from hundreds of rifles being fired joined the rattle of the machine guns.

The attack against the left wing of the II/R121 and the right wing of the I/R121 by the 1st East Lancaster and 1st Rifle Brigade was a disaster from the outset. At 7.26 a.m. the 1st East Lancashire formed in front of their trenches and began the attack. The men in the first wave soon came under accurate rifle and machine gun fire and began to suffer casualties.

The men in the first wave however were fortunate in that the German artillery fire had not yet started coming down on them.

Both battalions did come under deadly enfilade fire from Redan Redoubt in the center of the front opposite the division as well as heavy fire from the defenders in the front line and from reserves further to the rear on Beaucourt Spur. Heavy machine gun fire also came from the direction of the village of Beaumont. The German trenches were set up in a manner that allowed the men in the rear trenches to fire over the heads of the front line thereby increasing the level of defensive fire substantially.

When the assault began it was reported that some German machine guns were simply placed upon the parapet and the gunners fired belt after belt into the advancing British lines. The gunners simply swept the line from right to left and back again.

Support fire from the neighboring regiments would prove to be very effective in the defense of many German positions on July 1st. At least two machine guns from RIR 119, located directly south of RIR 121, opened fired on the advancing waves of 4th Division men.

Machine Gun No. 1 from the 2MG/R119 commanded by *Unteroffizier* Braungart fired at Sectors 40 and 41 (1st East Lancashire Regiment, 11th Brigade, 4th Division and 1st Lancashire Fusiliers, 86th Brigade, 29th Division). A captured Belgian Machine Gun under *Gefreiter* Bürk was also firing at Sectors 38, 39 and 40 at a range of 1,600 meters. His targets would have included the men of the 1st East Lancashire Regiment and possibly the left flank company of 1st Lancashire Fusiliers as mentioned in the previous chapter. Both of these guns contributed substantially to the successful defense of the trenches being held by RIR 121.[4]

At least two machine guns from RIR 121 had been placed on the German parapet and fired continuously, while another two in Ridge Redoubt fired throughout 1 July and were never silenced. The guns swept across no man's land and the British front line trenches.

Infantrymen – RIR 121. (Author's collection)

They not only shot down the leading battalions, but slaughtered the support battalions and prevented reinforcements and supplies moving forward and wounded men from making their way back to the rear.

Lieutenant-Colonel J.E. Green, commanding the 1st East Lancashire Regiment, was wounded during the attack and lay close to the German wire. He counted no less than eight German machine guns firing on his battalion. There was little that could be done in the face of such heavy fire.

The 1st Rifle Brigade in the center suffered heavy losses in the German fire even though the Riflemen were already at the German wire as the British shrapnel barrage lifted. The first lines of these battalions were literally mown down; according to the men from RIR 121 the British soldiers appeared to be terribly surprised by the strength of the German resistance and many of the attackers turned back. Most of the men from the 1st East Lancashire were stopped dead in their tracks before anyone had the opportunity of entering the German lines and the survivors looked for shelter in the numerous shell holes that covered no man's land.

2nd Lieutenant W.J. Page, the Intelligence officer of the 1st Battalion East Lancashire Regiment, accompanied his battalion as it crossed no man's land the morning of 1 July.

It is truly amazing that anyone could live in such a devastating fire, probably the heaviest artillery onslaught in history. Right, left and centre, shells were having their deadly effect. Cool marksmanship and MG bullets also found their numerous victims. Miraculously I advanced through this until I came to a slightly sunken road about midway in no man's land. Here I urged forward some men who were trying to find shelter from the deadly fire; they probably had right on their side. Later, as I approached the enemy wire, I saw and spoke to Lieutenant Layton ... A few seconds after speaking to Layton I was right against the German wire. It was quite intact on my immediate front. I should say we were about eight minutes after 'Zero', and the enemy was wholly and completely master of the situation, on the Battalion front at least. Though the Regiment had achieved little or nothing, I don't think any troops in the world could have done more under the circumstances. I distinctly remember a small group of enemy infantry standing on their parapet half left from where I stood. They were waving their caps on their wooden-handled grenades and shouting 'Come on English'. I commenced to empty my revolver into this group and as I did so one of our field guns – maybe from open sights – put its first shell right into the middle of them, so that target was disposed of.[5]

Many of the details of the attack are not known as some eyewitness accounts mention being unable to see more than a few yards to the left and right and the men had no idea how other parts of their own battalion were doing. One officer reported that as the companies came up to the German lines and could finally see the men from RIR 121 the battalion stopped and the men opened fire. As the second rank came up the men surged forward.

While the center and right companies of the 1st East Lancashire were held up in front of the German wire, B Coy, on the left, found most of the wire entanglements had been destroyed. It does appear that at least a small party of approximately 40 men from B Coy managed to enter the German lines near Ridge Redoubt. The men from the II/R121 immediately counter attacked and drove them back into no man's land. The survivors, some

Men from RIR 121 in the trenches. (Lawrence Brown)

10-12 men stopped near the German wire and opened fire on the *Württembergers*. There were simply too few men left and they were unable to establish a foothold in the German lines.

While the initial German reports indicated that the 1st Rifle Brigade had been stopped in its tracks it appears that the Riflemen had been slightly more successful in their attack. However it was short lived for the most part. The survivors on the right wing of this battalion advanced into the area known as the *Minenfeld*, the location of extensive mine warfare that contained numerous craters created by both sides in the last year and a half.

Heavy British trench mortar bombs had destroyed much of the German wire and badly damaged the trenches. Many of the dugout entrances had been either crushed or were severely damaged and difficult to exit quickly. The terrain was filled with smoke and dust making visibility difficult. The men of the 1st Rifle Brigade had been able to approach the former German front line in several locations. They did meet stiff resistance from small groups of *pioniers* from the 4/13th *Pioniers* but they were too few to prevent the men from the Rifle Brigade from entering the German lines.

One such penetration occurred in the sector held by the 1/R121, at the junction with the 7/R121. Almost immediately the huge leader of the 1st Company, *Hauptmann der Reserve* Gonsor, assembled a squad of his most capable men, including his runners and while throwing hand grenades he stormed out of the second trench over the open ground against the men from the Rifle Brigade. At the same time a reserve machine gun he had hastily set up stopped the following groups of British troops in their tracks.

His intrepid orderly, who had accompanied him through all of the fighting since the beginning of the war remained faithful and was beside him when he placed his hand upon the first captured machine gun.[6]

The neighboring 7/R121 on the left flank of the 1st Coy provided some welcome assistance. Bombing parties from the 7th Coy advanced from the left flank and after a short, vicious fight the position was free from the enemy. The invaders, if they were not dead or wounded, were driven back into no man's land. RIR 121 reported that after only an hour the entire position south of the *Heidenkopf* was back in their hands. The English Captain leading the advance was among those captured; he had been wounded in both arms by machine gun fire.

Reports came back to the British lines that a few men from the 1st East Lancashire and the right wing of the 1st Rifle Brigade had managed to enter the German trenches and in a few instances made it to the next support trench. Of these men only two were able to make their way back to the British lines safely once the fighting was over. This portion of the German lines, the sector held by the II/R121 and the left wing of the I/R121 were not seriously threatened for the remainder of the day.

One man, Captain M.G. Browne, an officer in the 1st Battalion East Lancaster Regiment, had been wounded by a rifle bullet in the right thigh shortly after reaching the German lines. He was waiting for the onset of darkness in order to make his way back to the British trenches. During the day he lay helpless directly in front of the German wire. Any noise or sudden movement could have resulted in having a hand grenade being thrown in his direction. Unfortunately, he did suffer additional wounds from hand grenade fragments, not from a German hand grenade but instead from a Mills bomb thrown from behind his position.

After waiting for several hours in the hot sun, a German soldier approached his position. All firing on this portion of the sector had ceased some hours earlier and all of the fighting was taking place further to the north by the *Heidenkopf*. The German soldier grabbed Captain Browne and dragged him back to the German front line trench.

Browne quickly realized that a German sentry post had been established only a few meters from his position. As he was helped into the trench he looked back over no man's land and saw that a broad stretch of it was colored khaki from the British dead and wounded that covered the ground.

Meanwhile the left hand company of the 1st Rifle Brigade and the right of the neighboring 1/8th Royal Warwickshire came to a swell of ground formed by Redan Ridge. While the men were exposed to enfilade fire from Ridge Redoubt, they received little direct fire. This would prove to be fortunate for many of the men, or at least it appeared so at the time. So far this part of the advance had gone according to plan:

07:30. Advance begins. Enemy first line reached and passed very quickly as also was the second. Only in one or two cases were any enemy seen in these two lines.[7]

According to the men from RIR 121 the terrain at the *Heidenkopf* and adjacent trenches was covered in smoke and dust that allowed the enemy to approach the German lines closely. Many of the dugout exits located in the sector held by the 3/R121 had either been closed or badly damaged from the heavy British fire. By the time the men of the 2nd and 3/R121 could make it out of their dugouts the British had already entered the position. The fighting was hand-to-hand in many places.

Few firsthand accounts exist from either side of the wire. Among those from the 4th Division was Company Sergeant Major Percy Chappell. He was in the 1st Somerset Light Infantry that was in the center of the second wave of troops in the 11th Brigade. While the first wave began the assault at 7.30 a.m. the second wave, including the 1st Somerset L.I. followed 10 minutes later.

CSM Chappell and his company did not wait for the allotted time and advanced toward the German lines earlier than scheduled. His company had almost reached the enemy wire entanglements when the German barrage fire came down well behind them.

According to Chappell the men of the 1st Rifle Brigade were held up at the German wire, and an indecisive bombing fight was taking place. Finally an officer stood up and shouted 'Come on lads, let them have it!'

The men rose up and rushed the Germans who bolted and fled. This freed the men from the 1st Somerset and 1st Rifle Brigade from being pinned down in no man's land. The survivors of the two battalions advanced into the damaged German trenches and found themselves inside the *Heidenkopf* but only in weak numbers. These men immediately started mopping up the position and consolidated the maze of trenches, searching dugouts and tunnels while others pushed on to the next line of German trenches.

Infantrymen – 3/R121. (Author's collection)

The men facing the *Heidenkopf* were quite fortunate. While delayed for a short time by the German garrison there were simply too few defenders to hold up the attack forever. The lone German machine gun located in the *Heidenkopf* might have suffered a jam and was no longer able to fire. It is also possible it was damaged or destroyed by the preliminary bombardment or during the infantry attack. Whatever the reason might be that the gun was not firing, the survivors of the two British battalions were still in sufficient strength to force the small trench garrison to retreat.

The actual events taking place inside the *Heidenkopf* with the German garrison will probably never be known as it has been reported that the defenders were all killed during the subsequent fighting. No firsthand accounts have been located during the intervening years as well. In any case the small numbers of Germans inside the position were not equipped to offer a sustained defense, they were assigned to detonate the four mines and then evacuate the position.

Leutnant der Reserve Beck watched the attack unfold by the sector held by the 3/R121:

> Elements of the first British wave had worked their way forward very close to our positions under cover of the artillery fire and general obscuration. At once they overran the dugouts of the left flank of the 3rd Company, which was located immediately to the left of the evacuated *Heidenkopf*. Following up in strength, the enemy broke through and began to attack 3rd Company from the flank and rear. Courageously the company began at once to defend itself.[8]

The left hand companies of the 1/8th Royal Warwickshire were less fortunate and quickly came under severe machine gun fire from their left flank. Many of the men were forced to take any cover they could find and only a few men managed to enter the German trenches. Their left flank was completely exposed by the failure of the troops of the neighboring 31st Division to successfully advance against Serre.

The Warwickshires continued to encounter heavy machine gun fire, especially from the direction of Serre. It was suspected that the Germans had hidden machine guns under the remains of burnt haystacks in the sector held by IR 169. The machine guns from the neighboring IR 169 had most likely just turned their guns to enfilade the advancing troops of the 4th Division after successfully repelling the attack by the 31st Division. They simply had too few targets left to fire at on their own front.

Observers in the German lines such as *Leutnant der Reserve* Beck had watched the British troops advance. Some telephone lines remained intact despite the British artillery fire and reports of the attack were quickly relayed to the artillery batteries in the rear. In other instances the observers used flares calling for defensive artillery fire on their sector of the front.

> Desperately I fired off red flares calling for defensive fire which would interdict the further move forward of the masses of the enemy. But only a few guns responded. Nevertheless, the advancing enemy was so thickly massed that every shell found its mark. Now I noticed the effect of some of the machine guns, which were cutting down the enemy in waves just like mowing machines.[9]

The German artillery, while not overly powerful, was still very active during the last

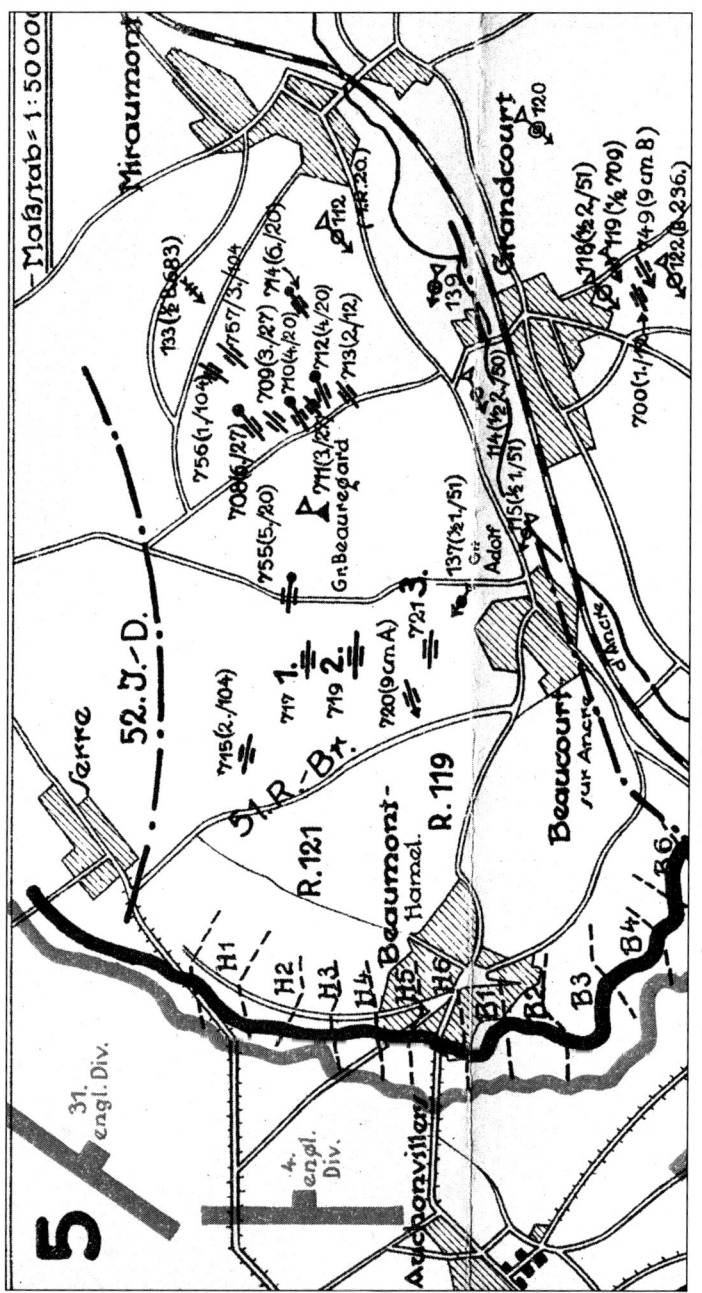

German battery positions behind RIR 121. The positions numbered 1., 2. and 3. in the center indicate batteries from the 26th RFAR.

seven days with some batteries firing up to 4,500 shells during this time. The fire from these guns continued on the morning of 1 July causing a number of losses in the British assembly trenches before Zero hour. One shell even managed to damage a 6-inch water main, badly flooding some trenches on the 4th Division front.

Red flares rose high up into the sky all across the German front line as the British infantry advanced. With the receipt of the reports of the British infantry attack combined with the numerous light signals it was obvious to the battery commanders that the attack had begun. Every available gun now fired on pre-arranged target areas. The lighter guns, the 7.7cm field guns and 10.5cm light field howitzers would concentrate their fire on the waves of British troops and across no man's land to form a fire barrier.

The heavier guns, the 15cm heavy field howitzers and the 21cm mortar fired into the enemy trenches and assembly areas where they would systematically search out and destroy the British trenches and subsequent assault waves. At this point the full effect of the German artillery barrage fell upon the advancing British troops and tore huge gaps in the their ranks.

The men of the 1st Hampshire Battalion came under fire from the 2nd and 3/RFAR 26 in Battery positions 719 and 721 respectively. The 1st Somerset Light Infantry following the 1st Rifle Brigade came under fire from the 1/RFAR 26 in Battery position 717 as well as from 10.5cm light field howitzers from the 5/FAR 20 located in Battery position 755.

The British communication trenches and assembly areas in the rear of these battalions were being systematically destroyed by the fire from the German heavy guns; two Russian 15cm heavy field howitzers from the 1/*Fuss Artillerie Regiment.* 51 located in Battery position 115 and one Russian 21cm heavy mortar from Battery 749 located in Battery position 139. All of the heavy guns were located in the vicinity of Grandcourt.

According to the British Official History, the barrage was put down in 'crumps' on small sections of trench and after about 10 minutes shifted fire to another section. The fire was so severe and systematic that for a distance of 50 yards from the front line no solid ground was left, nothing but a wilderness of shell holes.

Another unpleasant surprise occurred when the German artillery opened fire. It was apparent that some batteries located in the sector of the neighboring 52nd Division had also joined the barrage fire. 'The volume and accuracy of their fire disorganized the attack at the very onset.'[10]

Once the German barrage fire began to fall across no man's land and the British front line trenches in addition to the heavy machine gun fire all hope of any subsequent waves making it across no man's land was extinguished. The German defensive artillery fire missed many of the men involved in the first wave of the attack but caught the following waves as they crossed no man's land.

The few men who had made it safely to the German trenches were now cut off from nearly all support. Further reinforcements, supplies of food, water and ammunition could not make it across the open terrain in any appreciable numbers. Any attempt immediately came under heavy and accurate fire.

As soon as the attack started the *Minenwerfers* and other close range weapons quickly joined the fight against the advancing British troops, their huge shells causing heavy losses in the lines of British troops. *Leutnant der Reserve* Beck:

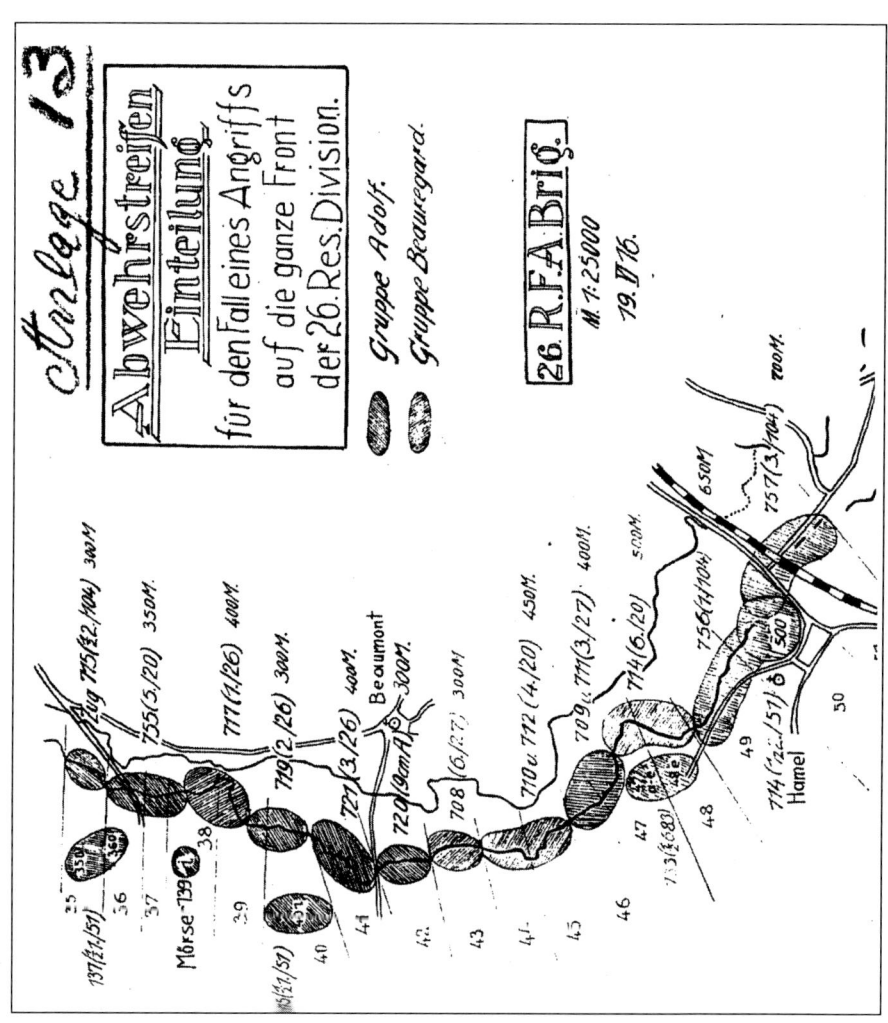

Sectors covered by the different battery positions on 1 July 1916.

Infantryman – 5/R121. (Author's collection)

Our somewhat primitive earth mortars also had an appalling effect, tearing great holes in the ranks of the British who were strolling happily forward. On one occasion I saw one of the barrel-like rounds curving up in a great arc to land next to a British section. The British stood stock still in surprise then one went over to see what it was and called the remainder to satisfy their curiosity. I could hardly have hatched a more diabolical plan if I had tried, because suddenly there was just a great black cloud there and bodies were flying in all directions through the air. One of them, a tall Scot, came down on a steel post which had been part of our destroyed barbed wire obstacle and was spitted straight under his lower jaw. Thereafter I was faced with the gruesome sight of a death's head staring at me.[11]

At least one *Minenwerfer* located in *Beaumont Nord* became placed out of action during 1 July. The gun crew quickly joined the trench garrison and took part in the defense of the trenches. They gave particularly important assistance to *Gruppen* Zorn, 5/R121.

The heavy German fire would have the most devastating affect against the battalions in the second British wave. At 7.40 a.m. three supporting battalions of the 11th Brigade advanced. On the right the 1st Hampshires, like the greater part of 1st East Lancashires in front, was unable to reach the German lines. The survivors took cover in the mass of shell holes between the opposing front lines and quickly became mixed together with the 1st East Lancashire men.

CSM Chappell recalled the German defensive barrage as it fell on the second wave of

Infantryman – RIR121. (Author's collection)

troops. While looking back from his position at the edge of the *Heidenkopf* Chappell saw the companies of his battalion advancing without hesitation into the line of shell bursts and reappear on the opposite side just as steady but pitifully reduced in numbers. Many of the wounded kept advancing until they were no longer physically able to continue.

The 1/6th Royal Warwickshire on the left of the attack advanced in support of its sister battalion a mere seven minutes after the first wave. In this brief period of time the battalion was decimated by German artillery and machine gun fire. While the right hand companies were able to make their way into the German lines and link up with their sister battalion the left hand companies came under the same machine gun fire from IR 169 that stopped parts of the 1/8th Royal Warwickshire a short time earlier. Unable to make any headway the men were forced to take cover as best they could in no man's land.

To many of the men of RIR 121 it seemed that a short time after the attack began nearly everyone on the British side who was still able to walk had flooded back to their starting position. The others were either killed or wounded and some of those that were still living had taken refuge in one of the many shell craters that dotted the landscape.

The survivors of both Warwickshire battalions advanced and established contact with the forward elements of the Rifle Brigade and Somerset Light Infantry. The Warwickshire companies on the left, continuing to suffer heavy losses from the fire of the machine guns near Serre were unable to make any progress despite repeated attempts to do so.

As the British troops pushed through the unfamiliar maze of trenches, small battles broke out as they came up against pockets of German resistance or trench blocks. As time passed there were fewer and fewer men available to continue the advance and German resistance stiffened as support troops moved into position.

> Having plenty of casualties from machine-gun fire in enemy third and fourth line. At the third line we were temporarily held up by machine-gun fire but took it by rushes. From this point the fighting was all with bombs, along trenches. 1/8th Royal Warwickshire battalion[12]

One of the delays experienced by the Warwickshire battalion was caused by the sudden appearance of a machine gun that, in the words of prisoners captured later in the fighting, was apparently completely unexpected. *Leutnant der Reserve* Wilhelm Bühler, who was wounded and bleeding from his hand and arm, had a reserve machine gun brought up from a dugout.[13] The machine gun placed upon the parapet opened fire into the attacking troops at close range. The effect was devastating as the men were caught in the open by the point blank fire from an unexpected source which caused them to hesitate.

At another location a platoon leader in the 3/R121, a *Leutnant* with a small group of his men, created a barricade inside a communication trench and blocked the route of the advancing Warwickshire battalions. In the ensuing fight the officer was killed by a hand grenade and some of his men also became casualties but the British were successfully stopped and could proceed no further at this point.

The remnants of the 3/R121 were being pushed back deeper and deeper into the German lines. However with each encounter the advancing British troops grew fewer and fewer and were eventually forced to halt. They had just enough men to hold the newly captured position and there were no reserves at hand nor was there any possibility of obtaining reinforcements.

The Warwickshire battalions eventually reached the third trench line and the near edge of the *Heidenkopf*. There was no support on the left where the 31st Division was hung up in front of Serre. The battalions made good their objectives, the *Heidenkopf* and the cutting beyond. By 11 a.m. 2nd Lieutenant J.G. Cooper was the only officer of the 1/6th Warwickshire not killed or wounded. The number of men still capable of providing a defense was pitifully small. The remainder lay scattered throughout the German trenches and no man's land, wounded or dead. The air was filled by machine gun fire and any attempt to move outside of the trenches would be fatal.

> We reached our objective probably in 35-40 minutes from zero hour and at once commenced consolidating and cleaning rifles under the directions of Captain Martin and 2nd Lt Turner. By this time the next battalion was arriving (1/6th Royal Warwickshire) but had had so many casualties that they could not go through us so helped consolidating. This happened with all battalions following us. 1/8th Royal Warwickshire battalion[14]

In the center, the 1st Somerset Light Infantry was forced to incline to the left while advancing. The Somersets should have crossed Redan Ridge but it was being continuously swept by machine gun fire. The men who had survived the crossing of no man's land entered the German trenches and reinforced the companies of the Rifle Brigade and the Warwickshires in the *Heidenkopf*.

Small parties of the Rifle Brigade and Somerset Light Infantry were able to penetrate separately into the German position, and enter the *Heidenkopf*. After crossing the front line they gained the support trench beyond it on a frontage of 600 yards.

Among the men who advanced deeper into the German trench system was CSM Chappell who, with a small group of men, reached the German 3rd trench. They found the trench free of German soldiers and began to consolidate their new position. Some of Chappell's men checked the nearby dugouts to make sure they too were empty. Barbed wire blocks were set up at both ends of their small section of trench. The party consisted of one officer and eleven other ranks, far too few to hold the trench very long in the face of a determined German counter attack.

As was the case with many small groups of men on both sides of the fighting, the noise of the battle appeared all around them but it was unusually quiet in their vicinity. From everything they could tell, there were apparently no Germans nearby. With the men occupying the deep trenches little could be seen of the surrounding countryside and visibility was limited to a few meters in places. It was impossible to tell if the next traverse was occupied by Germans or friendly forces and it was dangerous to stick their heads too far out of the trench due to the intensity of the fire.

For men such as *Leutnant der Reserve* Beck, sitting inside his observation post the war was to come all too close as a British party approached his position.

> The next few moments would determine my fate. A strong group came to the entrance to my turret and bawled 'Germans?' No reply! Two hand grenades came flying in, but were trapped by the timber framework. They exploded wrecking the timber and doing my hearing no good. A second group was hard on their heels, but when they saw the damage to the dugout entrance paid it no more attention. To check on the situation I crawled out later and looked over the edge of a crater towards the rear. Not ten meters behind my cupola I saw a British outpost armed with a machine gun and radio equipment manning a sandbag wall. Instantly I disappeared once more and waited for darkness so I could break through to our lines under the cover of darkness.[15]

The officer with Chappell, a captain, felt they needed to reconnoiter further and he ordered Chappell and a sergeant to accompany him. The three men went through an empty communication trench and reached the next German trench that was also empty. They felt it was odd being so deep into the enemy lines with no Germans about.

At this point the reconnaissance party met a wounded Somersets officer. The officers consulted for a short time and decided they would go to the rear and obtain new orders in light of their present circumstances. As the senior NCO Chappell was left in charge of the remaining men.

Chappell and his companion were discussing what to do next when the noise of a fierce bombing fight broke out behind them. It quickly became apparent that they were cut off from their men who were under heavy attack. At the same time a group of Germans appeared over a rise in front of them and started throwing hand grenades. Fortunately for Chappell and the sergeant, the hand grenades fell short of their position. Still, it was only a matter of time until the Germans could work close enough to their position where they would be in range of the bombers.

Chappell and the sergeant decided to make a run for it. They climbed out of the trench

Infantryman – RIR 121. (Author's collection)

and began to run across the open ground, taking cover as they moved from shell hole to shell hole. When Chappell dropped into an empty trench he looked back and saw no sign of his companion.

Chappell looked around and saw British soldiers some 150 yards distant. Between him and the soldiers was a trench occupied by Germans. He hesitated momentarily until a hand grenade burst nearby and this convinced him to go. He climbed up onto the parapet and ran toward the British soldiers while bullets whistled by him; he was not hit. He leaped over the German occupied trench safely while on the run and still was not hit by any fire. It is most likely he surprised the Germans who did not have time to react before he was gone. He made it to the British troops safely and found himself with a Lieutenant Colonel of the Seaforth Highlanders who was organizing a defense of the redoubt.

The position was vulnerable as it was overlooked by the Germans who could fire directly into the trench. The Lieutenant Colonel decided the threat had to be eliminated. His plan called for 5 rounds rapid and then a charge but as preparations were being made a Seaforth corporal collected an armful of hand grenades and started walking toward the German position, swearing and throwing hand grenades as he went. While he caused confusion and losses among the Germans he fell dead from rifle fire as he reached the trench. His actions inspired the rest of the British troops who then charged and cleared the German defenders. It proved to be the deepest point of penetration into the German trenches.

After the assault on the trench it grew quiet again. Now there were men from 5 different battalions inside the redoubt. In an attempt to organize the overall defense of the position each unit was given the responsibility of defending a specific portion of the occupied trenches.

Chappell found himself with about 50 men from the Somerset Light Infantry and he took charge of the group. He went about preparing his allotted sector for defense. The men were low on ammunition and searched the nearby dugouts for supplies. They found a large stock of German hand grenades. What followed were long periods of calm that were interrupted by several German attacks, all of which were repulsed.

By the time the British had been stopped almost the entire position of the 3/R121 had been lost. A small part of the 3rd Coy had been able to withdraw in the face of the enemy advance and still provided some resistance as they fell back toward the rear. However, the largest part lay trapped inside the numerous dugouts in the sector. These men were exhausted and thirsty; many were bleeding from their wounds as they waited deep under the earth for their comrades to rescue them.

Among the missing men of the 3/R121 was the company commander, *Oberleutnant* Max Lutz. Lutz had been slightly wounded and had taken refuge inside his dugout with some of his men. With the loss of virtually the entire sector held by the 3/R121, immediate steps needed to be taken in order to eject the British troops and restore the position. The closest troops at hand came from the 4/R121, the battalion reserve.

During the fighting the 4/R121 had been placed on alert and took up positions to contain the British penetration. However simply containing the enemy was not the objective, it was necessary to eject them from the German lines and drive them back to their own trenches.

Bombing parties supported by infantrymen began to advance against the British held trenches. An *Unteroffizier* from the 4/R121 who had already been awarded the Iron Cross I Class for his outstanding patrol work was among the first involved in containing the British advance and to take part in the counter attack. He took his detachment and advanced from shell crater to shell crater. It was difficult work as 'the brave adversary fought back with admirable tenacity.'[16]

As reports of the British penetration of the regimental sector reached the commander of RIR 121, *Oberst* Josenhans, he was determined to act decisively. He ordered an immediate counter-attack. The garrison in the rear trenches was already taking part, their machine guns mowing down the following British waves as they attempted to cross no man's land. Additional bombing parties had been established from the ranks of the III/R121 across the regimental sector, many of them advancing over the banks and across open ground or through the maze of trenches, all the while slowly driving the English back. The Warwickshires recalled:

> Many times we were bombed from this position and regained it until bombs ran out. We had to retire to the third line, line the parapet and hold on with machine and rifle fire. Parties were detailed to collect as many bombs as could be found (both English and German) and when we had a good store we again reached our objective. No supply of bombs was coming from the rear so could not hold on and retired again. Enemy machine-guns and snipers were doing great amount of damage all the while. Enemy artillery opened but fortunately their range was over.[17]

Inside the occupied German trenches the British reportedly placed sentries at the

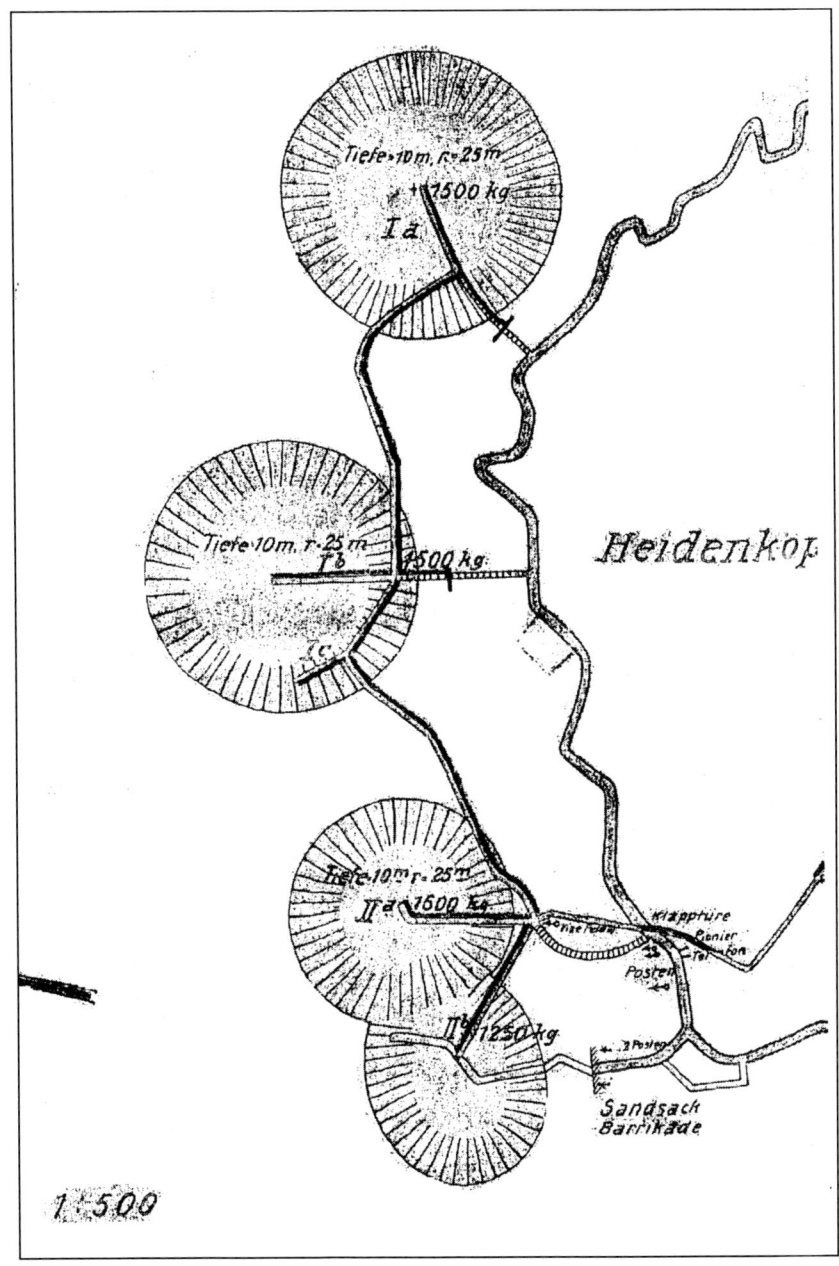

Sketch of the 4 mines placed in front of the *Heidenkopf*.

dugout exits but did not venture down into the depths. According to the men of RIR 121 they feared the unfamiliar world of the dugouts. There were simply too few British troops inside the German trenches and every man was needed to defend the position, no one could be spared to search all of the German dugouts. The occupants of the dugouts also reported that hand grenade and smoke bombs flew down from time to time. 'However no one who was trapped thought to surrender.'[18]

As the struggle continued deep inside the German lines the British commanders in the rear were in the dark as to what was happening. Visibility was very difficult in the heavy smoke and dust. Even observation aircraft flying barely 50 feet above the ground were unable to determine the exact location of friendly troops. From what it appeared portions of the 4th Division had successfully broken through the German front, which was confirmed by reports from the neighboring 31st Division.

While the men of the 11th Brigade were involved in heavy fighting inside the German trenches there had been several attempts to send reinforcements and supplies to the beleaguered men. The battalions of the 10th and 12th Brigades had prepared to move forward in order to advance as the second wave of the attack at 9.30 a.m. Given the uncertain situation at the front and the heavy German fire the 4th Division issued orders to postpone the assault until the overall situation could be cleared up.

The lead battalions of the 10th and 12th Brigades did not receive the message in time. They were actually slightly ahead of schedule and began the advance with 4½ battalions in extended lines on a front 1,500 yards wide. The 2nd Royal Dublin Fusiliers, 2nd Seaforth Highlanders (10th Brigade) were on the right and the 2nd Essex, 1st King's Own with half of the 2nd Lancashire Fusiliers (12th Brigade) on the left.

The 2nd Essex and 1st King's Own advanced on the original frontage of the left wing of the Rifle Brigade and the 1/8th Royal Warwickshire. They too suffered heavily from artillery and machine gun fire in no man's land. The King's Own also suffered losses when two of the mines in front of the *Heidenkopf* were detonated under the advancing men. Given the time of the mine detonations it would be reasonable to assume that somewhere within the *Heidenkopf* a small contingent of German soldiers had been missed when the redoubt had been overrun. The Germans not only could observe the advancing British troops, they were able to set off the mines as planned.

Attempts were made by the Germans following the recapture of the redoubt to determine what had happened with the four mines. A report from the *pioniers* indicated that they could find no trace of the security garrison of the *Heidenkopf* and the mined dugout containing the detonators used to set off the mines. There was no information concerning the fate of these men and the officer that had been left in charge was found lying dead inside the *Bayern Graben*. All that could be determined was that the mines did detonate, leaving four craters spread across the front of the redoubt.

Despite the mines and heavy fire some men still managed to reach the German lines. Once inside the relative safety of the German trenches the survivors made their way to the furthest trench occupied by the 11th Brigade.

The leading companies of the Dublin Fusiliers came under heavy fire the moment they started the attack, not only from Ridge Redoubt and adjacent trenches, but from Beaumont Hamel as well. Only a few men eventually reached the German position. The commanders of the companies following the Fusiliers observed what had happened to the lead companies and as a result kept their men back inside the British trenches.

The Seaforths and Lancashire Fusiliers inclined to the left under the relentless German fire and found some shelter under the north side of Redan Ridge. By this movement they were able to avoid machine gun fire from Beaumont Hamel. They crossed the German front line near the *Heidenkopf* and continued to advance and reinforced the weak remnants of the 11th Brigade.

Shortly before 11 a.m. the remaining two companies of the 2nd Lancashire Fusiliers and one company from the 2nd Duke of Wellington's (12th Brigade) had been able to cross no man's land while suffering heavy losses and reinforce the garrison in the *Heidenkopf* and the adjacent trenches; however little other assistance could be provided.

Soon after 11 a.m. German bombing parties had worked forward and around the flanks of the British penetration by making use of the numerous shell craters that scarred the ground. At the same time strong bombing parties attacked down the trenches from the north and from Serre, against the flank and rear of the surviving Warwickshire men.

By noon the remnants of the British troops fighting inside the German trenches were short of hand grenades and ammunition. The men were forced to fall back to the redoubt in response to the constant German attacks. The dwindling numbers of defenders left after each attack were simply done in.

Walter Ritchie, a drummer in the Seaforth Highlanders, was awarded the Victoria Cross for his actions on 1 July. The constant German pressure was apparently causing some men to retire without orders. He stood on the parapet of the trench in the *Heidenkopf* and repeatedly sounded 'charge' to encourage the men. Ritchie not only survived the fighting on 1 July, he also survived the war. Orders or not, the men who had survived the heavy fighting simply had enough. The trenches were disorganized and filled with wounded and dead.

Lack of food, water and especially ammunition were quickly becoming critical and there was little hope of fresh supplies of reaching the men fighting inside the German lines. The 11th Brigade and the two battalions from the 143rd Brigade had already suffered heavy losses by this point of the battle. 90 officers, 1,948 Other Ranks of the 4,500 officers and men who had gone into action were either killed, wounded or missing.

The men trapped in no man's land were in constant danger of being killed or wounded from the German shellfire and sweeping machine gun fire, unable to advance or retire. Only darkness would allow many of these men to make their way back to the British lines and that was many hours away. For some of the wounded it was too long to wait and many succumbed to their injuries before any rescue was possible.

British artillery observation posts could see some of the events unfolding on the other side of the wire. What they could see was that the men inside the German trenches were running short of hand grenades. Without hand grenades the men were forced to rely upon rifle fire to keep the Germans back. Since most of the fighting was from traverse to traverse inside the trenches the hand grenade was the most effective weapon and without them the British were gradually being forced to retire.

More bombing counter-attacks could be seen coming from the direction of Serre. The situation was confusing as no exact information could be established of the location and results of the 4th Division. The signals, 1 white flare for 'stopped by uncut wire' and 3 white flares for 'objective gained' could not be distinguished in the smoke, dust and debris that filled the air and proved to be useless.

Observers in the British trenches were still having great difficulties determining what

'Funf Weiden' Pionier Park. (*Die 26. Reserve Division 1914-1918*)

was taking place inside the German lines. It was believed that small parties of the 10th and 12th Brigades had managed to enter Munich Trench and pass beyond it to the edge of Pendant Copse. Other reports indicated that some British infantry had been seen entering the village of Serre. Considering what had happened to the neighboring 31st Division troops it is highly improbable any substantial numbers of British troops had reached Pendant Copse let alone Serre.

What did become known after the fighting was over was that a large number of men who had penetrated the German lines had been shot down by the Germans who came in from behind them from the trenches on both flanks where the 29th and 31st Divisions had failed in their attacks.

Additional attempts to advance across no man's land were made by the 10th Brigade, all ended up being stopped in their tracks. As the men exited their trenches they suffered huge losses from German shellfire and machine gun fire before making any headway at all. The level of fire was so great that all further attempts to advance were canceled.

At 2.55 p.m. Major General Lambton reported to Corps that his division had suffered heavy losses and that no further attack was possible that day. The reality is that two German battalions with support from a third had completely stopped the 4th Division cold. Shortly after 4 p.m. aerial observation finally discovered small pockets of British troops in areas previously thought to be held in force.

Reinforcements from the III/R121 had arrived on the scene from the rear support trenches during the course of the fighting. The constant counter-attacks by the battalion bombing parties, the 4/R121 and from a neighboring regiment gradually pressed back the

Infantrymen – 2/R121. (Author's collection)

stubbornly resisting adversary in bloody fighting.

The desire to help drive out the British seemed to grip everyone in the regiment. One man assigned to assist the regimental medical staff abandoned his duties in order to fight at the front. *Oberstabsarzt* Dr. Schwarz related a story of this man who had gone to the kitchen at the *'Funf Weiden'* [Five Willows] in the morning of 1 July with some mess kits to get coffee. On the return route to the medical dugout he looked for cover from the artillery fire. However when he found out that the English had penetrated into the position he dropped his full mess kits into the corner, tore a rifle out of the hands of a wounded man and rushed out with the words: 'With that I must be there!'

Reinforcements from the III/R121 continued to arrive on the scene from the rear support trenches during the course of the fighting. The constant counter-attacks by the battalion bombing parties, by the 4/R121 and finally detachments from the neighboring IR 169 gradually pressed back the stubbornly resisting adversary in bloody fighting in the I/R121 sector.

The enemy penetration in the 3rd Coy sector was now contained by the 4/R121 with additional support arriving from the III/R121. Trenches to the south were blocked off by the 1st and 2/R121 while any attempt to advance into the sector held by IR 169 was contained by trench blocks and by heavy machine gun fire. Every attempt by the British to bring up reinforcements or supplies was prevented and any attempt to cross the open fields was destroyed by machine gun, infantry and artillery fire.

The men from RIR 121 reported that each time they drove the British from one position they quickly settled in over and over again, setting up trench blocks behind piles of sandbags and installed machine guns and light mine throwers. Each attack resulted in more losses for the British troops as well as the attackers.

While RIR 121 was battling the men from the 4th Division assistance had arrived from the neighboring IR 169. This help was supplied without being requested. The officers of IR 169 had understood the need to protect their flank and prevent a possible breakthrough. If the enemy was allowed to occupy the *Heidenkopf*, also called the *Löwenrücken* [Lion's Back] by the Baden regiment, it could make the position held by IR 169 untenable.

There was a slight delay in sending support to the neighboring RIR 121. A small number of British troops had managed to penetrate the German lines in Sector S2 by Serre. This danger was resolved a short time later and was followed by a report from the 7/169 'that the Tommies in Sector S2 are not growing old'. *Feldwebel* Nold, holder of the Prussian Military Service Cross, commonly called the other ranks' Pour le Merite, and his platoon, had made short work of the invaders.

This was all that was needed to allow some of the men to proceed to the neighboring RIR 121 and offer their assistance. While preparations were being made the third platoon of the 11/169 under *Leutnant* Johannes Hoppe secured the left flank of IR 169 and prevented the English from penetrating it despite all of their efforts.

One platoon from the 11/169 under *Leutnant der Reserve* Gattner reinforced the 3/R121. Upon arrival they found only a few men left of this company who were involved in a fierce hand grenade fight. The company leader, who was reported to be severely wounded, was trapped inside a dugout along with several other wounded men in the area controlled by the British. Reports also indicated that all three of the platoon leaders in the 3/R121 had been killed or wounded.

20 year old *Leutnant* Friedrich Hoppe[19] and his platoon advanced toward the *Heidenkopf* that was covered in smoke from the impacts of British mines. Determined hand grenade attacks by *Leutnant* Hoppe slowly threw the English back and at the same time freed many of their wounded comrades from their dugouts. The leader of the 3/R121 and his comrades were among those rescued. Hoppe described the effect of the strain on Lutz, the leader of the 3/R121 'whose face appears to be no longer of this world from the inhumanly hard struggle.' Hoppe's platoon supplied ten men as reinforcements to the small group that *Oberleutnant* Lutz had with him.

Leutnant Hoppe was now faced with the task of attacking what was thought to be an entrenched English battalion with his one infantry platoon consisting of approximately 40 *Musketiers*. Despite these odds Hoppe and his men attacked each British trench block. Platoon Hoppe attacked four barricades inside the trenches. Each had been quickly thrown up utilizing sandbags, bodies of fallen men and any other obstacle at hand. Each barricade fell to the determined attacks of the men from IR 169.

By the third barricade the platoon consisted of *Leutnant* Hoppe, *Vizefeldwebel* Haid and approximately 17 men. Despite the small size of his force he still had orders to eliminate the British from the *Heidenkopf* and the attacks continued until finally their supply of hand grenades ran out.

At the last barricade the last of the hand grenades were used to dislodge the British defenders. A cheer rose from the throats of the men as they advanced with fixed bayonets and stormed the barricade. The British defenders had already run out of hand grenades and were unable to effectively defend their position.

When the fighting was over *Leutnant* Hoppe reported that the first platoon of the 11/169 had fulfilled its mission, the *Heidenkopf* was clear of enemy troops. His men had been fighting nearly non-stop for seven hours.

The *Swabians* of RIR 121 were also full of ardor and did not let up in their attacks. The bitter close quarter fighting lasted the entire day and the British defenders did not yield until the onset of darkness. Much of the lost position was back in German hands. The trenches were a shambles, filled with pieces of equipment and the dead from both sides.

> Our trenches were a horrible sight. Up to five and six lay on top of each other. Friend and foe, horribly mutilated by the hand grenades in the close combat that surged back and forth.[20]

The bombing parties continued to maintain close contact with the British, never relenting in their desire to drive the invaders from their trenches entirely. The British finally yielded to the rear at about 7 p.m. The remnants of Platoon Hoppe maintained heavy fire against the withdrawing British troops while standing upright. Hoppe and his men had captured approximately 40 prisoners and taken three machine guns. Only a small portion of the German lines in the *Heidenkopf* still remained in enemy hands. The fighting generally died down as darkness fell.

> The Tommies fall in the flanking fire of our machine guns on the northern slope of the hill. Again, the English soldiers have fallen to the earth in rows. Reaper's death![21]

When darkness fell no man's land suddenly became alive as many of the survivors of the morning attacks began to work their way back toward the British trenches. 2nd Lieutenant W.J. Page, 1st Battalion East Lancashire Regiment, was among the many men who had spent the entire day trapped in no man's land under the hot July sun. He was with a small group of men from his battalion and as they were so close to the German trenches they had to maintain strict silence and restrict all movement as they were well within German hand grenade range.

> The fall of a day like July 1st can bring no night in our accepted sense, just darkness on the same awful scene, like dusk coming down on a leaf strewn lawn in autumn time. But most of the leaves on the Somme fields lay still; some turned, some murmured in pain. Such was the scene as the last two men of the Regiment turned from their objective – and incidentally their home since 6.30 a.m. – the German wire. They stepped between the leaves. Occasional voices spoke a dying word. Some were tenderly placed in shell holes in the hope of just a little cover for a short time. But the position of the two fugitives themselves was difficult indeed; they were endeavoring to return to their 'taking off' trenches, but could do nothing but meander from one groaning figure to another, and give a word of hope and cheer, trying to take a course for the British lines, encircled in a perfect ring of verey lights and explosions of every kind. Taking this course was extremely difficult; a circle of lights, sudden bursts of machine gun fire, and salvos from guns, demanded rushes for cover to the nearest shell hole. Then darkness, then straying to help some wounded comrade, then to give water to another, all this made the return course extremely difficult.[22]

Page and his companion eventually made it safely to the British lines completely exhausted. They were among a very few officers of the battalion that had survived the day unscathed.

At the same time the British wounded were making their way to safety the men of RIR 121 were also using the cover of darkness to improve their positions. Small parties

British prisoners near the *Heidenkopf*, 1 July 1916. (Author's collection)

of Germans moved through the trenches trying to establish the location of the enemy so that the attacks could continue the following day. There was still heavy fire from numerous machine guns spreading across the terrain making it difficult to move at times. Overall, the situation on both sides was still unclear and it would not be until the sun came up on 2 July when the men could see once more.

> Just as it began to go dark there was a sharp exchange of artillery fire, which began to fall in my area. I made use of this to get past the British party. I crawled and slid across country towards the rear. Because I did not know how far the British had penetrated, I did not dare to speak or attempt to make contact with the occupants of a dugout until I reached the *Nagelgraben*. Here I linked up with comrades from the 12th Company and, when I discovered that the counter-attack was under way. I gathered a few comrades and headed off to deal with the block by my cupola. When we got to grenade throwing range, we discovered that the job had already been done. The bodies of three British soldiers lay tangled up with the damaged machine gun and the radio equipment. I then raced forward to join my company in the front line trenches, which had been captured by the 4th Company, supported by other companies of the regiment and a platoon of IR 169, our neighboring regiment to the right. *Leutnant der Reserve* Beck, 3/R121[23]

Following the day of heavy fighting it became obvious to the handful of British troops still inside German lines that the small section of trench still held by the 4th Division was untenable. Few supports or supplies could make it across no man's land as a result of the heavy German fire. Without supplies of food, water, ammunition and hand grenades it was only a matter of time until the men of RIR 121 recaptured the entire position.

Also, the Germans did not relent in their attacks as darkness fell, as it was imperative that the English nest still existing in the *Heidenkopf* was cleared as quickly as possible.

British prisoners and their captors on the Somme. (*An der Somme*)

Bitter close combat took place at numerous locations inside the *Heidenkopf* as one British trench block after another was eliminated.

During the night small groups of men were sent back to the British lines. As British began to exit the *Heidenkopf* the struggle took place for the *Bayern Graben*. The German counter attacks did lose some of their impetus when the supply of hand grenades began to run out. Fresh supplies were quickly brought forward along with additional support from the III/R121 and the attacks continued.

The remaining British garrison inside the redoubt was very hungry and several scroungers were sent out to locate any food in the dugouts. They retuned with dark bread, cold stew, cigars and several tins of British Bully Beef. The bread and stew were ignored, as it was feared they were poisoned. The men ate the Bully Beef, an item most likely captured in a trench raid, with water and afterward smoked the cigars.

During the night a company from the 1st Royal Irish Fusiliers crossed over to the redoubt as reinforcements. While searching for wounded men amongst the numerous bodies that littered the ground a sergeant heard German voices nearby. He threw a hand grenade in their direction and it apparently drove them off.

When it became light enough in the morning he saw that two machine guns had been set up that could have fired directly into the redoubt. He toppled one into a shell hole and he and another man carried the other back to his officer.

Early on 2 July the *Heidenkopf* had to be evacuated. The garrison was ordered to withdraw. Chappell gathered the Somerset survivors together, a mere 78 men including 20 walking wounded, and made their way back to the British trenches.

The Royal Irish Fusiliers were the last to leave. Determined not to leave empty handed they brought back piles of loot – German equipment, helmets, weapons, and three prisoners

Lutz

Leutn. d. R. i. Ref.=Inf.=Regt. 121,
gefallen bei Serre
am 1. Juli 1916

Bauer

Leutn. d. R. i. Ref.=Inf. Regt. 121,
gestorben am 3. Juli 1916 an den
bei Serre erhaltenen Wunden

Leutnant der Reserve Max Lutz
2/R121 killed on 1 July 1916.
(*Kriegstagbuch aus Schwaben*)

Leutnant der Reserve Emil Bauer 3/R121,
severely wounded 1 July 1916, died 3
July 1916. (*Kriegstagbuch aus Schwaben*)

they were reluctant to part with.

While the Irish Fusiliers returned with their three prisoners the Germans had taken a far large number of prisoners on 1 July. When the dugouts of the recaptured positions were searched on 2 July even more English soldiers were found inside several of them. More prisoners were taken from the men still taking cover in the shell holes close in front of the position so that the overall number of men captured amounted to 200.

In addition to the haul of British prisoners a number of men from RIR 121 who were already in English captivity were released during the counter attacks. To this number were added the men who had taken refuge in the deep dugouts and had not been discovered by the British during the fighting, such as the commander of the 3/R121 and many of his men who had been recovered earlier in the day.

Among the prisoners was Captain Brown, 1st Battalion East Lancashire Regiment. After being brought into the German trench he was taken down into what he described as an immense dugout, some 30 feet below ground and entirely untouched by the bombardment.

His wounds were dressed and as he spoke German fluently Browne had a conversation with his captors. The men of RIR 121 were apparently elated over the results of the day's fighting. One man apparently said, 'You English had to give the New Army that you have made a trial. You've done so and it has failed. Now we shall have peace!' Browne was of a different opinion and replied that he felt the fighting would go one for some time to come. The subject was then changed. One other German inside the dugout complained that his right arm was stiff from throwing so many hand grenades during the day.

Captain Browne was carried to the rear on the following day, accompanied by a German soldier who had been taken prisoner on 1 July and subsequently released. Browne's companion was not overly concerned about his slight wound, however he was extremely upset that he had been made to turn out his pockets after being captured and had lost all of his personal possessions.

Captain Browne went on to relate that all of his captors were loud in their praises of the discipline and order of the British advance and of the courage the British displayed. However they also expressed surprise at the slowness with which they had come on.

There was heavy traffic in the *Heidenkopf* Sector going to and from the front lines during 1 July and the days following. Prisoners and wounded were moving to the rear, new supplies and reinforcements were approaching the front line. Much of the route was considered dangerous as it was exposed to enemy observation and under constant shellfire. This forced the men to travel across open ground at times in order to avoid particularly dangerous locations.

On one occasion a returning wagon and team arrived in Miraumont at a gallop, the driver was found dead, the second man was also dead; his body had fallen off the wagon following a shell explosion. In the period from 24 June to 10 July 1916 the regiment lost 36 horses killed and many others wounded.

When the fighting was over at the end of 1 July there was a feeling of relief as if a great weight had been lifted from the shoulders of the men. The actions of the day had been physically and mentally exhausting.

By far the luckiest were the survivors who were alive at the end of 1 July, even if a few had suffered minor injuries or wounds that still allowed them to remain with their regiment. As *Leutnant der Reserve* Beck, 3/R121, surveyed the men who had survived the day he noted that:

> Sitting amongst comrades of other companies, tired and emotionally drained, were the remnants of my 3rd Company – thirty men and five *Unteroffiziers*. They slumped there, dog tired and spent. It had all been too much! *Oberleutnant* Lutz, the company commander had been seriously wounded in the first moments of the attack…The three platoon commanders *Reserve Leutnants* Seidel, von Gaisberg and Bauer had all fallen, along with three quarters of the company during the attack. Only a few had ended up in captivity; in part they came back to the company the next day.[24]

For many of the wounded men there was a good chance that they would recover sufficiently to be able to return to duty. During the intense fighting and in the relative quiet of the evening the stretcher-bearers searched the battlefield for wounded men and transported them as quickly as possible to a medical dugout located in a trench in the rear of the sector.

> There was plenty of life in the dressing station in one of the rear trenches. Most of the wounded had passed through the day before. All suffering and all the emotions of battle were reflected there. Next to the slightly wounded Englishmen, who were surprised by the good conditions where he had expected no more life to exist after the monstrous artillery fire, lay the severely wounded Germans who forgot their pain and worry in a dreamlike morphine slumber. The English Captain with both arms broken by bullets, who was still not bandaged, probably pondered how the British offensive had turned out at other places despite his pain. New wounded were continuously being carried up from the front by the indefatigable stretcher-bearers while the Other

Ambulances arriving at the dressing station behind the
Heidenkopf. (*Die 26. Reserve Division 1914-1918*)

Ranks of the Medical Company continued to take the wounded to the ambulances
that must stop one kilometer further behind.[25]

Oberstabsarzt Dr. Schwarz managed the regimental medical dugout located in *Feste
Soden* on 1 July 1916. It was located on the rise between Beaumont and Serre and the
location provided a wide panoramic view to the Ancre valley and to the hills of Thiepval
and Pozières on the other side. The medical service had little activity during the seven days
bombardment, only 35 wounded men from the I Battalion, almost all of which found their
way into the dugout at night. When the attack came on the morning of 1 July Dr. Schwarz
recalled:

> The slightly wounded first flowed toward us at 7.30 in the morning. It was not
> until the course of the afternoon and in the night that the severely wounded were
> brought in by the stretcher-bearers, some with terrible injuries. One saw head, lung
> and abdominal wounds as well as shattered bones of many different types. We were
> working in nonstop feverish activity. There was almost an alarming overcrowding
> in our small medical dugout and the strain of working in the blood and the thin,
> corrupted air, was no simple matter. Concerning the lightly wounded, who, for the
> most part had already been bandaged with a field dressing, had their bandages looked
> at by our medical non-commissioned officers and redone if required; then these men
> were placed in small groups after they had been refreshed with coffee, sausage and
> bread, and given instructions to march directly to the large dugout of the medical
> company behind Miraumont. There, fractured bones were splinted, bleeding was
> stopped and bandages were repositioned.

Dressing station behind the *Heidenkopf*. (*Die 26. Reserve Division 1914-1918*)

Several wounded men with head wounds in which part of the skull had disintegrated died in our medical dugout; however we could ease their ending through morphine injections or also by chloroform narcosis. We were especially careful in expediting the movement to the rear for the men with head, lung and abdominal wounds. However we could not begin their transport to the rear until the night from 1st to 2nd July. The division doctor, *Herr Generaloberarzt* Dr. Bihler, had placed twelve men under a very capable *Unteroffizier* from the medical company in our possession. These dependable men carried the seriously wounded in the communication trench from *Feste Soden* up to the artillery hollow at Beaucourt. It was a difficult and dangerous activity, and from this group one of the stretcher-bearers was killed and two were wounded in the first night.

The wagons from the medical company traveled to the front upon the Miraumont-Beaucourt road, which was lying under shellfire, to pick up the wounded from the artillery hollow that were not able to walk. Also, although there was a delay in transporting the wounded to the rear, which was understandable because of the extended front of the division on a day of a great battle, the regimental doctors must however gratefully acknowledge that the medical company had been managed as humanely as possible during these days and nights.

Within 48 hours from 1st July we had afforded assistance to over 200 wounded men in the medical dugout in *Feste Soden;* amongst them were more than 140 of our own wounded and approximately 70 wounded Englishmen. From 3rd July the access to wounded men became less daily, and a unique story to tell is how we bandaged the last Englishman on 6th July, who had lain between both positions without help since the morning of 1st July.

Our medical *Unteroffiziers* and Other Ranks as well as the regimental stretcher-bearers endeavored to assist their wounded comrades in an exemplary and often quite touching manner and they never recoiled to any danger they were exposed to if it was necessary in the interest of the wounded. Therefore the 26th Reserve Division also had no small number of bloody losses amongst their medical officers, medical Other Ranks and stretcher-bearers during that day of fighting.[26]

Decades later, while looking back at the fighting on 1 July 1916 Dr. Schwarz felt a sense of accomplishment and pride in the performance of the medical service on this momentous day.

When our hearts are moved by the feeling of pride and in mourning during the great memorial day, then we want to also thankfully remember that although they [medical personnel] stood under the sign of the Red Cross they shared their lot with their fighting comrades and have sacrificed their blood and lives for the Fatherland.[27]

For those who were slightly wounded or injured they would be dispersed among the numerous hospitals established in villages and towns on the Somme. Once the men were considered fit for duty they were returned to their regiment.

Among the less fortunate men, the ones who suffered severe wounds requiring extensive treatment and rest, it was the start of what could be a long journey to recovery or eventual discharge from service if their injuries proved to be too debilitating. For a few of the severely wounded men their journey to the rear may have been shorter than they expected. A number of the more seriously wounded died in the dressing station located in the rear trenches. Others made it no further than the II/R121 dressing station in Beaumont or the

British dead inside the German trenches near the *Heidenkopf*. (Author's collection)

RIR 121 mass grave behind *Feste Soden*. (Author's collection)

dressing station in Miraumont, the first stop for the ambulances arriving from the front.

Others managed to make it to the local hospitals in Vélu, Fremicourt or Bapaume before succumbing to their wounds while several survived long enough to be admitted to hospitals in Aachen and Köln-Lindenburg before dying. Regardless of their nationality, each man, British or German, was given the best treatment possible.

While the living received the best care available there was the question of the numerous dead that lay scattered in and around the position. Once RIR 121 had secured their sector an accounting was made of the fighting on 1 July. In addition to the prisoners taken 1,200 British dead were counted in front of I/R121, 576 British dead in front of II/R121.

Losses by RIR 121 on 1 July are not known in detail. The regiment followed the standard procedure of reporting losses every 10 days. Still, there was some attempt to determine just how many men had been lost in the preliminary bombardment as well as the heavy fighting on 1 July. According to the regiment the losses for the period from 24 to 30 June were: 24 killed, 122 wounded, 1 missing. For the period from 1–10 July the regiment reported losses of 179 killed, 291 wounded, 70 missing, the vast majority of which became casualties on 1 July.

The *Heidenkopf* had the appearance of a charnel house. Body lay next to body, and at individual positions there were piles of German and British soldiers lying in grotesque positions, intertwined, one under the other. The landscape was also filled with the debris of war, masses of weapons and material lying around. It provided a horrible picture of destruction. Approximately 150 German dead were found in the comparatively small area of the *Heidenkopf* and approximately triple that number of Englishmen.

The sector held by RIR 121 was reasonably quiet after 1 July and this allowed the men to make some repairs to the position. Progress was slow as the garrison was very tired and in some areas there were only enough men left to form a security guard. The II/186 arrived as support and did considerable work helping to carry away the dead.

Captured British equipment and weapons on display, including
the much-prized Lewis Gun. (Brett Butterworth)

Most of the German dead were buried in a mass grave behind *Feste Soden*. The grave site was later decorated with a large cross made of birch trunks where 150 German soldiers found a final resting place.

Most of the English dead were buried where they had been killed in the position. Some were interred in a separate mass grave adjacent to the German burials, most likely it contained the British dead who were found in the farthest reaches of the German position or who had been captured and died from their wounds before being sent to the rear. It took 10 days to recover all of the dead that could be located; many more lay in front of the position and fouled the air as they decomposed.

Of the 150 German soldiers buried in the mass grave none were officers. It was still considered proper to make a special effort to recover the bodies of the fallen officers and to transport them to the rear for a formal burial in Miraumont. One such officer was *Leutnant der Landwehr I* Kurt Seidel, a platoon commander in the 3/R121. He had served in the 3rd Coy since 5 August 1914 when he joined the regiment as a *Gefreiter*.

Seidel rose through the ranks and was eventually promoted to *Leutnant der Landwehr I* on 21 May 1915 when he was appointed as one of three platoon commanders in the company. The exact time of his death is not known; however he lost his life fighting in the German trenches of the 3/R121, more than likely while in action against the Warwickshire battalions. According to his records he was 'killed in action on 1 July from a gun shot wound to the stomach, killed in the field fortifications north of Beaumont.'

Unlike the men buried behind *Feste Soden* his body was recovered and sent back to Miraumont where he was buried in the new Soldiers Cemetery on 4 July 1916. His coffin was adorned with a flower and oak leaf wreath bearing his family name. *Pfarrer* Lempp conducted his funeral service.[28]

In the days following 1 July the groans and moans of the many wounded men could be

Seidel

Leutn. d. L. i. Res.-Inf.-Regt. 121,
gefallen bei Serre
am 1. Juli 1916

Schlösser

Leutnant i. Res.-Inf.-Regt. 121,
gefallen bei Beaumont-Hamel
am 1. Juli 1916

Leutnant der Landwehr Kurt Seidel
3/R121, killed in action 1 July 1916.
(*Kriegstagbuch aus Schwaben*)

Leutnant der Reserve Siegfried Schlösser
5/R121, killed in action 1 July 1916.
(*Kriegstagbuch aus Schwaben*)

heard coming from no man's land. Some who could be found were brought in for treatment while most were out of reach of the British medical teams. Every attempt to arrange for a truce in order to recover the dead and wounded was ignored by RIR 121. The German commanders felt the situation was still unclear and the position, while intact, required a great deal of repair and there were insufficient men to hold the position in the event of another determined British attack.

> Still all day long one heard the moaning and the shouting cry 'help' (Hilfe) by the wounded Englishmen in the foreground. However, despite all efforts only a few could be found and recovered in the night.
>
> It was completely quiet on the next day; the enemy had enough according to the punishment they received. The front sector there was deathly quiet, only now and then sounded the cry of a wounded Englishmen out of the foreground. I took over my post again in the turret and observed the enemy positions and the battlefield. On the fourth day a cloudburst came down and drove a few wounded Englishmen out of the shell craters that were filled with water. They were brought in as prisoners.[29]

The situation on 2 July was quite a contrast to the previous day. It was a sunny summer day, the calm that prevails after a storm. Only a few shells fell on the regimental front.

> You can ignore the battle, and truly it is a battleground, as even the old warriors who have been in the field since the beginning of the war have not seen it too often. In front of the position it is brown from the English covering the ground lying alongside and on top of each other, sometimes still alive. And also in the destroyed trenches

and shell holes! Everywhere the dead, maimed and half buried, friend and foe lying in confusion, as they were left by the hard fighting in the fate of war. Rifles, machine guns, various systems, apparatus and equipment was in disorder and in wild confusion and in between nimble soldiers, who begin to bring a little order again, stretcher-bearers who searched for the wounded and bandaged them. The numbers and type of booty the enemy had brought with him indicated the strength of the attack and their high expectations. More than 30 enemy machine guns and mortars, countless light signal apparatus, telephones and even a complete apparatus for wireless telegraphy lie around, truly a strange assault kit.[30]

The captured material included 28 machine guns, 4 mine throwers and a great deal of equipment: arms, ammunition, entrenching tools, signaling and telephone apparatus. The men of RIR 121 considered the English to be splendidly equipped. The prisoners made excellent impressions; large, strong, well maintained men. Each man had his shaving things with him and at least one was occupied with shaving during his capture in a dugout, as it was apparently very important to him.

On 2 July the regimental commander was able to walk over and survey the position held by his men in the hot fighting with pride, the regiment that he had led since August 1914. Regretfully he saw many that had been with him for nearly two years had been killed.

Some of the information provided by the prisoners gave an insight into the thoughts of the enemy. One British Lieutenant asked his captors if they were picked troops brought up from Verdun. Another Scotsman, 'dressed with a short skirt' reportedly said that they had marching orders for Miraumont, about 5 kilometers behind the front.

The highest praise, however, given to the regiment was found in an English army order that said:

British prisoners captured 1 July 1916. (*Die 26. Reserve Division 1914-1918*)

I want to convey my special thanks ... to the regular divisions, which were going on the attack between Serre and Beaumont. They had to make the most difficult part of the attack. There the Germans had concentrated their picked troops and therefore they could not achieve the expected success despite their proven prowess.[31]

The consequences of the action fought on 1 July 1916 near the *Heidenkopf* could be represented by the losses suffered by the 1/8th and 1/6th Royal Warwickshire Battalions. The survivors answered roll call at the end of 1 July in an area near the present day Sucrerie Cemetery. 1/8th could only muster 47 men; the 1/6th had 95 answer their names, only 25 of them unwounded.

Finally, on 5 July, there was a successful attempt to save some of the many wounded men lying in front of the German trenches.

A large Red Cross flag was slowly raised above the parapet. When, after a few minutes, no shots had been fired, two M.O.'s stood up on the parapet beside the flag. Still the enemy held their fire. The two officers then advanced across no man's land with the flag. A mass of curious heads appeared above the German parapet and a German M.O. and some orderlies came out to meet ours. The officers on both sides stiffened to a ceremonious salute. The Germans carried our wounded from near their wire to the middle of no man's land and handed them over to our bearers. This great work of humanity went on until all of the wounded were collected then, again, the officers saluted. Not a word had been exchanged all afternoon. Captain W. Carden Roe, 1st Royal Irish Fusiliers.[32]

The task assigned to the men of the 4th Division was simply beyond what could be expected with the tactics used in 1916. Even a badly damaged German trench system was a formidable obstacle. Add to this an integrated defensive system where the most was made of the terrain as well as mutual support between regiments and divisions and any idea of a breakthrough or serious breach of the German lines by a single division could not have been achieved. While there were numerous British divisions involved in the attack in essence each division was on their own during the fighting and they were unable to effectively support one another.

In March 1918 Brigadier General W.R. Ludlow visited the scene of the fighting on 1 July 1916. He was searching for the grave of his son, 22 year old Captain Stratford Walter Ludlow, commanding C Company, 1/8th Royal Warwickshire Battalion who was killed on 1 July. The areas encompassing the fighting near Serre and Beaumont-Hamel had not been cleared by the Graves Registration Department so his son was most likely in the spot where he fell almost two years earlier.

His son had been last seen while consolidating the German fourth line trench. Captain Ludlow and several other officers of the battalion had been shouting encouragement to their men, 'That's our objective,' while casually smoking cigarettes. After that there was no information to be found of his fate or whereabouts.

General Ludlow searched among the ruined trenches and heavily pockmarked ground. In his search he came across many signs of the heavy fighting that had taken place in 1916. Equipment, tunics, coats, rusty rifles and bayonets were scattered about along with full bully beef tins, boxes of hand grenades and shrapnel helmets.

He also came across numerous human remains; now just skulls and bones. Here and there were individual graves that did not identify the occupant. Most of the graves he found were hidden in the tall weeds and grass or in some cases destroyed by shellfire.

He continued his search and walked over to the old no man's land. While studying the terrain facing the old German front line from this position he realized that any attack over such ground was probably doomed to failure.

> I wondered how it was possible that any troops in the world could attack such a position in broad daylight on a lovely July morning. There was not sufficient cover for a mouse.[33]

General Ludlow never did locate the grave of his son. The Graves Registration staff promised they would continue the search but their efforts were disrupted a short time later when the German March offensive recaptured the very ground where his son was killed.

His name was placed on the Thiepval memorial to the missing following the end of the war. The remains of Captain Ludlow were eventually discovered and identified in the 1930s and he was given a burial in the Serre Road No. 2 cemetery, not far from where he had died.

The British Official History summed up the events of 1 July in a single sentence: 'The 4th Division also sustained disastrous losses in its assault.'[34] The official losses given for the 4th Division were: 136 officers, 1,747 Other Ranks killed; 134 officers, 3,429 Other Ranks wounded; 15 officers, 213 Other Ranks missing; 1 officer, 87 Other Ranks prisoners. Total: 286 officers, 5,466 Other Ranks. The ratio of casualties between the losses suffered by RIR 121 and the 4th Division was almost 10-1.

Notes:

1. Battalion war diary 1/8th Royal Warwickshire Regiment.
2. M. Middlebrook, *The First Day on the Somme*, p. 97.
3. J. Sheldon, *The Germans at Beaumont Hamel*, p. 86. G. Matthäus, *Treffen der 26.R.D. am 5 Juli 1936*, pp. 16-17.
4. Report of 2nd MG Coy, RIR 119, translation provided by Jack Sheldon.
5. 1st East Lancashire article, source unknown. It appears to have been taken from a magazine. It was sent to me some years ago and there is no indication of the author or publication on the documents.
6. 'Ein Württemberg Reserveregiment in der Schlacht an der Somme', *Kriegstagbuch aus Schwaben*, p. 1,390.
7. Battalion war diary 1/8th Royal Warwickshire Regiment.
8. Sheldon, op. cit., p. 86. Matthäus, op. cit., p. 17.
9. Ibid..
10. J. Edmonds, *History of the Great War. Military Operations France and Belgium 1916. Sir Douglas Haig's Command to the 1st July: Battle of the Somme*, p. 433.
11. Sheldon, op. cit., pp. 86-87. Matthäus, op. cit., pp. 17-18.
12. Battalion war diary 1/8th Royal Warwickshire Regiment.
13. Bühler, Wilhelm, *Leutnant der Reserve* in the Reserve Machine Gun Company, RIR 121 from Schorndorf. He was listed as slightly wounded on Württemberg *Verlustlisten* No. 464, 18 September 1916.
14. Battalion war diary 1/8th Royal Warwickshire Regiment.

15. Sheldon, op. cit. p. 87. Matthäus, op. cit., p. 18.

16. 'Ein Württemberg Reserveregiment in der Schlacht an der Somme', *Kriegstagbuch aus Schwaben*, p. 1,390.

17. Battalion war diary 1/8th Royal Warwickshire Regiment.

18. 'Ein Württemberg Reserveregiment in der Schlacht an der Somme', *Kriegstagbuch aus Schwaben*, p. 1,390.

19. *Leutnant* Friedrich Hoppe became a dentist in Berlin after the war.

20. Matthäus, op. cit., p. 19.

21. O. Lais, *Die Schlacht on der Somme*, p. 25.

22. 1st East Lancashire article, source unknown.

23. Sheldon, op. cit. p. 87. Matthäus, op. cit., p. 18.

24. Sheldon, op. cit., pp. 87-88. It should be noted that Beck had incorrectly listed the rank for Seidel as *Leutnant der Reserve* when in actuality he was a *Leutnant der Landwehr I. Leutnant der Reserve* Max Lutz, 3/R121, was listed as slightly wounded on Württemberg *Verlustlisten* No. 454, 5 September 1916.

25. 'Ein Württemberg Reserveregiment in der Schlacht an der Somme', *Kriegstagbuch aus Schwaben*, p. 1390.

26. Matthäus, op. cit., pp. 35-37.

27. IBID, p. 37.

Grave of *Leutnant der Landwehr* Kurt Seidel, Fricourt
German Military Cemetery. (John Sheen)

28. *Leutnant der Landwehr I* Kurt Seidel: Born 21 October 1886 in Möckmühl, Neckarsulm. He joined IR 180 on 1 October 1904 as an *Einjährig Freiwilliger* (1 year volunteer). On 30 September 1905 he was promoted to the rank of *Gefreiter*. He served 1 year, 5 months and 18 days before being discharged. He would have attended annual reserve training until the outbreak of the war in 1914. Between 1906 and 1914 he married Gertrud Kettenbach. Their last address was in Marbach am Neckar. He joined the 3/R121 on 5 August 1914. On 8 August 1914 he was promoted to *Unteroffizier*. After being in the field for two months he was awarded Iron Cross II Class on 4 October 1914. On 24 December 1914 he was promoted to the rank of *Vizefeldwebel*. He was then promoted to *Leutnant der Landwehr I* 21 May 1915 with pay from 1 May 1915. During his time in service Kurt went home on leave twice, the last time from 11 – 26 January 1916. On 2 June 1916 he was awarded the *Friedrich Ordnen* 3rd Class (awarded for Distinction in action in front of the enemy).

The news of the death of *Leutnant der Landwehr* Seidel reached his wife and family about one week after his death. His widow sent a letter to the Württemberg War Ministry on 12 July, the reply sent 14 July relates to his pay and pension benefits. There was an additional inquiry regarding pay and widow benefits from the Regimental *Zahlmeister* dated 20 July and a third document sent 7 August 1916 to Gertrud Seidel regarding the amount and payment of the War Widow pension.

Unlike most of the men killed in the fighting on 1 July Seidel not only received a burial service in Miraumont, his grave somehow survived the subsequent fighting in 1916 and once again in 1918 and his remains were eventually moved to the German Cemetery at Fricourt after the war had ended. His marked grave can be seen at Block 1, Grave 54.

29. Matthäus, op. cit., p. 19.
30. '*Ein Württemberg Reserveregiment in der Schlacht an der Somme*', *Kriegstagbuch aus Schwaben*, p. 1390.
31. Ibid.
32. Middlebrook, op. cit., pp. 227-228.
33. *The Birmingham Daily Post*, 1 July 1926.
34. J. Edmonds, op. cit., p. 437.

3

Serre

'Sehr haben sie gekriegt aber nicht Serre'
['They had gained a lot but they did not have Serre']

The village of Serre marked the northernmost portion of the main attack which stretched far to the south past the River Somme. The 31st Division was assigned to make the attack against the village and then to form the left flank of the British line. The attack against Serre would be executed by two brigades from the division – the 93rd on the right, the 94th on the left. The 92nd Brigade would follow in the rear as the division reserve.

The task given to this division was daunting at the very least. The men of the 31st Division would have to advance over 3,000 yards in some locations before even reaching the German position. Once the men had successfully broken through the German defenses the division would form the defensive left flank of the army. Anchored at John Copse in the British lines, it would extend through the village of Serre. The 31st Division would also simultaneously maintain contact with the 4th Division on its right. This was a very ambitious undertaking by any means.

Further to the north of Serre, a diversionary attack was also planned against Gommecourt. However the two attacks were not connected and could not rely upon one

The village of Serre. (*Zwischen Arras und Péronne*)

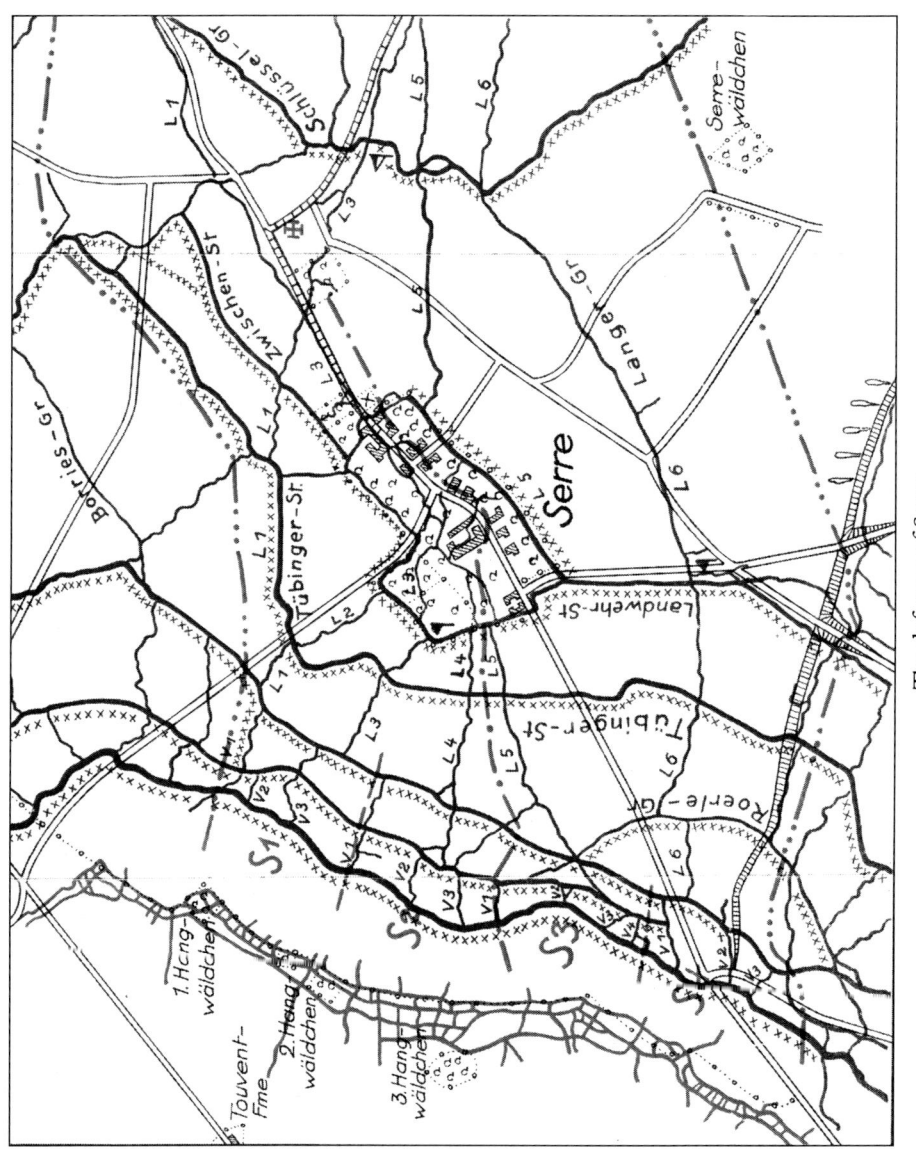

The defenses of Serre.

another for any support. A large gap existed between the 31st Division by Serre and the 56th Division by Gommecourt. The trenches between these two attacks were held by the 48th Division, a unit that would not take an active role in the heavy fighting on 1 July. This division was simply to hold the front line trenches and to provide whatever tactical support it could to the neighboring units.

In the week preceding the attack the 31st Division had sent out patrols on a daily basis to check on the condition of the German defenses and the trench garrison. In some instances these patrols returned, reporting that the wire entanglements appeared to be badly damaged at some locations while at others it still formed a formidable obstacle. Even in places where the wire had been badly damaged it was also often blown into thick piles and formed an impassable barrier to anyone trying to advance through it.

Instead of being cowed and hiding in their dugouts from the heavy fire the German garrison holding the front line trenches was found to be active and very alert, especially whenever a patrol approached their lines. Trench raids held by the British in the days before the attack were met with heavy fire and failed to penetrate into the German trenches in most cases. It would appear that not only were the men from IR 169 not hiding in their dugouts they were also eager to come to grips with their tormentors.

The raiding parties suffered heavy losses, including losing prisoners without accomplishing anything of real value. It would appear the fact that the German response was fast and deadly was ignored by the planners in the British rear. It was not the result that was expected by the British commanders and was apparently dismissed as being inconsequential.

The German defenders of Serre and the neighboring regiment IR 66 who were opposite the British 48th Division also sent out patrols on a nightly basis that checked on the activity taking place inside the British lines. The reports filed by these patrols also provided clear indications that an attack was going to take place shortly. In part this was deduced from the lack of repairs being made to the British wire entanglements, in part to the increased level of activity inside the British trenches.

The 48th Division was given the task of deceiving the Germans holding the trenches north of Serre into thinking their sector was also going to be attacked. In order to assist the 31st Division, a heavy smokescreen would be created on the morning of 1 July that was supposed to prevent the men of IR 66 from observing the advance by the neighboring division toward Serre and to reduce the effectiveness of their defensive fire against the left flank of the British line.

The heights by Serre were ideally situated to allow excellent observation over the British lines. Following the heavy fighting in June 1915 the new defensive position had been established in front of the village. The men from IR 180 that had created the new trench system used every technique they were aware of in an attempt to make the position as impregnable as possible. The excellent observation over the British lines meant that any movement in or near the enemy trenches could quickly be relayed to the artillery batteries in the rear and they could bring down accurate and deadly fire.

On 1 July the Serre Sector was being defended by the 8th Baden *Infanterie* Regiment Nr. 169 from the 52nd Division.[1] The regiment had been holding this portion of the line only a short time, since late May 1916 when the German divisions were shifted across the Somme front in order to provide the most protection against the expected attack. The trenches in front of Serre were divided into four sectors, S1 in the north through S4 at the

Deep trenches by Serre. (*Vom westlichsten Teil der Westfront*)

juncture with the RIR 121 on the left flank of the division.

The front line was held by two battalions, the I/169 on the right, the II/169 on the left. Sector S1 was occupied by the 4/169 in the front line with the 1/169 in the rear trenches as support. Sector S2 was occupied by the 3/169 in the front line with the 2/169 behind it in support. Sector S3 was held by the 6/169 with the 8/169 in support and Sector S4 was held by the 7/169 with the 5/169 close by in support. The companies of the III/169 occupied the *Tübinger Stellung* with the 10th, 9th and 11th and 12/169. IR 169 had two machine gun companies whose guns were positioned at various points in the German trenches. The guns from the 1st machine Gun Coy were distributed in Sector S1 and S2, while the guns from the 2nd Machine Gun Coy covered the trenches in Sector S3 and S4.

The machine guns of the 1 MG Coy/169 were distributed as follows: Sector S1, MG Wilhelm and MG Adelbrecht were in front line. MG Kölle was in the 2nd trench. MG Shumann was in the Intermediate line, the *Tübinger Stellung*. In Sector S2, MG Kaiser was located in the front line. MG Spengler was placed in the 3rd trench.

IR 169 could count on the men from *Pionier* Coy 103 and 104 as well as men from the 1/Bavarian *Pionier* Regiment for support in the upcoming battle. When it was discovered that many of the *pioniers* still working on the front line defenses were unable to move to the rear due to the heavy artillery barrage at the end of June it was decided they would fight alongside the infantry in their sectors and were absorbed into their ranks. Losses among the *pioniers* during the preparation fire were light. However, at least one *pionier* was killed at the end of the British bombardment when a mine penetrated the overhead cover of a

Trench by Serre before the
attack. (*Das 9. Badische Infanterie-
Regiment Nr.170 im Weltkrieg*)

Exposed machine gun post by
Serre. (*Das 9. Badische Infanterie-
Regiment Nr.170 im Weltkrieg*)

dugout entrance and exploded near where he was standing.

The Bavarian *Pionier* Company had a ration strength of 4 officers, 246 men and 30 horses of which 3 officers and 226 men were considered the battle strength. The company was distributed across the entire front of IR 169 when the attack occurred.

IR 66 stood on the right of IR 169, occupying the trenches between Serre and IR 170 that was located near Gommecourt. While the attack by the 31st Division would fall primarily against the trenches of IR 169 it would also affect the far left wing of the neighboring IR 66 in Sector M4. During the week-long preparation fire the trenches of IR 66 also suffered under the heavy bombardment. Patrols and trench raids were also conducted, as they were further south, all in the attempt to deceive the Germans. Losses in IR 66 were inevitable but very light in comparison to the number of shells falling on the regimental sector. The exact number of men wounded during the heavy bombardment is not known; however only 37 men were killed between 24 June and 30 June.

IR 66 had taken all possible precautions in order to meet the attack expected against their sector. The men were distributed throughout the trenches so that maximum firepower could be achieved against any attacking force. The guns from both regimental machine gun companies were also positioned in order to supply an optimum field of fire where needed.

The sector occupied by IR 66 was divided into four sections, M1 through M4. Two battalions held the front line while the third acted as the reserve. The III/66 was on the right with the 11/66 occupying the 1st and 2nd trenches of Sector M1; the 10/66 occupied the 1st and 2nd trenches of Sector M1b. The 12/66 occupied Sector M2 while the 9/66 occupied the 3rd trench and the *Gardegraben*.

The II/66 occupied the left of the regimental sector with the 6/66 occupying the 1st and 2nd trenches of Sector M3a, the 7/66 occupying Sector M3b and the 4/66 occupying Sector M4. The southern part of the third trench was held by the 8/66 while the northern part was held by the 3/66. The 2/66 was placed in the *Zwischenstellung* and along with

Infantrymen – IR 66. (Author's collection)

the 3/66 acted as the regimental reserve. The 1st and 4/66 along with two machine guns formed the brigade reserve.

Some time around 4 a.m. the Headquarters of IR 169 and IR 66 received news from the division HQ based upon a report from Moritz Station 28 located at La Boisselle that an attack would begin at 4.30 a.m. The time came and still no attack followed but the heavy fire continued. The men had been placed on alert as a result of the message and remained on alert even after the time had come and gone. Considering this was the eighth day of the bombardment many men suspected the attack would come soon as the British would eventually run out of ammunition.

Early on the morning of 1 July there were signs that the week-long bombardment had not been as effective as the British had hoped. At first light, 4.05 a.m., German artillery opened fire on John Copse and the British front lines. The fire was accurate and deadly and men packed inside the trenches started to take losses. One newly dug British trench that had so far been ignored by the Germans now came under extremely accurate artillery fire and was being methodically destroyed. In addition to the artillery fire the ominous sound of machine guns firing could be heard coming from the German lines.

Both IR 66 and IR 169 continued to send patrols out into no man's land during the cover of darkness to see if they could determine what the British were planning. The patrols reported seeing and hearing increased activity in the British lines on the night of 30 June/1 July, a clear sign that the enemy was up to something. One patrol found the tape set down to guide the attack later in the morning of 1 July. The patrol members quickly removed the tape in the hope of disrupting any enemy attack.

At 6.15 a.m. IR 66 reported that the entire regimental sector was under heavy bombardment. At 7 a.m. thick clouds of gas and smoke were generated in front of their position that effectively blocked all views of the British lines. Despite this obstacle great efforts had been made by the officers and men of IR 66 to remain vigilant and to watch the British lines carefully even in the heavy fire that still fell on them. It was critical that the moment the attack started was not missed so that the men could be called up from their dugouts to man the trenches.

The long awaited attack was about to begin. In the British lines the 94th Brigade, consisting of the 11th East Lancashire, 12th, 13th and 14th York & Lancaster battalions

Officers from IR 66 inside a large shell crater. (Author's collection)

made its final preparations. At 7.20 a.m. the men exited their trenches and passed through the British wire where they would lay on the grass in order to avoid any possible German fire being directed at their front line trench. The men would remain in this position for the final 10 minutes before the attack began at 7.30 a.m. However, as the men left the relative safety of their trenches they were already met by heavy machine gun fire and men began to fall to the ground, killed and wounded. Even lying flat on the ground, men were still being hit by the heavy German fire. To these men, the last few minutes before the actual attack must have seemed like hours.

The German artillery fire on the British trenches increased in volume just before the attack began. The front line trenches were targeted and the area 50 meters in front of and behind the trench was covered in high explosive shells. It was not too long before the ground was pockmarked by shell craters from the numerous impacts. Every attempt to silence or diminish the German fire by counter battery fire or Stokes mortars failed to have any effect. This was not the reception that so many had expected.

The level of dedication found inside the German lines by the trench sentries and officers inevitably resulted in losses from the heavy British fire. *Leutnant der Reserve* Waldemar Draheim, the company commander of the 5/66, was killed by a direct hit while observing next to his dugout in the 2nd trench of Sector M4. In order to be fully prepared for the anticipated attack the II/66 had been placed on alert and the men were at their positions inside the trenches before the artillery fire had lifted to the rear. While it resulted in some losses it also meant that the men could react to the attack without any delay.

Observation post *Scupin Weg* reported seeing large enemy reserves accumulating at the *Dreigiebelhaus* [Three Gable house], Toutvent and La Signy Farms. Immediate action was called for and the leader of the 1st Machine Gun Coy, *Leutnant der Reserve* Franz Seldte[2] made arrangements to bring these targets under fire. He placed a machine gun into position near the battalion battle headquarters and began to operate it himself. While he fired into the British assembly areas a shell fell near him that tore off part of his left forearm. The same shell also wounded *Leutnant der Reserve* Walter Mende, the company commander of the 8/66. Mende was in the act of alarming his company in the third trench when he was hit. The undamaged machine gun was then operated by *Unteroffizier* Ackermann with deadly effectiveness.

Destroyed 7.7cm field gun by Serre. (Author's collection)

Two other officers were also wounded at this time. *Leutnant der Reserve* Ebers was shot in the stomach while observing the British lines; he died a short time later. *Leutnant der Reserve* Kurt Rappold from the regimental Machine Gun Coy was also wounded. Some of the machine guns with the best field of fire were ordered to open fire on the British troop assemblies. The command to open fire was not really needed as many of the guns had already started shooting as the gun crews could also clearly see the mass of British troops.

While the initial smoke and gas clouds had made observation extremely difficult for the men of IR 66 it was short lived. The smoke quickly cleared and the opposing trenches became visible once more. It also became evident that no troops were preparing to advance from the 48th Division front so all of the regimental firepower could be directed against the men of the neighboring 31st Division.

While the one group of machine guns fired at the assembly areas and British trenches, the rest of the machine guns in the regiment were put to use firing into the left flank of the 94th Brigade as the men began their advance toward the German lines. The men in Sector M4 faced little opposition as the British artillery fire had already been lifted to the rear areas. Further north the sectors held by IR 66 came under desultory fire but this fire was too weak to prevent the trench garrison from participating in the defense.

As 7.30 approached the men of the 31st Division rose up and began their assault against the German lines. The trench sentries had alerted the garrison at the fall of the last shell and the remainder of the men quickly exited their dugouts and took up their positions. They immediately opened fire on the advancing British waves without fear of the British shells that were now falling several hundred meters behind them.

The level of fire directed against the British troops only seemed to increase at this time as the defenders of Serre rushed out of their dugouts and took up their assigned positions and also opened fire. Some of the Germans were even seen standing outside the trench in order to get a better shot at the approaching British troops. Other British observers watched

Leutnant der Reserve Franz Seldte (L) and Regimental Adjutant *Oberleutnant*
Dr. Korfer. (*Das 3.Magdeburgische Infanterie-Regiment Nr. 66 im Weltkriege*)

as machine guns were dragged out into shell craters where they would have a better field
of fire. As the British barrage had been transferred to the rear there was no effective way to
deal with these threats.

Red flares rose high up into the sky as the men in IR 66 and IR 169 called for artillery
barrage fire. The sight of thousands of British soldiers advancing toward the German lines
must have been daunting to the defenders who wondered silently if they would live to see
the next day.

> When the English started advancing we were very worried; they looked as though
> they must overrun our trenches. We were very surprised to see them walking, we had
> never seen that before. I could see them everywhere; there were hundreds. The officers
> were in front. I noticed one of them walking calmly, carrying a walking stick. When
> we started firing, we just had to load and reload. They went down in their hundreds.
> You didn't have to aim, we just fired into them. If only they had run, they would have
> overwhelmed us. *Musketier* Karl Blenk, IR 169[3]

After spending the last seven days sitting helplessly under the almost ceaseless impacts
of British shells and mines, many of the men in IR 66 and IR 169 were eager for the attack
to begin, even if it only meant an end to the shelling. Instead of demoralizing the defenders
or breaking their spirit, the bombardment had galvanized their resolve to give as good as
they got.

> If the English thought they could wear us out by the unprecedented fire of the past few
> days they were badly mistaken. Never was the battle enthusiasm and the camaraderie
> greater than during these days of terror and privation. The most ardent wish that we
> all cherished was that they would finally come. Everyone was aware of his duty. The
> look-outs were standing and when the shrapnel flew like hailstones, the actions of
> our Company leader Herr Hauptmann Haufer, acted as a shining example to us all.
> Almost constantly, day and night, he was in the trench and looked-out; went through
> the completely battered trenches and spoke in his fatherly manner to his 'children'

Infantryman – IR 169. (Author's collection)

and awakened the enthusiasm for battle. Who could have hidden their cowardice?
... Now everyone knows that the hour of retaliation will soon come. Cartridges and
hand-grenade reserves are made ready; everything is ready ...[4]

Oberleutnant Emil Schweikert, 6/169, was wounded in the head early in the fighting
by a shell splinter at the end of the final bombardment. Despite his wounds he continued to
command his company for some time. Later, during continued enemy attacks he stood high
on the side of the trench with a naked upper body, covered in bloody bandages encouraging
his men. He was finally convinced to go to the rear for medical treatment.

Nearby *Landsturmmann* Friedrich Essig was wounded in the right arm shortly before
7.30 a.m. He was in severe pain and unable to use his rifle. Instead he supplied his comrades
with ammunition and hand grenades during the attack until he too reluctantly went to the
rear for treatment.

The attack by the 94th Brigade consisted of the 11th East Lancashire and 12th York &
Lancaster in the front line. The advancing British troops were not only receiving heavy fire
from IR 169, they also reported receiving very heavy fire from their left flank coming from
the positions of IR 66. The German front line was positioned in a manner that allowed
many of the men from IR 66 to direct their fire into the left flank of the attacking units.
Early in the fighting *Unteroffizier* Kölle was ordered to fire against the British front line
trenches. He zeroed in on the British trench with deadly accuracy as he moved his gun back
and forth, hitting the men as they tried to leave their trenches.

Infantrymen – IR 169. (Author's collection)

Over there in closed file ranks, come the attacking English. Slowly, almost leisurely, they trot along, out of the third into the second, then into the first English trench. From there they proceed to the attack, their light cooking utensils flash in the gunpowder-impregnated air.[5]

The men of the 94th Brigade fell in rows, many before they had a chance to fully exit their trenches; others had not advanced more than 100 yards from their front line before being hit. The volume of fire that poured into their ranks almost seemed to destroy entire battalions to the last man. However, the losses were not all one sided.

One machine gun located opposite Luke Copse being operated by *Unteroffizier* Ludwig Adelbrecht was having a devastating effect upon the advancing British waves as they advanced from the British front line. The fire was so heavy and accurate the British troops were seen moving to left in order to avoid his fire. the situation changed rapidly when Adelbrecht's gun jammed, most likely the result of a faulty cartridge.

While attempting to remedy the jam Adelbrecht was struck in the head by infantry fire and died instantly. This annoying machine gun had become the target of numerous British troops who concentrated their fire at the gun crew. One shot probably struck a hand grenade being carried by *Schütze* Heinrich Pfahler that caused it to explode, killing Pfahler in the process. Four other members of the gun crew were also wounded as a result of the British fire or possibly from fragments of Pfahler's hand grenade. *Schützen* Wilhelm Buck, Ernst Gerbel, Jakob Stein and Karl Walter were all slightly wounded in the opening minutes of the attack.

Infantryman – IR 169. (Author's collection)

The surviving members of the gun crew sent a report to their company leader, *Oberleutnant* Faller, advising him of their situation. Faller quickly assessed the situation and ordered the machine gun crew under *Unteroffizier* Johann Wilhelm that was located inside the third trench to proceed toward the front line trench and resume firing at the advancing enemy waves.

Within moments of Wilhelm's gun opening fire he too fell victim to British fire, being struck in the head and killed. His position at the weapon was quickly taken up by the next man in the gun crew. The normal six man machine gun crews were all trained to automatically assume the duties of any man who became killed or wounded. This allowed for the uninterrupted fire of each machine gun that was especially valuable in situations such as the one facing the men of IR 169.

The advancing British troops had managed to advance so that they were in hand grenade range of the German machine gun. As Wilhelm's machine gun opened fire once again several Mills bombs exploded very close to the gun position. The machine gun crew remained calm and continued to fire into the British ranks with great accuracy. Considering how close the British troops were to the gun position it was almost impossible for the man operating the weapon to miss his targets. Within a short time the immediate threat of being overrun was eliminated as the exposed British troops fell in dense masses from the heavy fire. The battle report of the 1MG/169 went on to state that the wounded enemy soldiers were dealt with separately by the nearby infantry. Even wounded, an enemy soldier could remain a threat and had to be dealt with.

Another machine gun located in the German front line under *Unteroffizier* Fritz Kaiser was also the target of heavy British fire. Within a short time after the gun had opened fire four members of the gun crew had been placed out of action. *Gefreiter* Anton Bursch was severely wounded and later died; *Schützen* Bernhard Klein and Jakob Walde were both killed and *Schütze* Willi Keller was slightly wounded.

The remaining members of the gun crew continued to pour fire into the advancing enemy ranks when the gun suddenly stopped firing. It was imperative that the weapon be repaired and back into action as quickly as possible. The men immediately began to search for the cause of the problem. The entire crew was trained in how to recognize and quickly correct 36 different types of jams. This was an important component of the initial training given to machine gun troops in order to ensure that nothing would prevent the gun from firing at a critical moment.

Fortunately the jam in Adelbrecht's machine gun was located and corrected by *Unteroffizier* Schloss and he opened fire once again into the enemy ranks. Within a short time the firing pin suddenly broke. The broken pin was quickly replaced when suddenly the machine gun was hit by shrapnel on the water jacket causing the coolant water to escape. Without water to cool the barrel the machine gun would quickly overheat and seize up. The gun was carried back to *Leutnant* Bayer in the 3rd trench where repairs were made to the jacket. *Leutnant* Bayer and the gun crew returned to the 1st trench and opened fire once again.

Another defender left an account of his impressions of the start of the great offensive. *Unteroffizier* Otto Lais, 2nd Machine Gun Coy:

> The sun shines brightly. It is 1 July 1916. In the splendor of this summer's day the English columns advance to the attack. They have the certainty that their 8 days of bombardment, precisely calculated on every square meter of earth that every atom of life in our position has been destroyed.
>
> The enemy's artillery fire suddenly transfers to our rear positions, onto the grounds of the village of Serre, onto the approach roads and the villages in the rear. They advance to the attack 250 to 400 meters away from our destroyed trenches.
>
> They advance in columns, in dense, crowded assault lines, behind them are staggered the supports, the Indian lancers that after the English breakthrough at the wing of the attack front would create a crushing defeat of our center. The English infantry had their rifles hanging about their necks and over the shoulder, ready for the stroll to Bapaume, Cambrai, to the Rhine!
>
> The thought that any of us were still alive or could even afford any resistance (after the 8 days) appeared to be absurd to them!
>
> There he crawled out from half crushed dugouts, there forced themselves through shot up tunnels, through buried dugout entrances, through broken, shattered timber frames, now they rise up between the dead and dying and shouting and yelling 'Raus! Raus! Alarm! sie kommen!' [They're coming]
>
> The alarm sentries, who had to remain outside through the bombardment, rise out of the shell holes. Dust and dirt lie a centimeter thick on their faces and uniforms. Their cry of warning rings piercingly in the narrow gaps that form the dugout entrance. '*Raus....raus....sie kommen!*' Now they rush to the surface and throw themselves into shell holes and mine craters; now they fling themselves in readiness at the crater's rim;

now they rush forward under cover from the former second and third lines and shove themselves into the first line of defense, hauling boxes of hand grenades from shell hole to shell hole.

Everyone's throat is choking, a pressure which is released in a wild yell that becomes the battle cry: Sie kommen, sie kommen! Finally the battle! The nightmare of this week-long bombardment is about to end, finally we can free ourselves of this week-long inner torment, no longer must we crouch in a flattened dugout like a mouse in a trap.

No longer do we feel the dull impact of the dugout-breaker exploding downwards (an impact like a hammer blow on the helmeted skull).

We call for barrage fire. Red flares climb high then fade away as they fall to the ground. Destructive fire and barrage fire leave masses of green and red marks in the sky![6]

The batteries located in the rear of the German lines had been prepared for this very moment and as soon as the observers could see the numerous red flares rising up from the front line the guns were fired as rapidly as they could be loaded. Explosions tore across no man's land and the British front line trenches with deadly accuracy.

The level of fire from the defenders of Serre went against all predictions made before the battle started. No one should have survived the weight of fire directed against the Germans for the last 7 days yet the defensive fire was heavy and accurate.

As our infantry advanced, down came a perfect wall of explosives along the front trenches of my brigade and the 93rd. it was the most frightful display that I had seen up to that time and in some ways I think it was the heaviest barrage I had seen put down by the defense on any occasion. Brigadier-General H.C. Rees.[7]

Medium *Minenwerfer, Minenwerfer* Coy 52. (Author's collection)

The German artillery fired as rapidly as possible during the opening phase of the battle. Later they would settle down to a level of fire that the gun crews could handle without becoming completely exhausted. On the British side of the wire there seemed to be no reduction of the German barrage fire and it continued unabated. It was described as being 'so consistent and severe that the cones of the explosions gave the impression of a thick belt of poplar trees.'[8]

Just before 8 a.m. German observers noted the British were advancing from a copse of trees on their front, probably the 13th York & Lancaster Battalion. The men were heading directly into the heavy fire of the defending German machine gunners. At the same time the artillery observers noted the advance and quickly called for artillery fire. Within a short time a veritable curtain of fire descended upon the advancing men and cut them to pieces.

In spite of the heavy German fire, the men of the 31st Division continued to attack without hesitation. Men were going down in rows under the wall of artillery fire and seemingly endless machine gun fire. It could be considered almost miraculous that any men in the division even managed to reach the German trenches let alone enter them. However they did accomplish the seemingly impossible on this day. Small groups from different battalions had managed to reach the German front line trenches and once inside they were at least protected from the steady stream of rifle and machine gun fire they had faced in the open.

The majority of the men who had managed to reach the German wire found it almost impossible to enter the German trenches. While much of the wire had been damaged in the preliminary bombardment it had also been bundled together in large rolls that effectively prevented anyone from getting through unscathed, just as had been reported by patrols shortly before the attack on 1 July.

There were occasional gaps in the wire bundles that were at most the width of two men. Almost every one of these gaps however was covered by a German machine gun and infantry fire. When a man tried to make his way through the gap he was met with almost

Communication trench by Serre. (Vom westlichsten Teil der Westfront)

Feldwebel Hermann – 8/169. (Author's collection)

instantaneous machine gun and rifle fire. The survivors took cover in the numerous shell holes while bullets struck the ground all about them.

Looking back in no man's land the survivors could see their comrades lying in rows where they had fallen, the sun reflecting from the pieces of tin attached to their packs. So heavy was the fire that three of every ten men never reached their own parapet or left the front line trench when the attack started.

Against all odds some British soldiers had succeeded in penetrating the German position at the company boundary between the 4/ and 3/169. Most of the wire obstacles had been destroyed and the trenches and some dugouts had been crushed in by heavy British mines. The collapsed dugouts and blocked dugout entrances prevented these companies from occupying this portion of the line in time to meet the attack. Since the defensive fire was somewhat less here than in other portions of the German front line the men were able to reach the relative safety of the German trenches.

The first reports of the penetration of the German line reached the regimental Headquarters of IR 169 at 8.00 a.m. The response was immediate and decisive when it became evident that there were British troops between the German front line and Serre. At 8.04 a.m. the 12/169 was given orders to fall back into Serre as a security detachment. At the same time observers back inside the British lines could see the troop movement through the smoke and dust but they could not make out what was happening.

When the 12/169 was ordered to fall back the 1st and 2/169 were ordered to eliminate the British penetration and restore the front line. The plan called for the 2/169 to perform a counter attack against the British troops while the 1/169 would then occupy the trenches in order to prevent any further British penetrations. In order to ensure the success of this plan the 10/169 was ordered to support the 2/169.

The few British soldiers who had been lucky enough to enter the German lines advanced through the maze of unfamiliar trenches in order to reach their assigned goals for the attack. Despite the apparent disadvantage in numbers these men were determined to do their part. Their penetration of the German trenches continued to remain hidden to the British observers. The British were desperately trying to determine what exactly was happening inside the German trenches. The tin flashes on the packs of the men and the red and yellow marker flags used by the bombers to indicate their position were impossible to see in the smoke, dust and debris filled air and proved to be useless.

Depending upon the manner in which the trenches were occupied some of these groups made it quite deep into the German lines, including a few who reached the village of Serre. However, whether they were lucky enough to advance as far as Serre or simply to the next traverse, it was only a matter of time before they were discovered and dealt with by the German defenders.

The support companies in IR 169 had lost few men in the bombardment and even fewer in the attack as they remained under cover during the heavy fighting. As observers noted the location of the British penetration the support companies moved against them in force. They were determined to comply with their orders to eliminate all enemy detachments found within the German trenches.

By 8.30 a.m. reports made it back to the regimental headquarters of IR 169 that the entire front line was now in German hands again. The small detachments of British troops; cut off from their friends and much needed support, were slowly destroyed one by one as they ran into German bombing parties. The British soldiers did not give up easily and as long as their hand grenades held out they most likely inflicted as many losses as they suffered. Time and numbers were against them as their losses rose until there was no one left to offer any resistance.

While some men did manage to penetrate the German front line the vast majority of men in the 31st Division attack had become casualties during the advance or became trapped outside the German wire and under heavy fire, unable to advance or retreat. *Unteroffizier* Otto Lais left behind one of the most compelling accounts of these events and the part played by the regimental machine guns on 1 July.

> They fired, it whipped, it cracked wildly into the masses of the enemy, all around us, the rushing, whistling and roar of a storm, a hurricane; the paths of the British shells crashing down upon our few, bravely firing artillery, our reserves and our rear areas.
>
> Amidst all the rushing, this rumbling, growling and bursting, cracking and wild crashing of small arms fire, could be heard the firm, regular rhythm of our machine guns; tack-tack tack-tack … … … that one firing slower, the other in a faster rhythm! It was the precision work with materials and skill! A gruesome tune for the enemy, while providing our own infantry comrades, the *Musketen*, a high degree of security and reassurance.
>
> The machine gunners lived a privileged life in quiet times and were envied (excused from carrying heavy mortar shells!) They were earning their pay today.

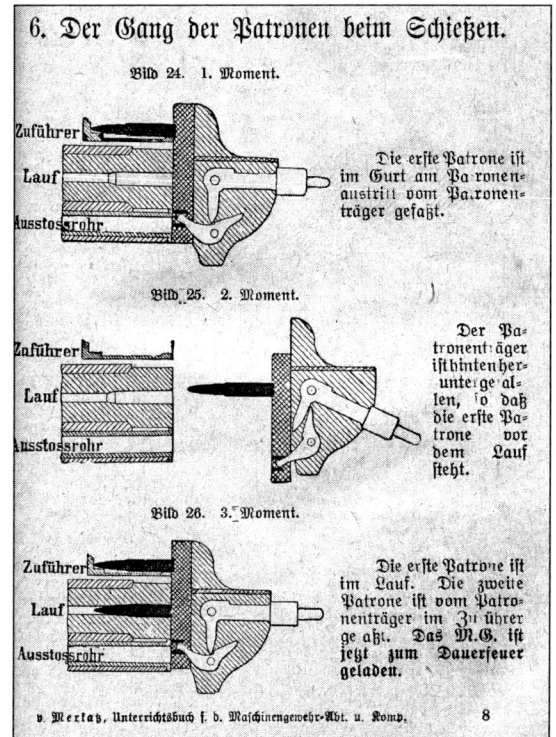

Loading and firing diagram for
the MG 08. (*Unterrichtsbuch für die
Maschinengewehr-Kompagnien Gerät 08*)

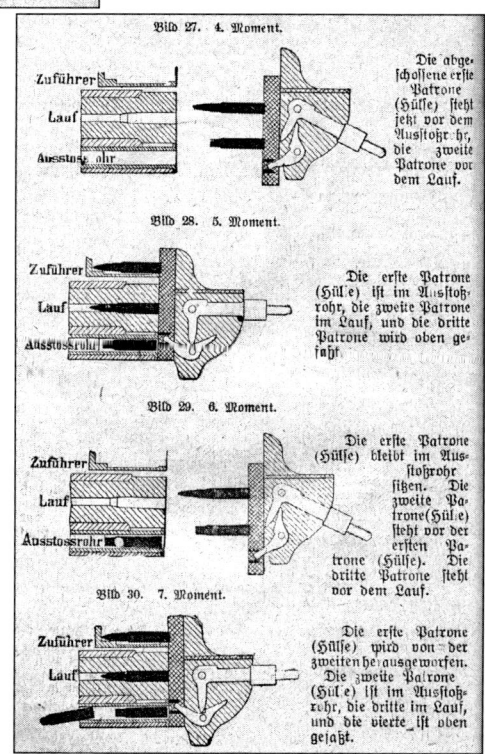

One belt after another raced through! 250 rounds – 1,000 rounds – 3,000 rounds. 'Bring up the spare barrels' shouts the gun commander. The gun barrel was changed. Continue firing. 5,000 rounds! The barrel must be changed again. The barrel is red hot, the cooling water is boiling – the hands of the *Schützen* operating the gun are nearly scorched, scalded. 'Keep firing!' urged the gun commander or shoot yourself!

The cooling water in the gun jacket was boiling, turned to steam by the continuous firing. In the heat of battle the condenser tube slips off the aperture of the water can, where it is supposed to re-condense. A tall jet of steam sprays upward, a fine target for the enemy. It is lucky for us that they have the sun in their eyes and we have it at our backs.

The enemy is coming closer. We fire on incessantly. There is less steam, another barrel change is urgent! The cooling water is nearly gone. 'Where's the water?' bawls the gunner. Get the *seltzer* [dugout iron rations] from down below in the deep dugout.

'There's none left *Unteroffizier.* The iron rations were all used up in the 8 day bombardment.'

The British still keep running forward, despite the fact that hundreds are lying shot down in the craters in front of us; fresh waves keep emerging from the assault trenches over there. We must keep firing!

A *Schütze* grabs the water can, jumps down into a shell hole and urinates into it. A second also pisses into the water can – it is quickly filled!

The English are already in hand grenade range; hand grenades fly back and forth. The barrel change is complete, the water jacket is refilled! Load! Hand grenades, rifle grenades explode directly in front of the gun. Only do not become unsettled and hinder the loading! Speak loudly, slowly and clearly to yourself; 'Forward – feed –

The devastated landscape by Serre. (Author's collection)

back (cocking lever pushed forward – belt advanced – cocking lever thrown back) the same again! Safety catch to the right! Press down, tack-tack tack-tack, once more rapid fire slams into the clay pit in front of us!

Tall columns of steam rise from almost all of the machine guns. The steam hoses of most of the guns have been torn off or shot away.

Skin hangs in ribbons from the fingers of the *Schützen* and the gun commanders, the hands are burned. The left thumb became a swollen, shapeless lump of flesh from the constant pressure on the safety catch. The hands felt like they were cramped from the slight vibrations of the handgrips of the gun.

18,000 rounds! The other gun in the platoon had a jam. *Schütze* Schw. falls from a shot to the head and falls over the belt that he was feeding. The belt twists, causing the cartridges to enter the feed opening at an angle and become jammed. The next *Schützen* forward! The dead man is laid to one side. The gunner takes the feeder out, removed the rounds and reloads. Firing, nothing but firing, barrel changes, fetching ammunition, laying the dead and wounded down in the crater ground. That is the hard, unrelenting tempo on the morning of 1st July 1916. The sound of machine gun fire can be heard right across the divisional front. The youth of England, the finest regiments of Scotland bled to death in front of Serre. The gun that was commanded by *Unteroffizier* Koch from Pforzheim and which was positioned directly on the Serre-Mailly road fired off the last belt! He fired no fewer than 20,000 rounds at the British.[9]

While the main action took place in front of IR 169 the men from IR 66 continued to provide critical support to their Baden comrades throughout the fighting. The machine gunners in IR 66 fired belt after belt of ammunition into the advancing rows of men from the 94th Brigade as well as pouring heavy fire into the assembly points inside the British trenches while still receiving little or no direct fire from British guns.

The German gun crews were able to maintain a steady supply of belted machine gun ammunition and fresh coolant water to keep the guns firing. The only reason to stop firing was in order to replenish the coolant water, clear an occasional jam or to change barrels after 5,000 rounds had been fired. The gunners had been issued a special woolen mitten that was used to pull out the red hot barrel in order to insert a fresh barrel. The entire process only took seconds and the gun was back in action.

The machine guns only stopped firing when they ran out of targets in no man's land. Even then a number of guns poured a steady stream of fire into the British trenches in order to inflict the maximum number of losses and to disrupt any fresh attacks. With the British trenches being well in range of the German machine guns and the gunners knowing the exact range of each enemy target area their fire was accurate and deadly.

There was a strong desire in the British lines to send over reinforcements to assist the men who had apparently entered the German trenches and were reportedly inside Serre. When the second wave of men were being sent over from the 93rd and 94th Brigades they were met with a wall of German artillery fire that caused numerous losses among the men and stopped the advance in its tracks. It was finally decided to suspend the attack.

At 9 a.m. observers in the British lines reported that the Germans opposite appeared to be massing for a counter attack. Brigadier General Ingles, commander of the 93rd Brigade, went against orders and directed the guns from the 170th Brigade RFA to fire upon the suspected German troop concentrations and disperse them.

Infantrymen – IR 66. (Author's collection)

There were several reports during the course of the morning that the German artillery was bombarding the German trenches and Serre with shrapnel shells. This is highly unlikely as the artillery fire plan called for the full effect of the artillery to be used to create a barrier across no man's land as well as bombarding the enemy trenches in order to disrupt any planed attacks and to destroy any troop concentrations. It is more likely that the observers saw British shrapnel shells bursting over the German lines.

General Ingles and the observers had apparently been mistaken. The German movement was not an attempt to mount a counter attack against the men of the 31st Division; it was either the shifting of available German reserves to meet the existing threat or possibly the movement of men from IR 169 heading toward the *Heidenkopf* to assist the men in RIR 121. The overall situation was still very unclear to the men of IR 169. There were far too few men available in the regimental sector to even consider the idea of a counter attack. In the meantime, the British continued to attack Serre despite the extremely heavy losses they had suffered and such little headway being made in the morning hours.

After the initial panic and confusion at the unexpected opposition, after terrible bloody losses of their dense attack columns the English reorganized. For two hours and longer wave upon wave broke against us.

They ran toward our craters with outrageous tenacity. In exemplary bravery and self-sacrifice they climbed up from the protection of their original assault positions and they have bled to death, barely reaching our shot up wire entanglements.

Twenty, thirty meters in front of our guns the bravest ones fall, the first and the last attack waves together.

Those that followed took cover behind their dead, groaning and moaning comrades. Many hanging, fatally wounded, whimpering in the remnants of the wire entanglements, over the bent iron stakes of the *Spanischen Reiter* [*cheval de frise*]. The survivors occupied the slight slope in and behind the remnants of our wire entanglements and shot at us as if possessed, without taking much aim. They create cover for themselves from the bodies of their dead comrades and some of our men fall in the fire. We fire into the wire stakes that wind down to the ground, on which the barbed wire hangs. The cone of fire breaks on the wire and strikes down in an unpredictable crossfire onto the protective slope. Soon the enemy fire dies down here also.

New waves appear over there; they half emerge above their cover and then sink down again behind the parapets. Officers jump up upon the thrown up earth and attempt to encourage their men to come with them by their example. Numerous flat helmets appear again only to disappear again immediately. The cone of bullets from the infantry and machine guns sprays on their cover over there.

The English officers no longer leave the trenches. The sight of the attack terrain takes the breath away from the attackers.[10]

While many of the machine guns and infantrymen in IR 169 concentrated their fire at the advancing British waves of infantry others took the support troops and British trenches under fire in a similar manner as the machine guns in IR 66. This long distance fire was solely designed to disrupt any new attacks by causing casualties among the men who were waiting for their time to advance. As men became wounded and killed in this heavy fire it must have brought a feeling of dread and doom to their surviving comrades before they even left the comparative safety of their trenches.

Meanwhile the English supports fared badly. Closely packed, caught between their jumping off positions and advanced columns of all types, they were unable to move forward, backward or sideways once the catastrophe had begun.

The machine guns firing from the sledge, lying higher than the first trench, with sights set at 600 to 1,000 meters, fired accurately into the English support troops. The modest destructive fire of the few German guns had a devastating effect on these masses. Two *Minenwerfer* still fired somehow in the sector and a makeshift mortar constructed by the *pioniers*, a so-called *Albrechtsmörser* (a wooden tube wrapped around with thick coils of wire or steel bands). With a low rate of fire but all the more terrible effect, this sent its shaky 'Marmalade bucket' filled with a high explosive charge, iron and thick glass, swaying through the air in the direction of Hébuterne. When one such monster exploded 3 to 4 meters above the ground the results were terrible to see.[11]

Brigadier-General Rees had already put an end to any further attacks once he had realized his brigade had been destroyed. The subsequent waves of men that should have advanced in support of the initial attacks were all canceled. This meant that any hope left for the men who had made it into the German trench system was gone. It was evident

Infantryman – IR 169. (Author's collection)

that some men had made it safely across and were still fighting against the men of IR 169 when British observers noted that German bombing parties were active inside their own communication trenches.

By noon most of the firing along the front of the 31st Division had stopped. There was only the occasional burst of machine gun fire or rifle fire. Some of the men from IR 169 were reported climbing out of their trench onto the parapet where they fired at the men trapped in no man's land in front of the German wire.

Bursts of machine gun fire from the British trenches effectively stopped this practice. At the same time any movement inside the British trenches resulted in German artillery fire from 15cm heavy field howitzers or 21cm heavy mortars.

During the fighting the defenders from IR 169 and two Groups from Platoon Stumpf, 1/Bavarian *Pionier* Regiment occupying Sector S4 could see the dense British columns advancing toward the *Heidenkopf* to their left. *Leutnant* Stumpf had assumed command of the 1st Platoon 7/169 during the fighting and his men had stood shoulder to shoulder with the infantry at the parapet. During the heavy fighting one *pionier* was killed by a German shell while another, *Gefreiter* Reinig, was severely wounded by British machine gun fire.

Since the 7/169 and *pioniers* from Platoon Stumpf had very few targets on their front they concentrated all of their fire into the flank of the 4th Division men advancing toward the *Heidenkopf* and neighboring RIR 121 and maintained their fire throughout the rest of the day. The men from the 1/Bavarian *Pionier* Regiment noted that the English advance was very slow, in part due to the heavy packs and equipment the men apparently carried and, in the opinion of the *pioniers*, in part due to heavy alcohol consumption just before the English attacked. It was most likely a reference to the standard issue of rum given to the British soldiers.

At one point *Leutnant der Reserve* von Drahten was ordered to take his platoon and counter attack against the British holding the *Heidenkopf.* His orders were changed at the last minute when it was determined that he should proceed to Sector S3 on his right and provide support for the 6/169. Von Drahten was killed in the fighting as he made his way to the commander of the 6/169. His body was recovered by his men and brought to the rear at the end of the day where he was buried in the soldier's cemetery in Miraumont.

When it had been determined that the attacks against the 6th and 7/169 had all been repulsed, the regimental commander, Major von Struensee still retained portions of the III/169 to be utilized as a sector reserve, ready to counter attack where he felt they were needed most.

During the height of the fighting it became obvious to the men in IR 66 that the only portion of their sector that was threatened by the British attacks was Sector M4 so the troops were shifted to meet the threat. During the attack the entire 5/66 occupied the front line trench. The battalion immediately ordered two platoons of the 8/66 to move up and occupy the empty 2nd trench in M4.

It was then decided to reinforce Sector M4 and once again one platoon from the 8/66 was sent into the front line while the remaining platoons continued to occupy the 2nd trench. The 2nd and 3/66 were then sent forward and distributed into the third trench of the sector thereby ensuring a strong defense in the event of any new attack directed against them. While the British fire had died down on the trenches held by the men from IR 169 it continued to fall on the sector held by IR 66 until 4 p.m.

IR 169 reported that by 5 p.m. the English who had occupied the German lines in the neighboring sector of RIR 121 were finally forced out and were flooding back to their positions. While they withdrew they remained constantly under heavy fire from RIR 121 and from IR 169 and the *pioniers* on their flank.

At the same time *Leutnant* Stumpf was approached by a runner with orders that he should also proceed to the 6/169 where a 'Russian Sap' was located a few meters in front of the German wire. He was to report to the battalion on his observations and the appropriate actions needed to be taken against it.

Stumpf's platoon was taken over at 6 p.m. by *Vizefeldwebel* Müller who had traveled to Sector S4. Müller was also placed in command of the company while at the same time he met with four groups of *pioniers* located in the front line position. The *pioniers* then received orders from the battalion to repair the badly damaged dugouts in Sectors S3 and S4.

Observers in IR 66 had noticed an accumulation of enemy troops inside the British lines in the late afternoon. The artillery was alerted to this new target and directed heavy fire to the coordinates. It was not known if this was the precursor of a new attack or not. No attack developed and the front eventually died down once again. There were attempts by the British to advance later in the day but all proved futile in the face of heavy defensive fire.

There was a wailing and lamentation from no man's land and much shouting for stretcher-bearers from the stricken English. They lay in piles but those who survived fired at us from behind their bodies. Later on, when the English tried again, they

Memorial card: Johann Schmid, 3/169. Killed 1 July 1916. (Author's collection)

weren't walking this time, they were running as fast as they could but when they reached the piles of bodies they got no farther. I could see English officers gesticulating wildly, trying to call their reserves forward, but very few came. Normally after 5,000 rounds had been fired we changed the barrel of the machine gun. We changed it five times that morning. *Musketier* Karl Blenk, IR 169.[12]

Late in the afternoon, reports arrived at the headquarters of IR 66 that portions of the line held by IR 170 to the north and IR 169 to the south had been penetrated by British troops. As a result of these reports the 1/66 was placed at its disposal of IR 170 at 4.15 p.m. Before the company arrived in the neighboring regimental sector it was discovered it was no longer required and the men returned to their former positions. By the evening the entire sector held by the 52nd Division was firmly in the hands of the division. The enemy had been repulsed at every point and the officers and men viewed the fighting on 1 July as a great victory.

While some British soldiers had managed to enter the German lines the vast majority had not. This aspect of the fighting in front of Serre was represented in the low numbers of British prisoners taken by the men of IR 66 and IR 169. Only 34 prisoners from six English battalions had been captured, in addition 5 machine guns were brought in. At the same time the 31st Division had prepared for large numbers of German prisoners that would be sent back after the successful advance that so many had expected and predicted. In fact the VII Corps only processed 22 German prisoners following the fighting of 1 July. It was another clear indication of the failure of the attack along the corps front.

Some of the 34 British prisoners captured on 1 July by IR 66 and IR 169.
(*Das 3.Magdeburgische Infanterie-Regiment Nr. 66 im Weltkriege*)

British losses in front of Serre had been devastating:

Our losses are very heavy. The enemy's losses are inconceivable. In front of our division's sector the English lie shot down in rows by companies and by battalion, swept away.[13]

On the other side of the wire IR 66 reported losses of 36 dead and 92 wounded. IR 169 reported losses of 141 dead including 5 officers – *Leutnants* Beck, Hoff, Jenisch, Neck, *Leutnant der Reserve* Imle; 219 wounded including 4 officers. One of these officers, *Oberleutnant* Welsch, died from his wounds on 16 January 1917.

The fighting may have ended at Serre but the suffering for many continued throughout the day and into the night.

The 'no man's land', the intervening field between both positions, is a great scene of misery. The battle falls silent; it seems to have frozen from so much misery and misfortune. Medics hurry into the foreground, an English medical unit appears from somewhere with many stretchers and unfurled Red Cross flags, a rare and powerful sight in trench warfare.

Where to start!? Whimpering confronts them from almost every square meter. Our own medics, those who can be spared, join forces on the battlefield and place the enemy just as carefully into the hands of his people.[14]

While not directly involved in the attack the men of IR 66 were a key factor in the destruction of the 31st Division. The small number of losses suffered by this regiment meant that in case of an emergency on another portion of the line a readily available pool of men could be sent at a moments notice.

At night patrols were sent out into no man's land. In front of Sector M4a a severely wounded English soldier from the 11th East Lancashire Regiment was found and brought back to the German lines for treatment. The different patrols also brought in numerous pieces of British equipment they found scattered throughout no man's land. They also

Minenwerfer crew following the battle, *Minenwerfer* Coy 52. (Author's collection)

counted approximately 150 British dead in front of Sectors M4 and S2.

One patrol from the 8/66 under *Leutnant* Kühne brought back a Lewis gun, a large number of rifles, numerous pieces of equipment of all types and a sack of mail that clearly indicated that the attacking troops found in their patrol area were from the 14th Battalion York & Lancaster Regiment.

The situation facing the men of IR 66 on 2 July was tense. It was not known if further attacks might take place or if the regimental sector would be attacked directly. The time was spent repairing the trenches that had been knocked about and replacing and repairing the damaged wire entanglements. Ammunition, hand grenades and rations were replenished in the front line positions while a close watch was kept on the British trenches.

The next days were quiet along the front held by IR 66. Patrols were sent out each night to keep an eye on the activity in the opposing enemy trenches. On 4 July one patrol from the 12/66 even went as far as entering the British front line but found it empty. They still came across pieces of British equipment that they gathered together and brought back with them. Reports from the patrols sent out by the III/66 indicated that the British had working parties outside of their trenches making repairs to the wire entanglements. The artillery was notified and the enemy troops came under fire from German artillery, *Minenwerfer* and machine guns.

The failure of the British guns to destroy or suppress the machine guns from IR 66 on 1 July was a major factor in the failure of the attack by the 31st Division. It is doubtful that any division could have obtained different results given the level of fire directed against the advancing units. It was also determined that the distance between each wave of men was too large. It allowed the Germans to deal with each wave individually and therefore bring all of their defensive fire on a relatively small target before worrying about the next wave of enemy troops.

British prisoners captured on the Somme. (Author's collection)

Brigadier-General Rees had nothing but praise for the actions of his men. They never wavered in their attempts to attack the German lines; they never wavered in the intense German fire. No other unit could have done any better under the circumstances.

General Rees also recognized the actions of the men in Field Grey on the other side of the wire:

> I can safely pay a tribute also to the bravery of the enemy, whom I saw standing up in their trenches to fire their rifles in a storm of fire ... [15]

When the fighting was over at the end of 1 July 1916 IR 169 reported expending 74,000 rounds of rifle and machine gun ammunition and over 1,000 hand grenades.

The entry in the after action report by the 7/169 summed up the events of the day: *'Sehr haben sie Gekriegt aber nicht Serre'*. ['They had much but they did not have Serre'.] The regimental history for IR 66 dedicated only a few pages to the fighting on 1 July. It summed up the events on the morning of 1 July in one sentence: 'The advancing English waves in front of M4 up to S2 (Infantry Regiment 169) were under combined fire so that only individual Englishmen reached the entanglements.'

Notes

1. Like many German regiments the 8th Baden I.R. Nr. 169 contained both the traditional regimental number from the former independent state of Baden (Nr. 8) as well as the number given to the regiment in the Prussian numbering system (Nr. 169).

2. *Leutnant der Reserve* Franz Seldte survived his wounds. After the war he became the 1st *Bundesführer* of the organization called *Stahlhelm*, an association of men who had served at the front during the war.

3. M. Middlebrook, *The First Day on the Somme*, p. 138.

4. J. Cooksey, *Barnsley Pals*, p. 197. The quote is from an extract of the war diary of the 6th Company, IR 169 and found in the Generallandesarchiv Karlsruhe, 456 EV 42 Vol. 114.

5. Cooksey, op. cit., p. 198.

6. Lais, Otto, pp. 16-17.

7. Cooksey, op. cit., pp. 198-199

8. Edmonds, op. cit., p. 443.

9. Lais, pp. 17-19. Lais' description of loading the MG: "Cocking lever forward, load belt, cocking lever back and then repeat once more. In order to load the MG 08 for firing the lever was moved forward, the belt was inserted and the lever moved back and then forward again, this brought the first round into the MG lock and brought the second to the ready position. The gun was ready for firing. Once fired the casing of the first round was ejected though a tube located at the lower front of the receiver. As the gun was fired the cocking lever moved forward and then back in a motion that ejected the empty cartridge case, moved the second bullet down to the firing location and fed a replacement into the lock." (See diagrams on page 124)

10. Lais, op. cit., pp. 19-20.

11. Ibid., p. 21

12. Middlebrook, op. cit., p. 185.

13. Lais, op. cit., p. 25.

14. Ibid.

15. Cooksey, op. cit., p. 203.

4

Gommecourt

While not part of the main Allied attack on the Somme; the village of Gommecourt would play an important role in the battle, or so it was hoped by the British. The German defenders of Gommecourt had long been anticipating the assault by the 46th and 56th Divisions. The activities of the enemy in the weeks before 1 July had made it quite clear that the village would be attacked. This is exactly what the British had hoped as it was meant to be a diversion to prevent German reserves from being sent to the south where the main blow would fall. It would be vital to prevent Germans artillery units from being allowed to shift their fire to the south, something that might prove critical in the imminent battle. The ruse had apparently worked. Four days before the attack Haig asked General Snow, commander of the VII Corps how he was getting on and he replied 'They know we are coming alright.'[1]

Gommecourt had been captured in early October 1914 during the opening phase of the 'Race to the Sea'. The village had been attacked by the 1st Guard Division and after several days of heavy fighting the 4th Guard *Infanterie* Regiment managed to capture and hold village against determined French counter attacks. Gommecourt was unique in that it represented the westernmost point of France being held by the Germans as noted by a tree called 'The Kaiser's Oak'.

The defensive system that began to encircle the village in late 1914 was slowly developed into a strong network of very deep trenches. They had been created in this manner as the position was exposed to fire from two directions, both from the north and from the west. The positioning of the defensive lines allowed many of the trenches to be enfiladed from the British lines.

In May 1916 the 2nd Guard Reserve Division arrived on the Somme and was assigned to the Gommecourt sector. This division was now part of the expanded XIV Reserve Corps. The four regiments that formed this division, RIR 15, RIR 55, RIR 77 and RIR 91 were all veteran units that consisted of men who had served in the ranks of Guard regiments before the war.[2]

The men of the 2nd Guard Reserve Division had an excellent field of vision over the opposing British lines on both sides of the village across an unusually wide no man's land. There were three main German defensive lines: 1st, 2nd Switch Line and Intermediate Line. Numerous communication trenches had been created that would allow the Germans to contain any breach in their lines and enable them to encircle any enemy penetration. A strongpoint was created in the eastern portion of the village called the *Kernwerk* by the Germans, known as 'The Maze' by the British. It was a large self-contained defensive work like many others scattered along the Somme front.

As in the other sectors on the Somme Gommecourt had numerous deep mined dugouts that could stand up to the heaviest shelling and many were also equipped with electric lighting. There were underground kitchens, living quarters that could hold large groups of men, each with several entrances. Many of the dugouts were also interconnected with one

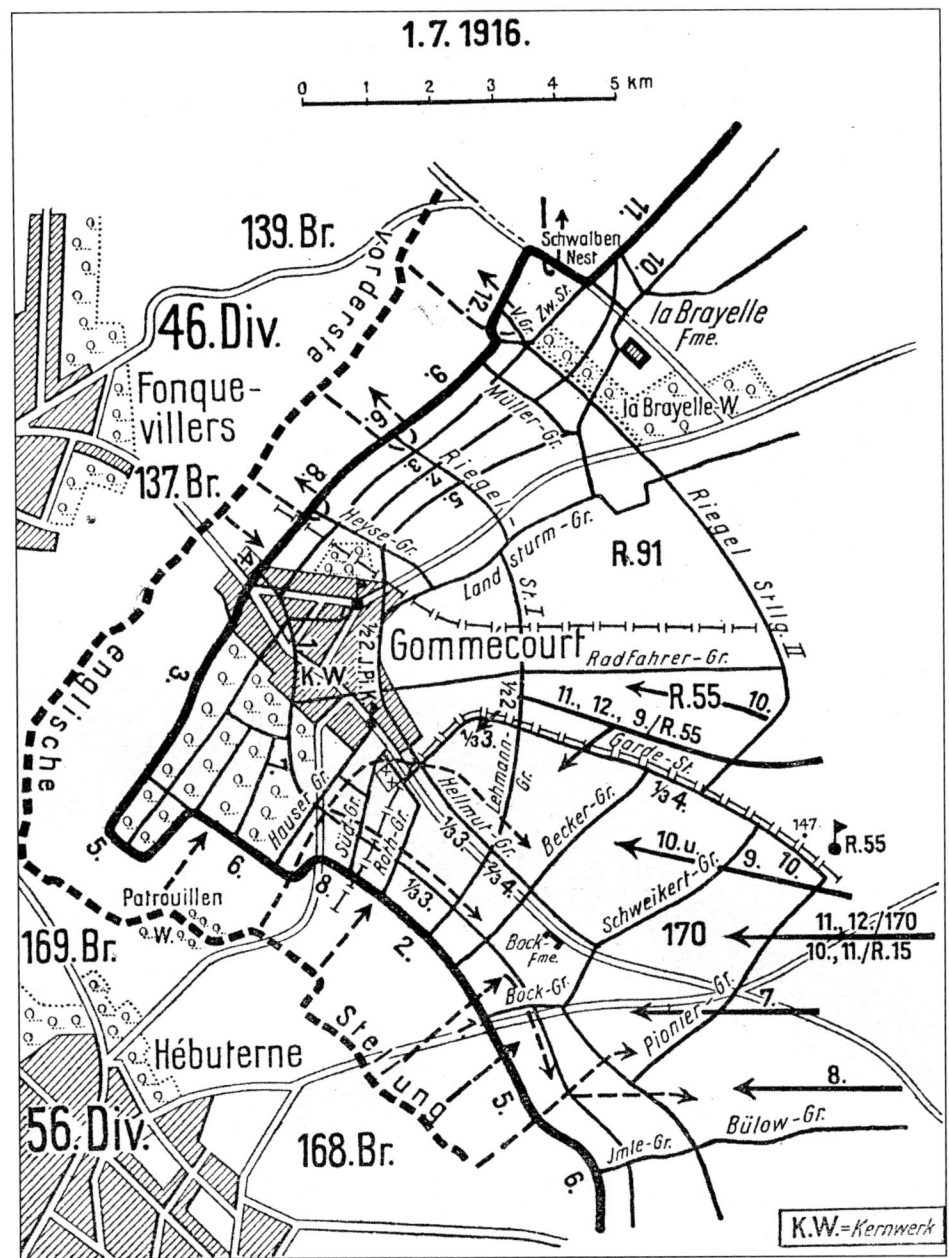

The attack on Gommecourt.

Communication trench near Gommecourt church. (*Vom westlichsten Teil der Westfront*)

another to allow a quick escape in case of an emergency as well as allowing safe movement of men and equipment throughout the sector even under heavy shelling. There were several underground passages leading back to the rear that allowed for safe movement of men and supplies to the front.

The activities by the British in the weeks before 1 July and during the week-long bombardment had made it very obvious to the German defenders that the village would be attacked. The men of the 2nd Guard Reserve Division made excellent use of the time given to them. Everything possible was done to make the position even more formidable in order to meet this threat.

Three regiments of the division were holding the front line on 1 July. RIR 77 occupied the trenches furthest north of the village on the right flank of the division, connecting with the neighboring 111th Division. The center was held by RIR 91 that occupied Sectors X1 through X6. The left flank of the division, the village of Gommecourt, was held by RIR 55 in Sectors G1 through G5. RIR 55 connected to IR 170 (52nd Division) that occupied Sectors N1 through N4. The boundary between the 2nd Guard Reserve and 52nd divisions was in the vicinity of the *Roth Graben*. RIR 15 was in reserve close behind the front line ready to deploy when needed.

The village and surrounding maze of trenches were the main targets for the British artillery fire that started on 24 June. The sector came under heavy fire on a daily basis up until the attack on 1 July. The British were evidently going out of their way to convince

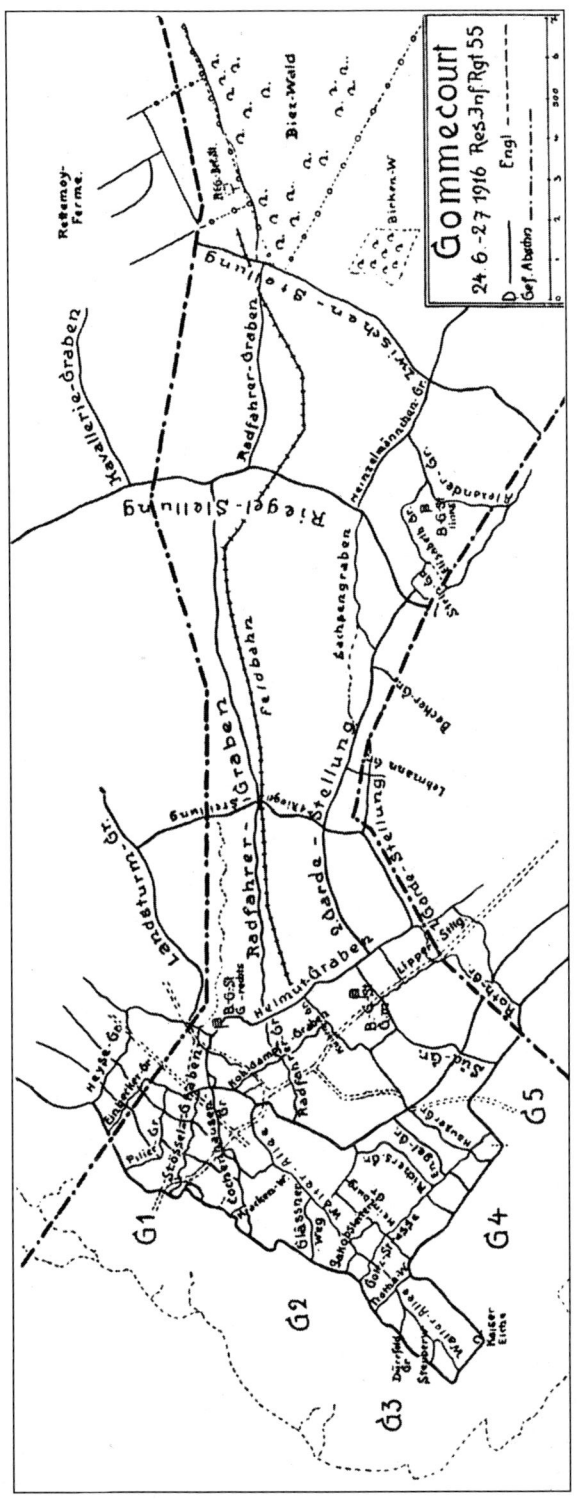

RIR 55 Sector G1 through G5.

Communication trench near Gommecourt. (*Vom westlichsten Teil der Westfront*)

the defenders of Gommecourt the attack was imminent. One clear instance of this can be seen on 24 June when RIR 55 reported the British had created a new trench north of the Gommecourt – Fonquevillers road but had not erected any wire entanglements to protect it, a clear indication it was going to be used to launch an attack and not simply for defense.

On 26 June the British used gas against the village that resulted in retaliatory fire from the German artillery. The III/R55 was placed on alert after receiving reports from RIR 91 that the British had been observed preparing sortie steps between Monchy and Sector X.2. On the same day the men in one dugout were feeling extremely relieved and quite lucky when a 9.2-inch British shell that penetrated their dugout turned out to be a dud.

27 June brought continued artillery fire and a report from the neighboring IR 170 that an enemy attack was expected according to statements made by a British prisoner. The III/R55 was placed on alert once again but no attack followed. Other reports however did mention that approximately 50 meters of the British wire north of the Gommecourt – Fonquevillers road had been removed, a clear indication an attack was forthcoming.

As the heavy bombardment continued there was inevitable damage to the German wire and many of the trenches in and around the village. Every attempt was made to maintain telephone connections with the different company sectors but at times runners had to be used after the buried telephone cables were cut over and over again in the shell and mine fire.

While the defensive system had been damaged by the constant shelling it was still a formidable obstacle to any attack. The months of hard work preparing the trenches and dugouts in the Gommecourt sector had not been in vain. The defenders of the village, RIR 55, had suffered remarkably few losses during the week-long bombardment and had reported casualties of 6 Other Ranks killed, 44 Other Ranks wounded despite the thousands of shells falling on their position.

The bombardment continued at varying levels of intensity until 1 July when Sectors

Deep mined dugout by Gommecourt. (*Vom westlichsten Teil der Westfront*)

G1 and G5 came under extremely heavy fire by guns and trench mortars of every caliber. It soon became evident to the officers in RIR 55 that the British were planning to attack the village on two flanks and then cut off the rest of the village after the two attack fronts joined together inside Gommecourt.

Gommecourt North – the 46th Division

Sectors X1 through G1 facing the 46th Division had been badly damaged in the week-long bombardment preceding the attack. Many of the trenches had been partially silted up; much of the wire entanglements had been damaged. However there were sections where despite the destruction the trenches still represented a serious obstacle to any attacking force and provided adequate cover to the defenders. Most importantly, the deep mined dugouts had withstood the bombardment intact and the men inside were ready to meet the British when the attack came.

The attack by the 46th Division would fall against the 4/R55, 12th, 9th, 6th and 8/R91. Trench sentries in these companies maintained a constant watch of the British lines despite the heavy fire. Their visibility was severely hampered on the morning of 1 July due to the dust filled air combined with the smoke of exploding shells and artificial fog being generated by the British.

When the British bombardment suddenly lifted from the German front line and shifted to the rear at 7.30 a.m. the sentries gave the alarm that the British were attacking. The trench garrison quickly exited their dugouts where possible and took their places in the trenches and shell holes. Some entrances to individual dugouts had been crushed in under the heavy fire and required more time to clear in order to allow the garrison to man the trenches.

Infantryman – 12/R55. (Author's collection)

Of the men who were able to exit their dugouts they quickly set up their machine guns while others brought up boxes containing thousands of rounds of belted machine gun ammunition or armed hand grenades. The seemingly endless training had paid off; the trenches were manned and most machine guns were in position and ready to open fire within 2 minutes of the alarm being sounded.

Red signal flares were fired, rising high into the air along the German front line as a signal for the field gun batteries located in the rear to provide immediate barrage fire. The guns had already been providing harassment fire in expectation of the attack but now they knew exactly what they had to do to cause the enemy the greatest damage and to provide the greatest protection for the German defenders.

At around 5 a.m. on 1 July, a terrible barrage was launched on the German positions, ranging from the Somme to the north up to the border between Sectors X and A of our divisional sector, where it suddenly dropped off. Dust and gas clouds darkened the atmosphere, a hellish spectacle made the air and the earth shake. At 7 a.m., it was obvious the assault was about to be launched when the enemy switched the barrage to our positions further back and to the areas in the rear. Groups Barnstedt and Niederstein replied with a steady barrage according to the prepared 'Gommecourt' fire plan.[3]

The artillery fired as rapidly as possible as shell after shell came down on the British trenches and in no man's land. 28 light and 22 heavy guns blanketed the 2-kilometer front facing 46th Division with destructive barrage fire:

At 7.30 a.m. the British launched their attacks against our Sectors X2, 3, 4, 5, G1, 2 and 5. *Gruppe Süd* laid blocking fire on the basis of direct observation, *Gruppe Nord*, which was unable to observe due to smoke until 8.45 a.m., fired and was directed by telephone.[4]

The guns fired salvos of shells among the advancing British troops while the infantry opened fire into the dense cloud of smoke and dust with rifles and machine guns. While the men found it difficult to identify individual shapes, the intensity of the infantry and artillery fire from the defenders could not fail but hit their targets.

Most of the German gun batteries had been targeted for counter-battery fire in the week before the attack and had suffered some damage. Thanks to the well-developed gun positions and deep dugouts losses had been kept to a minimum for the equipment and the gun crews.

The smoke and artificial fog generated by the British continued to plague the German defenders making it difficult to see anything along their front line in the opening phase of the fighting. What the Germans did not know was that the British also faced difficulties in the dense smoke and fog and found it almost impossible to orient on the German positions in some areas. The attackers also faced muddy ground conditions that made any quick advance almost impossible. Before the men of the 46th Division had made it half way across to the German lines they came under heavy infantry fire from the German trenches. It appears that not every German had been killed during the week-long bombardment as had been expected by many.

Despite the intense defensive fire small groups of British soldiers were able to enter the German lines at several places using the cover of the dense smoke and dust. In spite of what some accounts indicate not every foot of ground was occupied by the defenders. There were

Communication trench in wooded area near Gommecourt. (*Vom westlichsten Teil der Westfront*)

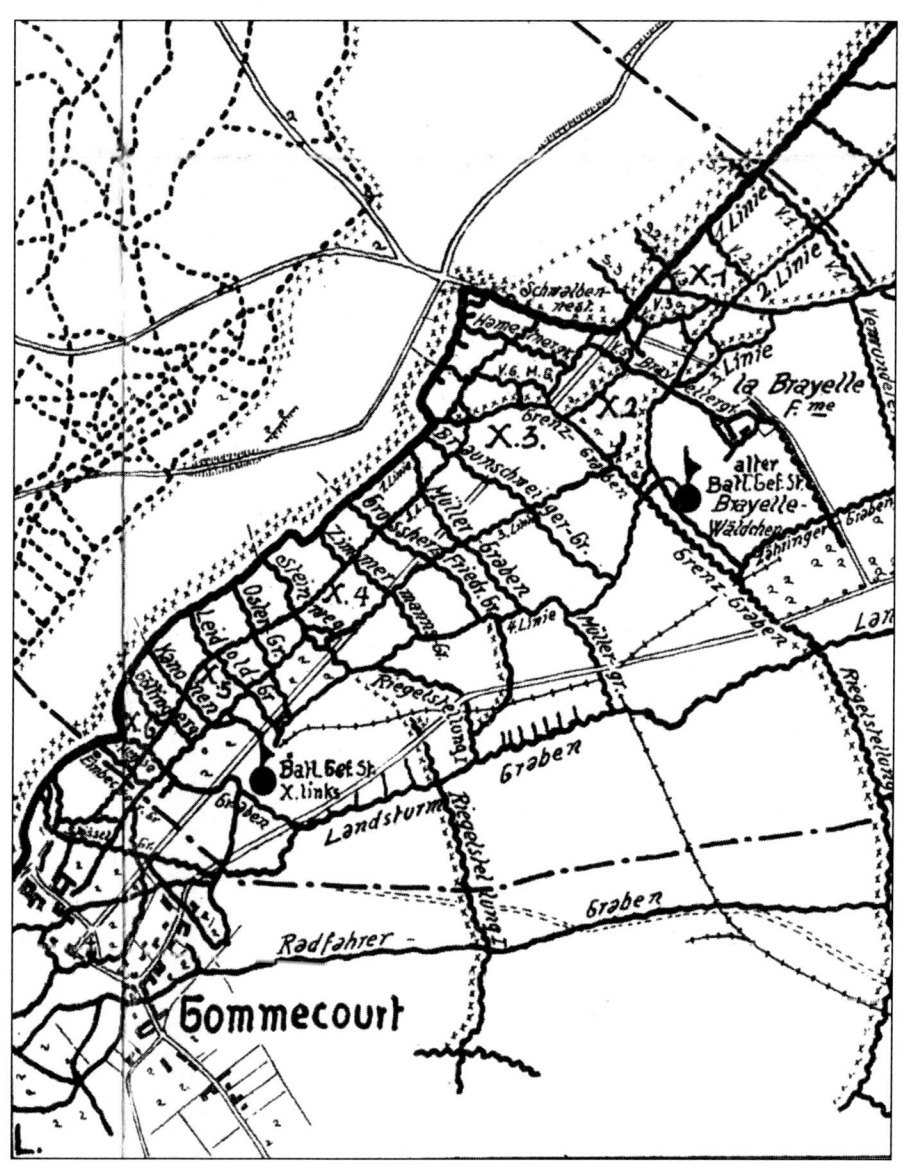

RIR 91 Sector X1 through X6.

Infantryman – RIR 91. (Author's collection)

areas where small gaps could be found that were not adequately protected or areas where the trench garrison was still having difficulty exiting their dugouts.

Also, while some German reports indicated that the wire entanglements had been destroyed and the trenches had been leveled many British reports provided a different picture. The wire had been badly damaged in many places but it had not been eliminated and many of the trenches still formed a major obstacle in their damaged condition. The British reported that the trenches were too wide to jump across and too deep to exit without assistance.

At the right wing of Sector X2 approximately 35 British soldiers managed to enter the German trenches near the *Schwalben Nest* [the 'Z']. The threat was quickly identified by *Offizier Stellvertreter* Mast, 12/R91 who attacked the invaders at the head of his platoon. The majority were killed or wounded by hand grenades thrown by Mast and his men while the survivors were forced back into the damaged entanglements where they were shot down by rifle and machine gun fire or captured.

Machine guns located in the *Schwalben Nest* now provided very effective enfilade fire against the following waves of attackers. When combined with the German barrage fire it proved almost impossible for anyone to make it across the wide expanse no man's land alive.

This seemingly impassable barrier of fire helped seal the fate of the few men who had been able to enter the German lines at other locations. Some German dugouts in the front line that still contained men had been passed over by the leading wave. These should have been mopped up by the following waves if all had gone according to plan. Instead the garrison was able to eventually exit their dugouts and join in the defensive fire against the

Men from *Pionier* Bn 10 in the trenches by Gommecourt. (Author's collection)

waves of men still approaching their lines. The small groups of British soldiers that had penetrated the German lines were now effectively cut off from all support or relief.

The limited visibility was probably also responsible for allowing about 25 men to enter the German lines at X3. It soon appeared they were attempting to widen their gain by flanking and cutting off Sector X2. The German response was quick and effective. The rest of the 12/R91 under *Leutnant der Reserve* Metzner and one group from the 9/R91 attacked the smaller British detachment and in a few minutes of close fighting had completely destroyed them.

46th Division troops also managed to gain entry to the German line at Sector X4 where they penetrated up to the second trench. They quickly installed a machine gun that could fire against the northwest corner of Gommecourt Wood. The fighting here was at close quarters and fierce.

When the commander of the II/R91 found out that the British had entered the German lines he ordered his bugler to sound '*Rasch vorwärts*'. The 5/R91, *Leutnant der Reserve* Kluckhohn along with the 6/R91, *Leutnant der Reserve* Rittmeyer left the safety of their trenches and advanced in the open against this new threat.

The British machine gun crew was destroyed and the surviving members of the detachment were forced back into the front line trench and then further into the wire entanglements under a hail of hand grenades and rapid rifle and machine gun fire. Only a few of the enemy managed to escape. The men back inside the British trenches could see their comrades taking cover in shell holes in front of the German wire through gaps in the heavy smoke and dust. They looked on helplessly as their friends were being bombed and slowly destroyed. There was nothing they could do to prevent it.

The men of the 4/R55, *Oberleutnant Graf* Matuschka at the right wing of RIR 55 in Sector G1 were able to exit their dugouts in time to meet the advancing British troops.[5] They quickly took up positions and opened fire into the advancing British waves cutting men down everywhere while others threw hand grenades as fast as they could into the dense masses. Two soldiers from the 4th Coy stood out during the attack, *Wehrmann* Siegmann and *Musketier* Tenbring both shouted 'hurra' while throwing hand grenade after hand grenade into the British ranks.

Despite the heavy artillery fire and devastating infantry fire some attackers managed to enter the German trenches near the *Einbecker Graben*. At 7.40 a.m. Platoon leader *Leutnant* Dobberke, 2/R55[6] who occupied the third support trench while in reserve recognized this threat and decided to advance over the open ground.

Dobberke and his men scrambled out of their trench and advanced in the open up to the second trench, crossed it and continued on to the first trench where they made a frontal assault against the small group of British soldiers. The invaders were quickly destroyed except for a few men that were taken prisoner. According to some German accounts at one point during the attack the British troops that had managed to enter the German trenches in Sector G1 gave the appearance of attempting to reform their ranks before continuing the advance despite the unprecedented volume of fire they experienced.

One machine gun located in Sector G1 was supposed to provide flanking fire for the front line but at the outset of the attack an English officer managed to get close to the gun in the dense smoke and dust and opened fire on the gun crew with his revolver.

The gun captain managed to fire back wounding the British officer twice with his Luger. Another member of the gun crew, *Schütze* Berns, brought the machine gun around to face the new threat and then threw a hand grenade that did not contain a fuze at the head of the British officer. The weight of the hand grenade alone apparently disabled the officer and the gun opened fire on the advancing British waves and mowed them down.[7]

A second machine gun located in Sector G1 with the 4/R55 opened fire on an enemy column advancing from Palier Farm and shot nearly all of them down. The subsequent artillery fire prevented any further attacks from this location.

Once the dense veil of smoke and dust slowly began to dissipate it allowed the defenders to finally see across to the British trenches. New waves of attackers were observed forming and advancing but the well-placed curtain of artillery fire quickly broke up this attack aided by heavy rifle and machine gun fire. By noon reports were received from the front line companies that the entire position was in German hands. The actual fighting had only lasted several hours and there had been only a few breaches in the German lines that had been quickly contained and then destroyed. The attack against this portion of the Gommecourt front had come to an end other than sporadic artillery fire for the rest of the day.

Gommecourt South – the 56th Division

The Germans facing the 56th Division south of Gommecourt included parts of RIR 55 and IR 170 (52nd Division). The defenders along this portion of the front line had experienced the same level of destructive fire as the trenches north of the village. The bombardment on the morning of 1 July on this front included 15-inch shells. Almost all of the wire obstacles in an area 50 meters wide in front of Sector G5 in had been destroyed in the heavy fire. Dugout entrances had been blown in and the trenches were badly damaged. The major problem facing the men holding this portion of the line was that the trenches in G5 were enfiladed from the direction of Fonquevillers. Nearly every shell fired at this target landed inside the trench making it almost impossible to maintain sentry posts or lookouts that could observe the start of an enemy attack.

The front was covered in smoke and dust and visibility was very poor during the final bombardment. When the attack came at 7.30 a.m. the men holding the right wing of the 6/R55 and the right wing of the 8/R55[8] were able to observe the enemy advance in time to exit their dugouts to meet the assault waves and drive them back with heavy rifle and machine gun fire while calling for barrage fire from the batteries positioned in the rear.

However, the men in the platoon at the left wing of the 8th Coy were unable to occupy their trenches in time due to the heavy damage to the exits to their dugout and the British overran the position. The first wave was soon followed by others and only a few men in the left wing platoon were able to prepare a defensive line under *Leutnant der Reserve* Hällander who set up barricades and blocked off the trenches leading to his position. This small group was able to repulse the succeeding British waves that were advancing out of *Patrouillen Wäldchen* [Patrol Wood] However, there were so few men who survived the initial rush they could do nothing more than hold their small section of trench and this only barely. The news of the penetration was quickly sent to headquarters, there was still hope help would be sent.

At 7.30 a.m. *Hauptmann* von Schroetter, 16/RFAR 20, made the observation 'The enemy has overrun sectors N1 and N2 and has pushed forward between *Süd Graben* and *Roth Graben* beyond Gommecourt Cemetery as far as the beginning of the *1st Garde Stellung* and the *Kernwerk*'.[9]

A large number of men from RIR 55 had been taken prisoner in the opening moments of the attack. Some British accounts indicate that approximately 300 German prisoners were sent back to the British lines as a result of the fighting on the morning of 1 July.[10] In one instance a captured officer from RIR 55 simply did not want to end up as a prisoner. *Leutnant* Gustav Feger, 8/R55 was among the men captured when his platoon was overrun by the British in Sector G5.

White linen tape had been laid down indicating the route from the German lines back to the British trenches that was to be used by the German prisoners making their way to the rear. Feger was able to escape from his captors while in no man's land and took refuge in a shell hole in all of the confusion. He was discovered by a British soldier at one point but apparently avoided being recaptured by feigning death. He remained in hiding until later in the day and was able to make his way back to his lines during the German counter attack against Sector G5, having suffered only minor wounds.

Approximately two companies of British troops had penetrated the German lines through the *Roth Graben* and *Süd Graben* and advanced toward the village via the Gommecourt cemetery up to the junction of the *Kernwerk* and *Garde Stellung*. The first

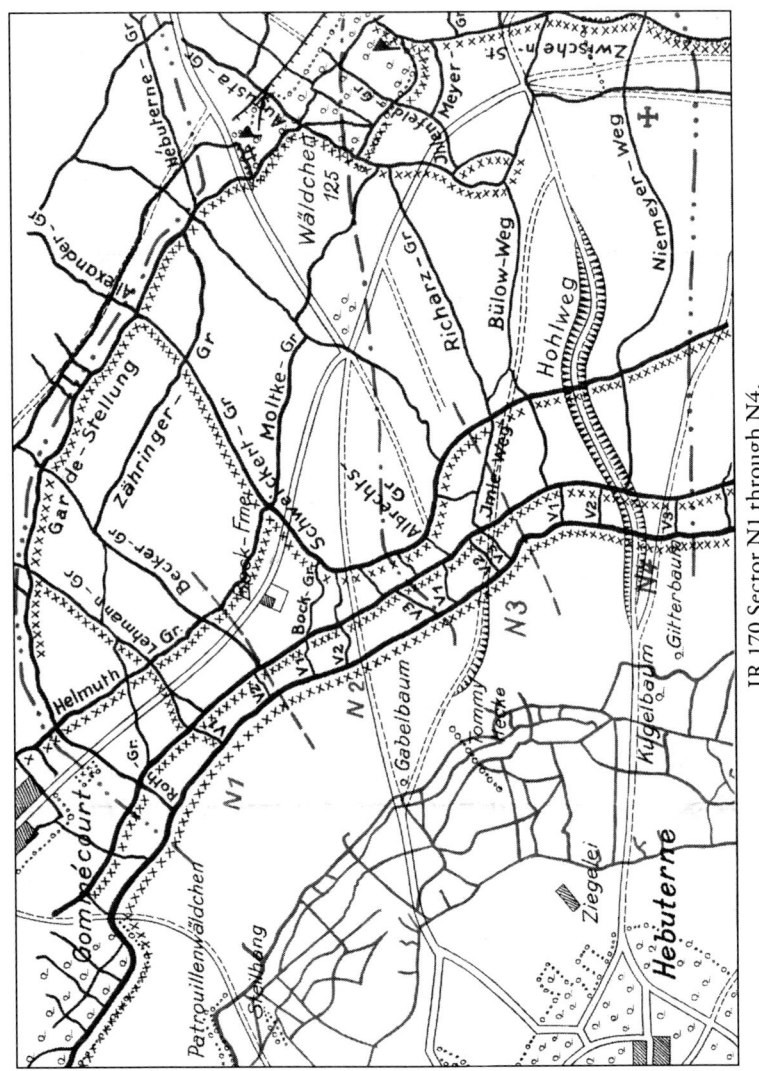

IR 170 Sector N1 through N4.

two trenches fell quickly to the advancing troops but the garrison of the third trench put up a stubborn defense. The British made some headway only after determined attacks through nearby communication trenches.

The attackers were eventually stopped by the Infantry *Pionier* Coy/R55 (150 rifles) and the *pionier* platoon of *Vizefeldwebel* Korthaus, 4/*Pionier* Bn 10 using rifle fire and hand grenades. The attackers were eventually driven back toward the cemetery. Afterward all routes leading into the *Kernwerk* were blocked off to prevent any further enemy advance in this direction.

One machine gun located in Sector G5 found itself in the middle of a battle where it was difficult to tell where the enemy was located. Even though the trenches around them were being overrun and most of the gun crew had been wounded or killed, this gun still provided much needed support against the British attack and continued to remain in use until the British were driven out of the position later in the day. Despite the loss of several guns, the machine gunners in MGSST 73 would play an important role in the defense of Gommecourt.

It should be noted that two *Schützen* from Machine Gun No. 8, who were still unhurt after their gun had been overrun (three [guns] in the first surprise) immediately dragged the gun into a dugout without being prevented by the British. They covered it with a groundsheet and sat on it. So they were able to place the gun in action against the withdrawing enemy at the right moment. The Gun Captain, *Unteroffizier* Schultheis, brought his gun into position (G5) in time to cause the attackers heavy losses. *Gefreiter* Freiberger acted as *Schütze* No. 3.[11] *Schützen* Hauptmeier, Hast and Gefreiter Berkefeld brought up the ammunition. Suddenly the enemy appeared in their rear and threw hand grenades. Freiberger was seriously wounded. Hauptmeier and Hast were also wounded. The Englishmen called upon *Unteroffizier* Schultheis to surrender. Schultheis, who was being supplied with cartridges by *Gefreiter* Berkefeld, refused. He threw his gun around and fired to the rear until hand grenades thrown by the Englishmen who came from all sides killed both men. Gun 7, commanded by *Gefreiter* Niemeyer, stood to the right of Gun 6. Niemeyer succeeded in repelling the enemy both frontally as well as the opponents who had penetrated into the trench from one side and from the rear. He caused the enemy heavy losses and prevented them from being able to expand their gains in the trench to the right. When Niemeyer was killed by a shot to the head, Hennig operated the gun in the same manner and fired with much success into the dense masses of fleeing Englishmen. Examination of the corpses indicated that he fired with great calmness and an excellent dispersal of fire. *Leutnant* Koch, Machine Gun Marksman Detachment 73[12]

All attempts by the British to expand their gains on both sides of the penetration were blocked by rifle fire and hand grenades. *Unteroffizier* Sieger from the 3rd Coy and *Unteroffizier* Laufermann from the 2nd Company were singled out for praise for their actions during the defensive fighting.

At 7.40 a.m. *Hauptmann* Minck, commanding II/R55, issued orders to the 7/R55 (158 rifles, 2 machine guns) positioned in the *Kernwerk* to attack the British and expel them from the German trenches.

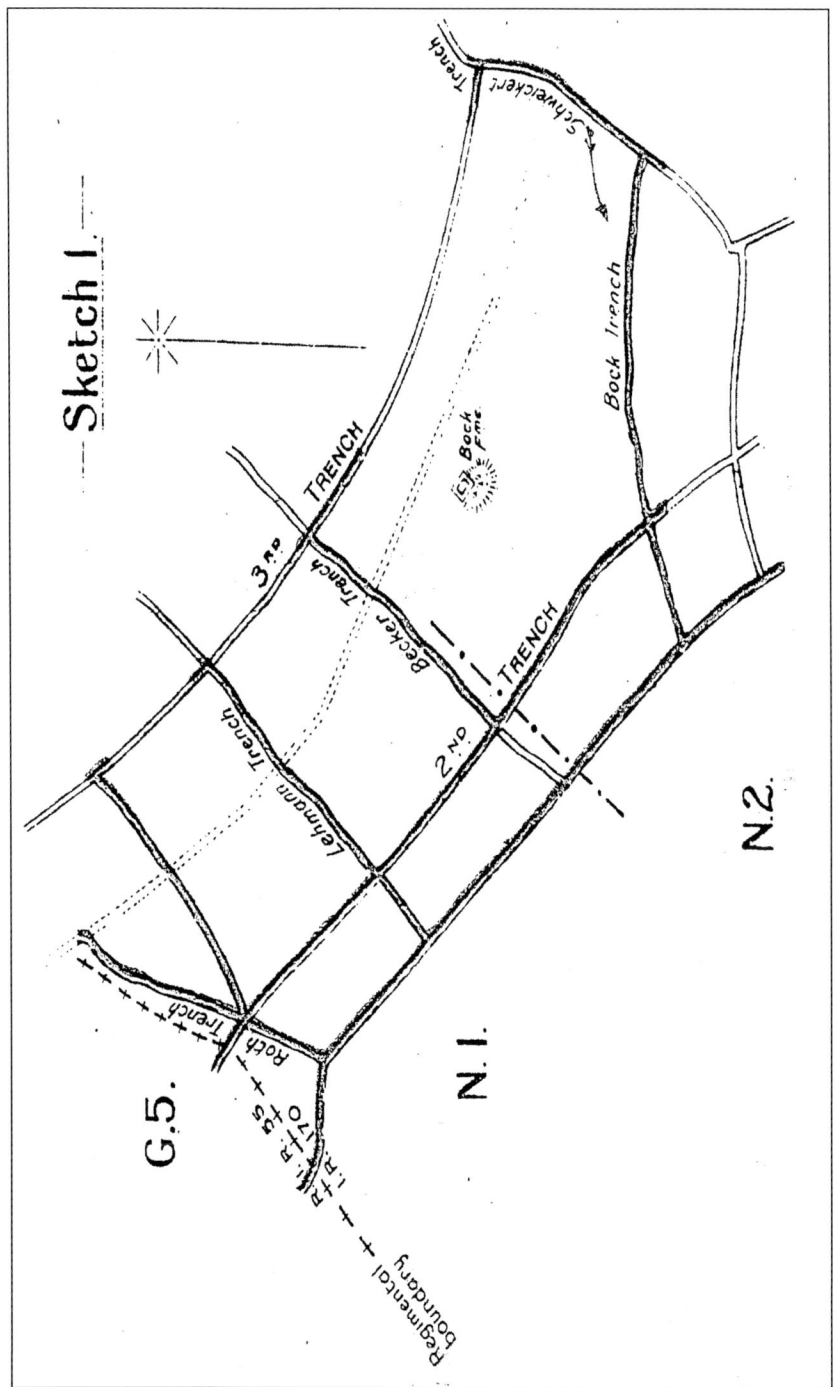

— Sketch I. —

Sketch I.

G.5.

N.1.

N.2.

British penetration into German trenches at G5, N1 and N2

No. 7 Company will at once attack the enemy who has penetrated into G5 and the sector of the 8th Company. The attack will be made through the *Süd Graben*.[13]

Hauptmann der Reserve Brockmann, 7/R55 did not feel his company was in a position to execute this order and instead assisted in holding the enemy in check with the assistance of a light *Minenwerfer*. The British eventually dug in approximately 100 meters in front of the *Kernwerk* and quickly installed two machine guns between the *Hauser Graben* and the *Süd Graben*.

Because most of the telephone lines had been destroyed in the preliminary bombardment and other forms of signaling were ineffective due to the dense smoke and fog there was no quick way to send a report about the situation to battalion headquarters and runners had to be used.

At 7.50 a.m. *Hauptmann* Minck issued the following order:

No. 10 Company will leave small parties in the *Riegelstellung* and will occupy *Kernwerk* Left. The 7th Company will attack the enemy who has penetrated into G5. Regiment informed![14]

Minck sent a report of his actions to regimental headquarters but it did not arrive until 10.25 a.m. due to the difficulties encountered by the runner. While still unaware of the events taking place in and around Gommecourt, the commander of RIR 55 issued new orders at 8 a.m.

One Platoon, 11th Company, 55th Reserve Regiment (Bucquoy), will advance through *Radfahrer Graben* and will occupy the *2nd Riegelstellung*. The 10th Company (*Riegelstellung*) will leave the *2nd Riegelstellung* clear. Acknowledge receipt to Regimental Headquarters.[15]

The neighboring regiment, IR 170, was also having difficulties driving off the British attack. The regiment reported extremely heavy bombardment starting at 6 a.m., especially on the 2nd and 3rd trenches that included mine throwers of the heaviest type. At 7 a.m. thick clouds of smoke appeared moving across the position from the southwest to the northeast and it was so dense that the normally good observation of the enemy trenches was completely blocked.

The men in Sector N1 in the 2/170 under *Leutnant* Bahl and the support troops from the 3/170 under *Oberleutnant der Reserve* Reinicke that were adjacent to the 8/R55, had not observed the British troops because the smoke cloud was so dense. The enemy had broken through the front near the *Roth Graben* and now was advancing toward Gommecourt cemetery. Shortly after 8 a.m. a large part of these troops turned to the south and rolled up the right wing of Sector N1. Faced with this threat the garrison of N1 vacated the 1st and 2nd trenches and moved into the *Helmut Graben* where the men formed a defensive line in conjunction with the 4/170 under *Leutnant* Itt.

British attempts to penetrate at the neighboring sector N2 were repulsed by well-aimed rifle and machine gun fire, as the garrison had been able to occupy the trenches in a timely manner. The garrison at the right wing of Sector N3 was also having some difficulties because the dense smoke allowed the attackers to approach the trench unseen.

Radfahrer Graben. (*Vom westlichsten Teil der Westfront*)

A large part of the 5/170 under *Hauptmann der Reserve* Mühlhaus at the right wing of N3 were forced back under the pressure of the advancing British troops until they had reached the 3rd trench. Once inside the German lines part of the British force turned north and attacked the left flank of Sector N2 at the *Albrechts Graben*. The hard pressed garrison of N2 had been forced to evacuate the first trench that had been largely leveled in the bombardment but held their ground against the attacks from both flanks and continued to hold the remaining trenches of the first position.

The remaining parts of the 5/170 holding the left wing of the sector as well as the 6/170 (*Leutnant* Thum) in Sector N4 held their ground against the attacks thereby limiting the British penetration to only two locations in N1 and N3 and the first trench of N2. The 7/170 under *Leutnant* Raapke was ordered forward to support the 6th and 5/170 effectively preventing the British from expanding their gains into the rest of N3 and N4.

The situation was serious at several locations but not hopeless. Many parts of the front line were still in German hands and the British penetrations were being contained for the present. The German artillery called up at the start of the attack had placed an almost impenetrable wall of fire in front of the British trenches making it extremely difficult to send reinforcements or supplies to the men inside the German trenches who needed them desperately.

At this time IR 170 sent the following message to RIR 55 informing the regiment of the situation on its left flank:

Infantryman – IR 170. (Author's collection)

At 8.35 enemy attack developed from Sectors 16-18. At 9.05 gas attack against Sector North. At 9.15 attack took place from Sector 19. At 9.30 the enemy penetrated into G5 threatening our right flank. We hold the third trench.[16]

At 9.30 a.m. RIR 55 issued the following order to the III Battalion in Bucquoy:

Major Tauscher with his battalion, including the Construction Company, should advance via the *2nd Garde Stellung* and expel the enemy who penetrated in G5. Report when ready to begin the operation. Machine guns will be made available. The battalion commander's post is to be on Hill 147.[17]

By 9.45 a.m. IR 170 had also made plans for a counter attack that would hopefully drive the British out of the German trenches. The 9th and 10/170 were in position to attack the enemy in the northern sector at N1. At the same time the hard-pressed RIR 55 sent a request for support. Despite the heavy fighting in their sector IR 170 was able to send two companies to assist RIR 55, the 11th and 12/170.

The 8th and 10/R15 from the brigade reserve were then moved forward to occupy the positions vacated by the 11th and 12/170. The companies from RIR 15 moved from the second position using the *Blücher Graben* and *Ihlenfeld Graben*. The 8/R15 remained as sector reserve while the 10/R15 with two platoons formed part of the counter attack along with detachments from *Pionier* Coy 103. The third platoon of the 10/R15 joined in the fighting with the II/170. In addition to the companies from RIR 15, the 8/R77 was moved to Bucquoy at 9.40 a.m. to assist RIR 55 if needed.

At 11 a.m. Major Tauscher went to the Reserve Battle Headquarters on Hill 147 west of the *Birkenwald* where he would be able to coordinate the efforts of the German counter attack. All the while these plans were being made; British troops from the 56th Division continued to press against the defenders in the *Garde Stellung*. The front line troops needed some relief or there was a possibility they could break.

The British were still firmly dug in at the left flank and still applying pressure against the *Garde Stellung*. It was decided that an attack directly south of the *Kernwerk* was not possible. In the meantime approximately 100 men from the 10/R55 (162 rifles) advanced into the redoubt from the *2nd Riegelstellung*.

Tauscher soon learned that British troops still occupied Sectors N1 and N3 by IR 170. Now that he had accurate information about the overall situation facing his regiment and IR 170 he issued orders for the 11/R55, *Leutnant der Reserve* Stolper to attack the British through the *Roth Graben* and the 12/R55, *Hauptmann der Landwehr* Winkelmann to attack through the *Lehmann Graben*. The 9/R55 under *Hauptmann Terberger* would remain in reserve in the *2nd Riegelstellung* as well as send men into the attack to support the 11th and 12th Coy when needed. The British had constructed barricades in both the *Roth Graben* and the *Lehmann Graben* as well as in the *Becker Graben* while at the same time occupying the ground in between all three trenches. It would prove difficult to force them back.

The 11th and 12/R55 began their attacks and slowly advanced against a stubborn adversary. Much of the fighting was at close quarters and both sides suffered losses as the British were being forced out of the German trenches traverse by traverse.

The 12th Coy advanced with *Gefreiters* Osthof and van Egeren at the front along with

Reserves moving up to the front – RIR 15. (*Das Königlich-Preussische Reserve-Infanterie-Regiment Nr. 15*)

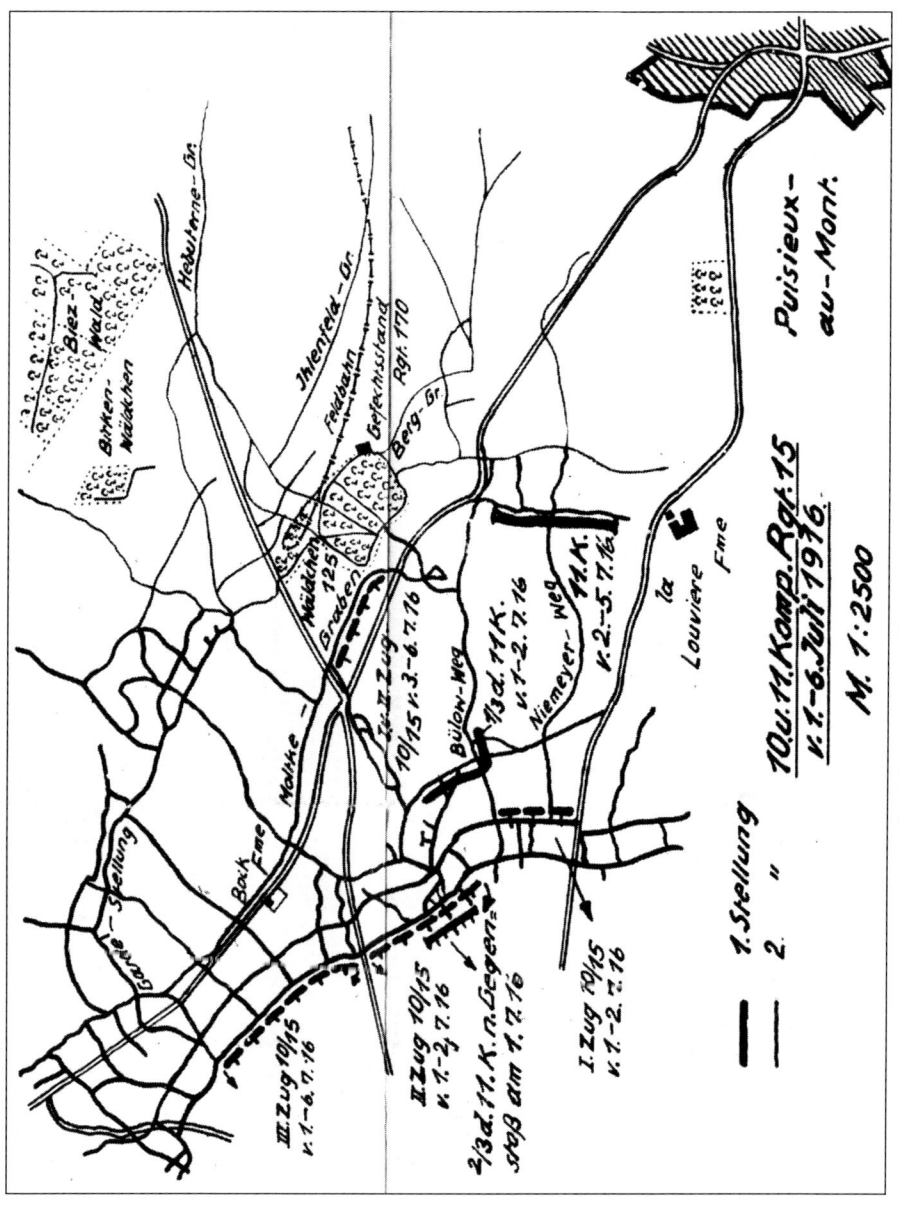

Positions occupied by RIR 15 on 1 July 1916.

Infantrymen – IR 170. (Author's collection)

Musketiers Breidenbach, Liebig, Elberfeld and Kochleida from the 10th Coy and three men from the 9th Coy. The first trench was captured along with the recovery of two German machine guns. A number of German prisoners were released and 50 British prisoners were taken. Many enemy soldiers who were forced to flee were shot down as they attempted to evade the German counter attack.

The 11th Coy advanced behind a hail of hand grenades. *Leutnant* Eilbracht, leader of the 2nd Platoon made sure that there were sufficient hand grenades available for the attack and ensured a constant fresh supply when they threatened to run out. *Unteroffizier* Manns assumed command over the bombing parties. During the advance *Landsturm Rekruit* Anton Tochtrop, *Musketier* Höwedes and several men from IR 170 received praise for their actions this day. It seemed as if the 11th Coy gained ground with almost every hand grenade being thrown as one barricade after another was captured and the British were forced back toward the old German front line. Tochtrop jumped out of the trench at the mouth of the third trench in order to signal the nearby assault detachments on their right of their presence and was killed when he exposed himself.

Gefreiter Oechler, who was considered an accomplished bomber, immediately took his place. While a large part of the company took up positions in the 3rd trench in order to secure their gains the attack went forward. *Unteroffizier* Manns was able to establish a connection to the left and in a short time the men had reached the 2nd trench.

Some of the troops from RIR 15 that had been sent forward to participate in the attack were having difficulty making any headway in the badly damaged trenches and were hindered by enemy machine gun fire. They were not able to participate in the fighting as a result.

Losses began to mount, many involving serious wounds from headshots that required other men to carry them to the rear for treatment. Manns and Oechler crawled closer to the position held by the British with the remaining men and succeeded in reaching the front trench while under the heaviest fire. *Musketier* Grodzki was hit in the head and killed during the attempt and others were wounded but there were still sufficient numbers to continue the attack. A machine gun was captured that was quickly put into use against its former owners. The front trench was taken and a number of prisoners belonging to IR 170 were released.

In order for the 12th Coy to enter the *Lehmann Graben* they first had to pass through the *Garde Stellung. Vizefeldwebel* Czibulka led the attack. Accompanied by two men they penetrated into the *Lehmann Graben* using four hand grenades to kill two British soldiers, wounding three others while also shooting five that tried to escape. The remaining enemy soldiers disappeared behind a nearby traverse. Czibulka threw the fifth hand grenade behind the traverse and within a short time a wounded Englishman came forth with his hands raised. Czibulka jumped up on the fire step holding another hand grenade and shouted loudly in the direction where the soldier had come from and in a short time 17 British soldiers surrendered. His actions this day brought praise from *Hauptmann* Winkelmann, his company commander.

Once this trench had been cleared *Gefreiter* Fritz Krüger along with *Musketiers* Heuermann, Fogoner and Helweg advanced toward the second trench where they were able to smoke out a number of dugouts and captured a machine gun. Once the British had been

Sketch of terrain near Bock Farm. (*Vom westlichsten Teil der Westfront*)

Infantryman – IR 170. (Author's collection)

forced back as far as they could go inside the German lines they attempted to run across no man's land back toward the British lines where many were killed by rifle and machine gun fire from the 11th and 12th Coy along with supporting fire from the 9th Coy.

Two groups from the 9th Coy under *Offizier Stellvertreter* Hau and *Vizefeldwebel* Steinmann joined in the attack. They advanced through the *Schweickert Graben* and *Becker Graben* up to the 2nd trench. Once here they were able to establish a connection with IR 170 on their left and soon determined that the British still held the trenches to their right. They moved against the British positions using rifle fire and hand grenades, forcing them out of the trench and then continued their advance to the old German front line. The defenders were apparently short of hand grenades but nevertheless put up a good fight. In the end they had to vacate the position because of the heavy fire and in particular because of the seemingly limitless hand grenades being thrown by the Germans. They were forced to leave behind 60 dead. The main fighting was over by 4p.m.

The companies from IR 170 had advanced at the same time as those from RIR 55. The fighting in Sectors N1 and N2 quickly turned into a fierce hand grenade battle. After a great deal of effort the enemy was cleared from the trenches in N2 by 4.30p.m. Over the next 90 minutes the British were also forced out of Sector N1 and the fighting was over in this sector about 6p.m.

At the right wing of N3 the British were in possession of all three trench lines. After capturing the German trenches they quickly prepared them for defense. A few reinforcements arrived after great difficulty due to the heavy artillery fire falling in front of the British lines and throughout no man's land. The British had every appearance of continuing their advance into the *Bülow Graben* and then on to the intermediate position. The 8/170 had been forced back toward Bock Farm [Nameless Farm] because of the heavy British pressure. However, the British were never able to capture the farm because of the determined German defense. The heavy fighting also sapped much of the British strength and quickly used up their supply of hand grenades.

In the early afternoon the British attempted to send further reinforcements across no man's land several times. These attempts proved to be disastrous on each occasion. The battalions suffered numerous losses in the heavy shell and machine gun fire before they could advance very far from their own trench. Soon the attempts had to be called off. There were so many wounded in no man's land calling for help and the survivors made great effort to bring them in.

At one point a German medical officer came out under a white flag and advised the British that the Germans had no objection to the removal of the wounded on the British side of the wire so long as no firing took place. The recovery of the wounded went smoothly until the truce was interrupted by a British field gun shelling the German trench. The battery had apparently been unaware of the unofficial truce. The men who had not been recovered by that time would have to wait for darkness before being rescued, for some this would prove to be too late.

Reports about the British advance in Sector N3 had taken a great deal of time reaching the regimental headquarters of IR 170. However the threat in this sector had already been spotted by the observation post located at the regimental headquarters and confirmed through a patrol by *Oberleutnant* Mayer and *Leutnant* Martin.

As a result of this new information the 11th and 12/170 were placed in possession of the II Battalion and an additional company was requested from the brigade reserve. The reserve company, 11/R15, arrived about 3 p.m. and was ordered to counter attack from

Light 7.6cm *Minenwerfer* and crew. (Author's collection)

behind Sector N2. *Leutnant* Petersen RIR 15 described their experience:

> Gas clouds covered the terrain and darkened the sun. On the road to Gommecourt R77er with combat packs rushed forward. Everyone was hurrying and making haste. The tubes of the still intact guns were cooled, then opened fire again. At Copse 125 we received instructions from the commander of the II Battalion IR 170; we received hand grenades, rifle and machine gun ammunition. The 11th Company was to eject the Tommies who penetrated into N3 and N2 and proceeds in a brilliant attack upon the Scottish and Yorkshire Fusiliers...unfortunately the long serving, proven *Feldwebel Leutnant* Stollberg was seriously wounded.[18]

Hauptmann von Busse, the commander of a light field howitzer battery located near the regimental headquarters, was asked verbally to fire upon the German trenches in Sector N3 that were occupied by the British starting at 4 p.m. and ending 5 minutes later. The howitzer battery opened rapid fire against the enemy occupied trenches causing a great deal of damage to the position and many casualties as dozens of 10.5cm shells rained down upon the British troops.

The Germans counter attacked immediately after the fire had ceased and by 6 p.m. Sector N3 was also clear of enemy troops. Many of the British defenders had been killed; others were shot down while attempting to escape back to their lines or were taken prisoner.

Leutnant Kaiser provided the after action report in place of *Feldwebel Leutnant* Stollberg:

> My report after the storm – sent at the same time with a captured machine gun – was delivered to the II/170. When the company reached Copse 125 around 2 o'clock in the

Infantrymen – RIR 55. (Author's collection)

afternoon I received instructions from the commander of the II Battalion to clear the trench in N3 with two saps and a communication trench to the 2nd trench that were occupied by the enemy. I requested artillery support. As soon as the howitzers began we began the storm at 3 o'clock in the afternoon on the completely leveled trench. Therefore the company did not make any progress with the procedure of rolling up the trench. So we attacked from the rear and out over the parapet over the open field with hand grenades. The enemy now moved quickly to the rear. Some Tommies already surrendered now. Our men behaved brilliantly. Within one half hour the trench was cleared under continuous cheering.

We captured a machine gun and an American quick fire rifle. *Leutnant* Stollberg lies in front with a stomach shot. *Feldwebel* Piepertz was killed; *Vizefeldwebel* Strohmeyer was wounded. Losses otherwise: 3 dead, 6 wounded, 3 missing. We were able to release many 170er from the dugouts. 1 officer, 60 men, mostly from the London Scottish Regiment, became taken prisoner. The artillery fired very well and accurate. All is in the best order. Kaiser.[19]

At the same time the attack was proceeding in Sector N3 the 7/R55 under *Hauptmann* Brockmann advanced through the second line from *Hauser Graben* with the aid of light *Minenwerfers* from the 6th *Garde Minenwerfer* Coy and several machine guns from Machine Gun Marksman Detachment 73 under *Vizefeldwebel* Lindemann. The 10/R55 and parts of the 6th and 8/R55 were also pressing forward.

Strong resistance by the British defenders held up their initial advance until the *Minenwerfers* were employed, which provided an opening in the enemy defenses. Afterward the advance went quickly with the men primarily using hand grenades.

Bombing parties joined parts of the 6th, 8th and 10th Coy and a platoon from the 4/ *Pionier* Bn 10 as these companies attacked the third trench in Sector G5 and the ground between the trench and the *Kernwerk*. During the attacks 2 British officers and 70 Other Ranks were captured. By 4 p.m. much of G5 had been recaptured but enemy troops still occupied the 2nd trench and the *Süd Graben*. The German soldiers were almost done in and did not have the strength needed to completely recapture the few remaining trench pieces.

At 7 p.m. the 11th and 12/R55, having been relieved by units from IR 170 that had reoccupied their old positions, were directed to assist in the counter attack in Sector G5. The attack was made through the *Roth Graben* along with 80 men from the Infantry *Pionier* Coy. Before the order could be delivered elements of the 11/R55 had already advanced into Sector G5, on their own initiative, and had recaptured much of the front line, nearly up to the *Süd Graben*. Major Tauscher, II/R55, provided support for these attacks by sending an additional 80 men and the Infantry *Pionier* Coy through the *Roth Graben*.

While the majority of the German trenches lost during the fighting earlier in the day had been recaptured there were still areas where small pockets of British soldiers were trapped in the German lines. The British troops were quickly running out of bombs including captured German ones. The German attacks were slowly pushing the British back toward the German front line and under these circumstances some of the British wounded who were capable of walking attempted to make their way back to their own lines in the hope of escaping capture or possible death.

Once most of the wounded were on their way back, the last organized party inside the

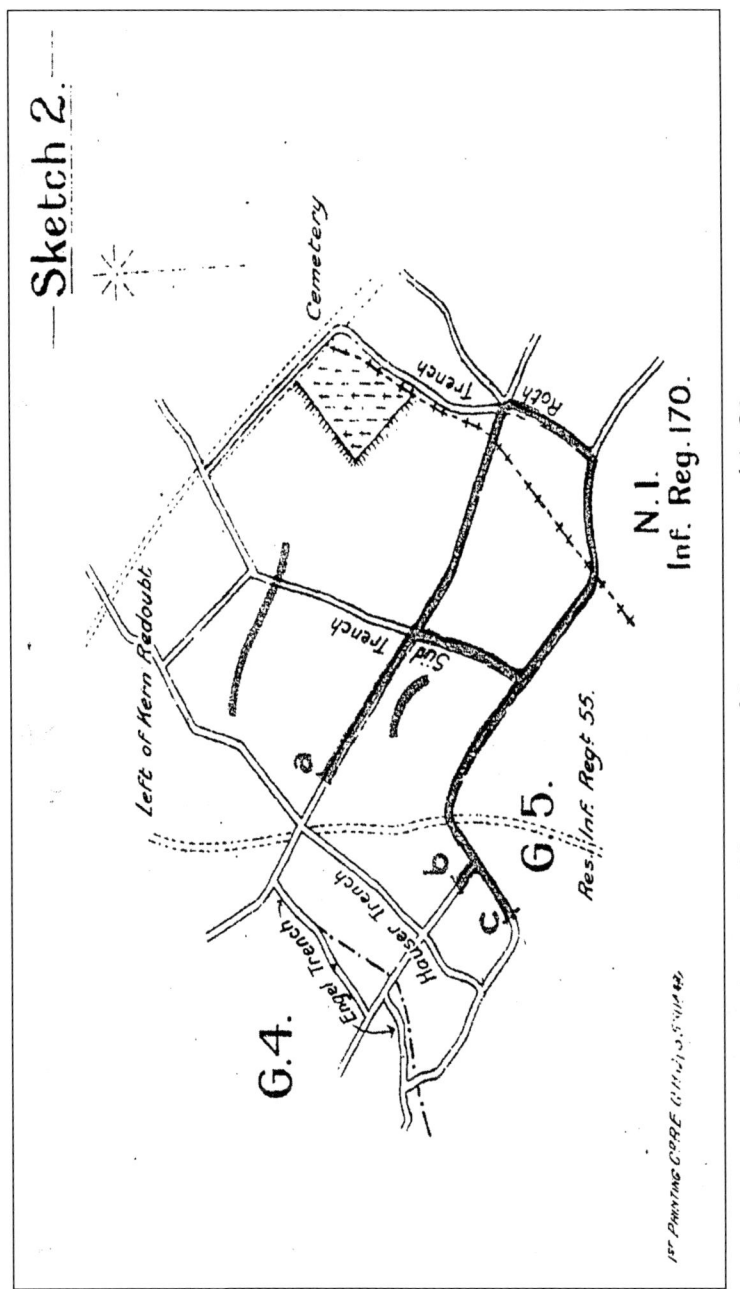

Sketch 2.

Cemetery

Roth Trench

Left of Kern Redoubt

Süd Trench

N.I.
Inf. Reg. 170.

Res. Inf. Regt 55.

G.5.

a

b

c

G.4.

Engel Trench

Hauser Trench

1ST PRINTING CORE (illegible)

Positions at start of German counter attack in G5.

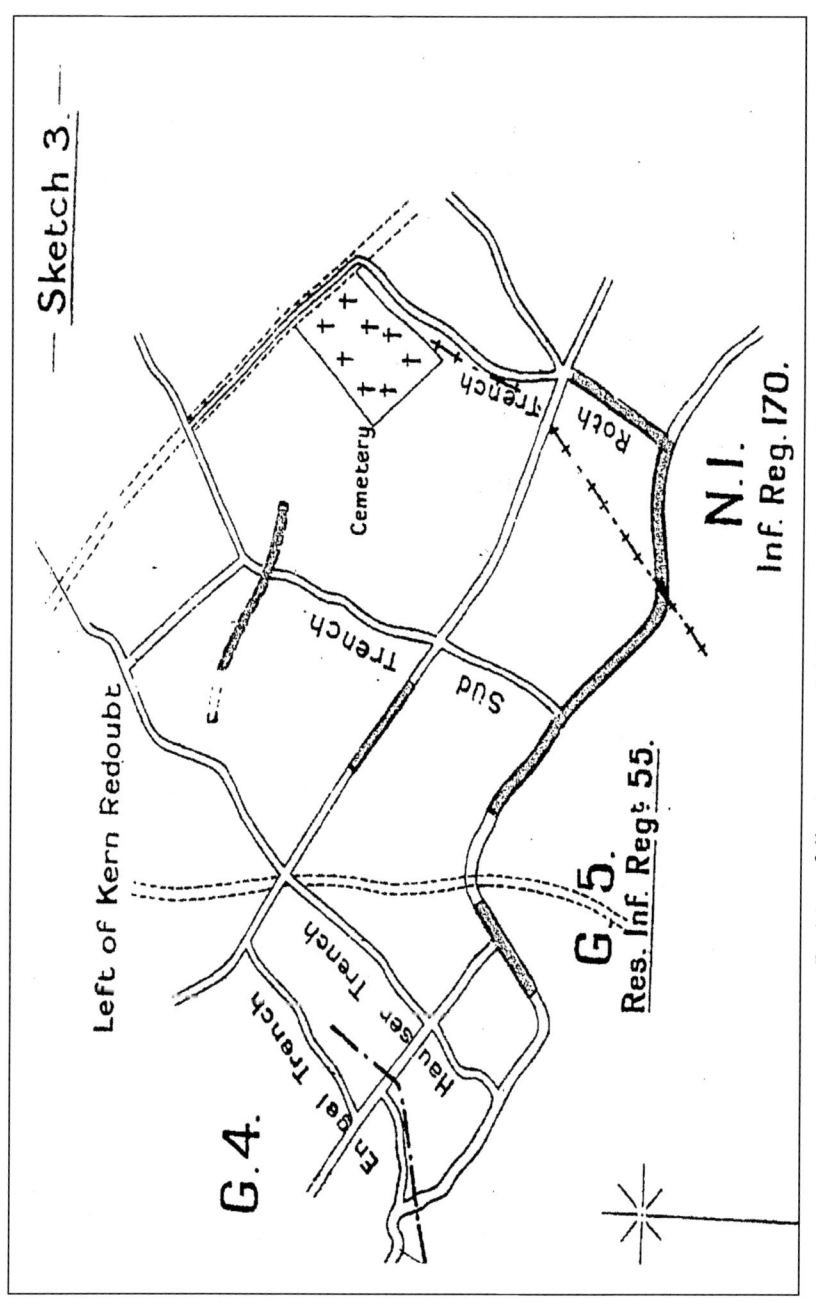

Positions following successful German counter attacks in G5

Zum Andenken
an unsern lieben Sohn

Martin Wassmer

Gefreiter im Feld-Art.-Regt. Nr. 103
Ritter des eisernen Kreuzes
geboren am 20 Juli 1893
gefallen im Kampfe fürs Vaterland am 1. Juli 1916.

Memorial card: *Gefreiter* Martin Wassmer, FAR 103, killed
in action 1 July 1916. (Author's collection)

German trench, code named Ferret on British maps, consisted of 5 officers and 70 men. These men provided cover while the remainder of the walking wounded withdrew to the British lines. Before too long the last survivors were finally driven out of the relative safety of the trench and into the barbed wire and shell holes.

Without anywhere to go and with the knowledge that the wounded had already started back the survivors began their withdrawal. The men came under rifle and machine gun fire as they attempted to return across no man's land, losing heavily in the process.

The last party did not reach the British lines until about 9.30 p.m. There was no one left in the German trenches other than some wounded, a few men who had become separated from their friends and the men who had already been captured. The Germans reported the position was in their hands once more at 9.45 p.m.

While the last organized British detachment had been forced out of the German trenches there were still individual soldiers that had to be rounded up. In one case the actions of a German officer would make the difference between becoming another name on the Thiepval Memorial or on a P.O.W. list. This incident occurred toward the end of the fighting, and could be considered almost comical if not for the immense tragedy surrounding the men on all sides.

> *Leutnant* Steenbock, 10/R55, now a director of a savings bank in Neustadt in Holstein, was a true *Frisian*, large and blond, who was admittedly a good sportsman and some months later transferred to MGSST 73. He was in the front line during the clearing of the position as well as his faithful orderly Haberstroh. Once, when a tall Englishman stood up behind a traverse in order to run to the rear, Steenbock shouted 'Don't shoot, I want to take him alive.' At the same instant he ran across the field between them after the Englishman and it now became a race, whereby Steenbock came closer and closer to the fleeing man. In addition, the orderly, who obviously did not want to leave his *Leutnant* alone, ran after him. In the moment when Steenbock had almost reached

the fleeing man Steenbock fell into a shell hole so that the Englishmen threatened to escape. However his orderly ran further and succeeded in seizing the Englishman and bringing him back to the rear. Thereby he proudly came to his *Leutnant* saying '*Herr Leutnant*, we caught him nevertheless.'[20]

At midnight the entire regimental position was reorganized and the tedious job of restoring the position was started. The enemy cooperated in this effort with most of the British artillery fire falling on the *Kernwerk*.

At midnight of 1 July new orders were issued regarding the makeup of the sector. Sectors G1, G2 and the right of the *Kernwerk* would be held by the I/R55. Sectors G3 and G4 as well as the left of the *Kernwerk* would be held by the II Battalion including the Infantry *Pionier* Company and the 4/*Pionier* Bn 10. Sector G5, *1st Riegelstellung* and left of the *2nd Riegelstellung* and the *2nd Garde Stellung* would be occupied by the III Battalion. The 8/R77 would hold the right portion of the *2nd Riegelstellung*.

After the fighting was over the commander of the 11/R55 mentioned several men in his company because of their courageous behavior in the counter attack. *Musketiers* Michels, Stawitzki, Köhler I, Niess, Kunz, Brinkmann and Weger were particularly mentioned in his after action report. An officer in IR 170 who prepared a written statement mentioning his courageous actions also singled out *Unteroffizier* Manns for his exceptional behavior.

Once the fighting had died down many of the surviving German soldiers had time to reflect upon the events of this momentous day. Above all else they were dirty and tired but very glad to be alive. Several men fighting near Gommecourt left a record of their thoughts on the fighting on 1 July:

We were hardened, experienced soldiers. It wasn't fair to send these young soldiers against us. Some of them were only students and we felt very sorry for them. *Gefreiter* Hugo van Egeren, RIR 55[21]

During the heavy fighting on 1 July the German artillery had been able to play an important role in the successful defense of the German lines as well as in several local counter attacks. Despite coming under heavy and often accurate fire from British guns the batteries assigned to the 111th, 2nd Guard Reserve and 52nd Divisions had been able to maintain a constant wall of fire between the opposing trench systems. They also effectively bombarded the British lines making it almost impossible to send men or supplies to the troops trapped in the German trenches.

The practice of inter-division cooperation and the concentration of artillery fire, especially from the flank, introduced from the lessons learned during the fighting at Serre in June 1915 apparently had been perfected.

When *Gruppe Süd* was ordered by the artillery commander to support the threatened sectors held by the 52nd Infantry Division, Major Niederstein reported that he was already laying blocking fire on those sectors, reinforced by batteries belonging to *Gruppe Nörd*. Despite repeated attempts by dense attack waves, British supporting troops that tried to follow through at 12.45 and 3 p.m. did not manage to pass through our artillery fire, which alternated between a rolling barrage and blocking fire. Troops gathered for fresh attacks, particularly at *Patrouillen Wäldchen* and in

Sector 10, were identified and engaged with complete success. Under the protection of this extraordinarily effective artillery fire, the reserves [from 2nd Guard Reserve Division Battalion Tauscher, III/RIR 55, which advanced through the *Roth Graben* and *Lehmann Graben*, and two companies of IR 170 from 52nd Infantry Division] deployed to counter-attack the infiltrating enemy forcing them to yield in heavy close quarter fighting. The fleeing British troops did not escape our artillery fire.[22]

This inter-divisional support did not go unnoticed by the British:

The manner in which the enemy managed to concentrate gun fire from a wide front on to the place where it could be most usefully employed deeply impressed British staff officers.[23]

The ammunition consumption by the artillery batteries of the 2nd Guard Reserve Division had been enormous. Large quantities of shells had already been fired in response of the week-long British bombardment at the end of June but by far the largest number of shells fired was on 1 July. In order to ensure uninterrupted fire the battery commanders were diligent in keeping track of the supply of shells available for each battery and bringing up fresh supplies as needed. Thanks to the foresight of stockpiling large numbers of shells near each gun none of the batteries were forced to stop firing for lack of ammunition.

The artillery ammunition supply columns delivered new shells to each battery position starting as early as 10.30 a.m. For the most part the routes they traveled on were not under heavy fire. The greatest danger they faced was as they approached the battery positions that were under constant shellfire. However they were able to maintain their deliveries of new shells throughout the day without suffering any losses or interruption in their duties.

The 40 field guns (7.7cm) in the division alone fired 11,683 rounds on 1 July. This

7.7cm field gun and crew, Bavarian FAR 19. (Author's collection)

was the equivalent of almost 117 tons of ammunition. In addition to the problems of maintaining a high rate of fire there was another matter to consider, the logistical issue of the large numbers of empty shell casings and wicker ammunition basket carriers, 3,894 that were needed to transport nearly 12,000 rounds.

Many of the gunners were needed to keep the gun emplacements free of obstructions on that long, hot day. As new ammunition was brought forward it became increasingly difficult to dispose of the empty casings and wicker shell baskets from around the guns. If the baskets were allowed to build up they not only created an obstruction to any movement inside the gun positions, they also created a potential fire hazard if they were set ablaze.

The other guns of the 2nd Guard Reserve Division fired the following number of rounds on 1 July:[24]

10.5cm Light Field Howitzers (12)	4,429 rounds
9cm guns (8)	2,070 rounds
10cm guns, '14 (2)	609 rounds
15 cm Howitzer '96 (4)	481 rounds
15cm Howitzer '02/13 (8)	2,821 rounds
Russian 20.5cm guns (4)	258 rounds
21cm Howitzer, Old Pattern (2)	252 rounds

By the morning of 1 July most of the battery positions had been pinpointed by low flying British aircraft that directed accurate fire onto them. Despite the enemy shells falling all about the battery positions the guns kept up a rapid rate of fire. While the fire did not interrupt re-supplying the guns with ammunition it did disrupt the evacuation of the wounded.

The overall losses suffered by Bavarian FAR 19 on 1 July were quite light, 2 killed and about 15 wounded despite the hundreds of shells that fell around the battery positions. In addition to these losses many of the men suffered nervous disorders and complained of impaired hearing. That was not unexpected considering the noise they had endured from shells falling about them as well as the sound of their own guns being fired all day.

The 3/Bavarian FAR 19 firing from the edge of a road north of Gommecourt near the ruins of the village of Essarts had been under heavy fire for some days but had suffered little damage and on the morning of 1 July the guns continued to fire. The battery observation post was in the so-called *Granathecke* [Shell Hedge] opposite Fonquevillers and Hannescamps. The maze of trenches there and those flanking it to the south towards Hébuterne were the main targets of the battery. The battery had suffered some casualties but could still provide rapid and accurate support of the German front line.

Many of the batteries did suffer losses to gun crews and equipment throughout the day. In one instance, the 4/Bavarian FAR 19 that was located close to the road between Bucquoy and the *Ziegelwäldchen* and open to observation from Hébuterne had one gun placed out of action at 11 a.m. after receiving four direct hits by heavy caliber shells. Later another gun was knocked out by two direct hits be heavy caliber shells. The last serviceable gun continued to fire despite losing 1 man killed and 7 wounded including one officer. Even with the high number of casualties among the gun crew the remaining men still provided a high rate of fire despite the battery being down to one gun.[25]

Several of the gunners from the 4/Bavarian FAR 19 that had been wounded in the heavy shelling just before the infantry attack started were evacuated to a dressing station

Men from Reserve *Sanitäts* Coy 2, 2nd Guard Reserve Division. (Author's collection)

in *Gruppe Nord* set up near the 6/FAR 103 close to the *Ziegelwäldchen*. They had been placed in the telephone dugout to await treatment when two heavy shells struck the dugout burying all of the occupants.

Men came from all sides to quickly dig out their comrades all the while under heavy fire. During the rescue attempt two guns from the 6th Battery were hit and placed out of action resulting in even more casualties. It was only 7 a.m., 30 minutes before the scheduled attack.

The rescuers finally managed to create a hole down into the damaged dugout where they found to their amazement that the wounded men had been left untouched by the shells. The men were quickly removed using boards and then sent further to the rear some 150 meters away to a kitchen located near the edge of the wood. During the journey the stretcher-bearers were forced to take cover in large shell craters in order to avoid machine gun fire from low flying British aircraft that swarmed above the position. All of the wounded eventually made it safely to the kitchen where they were once again under cover.

By the end of the fighting there were many wounded soldiers from both sides scattered about the trenches. Earlier in the evening, after the 9th Coy had participated in recapturing the trenches formerly held by IR 170 one man, *Musketier* Rabbeau noticed that a British soldier still lay out in the wire entanglements in front of the trench. Rabbeau, the company tailor, had spent little time in the front lines during his time with the regiment but now he would play a small part in the acts of kindness and humanity that would have lasting effects

British prisoners being interrogated by *General der Infanterie Frhr.* von Süsskind. (Felix Fregin)

on several British soldiers who might otherwise have died alone and in pain.

Rabbeau and several others went out of the front line trench and brought in the wounded man and four others they found at the same time. There were two men left out in the open, a badly wounded British soldier and a badly wounded German soldier who had been shot three times in the thigh and once in the chest.

Rabbeau was unable to get these men back to the German trench during daylight and he decided to remain with them until it was dark enough to carry them to safety. He waited with them for over two hours until darkness fell and he sent for a stretcher. The stretcher-bearers were unable to reach Rabbeau and the wounded men due to the volume of enemy fire so Rabbeau decided to bring them to safety by himself if possible.

He managed to assist the badly wounded German soldier back across the barbed wire and into the German trench where medical personnel were waiting to help him. As he left the wounded British soldier reminded him that he had promised to come back for him as well.

Rabbeau and another man started to crawl back to the wounded man in order to keep his promise when they came under heavy fire. Rabbeau's companion decided it was not safe and turned back. Rabbeau continued to slowly crawl toward the wounded man as shells

Wounded British prisoners being treated by medical
officers from RIR 91. (Author's collection)

burst randomly about him and machine gun fire played across the terrain.

He was able to reach the wounded Englishman and with great effort he carried him to the rear piggyback. Once inside the trench the medical personnel started to treat and bandage his wounds. The prisoner showed his gratitude to Rabbeau for his rescue through hand gestures before being led back to the rear for medical care.

Rabbeau was praised for his actions and was apparently very embarrassed by the attention. He felt it should not be mentioned again for he only had sympathy for the moaning wounded still lying out in the open.

Sanitäts Unteroffizier Bernhard Holtmann, 10/R55 also succeeded in bringing in two wounded Englishmen on the evening of 1 July. He was accompanied by a *Sanitäts Hund* that was trained to locate and recover wounded men. It appears Holtmann had the knack for finding live prisoners while several of his comrades including *Unteroffizier* Otto and another apparently were only able to recover corpses from the wire. Perhaps it was not Holtmann that should be praised but the unnamed dog at his side.

Many of the wounded men lying out in no man's land under the hot July sun were finally recovered once darkness had fallen, and the rescue attempts continued until first light on 2 July Early on the 2nd the Germans hoisted a large Red Cross flag on their parapet opposite the 46th Division. Both sides sent out parties to collect wounded and nearly all of the British wounded were recovered. There was ceremonial saluting on both sides, but there was no fraternization.

Several days later a German plane flew over the British lines and dropped a list of the prisoners taken at Gommecourt. A similar list was sent to the Germans a short time later in the same manner.

When it became obvious that the British were going to attack Gommecourt in force, the medical service made plans in order to meet any contingency. RIR 55 issued orders

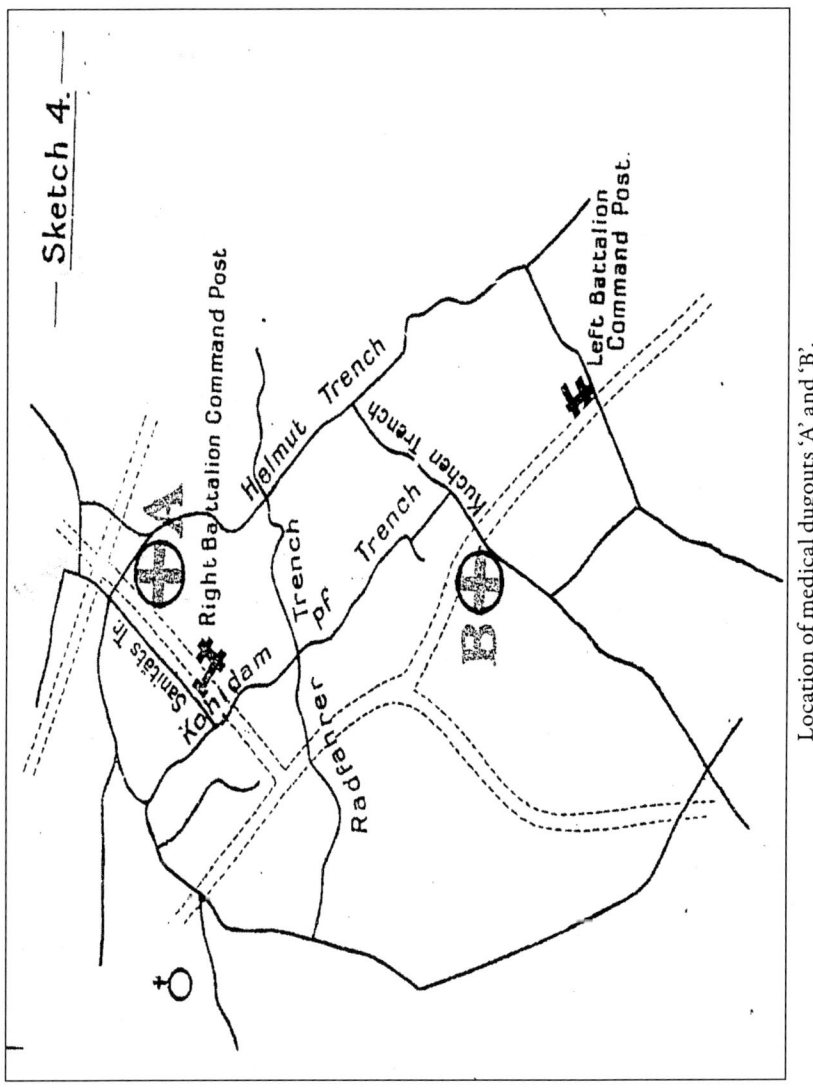

Location of medical dugouts 'A' and 'B'.

that the large medical dugout 'A' located near the right battalion command post near the *Sanitäts Graben* and *Helmut Graben* would be manned by three medical officers and the necessary support personnel. The dugout was fully equipped with large stores of medical supplies and dressing material as well as three wheeled stretchers.

This dugout had the capacity of holding up to 30 stretcher cases and 50-60 sitting cases for a period of several days if necessary. Sufficient supplies of food and water were stored inside the dugout and it was also able to supply nine stretchers for each company. Additional stretchers were created using poles and straw mats.

A second medical dugout, 'B' located along the *Kuchen Graben* was to be used as an intermediate point that would direct wounded to Medical Dugout 'A' after providing initial treatment of their wounds. It was decided to utilize the dugout in this manner when it was determined that dugout 'B' was difficult to access due to its location.

Medical Dugout 'B' would still be manned with one medical officer and the necessary support staff. The walls of both dugouts had been painted with a mixture of whitewash and carbide that was left over from the acetylene lamps. It was determined that this helped make the dugouts more comfortable and pleasant for the wounded men as well as reducing the odor of mildew and mold that was normally encountered in deep, mined dugouts.

Sanitary conditions were maintained throughout this period using an ample supply of disinfected latrine buckets and urine tubs that had been prepared in advance. These were emptied on a regular basis along with the removal of other waste in order to maintain a clean and sanitary environment.

The preliminary bombardment had caused most of the problems experienced by the medical staff. During the bombardment the nearby battalion headquarters was destroyed by heavy shells, forcing the battalion staff to take refuge inside Medical Dugout 'A'. The upper vaulted cellar of the dugout was also seriously damaged by heavy shells and evacuated after several shells blocked the entrance and threatened to collapse the cellar.

As a result of the damage additional supports were installed in the dressing station and all rooms and recesses of the dugout. With this added support the dugout remained intact throughout the following days of bombardment and fighting. Overall losses during the preliminary bombardment had been very light and the medical facilities had no problems dealing with the small numbers of wounded men that passed through the facilities.

The procedures to handle the sick and wounded put into place before the attack proved to be very effective. Any wounded cases brought in by the stretcher-bearers were examined at once and divided into categories depending upon their wound and ability to walk.

Slightly wounded men were assembled were collected in the medical company's dugout and divided into groups and marched back to Essarts in small parties under the command of the senior man present. The more seriously wounded were placed on stretchers and then after being treated they were evacuated to Essarts by ambulance. Normally this would be done by the medical company but circumstances prevented this from happening during the heaviest period of fighting and quite often men taken from the infantry companies were used to evacuate the stretcher cases.

After the heaviest fighting was over the medical company was able to resume its duties of transporting the stretcher cases to the rear. The staff in Medical Dugout 'A' provided services not only to the men of RIR 55 but also to those *pioniers*, *Minenwerfer* crews and prisoners that were brought in.

During the fighting on 1 July the *Hauptverbandplatz* (Main Dressing Station) of the

2nd Guard Reserve Division at Courcelles treated 739 wounded including 87 men who belonged to the 52nd Division and 157 English wounded. All of the walking wounded were collected in the medical dugout in Bucquoy and sent to the *Hauptverbandplatz* by trench tramway. The wounded that could not walk were transported in ambulances from Essarts to the *Hauptverbandplatz*.

All of the wounded treated at the *Hauptverbandplatz* were then sent to the 45th Field Hospital at Vaulx-Vraucourt and to the 17th Field Hospital at Fremicourt in ambulance wagons and specially prepared wagons. Because of the distance needed to travel to the Ambulance Section (*Krankentransport Abteilung*) in Vélu several rest stations were set up in Mory and Ervillers that could handle up to 200 cases at any one time.

The Germans were provided with a small piece of intelligence at the end of July that confirmed what they had already suspected, that London Regiments had attacked the 2nd Guard Reserve and 52nd Infantry Divisions. The details came from the *Morning Post* of 31 July 1916. The regiment also received a compliment, although a backhanded one at best:

> All of the English officers confirmed that the Germans had shown themselves as true Europeans in their behavior. The English litter bearers were permitted to come on the battleground and to fetch back the wounded, even ones lying in front of the position. Even some wounded who were already prisoners were delivered to them. We dealt with well-disciplined German troops. They were capable of such acts of philanthropy although they had conducted nearly two years of war with barbaric savageness.[26]

Shortly after the fighting on 1 July the 2nd Guard Reserve Division was able to take stock of the prisoners and materiel it had captured. The division was impressed by the level of preparation provided to the enemy soldiers as well as the quantity and type of equipment they had been given.

When the captured documents were reviewed the division found that the attackers had been provided with extremely detailed trench maps in which every German trench was systematically named and showed even the smallest details of the German position. Even

British prisoners captured on 1 July 1916. (Author's collection)

German soldiers displaying and wearing captured British
equipment, weapons and uniforms. (Author's collection)

the most recent work on the trench system had been added to the maps. The sectors taken
under attack were also shown on a very large scale including objectives for each unit as well
as detailed aerial photographs of the position.

The number of British prisoners captured on 1 July was given as 16 officers, 251 Other
Ranks. The amount of equipment and weapons captured was also quite large and consisted
of:

     10 heavy machine guns
     29 Lewis Guns
     95 drums of Lewis Gun ammunition
     5 machine gun mounts
     2 reserve barrels for machine guns
     2 shoulder pieces for machine guns
     6 trench mortars
     1 trench mortar bed
     915 rifles
     455 bayonets
     2 revolvers
     2 light/flare pistols
     65 steel helmets
     150 belts and frogs

1 pack
23 wire cutters including one used as an attachment to a rifle
10 knobkerries
97 spades
16 picks
6 telephone apparatus
3 reels of wire
1 signal apparatus
42 anti-gas apparatus
41 gas masks
4 gas helmets
4 sacks of English equipment

Ammunition:

11 boxes of S.A. ammunition
3,880 loose cartridges
44 boxes of machine gun ammunition
6,000 belted rounds of machine gun ammunition
2 sacks of machine gun ammunition
214 rifle grenades
381 hand grenades
52 trench mortar bombs[27]

Once the fighting had died down by Gommecourt at the end of 1 July 1916 several important questions needed to be answered. Had the planned diversionary attack against Gommecourt and the 2nd Guard Reserve Division been successful? Had German infantry and artillery units been prevented from being deployed further south where the main blow

Death notice: *Reservist* Eugen Klingler, 4/170, from his employer. (*Freiburger Zeitung*)

Mass grave of men killed on 1 July 1916 in the II/170. (Author's collection)

had fallen and were the overall losses acceptable for the results achieved?

While the British attack at Gommecourt did tie up German units, it did not have the desired results as hoped by the British staff. Once the fighting was over, only three of the five German regiments involved in the fighting had suffered any appreciable losses. IR 170 reported a total of 650 officers and men lost on 1 July, RIR 55 suffered a total of 455 losses while RIR 91 lost approximately 150 men.

Two of the regiments, RIR 15 and RIR 77, had suffered a total of twenty two losses, something they might have experienced on a daily basis by simply holding the line in a quiet sector. The result was that these regiments were intact and were available for deployment at any location along the German front. Since they were so close to the main area of fighting it would not take much time to deploy them as needed.

This failure to tie down or to inflict serious losses on the regiments in the 2nd Guard Reserve Regiment and IR 170 (52nd Division) could be seen in the fighting later in July. The I/R77 was sent to Pozières where the battalion was in action between 7 and 21 July. The II/R77 was stationed by Bazentin and Martinpuich from 8-23 July and the III/R77 was positioned between Pozières, Martinpuich and Bazentin from 14-23 July.

The men from RIR15 were placed in *Feste Schwaben*, Thiepval, Ovillers and Pozières from 8-22 July. The I/R15 fought in Martinpuich, while the II/R15 fought in *Thiepval-Süd* in August 1916. The rest of the 2nd Guard Reserve Division would see action on the Somme at various times until the end of the fighting in November. One regiment, RIR 15, ended up occupying the familiar trenches at Gommecourt from 1 September through 23 February 1917.

In looking at the British losses for the fighting on 1 July 1916 they were far higher than those suffered by the defenders. The British Official History gives the losses suffered by the 46th and 56th Divisions:[28]

Death notice: *Landsturmmann* Emil Bettinger, 5/170, killed
in action 1 July 1916. (*Freiburger Zeitung*)

46th Division:
50 officers, 803 men killed
71 officers, 1,340 men wounded
14 officers, 172 men missing
 2 officers, 3 men prisoners
Total 2,455

56th Division:
58 officers, 1,300 men killed
107 officers, 2,248 men wounded
17 officers, 356 men missing
6 officers, 227 men prisoners
Total 4,314

The unanswered question at the end of the fighting on 1 July was if the 1,257 probable German casualties were worth losing 6,769 British officers and men to achieve.

Notes

1.   Edmonds, op. cit., p 460.
2.   RIR 15 had men from: *Kaiser Franz Garde Grenadier Regiment* No. 2, *Regiment Franz und König in Augusta* (*Garde Grenadier Regiment* No. 4). RIR 55: *Infanterie Schiessschule* (Infantry Musketry School), 5th *Garde Regiment zu Fuss, Regiment Augusta, Regiment Alexander.* RIR 77: *Königin Elisabeth Garde Grenadier Regiment* No. 3, *Garde Grenadier Regiment* No. 5, *Infanterie Schiessschule.* RIR 91: *Kaiser Alexander Garde Grenadier Regiment* No. 1, 5th *Garde Regiment zu Fuss, Garde Grenadier Regiment* No. 5.
3.   Translation from http://www.zeltbahn.net/wehrpass/rar20.htm, maintained by David Gregory.
4.   Ibid.
5.   The 4/R55 consisted of three platoons. The company strength on 1 July was 126 rifles and 2 machine guns.
6.   The 2/R55 had a combat strength of 152 rifles and occupied parts of the Kern Redoubt and the 1st Switch Line on 1 July 1916.

7.   German hand grenades were transported without detonators in place. These had to be manually inserted before they could be used. It was not unusual for men to use hand grenades that had not been prepared properly beforehand.

8.   The 6/R55 had a combat strength of 134 rifles while the 8/R55 had a combat strength of 170 rifles and 3 machine guns.

9.   *Royal United Services Institution Journal* 62 (1917 Feb./Nov.), 'Report on the defence of Gommecourt on July the 1st, 1916', p. 540.

10.   The report of 300 German prisoners is not supported by the casualty lists compiled at the end of the fighting. RIR 55 and IR 170 reported a combined total of 199 men listed as missing or POWs for 1 July 1916. The status of many of the missing was not fully established until 1917 and 1918.

11.   Machine gun crews normally consisted of 6 men for each gun. There was a gun captain who was in charge of the overall deployment of the machine gun. A second man acted as the gunner, a third as loader. The rest of the gun crew would bring up fresh supplies of water and ammunition and act as observers. In the event of any one man being placed out of action the next man in line would take over their duties.

12.   Oberst von Wissmann, *Das Reserve Infanterie Regiment Nr. 55 im Weltkrieg*, p. 115.

13.   *Royal United Services Institution Journal* 62 (1917 Feb./Nov.), 'Report on the defence of Gommecourt on July the 1st, 1916', p. 540.

14.   Ibid, p. 541.

15.   Ibid.

16.   Ibid.

17.   Ibid.

18.   K. Frhr. von Forstner, *Das Königlich Preussische Reserve Infanterie Regiment Nr. 15*, pp. 304-305.

19.   Forstner, op cit, p. 305

20.   Wissmann, op cit, p. 118.

21.   Middlebrook, p. 138, p. 216.

22.   Gregory op. cit.

23.   Edmonds, op. cit., p. 461

24.   Gregory op.cit.

25.   The number of guns lost by the 2nd Guard Reserve Division on 1 July 1916 was minimal. Three light field howitzers were put out action and one 7.7cm field gun and one 9cm gun were knocked out by direct hits in addition to those Bavarian guns lost that had been attached to the division. Otherwise the artillery continued to fire almost undisturbed throughout the day. The gun positions prepared for the division proved to be very effective in reducing overall losses to guns and crews. The use of strong timber frames prefabricated in pioneer parks allowed a gun emplacement to be constructed and ready for use in a single night. The strong framework allowed the emplacements to have overhead and flanking protection and still allow for maximum lateral traverse for each gun.

26.   Wissmann, op cit, p. 119.

27.   *Royal United Services Institution Journal* 62, p. 545.

28.   Edmonds, op. cit., p. 474.

5

Thiepval

36th Division – the Morning

While two battalions of the 36th (Ulster) Division were involved in the attack north of the Ancre with the 29th Division, the main thrust of this division took place south of the Ancre. This portion of the attack was directed against one of the most heavily fortified locations on the Somme, the area between Thiepval and St. Pierre-Divion. The sector the Ulster division was responsible for included two heavily fortified locations; the village of St. Pierre-Divion and *Feste Schwaben*. The latter was located on Hill 151 and from this vantage point the strongpoint dominated the surrounding terrain. If this key strongpoint was lost it could jeopardize the entire German position far to the north and south. It was therefore considered imperative that *Feste Schwaben* be held under all circumstances by the XIV Reserve Corps.

The 36th (Ulster) Division consisted of three brigades – the 107th, 108th and 109th. The 108th Brigade under Brigadier General C.R.J. Griffith had been forced to split its attack with two battalions of the brigade advancing north of the river, the 9th and 12th Royal Irish Rifles as described in the earlier chapter on Beaumont-Hamel. The remainder of the 108th Brigade, the 13th and 11th Royal Irish Rifles would advance on the southern bank of the Ancre on the left flank of the 109th Brigade (Brigadier General R.G. Shuter). The 109th Brigade had placed the 9th and 10th Royal Inniskilling Fusiliers in the first line, supported by the 11th Royal Inniskilling Fusiliers and the 14th Royal Irish Rifles. The

Battalion Staff – IV/R99. (Author's collection)

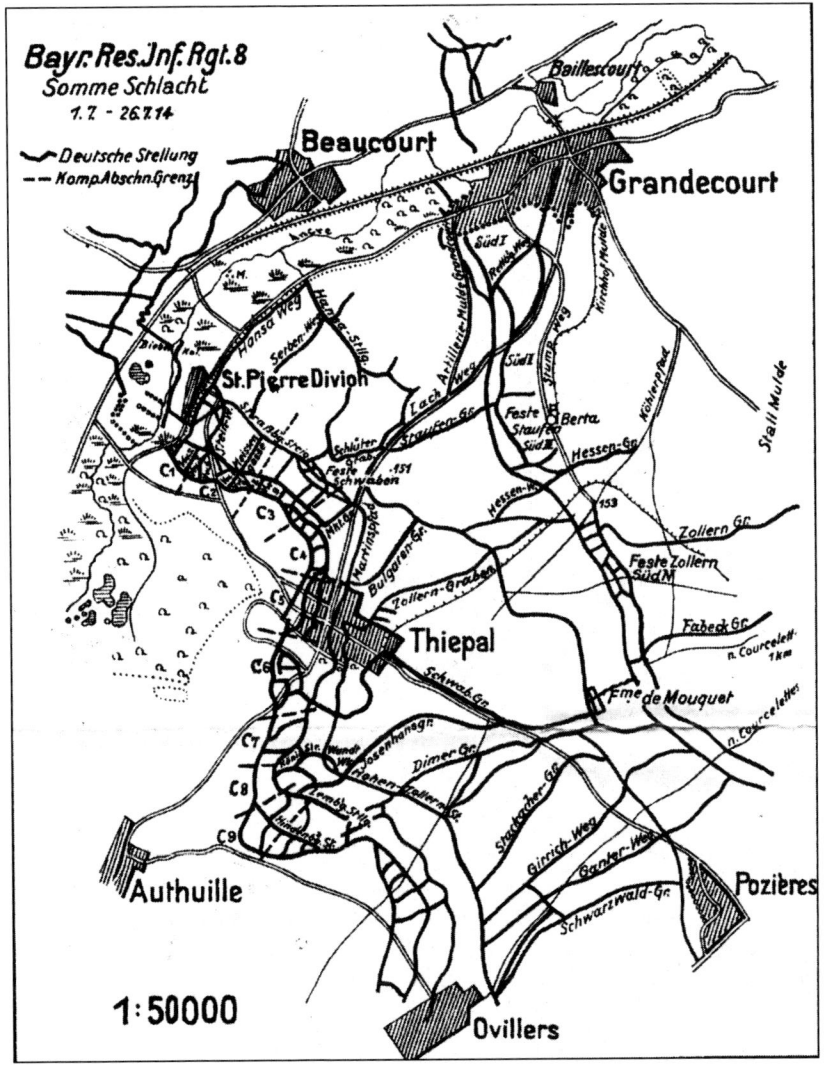

Map of Thiepval Sector.

107th Brigade would be kept back in reserve.

The Thiepval Sector had been divided into three sub-sectors by the Germans – *Thiepval-Nord* (C1-C3), *Thiepval-Mitte* (C4-C6) and *Thiepval-Süd* (C7-C9). Each of these sub-sectors was occupied by one battalion from RIR 99. The nine smaller sectors, C1 through C9, covered the area from St. Pierre-Divion on the southern bank of the Ancre in C1 through the *Granatloch* (Leipzig Redoubt) in C9 just south of Thiepval. Each of the sectors, C1 through C9 were occupied by an infantry company that garrisoned the front line trenches with the fourth company of each battalion located nearby in the rear in reserve. The fourth battalion of RIR 99 (Companies 13-16) were positioned close by the front as a regimental reserve force.

The men of RIR 99 had occupied the trenches in the Thiepval Sector since March and were very familiar with the sector when the attack came. Three battalions from RIR 99 had occupied the front line trenches while the IV/R99 was actively working on the extension of the II Line of trenches as well as supplying carrying parties that were bringing supplies up to the front lines.

Facing the six battalions of the 36th (Ulster) Division were the 9th, 10th, 11th and 12/R99 as well as the 1st and 4/8th Bavarian Reserve Regiment, a total of one and a half battalions consisting of some 1,200 officers and men. These companies occupied the sectors designated as C1 through C3 as well as *Feste Schwaben*.

The III/R99 was under the command of *Hauptmann* Mandel. The 12/R99 under *Oberleutnant der Reserve* Vollert held the right wing of the regiment along the Ancre and St. Pierre-Divion in C1 along with the 1/8th Bavarian RIR. The next company in line was the 10/R99 under *Oberleutnant der Reserve* Hessinger in C2. Sector C3 was occupied by the 9/R99 under *Oberleutnant* Hille while the 11/R99 under *Leutnant der Reserve* Wolff was positioned in the second line inside *Feste Schwaben*. The 11/R99 was also joined by the 4/8th Bavarian RIR.

Infantrymen – RIR 99. (Author's collection)

Dugout entrance in the cellar of Thiepval Château. (*Die 26. Reserve Division 1914-1918*)

Thiepval-Mitte and *Thiepval-Süd* were being attacked by the 32nd Division. The 32nd was responsible for the German lines from the village of Thiepval to the *Granatloch*. Two brigades were allotted to the task; the 96th Brigade on the left, directly in front of Thiepval, and the 97th Brigade on the right, south of the village up to the *Granatloch*.

Four companies of the II/R99 under Major Sauer defended *Thiepval-Mitte*. The 7th Coy under *Leutnant der Reserve* Schmidt held the right wing of *Thiepval-Mitte*, just north of the village followed by the 6/R99 under *Leutnant* Nehlig that held the trenches in front of Thiepval. The left wing of the sector was being held by the 5/R99 under *Hauptmann* Brée just south of the village with the 8/R99 under *Hauptmann* Mundt in reserve located in and around the Château and adjacent park. Both the village and the ruins of the Château were heavily fortified, with numerous interconnecting trenches and strong points that included the extensive stone cellars of the Château ruins.

The four companies of the I/R99 under Major *Frhr.* von Meerscheidt-Hüllessem occupied the trenches in C7 through C9 in *Thiepval-Süd*. The 2/R99 under *Hauptmann* Lingke was positioned on the right wing of the sector adjacent to the 5/R99. The next company in line was the 1/R99 under *Hauptmann* Hartbrich. The 4/R99 under *Leutnant der Reserve* Geist originally held the portion of the line designated as the *Granatloch* while the 3/R99 under *Leutnant der Reserve* Mechenbier was positioned inside the *Lemberg, Wundtwerk and Turken Stellung* in reserve. Due to the heavy losses reported by the 4/R99 during the bombardment, the company was replaced by the 3/R99 in the night of 28/29 June.

The IV/R99 under Major von Rettenberg was positioned in Courcelette and placed on alert. Just before the attack the four companies of the battalion were sent to Mouquet Farm and the intermediate terrain behind the front line to be used as reserves and carrying troops as needed.

RIR 99 had two machine gun companies attached to the regiment, commanded

Gefreiter Auer, MGSST 89 and dud 30.5cm British shell. (*Das K. B. Reserve-Infanterie-Regiment Nr. 8*)

by *Frhr.* von Babo and *Oberleutnant* Schöpfer. With additional German weapons and captured enemy machine guns the regiment had obtained, there were a total of 26 heavy machine guns spread across the front line that would provide substantial opposition to any enemy advance.

Due to the shape of the German line in the Thiepval Sector there were several areas that were particularly vulnerable to enemy fire. In part this was due to the line forming a right angle near the Village of Thiepval. This configuration allowed portions of the German line to be enfiladed by the opposing artillery. Another weakness in the line occurred near the Ancre where the trenches were fully exposed on terrain that sloped steeply down toward the river. The British were able to easily observe the German trenches and accurately direct fire into them. This was one reason why many of the trenches here were considerably deeper than the trenches at other locations in the sector.

Reports concerning the events of 1 July 1916 were being sent in from the moment the day started and would continue unabated for the entire day and the days that followed. The first report was made at 12.01 a.m. from the Sector *Thiepval-Süd*:

> C9 and *Königstrasse* are under constant shrapnel fire. C8 is suffering severely from the enemy battery firing in enfilade from the northern edge of Authuille Wood. The same applies to the *Lemberg Stellung* which is being enfiladed by a battery firing from the direction of Auchonvillers. The left flank of C9 received around 300 heavy mortar rounds during the previous day and *Thiepval-Süd* as a whole about 1,000.[1]

The level of shelling was having an inevitable effect on the garrison holding the Thiepval sector. At 12.30 a.m. Dr. Wittig sent an urgent request for additional stretcher-bearers as he was faced with evacuating at least 25 seriously wounded men. A short time later the men in *Feste Schwaben* reported the smell of gas in the air that caused their eyes to sting severely.

The dangers facing the men of RIR 99 and 8th Bavarian RIR did not come solely from the heavy British fire. A report sent at 12.14 a.m. indicated that German batteries were apparently firing on Sector C8 and shells were falling behind the *Wohngraben*. Sector *Thiepval-Süd* also reported at least one German shell falling short a brief time later.

It was far from quiet inside the German lines. Every man in RIR 99 and the 8th Bavarian

RIR as well as the artillery regiments and support troops were awake and anticipating the moment when the attack would come. Orders were issued and troops shifted closer to the front. For one man, *Leutnant der Reserve* Stahlhofer, 2/8th Bavarian RIR, 1 July 1916 was a lucky day. Not only was it his 23rd birthday, he would also cheat being captured or killed by a stroke of good luck.

> At approximately 12 o'clock at night on the 30th ... an orderly brought an order from Battalion with the instructions 'To transmit to the 4th Coy by the 2nd Coy.' Now almost no one knew the route to that place. *Leutnant* Schmeisser had probably been there, surely he would not get lost. He could not safely send *Unteroffizier* Heinlein with two men alone. I thought about it and then I offered to attempt it. On the one hand it was good if I got to know the terrain, on the other hand I tempted danger. The suggestion was gladly accepted. I persuaded Benedikt Wagner, who had already made the trip, to go with me and a second man, Brendl, went voluntarily.
>
> It was the first morning hours of 1st July, my 23rd birthday that I thought to consecrate in this manner. We danced on. Soon we ran as if possessed, threw ourselves along, puffing then hurried again. It was tolerably cold, we were sweating a lot. So it went on, for maybe an hour. On the right and left, in front and behind us the earth sprayed up, undermined from the damn sugar loafs so that we found ourselves with each step in the loving embrace of a different shell hole. The flash of the exploding shells blinded us. This cheap illumination was purely for cats. To appease the beating heart in the men's chest, from time to time I told a bad joke, but nobody laughed at it. After all we were comparatively lively and to once perceive the feeling of being amidst a hail of shells animated me oddly. Finally we bumped into something that probably had to have been a trench. We randomly curved to the right, and soon found something like a dugout entrance ... I shone the torch carefully downward. There were traces of men, but the smell indicated such that they were not socially acceptable, even if I could see nothing. Therefore, we moved further on. Again, at an entrance, and underneath a light. It was the medical dugout. I called for *Hauptmann* Schorer. 'Still somewhat further'. Finally we were there. 'Is *Hauptmann* Schorer below?' I called. 'yes' came up the answer. Now we sat down on the steps and drank out of the canteen. Then I crawled downward, came into an area completely filled with men, where I still met some well known friends and immediately following, near the front, was Schorer, who I handed over the battalion orders. People were amazed by us, as if we were like beings from another world. Actually, we provided an excellent specimen of Neanderthal man.
>
> In the order that I delivered, was a report of execution of orders demanded by the Battalion and I wanted to wait for it and then bring it back again. However Schorer said: 'It will be broad daylight before the order is executed, and then it will be impossible for you to return.' So I then clicked my heels together and left. He was quite right, because at that hour I would have been in English captivity like the entire 4th Coy.[2]

Stahlhofer, after leaving *Feste Schwaben*, made his way back to his company position where he was in for a pleasant surprise:

Battalion Staff – III/R99. (Author's collection)

I arrived in front of the dugout of *Leutnant* Traub and *Vizefeldwebel* Weinmann, where I spoke to his dog Fips. I saw both of them for the last time, the former is a prisoner; the latter is probably dead. At the entrance to the medical dugout we took a breather; then we began the return route. After a short time we left the destroyed trench, in the same way that we had come, and then curved to the right into one seemingly more spared that to be sure was full of water, but however allowed for easier movement. When we reached the second position, we puffed on. To be sure shell fragments still swished around in front of our noses, but the worst was over. I took the time to observe the trajectory of German projectiles, how they flew over us in a graceful arc like glowing meteors. About 3.30 I reached *Leutnant* Barz, I reported and wanted to begin trench duty that went from 3 until 5. However he said: 'you now have an official order, to sit here and drink a couple of draught beers and then to go to sleep,' 'To orders' I replied and drank. *Leutnant* Schmeisser slept on his bed and Forster sat beside me. After I got through a few cups of beer, I got myself up and went to my men. Gratified, I then stretched out on my bed and sank into a profoundly agreeable sleep.[3]

The British fire continued to fall along the entire Thiepval Sector throughout the night. *Thiepval-Süd* reported at 2.56 a.m. that the second trench in Sector C9 was being targeted by heavy mortars. Perhaps the most fateful report arrived at 4 a.m. from Headquarters XIV Reserve Corps. The 28th Reserve Division had passed along the report received from RIR 110 when the Moritz Station in La Boisselle had intercepted a British message that in part said that the infantry should hold on to all its gains obstinately and mentioned that they would be supported by artillery.

The regiment had evaluated the details in the message to indicate that a large-scale attack would take place at 4.30 a.m. A few minutes past the time set for the attack a

Men from RIR 99 in the trenches. (Author's collection)

thick fog bank was noted in the Ancre Valley that was drifting up toward Mesnil but no attack followed. The tense situation only grew worse as the men continued to wait for the inevitable moment the enemy would attack.

During this period of time many of the German guns continued to fire into the British trenches as they had done throughout the week-long bombardment. While not considered a serious bombardment the German shells inevitably found their mark inside the crowded British lines.

> We'd been drumming up a cup of tea and Jerry spotted us and sent over a 5.9 and blew the machine-gun up – our Lewis gun was totally beyond repair. I got up after the explosion and I wondered why the ground was all springy underfoot – it was my mate, and he was lying there dead under the rubble and dust. He'd been alive a few minutes ago. Now I was standing on him.[4]

At 6.33.a.m. the British artillery and mortar fire on *Thiepval-Mitte* had increased to a terrific level. The intensity of the fire resulted in a message being sent to the supporting batteries to open defensive fire immediately. Two minutes later three red flares rose up into the sky near the regimental headquarters, the signal for barrage fire. Three minutes later *Gruppe Zollern*; the I/RFAR 27 commanded by *Hauptmann* Wiedtemann, was ordered to provide the heaviest possible defensive fire in front of *Thiepval-Mitte* and *Thiepval Süd*. Further reports provided more detailed information showing that Sector C9 was under heavy fire while C8 and the right flank of C9 were experiencing somewhat lighter fire.

At 6.53 a.m. three companies of the IV/R99 and the 2nd Recruit Coy/R99 were placed on alert. Less than ten minutes later two reserve machine guns located at Mouquet Farm were also placed on alert. Messages to and from the front line kept the telephone operators and observers very busy monitoring the situation at the front and providing directions for

View of no man's land from the German trenches. (*Geschichte des Reserve-Infanterie-Regiment Nr. 99*)

the artillery batteries positioned behind the Thiepval Sector. The fact that the telephone wires were still intact was due in part to luck and in part to the extraordinary precautions taken in the weeks before the battle began when the telephone lines were buried very deep under the position.

At 7.24 a.m. a report was sent to *Reserve Infanterie Brigade* 52:

> The very heaviest defensive fire must be maintained in front of all sub-sectors. In particular extremely heavy fire is required in front of C6, because an attack there appears to be imminent.[5]

The first indication that actual fighting was taking place became known at headquarters when rifle and machine gun fire was heard above the din of artillery and mine fire coming from the front line at 7.39 a.m. *Leutnant der Landwehr* Matthias Gerster, in the neighboring RIR 119, described his impressions of the first day of the battle:

> The British horizon was filled with captive balloons, the air with the buzzing of enemy aircraft. Odd artillery shells ploughed up the ground here and there. Suddenly at 6.30 a.m. an unparalleled storm of artillery broke out. Initially this was directed at Thiepval. Soon at around 8 a.m. it began to fall on Ovillers and from 7.20 a.m. on *Feste Schwaben*. All hell seemed to have broken loose along the line, impact by impact, smoke column by smoke column. A monstrous line of geysers seemed to spring up as though the bowels of the earth themselves were being torn apart. Within moments everything was enveloped in dust and smoke and a pall of haze prevented observation of distant objects. It was impossible to distinguish one explosion from the other. There was just one great raging hammering, rumbling, crashing, heaving, trembling, whose rhythm was punctuated only by the gigantic impacts of the super-heavy caliber shells. All communications forward were severed, the telephone lines cut. Only a few deeply buried cables were still intact, but the brigade staff was completely cut off from the outside world. What was happening at the front?[6]

At 7.15 in the morning of 1 July the lead battalions of the 108th and 109th Brigades moved into no man's land and crept forward to a position about one hundred and fifty meters from the German trenches. In order to screen the two battalions of the 108th Brigade from German observers north of the Ancre 4-inch Stokes mortar batteries of the Special Brigade R.E. located in the Ancre valley fired numerous smoke shells that formed a dense smoke screen in front of the attacking battalions. Also, due to the nature of the

Officers – RIR 99. (Author's collection)

ground between the opposing lines there were sections where the Germans were unable to observe the concentration of enemy troops. This dead ground allowed the Irishmen to approach the German front line trenches unseen.

The first evidence that the week-long bombardment had not been as successful as hoped for came at 7.20 a.m. when Captain McConachie, Machine Gun Officer 109th Brigade, reported that a German machine gun had opened fire on them from the direction of Thiepval. The fire was reported to be steady and accurate.

At 7.29 a.m. McConachie reported that four additional German machine guns were firing from Thiepval, and that at least two of them were firing on the 36th (Ulster) Division troops. At 7.30 a.m. British artillery fire lifted from the I Line and moved to the II Line in accordance with the plan of attack. With buglers sounding the advance the lead Irish companies moved forward in four extended lines, each 50 paces apart. Support companies followed in artillery formation, lines of platoons in fours.

At 7.30 a.m. observers in the III/R99 reported that fire from enemy field guns, heavy artillery and trench mortars had risen to the level of barrage fire. At the same time the 10/R99 in Sector C2 reported that a large smoke cloud was forming near their line. The sentries had already alerted the trench garrison and the men that had been able to man the trenches opened a steady fire into the smoke cloud with their rifles and machine guns. The artillery batteries in the rear were contacted using colored flares that called for barrage fire on the British lines and support areas.

> I shall never forget for one minute the extraordinary sight. The Derrys, on our left, were so eager they started a few minutes before the ordered time, and the Tyrones were not going to be left behind, and they got going without delay – no fuss, no shouting, no running; everything orderly, solid and thorough, just like the men themselves. Here and there a boy would wave his hand to me as I shouted 'Good luck' to them

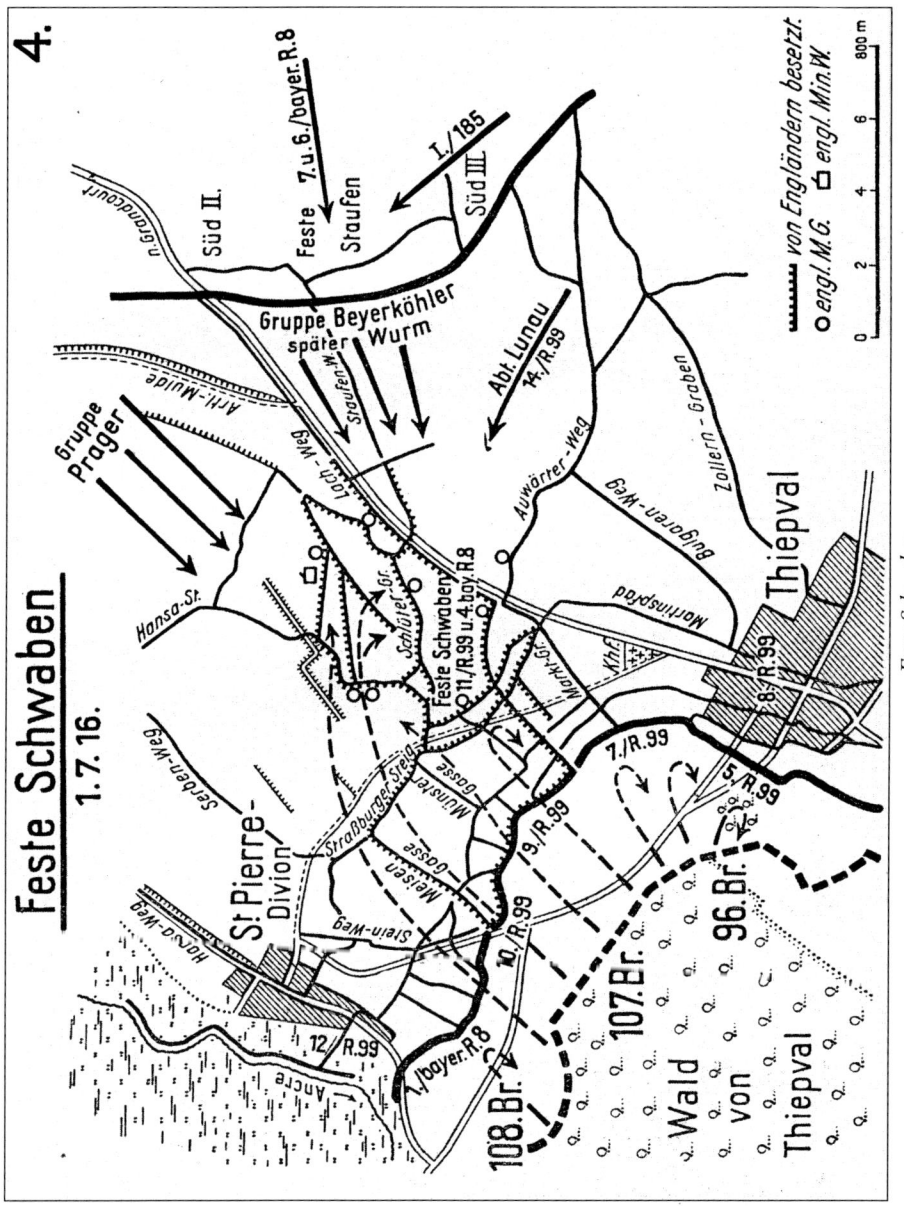

Feste Schwaben.

Anti-aircraft Machine gun post – RIR 99. (Author's collection)

through my megaphone, and all had a happy face. Many were carrying loads. Fancy advancing against heavy fire carrying a heavy roll of barbed wire on your shoulders.
Ricardo, Tyrone CO[7]

The 13th Royal Irish Rifles advanced alongside the Ancre as the left flank of the 36th (Ulster) Division attack south of the river. Almost immediately the battalion came under heavy and accurate rifle and machine gun fire from the direction of St. Pierre-Divion and from artillery fire from batteries of the 26th Reserve Division. The battalion suffered severe losses before much headway could be made and the attack was stopped before it could reach the German wire. The survivors were forced to move to their right as a matter of self-preservation and joined with the 11th Royal Irish Rifles who were having better luck with their advance. One of the defenders, *Infanterist* Wilhelm Lange, RIR 99, described the events of that morning:

I scrambled up the back of the trench, took up my position with my rifle on a small rise and opened fire into the crowd of English soldiers who were coming across No man's land. There were so many of them, they were like trees in a wood. We kept them out of our part of the line but they broke through on our left. I was standing up, firing, and my officer shouted to me, 'Come down', but in my excitement I told him, 'But they're not shooting', and the officer said, 'You fool, can't you hear the bullets whistling?'[8]

Despite the heavy German fire the 11th Royal Irish Rifles were able to reach the first line trench at the left wing of Sector C1 and with the aid of the smokescreen broke through the position held by the 10/R99 in Sector C2. Despite losing a portion of the front line in Sector C1 the defenders, the 12/R99 and 1/8th Bavarian RIR, continued to hold out in the second trench and prevented the British from expanding their gains further into Sector C1 from the flank.

Valuable assistance was provided by the men of the 2/8th Bavarian RIR in holding the trenches near St. Pierre-Divion. One platoon from this company under *Offizier Stellvertreter* Kamm occupied a critical trench barricade. Kamm and his men fought off numerous British hand grenade attacks despite being surrounded on three sides. Leading by example, Kamm prevented his men from considering a withdrawal or surrendering to the enemy during the heaviest fighting. At one point in the fighting, late in the day, he actually advanced against the Ulstermen during their withdrawal from the German lines and in doing so was able to take several prisoners. Kamm was later awarded the Gold Medal for Bravery for his actions on 1 July 1916.

Even if the Ulstermen had been able to force their way deeper into the German lines along the Ancre they would have come up against the 2/8th Bavarian RIR, and apparently there was only a single route the men of the 36th Division could have taken. Even while the heavy bombardment continued right up to the time of the attack, the noise and commotion apparently did not disturb the sleep of *Leutnant der Reserve* Stahlhofer.

> How long I slept, I do not know. Through the half-sleep all at once it seemed to me as if the drumming at the front became even stronger. I roused myself quickly and moved into the open. It was a day so bright and sunny, as if the heavens wanted to congratulate me on my birthday. I didn't have long to wait, as the gifts arrived and they were more plentiful than wished for. Suddenly an *Unteroffizier* hurried to me

Infantrymen – RIR 99. (Author's collection)

and shouted: 'Everyone in position, the English have broken through and are already on the way to us.' Quickly I urged the man out into the little piece of trench overgrown with grass that I was to have occupied. For the time being I saw still no Englishmen. Instead all at once a bumble bee (pilot) appeared and began to circle above us.

He didn't yield from the spot and continued to wave. The answer soon came. The first one hit about 200 meters in front of us, then one more, a couple of duds, now came more. He waved, he came closer; he waved further and ever closer moved the shells that pelted down on us. Now dirt flew up and broke on my nose. Then I followed the cries of the men, placed myself in the trench and looked out again from time to time. There was no activity, nor on the left; it was 9 o'clock, 9.30, no Englishmen far and wide; however the pilot was still there. They smashed in front of us, behind us, the men were nervous. Now I gave the order to go back individually as it was clear to me – because the English did not advance any more – that when they did come they could only advance on the road, where we were already ready for them. In the troubled Ancre ground, where we lay, they could not advance swiftly enough. Meanwhile the soldiers jumped and danced through the fire and came through.

Now a direct hit struck the trench. Fortunately only a few men were inside it. On a small traverse went fell heavy ones, burying the man lying right next to them. Just as I went back to extract him, he crawled out himself. A hot wind blew directly from the right on my cheek; barely 1 meter behind the trench smashed a big one. On the left a couple of men pulled themselves together and dug and dug. Water stood in the hole they sat in. I saw, according to the time it was 10 o'clock. Therefore 23 years ago, at about this hour, a little cry and whimpering greeted the world, later to be baptized Sepperl. And today, about the same hour, he sat here in the mud, a little curious, if his birth hour would not also be his hour of death. A strong rumble disturbed me from this thought. It moved with the clatter of a nearby express train.

Ah, I supposed, the Thirty Eights. Especially on the little road that led to Pierre-Divion, not 15 meters from where I sat. There were, however, more and more of the fat 38's. A completely hellish concert from the smallest up to the largest caliber shells. I could not just say that I had very much fun with it. Once I truly used the rosary to pray that they would not hit all of the men.

The feeling of responsibility lay heavy on my chest. Meanwhile the prayer was not very big, and too vivid impressions rushed at me. I was sitting there and then saw the black chunks rush up to the rooftops at lightning speed, the blood red brick dust swirled and flew up to the roofs, and then came the muffled bang. A deep calm came over me and I had the feeling that I was immune against death and wounds. The fire finally lessened about 12 o'clock. The plane vanished, no Englishmen showed themselves. I had trouble bringing the men out of their cover; there were only a couple of them.[9]

The German wire and trenches had been badly damaged in Sector C2 during the week-long bombardment, primarily by British 'ball' mines; also known as 'Plum puddings', and were quickly overrun in the initial advance. Many dugout entrances were blocked by debris from the heavy fire and their occupants were still busy trying to clear them when the attack began. After taking the front line trench the 11th Royal Irish Rifles continued to advance and quickly reached the *Steinweg* and *Meisengasse*.

Infantrymen – RIR 99. (Author's collection)

The parts of the 10/R99 that had been able to man their trenches continued to pour fire into the enemy ranks as quickly as they could load and fire. One machine gun placed into position in Sector C2 was only able to fire for a few moments before most of the gun crew was killed or wounded and the Ulstermen captured the gun. The 13th and 11th Royal Irish Rifles pressed their advance, driving the remnants of the 10th Coy further to the rear. The fighting was fierce as the Ulstermen pushed deeper into the German trenches towards the *Strassburger Steige*.

All the time the two battalions of the 108th Brigade south of the Ancre advanced, their left flank was under continuous heavy fire from the 12/R99 and 1/8th Bavarian RIR positioned around St. Pierre-Divion. When the 13th and 11th Royal Irish Rifles reached the *Strassburger Steige* near the *Meisengasse* they were unable to move toward St. Pierre-Divion due to heavy fire from a machine gun positioned further up the *Strassburger Steige* near the village. This gun crew fired belt after belt of ammunition into the ranks of the advancing Ulstermen. Unable to make any headway the Irishmen in the 108th Brigade continued to move further to their right where they remained in close contact with the 109th Brigade as the men from this brigade also advanced deeper into the German lines.

The fighting was brutal; men were killed and wounded on both sides as the fighting took place inside the damaged trenches. Hand grenades flew back and forth and small groups of men fought hand to hand at each traverse. While some of the German defenders surrendered when confronted by the onrushing Ulstermen, others were as equally determined to stop them in their tracks. Members of the Ulster Division described the scene:

> In one part of the B line, the trenches near the river, there was a carpet of dead and dying Ulstermen and Germans. Blood lay like a layer and, do you know, you couldn't tell one blood from the other ... in another part ... a party of the Skins [Inniskilling Fusiliers] left the B line and hid in shell-holes within bombing distance – the distance

a man could throw a Mills bomb. The Germans re-entered their own trench. The sound of the firsthand-grenade exploding was the signal to start bombing the two or three hundred yards of the trench where the Germans were collecting ... after the last grenade had been thrown there was a bayonet charge. There was not one German soldier left alive ... they collected all the grenades, ammunition, even rifles, water and food the Germans were carrying – a bloody messy job.[10]

At 7.30 a.m. the battalions of the 109th Brigade advanced against Sector C3 held by the 9/R99. The 9th Coy had been especially hard hit during the preliminary bombardment. Their wire entanglements were almost completely destroyed and many of their dugouts had collapsed or were blocked off by debris from the heavy British ball mines. The trenches were badly knocked about but still offered some protection for the few defenders who had managed to exit their dugouts in time.

The men from the 9/R99 had been unable to fully occupy their front line and there were many gaps in their defenses. The lead companies of the 109th Brigade exploited these weaknesses and were able to overrun the first line trench at many different points with minimal resistance from the German garrison, especially at the right flank of C3.

While the survivors of the leading companies in the first wave of the Ulster Division had successfully entered the German lines at various points, the rear companies of the first wave as well as the companies in the second wave were caught by the German artillery barrage and enfilading machine gun fire that had begun in earnest. The Ulstermen suffered heavy casualties as the men attempted to cross no man's land.

When the British bombardment lifted off of the German front line trenches it signaled the start of the attack. Flanking fire from German machine guns immediately targeted the attacking battalions from the dominating heights of Thiepval Cemetery. The 11th Inniskilling Fusiliers and 14th Royal Irish Rifles were hit by this withering fire and literally mown down as they emerged from Thiepval wood. The machine gun teams from RIR 99 had every position marked clearly in their target books and had spent months becoming familiar with every aspect of the terrain. They were able to bring a devastating level of fire against the British troops as they appeared in the sights of the gunners.

The 9/R99 had also managed to set up one machine gun at the start of the attack. However this gun only fired a few rounds before most of the crew was killed and the gun was overrun and captured. Many men in the 9th Coy were captured as they slowly emerged from their damaged dugouts only to discover that the Ulstermen were already in their trenches. Any attempt at resistance proved to be futile and most likely fatal.

Only the right wing platoon of the 9th Coy was able to hold its position in Sector C3. The men occupied their trenches just before the 9th Royal Inniskilling Fusiliers could overrun them. This platoon quickly formed trench blocks in all trenches leading up to the enemy occupied positions and engaged the Ulstermen with hand grenades, rifle butts, bayonets and daggers. This small group of defenders blocked any further advance to the east by the 36th (Ulster) Division for the time being. How long they could hold out was another question as their casualties were quickly rising under the constant pressure from the enemy.

No one back in the British trenches knew exactly what was happening with the attack. Visibility was poor due to the amount of dust, smoke and debris in the air. The Ulstermen knew that their continued success relied upon the ability of messages reaching the British commanders in the rear, usually carried by runners. One of the first messages to make it back to the British lines came in at 7.47 A.M. from the 9th Inniskilling Fusiliers:

> Have got telephone message from our signaling sergeant from the German 'A' line, saying 'all's well', have seen the junior captain of our left supporting Coy. Who said that all was going well, the enemy's machine gun fire is high but is very harassing.[11]

The 'A' Line (German front line) was reported as being taken at 7.48 a.m., the time the men were to have already taken the third trench. The combined Irish brigades continued to move further into the German defenses, forcing back the survivors of the 10th and 9/R99 into the support trenches. A few of these men from the 9th Coy were able to form another trench block in the *Hansa Weg* where the fighting was hand-to-hand. This trench block ultimately prevented the Ulstermen from advancing further north toward Grandcourt, forcing them to move further east into the network of trenches leading to the rear of *Feste Schwaben*.

> We had a young officer not as old as some of us, and as hard-faced, crooked a sergeant as ever walked on two feet. As we moved across no man's land a shell landed on our left. It could have been one of our own landing a bit short. Anyway it killed the officer and wounded the sergeant and a bit of it hit me on the upper part of my left arm and cut me, but not too badly. The old sergeant kept going till we reached the German lines. With the first bomb he threw the door off a deep dugout, and the next two he flung inside. He must have killed every German in it. We left him sitting just below the parapet with a grenade in each hand ready for the next live German that came along. We did not stay that long in that line but moved on to the next. Then to the 3rd line ... It was here that the real fighting started. I had never killed a man with a bayonet before and it sent cold shivers up and down my spine many's a night afterwards just thinking about it. It must have taken our lot about a quarter of an hour to clear a hundred yards or so of the trench. I was one of them left to hold the line because I had to get my arm bandaged. We found some food the Germans had and it was worse than our own rations but we were so hungry we ate them.[12]

The right wing of the 109th Brigade continued to push forward against the German II Line about 500 meters away; the front face of *Feste* Schwaben. As they moved forward the men came under fire from the *Schwaben* garrison, the 11/R99 and 4/8th Bavarian RIR. The two right hand battalions, the 9th and 11th Royal Inniskilling Fusiliers also came under heavy flanking machine gun fire from the direction of Thiepval, causing numerous casualties. There seemed to be no way to stop the German machine guns from firing into their ranks. The bombardment had long moved on from this sector leaving the machine guns intact. It was up to the infantry to take care of them once and for all.

Feste Schwaben had been heavily shelled throughout the bombardment, and as a result much of its wire entanglements were destroyed or heavily damaged. The trenches were badly smashed up and a large number of men in the garrison were trapped inside their dugouts. Many of the officers in the redoubt had already become casualties early on in the fighting.

A captured Russian machine gun positioned inside *Feste Schwaben* was brought out of its dugout and placed in position at the start of the British attack. A British shell burst next to it, burying the gun and most of its crew. The Gun Captain and his orderly quickly tried

Memorial card: *Vizefeldwebel* Franz Xaver Wildmann, 4/8th Bavarian RIR,
killed in action 1 July 1916 in Feste Schwaben. (Author's collection)

to dig them out but they were both killed by shrapnel fire.

Platoon Fassbender, 11/R99, was ordered to occupy the forward firing trench of *Feste Schwaben*. The platoon engaged the advancing 109th Brigade with the support of a machine gun positioned with the 9/R99 in Sector C3 and a machine gun located with the 7/R99 in Sector C4. During the attack by the 109th Brigade both of these machine guns were placed out of action by direct hits. The crews from these guns immediately moved to nearby machine guns and joined their crews, taking the place of men who had already become casualties in the fighting. Several of the *Schützen* also manned a captured British machine gun and continued to fire into the ranks of the advancing Ulstermen.

Sometime after 7.50 a.m. the 109th Brigade Headquarters received another message from the front:

> Message from 14th Royal Irish Rifles sent to Battalion from 'A' Line. (1) Believe German machine gun in Thiepval is causing us trouble. (2) Reached support line, very few casualties. Machine guns very prevalent on every side.[13]

Feste Schwaben was now being attacked by elements of six battalions, from three different sides. The remnants of the two companies of German infantry defending the redoubt put up a strong defense and the fighting was vicious. Hand grenades, rifles, bayonets and trench knives were used as the Irishmen moved deeper into the redoubt. However by 8.48 A.M. the C Line and *Feste Schwaben* had been taken. Several members of the Ulster

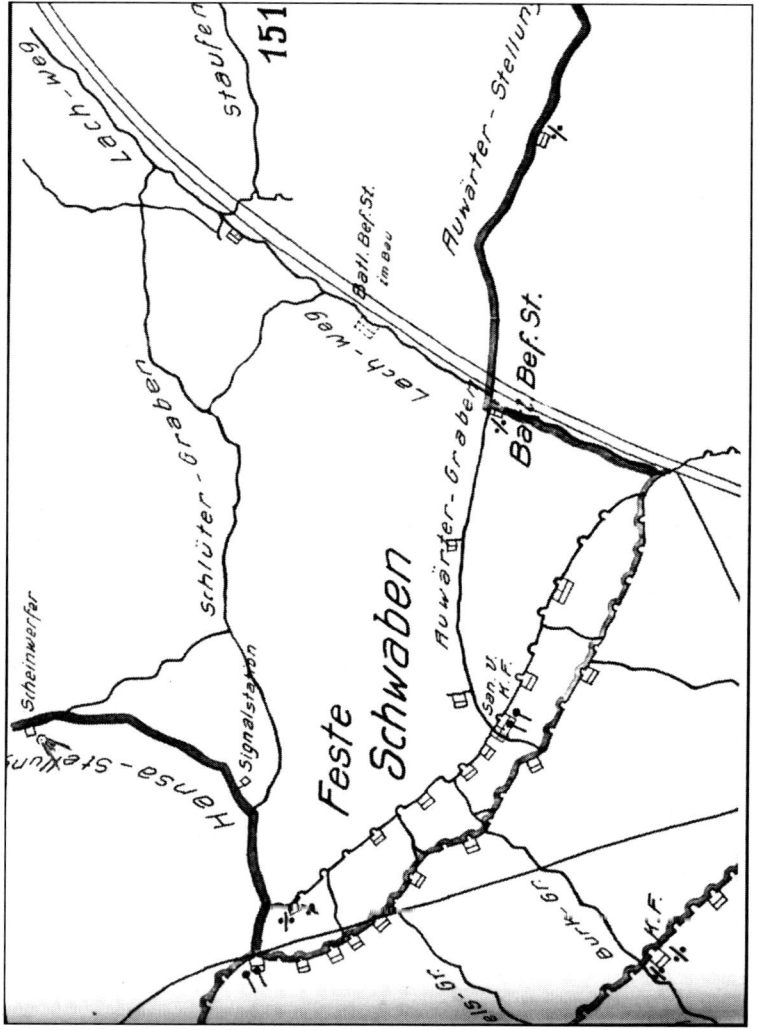

The *Schwaben* Redoubt (*Feste Schwaben*).

Division recalled the fighting around the redoubt:

> There was one soldier I'll never forget ... He made himself a special weapon for fighting
> in the trenches. It was about half the length of a pick shaft and on one end he screwed
> in a pear-shaped lump of cast iron, on the other was a leather thong which he kept tied
> around his waist. He used to parry a bayonet thrust with the rifle and then swing his
> lump of cast iron upwards. No matter where it hit a man it broke bones. He'd smash
> a man's wrist or hand, then when the rifle flew away from the man's hands he'd shoot
> him. I fought beside him in the 'D' line that day. He fought like a devil. He must have
> killed a dozen Germans ... I don't know how long we were in the 'D' line but while we
> were there we fought every second, there was no rest at all. The blood had got about
> the tongue of our boots and our socks were soaked with it.[14]
>
> I had a bayonet in one hand and a revolver in the other ... They had a kick like a
> horse but if you hit a man with a bullet from one of them he gave no more trouble ...
> we all made our way down to the third line ... here there was one young officer ... and
> he set about getting us set for a bayonet charge against the trenches in front of us – the
> Crucifix ... we fixed bayonets and charged. There was not many Germans left alive.
> Few of us got hit in the dash across, maybe we caught the Germans off guard ... we
> cleared the trenches right down to the Mouquet Switch – we settled down to hold the
> bit we captured. We took no prisoners and we had not to detail any men guard duty.
> First we gathered up all the bombs, the German ones as well as our own. (This meant
> going over the dead looking for bombs.) We had a lot of our own men wounded and
> we took care of these as best we could. Then we collected our dead and put them in
> two dugouts. We moved the German dead out of our way. It was warm and clammy
> and we were sweating in the heat. We had little or no water and we were very thirsty.[15]

Towards 9 o'clock in the morning reports stopped coming in to the British lines as a
result of the heavy machine gun fire from the area around Thiepval enfilading no man's
land. Runners attempting to get back with the messages were often killed or wounded
before making any real progress and any further attempts only resulted in more losses.

The Ulster Division reported taking between 400 and 500 German prisoners in the
opening attack. The prisoners were being sent back to the rear with 1 escort for every 16
prisoners. By 9.30 a.m. some 200 prisoners had passed through the 109th Brigade Prisoner
Collecting Post.

> One man, whose name we shall never know, could be seen walking across the open
> behind about sixty prisoners, some of them apparently wounded, holding them
> together as jealously as a sheepdog holds his flock, urging along the laggards, keeping
> ever behind the last man of his party.[16]

However not all of the Germans who were captured made it back to the British lines.
Major Crozier was watching the fighting from British front line:

> There is a shout. Someone seizes a Lewis gun ... I see an advancing crowd of field
> grey. Fire is opened ... The enemy fall like grass before the scythe ... 'Good heavens,' I
> shout, 'those men are prisoners surrendering, and some of our own wounded men are

Memorial card: *Infanterist* Georg Käsmayer, 4/8th Bavarian RIR, killed
in action 1 July 1916 in *Feste Schwaben*. (Author's collection)

escorting them. Cease fire ... The fire ripples on for a time. The target is too good to
lose. 'After all, they are only Germans,' I hear a youngster say.[17]

Others would fall victim to the very fire they had called up to defend their lines.
Among the men killed by German artillery fire was *Hauptmann* Schorer and *Vizefeldwebel*
Wald from *Feste Schwaben* along with others as they moved toward the British trenches;
Leutnant der Reserve Traub was reported among the missing, he was later found to be a
prisoner of war.

There would be no rest after the redoubt was captured and the exhausted men continued
their advance. The surviving Ulstermen sent patrols out on both flanks in order to get some
idea of their position. Losses in the Irish battalions had been heavy and reinforcements
were needed to maintain the forward momentum, and to consolidate their gains.

Since battalion and brigade headquarters along the British front were no longer
receiving regular reports from the men in the German lines, Lieutenant-Colonel Ricardo,
commanding 9th Royal Inniskilling Fusiliers, suggested that he should send out Major
Peacocke to determine what was going on in the German front line. At 9.20 a.m. a message
was received that Major Peacocke had gotten as far as one of the British front line saps and
reported that there was an enfilade of machine gun fire sweeping the sunken road running
from Thiepval to Hamel, and it was almost impassable. A wounded signaler who had just
arrived back at brigade headquarters confirmed this information. Later, Major Peacocke
was able to slowly work his way forward into *Feste Schwaben* where he helped to coordinate
the defense of the position.

Hauptmann Schorer, 8th Bavarian RIR. (*Das K. B. Reserve-Infanterie-Regiment Nr. 8*)

The reinforcements so desperately needed to continue the advance were to come from the 107th Brigade; the 8th, 9th, 10th, and 15th Royal Irish Rifles. While still in Thiepval Wood the 10th Royal Irish Rifles came under machine gun fire and among their casualties they lost their commanding officer, Lieutenant-Colonel H.C. Bernard. At 9.15 a.m. these battalions left Thiepval Wood and proceeded to cross no man's land. They were immediately met with heavy German artillery fire and heavy machine gun fire coming from St. Pierre-Divion on the left flank and from five machine guns in Thiepval on the right flank as well as machine gun fire from their right rear. It must have been demoralizing that the men could actually see the machine guns that were firing at them. Those men who were able to make it to the old German front line joined forces with the six battalions already in and around *Feste Schwaben*.

> There were two Lewis guns going over with the 9th Fusiliers – we got held up by the wire ... the other gun crew got set up in a good spot behind a natural rise in the ground and we got our gun going from a shell-hole. More ammunition had to be carried out to us as the men moved forward but we only got about a third of the supplies we should have had. Suddenly we realized there was no more men going past us, we were on our own. The crew of the other gun was either killed or wounded, and a big man called Hill from near Lurgan crawled to the pit and collected the good bullets, for the other Lewis gun was wrecked and no good to us. The German soldiers got back into their own trenches again and we started to fire short bursts at them ... we helped to cover the retreat of the Fusiliers and the Rifles. We ran out of ammunition completely. Gunner Hill and myself managed to trail the gun and two wounded back to our own lines. There was a big gap in our wire and we covered this with the Lewis. By dinner-time we had collected all the spare Lewis gun bullets and was ready for the Germans we thought would attack us.[18]

The survivors of the 107th Brigade passed through the lines of the 108th and 109th Brigades by the *Hansa Weg* and *Fabeck Graben* on their way to attack the next German line. After a brief time needed to reorganize the men, the 107th Brigade along with small parties from the other two brigades advanced toward the II Line, some 600 meters away.

At 9.25 a.m. the artillery liaison officer with the 109th Brigade reported that the 'C' Line had been taken and was being consolidated. At 9.45 a.m. the 109th Brigade successfully sent a message to Division Headquarters and reported:

That the right flank of the division was in the air, and that although the 9th Royal Inniskilling Fusiliers on the extreme flank were strong, they were anxious, and were endeavoring to get in touch with the 96th Brigade, which was the brigade on our right.[19]

The German II Line was virtually undefended at this time. A lightly armed artillery observation group from RFAR 26 watched helplessly as the British soldiers approached their position located in *Feste Staufen* (Stuff Redoubt). One member of their group, *Unteroffizier* Felix Kircher, later recalled:

We lay in our dugout and from time to time one of us went upstairs to watch the area. Suddenly, at 9 o'clock, an observer shouted down the dugout steps in an amazed voice, '*Der Tommy ist da, kommt rauf!*' 'Tommy is here, come up!' We rushed up and saw a lot of khaki-clothed men with flat steel helmets. They were the first Englishmen we had seen so near, running up and down in front of our barbed wire, searching for a breach in it. Most of them were young boys just like us – about 20 years old. We were in a desperate position. Being artillery observers we had no weapons and no ammunition. Each moment we expected a raid with hand grenades. But nothing happened. Then the English artillery began to shoot at our trench, but the shells fell too short and exploded among their own people. We saw corpses whirling through the air and the survivors stormed back down the hill.[20]

While Kircher thought that the Ulstermen had run into British barrage fire and having been caught in the open had suffered heavy casualties it appears that this was not exactly what was happening. At 9.15 a.m. reports came in to the German headquarters that 'the Englishmen were in the Artillery Hollow Grandcourt!' *Oberst* Erlenbusch, commander of RFAR 26 had already observed the enemy advance toward Grandcourt and had taken immediate action to counter the threat. Erlenbusch ordered the heavy field howitzers of 1/FAR 20 in Battery Position 112 that was close to the regimental headquarters located on Hill 131 south of Miraumont to open fire on the advancing Ulstermen.

Erlenbusch also sent *Radfahrer Gefreiter* Schmid to inform *Gruppe* Berta and *Gruppe* Adolf of the situation and ordered them to 'destroy the Englishmen in the Artillery Hollow!' The 3/RFAR had also noticed the enemy troops near *Feste Staufen*. *Leutnant* Häusermann ordered his guns to be taken out of their protective emplacements and they fired shell after shell into the advancing Ulstermen over open sights. The battery was soon joined by the guns from 2/RFAR 27 near the ruined mill. Artillery Survey troops in the *Staufenriegel*, some *pioniers* along with the gun crews from Battery Becker whose 9cm guns were out of ammunition also joined in with rifle and pistol fire helping to drive off the enemy soldiers. The attackers caught in the heavy fire attempted to take cover in the open grassland and wait for the fire to stop; it was now 10 a.m.

While it is possible the Ulstermen had run into a portion of the British barrage the main fire being directed against them was coming from German guns. Any hope of

Radfahrer – RIR 99. (Author's collection)

forcing their way through the German defenses under this withering fire was completely crushed when within a few minutes German reserves, a recruit company from IR 180 and a machine gun company, opened fire on the exposed Ulstermen from Grandcourt as well as from the *Feste Alt Württemberg* (Beaucourt Redoubt) on the northern edge of the Ancre. The surviving attackers were forced to make their way back toward *Feste Schwaben* or tried to dig in and find protection from the heavy fire all the while suffering further losses from the infantry and shellfire. The potentially disastrous breakthrough of the German line had been effectively stopped.

About 9 a.m. British officers were seen orienting themselves with the aid of maps and detachments of British soldiers were observed. Some were digging in and others were advancing into the area in front of Schnürlen's Company (1st Recruit Company Infantry Regiment 180). Fire brought to bear by Schnürlen's Company and one weapon of the 1st Machine Gun Company Reserve Infantry Regiment 119 caused the enemy to pull back into the *Hansastellung* and *Schwaben* Redoubt.[21]

At 10.10 a.m. the artillery fire lifted from the II Line and about 50 men from the 107th Brigade did manage to enter the German lines near *Feste Staufen*, which they found unoccupied. Another group entered the German trenches about 300 meters further north and formed a trench block facing Grandcourt. On the left, about 200 men worked their way into the *Artillerie Mulde* and occupied an unoccupied German battery position. The balance of the men remained in the open with both flanks unsecured. Heavy machine gun fire from Thiepval and St. Pierre-Divion, and the arrival of further German reserves in Grandcourt prevented any further expansion of these gains by the men of the Ulster Division.

For the time being the threat against Grandcourt appeared to be contained. *Gruppe* Bertha; the II/RFAR 26 under the command of *Hauptmann Graf* von Preysing advised headquarters of the situation:

> It appears that about 100 British have broken through to the western slope of the *Artillerie Mulde Grandcourt*. They are isolated and digging in by the barbed wire obstacle of Position 723. Our infantry in *Süd I* and *Süd II* are short of ammunition. Message passed immediately from Regiment to *Feste Zollern* for re-transmission.[22]

At the same time the Ulstermen were attempting to advance towards Grandcourt, elements of the 109th Brigade continued their attacks against the left wing platoon of the 9/R99 back in the 1st German position. The fighting was fierce and virtually non-stop, resulting in very heavy casualties for the defenders as well as the attackers. At 10 o'clock in the morning the exhausted remnants of the 9th Coy requested permission to give up their positions. They were finally forced to yield and the men bolted into the right wing of Sector C4.

The abandoned trench blocks in C3 were quickly manned by the men of the 7/R99 under *Leutnant der Reserve* Schmidt. The Ulstermen continued to push further into the maze of trenches where they soon came up to the *Martins Pfad* and *Markt Gasse*. The men of the 7th Coy took up position in the *Markt Gasse* and formed a key trench block where this trench joined the *Martins Pfad*, effectively preventing any further British advance towards Thiepval.

The credit for saving the right wing of the 7th Coy and Thiepval belongs to the right wing platoon of the 7th Coy, commanded by *Offizier Stellvertreter* Gelzenleichter. This platoon engaged the Ulstermen with hand grenades and kept them from advancing any further toward the village. During the fighting several Bavarians from 8th Bavarian RIR were released from captivity and they joined in the defense, using the rifles taken from the dead and wounded lying about. In the course of the fighting Gelzenleichter was killed, and many of his men became casualties.

> The 7th Company was surrounded. The situation was extremely critical, as weak remnants of the right hand neighboring company and a few completely crestfallen Bavarians came to us, giving up all for lost. This took all the fight and hope from many of us, I later discovered. Only the unprecedented courage and the most ferocious daredevil behavior of *Offizier Stellvertreter* Gelzenleichter, the platoon leader of the right wing platoon, saved our company through his example and thereby quite possibly Thiepval. However, he paid for the enthusiasm and courage he restored to his men through his deeds with his life.
>
> I moved from the left wing to the right wing, but only for a short period of time, then I became sent to block off the *Marktgasse* where it intersected the road that lead to the cemetery. Dark hours followed. Thirsty, hungry, listless and played out, the long, largely uneventful time waiting got on our nerves. Furthermore, hellish artillery fire that initially also included our howitzers and mortars that bombarded the previously lost trenches.
>
> English pilots circled directly over us, looking for the exact positions where the men in field grey were still holding out and fired into our small group with machine

Offizier Stellvertreter Gelzenleichter. (*Geschichte des Reserve-Infanterie-Regiment Nr. 99*)

guns, however without any damage. Whenever a steel helmet showed itself, it was dealt with just like at a hare shoot. The chaps did not seem to know where they were in our trenches, and we allowed many a group to calmly approach us and dealt with them with hand grenades.[23]

The men of the 36th Division continued to attack the positions held by the 7th Coy for the rest of the morning. Finally, two officers and two Groups with a machine gun were compelled to surrender as a result of the repeated attacks. This now meant that the *Markt Gasse* was now entirely in British hands. The loss of this position left the forward line of the 7th Coy nearly encircled and gave the British control of the area down to the cemetery overlooking Thiepval.

In order to contain the enemy penetration two *Musketen* from the 1st *Musketen* Bn, under *Hauptmann* Mundt, were set up in the *Martins Pfad* and *Bulgaren Graben* to support the right flank of the 7th Coy. The heavy fighting resulted in the need for fresh supplies of ammunition and hand grenades. The men of the 8/R99 were kept occupied during the morning filling these needs as they brought up boxes of hand grenades and ammunition to the forward firing line and then distributed it where it was needed the most.

While there had been a breach in the front line by RIR 99 there was hope that the penetration could be contained and the enemy could eventually be ejected. For now the survivors of the 9th Coy had set up new trench blocks in the *Hansa Strasse* only 400 meters in front of artillery positions by Grandcourt. St. Pierre-Divion was firmly held by the 12/R99 and 1/8th Bavarian RIR while reinforcements were moving into the sector as fast as they could be sent forward. It was only a matter of holding out until fresh troops arrived.

However, the Ulstermen kept up the pressure all along the line. *Infanterist* Wilhelm Lange:

> We built a block in the trench between us and the English who had broken into the trenches on the left. We couldn't see very well when they were coming, but some of our men behind us had better observation, so they would call out to us every time the English approached and then we threw grenades for all we were worth. I've no idea how many we threw; these people attacked us at least fifteen times. We had a big advantage because our grenades were on a stick and with the extra leverage we could throw further.[24]

Officer and canine companion – RIR 99. (Author's collection)

The commander of the 26th Reserve Division had learned of the attack on Thiepval by 8.05 A.M. from reports by observers in *Feste Alt Württemberg* (Beaucourt Redoubt) from RIR 119. The enemy penetration into *Feste Schwaben* was first learned an hour later.

Generalleutnant von Stein, commander of the XIV Reserve Corps, first heard of the capture of the *Feste Schwaben* at 9.40 A.M., and immediately issued orders to recapture the critical position using the II/8th Bavarian RIR, Machine Gun Coy/R119, men from the 13th Reserve *Pionier* Bn and Machine Gun Marksman Detachment 89.

Since 5.30 in the morning the II/8th Bavarian RIR, commanded by Major Roesch, with one machine gun company and one platoon from *Musketen* Bn 1 had been located at Irles, ready to march at a moments notice. About 9 A.M. orders from the 26th Reserve Division reached Roesch instructing him to take his men by the Ancre Ground and *Stall Mulde* and occupy the positions of that sector at *Süd I*, *Süd II* and the II Line.

Orders had also been issued to the artillery batteries of the division to take the *Feste Schwaben* and *Hansa Stetting* under fire from Artillery Section Pys commanded by Major Reiniger; RFAR 27 that consisted of Artillery Under Section Bertha, *Hauptmann* Frhr von Preysing, II/RFAR 26; Under Section Zollern, *Hauptmann* Wiedtemann, I/RFAR 27 and Under Section Cäsar, *Hauptmann* Jackh, II/RFAR 27. The batteries trained their guns on the Ulstermen in *Feste Schwaben* and *Hansa Stetting* while they still had to contend with British artillery fire and the ever-present danger of enemy aircraft.

The Royal Flying Corps engaged the German batteries with machine gun fire and bombs, which caused a small number of casualties among the gun crews, and, something considered far more serious, possible disruption of the ammunition supply. Despite the

Oberstleutnant von Bram, 8th Bavarian RIR. (*Das K. B. Reserve-Infanterie-Regiment Nr. 8*)

actions of the English aircraft the ammunition column for RFAR 27, *Oberleutnant der Reserve* Steurer and *Hauptmann der Reserve* Pischeck, were able to deliver shells to the batteries southwest of Courcelette and west of Miraumont with minimal interruption from British fire.

The German counter-attack being planned against the Ulstermen would consist of three assault groups, attacking simultaneously from the north, east, and southeast. Orders were prepared and sent to the battalion commanders who would command the attacks. Major Prager, I/8th Bavarian RIR, received orders to begin his attack from *Süd I* and *Süd II*. His group consisted of the 2/8th Bavarian RIR, 1st and 2nd Recruit Coy IR 180, 6/*Pionier* Bn 13, 1st Machine Gun Coy/R119, and Bavarian Machine Gun Marksman Detachment 89.

Major Beyerkohler, III/8th Bavarian RIR, received orders to attack from *Feste Zollern* (Goat Redoubt) located on Hill 153. His group consisted of the 3rd, 11th, and 12/8th Bavarian RIR. Major Roesch, II/8th Bavarian RIR commanded the third group. They would begin the attack first from *Feste Staufen* (Stuff Redoubt) with the II/8th Bavarian RIR, one machine gun company and one platoon from *Musketen* Bn 1.

While the three assault detachments were making preparations for the attack, *Oberstleutnant* Bram, commander of 8th Bavarian RIR, was directed to proceed to the Headquarters of the 52nd Reserve Infantry Brigade by Courcelette at about 10.20 a.m.

At 10.45 A.M. Major Beyerkohler issued orders to his group and to Group Prager located near *Feste Staufen*. During the attack the 9th and 10/8th Bavarian RIR and Bavarian Machine Gun Marksman Detachment 45 were supposed to occupy the II Line southwest of *Süd III* (*Feste Zollern* – Pozières) as a security garrison.

Maintaining communication between the three groups was very difficult as the II Line was deeply silted up due to the heavy bombardment and in many areas the trenches were barely knee deep. Runners and orderlies found it difficult to move across the shattered landscape and many were killed by the constant enemy fire or became disoriented in the unfamiliar maze of trenches.

The British troops were also having a hard time moving across the battlefield. At 10.55 a.m. a runner arrived in the British lines from the crucifix located near Thiepval. He had survived the heavy machine gun fire and was one of the few who had been able to deliver his message:

> There is no one on our right, that the 9th and 10th Royal Inniskilling Fusiliers are mixed there and are suffering from enfilade M.G. fire from S.E. presumably Thiepval, and were unable to say whether there were any troops in front of them.[25]

The British holding out inside the German trenches were also suffering from enfilading machine gun fire from Beaumont-Hamel. The heavy German fire and the confusing maze of trenches caused the Ulster battalions to become badly mixed together.

The German forces opposing the Ulstermen grew with each passing hour. At 11 A.M. von Stein assigned two battalions from Baden IR 185 as reinforcements for the 26th Reserve Division. The battalions immediately began to march from Beugny (about 12 miles east northeast of Thiepval) to Biefvillers. Shortly after, at 11.15 a.m., the overall command of the counter-attack was turned over to *Oberstleutnant* Bram.

General der Infanterie Frhr. von Soden impatiently waited for news of the counter-attack. Hill 151 controlled the entire position of the 26th Reserve Division, from the bank of the Ancre to Thiepval and beyond. The artillery positions could not be maintained if this important hill remained in enemy hands. The Germans felt that if they did not recapture the hill they could even lose the entire sector of the 26th Reserve Division. The fate of the division would hang on the success or failure of the planned counter attacks that were to begin shortly.

32nd Division – The Morning

The companies of the II/R99 facing the men of the 32nd Division reported the heaviest destructive fire they had ever experienced on 1 July. The British lines were still being kept under constant observation in spite of the heavy shelling. During the height of the bombardment German observers noticed enemy reserves moving through Thiepval Wood. The trench garrison in *Thiepval-Mitte* was immediately placed on alert and ordered to hold themselves ready on the steps of their dugouts. Shortly afterward all telephone lines leading to the observers were cut and further messages would have to be transmitted by runner or signal lamps. .

Unteroffizier Hinkel, 7/R99, described his experiences on 1 July:

> In the early morning of 1 July the enemy increased his fire to the greatest possible violence. Now they finally came! We were all mentally prepared. My post was secure. The night before we put up a framed piece of mirror in the trench. It was a wonderful

way to make observations of the enemy trenches from the stairs of the smashed entrances to our dugouts despite the violent fire on our position.

My group was in position, ready to spring up – rifles slung, hand grenades in their hands, full canteens and plump bread bags at their belt. Everyone knew his place – the first in the bend at the top of the path, the next in my favorite position at the crucifix and the rest in the sector of the 5th Coy. I can still picture him as sharply as in the past, my friend, the little *Leutnant* of the right wing platoon of the 5th Coy. We were talking for 5 minutes when suddenly a shell splinter went through his head.

I was not in the dark hole of the dugout. The inevitable excitement and frightfulness had made me come up. The piece of mirror that made observation safe was still not sufficient, besides I felt responsible for the 8 brave Westphalian young men, so I leapt out into my position at the crucifix. I took a quick look from the crucifix to the right side of the woods, and HUSCH – HUSCH, chalk and fragments of beams flew over to the rear. My magnificent young farmer, who stammered all of his life instead of speaking clearly afterwards described my actions to me, so that we should not become surprised.[26]

While Hinkel and the other trench sentries kept the enemy lines under observation the British trenches soon became covered by a smoke screen. The smoke grew thicker until the wood and trenches disappeared from sight. German artillery batteries began to shell the British trenches using the coordinates previously supplied by the Artillery Survey Section and the exploding shells created small openings in the smoke wall that enabled the observers to catch a glimpse of the advancing enemy infantry.

Hinkel recalled his reaction to seeing the advancing British infantry:

Raus! Raus! and my group is there. 'Give it to him hard!' Their Westphalian battle cry was bellowed, and in a blink of an eye all are in their place. The desire for battle and smoke allowed the ravenous men to shoot up onto the parapet. Three fell from the leaden hail of the shrapnel. I rushed to stop this! Standing and kneeling they were wounded and killed in the open gaps of the moving wall of smoky brew in front of us. They obeyed the instructions only reluctantly and unwillingly, and took cover. The range is great, set sights at 600 meters! And now the enemy leaped and turned somersaults over there, the correct range the first time. My rifle stock was knocked to pieces by a bullet, then in addition the rest of the infantry fire joined with us.[27]

Leutnant der Reserve FL Cassel, RIR 99, recalled that memorable day. While inside his dugout he heard the sentry shout 'They are coming!' Suddenly everyone was alert and realized that the attack had finally begun. The first thing that greeted the men as they exited their dugouts was the headless body of the trench sentry who had been killed by one of the last British shells falling on the front line trench.

When Cassel and his men reached the parapet they found that the advancing British troops were barely 20 meters from the trench. The enemy troops advanced slowly under the weight of their heavy equipment. Machine gun fire tore into their ranks and large gaps appeared in the orderly rows. As the British continued to advance toward the German front line trench the survivors took cover in the numerous shell craters while men from RIR 99 fired their rifles and threw hand grenades as fast as they could. Whenever ammunition ran

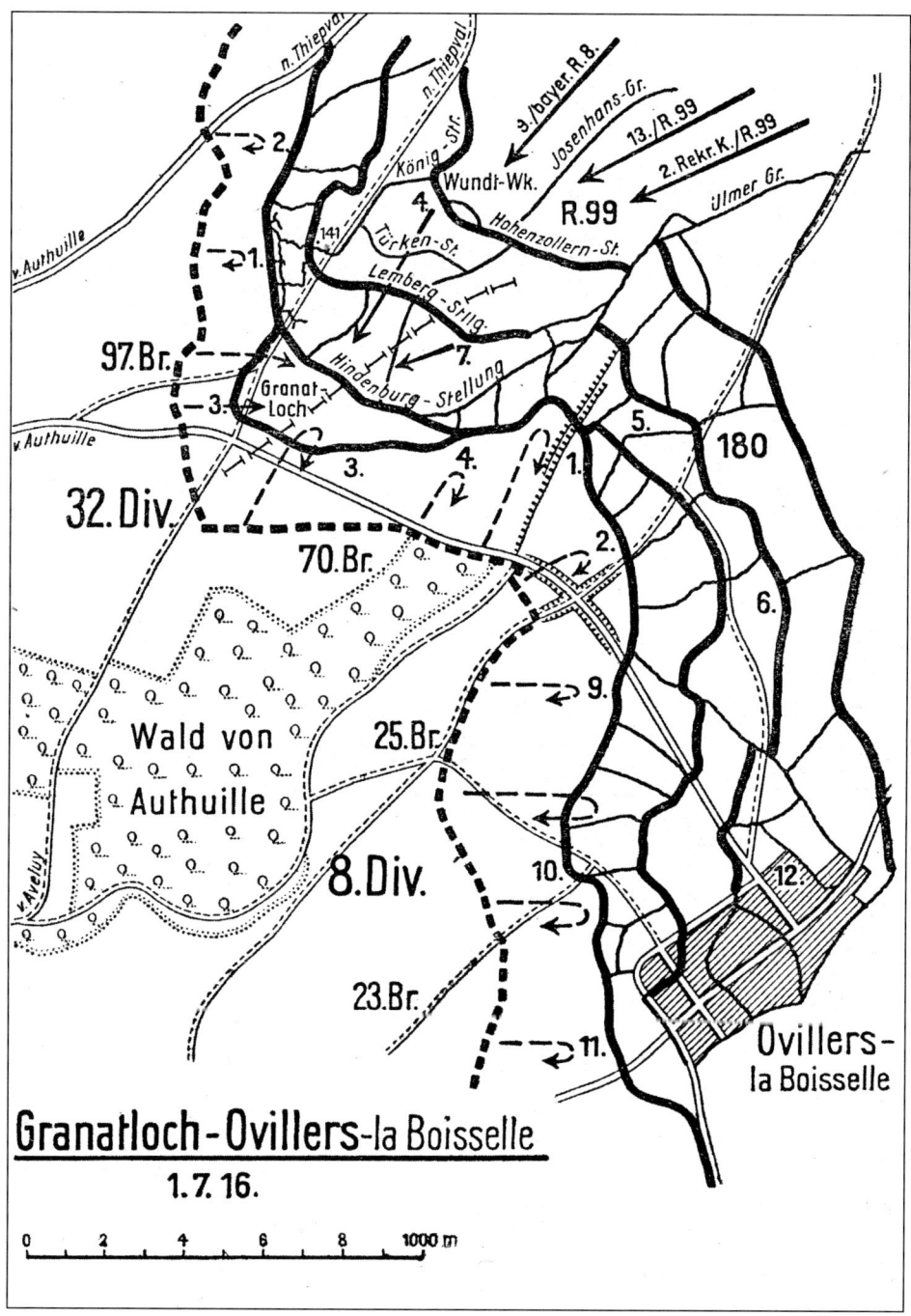

Machine gun positions by Thiepval.

short fresh supplies were brought up from the nearby dugouts.

All of the machine guns located in the positions held by the II and I/R99 had survived the bombardment. The two machine gun companies of RIR 99 had lost only 3 men wounded during the week-long bombardment. The British had attempted to neutralize this serious threat and had assigned two 9.2-inch howitzers to destroy the machine gun positions in and around Thiepval during the preliminary bombardment. The attempt failed when a premature burst in one gun placed both howitzers out of action.

The 16th Northumberland Fusiliers and 15th Lancashire Fusiliers, 96th Brigade, were met with a devastating hail of machine gun and rifle fire while advancing on the German lines; entire rows of men were being cut down. One member of the 15th Lancashire Fusiliers, Sergeant Bill Dutton, watched as his battalion was hit by intense machine gun fire as soon as the men entered no man's land. Men were being hit all along the line and dropping to the ground.

Finally, after taking cover in a nearby shell crater, one of the surviving officers realized that to continue would be futile and told the surviving men to remain where they were until darkness. Dutton recalled that any movement resulted in immediate German fire. It would have been suicidal to leave the safety of the shell crater.

A and B Coys moved forward in waves and were instantly fired upon by Enemy M.G. and snipers. The enemy stood upon their parapet and waved to our men to come on and picked them off with rifle fire. The enemy's fire was so intense that the advance was checked and the waves, or what was left of them, were forced to lie down. 16th Northumberland Fusiliers War Diary.[28]

The *Schwaben Graben* inside the village of Thiepval. (Lawrence Brown)

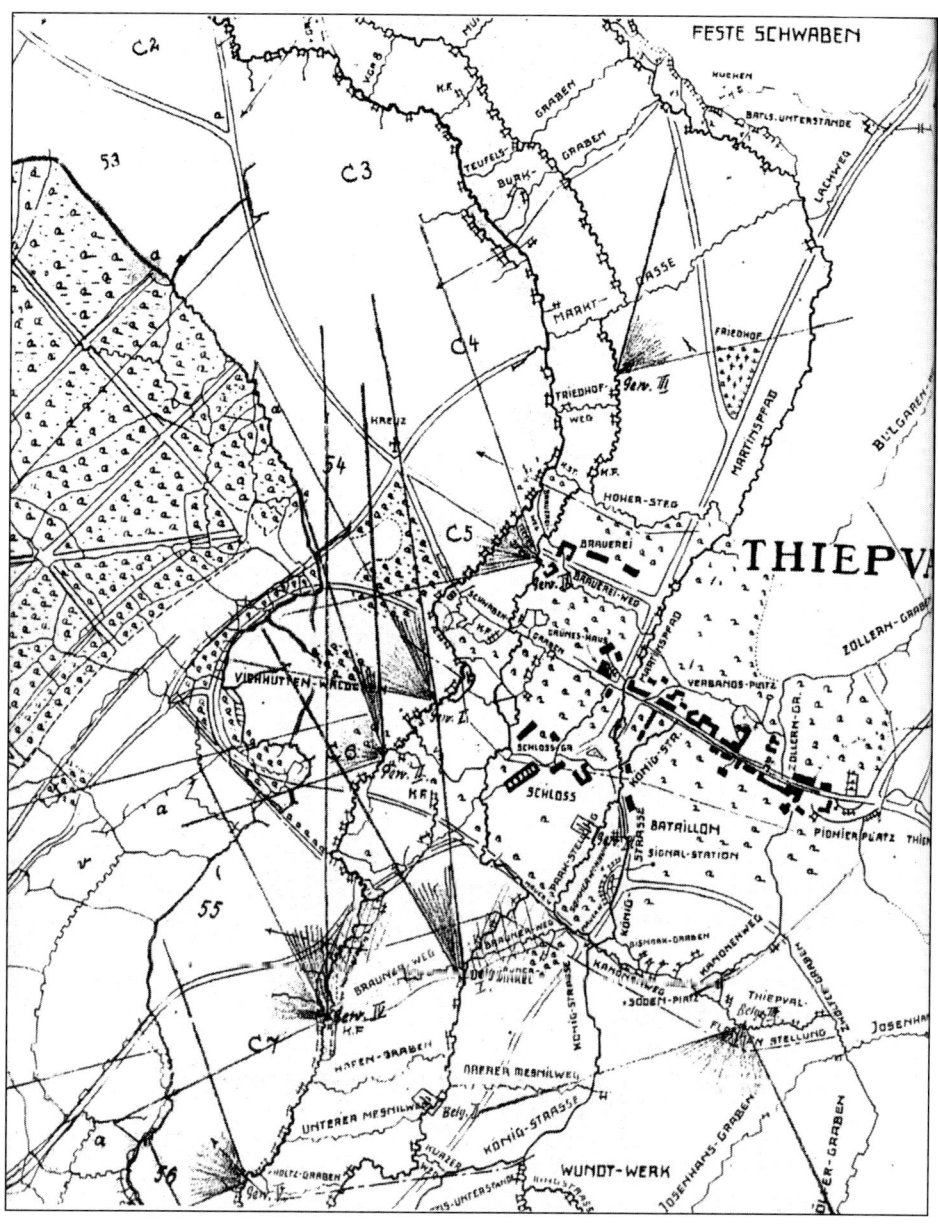

RIR 99 machine gun positions by Thiepval.

The German field guns and 15cm howitzers added their destructive fire and large gaps appeared in the British ranks. Each enemy wave seemed to simply disappear as the men slowly walked towards the German lines. Due to the slope of the ground the reserves in the rear trenches of Sector C5 and C6 were able to fire over the top of the forward trench, helping to eliminate any chance of a successful attack by the 96th Brigade.

> The situation of the Englishmen in no man's land was as if they were caught in a finely meshed net. The Englishmen did not come towards us! Still, where did the 5th Company dwell? They already ascended from the woods where their entanglements were placed. To the right to Sergeant Günther! 'Help! Throw them back with hand grenades!' Thank God! The 5th is at work in the attack with rifle and hand grenades, some of them in shirtsleeves, and not until afterwards was it recognized that the jumbled, destroyed trench delayed their dash towards the battle headquarters.
>
> The beginning of the tightly grouped, slow walking wall coming towards us was finished and soon came to a standstill. My best shot, the stammerer, was instructed to bring down the officer in the front of the advancing line carrying a pennon and stick by shooting him. He fired at the standing target. He missed and almost before he fired again Günther and many other reliable marksmen of the same kind fired. Soon, without their leader to rely upon they became a mass. They came to a standstill, there was confusion and then they flooded to the rear, when our machine guns rattled, our field guns flashed and our brave 15ers gargled. *Unteroffizier* Hinkel, 7/R99[29]

According to British observers about one hundred men from the 15th Lancashire Fusiliers had succeeded in entering the German front trench before the defenders had time to emerge from their dugouts. Without waiting to clear out the dugouts the Fusiliers went

Looking down the Thiepval-Hamel road, later known as the 'Bloody Road'. (*Die 26. Reserve Division 1914-1918*)

forward, past the northern edge of Thiepval. According to reports these men apparently continued on, moving to their left and eventually joined up with the right of the advancing 36th Division.

The only reference to the British from the 96th Brigade reaching the German lines came from RIR 99. They reported that the enemy was able to get up to the wire entanglements on the left wing of Sector C5 and the right wing of Sector C6:

> With a loud hurrah our people rushed out of our trench towards the enemy here and dealt with him with hand grenades and rifle fire in hand to hand fighting. The enemy that was not shot down at once became disordered and took cover in the ground and attempted to crawl back to the rear to the enemy's lines, became our targets through our independent fire, and were shot down.[30]

While the main attack was stopped, no man's land was still filled with British soldiers, many of who tried to push forward while others who were pinned down began to fire at the German lines. *Leutnant der Reserve* Cassel was firing his rifle when he felt a heavy blow to his right hand; a bullet fired from a distance of 20 meters had struck him. His rifle fell to the ground and he could see blood flowing from his wound.

Almost at the same time he watched one of the many British soldiers trying to evade a hand grenade thrown by *Infanterist* Kühnel, without success. The hand grenade exploded and most likely killed or seriously injured the enemy soldier. Cassel had his wound dressed by an orderly and once again resumed command of his platoon. Within half an hour it had become clear that the attack had been repulsed, at least in his platoon sector.

The survivors of the 96th Brigade could neither move forward or to the rear. Without any effective opposition and free from British artillery fire the machine gun crews from RIR 99 controlled no man's land. Extensive training, combined with the use of a prismatic sight enabled the German machine gun crews to fire accurately and quickly on any movement they spotted. Above all, it was the failure of the preliminary bombardment to destroy the German machine guns and crews in the Thiepval Sector that doomed the attack of the 96th Brigade.

The two battalions of the 96th Brigade were facing at least nine heavy machine guns in and around Thiepval. Two guns located in Sector C4 and C5 concentrated their fire on the sunken road leading from Thiepval to Hamel. Numerous British soldiers were caught in their fire and became casualties and after 1 July this road became known as the 'Bloody Road'.

When the attack of the 96th Brigade collapsed, five machine guns in Thiepval and Machine Gun No. 9, located in the *Brauner Weg*, turned their sights onto the right flank of the Ulstermen of the 36th Division still trying to cross no man's land. They were responsible for inflicting heavy casualties on the 9th and 11th Royal Inniskilling Fusiliers from the 109th Brigade as well as the reinforcements from the 107th Brigade. Another machine gun located near Thiepval set its sights at 1,200 meters and was used for indirect fire against suspected English reserves on a reverse slope at the eastern edge of Thiepval wood. It was suspected that this gun killed about 150 men in this manner. British troops located in Sector 54 inside the British trenches suffered heavily in the artillery, infantry and machine gun fire.

At 9.10 a.m. the 96th Brigade was ordered to push forward supports into Thiepval as reports persisted that some men from the first wave had entered the village. At 9.15 a.m. two companies from the 16th Lancashire Fusiliers and two companies from the 16th Northumberland Fusiliers advanced from their front line trench, but were stopped almost immediately by heavy machine gun fire and driven back into their trenches.

> Above our heads an enemy machine gun kept spitting away defiantly. Skillfully hidden behind a wood, in the ruins of a village which was to be taken by us, it had braved the bombardment and its team of – to be quite fair – very brave and capable soldiers, fired with a deadliness and accuracy which was amazing.[31]

Some British soldiers had managed to find their way into the German front line, but they were too few in number to be of any real threat. Nevertheless, they had to be removed. *Leutnant der Reserve* Cassel found that he had only a few men still capable of fighting. His men volunteered to drive out the intruders along with *Infanterist* Kühnel. The small group moved from one traverse to the next, throwing hand grenades as they advanced. The British troops put up a strong defense but they were outnumbered and had no hope of support. The trench was slowly cleared of the invaders with many badly wounded men falling into the hands of Cassel and his men.

The 97th Brigade was on the right wing of the attack by the 32nd Division. The 97th attacked on an 800 meter front with its right flank against the blunted end of the *Leipzig* Salient, its left flank just south of the village of Thiepval. The 16th and 17th Highland Light Infantry were in the first wave, supported by the 2nd King's Own Yorkshire Light Infantry. According to the plan as soon as the *Leipzig* Salient was overrun the 11th Border Regiment would move forward and continue the advance.

At 7.23 a.m. the lead companies of the 16th and 17th Highland Light Infantry moved into no man's land, the 16th HLI as close as 50 to 80 meters from the German wire, the

Kanoniers and medic – RFAR 26. (Author's collection)

17th HLI as close as 30 to 40 meters from the German wire.

When the barrage lifted at 7.30 the 97th Brigade quickly advanced. The bombardment had not done much damage to the trenches or barbed wire in Sectors C7 and C8 where the 1st and 2/R99 were positioned. Any gaps in the wire were covered by machine guns from nearby trenches as well as from the Château grounds. The 16th HLI and the left half of the 2nd KOYLI ran into heavy fire and suffered numerous casualties. The men who were not killed outright took cover among the shell holes in no man's land, where any movement brought down machine gun fire. The German trenches in sectors C7 and C8 were not reached.

The 17th HLI rushed forward at 7.30, crossed over the broken wire entanglements and entered the *Granatloch* (Leipzig Redoubt) before most of the 3/R99 could exit their dugouts. There was some fighting with the few Germans who did manage to get into position as well as heavy fighting with the 3/180 on the right of the 97th Brigade. Despite this resistance, in a short time most of Sector C9 was in British hands as well as part of Sector C8 along with a considerable number of prisoners from the 3/R99. At 8.10 a.m. the adjoining 3/180 reported the loss of the neighboring trenches by the *Granatloch* and that they had been forced to curve back their right flank in Sector P1 because of the enemy pressure.

The men of the 17th HLI continued the advance and immediately moved forward towards the *Hindenburg Strasse*. They were stopped by machine gun fire from the *Wundt Werk* as the Highlanders moved across the open ground. Two batteries of British guns were directed to assist the 17th HLI and the survivors retreated back to the Leipzig Redoubt under the cover of shellfire.

The right half of the 2nd KOYLI moved into the Leipzig Redoubt as support. Additional attempts were made to reach the *Hindenburg Stellung*; all were stopped by intense machine gun fire. The survivors had fallen back to the protection of the *Granatloch*, the 17th HLI and 2nd KOYLI now controlled a chalk pit approximately 60 meters long and 40 meters wide.

Units from the 14th Brigade were waiting in reserve in Aveluy Wood at 7.30 a.m. where they were supposed to move up after the initial attack to continue the advance. Things did not appear to be going the way they expected when heavy shrapnel fire and machine gun fire swept through the wood searching for troop concentrations.

While the men waited for the order to advance from the safety of the wooded area the men could clearly hear the call for stretcher-bearers from the front line. Soon lines of wounded men, some walking, some on stretchers, began to pass by the waiting infantry. When the 14th Brigade moved closer to the front the scene facing the men was less than reassuring. Large numbers of dead lay crumpled by the path. These were interspersed with seriously wounded men awaiting medical treatment. Things were not going well and the men of the 14th Brigade had not even started their attack.

At this time the men from RIR 99 was fortunate that the attacks had failed to reach the *Hindenburg Stellung* as it was only being occupied by about 20 men from the 4/R99, half of whom were busy digging out the leader of the 1st Coy from his collapsed dugout. Reinforcements were being sent forward from the 13/R99 and the 9/8th Bavarian RIR, in order to contain the breach in the line. Meanwhile trench blocks formed by the survivors of the 3/R99 and the 3/180 were containing the British advance for the moment.

The 17th HLI and 2nd KOYLI sent bombing parties north and east along the forward trench in the direction of the *Hindenburg Stellung*. They were stopped at the trench blocks and unable to make any progress as hand grenades flew back and forth from both sides.

At 8.30 the 11th Border Regiment moved into no man's land in order to cross over into the *Granatloch* and continue the planned advance. As the Border Regiment crossed the exposed terrain they came under heavy machine gun fire, especially from IR 180 on their right flank. Some men on the left of the advance did mange to reach the redoubt; the others were forced to turn back.

The 13/R99 and 9/8th Bavarian RIR worked their way forward from the area of Mouquet Farm towards the *Wundt Werk*, an uphill climb. Both companies suffered casualties from the constant shellfire as they moved forward. From the redoubt at the summit the men could see the panorama of the battlefield up to the British rear areas. At the same time the British troops in the *Granatloch* also received a small number of reinforcements as small parties from the 16th HLI and 2nd KOYLI continued to work their way into the redoubt from the left.

When the 97th Brigade captured the *Granatloch, Leutnant* Geist, commander of the 4/R99, ordered an immediate counter attack. The attack was to be led by *Oberleutnant* Mechenbier, commander of the 3/R99. However, the only men available for the attack were six Groups from the 4th Coy, two Groups from the 16/R99 and a small part of the 3/R99. This composite force began its attack from the *Wundt Werk* with one Group moving down the *König Strasse* to where it joined the *Hindenburg Stellung*. Another Group was to move along the *Hindenburg Stellung* from the right, to where it met the *Josenhans Graben*. Both detachments ran into heavy British fire and neither one could move any further along the *Hindenburg Stellung*. They were separated from one another for a distance of about 100 meters, an area that was controlled by the British in the *Granatloch*. Both groups suffered casualties as they moved against British trench blocks; hand grenades were used freely on both sides and soon the Germans began running out of this critical weapon.

At 8.45 a.m. the 14th Brigade sent one of its battalions forward to support the 97th Brigade, and, to continue the attack that would hopefully capture Mouquet Farm. The men in the 1st Dorsets knew something had gone wrong when they received heavy machine gun fire while they were still in Aveluy Wood, long after the German machine guns should have been silenced. Only 6 officers and 60 men of the 1st Dorsets made it across no man's land into the *Granatloch* from the two companies that had started off. The remaining companies stayed under cover in the British lines. While the Dorsets made their attempt, other men from their brigade awaited their turn.

The men patiently waited for their turn to attack while they could hear the sound of the German machine guns firing and the bullets whistling past their ears. Small branches fell around them as they were being cut down by the fire. It was accompanied by the dull sound a bullet made when it struck the tree trunks. The men hoped that their wait would be over soon and that they could get to grips with the enemy.

The next attempt to reinforce the *Granatloch* came from the 19th Lancashire Fusiliers. While some of the men did manage the perilous journey across no man's land, much needed equipment and supplies never made it.

One Lewis Gun was carried over into the German trenches, but of the others, the carriers were either killed or wounded.[32]

Of the bomb carriers, very few got across the fire-swept zone with their buckets. This

Hauptmann Mechenbier, 3/R99. (*Geschichte des Reserve-Infanterie-Regiment Nr. 99*)

was due to the fact that the men could not advance quickly enough with the loads they had to carry, and they, probably being more conspicuous, were singled out by the men from RIR 99.

The situation facing the Germans defending the area around the *Granatloch* was becoming critical. However, there was still a chance that if sufficient artillery fire could be brought to bear on the new threat the threat could be eliminated.

> 9.40 a.m.: To *Feste Zollern*. The enemy is being reinforced. Dense masses have been observed in Authuille Wood.

> 9.43 a.m.: *Thiepval Süd*, The edge of Authuille Wood is occupied by dense masses. The enemy is holding massed reinforcements there. *Feste Zollern* reports that our own artillery is not firing much, despite the fact that the Regiment is demanding the heaviest possible defensive fire in front of *Thiepval-Mitte* and *Süd* and on the edge of Authuille Wood.[33]

The large masses of men offered such a tempting target, if only the German guns could take the position under fire. However the men remained relatively safe under the light fire that was being directed against them. This was fortunate for the British troops waiting to cross no man's land. The *Granatloch* was now so full of men that there was no room for any more. The officer in charge sent a message to the rear to stop any additional reinforcements.

Eventually the two Russian saps had been run out into no man's land, one to serve as a trench and the other as a tunnel. These would allow reinforcements and communications to cross the exposed terrain in safety – the connection with the rear was now secure.

The news coming from the front shortly before noon was anything but good. The situation facing the men from RIR 99 and IR 180 holding the front line was critical and without fresh supplies of ammunition, especially hand grenades as well as fresh troops there was the chance the entire position could be lost.

> 11.40 a.m.: Report from *Thiepval-Süd* (written). *Granatloch* overrun at 8.00 a.m. Enemy in *Hindenburg Stellung*. *Oberleutnant* Mechenbier is conducting a counter-attack in front of C8 from the *Lemberg Stellung* via *Königstrasse*. 5 mass attacks have been beaten off.

11.40 a.m.: To *Feste Zollern*. Reinforcements required urgently. All troops in action (13th and 16th Coys in *Thiepval-Süd*, 15th Coy *Hansa Stellung* and 2nd Recruit Coy tasked to carry hand grenades forward.[34]

Perhaps the only good news came at the same time from the men holding *Thiepval-Mitte*: 'Everything under control. It appears that a new attack is being prepared in front of C6.'[35]

36th Division – The Afternoon Counter-attack

Until the village of Thiepval was captured the 36th Division would be unable to expand its gains. The division had made one of the furthest penetrations of the German lines so far in the fighting but the position being held was tenuous. When the majority of the attacks by the neighboring 32nd Division failed, the German defenders were able to concentrate their effort against the 36th Division, including its base of support in Thiepval Wood. Gas and high explosive shells rained down on the Ulstermen from artillery batteries and trench mortars.

The Germans also concentrated their machine gun fire against the Ulstermen from three sides, as well as forming an almost impenetrable curtain of fire across no man's land. Reinforcements found it impossible to cross over to the captured position; even lone runners still found it virtually impossible to cross. Most of the men carrying supplies, ammunition and messages became casualties in their attempts. Sappers had tried to dig communication trenches across no man's land but were forced to stop their work in daylight due to the volume of machine gun and artillery fire.

While the Germans prepared for their counter attacks the Ulstermen had sent out several patrols in the direction of Thiepval and Mouquet Farm in order to determine their exact situation. The patrol that went in the direction of Thiepval ran into stiff opposition and was driven back by Germans using hand grenades. Another patrol under the command of Lieutenant Sanderson went through the German trenches until they were within 500 meters of Mouquet Farm, where they stopped without seeing any German soldiers. The patrol returned to its starting point and reported their findings, but no attempt was made to occupy the empty trench, probably due to the critical shortage of men.

Between 1 and 2 o'clock in the afternoon bombing parties from the 12th and 4/8th Bavarian RIR came into the line at Sector C4 and reinforced the existing garrison. The replacements quickly captured an English machine gun and recaptured a German machine gun; both were then sent to the rear.

Starting about noon all available German guns and *Minenwerfer* fired on the captured

Machine Gun Marksman Detachment 89. (*Das K. B. Reserve-Infanterie-Regiment Nr. 8*)

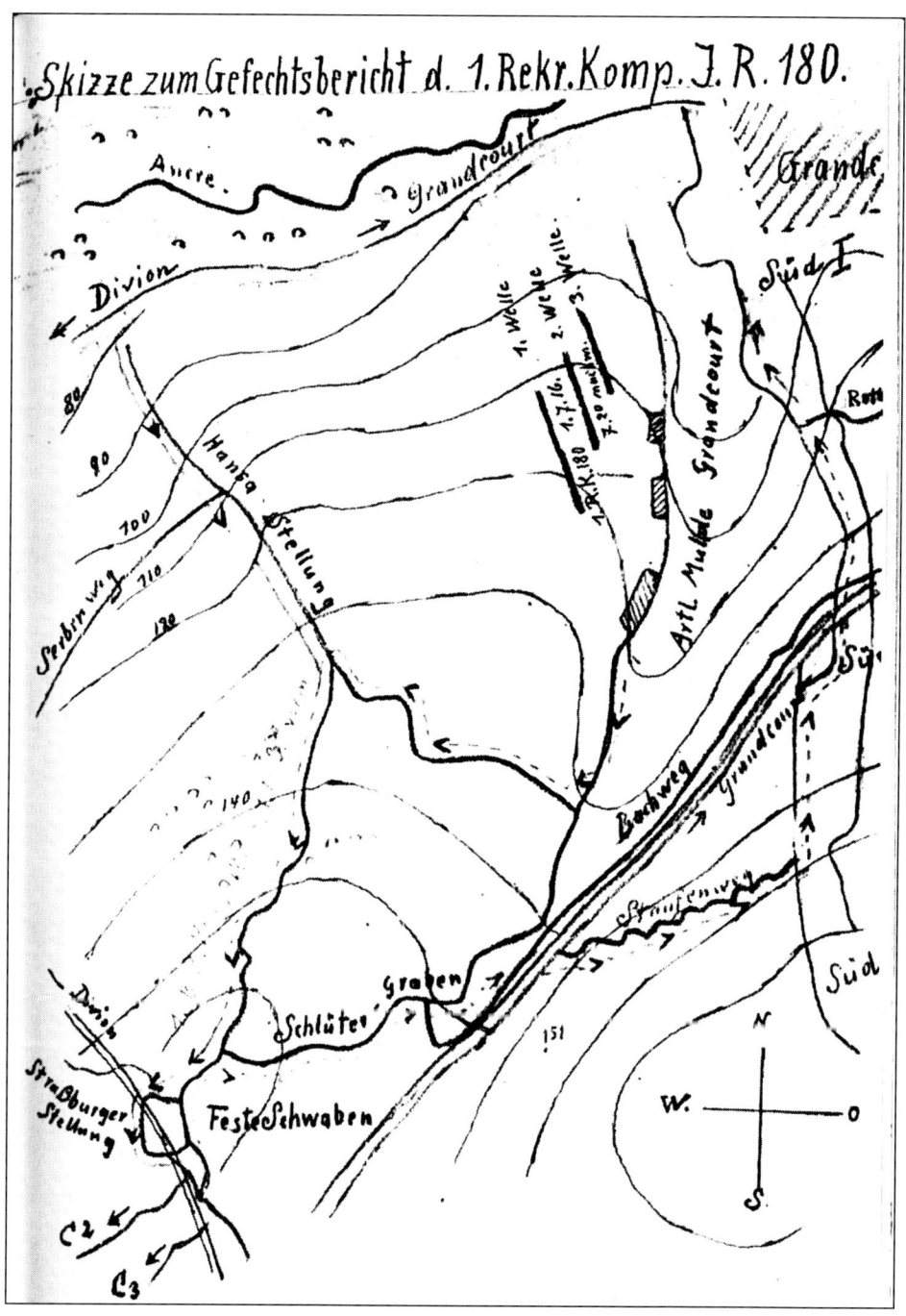

Route of attack of the 1st Recruit Company IR 180.

Memorial card: *Infanterist* Anton Mittermaier, 11/8th Bavarian
RIR, killed in action 1 July 1916. (Author's collection)

positions and the surrounding trenches in preparation for the first counter attacks. The guns from Artillery Sub-Group Bertha, with its battle headquarters in the *Stump Weg*, were already shelling the Ulstermen in *Feste Schwaben* and would continue to fire in support of the attack by Group Beyerkohler. Artillery Sub-Groups Zollern and Cäsar would also continue their bombardment and support the counter attacks being made by the other two groups. Due to the higher priority given to the recapture of *Feste Schwaben* few guns could be spared to support the situation at the *Granatloch* and surrounding terrain.

About 1 o'clock in the afternoon *Oberstleutnant* Bram and his regimental Adjutant *Oberleutnant* Grabinger left the headquarters of the 52nd *Reserve Infanterie Brigade* near Courcelette and moved forward towards *Feste Staufen* in order to look over the position that was to be attacked. Moving around in the position was extremely difficult due to the thousands upon thousands of shells that had ploughed up the land, the maze of unfamiliar trenches, the unclear nature of the terrain and the uninterrupted enemy fire. While completing their survey *Oberstleutnant* Bram and *Oberleutnant* Grabinger looked through one of the few surviving observation positions and saw an English patrol just in front of the II Line, therefore they realized that haste was needed and the attacks must be made as soon as possible, with or without the cooperation of all of the groups.

Other members of the Bavarian regiment were also having problems locating the positions they were supposed to occupy as part of the planned counter attack:

> On the right men came out of the house ruins and gardens, ducked, jumped and leapt to us in the trench. It was part of the 8th Coy. No platoon leader was with it. They wanted the second position. I chased them out of my trench, where they had lost nothing and needlessly exposed themselves to the fire and pointed out the main trench

Memorial card: *Infanterist* Franz Thurnberger, 12/8th Bavarian RIR, killed in action
1 July 1916 during the counter attack against *Feste Schwaben*. (Author's collection

to them; then I inquired after Ernst Martin and found out he was wounded. Finally, about 1 o'clock the trench was empty. I went off through the now quite moderate fire, coming back to my men again. However to my relief I found out that we had lost no more than one man (Pius Pfeiffer); Heinlein was also missing. Just as I went to the position again, where I had experienced the fair dance, I encountered him there. He had waited when I had left the trench.[36]

At the same time Major Beyerkohler was in the front line trench near *Feste Staufen* positioning three of his companies for the attack. The platoon of *Offizier Stellvertreter* Gottel, 5/8th Bavarian RIR and Machine Gun Marksman Detachment 89 were also located in *Feste Staufen*. They were waiting to join Group Prager, however under the present circumstances they were reassigned to Group Beyerkohler.

There was no sign of Group Roesch and it was reported that they had suffered heavy losses from enemy artillery fire and that a portion of the men apparently had gotten lost in the unfamiliar terrain. Group Roesch could not be counted upon in the upcoming attack. Another problem arose when *Oberstleutnant* Bram lost contact with Major Prager in Grandcourt, so he decided to lead the attack alone with Group Beyerkohler. It would be a hastily prepared attack with only the few men he had available, but Bram felt it was necessary in order to recapture the important position of *Feste Schwaben*.

The 9th and 10/8th Bavarian RIR were to remain in the II Line, occupying the trenches from *Feste Zollern* to Pozières as a security garrison in case of any possible reverses during the attack. Assembling the men in the trenches around *Feste Staufen* was very difficult. Persistent shellfire had choked up the trenches and dugouts; shell splinters were causing a steady stream of casualties. In one instance an important observation post occupied by the

Memorial card: *Infanterist* Engelbert Feichtner, 5/8th Bavarian RIR, killed 6 p.m. 1 July 1916. (Author's collection)

Bavarians was destroyed by a direct hit.

The Ulsterman's position was also becoming increasingly serious. At 1.45 P.M. the 10th Royal Inniskilling Fusiliers reported that the men of all the battalions were being raked by machine gun fire from Thiepval and they had suffered almost 60% casualties.

At 1.58 p.m. the German defenders in *Thiepval-Nord* reported that Sector C1 was firmly in their hands and the English had broken through in Sector C3 up to *Feste Schwaben*. Part of an English detachment had penetrated the front up to the *Artillerie Mulde* in front of Grandcourt but they were helpless and dug in at the western slope of the hollow.

Group Prager was completing preparations for the attack against the Ulstermen from the direction of Grandcourt. At approximately 2 p.m. the counter attacks began. The 1st and 2nd Recruit Coys from IR 180 attacked the British troops that were in the *Artillerie Mulde* just south of Grandcourt. Rifle and machine gun fire, along with artillery support from Artillery Sub-Groups Zollern and Cäsar, forced the British soldiers in the *Artillerie Mulde* to withdraw to the rear. At first the retirement was in good order and the British artillery provided barrage fire in an attempt to support them, but as the men had to cross open ground many were killed and others were cut off and captured. Group Prager then continued on until it reached the *Hansa Stellung*. The men of Group Prager also suffered a number of casualties as they advanced, including the leader of the 2nd Recruit Coy/180, *Hauptmann der Reserve* Hudelmaier, who was wounded.

Losses were heavy among the Recruit Companies who had been thrown into action before the men had completed their training. Regardless of this, every man was needed if the counter attacks were to succeed.

7.7cm Field gun and crew, RFAR 26. (Author's collection)

After the first wave had crossed the Artillery Hollow, Grandcourt, the second wave left the trenches. Although the right half of the first wave succeeded in forcing a way into the Hanseatic Position (*Hansa Stellung*), the left hand had to wait until the support of the second wave enabled it to get further forward. Despite heavy rifle and machine gun fire, this part of the Company also succeeded in working its way forward to within 100 meters of the Hanseatic Position, albeit at the cost of heavy casualties (twenty three killed and 100 wounded). In doing so, *Offizier Stellvertreter* Rädle, (who was severely wounded in the upper arm by a shell splinter), together with his platoon, took twenty prisoners and two Lewis guns. Simultaneously *Unteroffizier* Stumpf and four men (Gessmann, Reng, Georg, Bregizer and Dötlinger) launched an assault on about twenty British soldiers, who were attempting to hold out in shell holes in front of the Hanseatic Position. He captured one officer and two men. The remainder were killed. *Leutnant* Scheurlen, 2nd Recruit Coy, IR 180[37]

When they reached the *Hansa Stellung* the Württembergers from Group Prager moved up the trench towards the *Feste Schwaben*, mopping up the trench with hand grenades as they went. Group Prager managed to get within 600 meters of the redoubt before they were stopped. The Germans now knew the exact location of the British troops in this sector and were able to bring accurate artillery fire down on them.

The situation confronting the British troops in *Feste Schwaben* grew worse as each hour passed. Some runners were able to get through the heavy German fire, and they brought news of the plight of their men. The following report came in at about 2.15 p.m. from 2nd Lieutenant Hogg, 14th Royal Irish Rifles:

He was the only officer with a mixed party 40 men at *Feste Schwaben* left edge, his left was guarded by two machine guns, his right by 1 Lewis Gun, but was not in connection with anyone.[38]

Trench by Thiepval church. (*An der Somme*)

Another message was sent by the 14th Royal Irish Rifles at about the same time, but this one did not reach the 109th Brigade Headquarters until 6.30 in the evening. By then, the information was old and the situation had already changed for the worse. The message stated that:

A train arrived at Grandcourt at 2.03 P.M. – probably containing German reinforcements.[39]

Considering the size and duration of the preliminary bombardment and aerial activity, the rail line into Grandcourt should have been disabled long before 1 July. If this was not the case then the use of the rail line could only speed up the arrival of fresh troops.

Group Beyerkohler also began their attack against the Ulstermen in *Feste Schwaben*. The 3/8th Bavarian RIR in front with *Hauptmann* Wurmb in the lead and the 11th and 12/8th Bavarian RIR following. The watchwords were "Run at the enemy!" The Bavarians immediately suffered a number of casualties from British shellfire and from infantry fire. In a short time the 11th and 12/8th Bavarian RIR lost their leaders, *Leutnants der Reserve* Schiller and Klug, and many of their platoon leaders were put out of action. The 3rd Coy also lost its best platoon leader, *Leutnant der Reserve* Engelhardt, who was killed.

During one of the attacks some German soldiers met a particularly horrible death from an unusual source, a Bangalore torpedo:

A squad of German soldiers went from the trench to the dugout ... these soldiers of ours ... managed to get the tubes burning and pushed them into the dugout where the Germans were. We were a right distance away but we could smell the burning flesh as the Germans inside the dugout burnt to death.[40]

Memorial card: *Infanterist* Johann Duschl, 5/8th Bavarian RIR, killed in action 1.30 p.m. 1 July 1916 by an artillery shell. (Author's collection)

Two platoons from the 3rd Coy that were positioned on both sides of the *Staufen Graben* soon came up against a well entrenched enemy force, supported by a machine gun and a mine thrower. The men of the 3rd Coy continued to push forward, still out of sight of the defenders in the *Feste Schwaben* due to the terrain. They slowly forced the British back towards the redoubt. Eventually Group Beyerkohler had cleared the *Staufen Graben* up to the *Lach Weg*.

When they reached this point the attackers ran into a British trench block that was supported by three machine guns. Hand grenades flew back and forth and there was rifle fire everywhere. After bitter fighting the trench block was cleared and the Bavarians continued their advance. They had moved to within 200 meters of *Feste Schwaben*. When the men from Group Beyerkohler came into full view of the defenders of the redoubt they were brought to a stop by heavy rifle and machine gun fire.

During the advance by Group Beyerkohler, five Groups of the 8/R99 asked to be relieved because of exhaustion. *Unteroffizier* Hinkel, 7/R99, was sent to the right wing of the battalion sector where he and his men were to block off the *Markt Gasse* by the heights at the road. Hinkel and his men were thirsty, hungry, and weary but they obeyed the orders. Hinkel's group took up their position, which was under heavy British artillery fire. They also came under heavy howitzer and mortar fire from German guns that were firing on the communication trenches reportedly lost to the enemy.

There was no organized counter attack from the direction of St. Pierre-Divion, but there was still heavy fighting throughout the afternoon. Two platoons from 8th Bavarian RIR occupied the second trench near the *Meisengasse* where they formed a trench block, effectively preventing the British troops from expanding their gains towards St. Pierre-Divion. *Hauptmann* Mandel coordinated the defenses near the village. He had troops from the 12/R99 and 1/8th Bavarian RIR move into the trenches occupied by the Ulstermen

Hauptmann Herbert Ritter von Wurmb. (*Das K. B. Reserve-Infanterie-Regiment Nr. 8*)

and began mopping them up. They came up against parties from the Royal Irish Rifles, who were defending the left flank of the Ulstermen against the German bombing parties. During this action *Unteroffizier* Bronnbauer, 4/8th Bavarian RIR and *Unteroffizier* Schuler and *Infanterist* Biener, 1/8th Bavarian RIR were singled out for their actions during the day.

Bronnbauer had been given orders to perform a reconnaissance of the trenches leading up to *Feste Schwaben* from Sector C4. Even though the enemy had penetrated into the German position, their exact location was still unknown. Bronnbauer advanced toward the enemy held position with half of a platoon from the 4/8th Bavarian RIR. The men had not gone far when they came across several dugouts that proved to be empty. A third dugout was located and Bronnbauer noted that there was a light down below.

His men blocked off the entrances of the dugout while one man fired his rifle down the steps, followed by a hand grenade. *Unteroffizier* Zahn, who spoke English, then called down to anyone inside the dugout to come out. Within a few moments seven British soldiers came up and surrendered to Zahn. The men were searched and then led off to the rear by several guards while Bronnbauer and the detachment continued their reconnaissance. After several skirmishes involving hand grenades Bronnbauer was able to complete his assignment and return with an additional five prisoners. He would later receive the Gold Medal for Bravery for his accomplishments.

Another patrol in sector C1 consisting of an *Unteroffizier* and three men penetrated into the front line and reported the capture of 1 officer and 25 men. Later, the left wing of sector C3 was occupied by a platoon from IR 186 that had arrived at the front. It was the beginning of a long list of replacement units that would see service on the Somme over the next 5 months.

Much of the fighting inside the German trenches took the form of small skirmishes as groups of men from both sides stumbled into one another. It was often a matter of luck or in some cases resolve that allowed one side to overcome the other. The men could not see much of their surroundings as they kept to the deep German trenches. Visibility was measured in meters and the walls of the trenches muffled much of the sounds that the men could hear.

This type of fighting was evident in the small action fought by *Infanterist* Peter Rietzler, 12/8th Bavarian RIR in the afternoon of 1 July. Rietzler and a small group of men were participating in the attack against *Feste Schwaben*. One by one the men with Rietzler became killed or wounded. Still, his detachment was able to capture a British machine gun during the heavy fighting and take the crew prisoner.

Finally, after fighting against the British for an hour with only four remaining men Rietzler and his comrades bumped into a group of British soldiers that they estimated to be 100 strong. Rietzler's small band decided to attack and rushed toward the British troops while yelling, shouting and firing their rifles. Apparently the British were caught off guard and made a hasty withdrawal in the face of what appeared to be a determined attack by a large force, not just five men. The ruse worked, not only did the British force withdraw, Rietzler and his comrades managed to capture 16 British soldiers. For this action as well as making a dangerous journey in order to deliver an important message, Rietzler was awarded the Gold Medal for Bravery.

During a lull in the fighting around St. Pierre-Divion, *Soldat* Wilhelm Lange, RIR 99, heard an unusual sound:

> About 2.30 in the afternoon the attacks had stopped. I heard music from a bit farther along the trench where the English were. I told my mates and the didn't believe me. Then we all listened and sure enough we heard something like a zither or guitar. So I popped up my rifle and went along to have a look. At about 100 meters distance, I could vaguely see some people so I went back to my mates. We all took our rifles and fired off a few rounds at them. There was a short silence and then they replied with a machine gun. We didn't hear the music again.[41]

In the afternoon of 1 July the 52nd *Reserve Infanterie Brigade* issued orders: 'Reserve Infantry Regiment 99 must hold out, even if it is bled to death.' The brigade also reported to the division headquarters that half of RIR 99 was either already killed or wounded, and arrangements were being made to bring up an additional 10,000 hand grenades to the regimental sector.

Major von Fabeck was in his battle headquarters under Mouquet Farm, and he was still in telephone contact with the rear during the afternoon. He received a telephone call from General von Soden, who was inquiring about the situation of the regiment. Von Fabeck reported that the "regiment has had heavy casualties. The regimental sector would be held to the last man. The disposition and fighting spirit of the officers, non-commissioned officers and men was excellent!" Von Soden replied, "I shake your hand in spirit!"

At 4.50 p.m. *Oberstleutnant* Bram issued orders for RIR 99 to attack *Feste Schwaben* and capture it. The attack was to take precedence over any other attack. The overriding concern was *Feste Schwaben*. General von Soden fully realized that the position had to be recaptured at all cost. He issued orders that clearly indicated that the efforts to retake the strongpoint superseded everything else. Von Soden also considered it a matter of honor for the division to recapture this strategic position.

In order to ensure the completion of this task von Soden gave directions that all available artillery units should support the attack. This order would take precedence over

Contemporary German newspaper rendering of the capture
of Captain Craig MP. (Desmond Blackadder)

the existing fire plans the batteries had been following, leaving much of the 26th Reserve Division front without the level of artillery support they had expected at the start of the attack.

Despite the increased firepower this latest counter attack ran into difficulties almost immediately. Group Prager had received reports that *Feste Schwaben* had been recaptured several hours earlier, and the British troops had been driven out of it. As a result of this erroneous information Group Prager did not take part in the attack.

The British were still in control of the redoubt but their situation was rapidly deteriorating. One message made it back from the British defenders in the redoubt coming from Major Peacocke in the German 3rd trench:

> Please do all that you can to send up Vickers Machine Gun belts, bombs and S.A.A. I think we shall hold on only men are rather done up.[42]

Major Beyerkohler and his staff arrived at the assembly area and proceeded with the attack. Shortly after they started to advance a lone British soldier jumped up from a shell hole and fired at the advancing Bavarians. Major Beyerkohler was struck and killed; his batman picked up the Major's blood covered rifle and shot down the Ulsterman. *Hauptmann* Wurmb now assumed command of the attack. *Leutnant* Zimmerman from Machine Gun Marksman Detachment 89 acted as his adjutant since *Oberleutnant* Fritzsching, adjutant of the II/8th Bavarian RIR had command over the support garrison in the II Line.

Fresh troops from the British 146th Brigade now attempted to cross no man's land and reinforce the defenders in the redoubt. Two companies of the 1/4 West Yorkshires did manage to make it to the German lines but they had entered them too far to the west and they could not locate any friendly troops nearby. Without any contact with either British or German troops, they took over the trenches they currently occupied, an empty reserve trench northwest of the redoubt.

During the advance of the 3/8th Bavarian RIR, *Vizefeldwebel* Stolz captured a British sergeant and Captain Craig, a member of parliament, who had been wounded. Captain Craig was apparently a large man and the Germans were forced to transport him to the rear in a wheelbarrow, instead of a stretcher.

Ruins of Mouquet Farm. (*Geschichte des Reserve-Infanterie-Regiment Nr. 99*)

The attack slowed to a halt faced with the stiffening resistance of the defenders, and the growing exhaustion of the attackers. *Hauptmann* Wurmb sent one man forward on a reconnaissance through the *Schlüter Graben*. He returned a short while later and reported that he had encountered strong opposition. The advance now continued very slowly, the attackers advanced traverse by traverse, each one being taken from the defending Ulstermen with the use of hand grenades. The attack was being supported by *Unteroffizier* Haas, who was operating the English machine gun they had captured earlier, most likely a Lewis Gun.

As Group Wurmb (formerly Beyerkohler) moved forward, the men began to run short of hand grenades, food and water. Part of the problem was temporarily relieved when the men found a blue sack in the recaptured trench, which contained English provisions; they were quickly distributed among the men and consumed.

During the advance up the *Lach Weg* the different units became badly mixed together. Casualties began to increase until finally, there were only about 40 men left from the 3rd Coy under the command of *Vizefeldwebel* Zeissner and *Offizier Stellvertreter* Buckrees. The men were positioned in the *Lach Weg* and in shell craters on both sides of the trench. The rest of the men were either pinned down further to the north or in the rear, killed, wounded, or simply missing. During the advance *Hauptmann* Wurmb lost his batman, *Infanterist* Kniebert, who was shot down only two steps behind him. Finally, the latest attack on *Feste Schwaben* came to a standstill.

During this attack about 70 additional reinforcements arrived at *Feste Staufen*. With their arrival the 7/8th Bavarian RIR was ordered forward to support the flank of the attackers by establishing a barricade where the enemy was apparently concentrated. For some unexplained reason the men of the 7th Coy remained in the *Lach Weg* and failed to provide the much needed support.

When Major von Fabeck learned earlier that the attacks had stalled, he ordered *Offizier Stellvertreter* Lunau, 14/R99, to take two groups from the reserves near Mouquet Farm and carry out a reconnaissance of the Intermediate position in the direction of *Feste Schwaben*. Group Lunau advanced towards the redoubt without any other specific orders, the men taking the most direct route. It was not long before Lunau and his men ran into the Ulstermen and the reconnaissance mission turned into a counter-attack.

Lunau's advance was materially supported by the placement of a reserve machine gun in the Intermediate position that had a clear field of fire over the area from *Feste Schwaben*

Schnürlen
Leutnant d. R. i. Inf.-Regt. 180,
gefallen bei Thiepval
am 1. Juli 1916

Leutnant der Reserve Kurt Schnürlen, 1 Recruit Coy/180, killed 1 July 1916
during attack against *Feste Schwaben*. (*Kriegstagbuch aus Schwaben*)

to the village of Thiepval. The gun crew was given the task to seal off any escape route of the British troops that were occupying *Feste Schwaben*.

Group Lunau advanced up the *Auwärter Weg* and soon became involved in a firefight with the garrison of a British trench block. Group Lunau quickly broke through the trench block and captured a machine gun in the process, then continued to advance. They cleared a section of trench about 150 meters from the switch line and continued to advance towards the *Lach Weg*. Whenever Group Lunau met a group of Ulstermen it resulted in a sharp fight, mainly with hand grenades flying back and forth. When it was finished Group Lunau continued to advance. Group Lunau forced the Ulstermen out of a section of the *Lach Weg*, pushed into the *Martins Pfad* and cleared it of the enemy. By the time Group Lunau had run out of steam they had penetrated up to the *Wohn Graben* in front of *Feste Schwaben*. During this time they had captured an additional three machine guns and a machine gun sledge and mopped up 1,100 meters of trench.

Group Lunau had materially assisted the counter attack of the Bavarians on their right flank, and by doing so made it possible for the Bavarians to eventually capture the redoubt later in the evening. During this part of the fighting *Vizefeldwebel* Koch and *Freiwilliger* Pfeiffer, 14/R99, stood out from the rest of the men for their prominent part in the action.

In order to allow the counter attacks to continue unabated, new troops were required to fill in the gaps created by the loss of so many men. Fortunately, there were still Bavarian companies in reserve and by late afternoon orders were sent to have them move forward.

1 July. A state of highest alert exists, but everything is quiet. *Vizefeldwebel* Walcher and I stand in our trench with several people, watching a group of English airplanes off in the distance. Suddenly, they change direction and the entire group tears down from the sky toward our position. Dirt spurts up from the ground as the enemy

planes open fire with their machine guns. Walcher looks at me, feeling his back. 'I believe I am wounded', he says. A hole in his uniform and a somewhat bloody scratch – indications of Tommy's intentions? Or is this a small portent of far worse things to come? We put a bandage on Walcher. He smiles his ever-present soulful smile and remains with his platoon.

It is Sunday. Up at Thiepval the sound of steady, heavy shellfire can be heard. What's going on there? We don't know. Afternoon arrives lazily. We talk, smoke, sleep. Who knows what night will bring.

'Where is the company commander?' an excited voice shouts down from the trench. 'Who wants to know?' I ask. 'A messenger'.

Leutnant Meister appears in the dugout entrance and is handed a dirt-smeared piece of paper with the report: 'Enemy has penetrated *Feste Schwaben*.' The regiment's 1st and 2nd Battalions, along with the 11th and 12th Companies, must counter attack; the 10th Company will occupy the 11th and 12th's vacated position, and we are to take over the 10th's sector. Hurrying to our new destination, we find it in a sorry condition. The trenches are barely knee deep and there is no trace of dugouts. Some shell holes in the position's forward area have been fortified, however, and we seek cover in these from the enemy's increasingly heavy artillery fire. We find here the bodies of the regiment's and the 3rd Battalion's first casualties of the battle. How many of our own company will join them. *Offizier Stellvertreter* Heinrich Conrad, 9/8th Bavarian RIR[43]

Early in the evening, the 1st Recruit Coy IR 180, under *Leutnant der Reserve* Schnürlen, from Group Prager, attacked the Ulstermen in *Feste Schwaben* from the area of the *Hansa Stellung*. The recruits attacked recklessly and fearlessly threw themselves at the enemy. They were met by heavy fire and suffered serious losses, including their leader, who was killed. Their enthusiasm could not overcome their lack of training.

At 7 p.m., the company received the order to move to the Hanseatic Position and from there, together with Company Hudelmeier and the Bavarian troops, to capture Schwaben Redoubt...The Company advanced in three waves in the direction of the Hanseatic Position: First wave, *Leutnant* Arnold; second wave *Unteroffizier* Seitz; third wave *Leutnant* Schnürlen. There was 100 meter spacing between the waves. The first wave crossed the Artillery Hollow, Grandcourt, but as it moved up onto the heights it received such a hail of machine gun and rifle fire that further advance was out of the question for the time being. As the third wave appeared, heavy enemy artillery fire came down, causing the company very heavy casualties. *Leutnant* Schnürlen was killed, so despite being wounded in the arm, [I] took over the company, rallying the remnants in the Artillery Hollow. *Leutnant* Arnold, 1st Recruit Coy, IR 180.[44]

At about 6.30 p.m. a message arrived at the 109th Brigade headquarters from Lieutenant McClure, 10th Royal Inniskilling Fusiliers, who were in the 'B' Line just south of the crucifix. His report was short and to the point:

Very short of Lewis Gun ammunition and water. He had consolidated but the men numbering about 120 were rather done up. He was in touch with the 9th Royal

Oberleutnant der Reserve Schwarz, MGSST 89. (*Das K. B. Reserve-Infanterie-Regiment Nr. 8*)

Inniskilling Fusiliers and 14th Royal Irish Rifles, and that the casualties were fairly heavy.[45]

When darkness fell the Ulstermen were still occupying *Feste Schwaben*, and the men of RIR 99 and support units were reminded to continue their efforts to expel the British in another regimental order. The main obstacle to any further German advance from the direction of *Feste Staufen* was a particular trench block that was being supported by three machine guns, which were positioned to fire in front and on both flanks.

This formidable obstacle was overcome with the assistance of Machine Gun Marksman Detachment 89. *Oberleutnant der Reserve* Schwarz[46] from MGSST 89 was returning to his unit in the vicinity of Thiepval. He came across *Unteroffizier* Bauer, who was operating a machine gun. They positioned the machine gun against the British trench block and opened fire at point blank range. The fire from this gun opened a breach in the British line, which was expanded with the support of troops using hand grenades.

Three additional machine guns from MGSST 89 under *Offizier Stellvertreter* Bernd, combined with men from the II/8th Bavarian RIR opened fire on the left of *Oberleutnant* Schwarz. By 7.45 p.m. the three English machine guns were placed out of action. The actions of *Unteroffiziers* Haas, Klein, Muck and Schmelzer from the II Battalion stood out from the rest, as did the prominent action of *Gefreiter* Kerndl of the II Battalion and *Gefreiter* Bollwein from the MGSST 89.

Bollwein had already proven himself as an intrepid runner from earlier actions. The fighting on 1 July would be no different. He commanded a group of soldiers who were applying a great deal of pressure against the Ulstermen in an almost reckless advance. Traverse after traverse was taken by Bollwein and his men, it seemed as if they had an endless

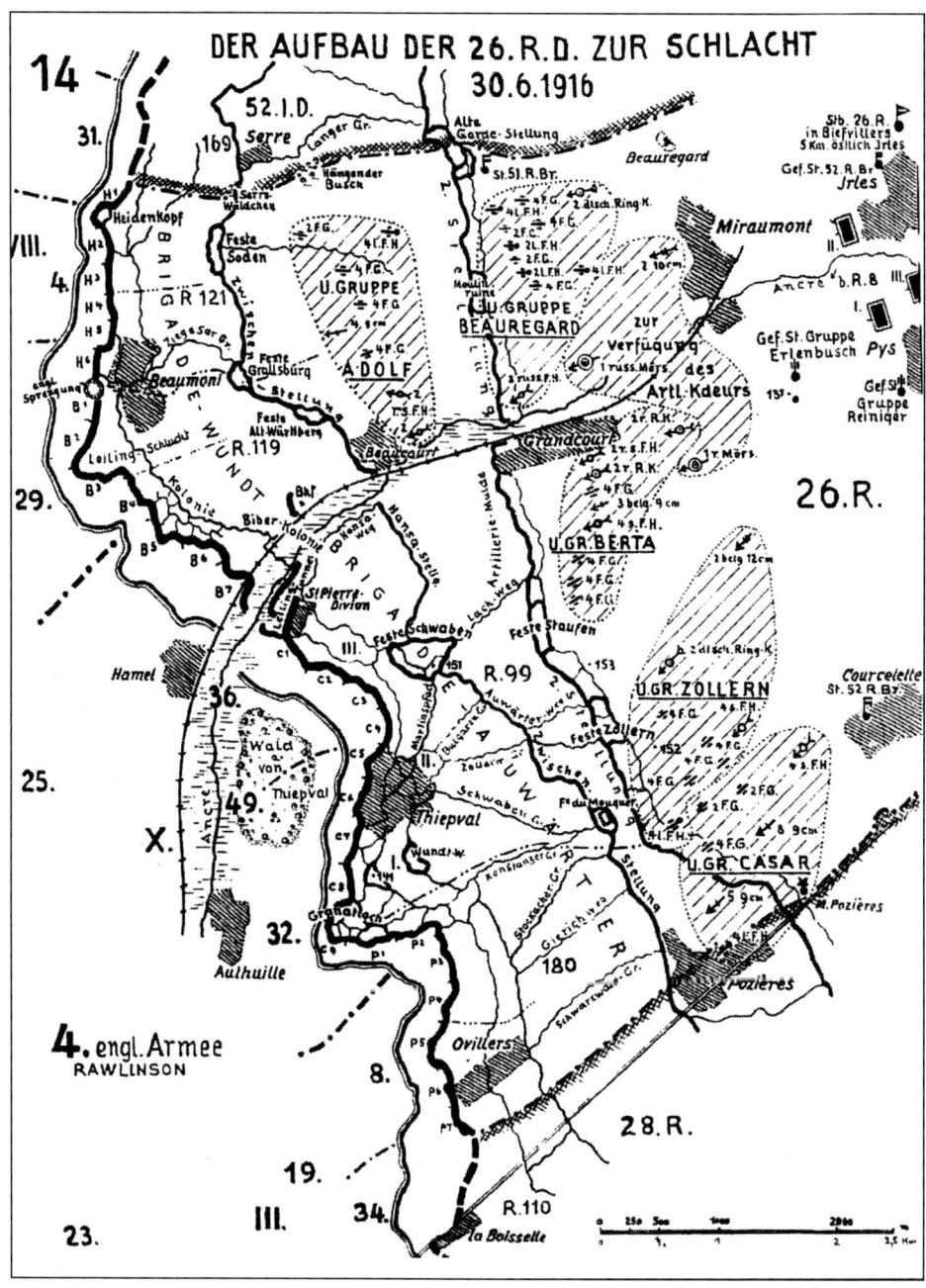

Battery locations for the 26th Reserve Division.

Officers from RFAR 26. (Author's collection)

supply of hand grenades. Finally, the redoubt was reached and the last enemy resistance was overcome. German losses had not been insignificant during the fighting. When Bollwein arrived at the redoubt he found that he only had 6 men left in his detachment.

During the heavy fighting the section of *Unteroffizier* Haas moved forward and attacked the three machine guns and mine thrower with hand grenades. They managed to kill the crew of one machine gun and the mine thrower as well as capturing both weapons. Haas then personally operated the captured machine gun as he fired at any British target that he could see, often at great personal risk as he exposed himself at a number of very dangerous locations. Haas continued to operate his machine gun and in doing so helped to prevent several enemy advances against his small force. Eventually his luck ran out and Haas was struck by a bullet in the neck and was forced to go to the rear for medical aid.

Haas was aided effectively by several men in his company. *Unteroffizier der Reserve* Klein also assisted in the fight against the entrenched Ulstermen. At one stage in the counter attack Klein and his men came under fire from the three British machine guns. Klein actively engaged the machine gun that was located directly in their front. He also fought courageously against the trench blocks set up by the Ulstermen and helped to drive them back deeper into the German lines. Haas and Klein were accompanied by *Unteroffizier der Landwehr* Mück and *Gefreiter* Kerndl, both of whom proved to be adept with throwing hand grenades. All four men were recognized for their actions on this day. Klein, Haas and Kerndl received the Gold Medal for Bravery while Mück received the Silver Medal.

At another location *Kriegsfreiwilliger* Egerer was pinned down in a shell crater with four comrades, Diehl, Hann, Justus and Hage. The small group remained in their makeshift position for the rest of the afternoon and early evening. Even the smallest movement by the men brought down rifle and machine gun fire on the edge of their crater from three sides. During the evening Egerer discovered the location of an enemy machine gun which was very close to them. He fired and killed the gun captain, and then sprang forward across the

Radfahrer Company – 26th Reserve Division. (Felix Fregin)

Major Prager near St. Pierre-Divion. (*Das K. B. Reserve-Infanterie-Regiment Nr. 8*)

open ground towards the gun followed by his comrades. Two members of the machine gun crew were placed out of action with the use of hand grenades, the remainder of the crew then surrendered.

It became evident that any further attack against *Feste Schwaben* would have been futile without sufficient artillery preparation. Accordingly, at 9 p.m. German batteries concentrated their fire on the redoubt while Wurmb made his final preparations for the next attack. He ordered *Leutnant* Zimmerman to take 20 men and branch off to the right and outflank the redoubt, and to breakthrough any opposition in their path.

The British troops in the redoubt were exhausted after fighting constantly for more than twelve hours. Heavy shelling, hot weather and lack of water had worn down the men. The pressure by the Germans was relentless and the Ulstermen were at the breaking point; about 150 of them started to move to the rear. Some of these men were temporarily rallied, but before long they too started to the rear again. It was reported that several British officers fired upon their own men, but if it was true it had little effect on their withdrawal. There were still scattered parties of men hanging on in the German trenches who were out of touch with any other friendly troops. While these men waited for the next German attack they collected ammunition and supplies from the numerous dead lying about.

The small detachment under *Leutnant* Zimmerman had orders to clear the enemy from *Feste Schwaben*. Zimmermann and his men began their advance and quickly came up against the entrenched Ulstermen. The Germans pressed forward across open ground under rifle fire and British hand grenades. The detachment broke through the resistance on their front, resulting in a number of casualties including Lory who received a hand grenade splinter in his right eye.

The detachment now consisted of Zimmerman and five men, including *Infanterist* Lory, who remained in action despite being slightly wounded. Zimmerman and his men continued to deceive the enemy about their actual numbers with lively fire and loud hurrahs. Once the Ulstermen had been cleared from *Feste Schwaben* Lory had his wounds dressed. Lory later received the Silver Medal for Bravery for his actions during the assault, despite being wounded. It was determined that he had effectively assisted in the capture of the critical strongpoint.

During this time Group Wurmb attacked the Ulstermen through the *Lach Weg* and finally penetrated into the trenches that formed part of the redoubt. Wurmb's men also experienced heavy fighting in the *Aüwarter Weg* and losses began to rise. Finally, the few remaining enemy soldiers in the redoubt, as well as four machine guns that had been firmly positioned at the southeast corner of the redoubt were outflanked. The position of the remaining Ulstermen had finally become untenable and at 10 p.m. Major Peacocke ordered the withdrawal of all troops to the old German front line.

While the men moved back, the long awaited reinforcements began to arrive; the 1/5 West Yorkshire, the 2nd Coy of the 1/7 West Yorkshire and the 2nd Coy of the 1/8 West Yorkshire. However by this time it was too late, *Feste Schwaben* was back in German hands.

About 10.30 in the evening, German soldiers in the trenches near Thiepval could see men moving from the direction of the redoubt towards the old German front line. The men moved along a wide front and it was impossible to tell which side they belonged to. A flare was fired from Thiepval and lit up the surrounding countryside. The Germans quickly recognized the flat steel helmets of the British troops and Wurmb gave the order, 'sustained fire'. Rifle and machine gun fire opened up along the German lines against the retreating

Feldwebel – RIR 99. (Author's collection)

Ulstermen, during which time Zimmerman called for the singing of the *Die Wacht am Rhein*.

During the numerous German attacks throughout the day the retreating British soldiers continued to move past the position held by *Unteroffizier* Hinkel, 7/R99, and his men. As each group approached, Hinkel and his men fired at them and drove them back into their old positions. With each small skirmish Hinkel's ammunition supply grew smaller and smaller.

During one brief lull in the fighting by their position, Hinkel's men could hear the sounds of fighting going on nearby, but could not see what was actually happening. The sounds appeared to come from the *Hansa Strasse* or from the fire trench. They could see men retreating, then the sounds of rifle fire for a time, then silence. Explosions from hand grenades followed shortly afterwards, the sounds getting closer to them each time.

Finally darkness came. With it the battle activity that had died down became active again, when many Englishmen tried to reach their own position under the protection of the darkness. They fall victim to our well-aimed fire. They were probably moving back in fear of our counter-attack... And so I knew our counter attacks would be employed for sure, and I was also certain of their success. And indeed! It had to come from the *Hansastellung* or from the trench, at times one could hear volleys of rifle fire and the bursts of hand grenades that were constantly coming closer. I also went through a portion of the *Marktgasse* with two *Gefreiten* to the battalion dugout. We eliminated a few groups of Englishmen with our hand grenades and drove others off. We turned back so that we did not end up in the hand grenade fire of the Bavarians who were mopping up the trench. There is also much work to do at the old position.

Individually, in groups, in entire swarms they hastened to the rear from *Feste Schwaben*. Once again our machine guns rattled and our rifles glowed red hot. Many an Irish mother's son lay down to the eternal sleep from which there is no awakening. The wild recklessness of the morning gripped the men again. Unfortunately, the sensitive shortage of hand grenades doesn't allow us to fully take advantage of the discouraged enemy. I have no doubt that otherwise we could have cleared the enemy from our entire position as far as the Ancre in the same night.

However we had also accomplished so much. We had the rear free of the enemy, we already protected the flank ourselves and we could courageously await a new assault by the enemy with confidence

The eventful 1 July had slipped into the past for a long time before we regained our old positions at the front. The new day revealed piles of dead and wounded as part of the success of our tremendous work that we had achieved in conjunction with the machine guns.[47]

While the fighting was going on by Group Wurmb, additional preparations were being made for an attack by Group Prager near St. Pierre-Division. The 2/8th Bavarian RIR under *Leutnant der Reserve* Barz received orders to attack the redoubt from their position near St. Pierre-Division.

The 2nd Coy worked forward through the village ruins and were positioned in the *Strassburger Steig* by *Hauptmann* Mandel. They were about 100 meters to the south of the *Meisengasse*. Considering the heavy losses suffered by the men of the 2nd Coy and the unknown situation in their front, it was finally decided to continue the attack against the enemy sitting in the old forward line of the 9/R99 during the morning of 2 July.

Now I went to the company leader, to make a report to him, crossed the ravine and saw a 38cm dud on the slope standing on the detonator. This sight scared me more than the entire shelling from this morning. Then I climbed into the trench and saw one of our men lying there dead. It was Fleischmann, a humble, brave *Landwehrmann*. Blood started to run out and he was turning blue in the heat of the sun. When I joined the company leader, I saw that he was very serious. I was immediately informed. The 2nd Coy had orders to attack. Therefore back down. In passing I took Fleischmann's rifle with me and trotted down to make my preparations. One could imagine the effect on the Other Ranks. The pale faces were still a shade paler. After the excitement of this morning I could probably understand that very well, however I could not help that it was also pleasing to me that I was not out of the dance. To a young *Münchener* Haseneder, I said 'Well Hasenöder now that comes together nicely today, but just between us our Lord God cannot allow this to remain!' 'No' he said quietly. During the preparations suddenly came counter orders 'Assault cancelled'. The men gladly moved back into the holes. They were scarcely gone when I became called to the Company leader. There I found out that the 2nd Coy had since penetrated the English position from the north and cleaned it out. So there. I did finish and was personally at the village exit, to see when the company would come out from the trench on to the road. I did not stand a man there because the place lay rather under fire and the chaps might be delayed. As I stood and watched I saw how one house roof after another went to pieces...

I saw the first men from the company coming on the road and joined my platoon onto it as the last and finally after everyone I came. Some shrapnel greeted us and now one burst slightly in front of me. A man cried out. I hurried there. It was Haseneder. He had a ball in the stomach. The shot seemed very grave to me. One poorly applies a bandage. '*Herr Feldwebel*, you will not leave me' were the last words that he directed at me. I asked if he could walk. He said he could and from there up to the next medical dugout was not far away, so I only placed one man with him. Unfortunately he later succumbed to his wound. A few of our men we encountered were already wounded. The shrapnel continued to grow thicker and we were glad when we finally reached the *Hansa Graben*. The joy was however of short duration. A little piece seemed undamaged, and then it began: crater-on, crater-off. Then again a piece of trench and so further on like this. Every moment the order, 'take cover, aircraft! Then, '*Feldwebel* Stahlhofer, come forward!' I pushed myself forward, the company was torn apart. So I went forward with the small party, found the flock again and called: 'Is the company leader in the front '? 'We have been separated,' was the reply. Again I scuffled forward, leading the squad and finally reached the company. We came to a fork in the trench. Now good advice was dear. Where was the company? No one had the slightest knowledge of the course of the position. I turned off to the left, in this direction must be the '*Feste Schwaben*' sector where I had been this morning, when I went to the 4th Coy, and lying in that direction perhaps I will meet the company that probably used it like us. However there was no trace of Barz with his men. The tapping of the machine guns sounded through the roaring and hissing of the shells. There was in any case something going on, so I could not go wrong. A young Englishman was in my way, a thin fellow. He lay there trampled to death like a cat, beside him a German. A man from our regiment met me. 'Is the 2nd Coy there somewhere?' 'Yes, the same over there.' Behind me eighteen of the Other Ranks I paid no attention to had foolishly departed, that annoyed me. Ever further! Now even more so, by something that had probably once been a traverse, and finally we were there, but just as the affair was over. That irked me ... I walked over to Barz and asked what was going on. He pointed at the disappearing Englishmen that had ducked down into a trench directly further to the left.

Now orders had come not to proceed any further. Commanders from Reserve Infantry 99 that had occupied the position led us into the second trench. The men became divided and then went back on the same road that we came on. They were formed out of two platoons, so that I had no one to lead and so I followed behind. A couple of prisoners were led past us. In the meantime it had become night. Fog came down, it took effort not to lose sight of the man in front. A couple of men come toward me, they hesitated. Finally at the end of the trench, and as if blown away by the wind the man in front of me was gone. I called, in vain, hurried along, finding no one. On the road I discovered a mined dugout, maybe I will find someone there. Nothing. Then I ran in the direction of Grandcourt. There I heard a voice call out 'Stahlhofer' 'Yes' I shouted, 'who is there?' '*Leutnant* Barz' came the reply. One asks the other about the company. No one knows where they are. Now it was a question of, where were Schmeisser and Kamm? Now good advice was costly. So I suggested we pass the night in the tunnel discovered by me. We crawled through under a destroyed tree, fell into a shell hole and now reached it. In front of the mined dugout was a small well, a

View of Thiepval Wood from the German lines illustrating the ideal field of fire the men of RIR 99 experienced during the battle. (*Geschichte des Reserve-Infanterie-Regiment Nr. 99*)

shell had damaged it and the water bubbled forth clear and bright. With the delicious moisture I satisfied up my dry throat. *Infanterist* Hanauer and Wilhelm Ignatz were still with *Leutnant* Barz. Hanauer offered me an English cigarette, I smoked it. Then I looked at my watch. It was 12 o'clock. 'So I have survived my birthday' I said. 'Well' said Hanauer, 'tomorrow is mine, I am curious to see whether I survive.' 'That was my 23rd cradle celebration and I am glad that it went as it did. Stahlhofer, 8th Bavarian RIR[48]

After the last attack was over and the Germans moved back into the trenches of *Feste Schwaben*, *Hauptmann* Wurmb sent a runner back to battalion headquarters with news of the capture of the strongpoint. The situation was still unclear, pockets of British soldiers were left behind and it would not be until the following days that they would be eliminated. One Ulsterman who spent the night in the German lines recalled:

> ... we collected all the ammunition we could from our own dead, a terrible task, but it was necessary, for we knew we would need every bullet we could get. In the big trench we set up sentries and some of us tried to get some rest. It was hard for we kept seeing the bits and pieces of the dead bodies and the terrible bleeding of the wounded, and the smell of the sweat and the hunger kept us from sleeping. Funny thing was we found ourselves taking orders from other privates and giving them ourselves ... it brought a lump to our throats when we thought of all the friends that was dead or wounded.[49]

Oberstleutnant Bram had set up his battalion headquarters in a dugout in *Feste Staufen* at the beginning of the first counter attacks. The dugout became filled with wounded almost immediately and the space became very crowded. Bram and his adjutant worked long hours, receiving and writing reports and orders, and were fully occupied in arranging for fresh ammunition, supplies, water and reinforcements. Bram was later praised for his clear judgment during the critical situation that faced him on 1 July.[50]

About 11 p.m. German reinforcements began to arrive in *Feste Schwaben*. The largest part of the 6th Coy, *Leutnant der Landwehr* Meyer, arrived. The men were completely exhausted from advancing in the unfamiliar territory, through trenches that were deeply silted up. The rest of the 6th Coy and the 7th Coy, *Oberleutnant* Illig, arrived in the early morning of 2 July.

The 52nd *Reserve Infanterie* Brigade had ordered additional reserves forward when the attacks on the redoubt did not appear to be moving forward earlier on 1 July. The I/185,

Leutnant der Reserve Rudolf
Beisenwenger, 3/180, killed in action 1
July 1916. (*Kriegstagbuch aus Schwaben*)

Leutnant Otto Borst, 3/180,
killed in action 1 July 1916.
(*Kriegstagbuch aus Schwaben*)

Hauptmann der Landwehr Leonhard, was sent forward from *Feste Staufen*. When it was determined that they were no longer needed, this battalion occupied the II Line south of Grandcourt and connected with the 6/*Pionier* Bn 13, *Oberleutnant* Schefold[51], in the defense of the Ancre Valley. The II/185, *Hauptmann der Landwehr* Josephson, marched from Courcelette and occupied the II Line between *Feste Staufen* and *Süd IV*. They came under the command of *Oberstleutnant* Krause. With the arrival of these reinforcements the Thiepval Sector had additional men to help prevent any further advances by the enemy positioned at Hill 141, south of Thiepval.

32nd Division – The Afternoon

The only gain made by the 32nd Division during the morning of 1 July had been the capture of the Leipzig Salient and the *Granatloch*. Now, plans were being formulated to expand their gains and continue their effort to capture the village of Thiepval and Mouquet Farm.

The plan that was adopted called for the 14th Brigade to reinforce the troops in the Leipzig Salient and then move forward against the *Hindenburg* and *Lemberg Stellung*. The 96th Brigade would resume their attack against Thiepval, where the brigade would work its way along the northern and southern edges of the village, and then would attack the Germans facing the Leipzig Salient from the rear.

The bombardment in preparation of the attack was ineffective. This was caused in part by the amount of area to be covered by the artillery and the shortage in the number of guns needed for the task. The artillery was also restricted by not being allowed to fire upon the village of Thiepval. This last condition was a result of earlier reports that placed troops from the 15th Lancashire Fusiliers in the village; actually the only troops in the village were German. The shelling lasted from 12.05 to 1.30 p.m., and did relatively little damage to the

German defenses.

At 1.30 p.m. two companies from the 2nd Royal Inniskilling Fusiliers and other sections from the 16th Lancashire Fusiliers (2nd Salford Pals) moved forward from Thiepval Wood towards the village. They were met by a wall of machine gun fire and immediately suffered heavy casualties. Due to the heavy German fire the attack was quickly abandoned.

At 1.45 p.m. two companies from the 2nd Manchester managed to reach the Leipzig Redoubt. They tried to bomb forward into the *Hindenburg* and *Lemberg Stellung*, but were stopped by the defenders of the German trench blocks. The Leipzig Redoubt was now filled to capacity with troops, including numerous dead and wounded. The exact situation along their front and flanks was unknown. Sergeant-Major Shephard (already slightly wounded) from the 1st Dorsets noted in his diary that the Germans were dropping heavy shells directly into the mass of men occupying the *Granatloch*.

Apparently a direct hit from one such shell wiped out a complete trench mortar battery. By now the small area occupied by the British was filled with numerous wounded and dead men. Any movement observed by the Germans quickly resulted in further fire. The position was in such bad condition that every movement could be seen by the nearby enemy soldiers. Efforts were made to recover some of the numerous wounded that were lying in the open. These men were brought into the *Granatloch* where it was not much safer than being out in the open. Many of the wounded men were struck by German fire for a second or third time and killed while waiting to be evacuated to the rear.

The German defenders desperately needed reinforcements and more hand grenades in order to contain the breach in their line. The only troops at hand were the 4/8th Bavarian RIR and 2nd Recruit Coy/R99 positioned in and around the *Wundt Werk, Lemberg Stellung* and *Türken Stellung*. One of the only other available reserves was the 9/8th Bavarian RIR, under *Leutnant* Meister.

The British troops in the Leipzig Redoubt were being contained on the right by the 3/180. Even facing constant British pressure at the trench blocks, the Württembergers from IR 180 had held their position, using hand grenades to keep the British back. In spite of their best efforts the men of the 3rd Coy were eventually forced to give up about 100 meters of their forward line at about 12.45 in the afternoon. During the hand grenade fight the company leader, *Leutnant der Reserve* Beisenwinger, was killed and *Leutnant* Borst assumed command of the company. By 3.10 p.m. the British occupied the entire line formerly held by the 3rd Coy. The Germans eventually stopped the British advance at a new trench block with the assistance of part of the 7th and 4/180.

In order to safeguard their right flank and help contain the breach in their line, the 4/180 firmly blocked off all trenches along their right wing. The rest of the 3rd and 7th Coys under *Oberleutnant der Reserve* Vogler, were positioned in the *Hindenburg Stellung*. Six sections of the 5/180 were placed with the 7/180 in order to maintain contact with RIR 99 for the duration of the fighting on July 1st.

By the middle of the afternoon the men from RIR 99 fighting in *Thiepval-Süd* desperately needed reinforcements and ammunition. Unless something was done soon it was doubtful they could maintain their positions.

Report from *Thiepval-Süd* (written): the remnants of the 3rd and 4th Coys are attempting to continue to work their way forward in the *Hindenburg Stellung*. With the exception of the 2nd, all the companies are completely exhausted. There is a lack

Riedel

Leutnant d. R. i. Inf.-Regt. 180,
gest. am 2. Juli 1916 an den bei
Ovillers la Boisselle erhalt. Wunden

Leutnant der Reserve Georg Riedel, 7/180, severely wounded 1 July 1916.
Died from wounds 2 July 1916. (*Kriegstagbuch aus Schwaben*)

of hand grenades. Reinforcement is absolutely essential. Only 20 men are left from the 13th (Reinforcement) Company. Strong columns are being observed constantly in the area of the Engineer dump in Target area 55. The 2nd Coy is holding one British POW. Further attacks are expected.[52]

The British planned additional attacks against Thiepval in the middle of the afternoon. Battalions from the 146th Brigade, 49th Division, were going to make a frontal attack against the village. At 3.30 p.m. the British guns opened fire on Thiepval and the Château grounds, covering Sector C6 and the left section of C5, which were being held by the 5th and 6/R99 respectively.

Shortly before 4 o'clock the British bombardment lifted and the men of RIR 99 knew that an attack would follow shortly. Due to congestion in the British lines and the limited advance notice of the attack to the troops involved, only the 1/6 West Yorkshire and one company of the 1/8 West Yorkshire were in their assigned places at 4 p.m.

The lead waves moved out of Thiepval Wood to cross no man's land in column of route. Much of the German wire was intact, as were the numerous machine guns in Thiepval, the Château grounds and nearby locations. Within minutes the Yorkshire men had lost nearly half of their strength, including Lieutenant Colonel H.O. Wade, who was wounded. The survivors took cover and slowly began to move back to the protection of the wood.

Report from II/R99 *Thiepval-Mitte* (written): Centre section firmly in our hands. Despite crippling losses the British are pressing on tirelessly with their attacks. Own casualties very heavy. Support needed urgently. Ammunition and red signal cartridges required. The British are currently attacking C5 in strength.[53]

As a result of this failed attack it was decided not to send any more men forward, and it was with great difficulty that the attack by the 1/5 West Yorkshire was stopped. It was apparent that the 30-minute bombardment and the subsequent shrapnel fire were ineffectual. One machine gun in Sector C6 had been put out of action from the shrapnel fire, but this had little effect on the defenders. This machine gun had been firing at long range most of the day. It had reportedly forced one British battery out of action due to its fire. The gun was quickly repaired and back in action once more.

At 4.50 p.m., *Oberleutnant* Gleis, 4/180, commenced a hand grenade attack against the 'Englishmen' on the right wing of their foothold in the German trenches, the old front line of the 3/180. The Württembergers from IR 180 maintained the pressure on the British defenders, capturing bay after bay, until about 5.35 p.m. when the greater part of the old front line of the 3rd Coy was mopped up, then they were forced to stop. The casualties had steadily risen in the 4/180, and they eventually did not have enough men to continue the attack and hold the recaptured line.

At the same time the 4th Coy was attacking, the enemy was applying renewed pressure against the trench blocks of RIR 99 in a violent hand grenade attack. *Leutnant* Borst, 7/8th Bavarian RIR received orders to reinforce the connections between the different regiments in the *Hindenburg Stellung*, and in order to comply with orders two sections were sent to the right wing. In addition one platoon from the 7/8th Bavarian RIR had already occupied the left wing of RIR 99.

Borst played a prominent role in the ensuing fighting until he was killed. *Leutnant* Wuterich then assumed command, but he was severely wounded a short time later, and *Leutnant* Riedel took over. Finally, the British stopped their attacks.

At 5.10 p.m. two battalions of the 148th Brigade were placed at the disposal of the 96th Brigade, but no further attacks were attempted. At the same time the Germans moved up additional reserves. Shortly before 5 p.m. the 9/8th Bavarian RIR received orders to immediately advance to the *Wundt Werk*.

We lay in the open, barely 200 meters behind Mouquet Farm. Shortly before 6 p.m. another messenger arrives, bringing new instructions: 'The 9th Company will advance immediately to the *Wundtwerk*'. 'Everyone ready! Let's go!'

With *Leutnant* Meister and I in the lead, we pass the ruins of Mouquet and move through Josenhansgraben, badly battered from shellfire. We encounter a large Württemberger going in the opposite direction, his hand bound with a bloody rag.

'What's going on up there?' we ask. 'Those dogs, those damned accursed dogs!' comes the reply. He thrust his injured fist into the air and continues on.

Just then a shell whizzes by a short distance over the trench, and is followed by a second. This one explodes in the vicinity of the 1st Platoon. Screams! Albin Bauer, our drummer, is badly wounded. A piece of shrapnel has torn into his chest. Stretcher-bearers quickly attend to him while the rest of us move forward again. The ground slopes upward. Seen from the shell-plowed summit the entire area is a grey-brown field of craters. But there, beyond the devastation, a river gleams in the shadow of a green wood. Is this where peace lives?

We lay in the *Wundtwerk*, bathed in sweat. Water! Water! The last drops are gone. My batman, Karl Guth, takes both of our water bottles and his boiler, then disappears. After a while he reappears completely breathless, but with a cunning smile on his face.

Senior NCO – RIR 99. (Author's collection)

All of the containers are filled with excellent coffee. The water boiler is passed from mouth to mouth until it is empty. Guth explains that along the way to our position he noticed a field kitchen, from which he 'liberated' the welcome antidote for our thirst. *Offizier Stellvertreter* Heinrich Conrad, 9/8th Bavarian RIR[54]

The urgent need for reinforcements such as those under *Offizier Stellvertreter* Conrad, could clearly be seen in a message sent only minutes after Conrad and his men started their journey toward the front line.

5.16 p.m. Report from *Thiepval-Süd* (written): Heavy casualties due to hand grenade battles. Further progress with the *Hindenburg Stellung* is currently not possible. At *Hindenburg Eck* it has been possible to work forward around the area of the barricade in the direction of *Königstrasse*. The men are very exhausted, tired out from throwing hand grenades. Reinforcements are essential. They are required urgently, as quickly as possible. The British are in the *Hindenburg Stellung* in strength. They are receiving reinforcements constantly.[55]

Most of the heavy fighting along the front of the 32nd Division was finished for the day. Artillery and machine gun fire was kept up for the rest of the night while the men on both sides of the line tended their wounded, cleared away the dead, worked on repairing their positions and brought up supplies and fresh reinforcements.

Due to the shortage of fresh troops, the Germans were unable to relieve the exhausted men of RIR 99, 8th Bavarian RIR and other units in and around the Thiepval sector. The

British did have fresh troops available, and units that fought on 1 July could be relieved wherever possible.

Sergeant-Major Shephard was in the Leipzig Redoubt when they received word that the 1st Dorsets were to be relieved by the 15th Highland Light Infantry, and that in the meanwhile they were to hold tight. Sergeant-Major Shephard was of the opinion that this relief was absolutely necessary as his men were very badly shaken from the constant German fire falling all around them.

Shephard noted that the wounded suffered from the heat, the shelling and lack of water. When the 1st Dorsets were finally relieved, Shephard led the remnants of B and C Coys to the rear: 10 NCOs and men.

Local attacks continued through the night when German bombing parties attacked several British trench blocks. Each attack was driven back and with each attack the casualty list grew on both sides. At 8 p.m. the British lines in the Leipzig Redoubt were heavily shelled, this continued on and off at intervals for the rest of the night.

The German lines were in a state of confusion; heavy casualties coupled with severe damage to most of the defensive works kept the survivors occupied in repairing their lines. The situation along the front by the Leipzig Salient was still unknown. The loss of the Leipzig Salient was recognized as a dangerous breach of the line that had to be retaken as soon as possible. Every attempt possible was made to determine the exact situation facing the defenders of the salient and surrounding sectors.

8.00 p.m. Report from *Thiepval-Mitte* (written): Request urgent support, also for *Thiepval-Süd*. *Thiepval-Mitte* is completely in our hands. The British are moving north within Thiepval Wood towards Sector Thiepval Nörd. Request immediate resupply of white and red signal cartridges. Plus drinks and tobacco. 1st machine Gun Coy Res. Inf. Regt. 99 requests the transfer of one replacement team from the reserve, because the entire team of a machine gun in C6 has been killed.

Report from *Thiepval-Süd* (written): Enemy located in the *Hindenburg Stellung* from the regimental boundary to close to *Hindenburg Eck*. We occupy: *Hindenburg Stellung* from the front line trench to the *Erdmörser* position in *Königstrasse*, then across to the *Josenhansgraben* just skirting the north of the *Hindenburg Stellung*. The first reinforcement company to arrive will be used to clear the *Hindenburg Stellung*. Own casualties are very severe. 1st, 3rd and 4th Coys are completely finished. All the platoon commanders of 3rd Coy are dead. Hand grenades, signal cartridges, water and rations are urgently required.[56]

Sometime after dark, the 9/8th Bavarian RIR received orders to participate in a counter attack, which was scheduled to begin at 3 a.m. on 2 July. The men moved through the badly damaged *König Strasse* towards the *Hindenburg Eck*, the place where the *König Strasse* and *Hindenburg Stellung* intersected. They reached their assigned position late in the evening where they found the remnants of the 3/R99, under the command of two officers. The men from the 9th Coy were placed in positions to cover a 250-meter front.

8.04 p.m. Report from *Thiepval-Süd* (written): Supply of hand grenades, green and red signal cartridges is required. Own artillery has dropped short into the front line trenches of C8 and C7 on numerous occasions. Water must be got forward. Battalion

Oberleutnant der Reserve Hans Dall – RIR 99 (formerly an officer in the 9th Hussars). (Author's collection)

(has suffered) heavy casualties. The remnants of 1st, 3rd and 4th Coys are completely exhausted. The 9th Coy Bavarian Res. Inf. Regt. has arrived as reinforcements, but needs to rest. For the time being it cannot be used to clear the *Hindenburg Stellung*.[57]

The 9/8th Bavarian RIR had no idea how far the British had penetrated into the lines, there was no sign of IR 180 on their left. The only thing they knew for sure was that the enemy occupied the quarry in Sector C9, and their task would be to recapture this critical position. Attack orders were issued and the men settled down and waited until it was time to begin the assault.

After dusk, an officer visits and orders yet another move. 'At 4 o'clock tomorrow morning we counter-attack'. I nod to him. The men silently proceed in the blackness through the *Königstrasse* to our newest destination, the *Hindenburg Eck*. Such is the appellation for the corner junction of the *Königstrasse* and the *Hindenburg Stellung*, named for the famous army commander to designate the first line trench here. The front line originally ran from Thiepval south-southwest to the Ovillers-Authuille road, then curved sharply eastward for some 800 meters until dropping south again toward Ovillers and la Boiselle. The point of this curved salient, known on our maps as Sectors C8 and C9, had been captured this morning by the English. The 9th

Company is meant to bolster the threatened Hindenburg position, whose barricaded corner section we reach at 11 p.m.. We find all that remains of the 99th Reserve Infantry Regiment's 3rd Company under the command of two officers. The 180th Regiment should be on the left, but where? No one is sure.

The entire company front measures about 250 meters in length. A delicate situation exists for no one seems to know how far the enemy has penetrated on our left. In the piece of line lost to the English there is a stone quarry which the enemy may now be filling with men and material. 'This quarry must be taken!' So reads our order. After a consultation with the two officers from the 99th's 3rd Company, *Leutnant* Meister issues orders. The 2nd and 3rd Platoons will attack: on the right, *Unteroffizier* Weindel with three sections of the 3rd Platoon; on the left, the rest of the 3rd Platoon under *Vizefeldwebel* Walcher; I am to lead in the centre with half of the 2nd Platoon. The 1st Platoon is our reserve and is to remain in dugouts of the *Königstrasse* and *Lemberg Stellung*. Bombers are selected and all other preparations are made. This finished, we then sit leaning or dozing against the wall of the trench to wait for the signal. Walcher, who earlier in the war at Soyecourt shared a dugout with me for nine months, is seated at my side and soon falls into a deep sleep, completely unconcerned with what the next hours might bring. *Offizier Stellvertreter* Heinrich Conrad, 9/8th Bavarian RIR[58]

During the evening the 16th and 17th Highland Light Infantry were relieved by the 2nd Manchesters and two companies of the 2nd Kings Own Yorkshire Light Infantry. The redoubt was consolidated with the help of the Royal Engineers. With the fighting all but over on this fateful day what of the thousands of men who had been wounded and left on their own for the most part.

All along the fronts of the 36th and 32nd Divisions men from both sides had been lying in no man's land or in the German trenches in the intense July heat. Those who were simply trapped due to heavy German fire began to move to the rear under the cover of darkness. Those who were wounded but still able to move made their way back to the British lines as best they could, while the more unfortunate ones would have to wait to be picked up. Many died of their wounds while they waited in hope of help arriving soon.

The regimental battle headquarters of RIR 99, located some 8 – 10 meters underneath Mouquet Farm, was a scene of frenzied activity since the opening of the bombardment on 24 June. The headquarters tunnel complex had been well constructed, and while the ruins of Mouquet Farm were being pulverized in the continuous shellfire, the staff and men of RIR 99 remained safe underground. The heavy bombardment had caused a great deal of damage to the trenches on the surface, and, many of the upper passages and entrances became blocked with earth. The men inside the tunnels would quickly clear away the fallen timbers and earth, and quickly repair any damage done to the entrances and passageway supports.

The shelling was so heavy that roof timbers deep underground occasionally cracked under the force of the impacts. And the tunnel complex was filled with a constant roaring noise from the bursting of the shells. The occupants reported that the floor swayed like a ship at sea as the heavy shells fell on top of them. Occasionally, all of the carbide lamps went out from the sudden change of air pressure caused by the shells, plunging the entire complex into darkness.

British prisoners captured by Thiepval. (*Das K. B. Reserve-Infanterie-Regiment Nr. 8*)

The regimental telephone exchange was constantly in use. Most of the telephone lines had been cut in the heavy fire but a few critical lines remained intact throughout the fighting including the main line to the headquarters of IR 180. These intact lines would prove to be invaluable in the defense of the Thiepval and Ovillers sectors.

During the course of the bombardment wounded men made their way to the protection of the medical dugout, where the medical staff treated them. These men left bloody trails along the corridors and stairs in the tunnel complex as they passed through it. As the day progressed every spare inch of the battle headquarters became filled with wounded men. The worst cases were the men who were gas sick. Blind and trembling, their faces were contorted in spasms from the effect of the gas.

There was a serious shortage of stretcher-bearers who were needed to bring in the men who were seriously wounded. The regimental under staff reported to the medical officer and volunteered their services as stretcher-bearers. Their actions saved many lives as they moved about the sector, picking up men on stretchers or assisting them back to the medical dugout. It was dangerous work and many of these volunteers were also killed and wounded in the heavy shelling.

During the course of the day, runners would suddenly appear in the tunnel entrances, catching their breath as they took cover from the endless shells. As soon as they were rested they were off to complete their errands. Food carriers arrived at infrequent intervals, also seeking relief from the heavy shelling before continuing their journey. It took them so long to arrive that the food was usually cold and most of it was spilled before it reached the front line troops, still it was always appreciated.

Based on the after action reports from the survivors of RIR 99, it was determined that each officer and man had fired an average of 350 rounds on 1 July. The machine gun companies reported that 21 guns had survived the fighting on this day. 20 of the guns had fired an average of 8,000 to 10,000 rounds each, machine gun No. 9 located in the *Brauner Weg*, south of Thiepval, had fired a total of 18,000 rounds. This gun was in a position that allowed it to enfilade the advancing and retreating waves of enemy soldiers in front of C2 and C3 throughout the day.

Following the heavy fighting the previous standard of having at least 4,500 belted rounds available for machine guns as directed by the Ministry of War was found to be inadequate. RIR 99 determined that at a minimum 8,000 rounds should be available and ready to fire for each gun. In the confusion of combat it could be difficult to provide additional ammunition for these key weapons and it would be better to have it at hand at the start of any attack.

Occasionally machine guns were forced to stop firing due to mechanical problems or a jam. Most of the stoppages experienced by the guns during 1 July were the result of faulty ammunition, a problem that was quickly corrected by the gun crews. There is no record of the number of hand grenades used by the defenders in the Thiepval sector, but it must have numbered in the thousands.

Major von Fabeck, *Oberleutnant der Reserve* Dall and the other officers of the regimental staff were commended for their untiring work during the seven days bombardment and the fighting on 1 July. Most of them had gone through this time with a minimum of sleep.

The casualties on both sides of the battle had been heavy. The men in both armies had given their full effort, and in many cases, exceeded it. The casualty lists reflected the intensity of the fighting.

The 36th Division suffered the heaviest casualties of the three British divisions in the X Corps that attacked the Thiepval Sector. They had also made the greatest penetration of the German lines, almost reaching the village of Grandcourt. The division losses were reported as:[59]

Killed:	79 officers	1,777 men
Wounded:	102 officers	2,626 men
Missing:	7 officers	206 men
Prisoners:	1 officer	164 men
Total:	189 officers	4,773 men

There were 142 other casualties, whose particulars were not available in detail. The total casualties amounted to 5,104 officers and men. Three battalions in the 36th Division suffered some of the highest losses of any troops fighting on the Somme that day: 108th Brigade: 13th Royal Irish Rifles (County Down) 17 officers, 578 men; 9th Royal Irish Rifles (Co. Armagh, Monaghan, Cavan) 14 officers, 518 men; 109th Brigade, 11th Royal Inniskilling Fusiliers (Donegal and Fermanagh) 12 officers, 577 men.

The losses in the 32nd Division were only slightly lower, having lost a total of 3,949 officers and men. The 16th Highland Light Infantry (Glasgow Boys Brigade) in the 97th Brigade, suffered the heaviest losses in the division – 19 officers, 492 men.

Other units in the division also suffered heavily. As previously mentioned, B and C Coys of the 1st Dorsets left the Leipzig Salient at the end of 1 July numbering 11 men. The 15th Lancashire Fusiliers (1st Salford Pals) ended the day with 3 officers and 150 men. B and D Coys of the 16th Lancashire Fusiliers (2nd Salford Pals) had only 18 uninjured men at the end of the day.

The total casualties suffered by RIR 99 in the defense of Thiepval on 1 July 1916 are not known in detail but they were very heavy. The casualty list for RIR 99 covers the period from 23 June through the end of July. While some of the casualties occurred after 1 July, the majority, by far, took place during the preliminary bombardment and the fighting on 1 July.

The casualty numbers for the bombardment period have recently been uncovered during research being performed by Jack Sheldon. According to the figures he discovered RIR 99 lost 5 officers, 92 men killed, 8 officers, 311 men wounded and 3 officers, 53 men missing in the time period between 24 June and 30 June.

The following casualty list provided in post-war accounts only reports the losses by the first three battalions of the regiment, it does not include the IV Battalion.[60]

Killed:	18 officers	367 men
Wounded:	22 officers	1,059 men
Sick: (mostly gas sick)	8 officers	423 men
Missing:	11 officers	624 men
Total:	59 officers	2,842 men

The casualty list for RIR 99 on the disc accompanying this book was published on 25 August 1916 and included the men who were casualties in the preliminary bombardment as well as the heavy fighting on 1 July and the weeks that followed. It also includes the names of the men who became casualties in the IV/R99, something omitted from the chart listed above. While it is possible to identify some men as becoming casualties on 1 July it is not possible at the present to do the same with the majority of the entries.

Notes

1. RIR 99 Report, courtesy of Jack Sheldon. In regard to the time used in this book I have altered the German accounts to show British time, one hour earlier than German time except in the first two instances to illustrate the frequency of reports flowing in to regimental headquarters.
2. H. Wurmb, *Das K.B. Reserve Infanterie Regiment Nr. 8,* p. 149.
3. Wurmb, op. cit., p. 150.
4. P. Orr, *The Road to the Somme,* p. 163.
5. Sheldon, op. cit., RIR 99 Report.
6. M. Gerster, *Die Schwaben an der Ancre,* p. 108.
7. Orr, op. cit., pp. 165-166.
8. Middlebrook, op. cit., p. 138.
9. Wurmb, op. cit., pp. 150-151.
10. Orr, op. cit., p. 183. The Ulster Division had assigned letters to the various portions of the German lines; 'A' was the first line, 'B' the second line, etc.
11. 109th Brigade War Diary. Courtesy of Graham Stewart.
12. Orr, op. cit., pp. 167-168.
13. 109th Brigade War Diary.
14. Orr, op. cit., p. 175.
15. Orr, op. cit., p. 171.
16. Orr, op. cit., pp. 171-172.
17. Orr, op. cit., p. 174.
18. Orr, op. cit., pp. 179-180.
19. 109th Brigade War Diary.
20. J. Sheldon, *The German Army on the Somme,* p. 151.

22. Sheldon, op. cit., p. 148.

23. P. Müller, H. Fabeck, R, Riesel, *Geschichte des Reserve-Infanterie-Regiment Nr. 99*, pp. 108-109.

24. Middlebrook, op. cit., p. 184.

25. 109th Brigade War Diary.

26. Müller, op. cit. p. 107.

27. Müller, op. cit., p. 108.

28. 16th Northumberland Fusiliers Battalion War Diary, NA WO 95/2398

29. Müller, op. cit., p. 108.

30. Müller, op. cit. p. 105.

31. Written by Lieutenant C.S. Marriot in 1964. Copy courtesy of Graham Stewart.

32. 19th Lancashire Fusiliers report on operations 1-4 July. NA WO 95/2394

33. Sheldon, op. cit., RIR 99 Report.

34. Ibid.

35. Ibid.

36. Wurmb, op. cit., pp. 151-152.

37. Sheldon, op. cit., pp. 151-152.

38. 109th Brigade War Diary.

39. Ibid.

40. Orr, op. cit., p. 183.

41. Middlebrook, op. cit., p. 215.

42. 109th Brigade War Diary

43. Wurmb, op. cit., p. 163.

44. Sheldon, op. cit., p. 153.

45. 109th Brigade War Diary.

46. *Oberleutnant der Reserve* Schwarz was wounded in the fighting on the Somme in the Fall of 1914, he subsequently lost his right arm.

47. Müller, op. cit., pp. 108-109.

48. Wurmb, op. cit., pp. 151-153. Johann Fleischmann was killed by artillery fire on 1 July. Andreas Haseneder died from his wound at 11.50 a.m., 3 July.

49. Orr, op. cit., p. 185.

50. *Oberstleutnant* Bram was praised for his critical use of his weak forces in the successful attacks against the Ulstermen. It was felt that his decisiveness was a strong influence in the victory in the Thiepval sector.

51. *Oberleutnant* Schefold was killed in action on 4 August 1916.

52. Sheldon, op. cit., RIR 99 Report.

53. Ibid.

54. Wurmb, op. cit., pp. 163-164. Albin Bauer remained in hospital until he succumbed to his wound on 3 April 1917.

55. Sheldon, op. cit., RIR 99 Report.

56. Ibid.

57. Ibid.

58. Wurmb, op. cit., pp. 164-165.

59. Edmonds, op. cit., p. 421.

60. H. Fabeck, *Im Orkan der Sommeschlacht, Ein Abschnitt aus der Kriegsgeschichte des Reserve-Infanterie-Regiment Nr. 99*, p. 44.

6

Ovillers

The Ovillers Sector was the target of the British 8th Division.[1] The village of Ovillers and the surrounding trenches up to the Nab located between Sectors P2 and P3 were the goals assigned to the Division. The attack would take place utilizing three brigades of infantry; the 23rd on the right, the 25th in the center and the 70th on the left.

Ovillers and the surrounding trenches were being defended by the men from IR 180. This regiment had taken over the Ovillers Sector in early June 1916 from RIR 109 that had been sent to Mametz and Montauban during the period of reorganization. The goal of these troop movements was to provide the best coverage possible for the entire Somme front in view of the imminent British offensive.

IR 180 occupied the trenches starting at the left flank of the Granatloch south of Thiepval to an area just south of Ovillers. The left flank of the regiment formed the boundary between the 26th and 28th Reserve Divisions. The Ovillers Sector was divided into smaller sub-sectors that were designated P1 (near the Granatloch) through P7 (just south of Ovillers). RIR 110 from the 28th Reserve Division occupied the trenches to the left of the regiment including the village of La Boisselle while RIR 99 occupied the trenches on the right flank. On 1 July the trenches between IR 180 and the village of La Boisselle were

Two men from IR 180 inside a trench. (Author's collection)

View of the British trenches from Ovillers. (Lawrence Brown)

manned by the 10/R110 and 1/R110. The 10/R110, on the left flank of the 11/180, would participate in the defense against the attack by the 23rd Brigade from the 8th Division.

Upon their arrival the men from IR 180 found their new sector had adequate defenses but certain improvements were needed before the regiment considered the sector to be ready for the expected offensive. The work was arduous and needed to be completed in the shortest time possible as the British could attack at any moment.

The Ovillers Sector was a formidable position, with thick belts of barbed wire and well-sited machine gun positions. Numerous communication trenches that had once been used to sap toward the enemy lines now provided easy access to the current front line trench. They also provided for quick movement through the German position and could be used as switch lines to quickly contain any enemy penetration.

Seven days of artillery bombardment had seriously damaged the German wire entanglements from what the British observers could see. However the deep, well-constructed front line and communication trenches, while damaged, still presented a major obstacle to any attacking force.

The heavy torpedo mines caused great devastation to the trenches, however the dugouts held up excellently against them, the losses through the bombardment remained miraculous low, the mood of the men was splendid.[2]

While some dugouts occupied by men from Infantry Regiment 180 had been crushed in by armour piercing shells most of them were still intact. The worst of the damage was caused to the entrances and these had been repaired from day to day during the shelling. Even if a particular section of trench was no longer suitable for defense the men had numerous shell craters that could be used in its stead.

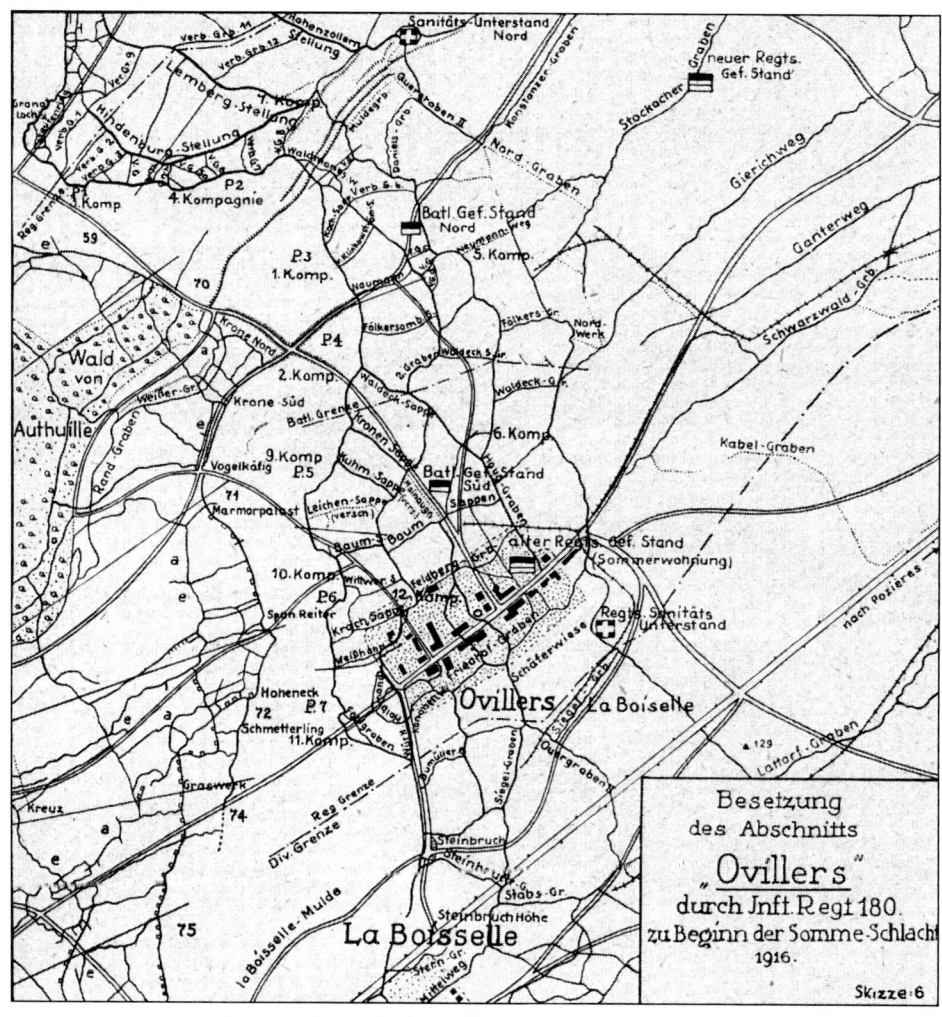

Granatloch-Ovillers-La Boisselle.

At 4.45 on the morning of 1 July a message arrived at the regimental battle headquarters of IR 180 from Army Headquarters that an attack was expected on the entire front. This message was then transmitted to all sectors of the regiment by runners. After enduring 8 days of shelling the men longed for an end of the bombardment and a chance to get back at the enemy, it seemed that this was to be their chance. As if to confirm the content of this message the British guns began firing the most intense bombardment the men in IR 180 had ever experienced. Shells as large as 24cm and heavy mines fell on the first and second trenches of the Ovillers Sector causing even further damage to the defenses.

The British soldiers in the 8th Division facing Ovillers could only hope that the bombardment had done its job and that few if any German soldiers were alive in the front lines. This belief was quickly shattered at 6.25 a.m.:

> At 6.25 a.m. the intensive bombardment commenced. To which the enemy retaliated on our front line and assembly trenches with high explosive and shrapnel. 2nd Lincolns report to Brigade HQ[3]

Further evidence of the dangers that would eventually face the 8th Division came at 7 a.m. when the British front line was swept by machine gun fire from at least two German machine guns. Many of the soldiers probably wondered how any of the defenders or their machine guns had survived such a terrible bombardment lasting over 7 days.

Shortly afterward, as some British troops moved out into no man's land in preparation for the attack they immediately came under rifle and machine gun fire. Obviously the Germans had not only survived the seemingly devastating bombardment, they were not even taking cover in the hurricane of fire falling about their heads during the final minutes before the attack.

Infantrymen – IR 180. (Author's collection)

At about 7.15 a.m. the enemy opened rifle and machine gun fire on our line. This fire was probably drawn by the 2nd Devon Regt. which at about this time attempted to line up in front of their parapet.[4]

The British had used every weapon available to them in preparing the German lines for the attack, including gas clouds. Finally, at 7.22 twelve 3-inch Stokes mortars joined in the bombardment that provided 8 minutes of rapid fire along the German front line. At precisely 7.30 a.m. the mortars ceased fire as the heavier guns shifted their fire to the rear trenches. Whistles were blown as the men from the 23rd, 25th and 70th Brigades advanced in waves against the German trenches.

The gas attacks failed, if the Englishman's gas sank into our own trenches we were not in them, our gas masks were very effective. The regiment had only two dead to record by gas, two telephonists that came back running from a wire patrol and through severe breathing partially annulled the effect of their masks. On the morning of 1st July the enemy increased the bombardment to the most extreme vehemence. Now, within two hours the forward trench was also leveled. At 7.30 the first English storm columns pressed forward, staggered in multiple rows, bent down sprinting across the field. At the same time the artillery transferred its barrage fire to the rear, in fact so far back that they apparently believed that after such preparation the entire first German position, with all three trenches, could easily be taken by the English infantry. However it turned out somewhat different.[5]

30.7cm dud and 7.5cm shrapnel shell case. (Author's collection)

30.7cm dud and 7.5cm shrapnel shell case. (*Das 10. Württembergische Infanterie-Regiment Nr. 180 im Weltkrieg 1914-1918*)

Infantrymen – IR 180. (Author's collection)

The trench sentries reacted quickly once the British fire lifted from the front line trenches. They sounded the alarm up and down the line and within a few seconds men poured from the ground and took up their assigned positions if they were still intact or occupied the nearest shell crater. Machine guns were dragged up from the deep dugouts and quickly made ready to fire.

> The telephone connection on either side never became disrupted, that to the rear only for a short time. The messages by flag signals that replaced the telephone were conveyed so well that within three seconds the requested barrage fire of our howitzers smashed on the given target points. The support of the sector through our severely bombarded artillery was altogether perfect despite their losses. The English tubes were finally played out to such an extent through the prolonged bombardment. That was clearly indicated by the duds found, which lacked any trace of the drive bands.[6]

When the telephone lines were disrupted the men in IR 180 used flares and signal flags to call up defensive artillery fire. Within moments of the alarm being sounded red rockets climbed high into the blue sky all along the German front line. Observers stationed further to the rear quickly spotted the flares and flag signals. The messages were rapidly relayed to the battery commanders. This was the signal the artillery was expecting in order to commence barrage fire in response to an infantry attack. The approaching waves of enemy soldiers was met with a withering volume of rifle and machine gun fire just as the first salvos of shells began falling on the British trenches and across no man's land.

The Attack of the 23rd Brigade

Of all the brigades on the 8th Division the 23rd had the longest distance to cross before reaching the German lines, 700 meters of open ground that was devoid of any cover. The German report of the fighting in the southern half of their sector was short and to the point. The attacks against Sectors P7, P6 and the right wing of P5 had completely broken down in the heavy defensive fire and the British losses had been extremely high.

> The Swabians poured forth out of every mined dugout. The trench was barely still able to be recognized, but each man, each group, each platoon knows their place and their defensive field. Nestled behind the destroyed breastworks and in shell craters, they awaited the superior strength of the approaching enemy. As if sprouting out of the ground, stand the machine guns. And now the deadly sowing begins. The left flank battalion knocks three dense English storm waves to the ground with machine gun fire. Every man and officer fires.[7]

The 2nd Middlesex and 2nd Devonshire battalions faced heavy rifle and machine gun fire from the start and it only grew more intense as they approached the German lines. The fire appeared to be coming from their front, primarily the second trench as well as from Ovillers on the left flank and La Boisselle on the right flank. The further the men advanced the heavier the fire grew until the men broke formation and started to bunch together while advancing toward the German lines in rushes.

Once the men came to within approximately 70 meters of the first German trench the intensity of infantry fire rose to the highest level. German batteries placed a curtain of fire

Machine gun crew – IR 180. (Author's collection)

behind the advancing men covering the British fire trench and communication trenches with heavy howitzer fire while bombarding no man's land with 7.7cm and 10.5cm shrapnel and high explosive shells.[8]

Almost miraculously, small groups of the 2nd Middlesex and 2nd Devonshire battalions survived the heavy fire and made their way through gaps in the front line being held by 10/R110 between the *Bumiller Graben* and the *Siegel Graben*.

These small forces then attempted to forge ahead and take the second trench about 180 meters away. Their advance was soon stopped by heavy crossfire coming from communication trenches and shell holes on both flanks and on their front from support troops holding the 2nd trench. The fire proved to be too heavy to overcome and there were too few men left to continue into the German trenches. The survivors were slowly forced back to the first trench.

The two German companies attacked by the 23rd Brigade had reacted quickly to the penetration of their front line. The routes leading up to the enemy occupied trenches were blocked off and manned by bombing parties while their comrades maintained their crossfire from rifles and machine guns from shell holes and the rear trenches. In addition German counter-attacks began almost at once from both flanks. These tactics had been the subject of numerous training demonstrations given by the men of IR 180 to the other regiments in the XIV Reserve Corps and each man knew exactly what to do in this situation.

Without support, the 2nd Middlesex and 2nd Devonshire could not enlarge their gains or even hope to hold for long the small sector they had taken. In an attempt to help the Middlesex and Devonshire battalions the 2nd West Yorkshire battalion moved forward and started to advance across no man's land at 8.25 a.m. The battalion immediately came under heavy German artillery fire and lost approximately 250 men before clearing the vicinity of the British front trench. As the survivors made their way across no man's land they came under fire including enfilade fire from La Boisselle on their right flank.

Only small parties from both battalions made it to the German front line, not enough men to make a difference. The 2nd West Yorkshire battalion alone lost 8 officers, 421 men on 1 July. The planned advance of the last battalion in the brigade, the 2nd Scottish Rifles, was cancelled when it became obvious they would not be able to reach the German lines intact and without suffering horrendous casualties.

On the German side of the wire the situation appeared to be under control so much so that the 10/R110 was able to assist the neighboring company by sending one platoon under *Leutnant* Wirthwein to assist the 1/R110 with the fighting near La Boisselle. The 1/R110 was occupied with repelling the attack against their position as well containing the penetration of their front due to the immense crater at the *Blinddarm* [Lochnagar Crater]. The sector had been breached on their left flank and the British had proceeded into the German trench system in La Boisselle held by the men from RIR 110.

> The Englishmen falter, waver, yield to the rear. The first storm is completely beaten back. In the second trench an officer ascends the parapet and full of spirit photographed the English battalions flooding back.[9]

During the advance by the 23rd Brigade, IR 180 received vital support from the neighboring regiment, in particular from *Vizefeldwebel* Laasch, III/R110 and his men. Laasch's group was part of the regimental reserve for RIR 110 and occupied positions in

Men from *Landwehr Brigade Ersatz Battalion 55* in the trenches. (Brett Butterworth)

the *Mittelweg* that overlooked the La Boisselle *Mulde*. Laasch did not have any contact with troops on his right or left flank and the situation had grown quiet after the initial British attack. Finally, he received orders to move forward and Laasch proceeded with his men to the front line where they overlooked the attack of the 23rd Brigade:

> Instructions had reached us and we swarmed into the foremost line. We did not meet any more Englishmen there also; they had probably all gone back to their assault start lines. However our trench garrison there lay shot down or struck dead. We distributed ourselves and placed the trench in good order. I found a machine gun still intact that a sandbag had served as a gun mount. The crew from Brigade *Ersatz* Battalion 55 lay dead beside it. There was a great deal of ammunition so we made the gun ready to fire because we could flank the sector of Regiment 180 up until Ovillers from our position.
>
> I could no longer determine if we had any connection on the right and on the left, then we observed movement in the English trenches lying further in the rear in front of Albert. The few guns of our division ready to fire had probably also discovered this assembly of men and provided well-placed fire on these trenches. There the enemy attack also broke forth, not against our *Granathof* of La Boisselle, but against the front of Regiment 180: dense, tightly packed lines poured out of the English trenches, strode across the wide foreground and ended up in the heavy defensive fire of Regiment 180. I also fired one belt after another into the flank of the ever-advancing English battalions with our machine gun: never in the war have I experienced a more devastating effect of our fire: the fallen were tightly packed in the entire hollow up

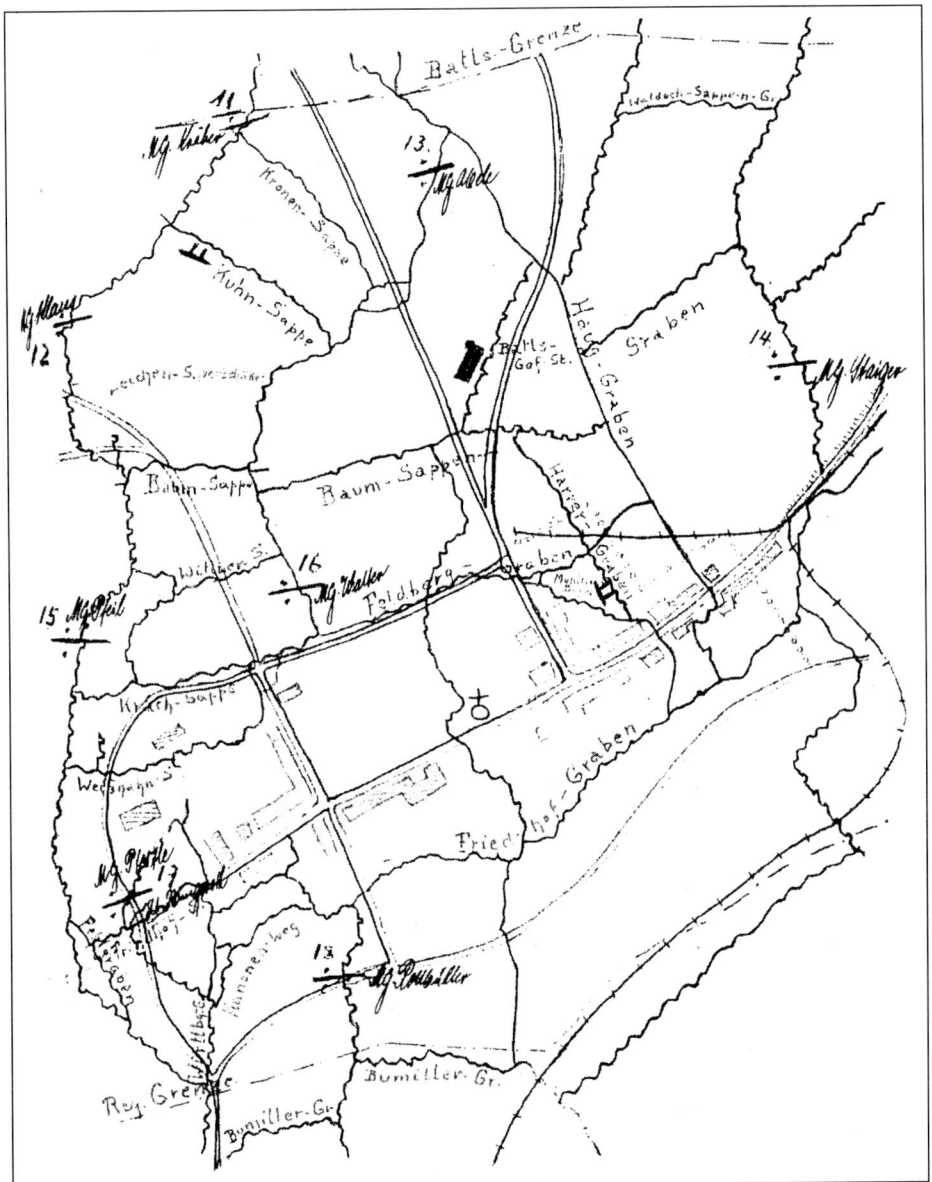

Machine gun positions of the 2MG/180 by Ovillers.

Contemporary artist's depiction of the attack against Ovillers on 1 July 1916. While there were no mounted British officers as depicted in the painting and the German

trenches lacked any parapets or parados the artist was able to capture the intensity of the events on this day. (*Illustrierte Geschichte des Weltkrieges 1914/16*)

to Ovillers! However our machine gun had also been discovered. The last water had been poured into the jacket. We first noticed that the white steam had betrayed our position when individual gunshots went through our helmets or caused the sand to spray up in front of us. It was bad luck that a low flying enemy plane discovered us and directed the fire of two guns on us. Now the shells swept into our trench from the left flank and caused us heavy losses. The men yielded into the *Stichgräben*. I crouched behind a traverse with a comrade when his head was torn to pieces by a large splinter so that his brains poured out over my tunic. The plane did not come there again and the guns fired on different targets. Then we fired at the still living Englishmen that were in front of our sector here and there.[10]

The survivors of the 23rd Brigade were eventually forced out of the German front line after they ran out of hand grenades. The men made their way back to their own line as best as possible using shell holes for cover. While crossing no man's land they found the remnants of the rear waves of their brigade pinned down by German fire. Everywhere they looked the ground was covered in dead and wounded men. The attack by the 23rd Brigade was over. No ground had been gained and losses were enormous. The casualties suffered by the three battalions of the brigade were reported to be 47 officers, 1,455 men killed, wounded or missing. The two German companies that defended against these attacks only show a total of 148 casualties for the fighting on this day. The 11/180 reported a loss of 80 men while the 10/R110 reported 68 casualties. It should also be considered that the losses reported by the 10/R110 would include men sent to assist the 1/R110 against the Tyneside Scottish in the fighting by La Boisselle.

The Attack of the 25th Brigade

The 25th Brigade, the center of the attack by the 8th Division, fared little better than the 23rd on its right flank. As soon as the brigade started to cross no man's land it was met with withering fire and the 2nd Royal Berkshire Battalion was unable to make any progress at all. The battalions on its left were able to advance despite the heavy losses they suffered. The lines quickly became mixed as men bunched together and started to move forward in short rushes, from shell hole to shell hole, while exchanging fire with the German defenders holding the front line.

The Germans facing the 25th Brigade included parts of the 10th and 9/180 that occupied the front line, with the 12th and 6/180 close by in support. The attack of the 25th Brigade finally broke down completely in front of the German lines with very heavy losses. The only success experienced by the brigade took place at the left wing of the 9/180.

The left wing of P5 that was occupied by the 9/180 had suffered the heaviest damage from the British fire and most of the wire obstacles had been damaged or destroyed. Many of the dugout entrances in the first trench had also been buried. The few men from the 2nd Lincolnshire and 2nd Royal Yorkshire Battalions that had survived the ordeal of crossing no man's land poured into this part of the shattered German front line where many of the defenders were unable to exit their dugouts and as a result there was little German fire coming from the front line.

Small parties of the 2nd Lincolns were able to reach the German line northwest of Ovillers at 7.50 a.m. They attempted to extend their penetration on both sides but the men of the 9th and 10/180 reacted quickly and made every effort to contain the British

Gefreiter Alfred Dessecker, 9/180 and his comrades. Alfred
was killed on 1 July 1916. (Author's collection)

foothold in their line. The Württembergers blocked off their front line with barricades and immediately sent bombing parties to the threatened areas.

The men of the 25th Brigade were not short of courage and despite their small numbers continued to advance even further toward the 2nd trench. The German lines appeared to be a warren of communication trenches and saps. While advancing toward the second trench the men ran into German reserves advancing along the communication trenches and came under heavy enfilade fire from the *Kuhm* and *Baum* Saps as well as from their goal, the 2nd German trench. The heavy fire eventually forced the surviving men back to the old German front line.

At this time approximately 70 men were still left in the German trenches from the entire brigade. They were under command of Lieutenant-Colonel Reginald Bastard of the 2nd Lincolnshire Battalion. For the time being, while the hand grenades held out, this small group was able to hold about 275 meters of the German front line. They blocked off all access routes to their trench with sandbags and barbed wire. The small band of survivors manned the trenches and fought back against the bombing parties from IR 180 as best they could. A few men were assigned to search the German dugouts, looking for supplies of food and water and in particular, hand grenades.

IR 180 was determined to completely expel the British troops from the German front line. The sector commander ordered one platoon from the 6th and supporting troops from the 10/180 to make a frontal assault. They would attack from the 3rd trench, cross the open ground between the Baum and Leichen Saps and advance against the British position. At the same time the seemingly endless bombing attacks continued on both flanks. The bombing attacks also included men from the 2/180 sent over as reinforcements. The bombing party from the 2/180 advanced through the front line trench beyond the *Kronen* and *Kuhm* Saps with an additional section moving into the *Kronen* Sap to act as close support.

The British were able to hold out in the German front line for slightly longer than 90 minutes, just about the time they ran out of hand grenades and small arms ammunition was becoming scarce. Finally, after being forced out of the front line trench the survivors took cover in the numerous shell craters covering no man's land where they came across the remnants of the support waves. The ground was covered by hundreds of dead, dying and wounded men. Many of the survivors became killed or wounded by machine gun, rifle and artillery fire while trying to make their way back across no man's land.

The men from IR 180 had successfully repelled the attack by the 25th Brigade with approximately four companies of infantry, the equivalent size of a British battalion. Two English machine guns that had been brought up into the sector of the 9th Company were also captured in the assault. Once the initial British penetration had been eliminated the infantry could once again direct all of their fire against the British front line and into the flanks of any nearby attacking force.

The men who had remained behind in support inside the British trenches during the initial attack were not much safer from the German fire than those who crossed no man's land. German artillery fired accurately along the British trench system covering the fire trench and communication trenches with high explosive and shrapnel shells from heavy 15cm field howitzers and 21cm mortars, the deadly 'Jack Johnsons' as they were commonly known. German machine gun fire was extremely accurate and covered the trench edges with a steady stream of fire. It was designed to effectively prevent any further British troops from joining the attack. The training given to the machine gun crews by instructors who belonged to Machine Gun Marksman Detachments had apparently been worth the time and effort.

The 1st Royal Irish Rifles was one of the battalions providing support for the first wave

Ersatz Reservist Friedrich Bühler, 5/180 (sitting) and his friends. Friedrich was a friend of Karl Losch, 3/R119. (Author's collection)

Infantrymen – IR 180. (Author's collection)

of the attack. 2nd Lieutenant W.V.C. Lake described the attack on 1 July:

> Punctually at Zero hour next morning the artillery barrage opened up. Never before or since have I heard such a din. It was accurate fire too and it was lifted after half an hour according to plan. This was the signal for the Infantry to go 'Over the Top'. We were supporting another company and were able to see how gallantly they leaped to it. But they got nowhere. The German machine guns had not been eliminated and at once they opened up accurate fire on our parapets. The men simply got up and fell back into the trench, either killed outright or badly wounded. Those who did get further were never seen or heard of again, as far as I know.[11]

The German artillery fire was so heavy and so accurate that A and B Coy were unable to leave their own trenches. The companies had taken so many casualties they were down to about 50 men by the time the fire trench was reached.

One eyewitness to the attack was Captain G.I. Gartlan, commanding A Coy in a report to Lieutenant Whitfield No. 1 Platoon:

> The attack commenced at 7.30 a.m. after an intensive bombardment of five to ten minutes. The Berks and Lincolns went over first and were met by a terrific fire which appeared to paralyse the attack. Our attack following faired no better, only two companies getting over and no one appeared to come back.
>
> Our company, coming up the communication trench, came right into the retaliation and your platoon, I hear, got two 5.9's right into the middle of it and hardly anyone escaped. Your servant was killed.
>
> The CO was terribly wounded – I saw him sitting down, he had lost an eye and was badly hit in the leg. He would not go until he had handed over command to

Gefreiter Alfred Dessecker 9/180 and his comrades at the Miraumont railroad station. Alfred is second from right, marked by a black X. (Author's collection)

Fitzmaurice. Dear old Dominick [the Adjutant] died in no-man's-land, shot through the femoral artery, so 'the faculty' told me. I believe Carroll [the RSM] knows where he is buried. I know he was brought in.[12]

The attack was a shambles from the outset as men were killed and wounded before even being able to leave their own trenches. The alert 2/180 quickly recognized the threat posed by the approach of fresh troops and the company commander gave orders to open a devastating flanking fire into waves of men. Once in no man's land the British ranks were thinned at every step as the men advanced into a wall of machine gun and rifle fire combined with dozens of high explosive and shrapnel shells falling everywhere. It was surprising that anyone was able to make his way into the German trenches at all. As it was only about 10 men from the original attacking force of the 1st Royal Irish Rifles actually made it to the German front line; far too few to be of any real help.

Lieutenant Colonel Bastard attempted to bring up fresh troops but after returning to the British lines but he found out that no further attacks were to be made. Even trying to reform the survivors of the original attack and make another attempt proved to be a disaster. The small group met withering fire before they could even clear the British trenches and the attack was called off.

There was not much to report about the events of the morning of 1 July, as most of the men involved had become casualties or were trapped inside no man's land. One of the battalions involved in the fighting from the 25th Brigade sent the following report:

At 7.30 a.m. the three assaulting Coys advanced to attack the German lines. They were met by intensive rifle and machine gun fire which prevented any of the waves reaching the enemy line. A little group on the left of the battalion succeeded in getting into the German trench but was eventually bombed out. At about 7.45 a.m. the parapet was swept by rifle and machine gun fire which prevented any exit from our trenches. The

Infantryman – IR 180. (Author's collection)

enemy replied to our intensive bombardment by barraging the front line from about 6.35 a.m. onwards. At about 11 a.m. the order came from Brigade HQ to stand by and await further orders. At about 12.30 p.m. news was received that the brigade would be relieved. Steel helmets proved very reliable and in many cases saved men's lives.[13] [2nd Royal Berkshires report to brigade]

It would take some time to determine the fate of most of the casualties suffered on 1 July as there were few survivors of the opening attack. Exact details about the fate of individual men or even company size units was lacking in the confusion following the attack. In the case of the men from C Coy 2nd Royal Berkshires it was not known if any of them ever made it to the German lines at all. It appears that the entire company was annihilated before getting very far from the British fire trench. Many of the wounded were apparently killed by shellfire where they lay exposed in the open.

The other battalion involved in the first attack provided a brief report on the events of 1 July: 2nd Lincolns report to Brigade.

At 7.25 a.m. companies started to move forward from their assembly positions preparatory to the assault.

The three assaulting companies [set off] getting their first two waves out into no-man's-land, and their third and fourth waves at Zero hour. The support company got into our front line trench but suffered a lot of casualties from shellfire. At 7.30 a.m. as soon as the barrage lifted the whole assaulted.

Memorial card: *Gefreiter* Karl Josef Buemann, 9/180, killed in action 1 July 1916. (Felix Fregin)

Memorial card: *Musketier* Adolf Schilling, 2/180 in civilian clothes. Killed in action 1 July 1916. (Author's collection)

They were met with very severe rifle fire and in most cases had to advance in short rushes and return the fire, this fire seemed to come from the German second line, and the machine gun from our left. On reaching the German front line they found it strongly held, and were met with showers of bombs, but after a very hard fight about 200 yards of German line was taken at about 7.50 a.m., the extreme right failing to get in and also the extreme left, where there appeared to be a gap of about 70 yards, although bits of platoons of the 70th Brigade joined them.

The Support Company by this time joined in. The few officers that were left gallantly led their men over the German trench to attack the second line, but owing to rifle and machine gun fire, could not push on. Attempts were made to consolidate and make blocks, but the trench was so badly knocked about that very little cover was obtainable, from the enfilade machine gun fire and continual bombing attacks which were being made by the enemy the whole time, and one frontal attack from their second line which we repulsed.

By about 9 a.m. this isolated position became untenable, no supports being able to reach us owing to the intense rifle and machine gun fire. And our left was being driven back, the remainder which by now only held 100 yards, had to withdraw.

On reaching our own lines all the men that could be collected were formed up and tried to push on again, but the heavy machine gun and rifle fire made the ground quite impassable. About 1 p.m. I received orders from the brigade to withdraw.[14]

Brigade and division headquarters were still in the dark when it came to any information on the progress of the attack. The 1st RIR report found in the 25th Brigade war diary summed it up in one short comment, 'Too few men to get a true picture yet.'

Zur frommen Erinnerung
im Gebete an
Adolf Schilling
von Nendingen
Inf.-Regt Nr. 180, 2. Komp.
geboren 17. Juni 1894; gefallen 1. Juli 1916
bei Oliviers (Nordfrankreich.)

✠

Memorial card: *Musketier* Adolf Schilling, 2/180 in his uniform. His date
of birth was incorrectly listed on the card. (Author's collection)

The progress of this battalion through our trenches was rendered exceedingly difficult by the wretched conditions of our trenches, which were moreover blocked by dead and wounded men, and by men of the assaulting battalions who had been unable to go forward, or had been driven back. The Commanding Officer was very seriously wounded and his Adjutant killed.[15]

No man's land was littered with individual soldiers, many of them wounded, who waited until darkness to finally make their way back to their lines or for the arrival of a medical unit that could dress their wounds and bring them to safety.

The Attack of the 70th Brigade
The 70th Brigade, the left wing of the attack, advanced against the 'Nab', the part of the line that was defended by the 1st, 2nd and part of the 9/180 with support from the 5/180 positioned near Battalion Battle Headquarters North. The week-long bombardment had caused a great deal of damage to the German defenses, in particular the first trench and the *Fölkersamb Sap* was leveled in Sector P4. Despite the damage caused by the bombardment the position was still formidable.

The 8th York & Lancaster battalion attacked alongside the 8th King's Own Yorkshire Light Infantry. The first few waves of the 8th KOYLI and parts of those from the 8th Yorks & Lancs had the advantage that the Germans on their left flank were distracted by the 32nd Division attack against the *Granatloch*. This allowed the attackers to overrun the 1st trench between the *Klinkowstrom Sap* and the *Kronen Sap* and then immediately press on to the 2nd trench.

What they failed to do was expand their gains to the trenches on their left flank, trenches that were not under direct attack by either the 8th or the 32nd Division. The

Zur Erinnerung im Gebete
an Kanonier

Albert Schilling

Reserve-Feld-Art.-Regt. Nr. 54, 2. Batterie
geb. 10. November 1892 zu Nendingen
O.-A. Tuttlingen
gefallen 1. Nov. 1918 bei Chennery (Ardennes).

✠

Eine größere Liebe hat niemand,
als daß er sein Leben hingibt
für seine Freunde.   (Joh. XV, 13.)

Barmherziger Jesus, gib ihnen die ewige Ruhe!
Jesus, Maria, Joseph !

Zur Erinnerung im Gebete
an Musketier

Adolf Schilling

Infanterie-Regt Nr. 180, 2. Kompagnie
geb. 15. Juni 1894 zu Nendingen
gefallen 1. Juli 1916 bei Oviliers (Nordfrankreich).

✠

O Jesus, um Deiner heißen Todes-
angst und um Deiner Verlassenheit wil-
len, erbarme Dich der Seelen Deiner
Diener A l b e r t und A d o l f und
laß Dein Leiden und Blut an ihnen nicht
verloren sein. Amen. Vater unser . . .

R. I. P.

The war would take another member of the Schilling family. Memorial
card: *Musketier* Adolf Schilling and his brother Albert, who was
killed only days before the war ended. (Author's collection)

garrison of this portion of the German line was then able to concentrate almost all of their efforts on containing the British penetration into the German lines and provide aid to the neighboring RIR 99 where the fighting was still surging back and forth. This was to have serious consequences in the next few hours.

While the leading waves had managed to reach the German lines the following waves came under the full force of the German defensive fire. Artillery, rifle and machine gun fire from the *Hindenburg Stellung* and the southern face of the *Granatloch* cut the attackers down by the dozens. Few men from the following waves ever reached the German front line.

Support fire from neighboring regiments was critical in stopping the British attack. One Belgian machine gun operated by RIR 99 fired into the left flank of the 70th Brigade while Machine Gun No. 6 from RIR 99 in the *Lemberg Stellung* also poured heavy fire into the unprotected left flank of the 70th Brigade causing numerous losses.

The men who had successfully penetrated the German front line reached the 2nd trench but were facing stiffer resistance as they moved deeper into the maze of the German defences. They were eventually able to advance further into the German lines and finally reached the area of Battalion Battle Headquarters North where the 5/180 was positioned in support of the front line. This proved to be the extent of their advance. Without reinforcements, ammunition and especially hand grenades, the men of the 70th Brigade would have a difficult time holding their gains.

While the 70th Brigade had penetrated into the 3rd trench the sector they held was narrow and unsupported on both flanks. The men of the 1st, 2nd and 5/180 reacted with the same determination and speed as their comrades had further south. The routes leading toward the trenches occupied by the British were blocked off and bombing parties were assembled and began to attack the British trench blocks. Machine guns, especially from

Artillerymen – RFAR 26. (Author's collection)

the area of trenches near the *Granatloch* and from the Thiepval Spur located on the British left flank and from the *Nordwerk* on the right flank poured streams of fire into the ranks of the 70th Brigade.

For the time being the British troops that had penetrated Sector P4 were contained. The men from IR 180 could pay full attention to any further attempts by the 70th Brigade to send over reinforcements to their beleaguered comrades. When the men of the 9th York & Lancaster did attempt to cross no man's land they came under increasingly heavy enfilading machine gun fire from the Thiepval Spur. With the failure of most attacks by the 32nd Division on the left flank of the 70th Brigade, several machine guns from RIR 99 continued to provide support for IR 180. It was reported that the 9th York & Lancs lost 50% of its strength almost at the onset of their advance from this heavy fire.

As the survivors continued to advance toward the German front line they had also to pass through the heavy barrage fire from the German batteries and came under increasingly heavy rifle and machine gun fire from their front as more and more Germans reoccupied portions of the front line originally lost during the first attack. The advancing waves of men soon lost all cohesion and the men began to bunch together as they approached the German front line. This only provided an easier target for the German defenders.

IR 180 described these events in a brief passage in its regimental history of the attack against Sector P4 through the sunken road by the *Naumann Sap* that led toward Mouquet

Farm. The defenders belonged to the 2/180:

> The attack against P4 faltered after the first shells of our own artillery barrage fire smashed into the first wave of riflemen. The enemy now tried to approach us using the sunken road; however they were prevented from doing this through the fire of a machine gun quickly thrown into position on the parados of the first trench. The detachment of approximately 150-200 men that were pressed together in the sunken road were literally mowed down. The enemy had brought a machine gun into position to protect his advance through the sunken road, however one of our patrols succeeded in shooting down the gun crew and bringing the gun in.[16]

According to the German accounts only 15 men survived the devastating fire inside the sunken road. This incident could refer to the party of 50 men, chiefly bombers, who attempted to reach the German lines using a sunken road that lead toward Mouquet Farm. They were checked 70 meters from the German trench by a German machine gun firing directly down the road at point blank range.

By this time the 70th Brigade only had one battalion left intact and it was decided to send it over in the hopes of helping the men trapped inside the German trenches. The 11th Sherwood Foresters had to make their way through the British communication trenches that were choked with wounded men from the earlier attacks. The battalion was finally able to begin the attack in two waves. While advancing over the open ground of no man's land the men had to step over the bodies of their comrades who had been killed or wounded in the earlier attack. It was a demoralizing sight to many.

The German defenders facing the 11th Sherwood Foresters had no direct communication to the batteries in the rear. Even if they did there was little that could be

Artillerymen – RFAR 26. (Author's collection)

Drebmann

Leutnant d. R. i. Inf. Regt. 180,
gefallen bei St. Quentin
am 1. Juli 1916

Leutnant der Reserve Johann Drehmann, 7/180, killed in
action 1 July 1916. (*Kriegstagbuch aus Schwaben*)

done to support them as most of the artillery covering their sector was now involved in the heavy fighting at the Leipzig Salient and *Feste Schwaben*. Under these circumstances the men from IR 180 had received orders to destroy any attack against their position with rifle and machine gun fire.

The first wave suffered heavily in the concentrated German fire and only a few men managed to make it to the German wire entanglements before being shot down. The second wave was virtually destroyed by heavy and accurate machine gun fire and only a handful of men actually reached the German trench where they were also shot down or forced to take cover.

The attack against Sector P4 was effectively destroyed, allowing the officer commanding the 2/180 the luxury of sending assistance to the hard pressed 9/180 on their left flank as previously described in the attack by the 25th Brigade. The men from the 8th York & Lancaster and the 8th KOYLI who were still holding a small portion of the German 1st, 2nd and 3rd trenches were completely isolated. There was no chance that reinforcements could reach them. All attempts to contact or re-supply the men from the British lines were futile; these men were on their own.

The Germans surrounded the men of the 70th Brigade and effectively contained the British inside the German lines with heavy enfilade fire from both flanks while bombing parties eliminated one British detachment after another. Finally, the last survivors were forced out of the German trenches and back into no man's land where they took shelter in shell holes among the dead and wounded. Observers in the British lines could see bombing fights going on inside the German lines. Some British soldiers were reported to have been standing on the parapet while throwing bombs at the Germans as late as 2.30 p.m. They were soon overpowered by German counter attacks pressing in from both flanks.

The companies of IR 180 and RIR 110 involved in the fighting by Ovillers had been able to eject the few British soldiers that had penetrated their lines. The entire position was back in German hands by the afternoon. The Germans had been able to accomplish this with the minimum use of reserves. During the course of the fighting one platoon from the 8/180 was moved from the *Harrer Graben* into the 3rd trench in Sector Ovillers-South. Another platoon from this company was moved into the *Harrer Graben* from the 4th trench. The remaining platoon from the 8/180 was transferred from the II Position into the *Nordwerk*.

Mutual support between regiments had been very effective in the fighting by Ovillers. This was amply demonstrated by the actions of *Vizefeldwebel* Laasch during the attack by the 23rd Brigade. Also, by the end of the day the Belgian Hotchkiss gun with RIR 99 had fired approximately 2,000 rounds while Machine Gun No. 6, also with RIR 99 had fired approximately 7,000 rounds. The low number of rounds fired by the Belgian gun was due solely to a shortage of appropriate ammunition. However both guns were extremely effective in breaking up the attacks made by the 70th Brigade and were instrumental in preventing any British gains along the front held by IR 180.

While most of the artillery in the Ovillers Sector had been directed against the Thiepval Sector where the breakthrough by the Ulster Division threatened the entire German line, some guns were still trained on no man's land facing the Ovillers Sector on this day. The battery positions were the scene of frantic activity as the guns were being operated at their maximum capacity. Fresh ammunition had to be brought up to the guns and the gun positions needed to be kept clear of the ever-growing piles of empty shell casings and wicker baskets. In the 5/RFAR 27, which was located just outside of Pozières, the problem of disposing of the empty wicker baskets would soon pose a threat to the battery.

The projectile baskets were now immediately brought into the ammunition dugout, as far as room was still available. Suddenly there was an impact. This

British prisoners captured on the Somme. (Author's collection)

causes the ammunition baskets to catch fire. Loud crashes throw projectiles and cartridges everywhere; all of the precious ammunition threatens to go up into the air. Ammunition *Unteroffizier* Kopp from Uttenhofen jumped up to the threatened position and despite the double danger from the enemy fire and the burning baskets he threw the burning baskets to the side where they were soon became harmless. So he saved the ammunition and the firepower of the battery.[17]

The availability of ammunition for the different batteries was apparently not an issue along the front held by the 26th Reserve Division. Ample supplies had been stored by each gun and additional ammunition was delivered to each battery as it became needed. In the period from 24 to 30 June the Light Ammunition Column of the I/RFAR 27 had already delivered 19,000 rounds to battery positions near Courcelette and Miraumont.

At 8 a.m. on the morning of 1 July the column received orders to deliver 1,600 rounds to Position 731, 400 rounds to Position 728 and 400 rounds to Position 733. Twenty ammunition wagons that were standing by fully loaded left from Grévillers to make their deliveries. They moved through Grévillers Wood toward the battery positions. Once they reached the positions each wagon stopped behind their assigned battery and the drivers and gunners sprang up and quickly unloaded the ammunition. The men of the Light Ammunition column helped the gunners stow it in the gun positions and attached dugouts. Everything was done as quickly as possible as the wagons were under constant aerial observation. The planes quickly directed the fire of the British guns against the battery positions and the ammunition wagons in the hopes of destroying both.

Once their task was completed the empty wagons quickly drove back along the same route they had taken to reach the batteries. Part of the journey went through locations that were heavily shelled and it took some time before all of the wagons reached an area of relative safety where they were out of sight of the enemy observers. A short time afterward an additional four wagons were sent forward to deliver more rounds to Position 733. The journey was simply described as being dangerous and difficult. Much of the road taken by the wagons was marked with craters and large holes. The ammunition wagons managed to reach the gun positions where a Bavarian *Gefreiter* showed the men where to place the wicker shell baskets. All the while the teams unloaded their cargo, British shells fell in front of, next to and along side the gun positions. At the same time the German batteries kept up a steady rate of fire toward the British lines.

As soon as each wagon was unloaded the men drove the horses at the fastest pace possible. They faced even more danger on the return trip as the wagons came under machine gun fire from low flying British planes. Luckily the trip was made without the loss of any men or horses. By midday an additional 1,500 rounds were delivered to Position 764 near Courcelette. The strain of each trip was starting to show as the men and horses were completely exhausted from their efforts in the morning of 1 July. By the end of the day almost 4,400 shells had been delivered to batteries across the front line.

The men in the light ammunition columns had lived charmed lives on this day. The wagons and men were under constant observation and heavy shellfire each time they ventured toward the battery positions. Almost miraculously, the total losses suffered by the columns consisted of three horses wounded on 1 July.

Much of the success experienced by the men in IR 180 had been the result of the extensive defensive system that had been created. The Ovillers Sector had been continuously worked on for nearly two years since it had first been captured. The trench system was formidable and the attacking troops would have little protection if any from defensive rifle and machine gun fire.

One of the key factors of the successful defense of the Ovillers Sector was the failure by the British in attacking the far right flank of IR 180. A portion of the sector and garrison had not been directly attacked by any forces from the 8th Division or the left flanking 32nd Division. This omission allowed the company to provide fire into the left flank of the 70th Brigade and to participate in the defense against the 32nd Division penetration into the German lines at the neighboring *Granatloch*.

> The Englishmen are apparently speechless. After the morning they no longer attacked. A later attack that, according to statements of prisoners, was ordered at 1.30 in the afternoon was no longer carried out by them. Our stretcher-bearer squads looked to save the wounded that were within reach. Reserves were brought up. Ammunition was brought up. Ammunition in masses, because each man has within the three-hour period fired several hundred cartridges. However no one has been lacking cartridges. Everything takes place in the bright light of day without any disturbance from enemy fire. The losses of the enemy were atrociously heavy. 1,500 to 2,000 corpses were mown down in entire rows lying there in the evening in front of the sector of the Swabian regiment. On the other hand, the losses of the regiment were fortunately small. According to the English estimates the ratio was 8:1, the few English prisoners taken belonged to eight different battalions.[18]

By the end of the day the fighting along the Ovillers front had died down once the attacks by the 8th Division had ended. The men of IR 180 did not have time to rest and were immediately put to work cleaning up the trenches and preparing for the next attack that they felt would surely take place. New wire entanglements were set up, trenches were dug out and in some places chains of craters were joined to make a cohesive defensive line.

The fighting on 1 July had consumed large amounts of hand grenades and small arms ammunition that needed to be replenished as quickly as possible. Despite the British artillery fire falling on the rear areas carrying parties from IR 180 had been able to keep a steady flow of supplies and ammunition to the front line and by 4 p.m. there were sufficient stockpiles of hand grenades and ammunition at hand to meet any renewed assault.

In at least one instance, the work being requested at the end of 1 July appeared almost ludicrous to the men who were exhausted after fighting all day. *Vizefeldwebel* Laasch, III/R110 and his men took a well-earned rest by the machine gun he had operated with such deadly effectiveness earlier in the day. The ammunition used when firing the gun had been enormous. Their rest was disturbed by an unwelcome visitor.

> A *Hauptmann* unfamiliar to me came through the trench and ordered that we should collect the empty cartridge casings.[19]

The reality of the battlefield soon came back into focus for Laasch and his men.

> Then came the night and the English first-aid men with lanterns fetched their groaning and crying wounded.[20]

The terrain between the opposing trenches was filled with the dead and dying men and hundreds of wounded. Once the fighting had ended the Germans made no attempt to hinder the British stretcher-bearers from going out into no man's land to recover their wounded and many men were saved because of this. However, not every wounded soldier could be rescued while it was still daylight and the moans and cries of those left behind could be heard throughout the night. The men from IR 180 did what they could for the wounded British soldiers that were close to their trenches and many men owed their lives to these acts of kindness. However, given the tense situation accidents were bound to occur.

> With the onset of darkness the terrain of dead in front of the obstacles becomes alive. The moaning sounds loudly, the wailing more desperate, the screams and yelling. Those frightened men who have been paralyzed by fear of creeping and jumping carefully watched and looked to escape again. Our *Jagdkommandos* cleared the field. A brave English doctor with his bearers inadvertently became wounded.[21]

The dead were given a quick burial usually near to the place where they fell. The only exception to this practice was if an officer had been killed. It was customary to carry the body to the rear where the deceased officer would receive a formal burial in one of the cemeteries that had been established in the villages behind the lines.

Numerous wounded men were collected and transported to dressing stations where they could receive proper care. Any unwounded prisoners were taken to holding areas further in the rear where they would await interrogation and finally transportation to a prisoner of war camp in Germany.

The losses suffered by the 8th Division had been enormous – 5,121 officers and men killed, wounded, missing and taken prisoner. In comparison, the defenders of the Ovillers Sector had lost few men. IR 180 reported losses of 4 officers and 79 men killed, 3 officers, 181 men wounded and 13 men missing. The 10/R110 had lost 10 men killed or died from wounds in the fighting on 1 July and approximately 25 men wounded.

Notes

1. The 8th Division consisted of the 23rd Brigade (2nd Devonshire, 2nd West Yorkshire, 2nd Scottish Rifles, 2nd Middlesex), 25th Brigade (2nd Lincolnshire, 2nd Royal Berkshire, 1st Royal Irish Rifles, 2nd Rifle Brigade), 70th Brigade (1st Sherwood Foresters, 8th King's Own Yorkshire Light Infantry, 8th Yorks & Lancaster, 9th Yorks & Lancaster), and Pioneers (2nd Durham Light Infantry).
2. 'Die Schwaben im Kampfe an der Somme', Kriegstagbuch aus Schwaben, p. 1341.
3. J. Taylor, *The 1st Royal Irish Rifles*, p. 84.
4. Taylor, op. cit., pp. 83-84
5. *Kriegstagbuch aus Schwaben*, op. cit.
6. Ibid.
7. Ibid.
8. 7.7cm field guns could achieve a rate of 15-20 rounds per minute with rapid fire depending upon the level of training of the gun crew and the availability of shells. This rate could only be kept up for a short time to prevent the gun from overheating. The guns could fire at a sustained rate afterward that would be from 4-6 shells per minute, more when needed due to an emergency

situation. The 10.5cm light field howitzer could achieve a rate of 10-15 rounds per minute with rapid fire but as with the field guns it could only be sustained for a short time.

9. *Kriegstagbuch aus Schwaben*, op. cit. I have searched for a copy of the photograph mentioned in the article. Unfortunately it has not shown up in any period publication or any subsequent publication that I am aware of.

10. Greiner, *Reserve-Infanterie-Regiment Nr. 110 im Weltkrieg 1914-1918*, pp. 132-133.

11. Taylor, op.cit., pp. 80-81.

12. Taylor, op.cit., pp. 82-83.

13. Taylor, op.cit., pp. 83-84.

14. Taylor, op.cit., pp. 84-85.

15. Taylor, op.cit., p. 86.

16. Vischer, *Das 10.Württembergische Infanterie-Regiment Nr. 180 im Weltkrieg 1914-1918*, p. 35.

17. E. Moos, *Das Württembergische Res.-Feld-Artillerie Regiment Nr. 27 im Weltkrieg 1916-1918*, p. 22.

18. *Kriegstagbuch aus Schwaben*, op. cit., pp. 1341-1342.

19. Greiner, op. cit., p. 133.

20. Ibid.

21. *Kriegstagbuch aus Schwaben*, op. cit., p. 1342.

7

La Boisselle, 1 July 1916

The attack against the village of La Boisselle was assigned to the men of the 34th Division (III Corps). The plan called for 12 battalions of infantry to be utilized in the opening phase.[1] This meant that every battalion in the division would be involved in the attack at the onset and there would no readily available reserves in case any part of the assault became held up or if needed to exploit any success.

The advance would take place with four columns, each consisting of three battalions. The two right hand columns were formed by the 101st Brigade in the first two lines and a battalion from the 103rd Brigade in the rear of each column as the third line. The right hand columns would advance toward the *Bécourt Mulde* [Sausage Valley]. The two left columns consisted of the 102nd Brigade in the first two lines with a battalion from the 103rd Brigade as the third line. The left columns would advance toward the *La Boisselle Mulde* [Mash Valley] and around the village of la Boisselle.

The tasks assigned to the men were very optimistic. The first objective called for the two leading waves of infantry to advance 2,000 yards into the German lines, capture four separate trench systems in only 48 minutes. It was almost as if the planners had forgotten about the presence of the German defenders as an obstacle to the advancing troops.

The 2nd objective would be reached only 10 minutes later. While the 101st and 102nd Brigades consolidated their positions the 103rd Brigade would pass through and capture the village of Contalmaison. Finally, the advance would proceed toward the German 2nd Position; this should be accomplished by 10.10 a.m. Once the men reached their final destination a new defensive line would be created that would be used as a starting point to continue the attacks in the days following 1 July.

The plan devised by the British III Corps was similar to those being used on other parts of the Somme front such as Gommecourt and Fricourt. The village of La Boisselle would not be assaulted directly; instead, it was to be flanked on both sides during the main attack and eventually pinched off.

The two left hand columns would advance on either side of the village. While passing along the flank of La Boisselle special bombing parties in the size of a platoon with support from Lewis Guns and Stokes mortars would split off from each column and clear the German trenches on both flanks.

One major factor in making the decision about the method of attack against the village of La Boisselle was that the III Corps staff considered that the preliminary bombardment would literally destroy the German defensive system as well as killing or incapacitating the German garrison inside the village. However their optimism was not shared by the infantry commanders on the ground who for the most part did not feel that the bombardment had been as effective as they had hoped, even with the additional firepower of eight Stokes Mortars that would fire at the village at zero hour. While appearing to have a considerable effect on the village defenses, in reality the Stokes mortars did nothing more than superficial damage to the well developed trench system and had no effect on the mined dugouts.

The village of La Boisselle had been the scene of numerous attacks and daily shellfire

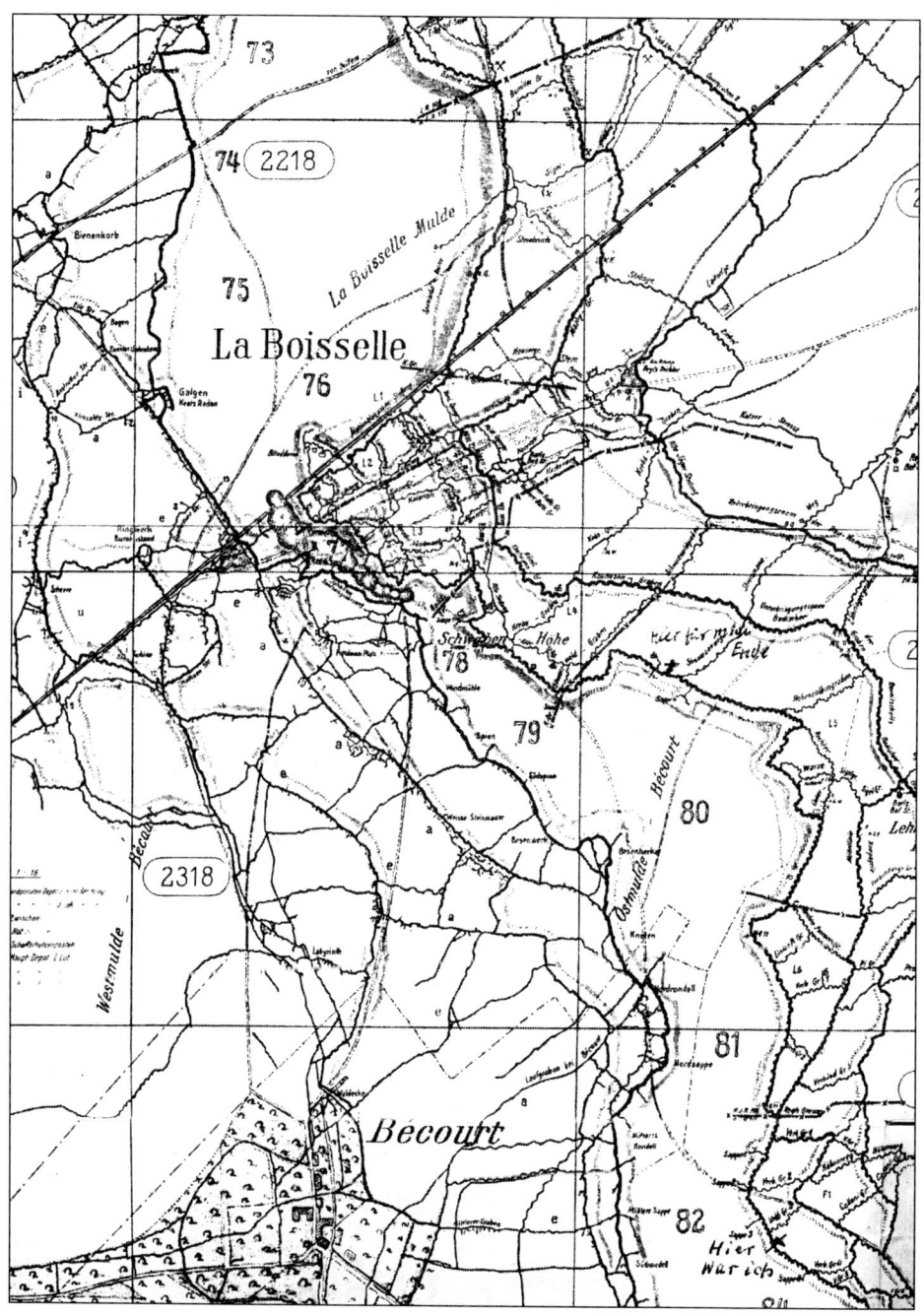

La Boisselle-Fricourt.

for the last 18 months as well as almost constant mine warfare since late 1914. Now, on 1 July 1916, the village was to fall within a few hours of the start of the battle if all went according to the overly optimistic predictions of III Corps.

The symbolic value of this small village far outweighed its strategic value. More effort and resources had been poured into its defense by the Germans and its capture by the French and now the British than most locations on the Somme. It had truly become a point of honour to possess the ruins of this small village for men on both sides of the wire, or perhaps just to the high commands on both sides and not to the average infantryman sitting inside his trench.

If there was one spot on the XIV Reserve Corps front that was prepared to meet the threat of the impending attack it was the village of La Boisselle. For more than a year and a half the once peaceful village astride the road to Albert was turned into a stronghold designed to withstand anything the enemy could throw against it. Already subjected to tens of thousands of high explosive and shrapnel shells the toil and effort by the men of the XIV Reserve Corps month after month had not been in vain.

The numerous mined dugouts that had been created since the winter of 1914/1915 were of sufficient depth to withstand even the heaviest bombardment the British could bring to bear on such a small target area. The proximity to the British trenches was also a factor in the upcoming attack. The opposing lines in the La Boisselle sector were at their closest point just at the tip of the village, some 50 meters or less. It was difficult for the British guns to accurately fire on the German defenses at this location without hitting their own men when the opposing trenches were so close together.

The Germans had also created an extensive mine system that was used, among other

Trench near ruins of church in La Boisselle. (*Zwischen Arras und Péronne*)

things, to house the Moritz 28 North listening station. Multiple mine explosions from all of the adversaries had created an extensive minefield by the tip of La Boisselle. The spoil thrown up by these mines effectively created a barrier that prevented direct observation of a large portion of the German line. Aerial photography and balloon observation had to be used in order to provide a clear picture of the extensive German surface emplacements.

The garrison of the village was used to heavy shelling and the myriad of trenches, saps, underground tunnels and switch lines should slow down an enemy attack and allow any penetration to be contained and then destroyed by prompt counter attacks. Still, the British III Corps staff thought the 'village would be untenable and the Germans in it "wiped out" by the preliminary bombardment, while the flanking shoulder on either side of it would be destroyed by the great mines.'[2]

There were two large mines being utilized in conjunction with the attack against La Boisselle. They had been under construction for many months and had eventually reached the locations that were being targeted for destruction. The mines would perform several critical functions in the attack. Both mines would naturally destroy a large portion of the German defenses at the positions flanking the village. Hopefully they would also kill or incapacitate the garrison at those locations.

The spoil from the mines, a lip some 10-15 feet in height would also provide cover for the attacking troops by protecting their flanks from enfilade fire. The plan called for the mines to be set off at 7.28 a.m. on 1 July followed by the infantry advance with a short delay to allow for the debris to settle. The 2 minute delay from firing the mines to the expected attack would not allow the Germans enough time to occupy and consolidate the mine craters before the attacking troops could overrun them.

The plan of the attack, the minute details and optimistic attitude, from the effect of the bombardment on the trenches to its effect on the average German soldier, was being

RIR 110 column marching toward La Boisselle, June 1916. (Author's collection)

German trenches looking toward *La Boisselle Mulde* (Mash Valley). (*An der Somme*)

prepared by British officers with the best intentions. However they often lacked the firsthand experience needed to make the decisions that would assure even a modicum of success. Many of the planning and the projected outcomes of the overall attack seemed to emphasize the positive over all other reasonable objections or observations made to the contrary.

The British observers facing La Boisselle and the infantry holding the front had a different perspective from being so close to the German lines. The former, tasked with observing the destruction of the German defenses, the latter sending out patrols and raids that tested the strength of the enemy defenses based their opinions on the reality they faced each day.

When patrols approached La Boisselle during the preliminary bombardment they found the defenses damaged but still very formidable. The wire, while in disrepair, still formed an impassable obstacle in most areas. The German infantry were alert and defended their trenches with tenacity, resulting in many of the patrols suffering numerous casualties. Most importantly the German machine guns were never fully silenced throughout the bombardment period. When men were sent out in the early morning hours to clear the British wire in preparation for the attack on the morning of 1 July they were fired upon by the German machine gunners. This did not bode well for the men going over the top a few hours later.

On the other side of the wire the men of RIR 110 were holding the village of La

Boisselle and the positions on both flanks. These men were eagerly waiting for the artillery fire to stop. The constant noise and vibrations from the bombardment was slowly eating away at them while deep under the ground. However, instead of causing the troops to become placid and numb the effect was actually the opposite. The desire to get back at their tormentors was becoming very strong in many of the Badeners who were stuck down inside their dugouts. It would soon be time to give back as good as they got.

At the onset of the battle the regimental battle strength was reported to be 70 officers, 2,500 men and two machine gun companies. In preparation to meet the expected British attack, the La Boisselle sector had been divided into three sub-sectors.

The right sector, the *La Boisselle Mulde* [Mash Valley], was commanded by *Hauptmann* Humricht. This sector ran from the regimental boundary by Ovillers and the neighboring IR 180 to the entrance of the *Kirchstellung* by the *Nationalstrasse*. The front line was manned by the 10th and 1/R110. They were supported by the 3/R110 that was garrisoned in the dugouts of the *Dorfbereitschaft* and the *Mathy Graben*. Humricht was given the task of defending the *La Boisselle Mulde*, to provide flanking protection to the western front of La Boisselle, to support the village garrison and protect the right wing of the regiment in the event of an enemy breakthrough by the neighboring IR 180.

The middle sector, the village of La Boisselle, was commanded by *Hauptmann* Heine. He had the 11th and 9/R110 on the front line, the support company, the 12/R110, was in the *Kirchstellung – Minenwerfer Stellung*. Heine was given the instructions to 'defend La Boisselle, the hinge point of the regimental sector'.

The left sector included *Bécourt Mulde* [Sausage Valley] and the *Lehmgrubenhöhe* under the command of Major Schröder. The left sector was defended by the 5th, 6th, 7th and 8/R110 in the front line. The sector ran from the *Kirchstellung* where it joined the *Blauer Graben* (front line trench). The left wing was the regimental boundary with RIR 111. The sector was supported by the 4/R110 that was located in the *Grüne Graben* on both sides of the *Zähringer Graben*. Schröder was given instructions to block any enemy advance through *Bécourt Mulde* and to safeguard the *Lehmgrubenhöhe*.

The last company, the 2/R110 was in reserve and was placed under the control of the regimental commander. The company was positioned in the *Völkerbereitschaft* with the instructions to protect the left flank of the regiment against any enemy breakthrough by Fricourt or Mametz.

Additional support was provided by the regimental entrenching company as well as a mining *Abteilung* of 70 men from *Landwehr Brigade Ersatz Battalion 55*. These units were accommodated in the *Alte Jägerstellung* and were placed under the command of the 1R/13th *Pionier* Bn. that was located in Sector Heine, the middle sector. Further support came from the 2/23 under *Leutnant* Hans-Joachim Schiefler and the 3/23 that were made subordinate to RIR 110.

Final troop movements were still taking place almost up to the moment of the attack. Schiefler's men had been positioned in the *Völkerbereitschaft* outside of Contalmaison when orders arrived in the night of 30 June to move the company into the *Alte Jägerstellung* and the *Weissbachgraben*. As the men of the 2/23 advanced toward the front through the *Frühlingsgraben* they received only a few scattered shells. Still, the company advanced by small sections in order to space out the men and prevent unnecessary losses from the shellfire.

When the men reached the third trench, the *Alte Jägerstellung,* and turned right toward

Men from *Landwehr Brigade Ersatz Battalion 55*. (Brett Butterworth)

La Boisselle the men discovered that the trench was at full depth and clear of obstructions. This allowed the company to reach their assigned positions much faster than had been expected despite the increased British shrapnel fire being directed on this portion of the German lines. The 2/23 was in its assigned positions by midnight on 30 June.

The third and final platoon of the company under *Leutnant der Reserve* Richter arrived at the *Weissbachgraben* early on 1 July. The company was in the new positions in time for the attack. Two additional platoons from the 3/23 under *Oberleutnant* Gerhard Fürstner remained in support at the *Völkerbereitschaft*.

The regimental machine guns were distributed across all three sectors, mainly in the second and third trenches where they could provide fire support to a wide area as well as effective flanking fire against any troops advancing upon La Boisselle. The regimental staff was in position behind the 3rd trench in *Bécourt Mulde* where they could overlook the entire regimental sector. The machine guns from the LBEB 55 were also distributed at key locations in order to provide additional fire support.

The staff of RIR 110 was fortunate in that a buried telephone cable running from the regimental headquarters to the Middle sector command post and then on to the tip of La Boisselle was still working. The subterranean tunnel at the tip of the village held the Arendt device codenamed Moritz 28 North that was still working. The Moritz stations scattered across the Somme front were quite good at picking up British and French radio messages. Moritz 28 North had picked up the now famous message in the early morning hours of 1 July that indicated an attack was imminent. Copies of this message were sent back to Division headquarters by *Radfahrer* troops and by runner to the neighboring battalions and battery positions. Division headquarters also sent copies of the message to corps headquarters and throughout the German line.

Patrols early on 1 July from the 9/R110 had firmly established that the enemy had set down tape from the southern edge of the *Galgen* [Keat's Redan] in a northeastern direction into the *La Boisselle Mulde*. It was evidently going to used to guide an attack, another clear sign the offensive was going to take place on this day. All preparations were complete; the

Machine gun and crew – RIR 110. (*Reserve-Infanterie-Regiment Nr. 110 im Weltkrieg 1914-1918*)

men had been placed on alert as were all regiments and companies across the German front after receiving word of the intercepted message. Everything was ready to receive the British attack.

On the British side the final preparations had also been made, nothing was left to do but wait for the two mines to be detonated. The mines were not a surprise to the Germans holding La Boisselle. They had been aware of their presence for some time but not their exact locations. In June 1916 the men of RIR 110 determined that the mine being directed against the *Schwabenhöhe* was within 50 meters of the German front line trench. However the final position of the mine was still unknown up to the time of the explosion.

The men in the 9/R110 had heard the distinctive sounds of mining approximately 10 meters from the *Blinddarm* [Y Sap]. As the *Blinddarm* was not considered to be a critical portion of the line and vulnerable to infantry attack as well as underground mining it was decided to evacuate the entire position. The *Blinddarm* would be guarded by regular patrols and a few trench sentries who would listen for enemy mining activity as well as remaining alert for any British patrols or raids.

In both cases the counter measures already underway were increased and every attempt was made to locate and disrupt the British mining activity. Additional men were given to RIR 110 for this purpose including a company from LBEB 55 but they had failed to locate or disrupt the British mining activities before the attack.

At 6.30 a.m. on 1 July 1916 RIR 110 noted that the entire regimental sector was

Unteroffizier Ernst Langerbach 9/R110. (Author's collection)

subjected to the heaviest bombardment yet seen. Guns and mine throwers of every caliber were being used. Almost an hour later the regimental sector was rocked by two massive explosions. The two British mines detected in the weeks prior to the attack had finally been detonated. Even knowing that mining was taking place, their size must have been a surprise to the men of RIR 110 as portions of the German front line simply disappeared in a mass of earth, debris and smoke.

> Our position at the *Blinddarm* that had been previously evacuated and the entire foremost position on the *Schwabenhöhe* flew into the air. A deep crater 50 meters in diameter had formed here. The stones rained down on the regimental sector for a full minute. Gas clouds were discharged.[3]

At 7.28 a.m. the first mine exploded with a gigantic roar, the earth heaved up as if in slow motion, a gigantic explosion erupted into the clear sky above. One British pilot had a clear view of the La Boisselle front and watched as the two massive mines were detonated.

> The whole earth heaved and flashed, a tremendous and magnificent column rose up into the sky. There was an earsplitting roar, drowning all the guns, flinging the machine sideways in the repercussing air. The earth column rose higher and higher to

almost 4,000 feet. There it hung, or seemed to hang, for a moment in the air, like the silhouette of some giant cypress tree, then fell away in a widening cone of dust and debris. A moment later came the second mine, again a roar, the upflung machine, the strange giant silhouette invading the sky. Then the dust cleared and we saw the two white eyes of the craters.[4]

The two mines that had been prepared by the 179th Tunneling Company R.E. had gone off as planned. The mine under the *Schwabenhöhe* was actually two mines set off simultaneously; one loaded with 36,000 pounds of explosives, the other loaded with 24,000 pounds of explosives. The two chambers were 60 feet apart and 52 feet below the surface. The mine under the *Blinddarm* consisted of 60,000 pounds of explosives.

Almost simultaneously the artillery fire on the German front lines suddenly grew silent and was then transferred to the rear areas. All gun positions, all routes leading to the front line now came under heavy fire.

As the smoke and gas cleared the enemy could finally be seen. The British advanced on both sides of *Bécourt Mulde* at a walk. Dense, deeply organized columns attacked out of Bécourt Wood, supposedly with staff and officers mounted on horses, with the apparent belief that everyone in the German lines was either dead or unnerved according to the official account provided by RIR 110. Under the circumstances it is extremely unlikely any British officers made the attack mounted on horseback. Mounted officers had not been seen on the Somme since the French attacks in December 1914.

Shortly after the mines exploded things began to go badly for the 34th Division. The preliminary bombardment on La Boisselle that was being counted upon to destroy the German defenses and trench garrison had not been as effective as the British had hoped for. Much of this was due to the unreliability of the shells being used at the time. Reports had already been received that many shells burst prematurely inside the gun barrels causing

Albrecht Mörser and crew, 28th Reserve Division. (Author's collection)

heavy damage to the weapons as well as numerous casualties among the men. Other shells fell short of their target where they either exploded or as in the case of numerous shells, never went off at all. One British officer crossing no man's land during the attack noted 'a dud shell every two or three yards over several acres of ground.'[5]

The German response to the attack was also probably not what the British planners had counted upon. The average German soldier should either have been killed or made ineffective from the weight of the bombardment; instead, the men of RIR 110 were ready to meet the attack head on:

> The moment of the attack, after long days and nights of unbearable tension, more longed for than feared, had come.[6]

The infantry attack was a failure from the start. The men had to cross an open area between 200 and 800 meters in most places. While the lines were much closer just outside the village of La Boisselle, no direct attack was taking place there. Within 10 minutes 80% of the men in the lead battalions had become casualties from the heavy German fire.

As soon as the bombardment had lifted from the German front line the alarm was sounded inside the German trenches. The men rushed up from their dugouts and took their places along the parapet while the machine gun companies lugged up their heavy guns and ammunition and had them set up to fire within 2 minutes of the alarm being sounded. The men from RIR 110 must have been amazed at what they saw through the smoke and dust.

> Wave after wave of riflemen came forth out of the 2nd and 3rd enemy trenches and advanced at a walk in and on both sides of the *Bécourt Mulde*.[7]

Once the wall of smoke had dissipated the men in Sector Humricht could see the advancing British waves. The attackers were met with a wall of machine gun fire as well as German artillery fire from Groups Leinekugel and Gericke whose guns were being fired as rapidly as the men could load them.

The batteries supporting the men in La Boisselle maintained their fire throughout 1 July in spite of being targeted by numerous British batteries that were intent on destroying them.

> At 6.30 a.m. strong bombardment from all calibers started; it lasted the entire day with only short pauses. The 6/RFAR 28 fired. Every hand there was needed, especially as the battery was almost smothered in empty materials (shell baskets, shell casings). The watchful aircraft immediately ordered fire, which also promptly came; from 10 a.m. on, including from heavy calibers, 12 and 15cm.[8]

The defenders in Sector Humricht reported seeing up to 10-20 lines of British troops advancing against the crater field and toward the German trenches, coming from the British front line trench as well as rear support trenches. At the right wing of the sector being defended by the 10/R110, the enemy was completely repulsed. The men attacking the 10/R110 were actually from the 23rd Brigade, 8th Division that was attacking the neighboring Ovillers Sector.

Some of the attackers from the left hand column of the 102nd Brigade did manage to

Death notice for *Ersatz Reservist* Gustav Hof, 5/R110. Killed in action 1 July 1916.
He was listed as Eugen Hof on the initial *Verlustlisten*. (*Freiburger Zeitung*)

penetrate the trenches of the 1/R110 by attacking up the *La Boisselle Mulde* as well as using the gap and the flanking protection created by the mine crater at the *Blinddarm*. They overran parts of the position and then advanced via the *Mittelweg* and *Grenzweg* toward the battalion command post La Boisselle.

There are British reports that indicate a German dugout was found close by the Y Sap mine crater that held 1 officer and 35 men 'thoroughly cowed'. The account continues by stating that the German officer felt that a further nine dugouts equally full must have been destroyed by the mine. These allegations are simply not supported by the reported casualties from the company holding the sector where the mine detonated, the 11/R110.

It is probably true that a large number of deep dugouts had been destroyed or seriously damaged by the large mine. As this area had been evacuated prior to the attack and was only being manned by sentries and patrols then the dugouts were more than likely empty at 7.28 a.m. when the explosion took place. This is supported further by the fatal casualties reported by the 11/R110 for the fighting on 1 July 1916: 8 men killed in action and approximately 18 men wounded, not the 324 officers and men that would have been killed, wounded or missing if the British report had been correct.

Hauptmann Heine with support from *Leutnants* Stradtmann, Bernhardi and Pommer and one platoon from the 12/R110 attacked the British frontally. Since the attack against the 10/R110 had broken down, the company was able to provide support to the endangered sector of the 1/R110. *Leutnant* Wirthwein (10/R110) accompanied by bombing parties attacked the British left flank. *Leutnant* Kircher and *Feldwebel* Hille with bombing parties from the 3/R110 attacked from the direction of the *Grenzweg* and *Steinbruch Graben*.

The fighting was severe inside the maze of German trenches and it was difficult to determine where the opposing sides were located as the fighting took place in the confines of the trenches. The fighting in the sector of the 1/R110 became very fierce as groups of men fought for control over each section of the trench. The company commander, *Leutnant* Gutjahr and *Leutnant* Kneer were among the men killed on 1 July. The fighting on this day would claim the lives of many company leaders across the La Boisselle sector. The fighting became even more difficult after the British had been able to set up a machine gun near the mine crater and opened fire at the German trenches at almost point blank range.

Machine gun fire from La Boisselle from the guns of the *LBEB 55* under *Hauptmann der Landwehr* von Rohr along with defensive fire from the 1/*Pionier* Bn 13 prevented the British flanking platoon from making any headway into the village. Additional long range support came from machine guns from IR 180 located near Ovillers. The fire from IR 180 was combined with fire from the 3/R110 in the support line, both of which assisted the men of the 1/R110 in preventing the British from expanding their gains any deeper into the German trench system. When the fighting died down somewhat it was determined that the British penetration had been confined to a narrow area inside the German trenches.

Vizefeldwebel Laasch, 12/R110 was a senior non-commissioned officer in the reserve platoon of the 12th Coy under *Leutnant der Reserve* Pommer when the attack began. His unit was positioned in the rear defenses of La Boisselle ready to be deployed as needed.

I belonged to the reserve platoon of the battalion that was led by *Leutnant der Reserve* Pommer that lay in the *Mittelweg* with 6 to 8 Groups. The seven days of bombardment had hardly caused us any losses. We felt extreme joy that the deep dugouts constructed by us with hard work also protected us against the heavy caliber shells. Admittedly, whoever went above as a sentry could barely still recognize the position; instead of the well-developed trenches he saw one crater alongside another; the last wall remnants of La Boisselle became crushed into powder in these days of innumerable shells.

When the English infantry began their mass attack with the huge explosion at the 5th Company on the morning of 1 July we immediately made ourselves ready to be deployed. The first command that reached us called for *Leutnant* Pommer to the head of the 12th Company and transferred the leadership of the reserve platoon to me. And then it came, how so often in the war; further orders did not arrive and the leader of the support became forced to deal with the developing situation independently. I observed the front from behind the remnants of a thorn hedge. The English artillery had already transferred its fire back behind the regimental crater. Very shortly I determined that the enemy had penetrated RIR 111 on the left of us. However who could describe our horror when I saw entire clusters of Englishmen suddenly behind us at the regimental crater! They flooded over the *Mathy Graben* and through the *La Boisselle Mulde* back into their old positions without being fired upon from anyone.

I had my groups out of the dugouts in an instant. We fired, partly standing upright, into the Englishmen at close range. Did the excitement race through my veins or was our success still not damning enough for me? I staggered around between the groups and shouted; 'Blast it, fire at them, fire at them!' until an annoyed *Landwehrmann* yelled at me while loading: 'By thunder *Herr Feldwebel*, I am firing!' I fired there with him and it grew quieter. How we knocked them over like hares! It attracted my attention that these Tommies who were flooding to the rear did not receive any sort of fire while crossing our foremost line (10th or 11th Company). Were they all dead, or prisoners? I was worried about the left flank of my platoon and ran alone down the

Reported to be a photograph of *Leutnant der Reserve* Josef Böhlefeld, 6/R110 taken on 1 July 1916. (*Reserve-Infanterie-Regiment Nr. 110 im Weltkrieg 1914-1918*)

Mittelweg in the direction of the forward line with only a hand grenade in my hand. When I curved around a traverse 3 Tommies were suddenly opposite me.

I threw my hand grenade in front of their feet and jumped back as fast as lightning. When I returned again with a few men I found only one severely wounded man in front of us and one dead (an English First Lieutenant, he had red hair and many freckles). During further advances the *Mittelweg* proved to be free from the enemy. Meanwhile my groups had since come up behind me.[9]

Laasch and his men were able to advance to a point where they flanked the attack on the nearby village of Ovillers as described in the previous chapter.

After several hours of heavy fighting, primarily with hand grenades, the German counter attack had succeeded completely and the entire *Blauer Stellung* (front line) was in the possession of RIR 110. There were inevitable losses to RIR 110 including more company leaders such as *Leutnant* Bernhardi who was killed and *Hauptmann* Heine who was severely wounded.[10]

The distance between the opposing lines in the attack by the 3rd Column, the 102nd Brigade south of the village and north of the mine crater by the *Schwabenhöhe,* was less than 200 yards. The first British waves quickly crossed the open terrain while under heavy fire from machine guns located along their front and especially from the left flank. Fire from the guns positioned inside the village had also been able to enfilade the attacking lines of men.

Thanks to the destruction of a large portion of the front line along with the garrison of the 5/R110 by the mine explosion the 3rd Column was able to penetrate the German front line and advance deeper into the German trenches.

At 5 a.m. [Sic] on 1 July a huge mine hit into the 8th [Sic] Company of our regiment, whereupon started a terrible bombardment by the English. Our trenches had been partly leveled anyway through the previous ten days of bombardment. Large losses had occurred to be sure, but the understanding by the English that everything short and small ought to be dead and that they no longer expected any opposition by the Germans, as they began the offensive on the 1st of July on the Somme, was very false. Resistance was encountered which the English had not expected. They became held up at most of the positions, including in the sector of the 6th Company.

Within the 6th Company the platoon of *Leutnant der Reserve* Böhlefeld commanded flanking positions, he the right wing, I the left wing. The company had suffered heavily during the bombardment, but did not yield even the width of a finger before the colossal superiority of the enemy. The English, apparently with the intention of deceiving us, waved cloths. I suspected this and quickly resolved to send a request to the artillery by an orderly to send a few shots on this target, whereupon the Tommies waving cloths ran away like hares. *Offizier Aspirant* Brachat[11]

The men of the 2/23 observed the British advance through the *Bécourt Mulde* from their trench and the company opened fire with their sights set at 800 meters. It was an experience the men appreciated after the never ending entrenching and ever-present danger when exposed to enemy fire.

One could clearly see the Englishmen wearing their packs using field glasses. Far shone the grey-green steel helmets. The lines became visibly thinner and thinner and 'Hurra', they went to the rear. However always new skirmish lines came up and filled up the big losses. The men of the 2nd stood and fired as if on the rifle range. They grinned at their *Leutnants* with pipes in their mouths and were happy. This was an opportunity to do something other than the endless entrenching. 110er, men from the 2nd Coy, a machine gun crew smoked at their guns. Although the *Alte Jägerstellung* was 700 meters distant from the foremost trench it proved almost incomprehensible that not a single shot from the English batteries fell on it.[12]

Once the trenches of the 5/R110 were overrun the advancing British troops moved forward against the *Grüner Stellung* [Second trench system]. It was here where they came up against the support company, the 4/R110, which held the enemy advance in check. The 4/R110 then mounted a counter attack using rifles, hand grenades and supporting machine gun fire. There were too few men left in the 3rd Column to withstand this attack and the men from the 34th Division were forced back toward the old German front line where they were able to hold out inside the trenches around the crater that was later named the Lochnagar crater.

Despite the heavy defensive fire coming from multiple trench lines and heavy losses the British seemed to have an unlimited reserve of men and inevitably they were able to make headway. The British advance continued and at 9.15 a.m. the first German trench fell to the attackers. A short time later the second trench in front of Company Schiefler also fell to the British onslaught. Now the enemy was directly in front of the 2/23.

At this time the British advanced toward the *Alte Jägerstellung* and ran into the platoon of *Leutnant der Reserve* Genzmer that was located at the area where the *Krebsgraben* joined the *Alte Jägerstellung*. A hand grenade fight broke out between the opposing sides as the British attempted to bomb their way deeper into the German lines. During the fighting Genzmer became severely wounded by a hand grenade and the platoon was turned over to

Death notice for *Ersatz Reservist* Ludwig Götzinger, 5/R110.
Killed in action 1 July 1916. (*Freiburger Zeitung*)

Vizefeldwebel Styrnal.

It soon became evident that the platoon under Styrnal was going to be overwhelmed in the fighting as more British troops arrived and placed even more pressure on the dwindling number of men still capable of fighting. It was determined that only a bold move could save the situation. *Leutnant der Reserve* Welzel and *Leutnant* Apfeld evaluated the situation and ordered a counter attack by the remaining men under their command. The men of the 2/23 rushed the British troops and quickly threw them out of the endangered section of trench.

The attack by the second column from the 101st Brigade was directed against the German line to the south of the Lochnagar crater at the *Schwabenhöhe*. The battalions that comprised this brigade delayed their attack for an additional 5 minutes in order to allow the mine debris to settle. It turns out that there was little danger from the debris; however the additional time did allow the men from RIR 110 to set up their machine guns and man the front line trenches in order to meet the attack.

The lip of the mine did present an obstacle to some portions of the German defenses but overall the men in the second column had to face the same dangers while crossing no man's land. German machine guns from their front and from both flanks poured fire into the succeeding waves of attackers. The failure of the first column to capture a feature of the German lines designated as Sausage Redoubt permitted the defenders to pour heavy fire directly into the right flank of the second column of the 101st Brigade with devastating results.

Oberleutnant Kienitz, the commander of one of the machine gun companies was positioned at the *Zähringer Graben* where it joined the *Badischer Graben* in the second trench of the first line system. Several guns were positioned close to one another and had a clear field of fire over the front line trench and dominated no man's land.

Our machine guns and infantry silently expected the close approach of the enemy. Not until he was meters distant from the trench did the fire from our machine guns and the individual fire of the riflemen roar like a hurricane into the close detachments of the enemy. Standing upon the parapet, individual men hurled hand grenades toward the enemy that had lain down and in barely one minute the battlefield seemed dead. However, soon individual small groups began to escape, then entire throngs, to Bécourt and finally it seemed as if the entire field of men wanted to flood back into the exit positions. There the pursuit fire of our infantry and machine guns struck into them and in a bold daredevil manner a few men stormed toward the Englishmen and brought back prisoners. The nonstop fire of our guns rattled for two hours; then the fighting in the *Bécourt Mulde* died down.[13]

The main thrust had taken place and other than some initial success north of the village and just south of the village of La Boisselle the British had little to show for their efforts. Losses continued to increase by the minute and there were no reserves at hand to offer assistance.

The greatest success found by the attacking troops of the 34th Division on this day came at the far left wing of RIR 110 where it joined RIR 111. The junction of the two regiments was the weakest portion of the German line in this sector. Here the British bombardment had been very effective. Heavy caliber mines had damaged or destroyed many of the dugouts being occupied by the 8/R110 resulting in numerous losses before the attack even occurred.

The damage had been so great and the losses so high for the 8th Coy that additional supports were needed. Shortly before the attack occurred the 8th Coy reported that only 80 men were still capable of action. The situation in the neighboring RIR 111 was not much different. The loss of so many dugouts required the men to be concentrated in the remaining usable dugouts but this left large gaps in the trenches. The gap between the two regiments would eventually grow to 150 meters in width.

Just hours before the attack began the sole support company in the regiment, the 2/R110 was moved from the *Völkerbereitschaft* and sent to the left wing of the regiment with orders to close the gap and secure the regimental flank.

One platoon from the 8/R110 under *Leutnant* Wölfle[14] was positioned inside dugouts in the *Totenwäldchen*. This platoon would help seal the gap by providing rifle fire from their position as well as helping protect the regimental left flank. *Oberleutnant* Kienitz, 2MG/R110 moved one of his machine guns to Platoon Wölfle in order to provide the small group with additional firepower. The remaining men of the 8th Coy were sent to the *Völkerbereitschaft* where they would join the 2/23 under *Leutnant* Schiefler.

The 2/R110 did its best to restore the integrity of the German line but there was simply not enough time or men to adequately close the gap. When the 2/R110 took over the former position of the 8/R110 it consisted of 130 rifles. The men were distributed in seven surviving dugouts and the three platoons were assigned their trench positions to await the expected British attack. The right was covered by Platoon Dumas, the center by the company commander *Leutnant der Reserve* Heine and the left by *Leutnant* Offenkop.

When it became light enough to see the men of the 2/R110 discovered that their position had an effective field of fire of between 15 to 40 meters. After these distances the ground dropped off slightly where the *Bécourt Mulde* started. The flank was also protected by a machine gun located in the 2nd trench under *Leutnant* Hauffe. *Leutnant* Heine had little time left to determine how bad the situation had become. He received a report a short time later and it did not contain good news.

> *Leutnant* Offenkop sent me a message shortly before the attack reporting: The adjoining company R111 did not occupy 150 meters, from the regimental border until Sap 1, has left only 4-5 Groups in the forward-most trench (by us, the 2nd trench) and moved back 9-10 Groups in their 2nd (for us 3rd) trench. Furthermore they have removed the machine gun from R111 covering our area. The machine gun inserted with Platoon Offenkop was no longer in service. *Leutnant der Reserve* Heine,
>
> At 8.30 a.m. [7.30 a.m. British time] followed an explosion that allowed the company to occupy their positions in time and to throw back the immensely superior attacker along the entire line, except Platoon Dumas (on the right and on the left of the *Pioniergraben*). Here attackers suddenly broke out of a sap (Russian) 10 meters distant and killed the Groups of the 2nd and 6th Companies that were lying in their dugouts with hand grenades. Immediately part of the enemy lugged equipment out of the Russian Sap and with it consolidated the right *Pioniergraben* for defense (towards La Boisselle). The other part moved in dense crowds along the *Pioniergraben* toward the 2nd position only to find no opposition. *Leutnant* Dumas came to me (Heine) in the middle of the company according to the alarm only to topple and fall to the ground dead. The company had held off the attacker approximately 1 hour, until they attacked on the right and on the left and from behind and were worn down. With it fell *Leutnant* Offenkop. I became forced back into a dugout by hand grenades with 3 unwounded men who had remained with me [at 9.30] in the morning and was taken prisoner. I could still see how the attackers near to R111 moved toward the *Totenwäldchen* (*Leutnant* Wölfle had also fallen here, from R110), furthermore how the enemy had already placed a telephone line from the *Lehmgrubenhöhe* to the rear. *Landwehrmann* Fehrenbach had particularly distinguished himself, he remained at his unprotected sentry post despite 1½ hours of bombardment and saved the company by timely alerting them before they could be overrun (he was wounded). The company has stoutly defended itself to the last. *Leutnant der Reserve Heine*, 2/R110[15]

As a result of the large gap that had appeared between RIR 110 and RIR 111 the British were able to penetrate the German front line shortly after reaching it. After occupying the first line trench the British continued to advance deeper into the German trenches as well as attempting to expand their gains both right and left. The men of the 2/R110 that formed the left wing of the regiment suddenly found themselves being attacked on their left flank as well as from the rear and the company suffered particularly heavy losses, especially in prisoners.

The heavy flanking rifle and machine gun fire against the left wing of the first British column forced some of the units to veer too far to the right and they eventually ended up headed toward the neighboring sector of Fricourt. Due to this unexpected movement the column subsequently failed to capture several key strong points inside the German lines at La Boisselle.

The British troops that had managed to penetrate the German front line now swarmed through the German trenches as they moved along the *Pionier Graben* and *Sigel Graben* and

Mounted officers and enlisted man – RIR 110. (Author's collection)

the *Kollonenweg*. The enemy advanced over the hill and had reached a spot on both sides of the Fricourt-Contalmaison road where he was in the vicinity of the *Völkerbereitschaft*. This advance now placed British troops in the rear of RIR 110 and could mean disaster for the regiment if the penetration was not contained and then quickly destroyed.

Every available man was needed to throw the enemy back. The British were now in the rear of the 3/RFAR 29, called Battery Fröhlich and the staff of Artillery Group *Scharfe Eck*. Once this threat was recognized by *Leutnant* Strüvy, 3/RFAR 29, he quickly assembled the battery runners, telephone operators and men from a nearby construction company. Strüvy's makeshift company advanced toward the British threat. One gun from the 3rd Battery was also dragged out of its emplacement where it could fire at almost point blank range into the British positions.

The 6/RFAR 28 and other batteries from RFAR 28 opened fire on the advancing British troops once they were made aware of how far the enemy had penetrated into the German lines. With all communication cut off between the batteries and the headquarters of RIR 110 the gun crews did not have any new information on where the opposing lines were located and as such continued to fire on previously known target coordinates.

An artillery officer, *Leutnant* Ehrenberg, made his way to the command post of RIR 110 in the *Kaisergraben* where he was advised of the current situation facing the regiment. Ehrenberg returned to his battery with the information that the British were occupying the *Pioniergraben* and had already installed several machine guns in the trench. The battery target map was consulted and the guns were directed to fire into the British ranks. Shell after shell was directed at the *Pioniergraben* as quickly as the men could load their guns. Later reports from nearby infantry groups indicated that the heavy fire had been very effective against the British soldiers.

During this time one machine gun that was positioned inside the second trench by *Oberleutnant* Kienitz was joined by *Leutnant* Hauffe who had recognized the danger

Death notice for *Vizefeldwebel* Walter Houben, 8/R110. Killed
in action 1 July 1916. (*Freiburger Zeitung*)

threatening the regimental position. Hauffe had the machine gun quickly placed into
position on the parapet and was about to operate it personally when the gun jammed after
the first shot was fired.

The advancing British troops were so close that it was impossible to clear the jam or
apparently to remove the gun to another position where it could be placed back in action.
Hauffe used a hand grenade and destroyed the gun so that it would not fall into British
hands intact. He then literally ran as fast as he could from his position in order to avoid
being captured. He was trying to reach the second machine gun in the sector that was
positioned by Platoon Wölfle. Hauffe ran across the open ground between the trenches and
whether as a result of British fire or simply losing his direction he missed Platoon Wölfle.
Finally, after evading the British troops swarming through the German trenches Hauffe
reached the command post of the neighboring RIR 111 by Fricourt where he apparently
collapsed 'as if he was half mad' as a result of his frantic dash to safety.

During Hauffe's escape the British advance encountered the position held by Platoon
Wölfle, and this small group of men and their machine gun were overrun and reportedly
killed to the last man while fighting against the superior enemy numbers. Nothing is
known of the actual circumstances of the fate of Platoon Wölfle.

Facing the imminent threat of a British attack into the rear of the regimental position
the men of RIR 110 took every step possible to stop the British advance. *Leutnants* Greiner
and Nothnagel quickly assembled every man they could find in the *Völkerbereitschaft*. The
Construction Company, one platoon from the 3/23 and approximately 60 men from the 8/
R110 under the command of *Leutnant* Scheifele counter attacked on their own initiative.

Additional troops were involved in this fighting from the neighboring RIR 111; parts
of the 9th and 11/R111. These companies attacked from the direction of Fricourt in an
attempt to stop the British advance into the gap that had formed where RIR 111 and RIR
110 had once connected.[16]

The counter attacks were working. The forward elements of the British advance
were forced back over the *Kolonnenweg* and *Sigelgraben* on to the *Totenwäldchen* and

Pioniergraben. During the fighting a field gun from the 1/RFAR 29 was recaptured and the gun crew was liberated from their captivity. The gun crew immediately opened fire on the enemy troops as they were withdrawing and fired upon the newly formed British front line south of the *Sigelgraben* and the *Totenwäldchen.*

At the same time a smaller British detachment attempted to press forward through the *Sigelgraben* by the command post of the II/R110 and had reached a medical dugout in the *Frühlingsgraben.* This advance was stopped and thrown back by a determined counter attack against the invading enemy troops by men under the command of *Leutnant* Reichwald, the adjutant of the II/R110. The bombing parties under Reichwald captured 18 prisoners that were then sent to the rear.

Following the successful counter attack *Leutnant* Reichwald, who had been slightly wounded during the fighting, rode down the hill on a horse at the gallop toward the regimental headquarters to report on the situation at the left wing of his battalion. *Hauptmann* Wagener from the regimental staff attempted once more to report to division headquarters about the situation facing RIR 110 and to request an additional two battalions and machine guns as reinforcements.

The first reports about the fighting at La Boisselle arrived at the regimental staff headquarters in Contalmaison at about 9 a.m. At the same time requests for more ammunition was received. The ammunition consumption was quite large and there was a danger that existing stockpiles could run out at a critical moment. Based on this request the infantry cartridge wagon north of Martinpuich was held ready to move forward when ordered.

The ammunition wagon for the machine gun companies received immediate orders to travel to the front at all cost and unload two-thirds of their load at the *Regiments Trichter* [Regimental Crater by La Boisselle] and one third at the *Völkerbereitschaft.*

After approximately one hour the ammunition wagon that was being conducted by older *Landwehr* men had broken through the British barrage fire at the gallop and had reached their destinations while still under heavy fire. The ammunition was unloaded as ordered and the wagon returned to the rear without the loss of a single man and with the loss of only one horse killed. The infantry at the front now had ample supplies of machine gun ammunition needed to keep up their high rate of fire.

However, not every attempt to re-supply ammunition to the front line was as successful.

At the midday time two ammunition wagons came at the gallop behind Position VI (6/FAR 50); there was a mighty cloud of dirt and a terrifying noise. When the view was free again, the eight horses and three drivers lay dead. A pilot had allowed the teams to drive up until they were behind the battery and directed a heavy mortar on them. Later the 6/FAR 50 and 6/RFAR 26 still each received three wagons of ammunition; fortunately the teams came and since went away safely.[17]

While the fighting continued in the morning hours fresh troops arrived at the *Völkerbereitschaft* that consisted of the 3/LBEB 55 under *Hauptmann* Stoll and parts of the 1/LBEB 55 under *Hauptmann* Kessler. These troops were immediately placed in possession of the regimental reserve in the sector commanded by Major Schröder. He was also given control over the 2/23.

The men from LBEB 55 arrived in the position about 11 a.m. Company Stoll was later given orders to proceed through the *Grüner Graben* up to the *Pioniergraben*. From there they would clear the *Pioniergraben* up to the *Blauer Stellung*, establish a connection with the 6/R110 and prepare the *Pioniergraben* for defense. The 2/23 also received orders to advance through the *Braun Graben* up to the *Pioniergraben* and clear out any enemy soldiers they found.

Both companies sent back reports at 3 p.m. that indicated the *Pioniergraben* was so strongly occupied by the British that it was not possible to capture it with the men at hand. The reserve units were then given new orders. Since the *Pioniergraben* could not be taken a new defensive line needed to be established. The connection with the 6/R110 was considered crucial for this plan and the different units were directed to establish a connection with this company.

The new line that would be formed had the 6/R110 occupying the *Blauer Graben* (old front line), the left hand portion of the *Sigelgraben* up to where the 3/LBEB 55 and parts of the 1/LBEB 55 were located. The *Landwehr* units would then occupy the *Sigelgraben* up to the II/R110 dugout. The 2/23 received orders to 'occupy the *Sigelgraben* to the left from there [the battalion dugout]'. Two platoons occupied this position up to the *Frühlingsgraben* while the third platoon was ordered to join Company Steinemann (RIR 110) and provide support. Finally, the Construction Company and the lone platoon from the 3/23 under *Leutnant* Greiner would occupy the *Frühlingsgraben* and *Kolonnenweg*. The latter units was also to establish a connection with the neighboring troops in RIR 111

The different companies took up their positions while under the heaviest artillery fire and were able to occupy their sectors with minimal losses. During the evening hours the two platoons in the *Sigel Graben* were attacked from the rear by enemy troops. Despite the seriousness of the situation they managed to drive off the British and hold their position. Since the orders called for the men to hold the *Sigel Graben* under all circumstances the men returned to developing it for defense against an attack coming from either side of the trench.

Earlier, the gap between RIR 110 and RIR 111 had greatly assisted the successful British breakthrough. Now, a new front had been established but with the weak German forces at hand it was doubtful that the men could withstand any serious British attack. The situation at the right wing of the regimental sector was unclear. It was difficult to know what portion of the trench system was occupied by German troops or British troops. Visibility from inside the trenches was limited and it was decidedly unhealthy to expose any portion of your body above the trench.

> It had become somewhat quieter in the course of the afternoon. I attempted to establish a connection with the 8th Company, however I found only a single double sentry post from a Platoon Group of 6/R110. I then gave the order that all of the people of this platoon had to occupy the trench. As I went further in the direction of the 8th Company, I suddenly heard 'Halt'. I stood in front of a barricade and firmly determined through listening and observing that it was occupied by Englishmen. I went back, to relate the news to my platoon, that meanwhile because of ongoing shrapnel fire had become even smaller. *Offizier Aspirant* Brachat[18]

The new front formed by the evening of 1 July consisted of the old *Blauer Stellung* (front line trench) from the right regimental boundary up to the southern junction of the

Reported to be a photograph of *Leutnant der Reserve* Josef Böhlefeld, 6/R110 taken
on 1 July 1916. (*Reserve-Infanterie-Regiment Nr. 110 im Weltkrieg 1914-1918*)

Kirchstellung in the *Granathof Stellung*. Hand grenade sentries occupied the *Blauer Graben*
to the south and the *'Alte Stellung'* toward the *Schwabenhöhe* crater. The new front line then
continued with the *Nagelgraben, Kaufmanngraben, Schwarzwaldgraben, Blauer Stellung*
up to the left *Sigelgraben, Frühlingsgraben* and *Kolonnenweg*.

After much effort *Hauptmann* Wagener managed to make contact with division
headquarters when a telephone connection was re-established late in the evening. While
the line still worked he provided details on the events taking place by RIR 110 and once
again urgently requested reinforcements. *Ordonnanz Offizier Leutnant* Pilger on the
division staff advised Wagener that all forces available to the division had been sent against
the British troops that had broken through at Montauban and that none were available to
assist RIR 110.

RIR 110 did learn that the neighboring regiment, RIR 111 was going to evacuate
Fricourt and occupy the Intermediate position south of Mametz Wood in connection to
the left wing of RIR 110. While this was their intent there was still no connection between
the two regiments. The regimental adjutant *Leutnant* Erb advised the division that no
connection could be established with RIR 111 and that the left wing of RIR 110 at the
Kolonnenweg was hanging in the air. In order to meet the threat of the exposed flank two
companies were ordered to move to Contalmaison and occupy the southern edge of the
village.

RIR 110 was determined to hold the second position between Bazentin le Petit and
Pozières. Help did arrive at midnight when the leader of the 2nd *Musketen* Company
arrived at the regimental headquarters and reported that he had been assigned to provide
support for the regiment. His men and *Musketen* were distributed in the line with the
majority being positioned at the southern edge of Contalmaison and approximately one
third sent to the 8/R110 at the *Kolonnenweg*.

The stage was set for 2 July. Only time would tell as to what the men from RIR 110 and
their support troops would face on the second day of fighting. It would not be long before
they found out.

One observation made by the men of RIR 110 during the heavy fighting on 1 July 1916
may explain some of the shortcomings of the overall British attack against La Boisselle. It

is not to say that the opinion is accurate or that it portrays the average British soldier, it is simply an observation made at the time of the heavy fighting that was important enough to be added to the regimental history..

> At the places where the trenches were completely buried by being blown up (*Schwabenhöhe*), or where almost all dugouts were destroyed (*Lehmgrubenhöhe*), the enemy was making good progress at first. The enemy machine guns and mine throwers in the captured trenches were inflicting heavy losses on us when rolling up our trenches. Smaller teams and individual men surrendered as soon as they saw that they would shortly lose out. The English officers, on the other hand led their Other Ranks from the front with considerable dash, but one had the impression of a more athletic than militarily educated leadership. Some opportunity to expand their successes was not recognized by them. Where the leadership was lacking, the Other Ranks completely failed to act. We often saw entire platoons bunch together so long until one after the other was shot down. Apparently the enemy was expecting the total destruction of our trench with its garrison through the artillery preparation.[19]

Notes

1. The 34th Division consisted of the 101st, 102nd and 103rd Brigades: 101st Brigade (15th Royal Scots, 16th Royal Scots, 10th Lincolnshire, 11th Suffolk), 102nd Brigade (20th Northumberland Fusiliers, 21st Northumberland Fusiliers, 22nd Northumberland Fusiliers, 23rd Northumberland Fusiliers), 103rd Brigade (24th Northumberland Fusiliers, 25th Northumberland Fusiliers, 26th Northumberland Fusiliers, 27th Northumberland Fusiliers).
2. Edmonds, op. cit., p. 376.
3. Greiner, op. cit., p. 123.
4. M. Stedman, *La Boisselle Ovillers/Contalmaison*, p. 43, from C.A. Lewis, *Sagittarius Rising.*
5. Edmonds, op. cit., p. 374
6. Greiner, op. cit., p. 123
7. Ibid.
8. A. Frick, *Elebnisse in den ersten Tagen der Somme-Schlacht (24 Juni bis 7 Juli 1916)*, p. 8.
9. Greiner, op. cit., p. 132
10. While it is not feasible at present to determine which men had been wounded on 1 July it is possible to identify the men who were killed fighting on this date. The overall losses of the III/R110 as well as the 1st and 3/R110 during the fighting on 1 July in the village and north of La Boisselle show that the defenders lost far less than the casualties suffered by the attacking battalions. The III/R110 suffered only 25 men killed on 1 July while the 1st Coy, where the initial breakthrough took place lost 33 men killed. The supporting 3/R110 lost the fewest men, 3 killed, during the heavy fighting, making the fatal losses suffered by the infantry in RIR 110 in the La Boisselle and right hand sectors 58 officers and men killed on this day. Most of the credit for the low number of men killed can go to the hard work performed on the trenches in the 18 months prior to the attack. Even if damaged the trenches were more than adequate to provide shelter and protection to the men defending them.
11. Greiner, op. cit., p. 304
12. P. Fiedel, *Geschichte des Infanterie-Regiments von Winterfeldt (2. Oberschlesisches) Nr. 23*, p. 123.
13. Greiner, op. cit., p. 125.

14. *Leutnant* Wölfle was reported killed on 28 June 1916 in the regimental records and does not appear in the various *Verlustlisten* associated with the fighting on 1 July 1916. The German Official History *Somme Nord Teil 1* indicates that he was fighting on 1 July and that he was killed along with his men on this date. In addition a report filed by *Leutnant der Reserve* Heine also confirms Wölfle's death on 1 July. His name was subsequently added to the *Verlustlisten* at the end of the book based upon the evidence presented. .

15. Greiner, op. cit., p. 303. The report on the events of 1 July 1916 submitted by *Leutnant der Reserve* Heine was received in a rather circuitous manner. Heine wrote the report in the English Prisoner of War Camp at Donington Hall. It was wrapped inside a cigarette and carried to Switzerland by a severely wounded officer who was being exchanged.

16. See Chapter 9.

17. Frick, op. cit., p. 9.

18. Greiner, op. cit., p. 304.

19. Greiner, op. cit., p. 302.

8

La Boisselle, 2–3 July 1916

2–3 July 1916

After the intense fighting on 1 July both armies desperately needed a period of rest and recuperation. However the circumstances only allowed for a brief respite for the men. Both sides needed to reorganize their units, recover the wounded and dead and to make sense of the situation facing them. Accurate intelligence was often difficult to come by and in many instances the men inside the trenches had no real idea of exactly where friend or foe was situated.

Fresh supplies of food, water and especially rifle and machine gun ammunition and hand grenades were needed as current stocks were critically low. The British casualties were far higher than had been expected and were simply overwhelming the medical facilities that had been created to handle a much smaller number of losses. Many of the British trenches were filled with wounded and virtually impassable which only added to the overall confusion that was present following the heavy fighting.

A British attack scheduled for late in the evening on 1 July was cancelled due to the inability to move men through the throng of dead and wounded in order to reach their starting point in time. No new attacks would take place until 2 July at the earliest.

The British attack for the most part had been a failure. Thousands of men were killed or wounded and there was little to show for such a sacrifice. However, while many of the attacks on 1 July did not accomplish anything of lasting value there were areas where the German lines had been penetrated and it would take some time to determine the location of friendly troops inside the German lines. It would also take time to determine just where

Slightly wounded men following the heavy fighting on 1 July 1916. (Author's collection)

to send reinforcements.

The batteries needed fresh supplies of ammunition and the gunners desperately needed some rest. New target coordinates were required before the guns could be used to their full effect.

While the German losses had been far less then their opponents the number of men wounded also placed a heavy strain on the medical facilities. The men from RIR 110, IR 23, Württemberg *Pioniers,* LBEB 55 and supporting artillery batteries, while suffering far fewer losses in comparison to the British, had still suffered greatly in the attack and many companies were drastically reduced in strength. In the week-long bombardment and fighting in the first day of July RIR 110 had lost more than a third of the regiment.

The men on both sides were simply exhausted. Stress, mental and physical fatigue brought on by the high levels of tension and the exertion needed to fight for most of a day in intense heat had taken a toll on the men on both sides. With the situation being so uncertain there was little chance of obtaining sleep in the German trenches as everyone was on alert.

Perhaps the biggest concern for the men from the 28th Reserve Division defending the La Boisselle sector was the lack of potable water. The heavy smoke and dust as well as the intense thirst most men experienced only compounded the problems faced and they had to recover as best they could. While some supplies were brought up to the front lines there were many instances where the men had not had any fresh water since the previous day. There was no indication that this would change in the near future.

The British had the luxury of knowing that reinforcements were at hand and that exhausted units could be relieved and replaced with men who were fresh. They also had ample sources of water for the troops and the ability to ensure that most men received adequate amounts each day. On the German side there were no reinforcements to be had. All of the units that had been in the vicinity of the Somme had been deployed at critical locations. The regiments holding the front line would have to rely upon the men still standing until additional reserves could be brought forward from more distant points.

Despite the exhaustion and heavy losses there was a feeling of accomplishment by the men of RIR 110 who had survived the heavy fighting on 1 July. They could look back with pride that they had inflicted far heavier losses on the British than they had experienced. Morale was high in many areas as it was evident that most of the enemy attacks had been beaten back and the British were in possession of only a few small sections of German trenches. There was also the expectation that the enemy could be ejected in a short period of time as long as fresh troops and supplies could be obtained.

Moritz 28 North was still operational early on 2 July deep under the ground at the tip of La Boisselle. The operators remained at their post intercepting British telephone messages for as long as they were able. One intercept probably raised the morale of the men in RIR 110 as it confirmed what many had already thought following the heavy fighting on 1 July. The message indicated that the 34th Division had been destroyed except for a few men. Also, the brigade placed in the *La Boisselle Mulde* from a different division had also been destroyed. It was quite an accomplishment for a single regiment to have inflicted such losses upon their opponent.

The situation in La Boisselle was serious but not considered critical by the sector commander, at least not yet. The defenders of the village had successfully beaten back most of the enemy attacks despite the overwhelming numbers thrown against them combined

Machine gun crew – RIR 110. (Author's collection)

with the use of two large mines. The right hand regimental sector was firmly in the hands of the garrison and the men were ready for action.

During the night *Hauptmann* Humricht reported that he had complete confidence that the right hand sector could resist any attack the enemy threw at them. The center battalion commander reported that his battalion had suffered moderate losses but was still an effective force. The biggest concern for the village garrison was the flanking fire coming from both mine craters. Losses were increasing with each passing hour and something was needed to be done to eliminate these threats.

The sector commander requested a fresh company as well as a *Minenwerfer* detachment in order to mount counter attacks against the crater on the *Schwabenhöhe*. The request had to be turned down as there were no men or *Minenwerfer* available.

The most critical area by La Boisselle was the left sector. The loss of men in the left hand battalion sector had been quite high, more than half of the 7/R110 had been killed or wounded when the *Schwabenhöhe* mine was detonated. The heavy fighting had reduced the 5/R110 to only 15 men under the command of a *Vizefeldwebel*. The 2/R110 reported that the company was almost completely worn out after the fighting on the *Lehmgrubenhöhe* and the 8/R110 was barely holding on. Already suffering heavy losses in the preliminary bombardment, this company had lost even more men in the fighting on 1 July.

The British resumed their attacks against the 6/R110 before dawn on 2 July. The platoon of *Offizier Aspirant* Brachat was still recovering from the heavy fighting on 1

July when a sentry noticed enemy soldiers close by their dugouts. Suddenly the alarm was sounded and a fierce hand grenade fight broke out between the opposing sides. Numerous brilliant flashes and loud explosions from hand grenades filled the early morning darkness.

> The Englishmen had crept up in the night under the cover of darkness until they were close to our dugouts, so that early on the 2nd of July an extremely violent death-defying hand grenade fight flared up between the Englishmen and the rest of the platoon remaining, 6-7 men, in the course we compelled the English to leave without any losses of our own.[1]

In light of the new situation facing the men of RIR 110 new ideas were needed that would allow the regiment to effectively resist the enemy pressure. By 3 a.m. on 2 July *Oberst* von Vietinghof had prepared plans that would allow each battalion commander to take the appropriate action needed in order to save the regimental strength and avoid the heavy losses from flanking enemy machine gun fire.

Each battalion commander was authorized to evacuate the parts of the front line trench that appeared unfavorable to them. In doing so they would have to consider the *Kirchstellung*, the *Grüner Graben*, *Frühlingsgraben* and *Kolonnenweg* as the main line of opposition. The only restriction was that this new position was to be held under all circumstances. Allowing local commanders the power to decide upon voluntary withdrawals would soon become prohibited along the entire German front on the Somme. At this time, however, local commanders still had some level of control over their fate.

Of all three battalion sectors Major Schröder considered his position on the left wing of the regiment to be the most critical. He felt that his battalion was no longer capable of meeting a determined British attack and one was surely expected to occur on 2 July. Schröder had surveyed the situation and determined that the best course of action to avoid additional losses and to preserve the combat ability of his men was to withdraw from their current positions immediately.

The British successes in the left hand sector of La Boisselle and the penetration of the German lines in the neighboring sector held by RIR 111 by Fricourt had created a serious situation. British machine gun fire could enfilade much of the German line and the numerous enemy guns were causing increasing losses among the defenders. Schröder sent his request to regimental headquarters for approval.

Major Schröder's request to withdraw was considered by *Oberst* von Vietinghoff. He too was concerned about the situation forming on the left flank of the regiment. The breach of the German lines by Fricourt, Mametz and Montauban had created a situation where the enemy could dominate and then overwhelm neighboring sectors. As each sector fell it endangered the next in line. The overall defense relied heavily upon the integrity of the entire trench system. This was something that the XIV Reserve Corps had always been concerned about since the corps arrived on the Somme in 1914.

A German counter attack was supposed to be taking place by Mametz and Montauban that if successful would restore most of the original German line. Von Vietinghoff realized that he had to hold his current defensive line until the situation by further south had been decided.

If events did not turn out as hoped, plans for a possible withdrawal had already been drawn up by von Vietinghoff's staff and was ready to be implemented. The line now held

Death notice for *Kanonier* Edgar Emil Deutsch, 3/RFAR 28. Killed 2 July 1916
while traveling from his observation post to his battery. (*Freiburger Zeitung*)

by RIR 110 ran from Ovillers in the north up to the *Frühlingsgraben*, then into the First
Intermediate position where it ended at the sector held by RIR 111.

Von Vietinghoff found himself faced with constant enemy pressure against his entire
regiment. Determined enemy attacks could break through his line at any time. The
situation was confusing and it was difficult to know exactly where each unit was positioned.
The left flank of the regiment was being held by a mixed force. The left flank was protected
by the 11th and two platoons of the 12/23, one platoon from the 1/LBEB 55 and one
platoon of *Musketen* from the 2/*Musketen* Battalion 1 that were positioned in and around
the *Völkerbereitschaft*.

The front held by the 28th Reserve Division was by far the most critical position in
the XIV Reserve Corps following the fighting on 1 July. Based on the current situation
Generalleutnant von Hahn decided that the front held by his division should be divided
into two brigade sectors. The left sector was considered the most important as it was faced
with the British breakthrough by Mametz and Montauban. This sector was given to
Generalmajor von Dresler und Scharfenstein.

The 28th Reserve Division would be under the protection of the approximately 65
remaining guns in the 28th *Reserve Feld Artillerie Brigade* that were still able to fire. While
offering some protection there were far too few guns left to be able to protect the entire
front of the division. It would take additional time before reinforcement batteries could be
brought forward and to provide effective defensive fire.

The biggest fear of the German commanders was further enemy penetrations if the
counter attack by Mametz and Montauban failed. The enemy would then be in possession
of critical positions inside the German lines and from there he could work eastward into
Bernafay and Trônes Wood. If the British then attacked Longueval and Guillemont
the entire position of the 28th Reserve Division to the west of these villages would be

Death notice for *Sergeant* Eugen Carl, 11/R110. Killed
in action 2 July 1916. (*Freiburger Zeitung*)

untenable. Everything depended upon stopping the enemy advance and preventing any
further expansion of the penetration.

The general fighting by La Boisselle resumed at dawn on 2 July. British artillery fire
that had never fully ceased during the night quickly grew in strength until it had increased
to a terrific level. About 5 a.m. the 9th Royal Welch Fusiliers and 6th Wiltshire advanced
up the La Boisselle *Mulde* and on both sides of the National road under the protection of
this fire.

The British were able to enter the village and occupy a portion of the German front line.
There was a rapid response to these attacks by *Leutnant der Reserve* Wirthwein and the men
at his disposal lying in the La Boisselle *Mulde* and at the western edge of the village. After
hours of hard fighting the British were thrown back and the danger averted, but not before
Wirthwein was severely wounded and many of his men became casualties in the fighting.

The defenders of La Boisselle under *Hauptmann* Heine including men from the 1R/
Pionier Bn 13 fought against the British invaders who had managed to advance up to the
battalion battle headquarters before being stopped. Additional attempts to penetrate the
German front line in the La Boisselle *Mulde* were prevented by infantry fire and by support
by Artillery Group Pozières whose fire helped to break up enemy troop concentrations
forming in the hollow. This was accomplished despite the ever-decreasing number of
operable artillery pieces still available.

At 4 a.m. *Leutnant der Reserve* Hübner and six Groups from the 12/23 arrived in La
Boisselle. The men were immediately positioned in the front line by the 9th and 12/R110.
The men from IR 23 had been marching all night in order to reach La Boisselle and had
not been provided with any food or water for some time. Their combat effectiveness was
not considered very high despite all of the good intentions of sending the men to the front.
After reaching La Boisselle Hübner received additional orders to send half of his 12/23

Men from *Landwehr Brigade Ersatz Battalion* in the trenches. (Brett Butterworth)

to occupy the trenches from the *Nagel Graben* to the *Schwarzwaldgraben* along with the remnants of the 9th and 11/R110.

By midday the situation on the left flank of the regiment was still considered critical. The constant fighting over the last 36 hours had resulted in such large losses that, 'as the III Battalion expressed it, only one man stood in every 4-8 meters of trench.' The main resistance line as outlined by the regiment was being occupied but the battalion commander still had no illusions that his men would be able to hold their positions in the face of any determined British attack.

The III/R110 now made the request that at the onset of darkness the battalion should be allowed to withdraw to the *Kirchstellung*. They would take with them the salvaged equipment from the *Arendt* listening post (Moritz 28 North) that had now been removed from the mine tunnel at the tip of La Boisselle.

About this time the regimental headquarters received bad news; the counter attack between Mametz Wood and Longueval had failed completely. In addition to this unsettling news the regiment was also advised again that no reinforcements were available. RIR 110 would have to rely upon the men of LBEB 55 that had been attached to the regiment shortly before the battle started as well as the few reinforcements from IR 23 and the platoon of *Musketen* from the 2/*Musketen* Battalion 1.

While Schröder waited for a reply to his proposal to withdraw, the British continued to apply pressure along the entire German front by La Boisselle. Some welcome relief did arrive at 12.30 p.m. in the form of 1 officer and about 40 men from IR 23 who arrived at the village ruins. They joined up with *Leutnant der Reserve* Hübner and his men to form Company Hübner.

Additional enemy attacks against La Boisselle took place about 2 p.m. The last available reserves of the III/R110 were thrown into the fighting as well as the men in the 12/23 under *Leutnants der Reserve* Hübner and Gach. This attack was also stopped but only after heavy fighting and numerous losses on both sides.

The defenders of La Boisselle were now considered to be spent and there was no hope of being able to remain victorious against any new enemy attack along most of the La Boisselle Sector. Still, with few reserves available the men who had survived the heavy fighting were expected to hold their ground to the very end.

The regimental staff of RIR 110 still did not know exactly where the new front line was located at any given moment with the front line changing slightly after each attack and counter-attack. Based upon reports received throughout the morning the staff assumed that the new line ran approximately north of Montauban to the southern tip of Mametz Wood and then was bent back in the Mametz *Mulde* to the south toward the *Edinger Dorf*.

At 3 p.m. the British attacked once more and this time succeeded in positioning mine throwers into shell craters close to the German lines by the *Schwabenhöhe*. The fire from the Stokes mortars and the infantry attack forced back the men from Company Hübner through the *Krebsgraben* and *Schwarzwaldgraben* until they had reached the *Braun Stellung*. A counter attack comprised of men from RIR 110 and IR 23 was able to force the British back and the lost trenches were recaptured. Losses were growing even higher and more serious with each attack. Soon there would be no one left to offer any resistance.

The defenders of the *Lehmgrubenhöhe* had been able to hold off the British attacks with rifle and machine gun fire but their situation also grew worse as the day passed. The British troops that had penetrated the German line by the neighboring RIR 111 had set up numerous machine guns that fired continuously into the flank of RIR 110 resulting in many losses and making it very difficult to move men about. The British were also bombarding

Infantrymen – RIR 110. (Felix Fregin)

the *Sigelgraben* with heavy caliber shells and the losses were rising as there were no dugouts or shelters for the men to use as cover.

A few additional reinforcements did arrive in the village about 4 p.m. when parts of the 11/23 under *Leutnants* Ueberascher and Lummer managed to work their way into the village and reinforced Company Hübner. Even a small number of men were a welcome addition to the sector defenses.

The regiment had to seriously consider that the enemy would continue to apply pressure against the German lines and advance to the north from Mametz Wood. In order to prevent the enemy from succeeding, RIR 110 might have to shift from its current position and move into the II Position that ran from Pozières to Bazentin le Petit.

This movement would require careful planning in order that it could be accomplished quickly and according to schedule. The regimental staff immediately started to work out a plan of action in order to meet this contingency.

The plan that was adopted would require all parts of the regiment acting in unison or the move could be disastrous. The right battalion, Humricht, would withdraw in the direction of Pozières. The left battalion, Schröder with LBEB 55 would move on a wide front into the position between Pozières and Bazentin.

The middle battalion, Gandenberger would be used as an assault unit and afterward would be positioned directly north of Pozières. If the British followed closely behind Battalion Schröder during the projected withdrawal they could be attacked in the flank by Battalion Gandenberger.

It was also critical that all nearby regiments were made aware of the possible withdrawal. Runners were sent to IR 180 and RIR 111 with details of the plan so that these regiments would know what was taking place in the event of a withdrawal from La Boisselle. Any move of this nature could adversely affect each of their sectors.

Copies of the plan were drawn up and transmitted to each of the three battalion commanders about 4 p.m. The regimental staff stressed that these were temporary plans and that they could not be implemented without express orders from the regiment.

Despite the safeguards and restrictions put into place by the regiment it was human nature that resulted in near disaster. During the transmission of the plans to the three battalions a telephone operator apparently forgot to add the last proviso that regimental approval was required before any move could be made.

When the instructions reached Battalion Schröder the plan was immediately interpreted to indicate that the battalion was to withdraw from the positions at La Boisselle. The battalion was completely worn down and fresh enemy attacks were barely being contained. Given these circumstances Battalion Schröder ordered a withdrawal to the north. If this was allowed then there would be a large hole in the German defensive line and the neighboring sectors could be outflanked when the British discovered the withdrawal.

Fortunately, the withdrawal was spotted by *Hauptmann* Wagener, a member of the regimental staff who was observing the front lines from the tower at the badly damaged Contalmaison Château. He reacted quickly to this potential disaster and he gathered every officer, runner, officer's servant and orderly he could find with orders to intercept the II/R110 and direct the men back into their old positions at all costs. The makeshift detachment proceeded along the Contalmaison-La Boisselle road and attempted to stop the exodus before it was too late.

Contalmaison Château. (Author's collection)

When Major Schröder arrived at the Château and was informed of the error he also reacted quickly. He drew his saber and began to rally his men around him while supported by his cane. Earlier in the war the major was severely wounded when his heel was shattered by enemy fire in 1914. Now, wearing a prosthetic device on his foot, Schröder gathered together some 100 of his men and advanced back toward their old positions.[2] Not everyone was happy about returning to the front line under the present circumstances. The small group of men under Schröder managed to reoccupy much of their old position with the exception of some sections of trench that had already been occupied by the enemy in force.

The garrison of the *Kolonnenweg* and *Frühlingsgraben* had also moved to the rear in error and were moving toward Contalmaison. The men had withdrawn once it was evident that there was no connection on their right wing. After the regimental staff by the Contalmaison Château explained the situation, *Leutnant der Reserve* Greiner led his men back toward their old positions.

The men advanced via the *Völkerbereitschaft* under heavy British artillery fire. As they approached the *Kolonnenweg* the British garrison that had occupied the trench was already being rolled up from the left by elements of RIR 110 that had remained in their position. As the British were forced back the survivors broke and ran or were shot down in close fighting. The advance by Greiner and his men and the clearing of the trench was also aided in a large part by the effective close range flanking fire of two machine guns from the 2MG/R110 under *Leutnant der Reserve* Gerstner.

This success was short lived when almost immediately a message was received that the British had successfully penetrated into the front line trench at the western edge of La Boisselle. There were no more reserves at hand and it appeared that the weak forces still holding the front line could not contain the British advance any further.

The confusion that existed inside the German lines was also evident on the left wing where the survivors of the 6/R110 still held their positions. The order to withdraw to the *Völkerbereitschaft* had arrived just as the British had penetrated into the second trench of the position. The officers of the 6/R110 suspected something was wrong and immediately turned their men around in order to reoccupy their old positions.

Offizier Aspirant Brachat and *Leutnant der Reserve* Böhlefeld, 6/R110, advanced with the remnants of their company, some 20 men in all. Brachat and Böhlefeld quickly made their way to their old position and waited for the rest of the company to arrive. After waiting some time the two officers began to suspect that something had gone wrong.

> *Leutnant* Böhlefeld and I took our former posts again, waiting for the Other Ranks, who looked to reach the first position again on a different route. They had met their fate and had been taken captive. Both platoon leaders were quite alone, no sentries could be seen far and wide. Suddenly, large, stealthy columns suddenly emerged out of the terrain and started to advance toward us. Because of this we went back up to the *Badischen Graben*, and there the enemy followed us, always close on our heels and since I was not otherwise able to defend myself I threw two Bunsen wire coils into the trench to block it. I succeeded in reaching the battalion dugout, where the rest of the company was found with *Leutnant* Böhlefeld.[3]

Almost miraculously the telephone connection from the tip of La Boisselle to the regiment and then back to division headquarters was still intact after all of the shelling and fighting over the last few days. A message was sent advising the regimental staff of the situation inside the village and asking for instructions. There were apparently two courses of action open to the defenders of La Boisselle. The battalion commander posed the question whether it was worth the effort of defending an untenable position with weak forces up to the last man in order to prevent an enemy breakthrough, or, if it was not better to transfer the defenses to the II Position as mentioned in the earlier plans issued by regimental headquarters and save the men from total destruction.

This request was relayed to division headquarters where a reply was sent back a short time later. The regiment was to hold its position under all circumstances, no withdrawal would be considered. The division informed the hard-pressed RIR 110 that reinforcements were on their way. The lead elements of IR 190 should arrive at the onset of darkness. With the expectation of additional troops RIR 110 would continue to defend the *Grüner Stellung* and make preparations to be relieved.[4]

Just as it appeared that reinforcements were approaching, the regiment received bad news regarding artillery support. While the defenders of La Boisselle had been fighting with little artillery support for most of the battle even the few serviceable guns were helpful. Now even that small support was gone. The artillery commander reported to the regiment at 5 p.m. that his last gun had been destroyed by a direct hit. He had also allowed the guns of the older types in Mametz Wood to be blown up because the enemy had already

Infantryman – RIR 110. (Author's collection)

penetrated into the position and there was the danger that the guns could be captured intact. No horse teams were available to remove them and the current circumstances would have prevented it even if they had been on hand.

At 6.30 p.m. Major Schröder sent back several officers from his staff to act as guides for the approaching companies of IR 190. There had been so many casualties among the officers that even the loss of a few could have a negative impact on maintaining the current position. Every officer and senior non-commissioned officer was needed at the front to keep the men focused on defending their positions.

Despite all efforts the constant enemy pressure had proven to be too much for the weakened companies. A short time after being ordered to hold their positions the survivors were forced back into the *Braun Stellung*. When Schröder heard of the withdrawal he also ordered the *Granathof* position to be abandoned. The men moved back as best they could through the badly damaged trench system while under heavy artillery fire. Small fights broke out at the left wing as the men attempted to disengage from the enemy and make their way to safety. For some it was too late:

When the Englishmen approached the dugout I called 'quickly, out of the hole' and to move against the enemy! I stood at the entrance to observe when I was wounded by a hand grenade and the dugout was set on fire. I stood between the English and the burning dugout, in which ammunition piled up was exploding. There was wailing and screams, a large number of dear comrades suffocated or were set on fire. I was only animated by the thought, not to fall into the hands of the English. After a quick prayer I jumped through the flames that were becoming greater in order to reach the 2nd exit. I was lucky despite my wound; how it was possible is a mystery to me. The way

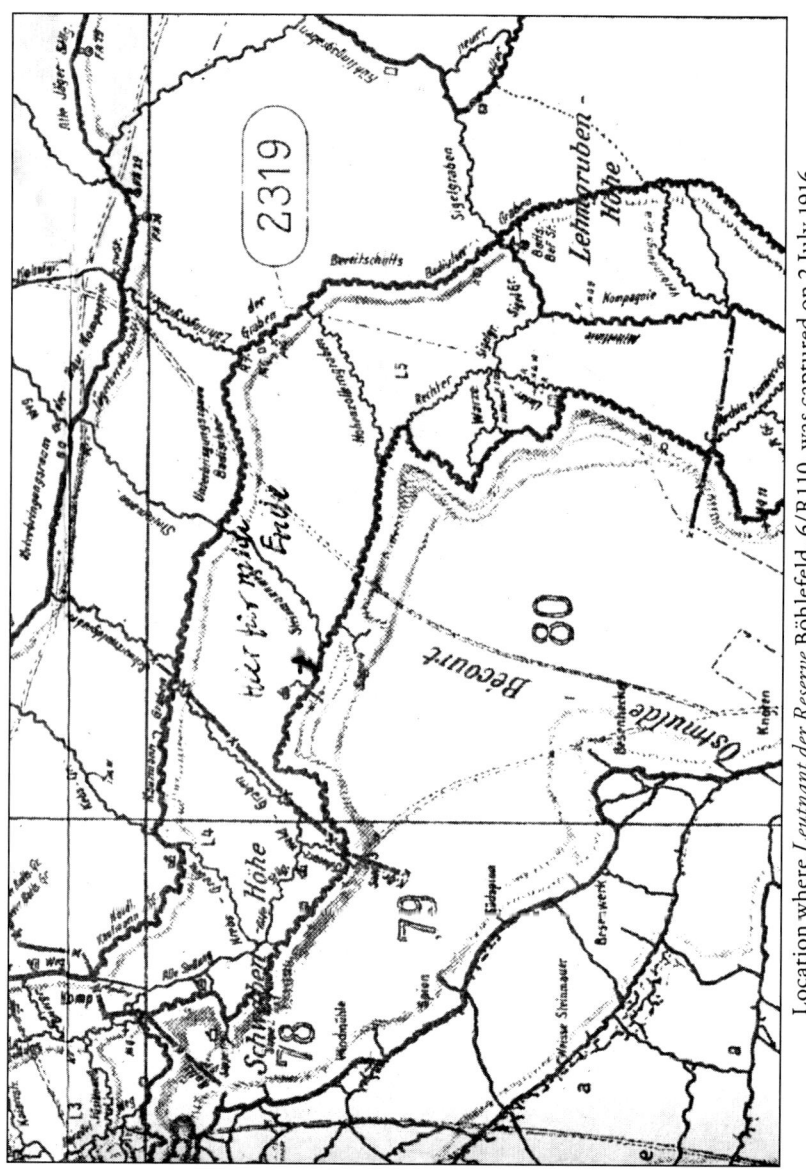

Location where *Leutnant der Reserve* Böhlefeld, 6/R110, was captured on 2 July 1916.

out went across the corpses of my comrades, up the dugout steps where Böhlefeld was coughing. An English officer pointed a pistol at me; however he was prevented from shooting by the discharge of a fatal shot by my good comrade Förster. I quickly put my pistol away and I was surrounded by hundreds of Englishmen. I was taken prisoner at 8.30 in the evening. *Offizier Aspirant* Brachat, 6/R110[5]

The much anticipated relief by IR 190 did not take place as planned. Darkness fell and the regiment had not yet arrived. The loss of officers was growing larger with each passing hour and every one was needed at the front. To lose even a few to guide the relief troops forward was potentially dangerous. It was feared that without firm leadership the men would simply break and abandon their positions. Officers could still inspire their men to perform at their best despite the hardships and danger that they faced.

Towards evening my platoon had become very small and was extremely exhausted. There came a *Leutnant* from the Silesian Regiment 23 with about 20 men and helped us. Nevertheless we were pressed back almost until the *Heckenweg* by a new violent English attack. While we prepared for the counter attack, we saw closely behind us, only a pistol shot distance from the enemy, our Major Gandenberger von Moisy with his Adjutant, *Leutnant der Reserve* Stradtmann standing between ruined houses and observing the front. He could, like us, become overrun at any moment by the Tommies from the flank. However his presence and his calmness and resolved attitude were strengths for us. Our counter attack succeeded. The enemy no longer attacked the newly erected barricade.

The *Leutnant* from the 23rd undertook the command alone. I and the above still remaining 12 men were sent by Major von Gandenberger to *Leutnant der Reserve* Hänlein with the order, because of the danger of becoming cut off from the left flank, the 9th Coy had to evacuate the *Granathof.* The *Kirchstellung* sector that had become unattached was to be occupied by me for the night. Connection on the left was with the 12th, on the right to the 1st Coy. *Leutnant* Hänlein didn't curse too badly: 'he has held his position against all attacks and now should evacuate it!' I distributed my few people in that long trench. Darkness fell. *Vizefeldwebel* Laasch, II/R110[6]

Midnight came and still no relief. No one seemed to know where the lead elements of IR 190 were located. Something needed to be done in La Boisselle, if the relief troops did not arrive soon then the village would be lost. The front line had stabilized for the time being but there was no expectation that the new front could be held against even a weak enemy attack. The fact that the defenders had held out to this point was considered almost a miracle. No one expected that their luck would continue to hold.

There appeared to be no end in sight for the suffering of the men defending the ruins of La Boisselle with seven days of shelling and two days of heavy fighting behind them. The British had been able to capture approximately half of the village in heavy fighting on 2 July, reaching a position just short of the church ruins.

The new line held by the defenders of La Boisselle consisted of the *Blauer Stellung* from the right wing of the battalion sector up to the *Kirchstellung*, then up to the *Beiergraben*, the upper *Heckenweg*, the *Beobachterweg*, *Alte Jägerstellung* (*Braun Stellung*), the *Schläfergraben*, *Frühlingsgraben* and *Kolonnenweg*.

The men eagerly awaited the promised support and the possibility of being relieved, but as the minutes and hours passed there was still no sign of the much-needed help. The regiment had been ordered to hold out at all cost but even this was proving to be unrealistic as fresh British troops continued their relentless pressure against the regimental sector.

On the 2nd of July the English repeated their attacks with fresh troops by Regiment 180 and by us unsuccessfully. However by the afternoon they were able to enlarge the pressed in position by RIR 111. From there since now came constantly increasing pressure on the left flank of our regiment. My platoon received orders to press back the English from out of the *Heckenweg*. It turned into a very fierce hand grenade battle. We threw salvos of hand grenades under the protection of the traverse and then jumped forward until at the next traverse. There were losses on both sides. Suddenly our situation became serious as again a low flying enemy pilot directed the fire of a battery on the trench piece occupied by us. The number of our dead and wounded grew. We closed off the trench through a sandbag barricade towards the English, but this was attacked again despite our hand grenades. We were pressed back, however we pushed forth again. This back and forth repeated itself many times. My servant fell next to me severely wounded and afterward ended up in an English prisoner of war camp. *Vizefeldwebel* Laasch, II/R110[7]

The entire regimental position was kept under heavy fire throughout the hours of darkness making it even more difficult to shift men around or to bring up fresh supplies, what little was still available. Large portions of the front line were being held by only a few scattered men. Under the cover of darkness, men shifted from one position to another while firing at the British, creating the impression that the German lines were occupied in force. Despite the subterfuge the men from RIR 110 were slowly being forced back from one trench to another as the British penetrated deeper into the German lines.

I went from one man to another and ordered them to simulate a strong trench garrison through continuous firing, always from new positions. Numerous English patrols felt about the front in the night; however they moved back as soon as we threw hand grenades at them, of which fortunately the dugouts still had stockpiles. On the right I found a connection to *Leutnant der Reserve* Hölzer from the 1st Coy, who I urgently, but naturally in vain, asked about reinforcements for my weak sentry line. The impossibility of holding the sector even against a weak enemy thrust was a heavy burden to me. It was a nasty night. It was a consolation for me that the little terrier of *Leutnant der Reserve* Hänlein that had not followed him now staunchly accompanied me on my endless walks from one sentry to the other. Some *pioniers* that were still in the mined tunnel that lay in the *Kirchstellung*, moved off to the rear towards midnight, and this became very suspicious to us. We should not have been so, because they had orders to bring back the listening apparatus 'Moritz'. We still found a few bottles of water; however we have not had any food for probably 36 hours. Heavy English bombardment came down in the morning dawn. At intervals we heard rifle shots from the Englishmen advancing again against the *Heckenweg* on the left behind us. Our fate, cut off and being taken prisoner, seemed sealed. While I was at the left wing of my platoon speaking with *Leutnant* Pommer from the 12th Coy two of my men came running from the right, reporting 'large masses of Englishmen are in the trench', and hand grenades in our immediate proximity confirmed that. We moved back with the rest of the 12th Coy, shooting and throwing hand grenades in the direction of the *Kaisergraben* by the regimental crater. The *Heckenweg* was soon in the hands of the English. It is still a miracle to me today that we have come back out of the sack! We occupied the *Alte Jägerstellung*. We had to evacuate our position against the threatening pincer movement, however the English had only gained some 100 metres in the day-long attack despite the use of the strongest forces. And they did not come any further. *Vizefeldwebel* Laasch, II/R110[8]

About 2 a.m. on 3 July the first platoon from IR 190 finally arrived and was able to relieve the right wing of Battalion Schröder. It had taken the men from IR 190 a great deal of time to make their way forward under the constant British fire. The platoon arrived in small groups, spread out over a considerable distance in order to minimize losses.

The III/190 arrived shortly afterward, followed by the other battalions later in the morning. The men from IR 190 apparently made quite an impression on the battle weary men of RIR 110. The new troops were mostly younger men who were full of energy and considerable enthusiasm as they moved toward the front. The pitifully few survivors of RIR 110 must have made quite a sight to the relief troops, covered in dust and dirt, sporting several days' growth of beard and with torn and ragged clothing as a result of the heavy fighting while the men from IR 190 were fully equipped and wearing fresh uniforms.

At 2.30 a.m. the village of La Boisselle and the right hand sector up to the Village of Ovillers came under strong bombardment. It lasted for an hour when the fire lifted and another British attack took place. The British were finally able to enter the *Kirchstellung* at the left wing of Sector Humricht. The fighting was fierce as the attackers attempted to clear out the maze of German trenches and numerous dugouts. The enemy continued to gain ground and losses to the men defending the village continued to grow, including the death of *Leutnant* Kirchner. The fighting surged back and forth as bombing parties from both sides tried to gain the upper hand at each traverse. Considering the close confines of the village trenches the hand grenade became the weapon of choice for both sides. Parts of the newly arrived IR 190 became caught up in the fighting along with the few survivors from RIR 110 and IR 23.

The fighting evolved into a long drawn out hand grenade battle as both sides tried to gain dominance over the other. It was not long before men from IR 190 became fully involved in the fight as the British pressure continued to shift until the fighting spread through most of the village of La Boisselle. *Leutnant* Wirthwein and his men from the 10/R110 continued to hold out despite the growing odds against them. Each time the British managed to gain a foothold inside the village, Wirthwein and his men were able to force them out once again.

Finally, the stock of hand grenades became used up and the 10/R110 was forced to abandon its positions in the *Blauer Stellung* from the *Grenzweg* up to the *Steinbruch*. A small portion of the old sector was still being occupied with a handful of men. Wirthwein was among the wounded following one of the hand grenade attacks, his presence would be sorely missed.

The *Bumiller Bereitschaft* and *Mathy Graben* now became strong points in the German lines because of the presence of five machine guns. The machine guns inside the *Bumiller*

Death notice for *Ersatz Reservist* Peter Bechtold, 9/R110. Killed in action 2 July 1916. (*Freiburger Zeitung*)

Bereitschaft were given instructions to provide flanking fire against any enemy advance into the *Blauer Stellung*. The men were also given orders that the *Blauer Stellung* by the *Steinbruch* had to be held under all circumstances. The concentrated fire from so many machine guns would be difficult for the British to overcome.

The situation was even more confusing than before as no one really knew where the neighboring companies were located or how far the enemy had actually advanced into the village. Patrols were sent out to see what they could learn. These patrols were able to establish that two companies from IR 190 occupied the *Lattorfgraben*. Since these companies were at full strength two platoons were sent to the 3/R110 (Thietje) as reinforcements. With the infusion of fresh men the 3/R110 was able to force the British out of the left wing of the position and clear the *Grenzweg, Mittel Querweg* up to the *Grüner Stellung* by midday. Despite this success there were still too few troops available to occupy the *Blauer Stellung* up to the *Steinbruchgraben*.

The British were able to penetrate into the village of La Boisselle during the morning fighting and advanced through the twisted wreckage and maze of trenches into the *Kirchstellung* and through the *Kaiserstrasse* until they had reached the battalion command post at about 5.30 a.m. Almost at the same time *Leutnant* Stradtmann, the Adjutant of the III/R110, arrived at the head of the lead elements of the II/190. Stradtmann did not stop to assess the situation but instead he and the men from IR 190 advanced toward the British troops, the men from IR 190 still wearing their field packs.

Stradtmann and his men managed to force the British back out of the village up to the *Kirchstellung* where he fell dead, shot through the head. *Leutnant der Reserve* Schirmer, 9/R110 also fell about this time near the regimental crater through enemy machine gun fire. Once the fighting died down again the relief of the village garrison could take place. It would take the entire day to accomplish the relief with the 3/R110 not being able to march

German trenches in La Boisselle near the *Kirchstellung*. (*Die 26. Reserve Division 1914-1918*)

to the rear until 9 p.m. that night.

This was also the time that the official British History gives for the capture of the village of La Boisselle after three days of heavy fighting. According to the Official History it was a regular 'soldier's battle' involving bombing attacks, hand to hand fighting and small group encounters as both sides struggled in the close confines of the German trenches. When the Germans were finally driven back from the village the British reported taking 153 prisoners from RIR 110 and IR 23.

For the time being this was the end of the fighting on the Somme for RIR 110. The regiment had been engaged in heavy fighting for the last three days and needed to be relieved. Following the fighting on 3 July the regiment was moved to the rear where the losses could eventually be replaced and the survivors could recover from their experience. Weapons and equipment all needed to be cared for, replaced and repaired before the regiment could be ready for further action.

Even as the men were leaving the battlefield of the Somme behind them it was inevitable that new rumors spread among the survivors, promises of better times ahead.

> The long-awaited reinforcements in the form of a battalion of 190er arrived. They were led forward by our *Leutnant der Reserve* Stradtmann, who unfortunately fell with them. The rest of our regiment was extracted in the course of 3rd July and re-assembled in a village in the rear. Still, under the outrageous impressions of the huge battle could the rumor arise that we would all receive 4 weeks leave giving us a new life. Only the quiet mourning for the many fallen stout comrades made us still quiet. *Vizefeldwebel* Laasch, II/R110[9]

For many of the men from RIR 110 who were fortunate enough to be alive the next few years would be spent inside a prisoner of war camp.

In Méaulte I counted approximately 35 prisoners from the company amongst them 25 wounded. *Leutnants* Manecke and Böhlefeld were also here.

As the first captive officer from RIR 110 I was brought before the English general. I refused to talk. A grinning English Orderly officer explained the attack plan to me:

1. The XIV Reserve Army Corps and especially the 28th Reserve Division were attacked with tenfold superior strength, because they had the longest defensive sector.
2. Because we had the least expectation of an attack here.
3. Because the division had almost only old *Landsturmmann*.
4. Because the division was used continuously since the beginning of the war, and therefore was 'mellow'.

The English wanted to take our first trench on the first day and to drive forward a so-called wedge between the strong fortified villages of Mametz-Fricourt-Boisselle throughout up to our 2nd Line, and on the second day also take these villages from all sides and our 2nd Line as well, with the 3rd Line taken on the third day, and the fourth day bringing the entry into Bapaume. It was said to me that they had encountered an especially energetic opposition from RIR 110. *Leutnant der Reserve* Heine.[10]

Offizier Aspirant Brachat, 6/R110 was also fortunate in that he had survived the heavy fighting on 1 and 2 July and now would wait out the rest of the war as a prisoner. He had one further adventure while on the way to the British rear.

On another morning, as I was going to be taken away on the Moulin d'Albert, I clearly heard my name called. I was tapped on the shoulder. I turned around to the caller and recognized the French Lieutenant Roger Pillet, who, because he could speak German, was apparently employed by the English as a translator. A year before the war Roger Pillet was learning to speak German as a boarder in my parental home. A friendship had formed between us as young men, and two years before he was even a guest at my wedding. I must thank his intercession that I was not made accountable for having ammunition for my pistol even though it had been discarded. *Offizier Aspirant* Brachat, 6/R110[11]

The official accounting of losses suffered by RIR 110 during the period from 23 June through 3 July 1916 were given as: 9 officers, 184 Other Ranks killed; 12 officers, 385 Other Ranks wounded; 8 officers, 491 Other Ranks missing for a total of 1,089 officers and men.[12]

Notes

1. Greiner, op. cit., p. 304.
2. Accounts differ on what Major Schröder was wearing as a result of his wound from 1914. Some accounts indicate it was an artificial foot, in other accounts only an artificial heel.
3. Greiner, op. cit., p. 304.
4. IR 190 was part of the 185th Division, formed in May 1915. The men from IR 190 had prior service at Hébuterne, Alsace and the Champagne before being sent to the Somme. The regiment was formed from men who came mainly from Westphalia.
5. Greiner, op. cit., pp. 304-305.
6. Greiner, op. cit., p. 133.

7.   Ibid.
8.   Greiner, op. cit., pp. 133-134.
9.   Greiner, op. cit., p. 134.
10. Greiner, op. cit., p. 303.
11. Greiner, op. cit., p. 305.
12. Over the following months the fate of many of the missing would be resolved and the original loss numbers would change as the true status of the men became known. Of the 1,089 officers and men reported as casualties in this time period the printed *Verlustlisten* listed 1,234 officers and men. The original loss numbers indicate 499 officers and men were missing. The *Verlustlisten* shows 503 officers and men under this category. The differences in the numbers can be accounted for when the reader realizes that the dates used for each list differ slightly. The *Verlustlisten* generally contained casualties that occurred over a 10 day period of time while the losses reported for the opening fighting on the Somme could be for one day up to three days in the case of RIR 110. By the end of 1916 only 156 names were still listed as missing. 170 of the men were found to be killed in action or died from wounds. 171 men were prisoners of war. 1 man was shown as having returned to the regiment and 5 entries were changed to wounded in action. The status of the remaining 156 officers and men still listed as missing at the end of 1916 would eventually be corrected during 1917 and 1918 as new information was obtained.

9

Fricourt

The portion of the attack against the Fricourt Sector would involve regiments from two British divisions; the 21st and 7th.[1] The boundary between the two divisions was located just below Fricourt near Hill 110. The main thrust by the 7th Division was actually directed toward the village of Mametz lying just south of Fricourt.

The German defenses in the Fricourt Sector had been developed over nearly two years of occupation. There were three separate lines of defense, the rear lines not being as well developed as the main defensive line but still a substantial line of defensive works. There were numerous deep dugouts, extensive wire entanglements and strong points. It was quite a change from the early days in late 1914 when only a few rudimentary trenches ringed the village; many of these not even connected to one another.

When RIR 111 took over this portion of the line in March 1916 the men went to work on improving the already strong defensive works using all of the experience the men had experienced in the last two years of fighting. Additional work was done to ensure a successful defense of the sector up to the last minute before the bombardment started on 24 June 1916.

The regimental front was divided into two sectors, Fricourt North and Fricourt South. The trenches in Fricourt North were manned by the companies of the I/R111 commanded by *Hauptmann* Mayer. The 4/R111 was on the extreme right wing of the regiment, followed by the 2nd and 1/R111. One platoon from the 3/R111 was positioned in the rear of each

View of Mametz from Hill 110. (*Reserve-Infanterie-Regiment Nr. 111 im Weltkrieg 1914 bis 1918*)

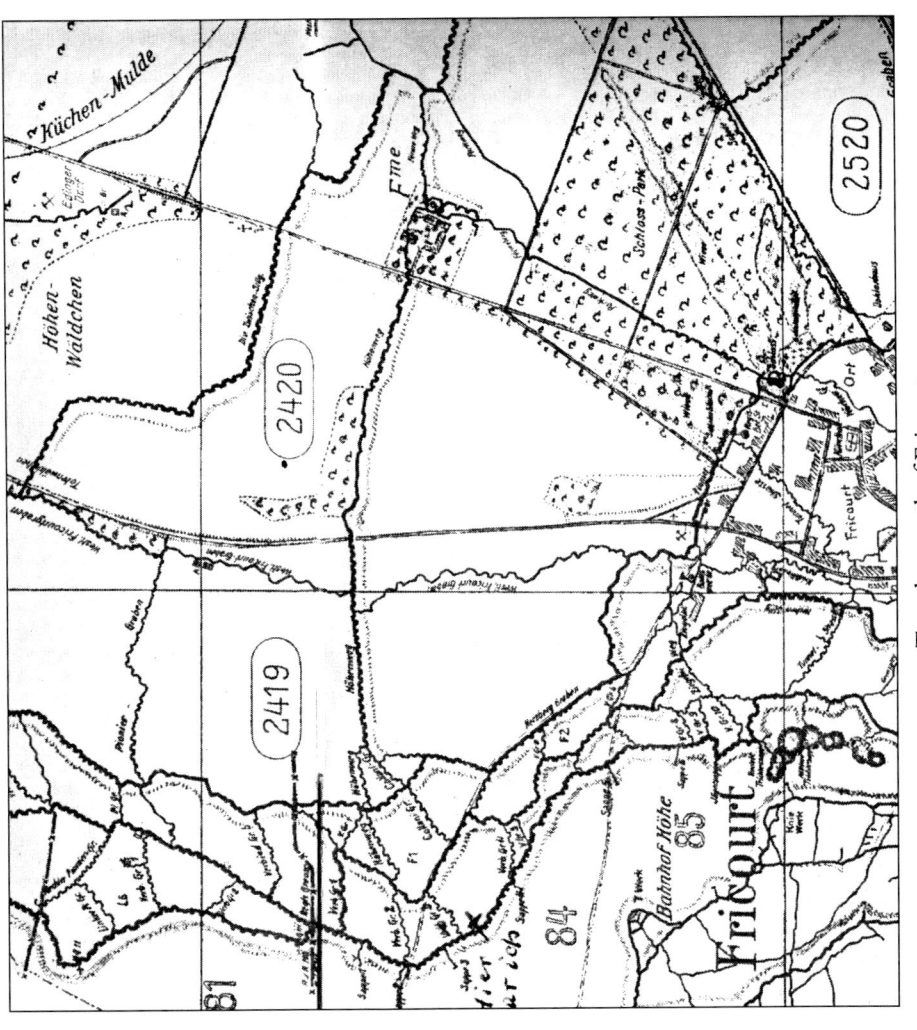

Trenches north of Fricourt.

German machine gun crews. (Author's collection)

company as support.

Fricourt South was occupied by the men of the II/R111 under *Hauptmann* von Neuenstein. The 7/R111 was adjacent to the 1/R111 followed by the 6th and 5/R111. one platoon from the 8/R111 was positioned behind each company as support. The III/R111 was positioned at different areas further to the rear and would act as support as needed during the attack.

During the week-long bombardment the III/R111 had been moved closer to the front where the 9/R111 was quartered in the *Edinger Dorf.* The 11/R111 was placed in the *Nestlerhöhlen* and the 12/R111 was placed in the Château Park. The 10/R111 had already been sent forward early in the bombardment and parts of this company had been placed behind both the I and II/R111 positions.

The regiment had two machine gun companies ready for action during the attack. Shortly before the attack additional firepower was provided when the Machine Gun Marksman Detachment 131 was assigned to the regiment. The three machine gun companies were then distributed across the front lines with the MGSST 131 in the right hand sector, the 2MG/R111 in the center of the regimental sector and the 1MG/R111 on the left. The regiment was further strengthened when the Machine Gun Marksman Detachment 161 was placed in the rear of the regiment with guns positioned in the *Edinger Dorf* as well as scattered in dugouts of the III/R111.

Two Bavarian *Pionier* companies were positioned at the minefield near Hill 110; the 2nd and 1st Reserve Coy of the Bavarian *Pionier* Regiment. *Pioniers* from the 2R/13th *Pionier* Battalion also occupied positions in the Fricourt Sector as well as a medium *Minenwerfer* platoon from *Minenwerfer* Coy 228.

Further to the rear the Recruit battalion of the 28th Reserve Division, which included the Recruit Company for RIR 111 under *Leutnant* Holzhauser, was positioned south of Bazentin le Petit and Longueval. Field guns from several different artillery regiments including RFAR 28, RFAR 29, FAR 57 and FAR 21 provided support along with a number of heavier guns positioned behind the front.

The defenses of Fricourt were formidable and had withstood all attempts to capture them for nearly two years. Now the men of RIR 111 and the supporting troops faced their ultimate challenge as they came up against units from two enemy divisions. Everything possible had been done to prepare for this day. Almost every member of the regiment was certain that the great offensive would take place some time on 1 July. As each tense minute passed in the pre-dawn darkness every officer and man was ready to defend their trenches.

There was one event that could have cast a shadow over the coming events for the men of RIR 111. The regimental commander *Oberst* Ley had left the regiment in May due to illness. In his absence the regiment was being commanded by Major Gandenberger von Noisy from RIR 110. While von Noisy was a competent officer, the men of RIR 111 had hoped they would be going into action with their own commander who had been with the regiment since the start of the war.

The week-long bombardment at the end of June had resulted in heavy damage to the overall position as well as casualties among the officers and men. However, the losses were quite low in comparison to the number of shells and mines fired at the Fricourt Sector over 7 days – 1 officer, 16 men killed and 3 officers, 67 men wounded. Most of the losses were confined to trench sentries as well as carrying parties who had necessarily been exposed to the enemy bombardment more than most. When the attack came on the morning of 1 July the regiment was nearly at full strength. On 23 June 1916 the regiment had consisted of 59 officers and 2,997 men.

Only hours before the attack would begin, the morale of the men in the regiment was raised when the trusted *Oberst* Ley returned and assumed command once more. Ley had barely recuperated from his illness when he received reports of the impending British offensive. He made arrangements to return to the regiment and had hoped to arrive before the attack had started. Late on 30 June he made his way to the regimental battle

2MG/R111. (*Das Reserve-Infanterie-Regiment Nr. 111 im Weltkrieg 1914 bis 1918*)

headquarters located in the cellar of the Fricourt Château where the regimental officers enthusiastically greeted him. Now the men of RIR 111 were ready to face the enemy.

The position of the 4/R111 at the extreme right wing of the regiment had suffered considerably from the bombardment. Some dugouts had become severely damaged and needed to be abandoned. The men were then consolidated into the few remaining intact dugouts. This redistribution of men helped to create the gap between the 4/R111 and the neighboring 8/R110.[2] The gap was to have serious consequences for both regiments in the upcoming fighting. As it grew light on the morning of 1 July the terrain in front of RIR 111was shrouded in dense fog making visibility difficult. Smoke and gas released from the British lines only reduced visibility even more.

There was no doubt that the attack was going to take place. The fragmentary message intercepted by Moritz 28 by La Boisselle had already been passed to each regiment and then down to each company. Trench sentries in the 4/R111 noticed that the British in the opposite trenches were clearing openings though their wire entanglements, another sure sign of the coming attack.

As a result of these observations the rest of the men of the 4th Coy were called up from their dugouts and took up positions in the front line trenches. The men opened fire into the opaque fog in front of them. Close range weapons, *Minenwerfer* and *Erdmörsers*, which were located nearby also opened fire, adding their din to the already very loud British bombardment.

Light signals were used to alert the artillery batteries in the rear to open fire. Most of the telephone lines had been destroyed and the smoke and dust made it difficult to use flares. The only methods that still seemed to work were the use of light signal stations and runners.

The artillery opened fire as requested but the level of fire was far less than what had been expected. The practice of allowing the front line regiments in the 28th Reserve Division to control the batteries in the previous week had resulted in unexpected consequences. Numerous batteries had suffered losses of men and equipment in the British counter-battery fire when many of the gun positions were discovered by their muzzle flash or through sound detection. As a result there were too few guns still in action needed to create a wall of fire that would seriously disrupt any attack.

Even with the reduction in German artillery fire the British troops inside their trenches suffered under the shelling. Casualties grew as the German high explosive and shrapnel shells fell among the densely crowded trenches. Perhaps the most disturbing aspect of the German bombardment was that the guns were able to fire at all. The previous seven days of shelling should have destroyed the German defenses and killed or incapacitated the defenders, yet German shells were falling on the British trenches and the distinctive staccato sounds of German machine guns could be heard coming from several locations along the front. The presence of undamaged German machine guns being operated by competent gun crews would have serious consequences for the men trying to cross 200-300 yards of open ground in no man's land.

The attack against Fricourt by the 21st and 7th Divisions was to take place in two phases. First, there would be an advance on both flanks of the village by brigades from each division. The plan called for the two wings of the attack to meet behind the village and thereby cut it off from the main German line.

The second phase, of the attack against the village, was not on a fixed timetable. Once

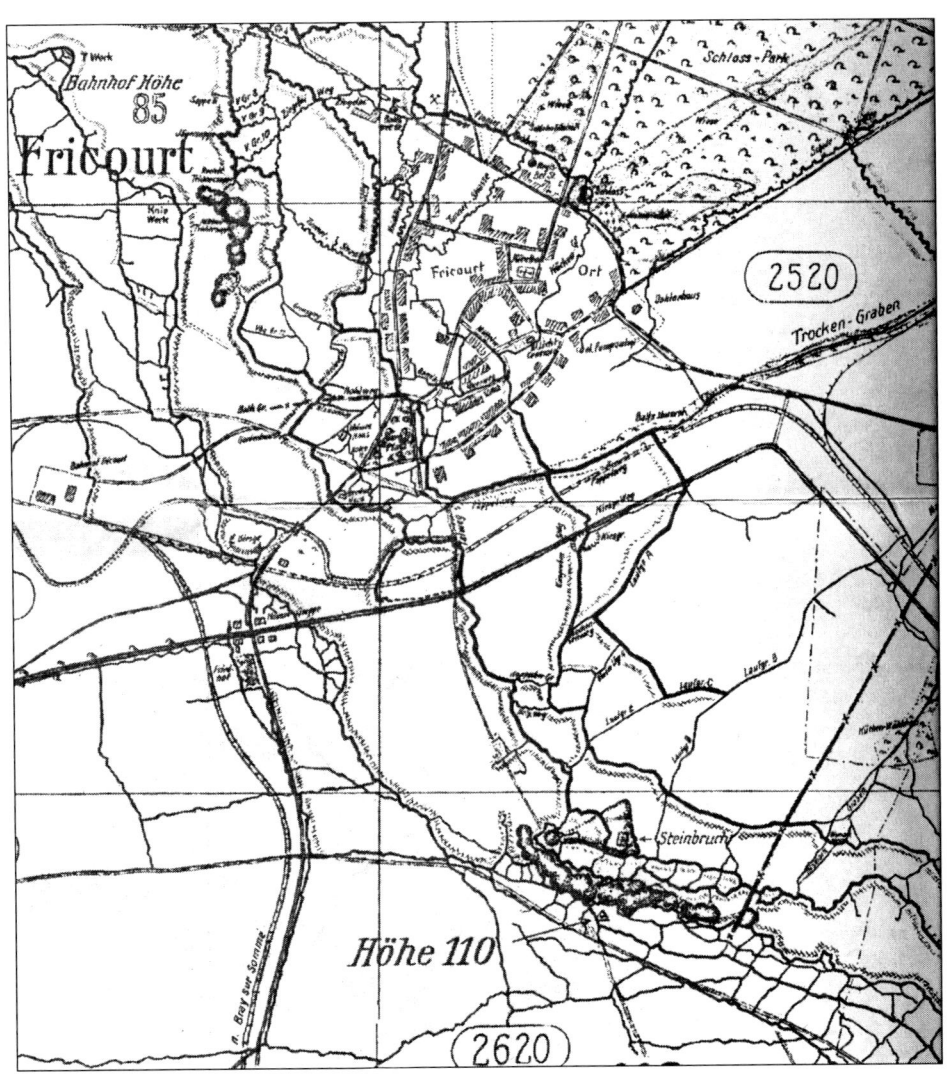

Fricourt Sector.

the first phase was deemed successful then the commanding general would order the attack against Fricourt, but only if the existing circumstances called for it. Once the Fricourt position was captured then it would be consolidated and used as the starting point for additional attacks against the German defenses.

At 6.25 a.m. the British artillery brought down the most intense bombardment yet seen on the German front lines. Between 7.15 and 7.25 a.m. the remaining gas supplies were also released at several points as a deception but no attack was to take place at these locations, yet. At 7.22 a.m. the Stokes mortars placed a hurricane bombardment across the German front line, the men firing as fast as they could manage. Finally at 7.26 a.m. a smoke barrage was created by the 4th Mortar Coy of No. 5 Battalion. This smoke was intended to screen the inner flanks of both attack wings facing Fricourt as well as form a cloud that would cover the German support line and mask the direct assault on Mametz by other elements of the 7th Division.

The final act of the preparation for the attack was the detonation of the mines at 7.28 a.m., just two minutes before zero hour. The men of RIR 111 clearly heard the mines go off by Fricourt and Hill 110 as well as the larger mine just south of La Boisselle on their right flank. The three mines set off by Fricourt[3] were designed to block the Germans from enfilading the right flank of the attack by the 21st Division that was being directed against the right flank of RIR 111. The debris thrown up by the mines should effectively screen the advancing troops and prevent many of the German machine guns from firing as the waves of men advanced across no man's land.

The German defenders noted that almost at the same time the British fire was lifted off of the front lines it was immediately transferred to the rear areas where it fell on the battery positions and the rear defenses. This was clearly the signal for the attack and the sound of sentries shouting to alarm the garrison went up across the German front line.

As in the other sectors on the Somme the British artillery plan was very detailed and rigid. No exceptions to the plan would be tolerated and it was up to the infantry to keep pace with the guns. The artillery plan was also only effective once the attacking troops actually reached the German front line and was of little help while the men were crossing the open terrain of no man's land. The advancing troops quickly fell behind the rigid timetable of the barrage they were to follow. These problems were quickly noted by British artillery observers but they were helpless to make corrections and could only watch the battle unfold.

On the left of the British line were three brigades of infantry from the 21st Division – the 50th (borrowed from the 17th Northern Division), the 63rd and 64th. The 62nd Brigade was held in reserve. Most of the 50th Brigade remained in their trenches facing the village of Fricourt and were scheduled to participate in the second phase of the attack plan. Only the 10th West Yorkshire would advance alongside the other brigades and form a defensive flank facing Fricourt.

The 63rd and 64th Brigades were assigned to take the German front line and advance and capture the intermediate line they designated Crucifix Trench. It was designated as the I *Zwischen Stellung* by the German defenders.

The second objective that the two brigades were expected to reach included *Mametzer Wäldchen* [Bottom Wood], part of *Nadelholz Strasse* [Quadrangle Trench] and the Second Intermediate Trench. Once reached the men of the 21st Division would join up with the men from the 7th Division and completely encircle the village of Fricourt and the remaining

German positions.

Starting the attack from the newly constructed Russian Sap that had been opened on the night of 30 June/1 July provided the 64th Brigade on the far left of the division some additional assistance. It allowed the brigade to attack the curved German positions in a straight line and without having to cross the British wire obstacles. Despite the advantage provided by the use of the Russian sap the brigade suffered heavy losses while crossing no man's land from enfilading machine guns located south of La Boisselle as well as from machine guns set up on the parapets of the German front line trenches opposite the attackers. German barrage fire was very weak and while shells did fall among the waves of men it did not form a barrier that would prevent them from advancing toward the German trenches.

In spite of the heavy losses the brigade reached the German front line where they found the wire obstacles badly damaged and destroyed in many places. The 9th and 10th KOYLI were greeted with a hail of hand grenades from the defenders of the German trench, the 4/R111. German hand grenades and infantry fire did not prevent the survivors of these battalions from rushing the German trench and overrunning it.

After entering the German front line the 9th and 10th KOYLI also overran a large portion of the second German trench. The 15th Durham Light Infantry and 1st East Yorkshire had followed close behind the lead battalions and now all four battalions of the 64th Brigade were inside the German front line. While this only took approximately 10 minutes it had cost the two lead battalions over half of their men.

The 4/R111 had already withdrawn from portions of their front line due to the destruction of many dugouts. The small pockets of defenders scattered across the company sector were simply too few to stop even the badly mauled British battalions.

Once inside the German trenches the British were able to surround the far left platoon of the 4/R111 along with the company commander *Leutnant* Winkler. This platoon had already been reduced to the size of a Group from the heavy fighting. The supports located in the 2nd and 3rd trenches; five Groups of the 4/R111 and the 1st platoon of the 3/R111, quickly opened fire in an attempt to stop the British advance.

The support the men of the 4/R111 had expected from two machine guns located inside the *Höhenweg* was no longer available. Both guns had been placed out of action just before the start of the attack when they were hit by some of the last artillery shells falling on the German lines. In this instance having the machine guns in position before the end of the bombardment proved to be a disaster; however it was a calculated risk that had been successful elsewhere. Their absence resulted in severely reducing the German defensive fire. If these guns had survived the initial bombardment it is very possible that the situation at the end of the day would have been far different than it turned out to be.

The British quickly began to roll up the German front line. The left wing platoon of the 4/R111 under *Leutnant* Göbel was forced to move to the left toward the 2/R111 in the *Hertzberggraben*, the second German trench where they blocked any further British advance in this direction. The men of the 2nd and 4/R111 quickly became embroiled in hand to hand combat with the men of the 64th Brigade. Rifles, pistols and especially hand grenades were used freely on both sides as the defenders attempted to hold back the British advance.

The British had a distinct advantage in the fighting; the availability of Stokes mortars and numerous Lewis Guns the men had brought into action with them. The defenders could not match this firepower and would eventually become overwhelmed. Finally, the survivors of the two companies were slowly forced back toward the village of Fricourt while under fire the entire time. Some support fire came from one platoon from the 3rd Coy and one platoons from the 10/R111, both located in the trenches behind the 4th Company sector. Despite the increased firepower they were unable to prevent the British from advancing.

The attack by the 63rd Brigade was also having some success despite heavy losses from German machine gun fire. Two companies from the 4th Middlesex had exited their trenches at 7.25 a.m. and formed up in front of their wire entanglements. The companies came under such severe machine gun and rifle fire they were forced back inside their trench. The losses had been so heavy that when the attack took place a few minutes later the Middlesex could only form a single line.

The Middlesex then came under fire from at least six German machine guns during the advance. Only scattered groups of men from the first two companies managed to reach the German trenches, some 40 men. The rear companies also suffered under the heavy fire but 4 officers and 100 men finally managed to reach the safety of the German front line.

One of the machine guns firing at the advancing British troops was being operated by Rudolf Stadelbacher and *Unteroffizier* Otto Schüsele Machine Gun Company, RIR 111:

When early on 1 July the enemy lifted the fire, we knew that the attack was not far off. Schüsele then discovered that we did not have enough water for the machine gun and said 'I'll go and get some water! Who's coming too?' Stadelbacher spoke up and we went and fetched about fifty liters of water from a damaged well in Fricourt. Going there was an unpleasant experience, but we returned safely to our dugout.

'Right', said Schüsler, 'let's get a dixie of water on the stove and make some coffee!' we did this and had another cup of coffee with biscuits. After that we put another pan on the stove and boiled up the last tins of rice and beef. We had no bread left for several days. That was a good nutritious preparation for battle. In the meantime the enemy had launched a gas attack. Schüsele was on guard and the machine gun was ready to fire. As the gas slowly drifted away, we saw the enemy assault out of all trenches. Our machine gun was in full working order. There was nothing to stop us from opening fire. Schüsele acted as gunner and I was his Number 2. Stadelbacher handled ammunition re-supply. *Unteroffizier* Ehret from Marksman Detachment 131 acted as observer. So we put down a hail of fire on the attacking enemy. Two companies of British who attempted to assault from the area of Fricourt Railway station were quickly caught by our machine gun and suffered dreadful casualties. We were not untouched, suffering two wounded and one killed.[4]

The 8th Somerset attacked on the left of the Middlesex and like the other battalions had also come under heavy machine gun and rifle fire as they crossed no man's land. The German artillery was still unable to provide an effective barrage and while causing some losses it was not considered a major obstacle in the advance.

When the Somerset reached the German front line they found the wire obstacles badly damaged and there were numerous paths that allowed the men to enter the German front line trench. They showered the men on the left flank of the 2nd and the 1/R111 with hand grenades and then rushed the position. The defenders were unable to stop the British with rifles and machine guns alone and were eventually forced to withdraw from the front line.

Ruins of Fricourt Railway station. (Author's collection)

Men from both sides of the wire fought in the close confines of the German trenches as each attempted to gain the upper hand. Even with the heavy losses the British had the advantage in numbers at many locations.

By 8 a.m. the 63rd Brigade was able to capture the *Jäger* Sap as well as the forward portion of the *Ziegelei Weg* before being stopped. During the attack the Bavarian *pioniers* under *Leutnant* Cuno from the 2/Bavarian *Pionier* Regiment attached to the 1/R111 were reported to have set off a mine chamber under the British advance thereby burying 80 enemy soldiers but the author was unable to be verify this using any of the available sources. Still, with the confusion of the opening attack and heavy losses suffered by both sides it is very possible something like this did take place. The number of British troops actually affected by this mine blast was apparently an estimate and the actual number could be much different.

The right wing of the 2/R111 managed to drive the enemy back but the platoon defending the center of the company was overwhelmed in the first attack and the British were able to penetrate the German front line. The British had also been able to penetrate the German front line at the right wing of the 1/R111. The fighting was intense as both sides tried to gain the upper hand.

The men of the 1st and 2/R111 had the support of two platoons of the 3/R111 and *Pionier* Platoon Cuno from the second and third trenches that allowed them to hold the 63rd Brigade troops in the front line. The Middlesex and Somerset troops also had another concern. Their numbers were very small and it would take more men to consolidate the captured trench and to continue their advance. While the Middlesex consolidated their gains and created trench blocks some of the Somerset troops continued their advance by bombing their way up nearby communication trenches toward the German rear. The potential danger of a German counter attack on their right flank was always present. During the fighting the Middlesex noticed large number of Germans moving about in the vicinity of Fricourt. These troops could pose a serious threat to the small garrison of British soldiers if these men advanced in their direction.

The fighting in and around the trenches of the 1st Coy sector continued. Reinforcements arrived on the German side in the form of a *Pionier* Platoon of *Leutnant* Krieg that was ordered into the threatened area By *Hauptmann* Meyer, I/R111. Eventually the 1/R111 managed to gain the upper hand and as a result of the fighting most of the British troops were killed, wounded or taken prisoner. *Pionier* Platoon Cuno was heavily involved in the fighting by the 1/R111 and had captured a total of 1 officer and 50 men.

The final part of the opening attack came from the 10th West Yorks (50th Brigade) that was supposed to advance toward Fricourt where the battalion would create a defensive flank to cover the advance of the 63rd and 64th Brigades on the left. At first the attack went smoothly, the battalion advanced with its right flank just north of the two mines detonated in front of the village. The two leading companies reached the German front line with few losses by utilizing the protection offered by the mine debris that blocked off much of the German positions nearby. They were also assisted when many of the defenders at the left wing of the 1/R111 were not able to exit their deep dugouts in time to oppose the attack.

When the 3rd and 4th Companies of the 10th West Yorks advanced in the second wave most of the defenders had been able to occupy their front lines, set up their machine guns and open fire on the advancing waves, especially from positions in Fricourt and the German Tambour that had not been affected by the mine explosions. If the British artillery barrage could have been brought back to the front line the fire from these machine guns could have been suppressed and the losses suffered by the West Yorks could have been reduced substantially.

The attack against Fricourt involved the 6/R111 commanded by *Leutnant* Wittwer and the 7/R111 commanded by *Hauptmann* Engländer. These companies holding the front line had several machine guns located in their sectors that caused the majority of the British losses. They were provided with additional fire support from the 1st Platoon of the 10/R111 under *Leutnant* Hugo Mayer. This platoon was located inside the *Marktplatzstellung* and directed level fire against the enemy waves. Among the losses suffered by the defenders was *Leutnant* Stöffler, who was killed by a shell from a mine thrower while directing the fire of his men

All the while these events were taking place the British artillery observers could only sit and watch helplessly as the men from the 3rd and 4th Coy, 10th West Yorks were nearly annihilated, the men being shot down in waves. Only a few small groups from this portion of the attack actually made it to the German front line. The survivors held the captured German front line trench while the lead companies continued to advance toward 'Red Cottage' at the northern edge of Fricourt. Their advance was slow due to increased German resistance and the men were forced to bomb their way at nearly every traverse through the German trenches.

A Company from the 7th Green Howards that was holding the line just north of the Tambour mines also joined the attack at 7.30 a.m. They had not been scheduled to take part in the initial attack and their actions proved to be disastrous. German machine gun fire was so accurate and devastating that barely 16 men made it any further than 40 yards from the

Officer in RIR 111. (Author's collection)

British front line. Very few managed to make it to the German trenches.

The West Yorks managed to reach 'Red Cottage' but there were far too few men left to maintain their position. Deep inside the German defenses the West Yorks came up against the men of the I/R111 as well as supporting troops from the III/R111.

The response to this enemy penetration was swift and sure. A bombing party assembled by the 2R/Bavarian *Pionier* Regiment quickly cleared the *Jäger* Sap of British troops. The 1/R111 accompanied by *pioniers* quickly recaptured the *Ziegelei Weg* near the I Battalion Headquarters and with it captured 1 officer and 56 men. The situation inside the first trench was restored under the energetic actions of *Unteroffizier* Jäger, 2/R111. Later in the afternoon the invaders were almost completely destroyed except for small groups that somehow managed to reach the 63rd Brigade positions further to the north.

The British troops holding out in the front line near Fricourt desperately needed reinforcements but the volume of German machine gun and rifle fire made it impossible to send any men across the open terrain of no man's land. These men would have to hold out until dark when reinforcements could be sent over with some chance of success. By the end of the day the 10th West Yorks had lost 22 officers and 688 Other Ranks.

The situation facing the men of RIR 111 on the right flank of Fricourt was very confusing. There was no single defensive line. The British occupied portions of the front line and Fricourt was threatened from the front as well as the flanks. The survivors of the 4th and 2/R111 from the far right flank had managed to establish trench blocks near the command post of the I Battalion located by the brick works under the command of *Leutnant* Dusbbach. Two machine guns from the 2nd Machine Gun Company were set up to cover the right flank of the regiment and these guns effectively fired upon the British troops inside the *Hertzberggraben*, *Höhenweg* and the *Totenwäldchen*.

The British troops in the second wave were supposed to begin their attack at 8.30 a.m. Confusion inside the British trenches and the heavy losses already suffered by the first wave caused the attack to be postponed. However, the concern that the surviving troops trapped inside the German lines would not be able to hold without reinforcements resulted in the attack being ordered to start at 8.40 a.m. This quick decision to provide additional support to the men fighting inside the German lines would mean the difference between success and failure of the attack in this sector at the end of the day.

The second wave also came under strong machine gun fire, especially from Fricourt and Fricourt Wood. Fortunately many of the machine guns that were once directed toward the front line were instead firing at British troops scattered throughout the German trenches.

The remnants of the men of the second wave quickly entered the German trenches and joined up with the men from the first wave and continued to advance deeper into the German lines. On the left flank the 8th Lincolnshire reinforced the 8th Somerset. As both battalions moved through the German communication trenches, bombers led the way. Progress was slow as they met with stubborn resistance by the men of RIR 111 at every step. Despite this the Lincolnshire and Somerset managed to gain ground by using bombs and bayonets to either kill or force the Germans to withdraw.

The British managed to capture the *Höhenweg* [Lozenge Alley] as far as the sunken road. The trench was occupied and prepared for defense so the left wing of the attack could be secured. Other small groups continued to advance along the sunken road and managed to enter the I *Zwischen Stellung* [Crucifix Trench]. A small party advanced to the east toward Fricourt Farm but they soon came up against stiff resistance and were forced back to the *Höhenweg*. In the advance the British overran a mountain gun position and reportedly found several boxes of soft nosed bullets.

Shortly after occupying the *Westlichen Fricourt Graben* [Lonely Trench] approximately 100 German soldiers came running toward them from the *Höhen Wald* [Shelter Wood]. It was noted that the men were wearing their overcoats despite the very warm weather. The

Musicians – RIR 111. (Author's collection)

men were quickly gathered up and sent back to the rear. Early in the fighting the 64th Brigade alone reported sending back some 200 prisoners.

The prisoners taken from the *Höhen Wald* could very well be rear echelon troops such as clerks, orderlies and labor troops; not combat troops who more than likely would not have access to their overcoats at such a critical time. The *Edinger Dorf* was located in the *Höhen Wald*. Many of the men who were quartered at this location had long ago been found less than suitable for front line service due to many issues including age, illness or physical impairments. Their contribution to the war effort was better served by performing essential duties needed to support the men at the front and to maintain the position.[5]

Before the attack took place *Oberst* Ley had one simple order in response to any possible British penetration of his position: 'Where the enemy has penetrated into a trench piece, he must be thrown out again immediately in a counter attack'. All telephone communication between regiment and battalion and the battalions and companies had completely broken down. Runners established communications but many were killed or wounded trying to carry their messages, others took hours to make the round trip and in that time the situation had often changed considerably. This placed a great deal of responsibility on the local company and platoon commanders who needed to act on their own initiative, and they did.

Leutnants Dusbach and Mencke, the Artillery Liaison Officer (AVO) had been providing effective fire against the British attempts to expand their gains to the north. Dusbach and Mencke then assembled several Groups who were manning the trench block near the I Battalion Headquarters and proceeded north along the *Hertzberggraben*. Their movements were covered by two machine guns that directed their fire at the enemy occupied trench pieces.

German bombing party managed to clear the third trench of the I Battalion sector up to the area behind the 4/R111 position. During the advance two British machine guns were captured. Weapons such as a Lewis Gun were prized items and were often placed in action against their former owners within a short time of being taken. Additional bombing parties formed from the Bavarian *pioniers* advanced toward the 2/R111 and cleared a trench behind the 2/R111 up to the *Höhenweg* from the enemy. During this attack the *pioniers* were able to capture another machine gun and during the mopping up operations cleared a dugout and captured 1 officer and 30 men. At the same time three Groups of *pioniers* cleared the third trench behind the 2/R111.

Gefreiter Haller and two Groups from the 2/R111 that were still holding out inside the first German trench joined the attack by the Bavarian *pioniers*. Haller and his men had observed the progress of the attack and worked back from their position until they were able to make contact.

In the course of the attack Mencke was killed and Dusbach became wounded, losses were also heavy among the Other Ranks. Finally, when the men ran out of hand grenades they were forced to retreat back towards the northern edge of Fricourt where they effectively prevented the British from advancing into the village. Once the German bombing parties had withdrawn the men of the 63rd Brigade holding parts of the *Westlichen Fricourt Graben* constructed a sandbag barricade in the expectation of further German attacks.

With the withdrawal of the Germans toward Fricourt it was time once more for the British to advance toward the village. It was not long before the opposing forces met in a violent clash. The advancing British troops first ran into opposition by a platoon from the 3/R111 that had been forced back into the *Fricourt Graben* [Lozenge Trench], as well as Platoons Baur and Schlageter from the 10/R111 in the *Höhenweg*. The opposing sides quickly became embroiled in hand grenade battles in the close confines of the trenches.

The German platoons planned and executed several further counter attacks with the goal of forcing the British back toward the former front line. All the while the men of RIR 111 were supported by rifle and machine gun fire from trench positions further in the rear. With each hand grenade fight, with each counter attack, the losses on both sides began to mount.

Finally, the threat of being outflanked on the right wing as well as being completely exhausted from the constant fighting forced the surviving Germans further back in the *Fricourt Graben*. When this happened, the route toward the *Edinger Dorf* located in *Höhen Wald* [Shelter Wood] was open.

Much needed support came from the 9/R111 when the company learned of the British breakthrough. The artillery observer from the I/RFAR 29 in the *Totenwäldchen* [Round Wood] had informed the company of the enemy advance. In response to this threat the 9th Coy occupied both sides of the slope north of the *Sigelgraben* near the Contalmaison-Fricourt road with two platoons and the wood position by the *Hohenwäldchen* with one platoon. The company was being supported by several machine guns from Machine Gun Marksman Detachment 161.

When the British advanced, the 9th Coy opened fire with rifles and one machine gun from Machine Gun Marksman Detachment 161. Under the protection of this fire the 9th Coy counter-attacked. The advancing enemy troops were quickly thrown back across the road. This small victory was very costly to the 9th Coy. Both officers, *Leutnants* Musselmann and Bill had been killed. All *Portepee* wearers (senior non-commissioned officers) and *Unteroffiziers* had been either killed or wounded.

The pursuit had to be called off despite the initial success the men enjoyed. This was primarily because of the heavy losses suffered by the 9th Coy. The men also found that they were isolated in their new position with no supports nearby; the nearest friendly units were in the *Sigelgraben* and on the right of this trench. The enemy was only 50 meters away on both flanks.

The 9/R111 attempted to remain in their newly captured position but they soon came under fire from their own field guns and howitzers that they suspected of firing too short. It is more likely that the few remaining German guns simply did not have exact information on the location of friendly and enemy troops and were firing on areas based upon old information or were firing blind. It was not too long before the last remaining officer, *Leutnant* Lieb, the commander of Machine Gun Marksman Detachment 161, was killed. *Vizefeldwebel* Reitze now took command as the most senior non-commissioned officer still standing.

The situation was very fluid and confusing as both sides took stock of their situation. Communications with the rear were spotty at best on the German side and almost non-existent on the British side. The opponents were relying upon the decisions and actions of local commanders to react as needed to the situation facing them. Some observation was possible due to the nature of the terrain but even this was suspect at times. Most of the men on each side had taken cover inside the many German trenches and were often not visible. In many instances the companies units had some reliable intelligence of the opposing adversary but only those that were within 50 to 100 meters away.

Men from RFAR 29. (Felix Fregin)

The British units inside the German trenches continued to apply heavy pressure across the newly captured front in the hope of reaching their objectives. The repeated attacks required additional support from the rear if the men from RIR 111 were to be successful in containing the British advance.

Leutnant Beyler, leader of the 11/R111 whose command post was in a mined dugout northeast of Fricourt farm placed two of his platoons under *Leutnant* Clouth and *Vizefeldwebel* Buntru on the left of the 8/R110 that had also become involved in stopping the British. The platoons provided much needed fire support in order to stop the latest British thrust.

Finally, the increased German resistance and presence of additional German troops including parts of the 2/23 that were fighting in the *Alte Jägerstellung* under *Leutnant der Reserve* Welzel and *Leutnant* Apfeld caused the British to cease their attacks for the time being.[6] The machine gun fire coming from the brick works north of Fricourt against the British right flank had been particularly effective in slowing and finally stopping the British attacks.

The British attacks up the *Höhenweg* toward Fricourt Farm broke down completely when the commander of the 12/R111, *Leutnant der Reserve* Jacob ordered two platoons from his company under *Vizefeldwebel* Benninger and *Unteroffizier* Kollenberger and half of a platoon from the 11/R111 under Winterer on their left to advance from the ruins of Fricourt Farm. The British were slowly pressed back from the small copse west of Fricourt farm and north of the *Höhenweg*. While the enemy had been forced back slightly it was not without the loss of many good men. The British casualties were also heavy, in part due to the support fire provided by the other parts of the 9/R111 and the machine guns from Machine Gun Marksman Detachment 161 located in the *Höhenwäldchen*.

A defensive line had finally been formed that appeared to contain the British advance.

Death notice for *Musketier* Heinrich Hauser, 1/R111. Killed
in action 1 July 1916. (*Freiburger Zeitung*)

The new line ran from the *Sigelgraben* to the *Höhen Wald* and then on the slope leading
from the *Parkweg* to Fricourt Farm. *Feldwebel* Reitze had been able to contact regimental
headquarters with runners and advised *Oberst* Ley of the situation facing his men.

The regiment immediately ordered Reitze to attack the British at the *Totenwäldchen*
with the units located on the right and left of Reitze's position. Reitze considered this order
to be impossible to carry out. The enemy forces appeared to be superior in numbers. Reitze
was also well aware of the presence of numerous machine guns the British had brought into
action and there was always the threat of renewed British attacks.

However orders were orders, the enemy had to be destroyed so Reitze looked over the
situation and came to the conclusion that a limited attack could be undertaken that had
some chance of success. He assembled a small party of men and prepared to attack the
British where the *Sigelgraben* passed under the road to Fricourt:

> The detachment went forward in the destroyed *Sigelgraben* and occupied a large shell
> crater approximately 20 meters in front of the underpass. At the moment when the
> enemy machine gun sentry this side of the underpass bent down, the troops jumped up,
> drew their hand grenades, and before the Englishmen on the left and the right knew
> what had happened here we were back in the shell hole again under the protection of
> huge smoke clouds with a captured machine gun and a floodlight. With this we had
> lost only one man (nervous shock). The English outposts before and in the underpass
> were killed in the attack.[7]

The British were now deep inside the German lines and slowly trying to expand their
original gains. Groups of German bombers holding improvised trench blocks and the ever-
present machine gun fire were holding up further enemy advances for the time being. Most
of the German machine gun fire appeared to be coming from an area some 500 meters in
front of the British line and from Fricourt Wood, Shelter Wood and Birch Tree Wood.
Little could be done until these guns were silenced. The artillery barrage had long since

Death notice for *Musketier* Heinrich Hauser, 1/R111 from his bicycle club. (*Freiburger Zeitung*)

moved on and any movement in the open terrain was suicidal to both sides.

The continued enemy attacks began to wear down the companies of the III/R111 and the ranks of the men were growing thinner all the time. During the fighting *Leutnant* Clouth had become wounded and the 12/R111 was reinforced with the last remaining platoon of the 11/R111 that was commanded by *Leutnant* Beyle. His platoon was quickly deployed into the front line.

The 9th, 11th and 12/R111 under *Hauptmann* Greininger were responsible for bringing the British advance to a halt on the right wing of Fricourt and prevented the enemy from exploiting their successful advance by the *Lehmgrubenhöhe*. The sacrifices made by these companies prevented the rest of the regimental sector from being isolated and destroyed.

More British troops were able to make their way through the gap between RIR 111 and RIR 110 and advanced via the *Totenwäldchen* and the Contalmaison-Fricourt road toward the *Höhen Wald* [Shelter Wood] where the *Edinger Dorf* was located. The British force was making preparations to continue their advance but until the flanks were secured it was considered too risky.

Fricourt was one of the few locations on the Somme battlefield where senior British commanders were able to move forward into the former German lines and personally assess the situation. On the 21st Division front Brigadier General Headlam, commanding the 64th Brigade worked his way into the German trenches that had been captured.

He immediately sent men to the left to fill in where the 34th Division should have been on their flank. Headlam sent parties forward to establish contact in Crucifix Trench. Lewis Gun detachments moved out to hold Lozenge Wood to the south and it was soon discovered that the Germans were still holding Round Wood. Headlam joined a party making a reconnaissance to Round Wood but was stopped by machine gun fire that resulted in heavy losses to the reconnaissance party.

The British left flank was made secure when Crucifix Trench was occupied where it intersected with the sunken road. Another nearby trench was occupied an hour later by the 1st East Yorkshire. At the same time a local German counter attack occurred against detachments from the 15th and 16th Royal Scots (34th Division) that were supposed to be involved in the attack against La Boisselle but had veered too far to the right and ended up in the 21st Division sector. The attack was brought to a stop and the Germans were eventually driven back.

Memorial card: *Kanonier* Johann Kagerer, LMK II Abteilung RFAR 28. Killed in action 1 July 1916 by an artillery shell. (Author's collection)

When taking stock of the situation at 11 a.m. the British found that both flanks were still in the air. The small parties of the Royal Scots had disappeared just as quickly as they had appeared. Further battalions moved forward from the 62nd Brigade as reinforcements and thereby helping to maintain the gains already made in heavy fighting throughout the morning. The fighting had died down while both sides tried to determine the status of their men and where the opposing side was positioned.

On the southern flank of Fricourt events had taken a different turn. There was no direct attack against the village by the 7th Division. The plan had called for the advance of the 7th Division against the village of Mametz with a defensive flank being formed facing Fricourt.

The attack against Mametz will be discussed in detail in the next chapter. However, the advance against Mametz had gone better than expected and while the defensive flank facing Fricourt was not fully established it was not long before the British had advanced deep into the German lines and had established positions south of Fricourt Wood almost to *Mametzer Wäldchen* [Mametz Copse]. While the men in the II/R111 had not suffered crippling losses they had lost a portion of the front line and numerous men with it. The battalion had participated in the fighting with some very effective long-range fire into the left flank of the 7th Division as well as the right flank of the 21st Division.

The attacks by the 7th Division involved the left wing of RIR 111 on Hill 110, in particular with the 5/R111. The local fighting was intense at some locations and losses began to mount as the British made inroads into the German positions. One man, Wilhelm Seebacher, inside the German trenches with the 5th Coy near the *Steinbruch* on Hill 110, had a close call during the fighting in the morning hours.

Hill 110. (*Das Reserve-Infanterie-Regiment Nr. 111 im Weltkrieg 1914 bis 1918*)

During the major attack by the English on 1 July 1916 I found myself in the front position by the 5th Company in the *Steinbruch* on Hill 110. After the enormous bombardment of the English had ceased, *Leutnant* K[8] and my few men hurried out of our remaining dugouts that were fortunately spared, in order to establish a connection with our men – if any of them were still alive. We jumped into the shot-up communication trench, however we found only dead and wounded. Immediately following I saw *Leutnant* K fall, whether hit by a bullet or only stumbled, I could no longer determine, because as I climbed over the trench and tried to jump after *Leutnant* K I also saw the arrival of the English. I immediately turned around and crept away about 100 meters further back into a shot-up dugout, in the expectation however of still finding straggling comrades. Not five minutes had passed when an English detachment came over to my dugout, but the same ran back directly again. I already decided upon a course of action, to take cover in a dugout lying further to the rear, when I heard footsteps and voices again, this time it was only two men. They both patrolled, especially in front of my prison, as if they had to guard me. How it felt being down underneath in the hole anyone could probably imagine; however here I was, not safe for a minute from becoming buried alive. Fortunately it had not occurred at all to both Tommies to look in my dugout; probably they believed there was no more living Germans inside.[9]

Seebacher would remain inside his makeshift prison well into the afternoon without ever being discovered by his jailers. At the same time Seebacher was trapped inside the dugout, the fighting continued to rage near the crater field by Hill 110.

Part of the garrison on the left wing of RIR 111 belonged to the 1st Reserve Company of the Bavarian *Pionier* Regiment. The 1st Reserve Coy started the battle with a total of 4 officers and 229 men under the command of *Hauptmann* Kellner and *Leutnant der Reserve* Bauer. Just before the end of the preliminary bombardment the last working telephone line in the sector was cut by the intense shellfire. A short time later the telephone line was working again, at least to the nearby company, thanks to a rather unconventional method.

About 7.30 the fire reached a colossal strength. It lingered until 8.30. The telephone connection (re-established on the 28th and 29th) had already been completely destroyed about 7 o'clock. I relate the following that during the fire an aerial line that was made out of ignition cables (mine) was laid down by *Infanterist* Keller, 5/R111 (Telephonist) and *Pionier* Braun of my platoon (Electrician), so that at least I had a connection with the company leader (5/R111). At 9.15 I heard through the telephone that the Englishmen had attacked the right battalion, but had been thrown out of the trenches again by the III/R111. At 11 a.m. I heard through the telephone that the Englishmen had broken through at the 7th Company (R111). *Leutnant der Reserve* Bauer[10]

The Bavarian *pioniers* had front row seats of the battle unfolding along the left flank of the Fricourt Sector. The company had previously been engaged in mining on Hill 110. When it became evident that an attack was to take place, the company was reassigned to act in an infantry role and assist in holding the front line of RIR 111.

On the morning of 1st July the enemy artillery and mine fire reached its highest strength and about at 8 a.m. the attack began. The distribution of the strength at the left wing of the regiment at the time of the attack was approximately the following: The forward most trench at the mine field up until the left regimental border was occupied by the 5/R111, here *Leutnant* von Horstig with his *pioniers* stood at their side. In the second trench behind the *Steinbruch* lay part of the 5/R111 with the company leader. In the connection to the right on the minefield stood the 6/R111. On the left of the 5/R111 was RIR 109.

I held the *'Küchengraben'* with my men up to the regimental border, occupying the connection-border to the *'Küchenmulde'* and the *'Ulmergasse'*. I had contact with the left wing of the 5/R111 through the *'Ulmergasse'* and *'Ostendweg'*.

I was able to observe from my point of view the main attack against the regiment's junction with the connecting regiment on the left. In the shortest time the forward line of the latter was overrun.

The Englishmen penetrated into the *'Küchenmulde'*, established themselves there, and now looked to press in our left flank in repeated attacks from the east and south. However all attacks failed with bloody losses for the enemy against my men. A group of Englishmen went through the *'Küchenmulde'* and penetrated up to the *'Mauzengasse'*, the connection with Mametz, and tried to bring a machine gun into position there. A surprises advance from the *Küchengraben* through the *Mauzengasse* succeeded, the garrison was knocked out of action. Despite our repeated requests through our still-functioning light station to our artillery, shortly after the attack there was not much shooting from them.

Wave upon wave of Englishmen penetrated forward through the Carnoy hollow on the left of us, so that the danger of circumvention became ever greater. It was reported that the left wing of 5/ R111 was hard pressed, so I sent a group of well-trained hand grenade throwers in the *'Ostende Weg'* and they succeeded in expelling the Englishmen that had already penetrated there again. I sent two Groups further into the connection trench between Communication trench B and the *Ulmergasse*.

The *Küchenmulde*. (Author's collection)

At this time there was no more knowledge about the events in the quarry and in the minefield. Now we became taken under strong artillery fire from the southeast, as well as from the enemy who had already broken through. *Leutnant der Reserve* Bauer[11]

The men of the 5/R111 supported by the Bavarian *pioniers* quickly mounted a counter attacked against the British who had penetrated their position. After 30 minutes of close combat with hand grenades and point blank rifle fire most of the enemy had been forced out of the German front line and the situation was temporarily stabilized.

Even with the limited action and relatively small losses the overall situation of the II Battalion as well as the entire regimental sector was in serious jeopardy. The enemy was well established on the left flank of the regiment and growing stronger on the right flank as each hour passed. RIR 111 had lost many men and there was no possibility of receiving any further support as the limited reserves available to the Germans were being utilized in other critical sectors.

At the headquarters of the II Battalion *Hauptmann* Bumiller was observing the enemy's progress when he suddenly saw a group of British soldiers carrying wood in a trench to the left and rear of the battalion dugout. What the wood was needed for was a mystery but the fact that the enemy was occupying such critical trenches could spell disaster for RIR 111. The situation by RIR 109 and what actions or plans the regiment was considering to counter the enemy advance was unknown. All communication between RIR 111 and RIR 109 had broken down. All communications between the II/R111 with regimental headquarters or division headquarters were also lost. If the British continued on their present course then Fricourt was sure to fall and the remaining men in RIR 111 with it.

Finally, a lamp signaling station was able to make contact with the 28th Reserve Division headquarters and transmit the urgent request for reinforcements. The response arrived a short time later, 'Persevere, reinforcements were approaching'. Even now it was almost too late. Shortly after communicating with the division, the II Battalion headquarters had to be evacuated due to the proximity of the enemy.

Despite heavy fire falling all about the battalion dugout, all of the staff and valuable maps and papers were successfully moved to a new location, safe from the enemy for the time being. *Telephonists* Fink and Dehmer also managed to dismantle and carry all of the heavy telephone equipment to the new location. It was still just dead weight as there were no working telephone lines to the rear and no one left to lay one down.

A further review of the situation revealed that the right flank of the regimental sector was secure for the time being, the enemy break in was being contained. The old front line by Fricourt was intact and all attempts to force their way into the village had been repulsed with disastrous results for the enemy. The situation on the left was still the most critical. The II Battalion had reported that the former position held by RIR 109 had been overrun and the situation was uncertain. However there was still hope that RIR 109 would be able to recapture the lost ground and relieve the pressure on RIR 111, but there was no sign that this would take place soon. Artillery support was almost non-existent with few German shells falling anywhere on the battlefield. The loss of all phone lines and the disruption of the artillery observers had effectively blinded the few artillery batteries that were still partially intact.

Some effort was being made to provide the II/RIR 111 with the support it required but all that could be spared was a single platoon from the 12/R111. Even this small number of men was a welcome addition to the overall defense. The platoon only arrived by Groups

Infantrymen – RIR 111. (Author's collection)

over a long period of time. The once quickly traveled route through Fricourt Park was now under constant enemy artillery and machine gun fire. While moving through the badly damaged trenches leading toward the II Battalion the platoon became separated and this slowed the advance even more.

Shortly before noon *Oberst* Ley made his way to the front line north of Fricourt where he made a personal assessment of the overall situation at the *Lehmgrubenhöhe*. His goal was to recapture all lost ground. After he had time to look over the situation he issued orders to the I Battalion to advance north through the *Fricourt Graben* and *Hertzberggraben*. Ley also established contact with division headquarters through light signals and again sent a request for additional reserves to be inserted on the right wing of his regiment

At 12.30 the attack by the I/R111 began with the addition of several Groups from the 10/R111. The number of men available for the attack was considered too small for it to have any success so additional units were ordered to move up and assist in the attack. Two platoons from the 2/Bavarian *Pionier* Regiment and half of two platoons from the 12/R111 were subsequently ordered forward from their positions by Fricourt farm.

Ley had counted on additional support from the III Battalion who had received orders to advance against the *Totenwäldchen* in conjunction with the I Battalion. Unfortunately, the III Battalion somehow did not become involved in the fighting for reasons unknown. Under these circumstances the full weight of the British response could be directed against the weak forces of the I Battalion alone. Losses on both sides of the fighting were increasing rapidly.

Unteroffizier Fuchssteiner and his Group from the 2/Bavarian *Pionier* Regiment was part of the detachment assigned to clear the *Hertzberggraben*. *Unteroffizier* Geiger and *Gefreiter* Gruber with their Groups followed him in support. Their advance was successful and the Bavarian *Pioniers* captured two machine guns and recaptured a German machine gun, whose crew had been killed. However there were too few men to continue the advance and the momentum of the attack was eventually lost as casualties increased.

Elsewhere, small detachments of men continued to offer resistance against the advancing British troops. However most of these detachments did not have enough men to be able to make any difference in the eventual outcome of the fighting in this sector of the front. One officer who had little experience leading men into combat was still willing to give it a try despite what his men thought.

> The liaison officer *Leutnant der Reserve* Menche fell on this day. He had volunteered to undertake the duty [of observation officer for the 4/RFAR 29] and the entire week of the pounding he brought daily reports to the battery. When the infantry by Fricourt had been thrown back, he remained with the battalion when it withdrew. However, during the retreat he gathered together a handful of *pioniers* from our 2nd Coy that were fighting there in shell craters in order to throw themselves against the British that had broken through. One said to him that it was futile; nevertheless he continued to fight on until a couple of minutes later when a bullet pierced his heart.[12]

When the attack stalled it quickly turned into a prolonged hand grenade battle along the entire front from Fricourt to the *Höhenwäldchen* that continued into the evening hours. The attacks accomplished very little. Most of the available strength of the I/R111 was lost when many of the men became casualties. The fighting required large quantities of

Menche

Leutnant d. R. i. Res. Feld-Art.
Regt. 29, gefallen bei Fricourt
am 1. Juli 1916

Leutnant der Reserve Walter Menche, 4/RFAR 29. Killed in
action 1 July 1916. (*Kriegstagbuch aus Schwaben*)

ammunition that could not be easily replaced. The issue of obtaining fresh supplies of hand grenades and rifle ammunition was becoming critical given the pace of consumption so far. The regiment had started the battle with large stockpiles on hand but the unexpected fighting at so many locations was quickly using it all up.

In the fighting that followed the British managed to temporarily penetrate the German trenches in the rear of the 2nd Reserve *Pioniers*. After further fighting the hard-pressed *pioniers* were relieved by an infantry platoon and were able to move to the rear for some much needed rest. The remainder of the *pioniers* in the strength of two Groups with *Leutnant* Knorr and *Leutnant* Krieg eventually were withdrawn with the remnants of the II/R111 to the Intermediate position north of the *Küchenmulde*. Knorr and Krieg remained on duty as Orderly Officers for RIR 111 because the connection between the different battalions and the neighboring RIR 110 had broken down and every officer was needed.

Oberleutnant Sorge, commander of the 2/Bavarian *Pionier* Regiment, remained for the support of the Battalion Commander I/R111 with the staff in the *Nestlerhöhlen*. The regimental staff moved into a dugout in the Intermediate position north of the *Küchenmulde* towards evening. Just before darkness fell the enemy was able to advance up to the *Totenwäldchen* at the Contalmaison-Fricourt road and occupy this position and the *Höhenweg* with strong forces.

Leutnant Rupp, 10/R111 and a few men went back to the *Nestlerhöhlen* to obtain new supplies of ammunition and carry it forward to the 2/R111. On the return journey the heavily-laden men were moving slowly through the shell-torn terrain while trying to find the position of the 2nd Coy. The exact location of the opposing forces was still unknown and in the time needed to obtain the ammunition the positions of both sides could have changed even more.

Rupp and his men suddenly bumped into a group of English soldiers inside a communication trench. The response from both sides was immediate and deadly as Mills bombs and *Stielhandgranaten* flew back and forth, exploding in the ranks of the opposing sides. Rupp and his men quickly got the upper hand and in a short time the fight was over and Rupp had managed to capture 1 non-commissioned officer and 10 privates. Rupp's party continued forward and successfully dropped off their heavy load.

The men of the 1R/Bavarian *Pionier* Regiment were also called upon to carry ammunition into the front lines. *Hauptmann* Kellner, commanding the 28th Reserve Division *Pioniers*, issued orders to the *pioniers* of the 1st Reserve Coy located in Martinpuich to carry ammunition and hand grenades into the front lines by Fricourt.

I was on the road myself with 3 Groups, at 3 o'clock in the afternoon [2 p.m. British time]. This ammunition transportation was an achievement for the men because the route had to be attained largely across open terrain due to the continuous and very severe artillery fire. I succeeded in coming forward with only 4 men.

According to a message from the regimental staff of RIR 111 I received the task with my men, together with the 2/Bavarian *Pionier* Regiment, to hold the *Schadeweg* [in the Château Park Fricourt, front toward Mametz]. *Unteroffizier* Stocker and *Gefreiter* Greiner succeeded in delivering this important regimental order to the leader of the 2nd Company. *Leutnant* Wendler[13]

Phase 2 of the British attack upon Fricourt was now set to take place. The original plan had called for the direct assault upon Fricourt once the 21st and 7th Divisions had met up behind the village and defensive flanks had been established. While none of these prerequisites had been met it was still decided to implement Phase 2 without delay.

At 12.50 p.m. the 22nd Brigade (7th Division) and 62nd Brigade (21st Division) along with parts of the 50th Brigade (on loan to 21st Division) were ordered to attack Fricourt. The actual attack would begin at 2.30 p.m. following a 30 minute bombardment. The bombardment was not as effective as hoped and the men of the II/R111 holding the lines in front of and south of the village to Hill 110 suffered few losses.

The leading wave of the 22nd Brigade managed to gain the German front line with few losses. They had the advantage of making it across the open ground of no man's land before the main German defenders could fully respond. The following waves suffered far more as the German infantry opened fire with rifles and machine guns, especially from the left flank.

All available men capable of using a weapon were called upon to repel this latest British attack. Men from the 5th, 6th, 7th, 8th, 10th and 12/R111 as well as portions of the 1st and 2MG/R111 directed their fire against the advancing British troops. With most of the defenders being situated in individual shell craters or small sections of trench there was little cohesiveness in the defensive position but the volume of fire quickly brought the attack to a halt. Despite the heavy fire the British did manage to penetrate the German lines between the 5th and 6/R111 and the fighting spread into the German trenches and shell crater positions.

While the leading troops of the 22nd Brigade managed to enter the German lines there was still hard fighting facing the men. On the left, bombing parties were sent down two support trenches toward the valley and the village of Fricourt where they were practically wiped out a short time later.

In the center a bombing party entered the area known as the 'Rectangle'. The men encountered heavy resistance from German bombing parties from the 5/R111 and were forced back to their starting point. There were attempts to advance over open ground but these came under very heavy fire from the left and were quickly abandoned. While establishing a foothold inside the German front line, the British were unable to make any headway for the present.

The 1st Royal Welch Fusiliers also managed to reach the German front line. They sent bombing parties forward along the German front line toward Fricourt. The Welch Fusiliers made good progress and reached Apple Alley with some men even making it into the village of Fricourt where they remained for a short time before being forced to retreat. Their success provided relief to the 20th Manchesters that allowed this battalion to maintain its position. While in Apple Alley the Welch Fusiliers were able to make contact with the 20th Brigade that had been fighting since the morning attack.

The attack by the 50th Brigade was far less successful. The 7th Green Howards attacked with only three companies, the fourth had already advanced at 7.45 a.m. in error. The battalion was almost completely destroyed in the first few minutes of the attack by a single German machine gun. The German defenses were at their strongest at the point of attack and much of the wire was intact with only a few gaps. The preliminary 30 minute bombardment had failed to destroy the German positions and additional support from the fire of Lewis Guns behind a railway embankment had little effect on the defending German garrison.

Entire lines of men were shot down before they could advance 50 meters under the deadly rifle and machine gun fire that tore through their ranks. Much of the German fire came from the front and left flank where the German line was not under attack. Many of the defenders could be seen standing on top of their parapet in order to get a better shot at the Green Howards. Within three minutes 15 officers and 336 men had become casualties and the attack was a shambles.

A few men did manage to reach the German front line but with the exception of a small group that had taken refuge in a cellar the rest were either killed or captured. Some survivors managed to hold out in shell holes across no man's land where they awaited darkness before attempting to return to the British lines.

The 7th East Yorkshire also attempted to attack Fricourt shortly after the disaster that befell the Green Howards. They suffered much the same fate. In the first two companies 5 officers and 150 men were killed or wounded within the first few minutes after leaving the British trenches. With such heavy losses the rest of the attack was quickly canceled as being impossible in the face of such heavy fire.

Now, with renewed attacks against Fricourt as well as intense pressure being applied by the 7th Division in the south, the 21st Division received orders to assist in the attack. The 21st Division had been consolidating its position since most of the heaviest fighting north of the village had ceased in the morning. The division had managed to create a unified flank facing the village of Fricourt.

The new orders called for the 63rd and 64th Brigades to support the attack that was scheduled for 2.30 p.m. Both brigades were instructed to press forward toward Fricourt farm and Shelter Wood from their positions in the sunken road and Crucifix Trench. If successful, this movement could cut off any retreat by the men of RIR 111 still in Fricourt.

However, when the men of the 63rd Brigade began to advance they were immediately checked by heavy and accurate machine gun fire coming from the direction of Fricourt farm and positions just to the north of the farm.

The 64th Brigade never had a chance. The orders to attack did not reach the brigade until 10 minutes after the brief artillery preparation barrage had ended. Without any protection at all, the brigade suffered losses from machine gun fire and rifle fire that effectively prevented any ground being taken. Some relief was at hand when at 5.33 p.m. the remaining two battalions of the 62nd Brigade were sent across no man's land from the British lines and reinforced the newly captured positions north of Fricourt.

The normal stress of combat was compounded by the lack of potable water. The British troops had been in action for hours in the hot July sun. Dust and smoke and the physical and mental exertion of constant fighting had made the men exceedingly thirsty and most water supplies had already been used up. The troops were in desperate need of fresh water – and soon. Ammunition was also being used up at a rapid rate and fresh supplies were also desperately needed. Most of the ammunition carried by the British in the attack had been expended.

Still, the fighting south of Fricourt had not let up as new attempts were made to capture the village from the west and from the south. The defenders along the extended left flank of RIR 111 were growing dangerously thin. Many of the reserves that could have been helpful in keeping the enemy back had already been deployed in the heavy fighting in the I/R111 sector.

Constant British pressure from the 7th Division used up the last of the available reserves; a few Groups from the 5/R111 and one platoon from the 8/R111 were now being used to block off the quarry on Hill 110. Now there were no more men to insert into the fighting. Messages came back from the front line on a regular basis urgently requesting

Infantrymen – RIR 111. (Author's collection)

Stone quarry on Hill 110. (*Das Reserve-Infanterie-Regiment Nr. 111 im Weltkrieg 1914 bis 1918*)

reinforcements but they had to be ignored. *Leutnants* Kleinjung and Kaufmann defended their trenches traverse by traverse but it was growing increasingly difficult as losses mounted and the supplies of hand grenades grew smaller.

There were occasions where the actions of individual men made a difference, even if only for a short time. After sitting inside his dugout for several hours *Infanterist* Seebacher was finally determined to attempt an escape.

> Now what to do? I watched the two for an hour, who regularly every 2 minutes, their rifles under their arms, walk leisurely up and down. However, gradually the situation grew too silly to me. I did not want to be taken captive; I could not remain sitting here forever, so I made the decision to escape. I waited for the moment, until both of them approached their position again and curved around the corner. Quickly I took to both of my legs and vanished in the opposite direction. For the time being I was saved.
>
> To break through to my unit in broad daylight was naturally impossible; so I decided again to vanish from the surface into a shot-up dugout. I hoped I would be able to make my way to safety in the night. Suddenly I heard footsteps again. This time it was not an Englishman, but a Bavarian pioneer straggler. Our joy was great! We held a council of war and then crept up to the position, where the two Englishmen still patrolled up and down. They were probably not particularly pleasantly surprised when our firsthand grenades came flittering past. However we now also had the Tommies by the neck and immediately a lively hand grenade battle developed. This fighting must have been observed by the Battalion or Regimental staff, because soon after we received reinforcements from the 8th Company with 6 men (amongst them also a Stockacher, K. Krumme).
>
> I immediately distributed these 6 men in the trench, while the *pioneer* and I together looked for hand grenades in the dugouts. The fighting surged back and forth, but we maintained the position. Unfortunately a comrade fell by a headshot. As a diversion the English artillery was still active, intervening from the flank, the

shells flew over our heads. Pilots circled quite low above us; fortunately they left us unmolested, likely because friend and foe were too close to one another.[14]

Leutnant Rothacker, 5/R111, had already placed every available man into the front line and could not spare anyone in spite of the call for reinforcements from every corner of the company sector. His one hope was that the neighboring RIR 109 could mount a successful counter attack in the Mametz Sector and thereby relieve the pressure against the left wing of his company and RIR 111. His hopes were dashed as the British continued to gain ground against RIR 109 and moved even further in the rear of the 5/R111. It was only a matter of time before the II Battalion sector would be surrounded and completely cut off from all assistance.

The fighting continued on both flanks of Fricourt throughout the afternoon and early evening hours. Constant pressure was being applied along the exposed left flank of the regiment. Stop-gap measures had been used to fill critical portions of the line but more men were desperately needed. North of the village the situation was not much different. The British applied pressure to the east and south in order to break the German resistance and hopefully to make contact with the 7th Division troops as originally planned.

It was often fate that spared one man over another, simple luck that one soldier would survive to fight another day while others fell around him or ended up as a prisoner of war. In one such instance the fate of three badly wounded men rested upon the need of a senior non-commissioned officer for something as insignificant in the scheme of the battle as his *Stammrolle* (company nominal roll book). With all of the death and destruction swirling around the men this *Feldwebel* did not want to leave his book behind.

On 1st July, towards 8 o'clock in the morning, the 12th Company became alarmed and distributed amongst the different position companies. I remained with the Battalion as a runner. Towards evening the Battalion moved back into the *Nestlerhöhlen*. At the onset of darkness I received orders from *Feldwebel* Kaufmann, to go to the park and to get the leather pouch, in which was the small *Stammrollen* book. *Musketier* Freitag went with me. We carefully went forward, because we didn't know if the park was already occupied by the Englishmen. I went into the dugout and got the pouch. As I was going to leave, I heard moans. I went to the other side of the dugout; there lay three severely wounded men, who had apparently been overlooked. My comrade Freitag and I brought one into the *Nestlerhöhlen*, where I made my report. The other two were fetched by the medics. *Ersatz Reservist* Joseph Würz, 12/RIR 111[15]

Apprehension grew in the regimental battle headquarters in the late afternoon. At 4.30 p.m. the II Battalion reported to headquarters that every connection to RIR 109 was gone and that the pressure against the left wing of the battalion was growing stronger all the time.

As the hours passed in the afternoon and early evening the British were able to make headway through the maze of trenches between Mametz and Fricourt. The 5/R111 had been forced to extend its lines along the regimental boundary that had once faced RIR 109. The problem was that they did not have enough men to extend their line far enough to prevent the British from flanking the German defenses on the left wing of the company and attacking them in the rear.

Once the British had been able to advance on both flanks of the 5/R111 the fate of this

Trenches on Hill 110. (An der Somme)

small company was sealed. It had cost the enemy dearly, however he still took Hill 110 after much hard fighting and losses to both sides.

Leutnant Rothacker realized that further resistance in the front line was pointless. He gathered the remaining survivors of the 5th Coy and moved back through a communication trench that led in the direction of Fricourt. He took up a new position and continued to hold back the enemy for as long as it was possible.

Rothacker and his men continued to resist all enemy attacks and held on to their small section of trench. The men had no idea what was happening around them and had no contact with the other companies that were supposed to be nearby. As far as Rothacker and his men knew, they were the last survivors of the II Battalion.

The fighting raged until almost 9 p.m. The 5th Coy repelled all enemy attacks against their position from the front and from both flanks. Then it was finally over, the men no longer had any strength left to continue the fight and little ammunition; it was time to surrender before every last man was either killed or wounded. Most of the survivors were taken prisoner; almost every one of these men was also wounded from the heavy fighting and required medical attention. *Leutnant* Rothacker was among this group, he had suffered a wound to the head.

Other troops from Hill 110 under *Leutnant* Kauffmann and *Vizefeldwebel* Wünsche tried to find a route through the enemy lines toward the spot where the 6th Company had been located earlier. From there the men would retreat further into the village of Fricourt. They were unsuccessful in their attempt and were blocked by the advancing British troops.

It was not until the early morning hours of 2 July that this small group was finally overwhelmed and taken prisoner. *Leutnant* Kauffmann and a large number of his men had been killed; *Vizefeldwebel* Wünsche and most of the others were wounded. The odds of successfully making it back safely to the rear were quite small. The regimental history relates that the men of RIR 111 could look back on this day with particular pride because of the men's devotion to duty and the stand of 5th Company and the support by the *pioniers* on Hill 110.

The battle had turned into small pockets of men desperately fighting for their lives. Parts of the 6th, 8th, 10/R111 and Bavarian *pioniers* moved to the left wing of their position and created a barricade in the second trench behind the 6th Company sector in order to prevent the British from advancing from the quarry toward Fricourt. The situation remained critical. There were no reserves left, ammunition was running out and water was urgently craved by the men. All wells that could have been used were destroyed by the heavy shelling and all stockpiles set up before the attacks were long gone.

Most of the commanders of the different companies as well as most non-commissioned officers had either been killed or wounded. The leaders of the 7th and 8/R111, *Hauptmann* Engländer and *Leutnant* Luhr, had been killed when a mortar shell exploded near both officers. The trenches had been badly damaged and most of the men were positioned inside the numerous shell craters. The ranks of the remaining men were growing thinner with each passing hour. There were serious doubts among the survivors that they would be able to hold out against a determined enemy attack. The only hope left was to wait for the cover of darkness when it might be possible to break out of the trap and reach the safety of the rear. The only other chance they had was if reinforcements would arrive and relieve them. At the very least, the heavy fighting would die down once darkness fell and that would be welcomed by all.

The fate of a large part of the defenders of Hill 110, in particular the *pioniers* in the 1st Reserve Company from the Bavarian *Pionier* Regiment, was derived from the report given by three *pioniers* that had managed to make it back to safety, the only ones to do so. These *pioniers* also provided critical information about the movements of the enemy. They had observed the English advancing in dense columns in the area between Hill 110 and Mametz. Shortly afterward they also saw the enemy advancing from Mametz toward the *Granatschlucht*.

This was a serious threat to the left flank of the entire Fricourt sector and required immediate action. Every man possible from RIR 111 as well as half of a platoon gathered together by the leader of the 2/Bavarian *Pionier* Regiment was assembled. The troops were placed in position at the southeastern edge of the Park of Fricourt. It was quickly determined that there were not enough men available to prevent the enemy in Mametz from advancing north and west and completing Phase 1 of the attack, the link up of the 7th and 21st Divisions in the rear of Fricourt.

If this was allowed to occur RIR 111 would be completely cut off and destroyed unless the regiment was able to force its way through enemy lines to the north. The big decision now facing *Oberst* Ley was if he should allow these events to take place. He was determined not to voluntarily give up a single foot of ground. On the other hand, his losses were increasing each hour and they had been involved in fighting for the last 12 hours, much of it hand to hand fighting.

Ley realized that if events continued along the same lines that his men would eventually

Pionier – 2R/13th Pionier Battalion. (Author's collection)

become so worn down from fatigue that their resilience would be gone. There was no food left, water was needed immediately and the shortage of ammunition and hand grenades was almost at a critical level. There was no prospect of any fresh supplies in the foreseeable future. Artillery support had been lacking for the entire day and there was no sign that this would change any time soon.

Some held the overly optimistic point of view that fresh troops positioned nearby. With the support of strong artillery forces they would counter attack and release RIR 111 from its difficult situation. Most felt that the enemy would also continuously insert new forces into the fight, and then it was only a matter of time until the British would overpower the weakened remnants of RIR 111 if the regiment did not receive any reinforcements.

At the front along Hill 110 the fighting raged while the regimental commander was considering his options. Cut off from all communications the small pockets of defenders did their best under very trying circumstances. The situation facing the commander of RIR 111 was very confusing. Some reports that arrived mentioning the approach of reinforcements were more likely to be rumors than fact as there were no reinforcements anywhere to be found.

Englishmen penetrated here from the east and the north, without finding any opposition in Mametz. Soon the trench in our rear was densely occupied by the English and we now received strong machine gun and rifle fire in the rear. *Offizier*

Stellvertreter Birkmann fell, after he was already previously wounded through a grazing shot to the head, through a head shot from behind.

I cannot let it be unsaid that Birkmann, during the entire battle action through his exceptionally intrepid and brave behavior, was invaluable and therefore had a large share in the successful defense against the repeated English attacks.

Connections with the neighbor (RIR 109) were lost. The difficulties of my own defense grew from minute to minute, because the trenches – generally those that could still be described as such – were cut into the hillside and did not have any rear cover. Attempts to contact the Battalion failed. There were no orders because of mix-ups. Connections were broken. I had already given the order to retreat to Fricourt on own responsibility, when out of *Laufgraben* C that the Württemberg *pioniers* occupied, verbal orders became passed through, to hold the position under all circumstances because the III/R111 already was advancing to reinforce Hill 110 in spite of the existing ammunition shortage. Trenches had almost disappeared. *Leutnant der Reserve* Bauer 1R/Bavarian *Pionier* Regiment[16]

Ley doubted highly that his men still had the strength left if they had to force their way through the British lines. He now had to decide if he was going to sacrifice his regiment, his men that had been with him almost two years. If he did, then whose interests would this serve? Should the regiment continue to resist the British advances against the right flank of the regiment north of Fricourt and on the left flank by La Boiselle, or withdraw to the I *Zwischen Stellung*?

Fortunately, because of the stubborn resistance by the I and III/R111 to the north of Fricourt there was an escape route still open to the rest of the regiment. It was only a narrow route that could be closed at any time. The path was outlined by fires the British had lit that were apparently designed to provide the British artillery with exact knowledge of the new front line.

Finally Ley made a decision, one he found difficult to issue. He would take his worn down regiment out of the precarious position it found itself in by withdrawing from Fricourt. He was aware that an alert enemy could easily take advantage of this situation and result in serious losses to RIR 111. The men would be most vulnerable as they withdrew from their defensive positions and moved across open ground.

He issued orders that all remnants of the regiment were to withdraw from their current positions at darkness. The regiment would then occupy the I *Zwischen Stellung* that was being held by parts of the III/R111 where the regiment would extend to the left up to the flank by Mametz. In order for this important move to take place it required the use of runners.

All telephone lines had been destroyed and light signals would not reach every portion of the regiment at the front line. The runners were given their orders and fanned out in order to reach every man in the regiment. It was difficult moving through the badly damaged position while under enemy fire but the men managed to complete their task. *Musketier* Löffler was unable to locate a central command point in the II Battalion Sector and instead he went from shell crater to shell crater and informed each man individually that he came across.

The relief began at 11 p.m. The bulk of the infantry would break off from the enemy and move toward the rear under the protection of blocking parties that would prevent the enemy from following.

The men withdrew in small detachments, in good order and taking back the majority of the wounded. Only the men who were severely wounded and could not be moved had to be left behind for the British to care for. There was no other option present. The fighting continued on Hill 110 and the sound of hand grenades exploding could still be clearly heard. For many the order to withdraw had either come too late or the runners carrying the message were unable to reach them.

> About 7 in the evening the Englishmen had Communication trench 'A' and the position of the 6/R111 in their hands. A retreat on this line to Fricourt was now impossible. It was now further absolutely clear to me that I was fully alone with my men on the open field, especially as also an attempt to establish a connection with the quarry company had resulted in learning that the area of the 5/R111 was also in the hands of the enemy. We were now literally surrounded on all sides. Nevertheless the Englishmen did not dare to attack. I recognized the hopelessness of the situation – ammunition and hand grenades were lacking – however I fired up my men over and over to endure, because however I still hoped to strike through to the rear between Mametz and Fricourt under the protection of darkness, with at least part of the Other Ranks. However before the onset of darkness, approximately 8.30 in the evening, strong mine fire was placed on our completely shot-up position and an attack against us from all sides with unbelievable superiority allowed us after brief opposition to realize that the rest of Hill 110 had fallen in the hands of the enemy.
>
> The superior strength of the enemy had been so overwhelming that there was no longer a need for a formal surrender, but we were simply assembled in the middle under masses of Englishmen who then took us away. The troops had given everything a man could possibly be expected to in this fight, especially when considering that there was little food and water. *Leutnant der Reserve* Bauer.[17]

The sounds of fighting on Hill 110 could clearly be heard until about 2 a.m. on 2 July, then it became eerily silent. It did not take much imagination to realize that all German resistance on the hill was finished. Still, a few men did manage to make their escape. One of the few men from the 5th Company that had managed to make his way safely to the rear was Wilhelm Seebacher. The runners had apparently not been able to reach Seebacher's position earlier in the evening.

> About 10.30 at night a battalion orderly came shouting 'We are surrounded, whoever can, save yourselves!' The pitch-black night came in very useful in our retreat. Five men succeeded in sneaking back through the enemy lines with tremendous effort. When the few remaining men of RIR 111 had assembled, the Regimental commander *Oberst* Ley congratulated us and promoted me to the 'Hand grenade General'.[18]

A large number of the defenders in front of the village of Fricourt had successfully held their position throughout the fighting on 1 July only to find that they had been cut off by the British from the flank or the rear. Unlike the *pioniers* fighting on Hill 110, some of them were fortunate and made their way back to safety. In the confused situation it had literally become every man for himself.

On one occasion a shell burst right in front of the machine gun and blew it into the trench. However that did not stop us. Altogether we fired 22,000 rounds during the day. As the assault ceased, we could see that we were already surrounded. Our telephones were still working. Schüsele rang up the Regiment and received the order 'Hold the position until it gets dark, then reinforcements will arrive'. During the night we received the order to withdraw and despite the fact that the British were so close that we could hear them talking, we got through unharmed to the Regimental staff in Bazentin Wood. We were each given a bottle of sparkling mineral water there, which cheered us up; then we moved off to the Divisional Intermediate Position, where we stuck it out until we were relieved. Rudolf Stadelbacher and *Unteroffizier* Otto Schüsele Machine Gun Company, RIR 111[19]

Many of the men who had been able to withdraw from Hill 110 where the worst of the fighting was raging felt remorse at leaving their comrades behind. Based upon the sound of heavy fighting it was obvious that their friends were in a bad spot, yet there was nothing they could do for them. It was recognized that the sacrifice of the men left on Hill 110 who fought to the end allowed the other parts of the II Battalion to successfully withdraw without being disturbed by the enemy.

The men moved over the broken ground, stumbling and cursing quietly as they moved through the damaged terrain toward the rear. There was a constant fear that they would bump into the British at any time as no one knew where friend or foe was located. At approximately 3 a.m. on 2 July the II/R111, or what was left of it, reached the *I Zwischen Stellung*. The 9/R111 formed the right wing of the battalion sector that reached up to the Contalmaison-Fricourt road. Lying north of this road was a company from IR 23 that was subordinate to RIR 110. Next to the 9/R111, about 50 meters south of the *Höhen Wäldchen*, was the 11/R111 under the command of *Vizewachtmeister* Schrempf who was standing in for *Leutnant* Beyle who had been wounded. The 12/R111 was in position north of Fricourt farm up to the Park road. Parts of the 10/R111 were placed in the line where they were needed, where there were too few men.

The last of the reserves from the 1/R111 had been ordered forward late in the afternoon. *Feldwebel* Robert Hauschild left behind an account of his experiences of this time.

From the evening of 24 June until 1 July [my platoon of replacements] lay under raging bombardment in a reserve position behind Contalmaison-Fricourt. Until 1 July the 109th, 110th and 111th [Reserve Regiments] held positions in front of us. The enemy's superiority was great, but the English wasted an enormous amount of large and small caliber ammunition, and one must wonder why greater devastation wasn't caused by such superior firepower. Although morale was splendid, the English main attack on 1 July near Montauban forced back the regiments of our division toward the second line of defenses.

That afternoon [1 July] at 5 o'clock I received orders to go forward with my platoon as support. For the past week the English had bombarded our trenches with such frightful intensity that in the surrounding area one could not walk 10 paces without encountering a crater. Shells were still falling, and to take a large platoon of 80 men through this hell would be quite a feat.

On the way I had to pass through a part of a large wood [Mametz Wood], which lay under pounding artillery fire. Debris was everywhere – there a destroyed gun, there dead and badly injured horses, here a moaning wounded man, there a dead one – with no discernible path through the smashed branches and tree stumps. The English had fired into it day and night without interruption. Wounded met us on their way to the dressing station, which in a masterful way was established and concealed with all necessary medical supplies. The air was thick with powder smoke and the odor of decay, yet I was amazed that in this wilderness at least some regard was paid to sanitation. Unburied horse cadavers had been covered with chlorine chalk. There was little time here for contemplation, so on we went.

About a half hour one of my people called out that he was hit. Two men bound the wound and accompanied him rearward. The farther we went the more vexing became the shell and shrapnel fire, which screamed hellishly in the wood like a herd of demons. Finally I reached a trench and allowed the men a short rest before moving forward again to another trench at the wood's edge, occupied by our 2nd Company. These comrades also were mostly from the Baden city of Pforzheim; we greeted them warmly and wished each other luck. It is difficult to describe thoughts that enter one's mind during such an unexpected, if short, meeting. For a few moments one forgot all danger. 'Everything is well,' we heard. So it was by us. Unfortunately, the reunion was short. I moved on further left to my assigned destination, where my people and I pressed ourselves flat on the ground.

Thirty minutes later an order arrived for the platoon to change flanks to the right. So, back to the trench we went. From there to the new position the route was overland and in the open. Each second above ground courted death, but finally it was reached. Disappointed, we found a trench only a meter deep with no dugouts. We could only lie down and barely stir. Within the first hour I already had six men wounded. Finally, as shadows lengthened it became darker, the shellfire lessened.

Soon an unfamiliar officer showed up and informed me that this position must be held at all hazards. 'Oh, fine!' I thought. We barely had a trench, no dugouts, my people had just endured a week-long bombardment and the advance to the front with some casualties. My current numbers were like a finger stuck in the hole of a dike. But orders were orders, and I gave instructions to my men to scrape small protective holes in the forward side of the trench. This was done with knives and bayonets. Then we laid down or took turns at watch, for not too far away we could hear the English likewise entrenching. After two hours the enemy's shelling increased and the English sought to breach my left flank. Several hand grenades and rapid fire drove them back.[20]

The 1st, 4th, 3rd and 2/R111 were placed in line to the left of the III/R111 up to the Mametz flank. This flank was open and unsupported by any nearby troops. In order to provide some protection a hand grenade blocking party was formed. The entire garrison of the new defensive position numbered only 400 rifles and 5 machine guns, far fewer men than had started the battle only a day before.

The II Battalion staff was located at the *Nestlerhöhlen* where approximately 50 men from different companies, *pioniers* and the rear echelon were assembled. This hastily formed detachment served as the only reserve available to the regiment.

The second line consisted of an unfinished position between Contalmaison and

Mametz Wood. The position was occupied by the II Battalion with parts of the I/R23 and the LBEB 55. The regimental staff was set up inside a dugout at the western edge of this wood. The staff was kept extremely busy trying to piece together the events and losses of the previous day as well as trying to organize the regimental forces for the anticipated enemy attacks that should follow shortly.

While the withdrawal from the Fricourt sector had been handled successfully and with little loss of men there were still massive shortages of ammunition, food, water and materiel. Everything from cooking equipment to machine guns needed to be replaced. The withdrawal from Fricourt was probably the largest and the last voluntary relinquishment of territory on the Somme by the Germans during the battle.

The new position occupied by RIR 111 was in poor condition and it was doubtful that it was sufficiently developed to be able to withstand any new enemy attack. The trenches were still in a rudimentary state, there simply was not enough time or manpower in the months before the attack to create a defensive system to rival the former front line position. In their present state it would not take much effort by the enemy to overwhelm the defenses. In addition the new position had also suffered damage in the week-long bombardment thereby weakening it even more at such a critical time.

The garrison was physically and mentally exhausted yet the men rose to the occasion as needed. The men went to work as if they had fully recovered from their ordeal on July 1st. They used whatever tools were available to improve the trenches to a state where they might have a chance against a determined enemy attack. While they worked the new line was kept under constant British artillery fire, a further incentive to make improvements to the position.

The only fortunate aspect of the situation was that the enemy infantry also appeared to be at the end of their strength and was only attempting very weak, indecisive attacks by the *Totenwäldchen*. This could all change in a minute once fresh enemy troops came into the line. Until then the men of RIR 111 had to persevere until relieved or reinforced.

Most of what we know about what took place by Fricourt in the final hours of fighting comes from the personal accounts of the men lucky enough to have made it back safely. The

British prisoners captured on 1 July 1916 by the men of RIR 111. (*Das Reserve-Infanterie-Regiment Nr. 111 im Weltkrieg 1914 bis 1918*)

fate of many would not be known for weeks or months as official reports were completed, casualty returns were created and lists of prisoners were exchanged through the Red Cross.

Some details also came from the personal letters of the men who had been taken prisoner, such as *Gefreiter der Reserve* Neuhäuser. He was amongst the men captured in the early morning hours of 2 July. Some months following the battle, Neuhäuser provided a sworn affidavit that outlined the fate of a fellow pionier, *Unteroffizier der Reserve* Georg Kappelmeier, 2/Bavarian *Pionier* Regiment:

> On the morning of 2 July *Unteroffizier* Kappelmeier and several other men were inside dugout 17 in the *Heckenstellung* Fricourt when an English detachment approached nearby and threw hand bombs into the dugout. An infantryman from the 111th Regiment [sic] was able to run out but no one else from the others inside came out, then the English threw in still more hand bombs.[21]

While the affidavit did not specifically mention the death of Kappelmeier there was never any other contact with him after 2 July 1916 and he was officially declared dead.

Leutnant Wendler, 1R/Bavarian *Pionier* Regiment, left a record of the final moments of his company in the company war diary:

> The Englishmen now also attacked the hill frontally. The company afforded desperate opposition against the superior enemy until 11 at night, without any artillery support, according to the statements of 3 *Pioniers* that were able to make it through at night. Then what of the company that was still remaining was taken prisoner.
>
> *Offizier Stellvertreter* Birkmann had already fallen in the trench fighting through a head shot. *Leutnant* Bauer and *Leutnant* von Horstig, as well as 133 *Unteroffizier* and Other Ranks were missing.
>
> 3 *Pioniers* – Feldlein, Irrgang and Winklmann – together with an infantry sergeant were able to make it through after several hours of hand grenade fighting that inflicted heavy losses on the Englishmen. Otherwise nothing would be known about that fate of the largest part of the company.[22]

Leutnant der Reserve Rudolf von Horstig D'Aubigny von Engelbrunner also provided details of the final moments of the 1st Reserve Company. He had sent a letter home while a prisoner of war at Donington Hall dated 9 July 1916 where he outlined many of the details of the events that occurred on 1 July and of his particular appreciation of the men who had fought by his side.

> … to mention the names of the ones belonging to the 1st Reserve Company who faithfully stood by the side of the very courageous, brave *Leutnant* von Horstig up to the final capture. This honorable conclusion of the drama followed after eight hours of bitter fighting, in view of the total exhaustion of the men and because, with the exception of 12 hand grenades and a few cartridges, the small brave flock were dependent alone upon the bayonet and rifle butt, surrounded by enemies, who continuously increased.
>
> Above all, *Pionier* Kist should be mentioned, who up to the last second fought beside his *Leutnant*. Only with difficulty did he decide to place his rifle at rest, as

did *Unteroffizier* Zeh, who found a hero's death in the close fighting, besides *Pioniers* Drexel, Ebentheuer, Gruschwitz, Schülein and Hempel.[23]

Von Horstig mentioned that after the surrender his men were in the trenches among dense masses of the enemy and then transported to the rear. The behavior of the enemy was throughout worthy and decent. Also the treatment of the Other Ranks was humane and that the officers everywhere were 'gentlemanlike'. This was in contrast to the reception the men received when encountering the French who apparently cursed and spit upon the captured men as they were led past.

Some of the men captured on 1 July were marched through France to Le Havre. Von Horstig did acknowledge that the prisoners were guarded against the outbursts of hatred by Frenchmen. However, he felt that the interrogation of the prisoners had not been made very pleasant through crudities and threats. Perhaps his biggest complaint was that the officers and men had their hair cut in the same manner as convicts.

When he arrived at the first assembly camp he found that the leader of the 1st Reserve Company, *Leutnant der Reserve* Bauer was also present. In their discussions of the events of 1 July they firmly established that 87 men belonging to the company were in the camp as well and that according to their perceptions and those of the Other Ranks a further 18 men were dead and 17 were wounded. They determined that the company had definitely lost 122 men in the fighting on 1st July.

2 July

While the first day of the battle was finished it did not mean that the fighting had stopped. The exhausted men from RIR 111 occupied their new positions and tried to get as much sleep as possible while some of their less fortunate comrades stood watch, always on the

Transporting the wounded on the Somme. (Author's collection)

alert for a new British attack.

The sun rose early on 2 July and the ever-present artillery observation aircraft were already in the air, circling over the German lines. The British had used the cover of night to bring up a number of artillery batteries. Some had been placed in position north of Hill 110 and were able to provide deadly flanking fire against the new German positions, all the time having their fire directed by the circling British planes.

The German troops on the ground did not have the benefit of a trench line that had taken months to create and the lack of sufficient protection was soon manifesting itself in ever increasing casualties. The artillery fire was supplemented by newly set up mine throwers that had been put into positions by the *Toten Wäldchen* and Fricourt farm. The added weight of fire was causing even more losses among the dwindling number of defenders.

The men from RIR 111 desperately hoped for some support from their own artillery but there were too few guns still capable of firing and they had to be moved in order to direct their fire against the new British targets. It seemed the men from RIR 111 would have to rely upon their own efforts to survive the second day of fighting.

Most of the close range infantry weapons – the *Minenwerfer, Priesterwerfer* and machine guns – had been destroyed, damaged or captured in the heavy fighting of 1 July. Fortunately for the men there were alternative sources of weapons close at hand. During the fighting on the previous day a number of British weapons had been captured and were now being used against their former owners.

Vizefeldwebel Eckert, 9/R111 brought up a Stokes mortar and began firing at the British positions. *Feldwebel* Reitze and *Ersatz Reservist* Baur manned a captured British machine gun and opened fire against the enemy positions by the *Toten Wäldchen*. The use of captured weapons proved to be very useful as the men also had plentiful amounts of ammunition for these weapons while supplies of machine gun ammunition for the German MG 08 had almost been completely used up the previous day.

15cm heavy field howitzer position on the Somme. (Author's collection)

The defenders experienced small successes as the British attempted to expand their gains made on 1 July. Morale remained high among the men from RIR 111 despite the casualties and physical hardships the troops experienced. Numerous small attacks made by the British in the morning were stopped one by one. Many of the defenders felt there was still a chance that the events experienced on 1 July could be reversed and the original German front line restored. However, it could only happen if enough fresh men could be found and if they were supported by artillery.

The night passed slowly until dawn of 2 July broke with the promise of more beautiful weather. Straight ahead lay the village of Mametz, with Fricourt to the right. The English occupied Mametz, and through my binoculars I could see many soldiers moving about. My observations were of short duration, however, for once again bombardment began falling in the vicinity of our trench. 'They're softening us up', I thought, 'for another attack'.

About 9 o'clock I could see the trench opposite me was full of English. I reported back the fact before one or more guns of our artillery began shelling the trench. The assembled enemy vacated his refuge for the rear, having to cross some 100 meters of open ground. We had been allotted two machine guns, so I signaled to the corporals in charge to fire. The others added their weight of fire with rifles, and through my binoculars I could see one, two, then more of the enemy falling. '*Nur drauf!*' I yelled to those around me, joining in with a rifle. I believe that I personally promoted two Englishmen to the 'other side.'

Once the English infantry pulled back, their artillery opened on our trench with such violence that hearing or seeing was virtually impossible. Small and still we huddled against the earth. Six enemy airplanes flew overhead, directing the artillery fire on our piece of trench. Never in my life will I forget the next hours spent in this furnace, powerless to do anything. So it went until evening, we lying in the shallow trench with nothing to eat or drink. My people clamored for water; all were hungry. I myself was consumed by thirst. One of the wounded crawled to me, pleading, '*Herr Feldwebel*, have you nothing to drink?' Unfortunately, I did not. Shells continued dropping all around us. Eventually, my corporals worked their way to me and said the position could not be held. I told them to be quiet, at least for a while longer. Convincingly, I put them off, explaining that our lack of provisions was only temporary. At such a moment the right words had to be found in order to raise the spirits and encourage the men. *Feldwebel* Robert Hauschild, 1/R111[24]

Hauschild and his platoon were experiencing the same heavy fire that was falling along the entire front line held by RIR 111. At least Hauschild and his men had been spared the worst of the fighting on the previous day but the lack of food and water was quickly becoming critical regardless of how long a man had been at the front.

The men from RIR 111 monitored the British activity all morning. It was evident that a new attack was going to take place some time during the day. By noon the men from RIR 111 had come to the conclusion that the British preparations to continue the attack were finished, but there was something different in the manner in which the assaults took place.

Instead of the large scale, well-coordinated assaults of the previous day, the attacks were smaller, seemingly splintered with less cohesion. The first attack waves advanced from

Mametz against the new German front line. The attackers fell in waves and were stopped cold by the concentrated defensive fire from the infantry and machine guns located in the front line and from positions in the rear from the II/R111.

Despite this setback the British were able to establish machine gun positions north of Mametz where they could spread fire on the hill by Fricourt farm and the hollow by the *Nestlerhöhlen*. The British attempted to advance from the northern edge of the Château Park under the protection of the machine gun fire. The British troops quickly came under heavy defensive fire and the attack was stopped in its tracks.

Each subsequent attack against the German lines was accompanied by ever increasing artillery fire. If the infantry was unable to dislodge the men from RIR 111 then the artillery would obliterate them. Like Hauschild and his men, the rest of the defenders also found themselves occupying shallow trenches that offered little protection against the heavy fire. Dugouts were almost non-existent and losses began to increase with each hour.

Command and control over the defensive positions was growing more difficult as time passed. Communication between the different units at the front was difficult at best as runners attempted to cross the exposed terrain while numerous shells exploded around them. The commanding officer of the I/R111, *Hauptmann* Meyer was killed while standing in front of the *Nestlerhöhlen*. *Oberleutnant* Haug took command but soon he was wounded in the shellfire and the command now fell to *Oberleutnant* Sorge, the leader of the 2/Bavarian *Pionier* Regiment.

The few trenches that had existed were slowly being destroyed under the weight of British fire as hundreds of shells plowed into the ground, erasing most signs that a trench

The officers from RIR 111 that survived the fighting on the Somme. (*Das Reserve-Infanterie-Regiment Nr. 111 im Weltkrieg 1914 bis 1918*)

once existed. New attacks occurred in the afternoon following the intense bombardment and the level of resistance the British encountered must have surprised them, almost as much as the opposition they encountered on the morning of 1 July. Surely, after such heavy shelling, the Germans must all be dead or wounded? Or so many hoped.

The British attacks continued south of the *Edinger Dorf*. British troops advanced against the German position from the *Sigel Graben* and north of Fricourt Farm. The attack was met by the remnants of the 12th, 11th and combined groups from the 1/R111 under *Leutnant* Eberenz. The fighting was intense and the British managed to penetrate into a section of trench some 200 meters wide between the 11th and 12/R111, *Leutnant* Eberenz was among the men killed in the fighting. All available men from RIR 111 and *pioniers* found at the *Nestlerhöhlen* were assembled and sent toward the enemy break-in.

Leutnant Jacob, 10/R111 quickly brought up a machine gun on the right wing of the threatened sector but it was soon destroyed and Jacob was killed. Losses among the men increased as the fighting continued. The problem of coordinating the defense grew more difficult as the few leaders remaining became wounded or killed including *Feldwebel* Kaufmann.

News was already spreading in the rear that the *Edinger Dorf* and the hill by Fricourt Farm had been captured by the British. Orders arrived soon after from the 28th Reserve Division that directed the men to recapture these positions. The few remaining German artillery pieces directed their fire onto these targets in anticipation of the counter attack.

The men from RIR 111 found themselves in a difficult position. The exact trench line was not known and the artillery from both sides was not firing as accurately as they might have done the day before. The remaining men from RIR 111 were engaged in close combat with their British opponents while under shellfire from friendly and enemy guns. It was fortunate that the British soldier was not the same tenacious attacker that he had been only 24 hours earlier. This was most likely due to the same reasons so many of the German defenders were at the end of their strength; the constant stress of combat coupled with heavy losses, lack of food and most importantly the lack of water.

Some water had managed to reach the men in RIR 111 but it was not enough to satisfy the needs of the entire regiment.

Finally, near nightfall, we received 10 large flasks of seltzer water, which extinguished our worst thirst. These were brought up from the rear only under the greatest difficulties and danger, but no food.

From battalion I received the order: 'The position will be held to the last man.' To my inquiry and request for reinforcements came the answer: 'Reinforcements and relief underway, perhaps tonight.' The night, however, passed slowly under artillery fire with nothing to eat and only a little soda water to drink. I began to think we would not live to see the morning.[25]

RIR 111 sent out bombing parties to recapture the lost trenches in accordance to orders. The bombers encountered some resistance but soon were able to force the British out of the newly captured trenches. Now the men from RIR 111 faced another problem; they did not have sufficient strength to hold the recaptured trench permanently. If reinforcements did not arrive soon they would have no choice but to withdraw to their starting position.

It was recognized that many of the men in RIR 111 still had fighting spirit and that their overall morale was still quite high. But, with each passing hour more and more men were killed and wounded. Almost every man in the regiment had reached the limits of their endurance and the regimental commander came to the conclusion that every man in his command was more or less physically exhausted.

Oberst Ley also knew that the men had gone two days with little or no food but perhaps the worst privation the men suffered still was the complete lack of water. Some men had taken to drinking from small pools found on the ground but this was not only dangerous, it was also not sufficient to satisfy the demands of the men. Ley finally sent his report to headquarters advising the brigade commander his men were at the end of their capabilities and needed to be relieved.

Relief of the regiment was to take place as quickly as new troops could be guided to the positions but it would not be until 3 July at the earliest. For many, their ordeal would not be over until the early hours of 4 July.

Barely had dawn's light illuminated the eastern sky when we heard the hated drone of English airplanes, which always made us nervous. In order to reconnoiter our position, the airmen dove steeply and flew low overhead. We kept still as mice. Once they again attained altitude the fliers fired red flares, signaling to their artillery, which reacted promptly. The whirring rush of a heavy shell left us startled and hope of a speedy relief quickly receded.

The uneasiness of my people grew greater, with good reason. It was no trifling thing to endure nearly 50 hours of such hell. Hunger and thirst left no one in happy humor, so once more I appealed to their sense of duty and upheld them with encouraging words. As for me, I cannot describe my thoughts as the morning of 3 July arrived with no relief. Around 7 o'clock some provisions turned up – a small amount of noodle soup and a few tins of meat. The carrying party had brought the soup from the rear with great effort. Some of the carriers were killed along the way, sacks of bread or water flasks still clenched in their hands. Although the shelling resumed, it did not seem to trouble the men as much after getting a bit to eat and drink. Once fed, their mood improved.

The enemy on the other hand, wanted to annihilate us by increasing his shelling on our piece of trench. I shudder when I think back on the following hours. Explosions, one after the other, pounded our position. Each man sought the best cover he could, holding his breath as the heavy shells tore up the ground. Some were direct hits and wreaked frightful damage amid the trench's scraped-out holes. For three uninterrupted hours this went on and my wounded multiplied. I, too, had been injured in several places by shell splinters.

My left wing crawled to where I was, excitedly reporting that its section of trench was completely destroyed and no longer tenable. I was sympathetic. Six days under bombardment in the second line and three more in the front line were quite enough to drive anyone mad. But the order, ringing in my ears, was implicit: 'The position will be held to the last man.' As quietly as possible, I admonished these men to persevere.

Personally, I already had given up hope for rescue, but I could not say or show that to my people. I tried to cheer them up with words and, singularly, they obeyed me and remained lying there. In effect, I told the men as they became more restless and impatient: 'Think, people, when we all get back with a little luck, we will happily say that these indeed were difficult days, but proud ones too, for we have held our ground.' And this makes me proud today. If I had given up my position I believe I never again would have had one moment's peace.

After anxious hours which seemed an eternity, a message came for us to hold until the coming night when we would be relieved. I communicated this to my people, who were buoyed by the prospect. During the evening of this day the artillery fire intensified. A shell splinter struck a half dozen hand grenades in the trench just 10 meters right of me, and the resulting explosion killed two and badly wounded two of my men.

Night settled in. Between the shellfire and watching for another English attack our nerves were kept taut. At 4 a.m. the relief arrived. To the commanding officer I turned over the position with a proud and joyful feeling that not one hand's breadth of it had been lost. When I accompanied the officer to the left flank of my trench, I saw for the first time just how wrecked and torn up it was. I silently pitied the newcomers who would have to defend it. But that was the rough reality of war.

In haste I showed the company commander the rest of the position, then I led my platoon out through the undiminished fire. About 6.30 I arrived with 52 men at our former rest quarters, stopping at the draw-well outside. Here we strengthened ourselves with fresh water and commissary bread before moving on. During our absence the enemy had shelled the village heavily and continued doing so. We halted after an hour's march. Exhausted, my people had reached their limit. I shook the hands of my corporals. Each said to me, with tears in their eyes: 'Yes *Herr Feldwebel*, difficult but proud days.' Hauschild, 1/R111[26]

It would be three months before the men from RIR 111 would step foot on the Somme again.

Notes

1. 21st Division consisted of the 62nd Brigade (12th and 13th Northumberland Fusiliers, 1st Lincolnshire and 10th Green Howards), the 63rd Brigade (8th Lincolnshire, 8th Somerset Light Infantry, 4th Middlesex and 1st Royal Dublin Fusiliers), 64th Brigade (1st East Yorkshire, 9th King's Own Yorkshire Light Infantry, 10th King's Own Yorkshire Light Infantry and 15th Durham Light Infantry), 50th Brigade, from 17th Division (10th West Yorkshire, 7th East Yorkshire, 7th Green Howards and 6th Dorsetshire). The 7th Division consisted of the 20th Brigade (8th and 9th Devonshire, 2nd Border, 2nd Gordons), 22nd Brigade (2nd Royal Warwickshire, 2nd Royal Irish Rifles, 1st Royal Welch Fusiliers and 20th Manchester), 91st Brigade (2nd Queen's, 1st South Staffordshire, 21st and 22nd Manchester).
2. The 8/R110 had suffered heavily in the weak long bombardment as mentioned in the La Boisselle chapter. The losses had been unusually high as a result of the shallow dugouts. Much of the position had to be evacuated thereby creating a gap of approximately 150 meters between this company and the 4/R111 on the morning of 1 July 1916.
3. The three mines had been positioned under the Salient called the Tambour by the British. The mines contained 25,000, 15,000 and 9,000lbs of explosives respectively. They were created by the 178th Tunneling Coy R.E. in the weeks before the attack.
4. E. Bachelin, *Das Reserve-Infanterie-Regiment Nr. 111 im Weltkrieg 1914 bis 1918*, pp. 291-292.

5.   The *Edinger Dorf* was a large tunnel complex driven into the hillside in *Foureaux* Wood. It contained the main regimental medical facilities including housing for the medical staff, a field kitchen, storerooms for supplies and ammunition, a horse stall and a generator from which electricity was produced to light the nearby dugouts and mine tunnels.
6.   See the chapter on La Boisselle for further details on the 2/23.
7.   Bachelin, op. cit., pp. 100-101.
8.   'K' could be *Leutnant* Alfred Kaufmann from Kreuzwertheim. He was listed as missing in action on the regimental *Verlustlisten* of 23 August 1916, or *Leutnant* Otto Kleinjung from Eupen who was listed as being taken prisoner on the same list.
9.   Bachelin, op. cit. pp. 286-287.
10.   A. Lehmann, *Das K.B. Pionier-Regiment,* pp. 397-398.
11.   Lehmann, op. cit., pp. 399-400.
12.   Silbereisen, Ehrler, Eisenmann, Alexander & Schulze-Etzel, *Schwäbische Kunde aus den grossen Krieg,* p. 65.
13.   Lehmann, op. cit., p. 394.
14.   Bachelin, op. cit., p. 287.
15.   Bachelin, op. cit., pp. 295-296.
16.   Lehmann, op. cit., pp. 400-401.
17.   Lehmann, op. cit., p. 401.
18.   Bachelin, op. cit., p. 287.
19.   Bachelin, op. cit., pp. 292-293.
20.   Baumgartner, op. cit., pp. 89-91.
21.   Stammrolle affidavit by *Gefreiter der Reserve* Neuhäuser.
22.   Lehmann, op. cit., pp. 393-394.
23.   Lehmann, op. cit. p. 398.
24.   Baumgartner, op. cit., p. 91.
25.   Baumgartner, op. cit., pp. 91-92.
26.   Baumgartner, op. cit., pp. 92-94

10

Mametz

The men in RIR 109 holding the front line trenches by Mametz at the end of June were wondering just how long the enemy could keep up the heavy bombardment that had been going on since the 24th of the month. While the intense shelling had caused losses and strained the nerves of the men sitting helplessly under the weight of tons of shells, the overall mood in the regiment was confident. As in the other sectors on the Somme, the men had become increasingly impatient with their current circumstances. There was a growing desire to get to grips with the enemy and to give back some of the torment they had been suffering.

The Mametz area had recently been under the control of the 12th Division, before them were the Bavarians that had fought on the Somme in 1914 and 1915. When the German command had the opportunity to shift troops in the face of the expected enemy attack in 1916, Mametz came under the control of the 28th Reserve Division. It was determined that the new placement of the divisions would provide a stronger defense when the enemy attack eventually came.

Under the new plan, RIR 109 was assigned to occupy the Mametz sector. The regiment was relieved from the Ovillers Sector and arrived at their new home on 16 June. When the regiment occupied the trenches at Mametz it was quickly realized that the position was not up to the standards the regiment had been used to on other portions of the front. To compound the issue, the regiment would ultimately have only eight days before the start of the bombardment to make any improvements in the defenses that were felt to be necessary.

Upon inspecting the new position it was discovered there were too few deep dugouts, not even a sufficient number to house the trench garrison. On top of that problem, most of the existing deep mined dugouts were found inside the front line trench. There were almost

Mametz in 1915. (*Das Reserve-Infanterie-Regiment Nr. 109 im Weltkrieg 1914 bis 1918*)

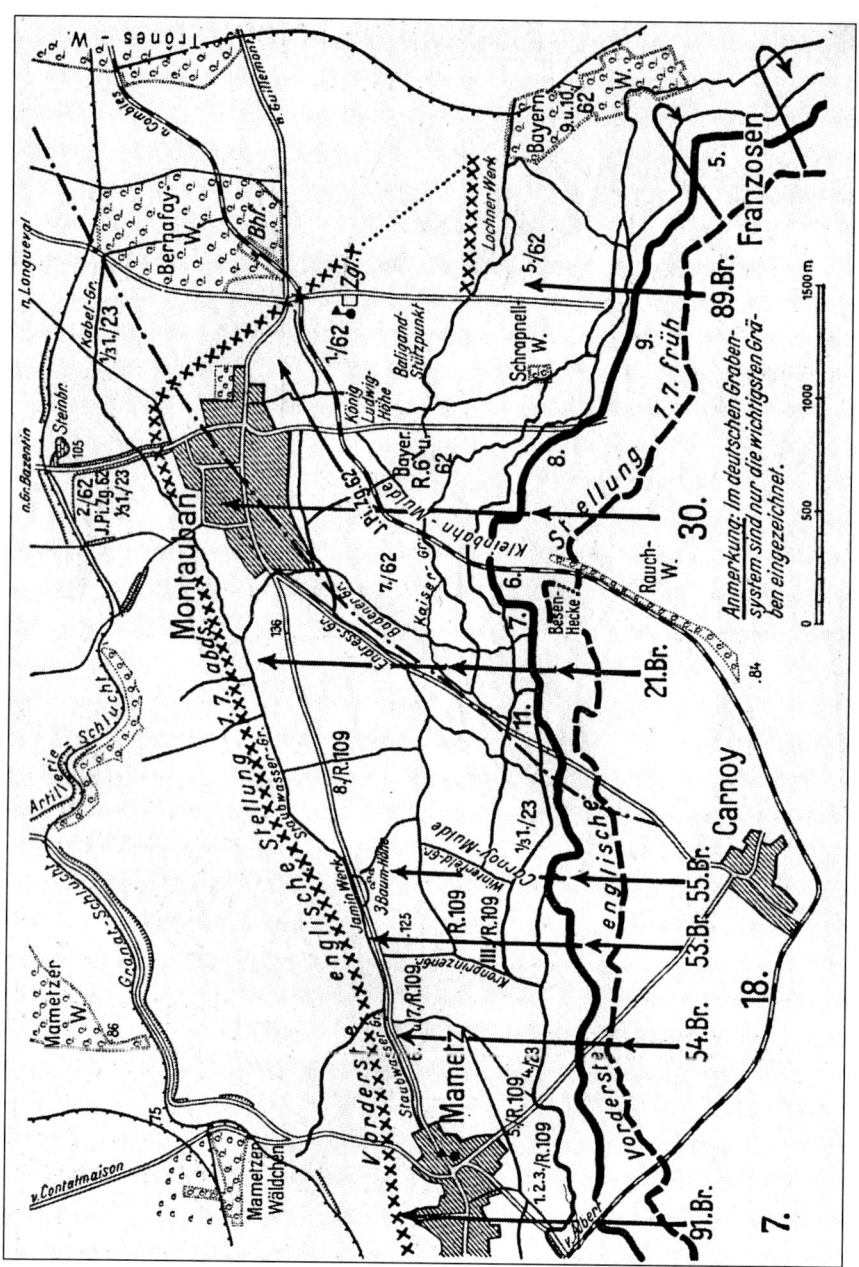

Mametz-Montauban.

no deep dugouts found in the second and third trenches at all.

Construction of new mined dugouts began immediately but there simply was not enough time to construct the numbers required by the garrison that could withstand the impact of a heavy shell. The lack of sufficient dugouts also meant that a large portion of the trench garrison was forced to find alternative quarters in the rear while construction was taking place. This forced the men to move in and out of the front line on a daily basis and therefore increased the risk facing the men of being killed or wounded by enemy shellfire. It also required a great deal of time to move large bodies of men in and out of the trenches as well as taxing the strength of the men.

In addition to the dugout problem there were too few communication trenches. In order to allow for the speedy movement in and out of the front lines the men required a reasonable number of communication trenches. Some of these would be designated to be used by reinforcements and supplies approaching the front line while others would be used to evacuate wounded and for transfer of men out of the front line. The existing communication trenches would have to perform both functions and this could quickly result in bottlenecks at critical times.

There were insufficient wire entanglements protecting the trenches and very few switch lines. All of these deficiencies required a great deal of hard work in order to improve the defenses of the Mametz Sector. Stocks of 'iron rations' of food and ammunition were completely lacking in the trenches. Much needed stockpiles of these items were hastily stored at key locations inside the trenches. This forced many of the men in the front lines to take part in carrying parties at night when they should have been resting. This extra duty only served to wear the men out even more as the work continued day and night during the short time before the British attack took place.

By the start of the bombardment on 24 June the men in RIR 109 had done what they could physically do to remedy the shortcomings of the position. New communication and switch trenches had been created; the size and depth of the wire entanglements had been increased. There were more dugouts available to house the men than only a short time earlier. In regard to the latter there were still too few deep mined dugouts available for the entire front line garrison. Many of the men were forced to utilize older, shallower dugouts that were vulnerable to medium and heavy caliber shells.

In order to make the most improvements to the position possible the men of Bavarian *Pionier* Coy 20 and the 1R/13th *Pionier* Battalion worked night and day. Both *pionier* companies were assigned to assist the regiment and to act as advisors and supervisors while the majority of the physical work was performed by the men from RIR 109.

One key trench that ran between Mametz and Montauban was called the *Staubwasser Graben*, an 8-foot deep communication trench that had been named after an officer from a Bavarian regiment that had once occupied the sector. The *Staubwasser Graben* could have been used effectively as a switch line in order to contain any enemy penetration but there were some major flaws with its construction. The trench was long and very straight and while deep, it lacked sufficient traverses that would prevent the enemy from dominating the full length of the trench with fire. It also had very steep sides and lacked fire steps and points of exit and entry. The wire entanglements in front of this trench were also inadequate according to the standards in place by mid 1916.

If the men became caught inside this trench it could prove to be a death trap. As such it could not be relied upon to adequately support the overall defenses. It was a glaring example of where specific orders and instructions recently issued several months earlier by the XIV Reserve Corps were ignored by some regiments or divisions that came under the control of corps headquarters. This oversight would have a profound effect during the fighting that followed.

While many improvements had been made in the position when the bombardment started on 24 June all work quickly came to a halt. In the opinion of the men from RIR 109 the Mametz sector and the regiments that had occupied it had not seen very much action. Consequently the men who had preceded RIR 109 had not see the need to create the strong defenses that existed at locations such as Ovillers and La Boisselle. As it turned out, some these were the same men who would soon be fighting alongside RIR 109; the men from IR 23.

Perhaps one of the most distressing discoveries made by the men from RIR 109 was the lack of sufficient telephone lines to nearly every portion of the front line. The I/R109 discovered that only one telephone line existed to the 1st Coy holding the far right wing of the regimental sector. Two other companies in the battalion sector had no communications to the rear other than by runners. Many of the men cursed the day they were forced to leave their former trench system by Ovillers where they felt the defenses were well developed and they had a real chance of repelling any enemy advance.

The Mametz Sector was divided into two parts, each being held by one battalion from the regiment. Each battalion sector was further divided into three company sectors. The right battalion sector was being held by the men of the I/R109 under *Hauptmann* von Schirach. The 1st, 2nd and 4/R109 were holding the front line trenches with the 3/R109 being held nearby in reserve in the *Bismarck Graben* [Danzig Trench]. The battalion

Trench by Mametz, similar to the *Staubwasser Graben* without fire steps or any means to enter or exit the trench. (*An der Somme*)

Trenches near Mametz. (*An der Somme*)

command post was originally located in the *Stall Graben* at the northern exit of the village of Mametz.

The left battalion sector was being held by the III/R109 under Major Schmidts with the 11th, 12th and 9/R109 holding the front line. The 10/R109 was located in the rear trenches as the battalion reserve.

The II/R109 under Major Collani was positioned at different locations across the regimental sector. The placement of the men would allow the battalion to provide support to any portion of the front line as needed. The 5/R109 was placed southwest of Mametz by the *Zeppelin Graben*. One platoon each from the 6th, 7th and 8/R109 were positioned in the *Staubwasser Graben* and the trenches connecting to the north of this trench. Two platoons from the 6/R109 were located in the *Granatschlucht* [Willow Stream] while one platoon from the 8/R109 was assigned to defend the quarry north of Montauban. The third platoon of the 8th Coy occupied the brigade dugouts along the Longueval-Maricourt road. The remainder of the 7/R109 was positioned nearby.

Just before the attack, the commander of RIR 109 realized that the regimental headquarters dugout was poorly positioned. Only a small portion of the regimental sector could be overseen from the dugout. In order to remedy this situation, the regimental staff took over the headquarters dugout of the I/R109 in order to have better command and control over the entire regiment. The staff of the I/R109 was forced to move to a new location inside the *Bismarck Graben* just to the west of the point where it was joined by the *Zeppelin Graben*.

The staff of the II/R109 occupied a dugout in Longueval and in addition to the duties of the regimental reserve the battalion was also responsible for carrying parties used to supply the front line. One Group each from the 5th, 7th and 8/R109 were assigned to this duty as

Machine gun crew – RIR 109. (Author's collection)

well as the men who worked in the regimental construction detachment, the *Ganterwerk*. Just before 1 July parts of the 7th and 10/R109 were assigned to occupy the strongpoint known as the *Jaminwerk* that was connected to the *Staubwasser Graben* midway between Mametz and Montauban.

The regimental machine guns, 16 heavy MG 08s[1], were positioned across the front lines of the Mametz Sector at key locations designed to provide the best possible field of fire against any attacking force. Seven machine guns belonging to the 2MG/R109 and two more from the 1MG/R109 were distributed to cover the left hand battalion sector. The remaining seven machine guns were positioned across the right battalion sector where they could provide support to the trench garrison.

The regimental firepower was substantially increased with four additional machine guns from Machine Gun Marksman Detachment 132. These guns were located in the *Staubwasser Graben*. 20 *Musketen* from the 2/*Musketen* Battalion 1 were also distributed in the *Staubwasser Graben* and the trenches that connected to it from the south.

The preliminary bombardment had caused a number of losses in the battalions holding the front line sectors. Much of the losses revolved around the carrying and working parties that worked in the open and had little protection against the shrapnel and high explosive shells. Trench sentries were also very vulnerable to losses as the men needed to remain vigilant at all times. This meant that men would have to physically watch the opposing trenches and in doing so become exposed to the heavy fire falling on the regimental sector.

In response to the increasing number of losses being reported by RIR 109 there were discussions at division and corps level of possibly relieving RIR 109 from the Mametz Sector. At first the idea of replacing the regiment was dismissed as being unnecessary. However, several days later, following a review of the increased losses suffered by RIR 109 the decision was made to relieve the entire regiment and insert fresh troops in their place. Theoretically this would ensure the strongest possible defense once the attack began. Once safely in the rear, RIR 109 could act as a sector reserve ready to be deployed where needed.

The orders for the relief arrived at regimental headquarters late on 30 June and apparently came as a great surprise to the staff of RIR 109. The regimental officers felt certain that their men were up to the task to provide a solid defense against any enemy attack even considering the losses the companies had reported. The overall mood of the

Danish Madsen Automatic rifles (*Musketen*). (Author's collection)

men was deemed to be very confident and they too saw no need to hold the relief.

Still, the orders had been issued and arrangements were made to comply with them. The initial relief would consist of two companies, the ones deemed to have suffered the most losses during the bombardment. The 4/23 would be sent forward to relieve the 4/R109 that according to reports from 29 June had been reduced to 142 men as a result of the shelling. The 1/23 would replace the 12/R109 that had suffered the most losses in the III Battalion sector.

The relief of even two companies at this juncture of the battle would prove to be very difficult. Most of the routes to the front were under constant fire and losses would be inevitable. Many of the trenches were badly damaged and movement was extremely restricted at many locations. Despite these obstacles the two companies from IR 23 moved forward to replace the two companies from RIR 109 in the course of the evening of 30 June and early morning hours of 1 July.

IR 23 had been chosen to replace RIR 109 in the Mametz Sector. The most likely reasons would include the fact that this regiment had previously occupied this sector for some months prior to the arrival of RIR 109 and was therefore familiar with the defenses.

Regimental Staff – RIR 109. (*Das Reserve-Infanterie-Regiment Nr. 109 im Weltkrieg 1914 bis 1918*)

IR 23 had been designated as a support unit in the upcoming battle. Since Bavarian IR 16, the only other regiment on hand, was already scheduled to replace RIR 99 by Thiepval this left IR 23 as the only possible choice. There were no other regiments available.

The Silesian regiment had received its orders in the evening of 30 June and two companies were sent forward as the first replacements for RIR 109. The 4/23 under *Leutnant der Reserve* Bobislawsky arrived at the horse stable of Mametz at approximately 11 p.m. This company would eventually take over Sector 'c', just south of Mametz.

Two platoons from the 4th Coy advanced via the *Matratzenweg* while the third platoon used the *Sigelgraben* to reach the front line. The men were able to reach their final positions by approximately 2 a.m. The continuous heavy shelling forced most of the men in the 4/23 to take shelter in the few remaining intact dugouts and wait for the fire to end before taking stock of their current situation. Fortunately the losses suffered by the company during the relief had been very low. After reaching the front line the men rested as best they could as dawn was only a short time away.

The 1/23 was scheduled to take over Sector 'e' that was located almost midway between Mametz and Montauban. The company should have reached the quarry north of Montauban by 10.30 p.m. on the 30th, but, instead did not reach the destination until 2 a.m. on 1 July due to the extremely poor condition of the *Kabelgraben* the men were using to move toward the front. Much of the trench was blocked by debris and large sections were almost leveled because of the amount of earth thrown up by the exploding shells.

Shortly after arriving at the quarry the company leader *Leutnant der Reserve* Preuss had continued to move toward Sector 'e'. He was accompanied by four Groups from the first platoon to act as an advance force for the remainder of the company. Just after Preuss and his small party had departed, the 1/23 received orders from RIR 109 to stop the relief because of the long delay in reaching just the quarry. The regiment had decided that there was not enough time to complete the exchange before dawn. The level of shelling made it impossible to move men in the open during daylight and to do so would result in heavy losses. While the bulk of the 1/23 remained in the support trenches, it proved to be impossible to advise Preuss of the change of orders, so he and his small band of men continued toward the front line.

The remainder of the 1/23 was now ordered to send one platoon each to Montauban and the Brigade battle headquarters, while one was to remain at the quarry. The first platoon of the 1/23 came under the command of Sergeant Kompalla in the absence of the company leader and he occupied the northern edge of Montauban with his men.

There had been no contact with Preuss after he had continued toward the front line. At first, nothing was known of their fate following the fighting on 1 July. It was determined some days later that Preuss and his men did reach Sector 'e' and joined forces with the men from the 12/R 109 that were holding the front line just before the British forces attacked.

At 3 a.m. on 1 July gas and fog clouds were observed rolling toward the German lines by Mametz. The presence of gas was interpreted to confirm that the enemy was going to attack soon. The stress on the men over the last seven days had been severe but the overall desire was still to get to grips with the enemy. This desire had not lessened in the final hours of the bombardment.

The suspicions that the attack was imminent were confirmed when a message from division headquarters arrived at regimental headquarters at 5.45 a.m. that an attack was expected about 6 a.m. While additional gas clouds were observed moving toward the

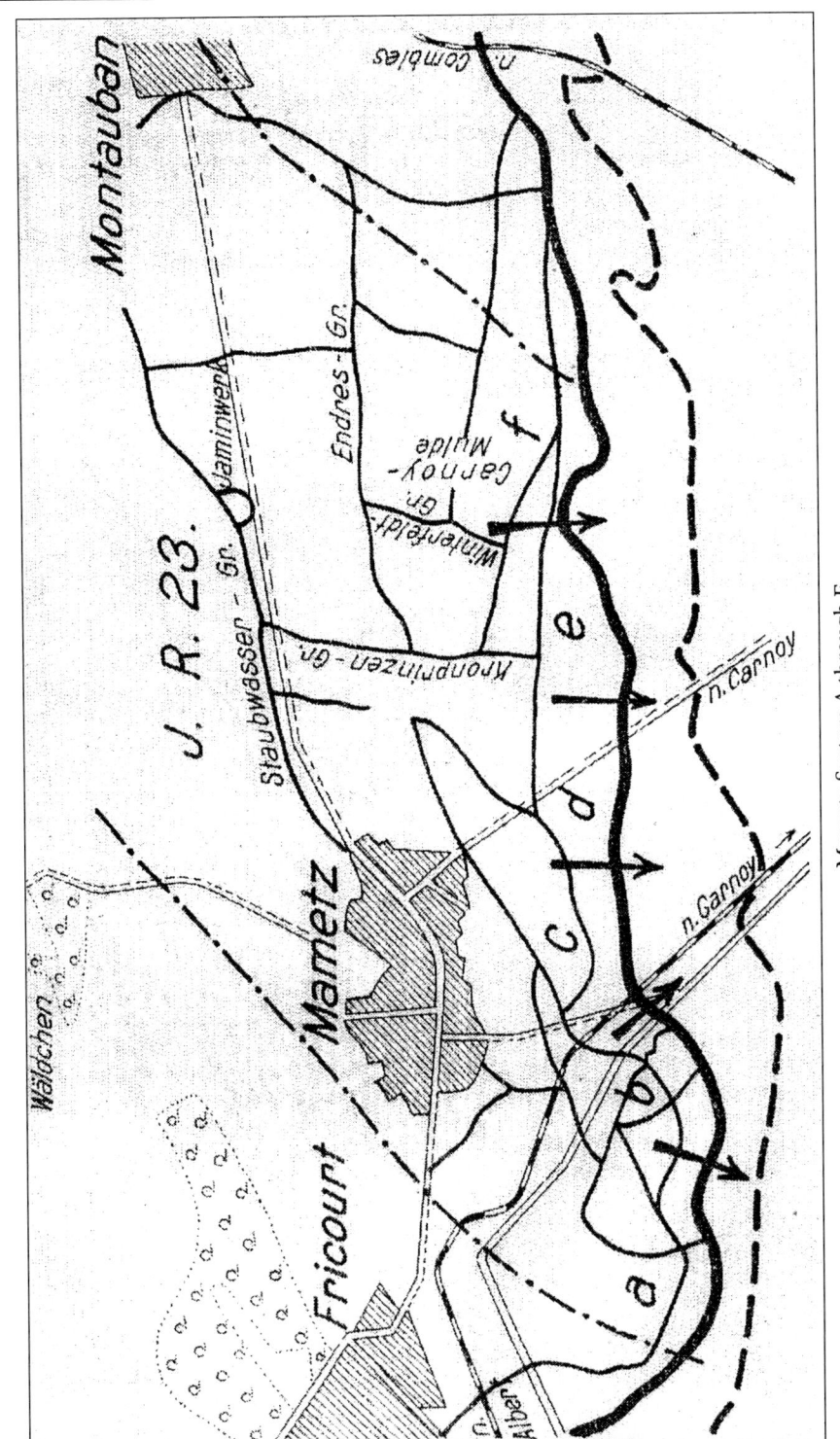

Mametz Sectors A through F

Mametz Sector at 6 a.m., no infantry attack followed.

For at least one man, *Grenadier* Emil Kury, 1 MG Coy RIR 109 the date of the attack was not a mystery. He had apparently received inside information about the British intentions from a very reliable source, the men running the field kitchens.

> We ran out of food that night [30 June] and I was sent back to get some. At the field kitchen I was told, 'Tell your comrades the English will attack tomorrow morning.' It took me seven hours to fetch the food and when I got back I couldn't find my dug-out because the ground was so torn up. Then I saw one of my friends signaling me.
>
> I told my comrades, 'We must be prepared; the English will attack soon.' We got our machine gun ready on the top step of the dug-out and we put all our equipment on; then we waited. We all expected to die. We thought of God. We prayed. Then someone shouted, 'They're coming! They're coming!' We rushed up and got our machine gun in position. We could see the English soldiers pouring out at us, thousands and thousands of them. We opened fire.' *Grenadier* Emil Kury, 1 MG Coy, RIR 109[2]

On the British side of the wire, the men awaiting orders to begin the attack were, like so many others along the entire front, confident that that bombardment had been so devastating that no German could possibly be left alive. Once the shelling had ended all that would be needed was to advance at a walk and capture the pitiful remnants of the German defenders. All serious opposition would have been crushed and the British losses would be low accordingly.

The British attack against the Mametz Sector involved parts of two divisions; the center and right hand brigades (20th and 91st Brigades) from the 7th Division and the center and

Infantrymen – RIR 109. (Author's collection)

2nd Coy, RIR 109. The casualties suffered by this company on or shortly before 1 July 1916 exceed the number of men shown in this photo taken a short time before the battle. The fighting on the opening day of the battle effectively destroyed the entire company. (Author's collection)

left hand brigades (54th and 53rd Brigades) from the 18th Division.[3] The attack was part of a larger plan that called for the integrated efforts of several divisions attacking the villages of Mametz and Montauban, all of which should have the desired effect of breaking through the German defensive line.

At 6.25 a.m. the bombardment of the German trenches reached a level the men had never experienced before since the start of the war. In the minds of the average British soldier, if the 7 days of artillery fire had not destroyed all German opposition, this surely would. The full effect of the heavy shelling was still unknown to the British observers as the front was shrouded in dense mist, fog and smoke, severely curtailing almost all visibility. If 1 July was going to be similar to the last few days of June, then the mist would slowly dissipate in the morning and eventually clear. The recent rains did not help the situation as the increased humidity and moisture in the ground allowed the mist to remain longer than if the weather had been bright, sunny and dry.

The mist did begin to clear somewhat about 7 a.m. At 7.22 a.m. Stokes mortars fired at the German lines at a rate of 30 rounds per minute, a rate of fire that neither the men nor the equipment could keep up forever. 8 minutes later the fire stopped; the sound of whistles being blown could be heard along the British lines and waves of enemy troops could be seen advancing across no man's land.

For the men in RIR 109 that were crouching inside their dugouts, it seemed that the bombardment would never end. The heavy fire continued to fall on the German trenches in the morning hours, just as it had for the last seven days. Then, suddenly, there was the instant when the shelling lifted from the front line and was transferred to the rear areas. Within moments the German trench sentries could see British troops climbing over the parapet of their trenches and forming in no man's land. The moment so long awaited had finally come, the attack had begun. The exact date and time of the attack was no longer a mystery to the men of RIR 109.

At almost the same time the heavy fire was lifting off the front line, two large mine explosions occurred at the far right wing of the I/R109.

Men from RIR 109 manning a trench. (Author's collection)

We had lain for seven days under the bombardment, in a mood of blind fury because we felt so defenseless; so that, when the moment of attack came, we felt good. At least we could get our own back. None of us thought we would be killed or wounded. Now we'd pay them back in their own kind.

We heard the mines go up; then it was deathly quiet for a few moments. The English came walking, as though they were going to the theatre or as though they were on a parade ground. We felt they were mad. Our orders were given in complete calm and every man took careful aim to avoid wasting ammunition. *Unteroffizier* Paul Scheytt, RIR 109[4]

The British infantry were able to cross no man's land quickly in some areas. This was in part due to the short distance between the opposing trenches; in some cases as little as 100 yards separated them. Also, both the 7th and 18th Divisions utilized Russian Saps that had been extended almost up to the German front line. These were opened just before the start of the attack and allowed some of the men to approach the German defenses in relative safety.

The opposition met by each battalion differed widely over the battlefield. While some continued to meet heavy fire that often slowed or stopped any forward movement, others were met by groups of German soldiers who freely surrendered to the advancing British troops.

The defenders holding the right battalion sector, the I/R109, were faced with a major problem. Because so many of the dugouts located in the front line had collapsed or had been badly damaged during the week-long bombardment, the survivors of two of the three front line companies had been forced to find cover inside the few remaining intact dugouts. At least two-thirds of the dugouts located in the sector held by the 2/R109 alone had been heavily damaged or destroyed by 1 July.

While still offering a safe refuge for the men, the reduced number of deep dugouts also had the effect of severely compromising the distribution of the troops across the sector. Large gaps appeared along the front line where there were no troops at all. In these locations, little or no opposition could be afforded against an enemy force advancing against this portion of the German line.

The physical distribution of the dugouts was a problem the regiment had not been able to remedy in time for the attack. The front line contained a moderate number of deep, mined dugouts while a few more had been prepared in the second and third trenches. Still, there were not enough to meet the demands of the companies. The lack of adequate dugouts in the second and third trenches also meant that a large proportion of the defenders were crammed together inside the first trench. In short, there was inadequate defense in depth.

Everything now depended upon the garrison preventing the enemy from penetrating the German front line and to accomplish this by utilizing a single trench. This was more reminiscent of the fighting near Mametz in late 1914 during the French attacks in December of that year than what should have been in place in mid 1916.

In the opening phase of the attack, the 20th Brigade would form the left flank of the British advance against Mametz with the brigade front facing Fricourt. There was a large mine field between the left wing of the attack against Mametz and the right wing of the

Mametz. (*An der Somme*)

Trenches inside the village of Mametz. (*An der Somme*)

attack against Fricourt. The area was heavily cratered from months of mine warfare on both sides of the wire. It would be up to the 2nd Border Regiment from this brigade to clear this area and then move on to the primary objective, Apple Alley. Fairly quickly after the start of the battle the 2nd Border Regiment was able to advance up to Hidden Lane, located near Hidden Wood, almost reaching the objective assigned to the battalion.

The experiences of the other three battalions of the 20th Brigade that were involved in the attack were quite different from each other. The 2nd Border Regiment and 2nd Gordon Highlanders were apparently able to cross no man's land rather quickly and suffered relatively few losses. However, there was an exception, the left hand company of the 2nd Gordon Highlanders. The advance by this company was held up by a section of uncut wire hidden in a dip in the ground. Many men in this company become casualties from the heavy German fire. The survivors of the Highland company were eventually able to advance into the German lines once the trench garrison had been taken in the flank and forced to withdraw.

The remaining companies of the 2nd Gordon Highlanders reported being able to reach the German front line as the defenders, part of the 4/23, were preparing to meet the attack with a shower of hand grenades. The attack was reported to be so swift that the front line was overrun before the defenders had a chance to throw them.

The Highlanders successfully breached the front line being held by the 4/23. Like the other companies on this portion of the front, the men in the 4th Coy had been packed into the few remaining intact dugouts. This left large portions of the front line unoccupied and as there were too few dugouts located in the 2nd or 3rd trench, it was up to the front line garrison to stop the enemy advance.

Little is known of the fighting by the 4/23. Subsequent reports from the few survivors stated that the company losses had been heavy but the men had held their positions as long as ammunition and hand grenades were available. Many of the men that survived the initial assault were apparently pushed back or overrun and captured. There are no known firsthand accounts from this company. This should not be surprising, as only nine men from the 4/23 returned to the rear on 4 July.[5]

The casualty returns for the 4/23 support the reports that the company had been involved in heavy fighting and suffered catastrophic losses on 1 July 1916. When looking at the losses suffered by the company in the period covering 1 July it is likely that the accounts of the fighting from both sides of the wire have a basis in fact. Some men in the 4/23 did surrender, under what circumstances is not known. However, the company did report a loss of 120 men that were captured. This number would lend credence to the British reports of quickly overrunning portions of the German front line.

It is also apparent that some members of this company did put up a fight, as described by the few survivors of the company. The company reported 44 men who died in the fighting with several more who died as a result of their wounds in the days that followed. The loss reports also show 50 men from the company becoming wounded. When these losses are combined it would also appear to support the German reports of the company putting up a good fight. As in many instances, the historian needs to look at all sides of any event, read all accounts and try to come to a reasonable conclusion of what happened so many decades ago. In the case of the 4/23 I suspect that the events the company experienced on 1 July were actually a combination of the two points of view, British and German.

When the Gordons advanced deeper into the German lines they were met with heavy fire coming from the maze of support trenches as well as from Mametz and a machine gun post located near the *Matratzenweg* [Cemetery Trench] that was known to the British as

Mametz under bombardment. (*Der Weltkrieg 1914-1918*)

'The Shrine'. The British troop also came under sporadic artillery fire from the few German guns still capable of being operated.

> The fate of the platoon of the 6th, which under leadership of *Leutnant der Reserve* Rees of the 3rd battery RFAR 29 had been assigned to Battery Fröhlich. They were in a position west of Contalmaison, already shot up and torn apart shortly before 1st July by the English shells.
>
> On 1st July, the day of the attack, the platoon at the right gun again received a direct hit. The 1st Battery of the 29th pushed a tube up on to the road, to greet the enemy coming up through the hollow between Mametz-Fricourt. Three men of the crew fell; the others, all wounded, had to go back. The Englishmen had already taken the gun in order to turn it against us, but the men of the battery and infantrymen stormed it and fired off the remaining ammunition.
>
> The crazy shooting on this day therefore cost three guns disabled, so that finally only one was able to fire. This gun was then also brought on to the hill in front of the battery, to bombard the enemy that were situated in the copse of Fricourt at 900 meters. However a pilot directed the guns of a heavy battery at the exposed gun, and it had to yield.
>
> In the evening it was likewise unserviceable, after 2,300 shots had been fired throughout the day. Hand grenades and rifle ammunition was distributed, in order to make the shot-up position as defensible as possible. *Hauptmann* Fröhlich emptied his wine cellar for the stalwart Other Ranks.[6]

One major obstacle that could have seriously affected the advance of the 91st Brigade, on the right of the 20th Brigade, was eliminated just before zero hour. Two mines were detonated under Bulgar Sap by Bulgar Trench. The larger of the two mines was set off under a spot called Bulgar Point on the right flank. The mines destroyed a machine gun emplacement as well as several mined dugouts in the German front line.

By 8 a.m. the 22nd Manchesters had advanced up to Bucket trench east of Mametz. The 1st South Staffordshire had also penetrated the German front line, coming up against the left wing of the 4/23. The Staffordshires had been able to push through the German front line and moved toward the village. As the British advanced deeper into the German lines and advanced up the shoulder of a spur they came up against heavy fire coming from Mametz on their left and from the *Staubwasser Graben* on their front.

Despite the German fire and heavy losses, the Staffordshire Regiment reached the *Matratzenweg*. It was reported that a few men had also managed to enter the village of Mametz. Finally, the advance slowed to a halt in face of continued German resistance. While the British units had reported that overall German resistance was half hearted and surrenders came freely, the German fire could be heavy enough at times to force the attackers to halt. Finally, the advance was held up at the southern outskirts of Mametz at the *Matratzenweg* at 7.45 a.m.

The 9th Devonshire had the farthest distance to travel in order to reach the German front line. The battalion had been forced to start its attack 250 yards behind the British front line. This was the result of the front line trench and support trenches having been badly damaged previously by German artillery fire. The battalion would be exposed to German rifle and machine gun fire far longer than the other battalions in the brigade.

MG 08 and crew. (Author's collection)

For many weeks before the attack, one officer in the 9th Devonshire had been very concerned about a German machine gun position that had been positioned in 'The Shrine', in front of the *Matratzenweg*. This machine gun would have an excellent field of fire across the very ground being crossed by the 9th Devonshire and it was in a reinforced position that made it difficult to place out of action without a direct hit from a heavy shell. The Devonshires would be only 400 yards from this machine gun position, point blank range for any competent gunner.

When the 9th Devonshire advanced across no man's land the concerns about this machine gun proved to be true. In addition to this machine gun, the men also came under heavy fire from machine guns located in Fricourt Wood and from trenches south of Mametz. The heavy German fire caused at least half of the casualties the battalion suffered on 1 July before it had reached Mansell Copse in the middle of no man's land. The survivors pressed on and successfully entered the first German trench and then continued on to the support trenches.

The fighting inside the front line trench was fierce and deadly as both sides struggled to obtain the upper hand. Small groups of defenders were scattered throughout the trenches where bombs and bayonets were used freely. The fighting continued throughout the maze of communication trenches as the men from RIR 109 withdrew to the rear. Small groups of Badeners continuously took up new positions inside the second and third trenches where

Infantryman – RIR 109. (Author's collection)

they offered further resistance to the British advance.

In spite of the heavy losses suffered by the British troops they had taken the front line trench and were firmly established inside the *Belgrade Stellung*. Some of the British troops had even managed to advance toward the support trenches where they established small footholds. These small groups were finally forced to stop in the face of heavy German infantry fire, particularly by the fire coming from the men of the 3/R109 inside the *Bismarck Graben*. The 3rd Coy had also effectively prevented any British advance from the direction of the *Kuchenwäldchen* [Hidden Wood] into the right flank of the regiment, at least for the time being.

Shortly after the attack began, the I/R109 suffered a loss that could hinder any well-coordinated defense. The battalion commander, *Hauptmann* von Schirach was outside of his battalion headquarters surveying the situation when he became severely wounded in both thighs by machine gun fire. As a result of his wounds he could no longer direct his men and he required immediate medical attention. The burden of command of the vital right battalion sector now fell to his subordinates.

The men from the 20th Brigade were now held up by groups of men from RIR 109 holding out in small sections of trench or in shell holes. The Badeners were aided by the excellent support provided by the machine guns and *Musketen* located further to the rear, including one machine gun that had been positioned inside a ruined house in Mametz. The house had been reinforced with concrete and the gun fired through slits cut into 4-inch armour plate. It proved to be a serious obstacle to any further advance.

Many of the machine gun positions located in the sector held by RIR 109 flanked the initial British advance. Their fire was very effective, however one by one the machine gun positions were discovered by low flying aircraft and came under heavy fire directed by the pilots or were eliminated by the advancing British troops.

Some guns were placed out of action when enemy infantry was allowed to approach the gun positions too closely. While the machine gun was an effective weapon, in order to use it properly it required the gun crews to become exposed when firing. Without adequate infantry support the gun positions and gun crews could become outflanked and thereby vulnerable to enemy fire.

> There were five of us on our machine gun when I saw an English soldier about twenty meters away to our left. Then our eldest soldier, a painter who came from Pforzheim and had five children, was shot in the forehead and dropped without a word. Next I was shot in the chest. I felt blood run down my back and I fell; I knew the war was over for me. He shot three of us before I even had the chance to use my rifle. I would like to meet that English soldier. He was a good shot. *Grenadier* Emil Kury, 1 MG Coy, RIR 109[7]

Reports of the British advance toward Mametz had eventually reached the regimental headquarters of RIR 109. There was sporadic telephone contact with various portions of the German lines as the telephone troops were kept busy constantly repairing damaged telephone cables. Once the overall situation was assessed by *Oberstleutnant* von Baumbach, he ordered *Leutnant der Landwehr* Ochel, 5/R109, to take a few detachments from his company along with a machine gun and take up positions at the southeastern exit of Mametz. His men were to take the enemy troops in the flank and stop their advance.

Ochel and his men made their way to the assigned location. Once there, four detachments of men were sent off to establish a connection with the I/R109 that should be located at the southern edge of the village. Other detachments were sent to occupy the

Infantrymen – RIR 109. (Author's collection)

shell craters and remnants of the trenches still remaining to the east of the village. Once in position the men opened fire and joined in with the heavy fire from machine guns and *Musketen* located at the eastern edge of the village as well as the western half of the *Staubwasser Graben*. The combined fire from all of these guns reportedly caused heavy losses among the attacking British troops.

Little had changed following the capture of the German front line and the establishment of footholds deep inside the German defenses. The overall situation in the right sector held by the I/R109 did not change much for the rest of the morning. Until the German machine guns and *Musketen* were eliminated the men of the 7th Division were unable to continue their advance.

The British attack against the left battalion sector of RIR 109 was directed towards the *Kronprinzen Graben* and *Endress Graben* held by the men of the III/R109. One portion of the British advance appeared to be directed toward the *Jaminwerk* [Pommiers Redoubt] located alongside the *Staubwasser Graben*.

The British were able to quickly penetrate the German front line occupied by the III/R109 and once there continued to advance deeper into the German trenches. The distribution of the defenders along this part of the front line was not continuous as a result of the loss of so many dugouts during the preliminary bombardment. The lack of adequate numbers of dugouts in the second and third trenches also made any defense in depth nearly impossible here as it did in the I Battalion sector.

When the men of the 54th Brigade crossed no man's land the men noted that while German artillery fire was sporadic the number of machine guns firing at them was quite large. Most of the losses suffered by the first waves came from the latter. Between the mine explosions set off at the start of the attack and the heavy damage caused by the preliminary bombardment, the wire along the German front line, known as Austrian trench by the British, was badly damaged. The 54th Brigade was able to enter the German trenches at numerous places.

Bombing parties spread out through the newly captured trench in order to consolidate the position and clear out any Germans hiding below in dugouts. Other groups continued to advance deeper into the German lines. While pushing deeper into the trenches the advancing British troops came up against a particularly annoying machine gun positioned at the junction of three trenches, known as the 'Triangle'. This particular machine gun apparently caused numerous losses for the men of the 7th Bedfords, until it was finally knocked out.

Parts of the 54th Brigade managed to advance deep into the German defenses and reached an intermediate line designated Pommiers trench by the British troops. Here, the men were forced to wait until the British artillery fire lifted on to the next target. By 8 a.m. the artillery fire moved on and Pommiers trench was captured with help from the neighboring 53rd Brigade.

The next major obstacle facing the British was the strongpoint the *Jaminwerk*. When the British troops advanced toward it one platoon each from the 7th and 8/R109 opened fire and put up strong resistance. The garrison was aided by several machine guns from Machine Gun Marksman Detachment 132 and three *Musketen* Groups.[8]

The heavy automatic weapons fire forced the attackers to seek cover. The British found that the *Jaminwerk* was protected by several large belts of barbed wire that were completely intact. Much of the wire was apparently hidden from observation by long grass. Every attempt to attack the *Jaminwerk* was quickly destroyed in concentrated machine gun, rifle and *Musketen* fire.

While German artillery fire was sporadic at best along this portion of the front line, the men inside the *Jaminwerk* were fortunate that several batteries of field guns located just to the rear of the strongpoint were still capable of providing fire support.

One sees our infantry threatened. The Battery leader independently opens barrage fire on the endangered sector, it goes back and forth. *Oberleutnant* Körner becomes wounded on the head, however he does not allow himself to be sent out of the position; Non-commissioned officers and Other Ranks bleed; they remain. Tunics and shirts fly off; the crews work only in their trousers.

Towards midday the battery leader suddenly notices through the stereo telescope: the enemy is 1,000 meters distant on the left flank, penetrating into our trench on the *Dreibaumhöhe*. A weak German force defends itself there against the superior strength in the close combat; soon the brave men would be overwhelmed.

There could be no hesitation. *Hauptmann der Reserve* Weber runs from the observation post to his battery (the telephone connection was lost a long time ago), gets the guns out of their emplacements that were masked from the endangered position through a gradient and moves them up onto the slope. A couple of moments and the row stand above in an open firing position.

'Entire battery – advancing riflemen directly ahead – 800 meters – one salvo!' The salvo hits the Englishmen. Officers and gunners perform the work furiously. After a few minutes the English dig in. He uses flag signals; his artillery places down fire.

Dreibaumhöhe. (*An der Somme*)

Nevertheless, after a further 10 minutes his work is also done. He vanishes into his communication trench.

Then he dares to advance again, a machine gun plays against the battery. It is soon silenced, placed out of action. About midday shrapnel and shells literally pour down on the position. The gun crews hold. The gun layer often sits alone on the gun and fires further, meanwhile his wounded comrades are carried away. A direct hit destroys the second gun. The sound of a machine gun from a plane diving down from above. *Leutnant der Reserve* Maag is hit in the upper arm by one of their bullets. He does not go back immediately like his comrade Körner. The ammunition needed to fire cannot be brought up quickly enough; two further [guns] have burst or were hit. With the last one continuing to fire, the gun layer falls over, *Oberleutnant* Körner jumps in his place, the battery leader undertakes the direction of the gun. The small group of good men continue to lug up projectiles to the only gun that fired. After a further half hour the enemy brings another machine gun forth that continuously raises dust around our final firing gun. It also suffers a jam now. With each shot the brave Gunner Elser exposes himself to a large number of bullets when he shoves out each shell casing with the barrel sponge from the front.

About 11.30 a.m. the last gun is also unserviceable. 20 rounds of ammunition were still there from 4,600 rounds we began with.

The enemy had penetrated a neighboring division and thrust on the left flank of the 28th Reserve Division. The 4th was the most extreme left battery of the army. 4/RFAR 29[9]

The British sent out bombing parties and Lewis gun teams that managed to gain ground on the left of the *Jaminwerk* and from there, work their way toward the rear of the strongpoint. They were temporarily held up by German infantry fire coming from a trench located just beyond the *Staubwasser Graben*. This trench was soon cleared and the bombing parties and Lewis guns were able to take up position where their fire could enfilade most of the German trenches inside the *Jaminwerk*.

The commander of RIR 109 knew that immediate action was needed if the British advance was to be stopped and the lost ground recaptured. The II/R109 was contacted by regimental headquarters in order to provide assistance to the hard pressed men of the III/R109 inside the *Jaminwerk* and surrounding trenches. Reinforcements from the II Battalion quickly moved up into the intermediate line. The remaining platoons of the 7/R109 were given orders to clear the *Kronprinzen Graben* while the 8/R109 was ordered to provide support and to help defend the Intermediate line.

Leutnant der Reserve Markwitz, 7/R109, pushed forward one platoon from his company into the *Kronprinz Graben*. The other part of the 7/R109 along with the 6th and 8/R109 under *Hauptmann der Reserve* Waldmann and *Oberleutnant der Reserve* Faber occupied the *Staubwasser Graben* and *Endress Graben*. As both latter trenches lacked any form of fire step or traverses, much of the defensive fighting took place out in the open on both sides of the actual trenches.

While the defenders were able to hold back part of the British advance for the moment, the situation facing the III/R109 was growing critical. From the start of the attack the British had been able to drive a wedge deep into the position by Montauban at the left wing of the regiment. The British continued to advance toward Montauban until they were able

Infantrymen – RIR 109. (Author's collection)

to enter the village and in doing so threatened the left flank and rear of RIR 109.

Machine guns and *Musketen* severely thinned the ranks of the advancing British troops as they crossed the open terrain. In addition, the flanking machine gun and rifle fire from an area known as 'The Pulpit' also caused numerous losses to the British troops. However, the machine guns were detected by low flying aircraft that quickly directed artillery fire on their positions and they were soon silenced.

The greatest threat to the British troops by Mametz came from the fire of the machine guns and *Musketen*. The heavy fire coming from these weapons formed the greatest barrier to any further British advance and caused the highest number of losses. German rifle fire was also very effective, but without the aid of the automatic weapons, the men of RIR 109 would have found it difficult to hold back the British troops.

Two machine guns and the *Musketen* that had been inserted into the *Ostring* joined forces. The combined fire of so many automatic weapons made any attempt to move forward in the open almost suicidal. For the time being the British advance was stopped in its tracks.

At the same time, parts of the 5th Coy that were still located inside the *Staubwasser Graben* attempted to establish a connection with the platoon of the 7/R109 that was fighting inside the *Jaminwerk*. The 8/R109 now had men fighting in the *Jaminwerk*, *Staubwasser Graben* and *Endres Graben*. These units became caught up in fierce fighting with approximately four British companies that had broken through the front line and that were advancing on the German left flank.

The pressure coming from the left flank was increasing each hour. By 10.15 a.m. the British had become firmly established at the northern and western edge of Montauban and from their new positions they opened fire upon Mametz with machine guns and mine throwers.

In addition to the Lewis guns and bombing parties that had been used against the *Jaminwerk*, the British also brought up Stokes mortars that could be used to dislodge particularly stubborn pockets of German resistance. While the fighting was taking place in and around the strongpoint the Stokes mortars were able to provide effective fire against

Trench near Mametz. (*An der Somme*)

many of the surrounding trenches. The German defenders were unable to silence the mortars and many of the Badeners had reached their breaking point.

To many of the men in RIR 109 it appeared as if all was lost. The British were not only deep inside the German trench system, they had also brought up numerous close range weapons that provided accurate fire wherever it was needed. Many of the men from RIR 109 broke under this concentrated fire and made their way toward the rear as rapidly as possible. Some men used the existing communication trenches; others simply climbed out of the trenches and shell craters into the open and ran toward the rear and hopefully to safety. Many did not make it to safety as large numbers of fleeing Germans were cut down by the fire from Lewis guns.

With much of the German resistance starting to crumble, the British troops made a concerted effort to capture the *Jaminwerk* once and for all. They were finally able to breach the defensive belts of wire and enter the maze of trenches. The defenders that were still inside the strongpoint did not surrender easily and the fighting soon became hand to hand as each traverse was fought over with great determination on both sides.

Finally, after close quarters fighting inside the strongpoint for almost an hour, the *Jaminwerk* fell. Most of the defenders had been killed, wounded or taken prisoner. Some survivors did manage to escape and these men quickly retreated through the *Artillerie Schlucht* [Caterpillar Alley]. By 9.30 a.m. the *Jaminwerk* was under British control.

The British had managed to advance some 2,000 meters into the German lines and by late morning occupied positions near the *Artillerie Schlucht*. The German trenches were found to be in a deplorable state. Many sections of trench had been badly damaged and in some cases had been obliterated.

Morale must have been high among the British troops as they observed numerous German dead scattered throughout the position. Prisoners being led out of shattered dugout entrances were often visibly shaken from their week-long ordeal and many looked exhausted and in some cases almost incoherent. It appeared that many of the Germans simply wanted to make it to the British rear and the safety of a P.O.W. cage.

The attack by the 53rd Brigade (18th Division) in the morning had also succeeded in breaching the German defenses. This brigade was facing a German position called Casino Point by the British. It was a portion of the German line that extended out into no man's land. The Germans had placed a well-fortified machine gun post at this spot that was able to provide enfilade fire against any attacking force.

Shortly before 7.30 a.m. this machine gun opened fire and immediately resulted in numerous losses to the leading British waves that had assembled in no man's land. Then, suddenly, at 7.27 a.m. there was a huge explosion as a 5,000 pound mine was detonated under the machine gun position.

A captain in the 6th Royal Berkshires described the events of that morning. He reported the event as a blinding flash accompanied by the ground shaking as the mine detonated nearby. The mine devastated the German defenses opposite the 6th Royal Berkshires. The air was filled with large pieces of debris as earth and chalk flew into the air mixed together with pieces of timber and chunks of concrete.

Any German defenders from RIR 109 that were unfortunate enough to be caught in the blast were literally blown to pieces by the explosion. When the debris settled there was a gaping hole of smoking earth estimated to be 40 feet deep and 120 feet in diameter. The threat posed by Casino Point was eliminated in a split second.

Some of the debris fell among the leading waves of British troops and caused a few injuries, however the mine did destroy a dangerous obstacle that allowed the British troops to enter and cross over the German front line with far fewer casualties than could otherwise be expected. The men of the 53rd Brigade were able to successfully move through the German trench system and reach an area close to the *Staubwasser Graben*. The only real resistance the men faced came from German machine gun fire from the rear trenches and from two fortified trench positions known to the British as 'The Loop' and 'The Castle'.

Once the Loop was captured it allowed the attackers to continue toward the *Staubwasser Graben*. The advance was slowed somewhat by German snipers, but they were soon cleared out one by one or forced to withdraw as the British moved deeper into the German trench system.

In some areas the men of the 53rd Brigade met stubborn resistance that hindered the advance. At other locations the defenders appeared to have fled, allowing the British to consolidate their gains inside the German defenses. The men from RIR 109 had been able to delay the British advance in some areas of the front with the assistance offered by each strongpoint or machine gun emplacement. The British advance was soon broken up, with some units being further ahead of the battalions on either flank. British troops now occupied a large portion of the German trench system.

The men of RIR 109 made every attempt to stop the British from taking any more ground but the situation was growing even more ominous as the enemy advanced deeper into the German lines. Parts of the III/R109 joined with a platoon from IR 23 and a number of groups from the neighboring IR 62 that had been driven back from the front line trenches. Together they occupied the quarry north of Montauban. From here they continued to oppose any further enemy advance but their ammunition was limited and no further reserves were at hand. The hard-pressed defenders sent runners to the rear to inform division headquarters of the situation and to advise the artillery of their position.

The artillery support that the regiment had relied upon to assist in the defense did not have sufficient strength to stop the British advance. On 1 July RIR 109 was supposedly being protected by the fire of 10 field and 13 heavy batteries, or so it appeared on paper. In reality many of the batteries had suffered losses as guns had been destroyed or damaged and placed out of action during the week-long bombardment.

The loss of many of the guns can be traced to two factors. First, the location where the batteries could be located was limited and it did not take long for the British to determine where the guns had been placed. The next step was to cover each suspected battery location with heavy fire. Second, the guns had been firing throughout the week-long bombardment period under the direct control of the local regimental commanders. The fire from the guns also made it easier for British observers to locate their positions and this made them even more vulnerable to British counter fire.

Allowing the local infantry commanders to control the use of the artillery did not allow for a coordinated defensive effort by the 28th Reserve Division when the actual attack occurred. It would have been far better if the guns had been controlled at division or corps level. This would have allowed them to be saved until the critical time of the attack when the full weight of their fire could be utilized. Despite these shortcomings the remaining artillery batteries did their best to stop the advancing British troops.

There was an attempt to increase the overall effectiveness of the artillery when two light field howitzer batteries and one mortar battery were assigned to support RIR 109 on 1 July. There were delays getting these guns into position and they did not start firing on

Destroyed 10.5cm Light field howitzer, 5(F)/RFAR 27. (Author's collection)

British positions until later in the day. Until these guns could join the fight the regiment had to rely on an ever-shrinking number of serviceable artillery pieces.

In order to effectively utilize the existing artillery pieces, it was critical to have a secure line of communications from the front line to the rear so that new target information could be relayed to the batteries quickly. By now, almost every telephone line leading to the rear had been cut making it almost impossible for the forward artillery observers to provide fire direction orders. Many of the observation posts had also been overrun or the observers had been forced to withdraw or face capture from the swift British advance.

All communication between the front line and the batteries had to rely upon runners and signal flags that proved to be very slow. The heavy smoke and dust often made signal flags useless and it was not unusual for runners to take a long time in reaching the batteries, if they survived the journey at all.

The British reports all continued to indicate that the German defensive barrage was extremely weak and poorly directed with only a few shells falling intermittently across the terrain. Without any protective fire barrier the British were able to move reinforcements and supplies across no man's land with relative impunity once most of the German machine gun and rifle fire had been eliminated or forced to withdraw further to the rear.

The fighting around the village of Mametz flared up once again shortly after noon. At about 1 p.m. several British bombing parties managed to work their way into the village from the southeast. German resistance prevented any further progress and the men soon entrenched in the area of the cemetery and the southern edge of the village.

Elements from the I/R109 sent bombing parties against this new threat, both on their own initiative and also following orders sent down from regimental headquarters. The fighting surged back and forth as parties of German and British troops fought in the narrow confines of the German trenches while hand grenades flew through the air from both sides.

This enemy threat was neutralized for the present by the German bombing parties from RIR 109. Many of the British soldiers that had entered Mametz were forced to withdraw. However, not all of the British footholds could be eliminated. Once the fighting died down

Infantrymen – RIR 109. (Author's collection)

the British were able to consolidate some of their gains. They were prevented from making any further advances for the time being despite repeated efforts.

It began to look doubtful if the forces available to RIR 109 around Mametz would be able to hold the village ruins let alone force the enemy back completely. The British continued to apply continuous pressure against the southern edge of the village. With each passing hour the number of defenders grew smaller and smaller as the number of losses continued to mount.

As a result of the latest British attacks the 3/R109 under *Leutnant der Reserve* Vohl found itself attacked on the right flank and from the rear. Further enemy attacks often led to hand to hand fighting throughout the sector held by the I/R109. The defenders barely managed to stop the British once more with heavy fire from the 3rd, and parts of the 5/R109 as well as from machine guns and *Musketen* positioned in and around Mametz.

Some time around 2 p.m. the eastern part of Mametz as well as the western half of the *Staubwasser Graben* came under increasingly heavy British artillery fire. Even subjected to heavy shelling, the machine guns from Machine Gun Marksman Detachment 132 and several *Musketen* positioned at these locations continued to have great effect on the British columns attempting to advance between Mametz and Montauban.

The British continued to attack the defenders of Mametz and gradually moved deeper into the German trenches. The pressure against the small group of survivors from the 3/R109 and 4/23 in the *Küchenwaldchen* and by Mametz Cemetery continued to increase each hour. It was not long before the British had effectively closed any passage through the *Matratzenweg* and the *Zeppelin Graben*, the only routes still available in the event the German defenders had wanted to withdraw to the rear.

This also had the effect of cutting off the right flank of the regiment from any further support from the rear. The men of the 3/R109 who were still fighting in the *Bismarck Graben* facing Hill 110 along with the remnants of the 4/23 on their left flank were facing an enemy on their right flank and from the rear. There was no hope for these men; no reinforcements could reach them even if any could be spared.

The British facing Mametz also made good use of the attack that was being made against the neighboring Fricourt at 2.30 p.m. It was hoped that the attack against Fricourt would distract many of the German defenders. An advance was ordered against Mametz at the same time, which resulted in more ground being gained and a number of German prisoners being taken.

At 3 p.m. the machine gun located inside the *Staubwasser Graben* just outside of Mametz was knocked out of action. At the same time the British concentrated their artillery fire on the village and the trenches running to the north from it. After a 30 minute bombardment the British advanced toward the village once more. One of the few remaining machine guns still in operation was located at the northern edge of Mametz. This gun continued to fire into the British left flank at a range of 600 meters with great effect.

During this latest attack the men of the 20th Brigade crossed Shrine Alley and bombed along the *Bismarck Graben*. They eventually reached Orchard Alley and Orchard trench west of Mametz later in the evening. At about 4 p.m. British artillery fire was again directed against the village of Mametz and the trenches connecting to the German rear. The particularly annoying machine gun at the northern edge of the village was struck by a direct hit and completely destroyed. With the loss of each machine gun or *Musketen* the overall effect of the defensive fire weakened considerably.

Covered trench near Mametz. (*An der Somme*)

Many of the survivors of the I/R109 had come to realize that their position was hopeless. It appeared that all lines of retreat had been cut off and stocks of ammunition were running very low. There was no food, but worst of all there was no water. Any wells found in the sector had all been destroyed and rendered useless by shellfire. The men had to rely on the water in their canteens, if they had any left at all. Most of the stocks of water prepared before the attack began had either been used or destroyed during the preliminary bombardment or overrun by enemy troops during the advance on 1 July.

The strain of the week-long bombardment and the effect of the heat and dust proved to be too much for some men. Even in areas where it might be possible, there was little that could be done to provide either reinforcements or fresh supplies of water while the heavy fighting raged on. One man in RIR 109 had apparently reached the breaking point.

> One of the men in my group went completely mad from thirst during the day. He was foaming at the mouth and, despite our shouts, he ran blindly out of our trench towards the English and was shot down. *Unteroffizier* Paul Scheytt, RIR 109[10]

The defenders of Mametz could point to at least one successful incident in the heavy fighting. A small detachment from the 3/R109 advanced into the cemetery and was able to knock out a British machine gun that had become particularly annoying to the Badeners. The gun was captured and brought back to the German lines as a trophy. Losses had been

Trench near Mametz. (*An der Somme*)

light for the 3rd Coy with one man, *Landwehrmann* Loos, being injured during the undertaking. He had been severely wounded in both legs from hand grenade fragments.

By late afternoon elements of RIR 109 still held out inside Mametz but the number of men was too small to offer any real resistance. The British also had detachments inside Mametz as a result of several strong bombing parties that had forced their way into the village ruins. Despite this success the bombing parties were still unable to make any further headway as a result of a machine gun inside the village that fired at point blank range. As long as this gun was operational any forward movement would be difficult. Further British advances coming from the Mametz Railway station suffered heavy losses from this gun as well.

By late afternoon many of the men from RIR 109 realized that they could no longer hold onto the village against the increasing enemy pressure. It was decided to abandon Mametz and head toward the rear. By now the village garrison had been reduced to only 32 men, not including the regimental staff located inside their headquarters dugout. While the men retreated along the road that lead toward Bazentin le Petit, the regimental commander and his staff forced their way through the British lines in a running hand grenade fight.

During the withdrawal the regimental adjutant *Oberleutnant* Krebs became severely wounded and had to be left behind. He was eventually picked up by the British and sent back for medical treatment. His wounds proved to be too serious and on 5 July he died from his injuries.

The fighting around Mametz continued almost non-stop until 5.30 p.m. Finally, the

British advanced in force against the *Bismarck Graben* and the southern edge of Mametz as well as from Hill 110 towards the village. The men from the I/R109 could not stop this attack. The last rifle cartridge had been fired and the last hand grenade had been used up, the men were at the end of their strength. The British were able to overrun the all resistance by Mametz and the pitiful remnants of the I/R109 as well as the men from the 5/R109 and the few survivors of the 4/23 were either captured or killed.

The men in the III Battalion were also fighting for their lives. In the left sector the 10/R109 had been designated as the battalion reserve and the men had been assigned to the trenches in the vicinity of the *Jaminwerk* and *Kronprinzen Graben* [Black Alley]. By late morning the sector held by the 10/R109 had been involved in continuous heavy fighting and losses were high on both sides.

The successful advance by the 54th and 53rd Brigades had dealt a serious blow to the cohesive defense of the trenches occupied by R109. Men on both sides often did not know where friend or foe was located or for that matter where any troops were located other than those they could see in their limited field of vision. The sound of firing could be heard coming from every direction and it was difficult to know what was happening.

For one party of German soldiers in the 10/R109 their participation in the battle was soon over. The men were putting up a good fight until they came under 'friendly fire' from the rear, or so they first thought.

We were being fired on from the rear. We thought this was our own infantry, so we jumped out of our trench, all waving and shouting 'Higher! Higher!' Then we saw two or three of our men drop wounded and we realized it was the English who were behind us, so we jumped back into our trench. There we had a conference as to whether to surrender. One or two wanted to fight on but there were many in our regiment who were over forty and, unlike the younger men, these had families and were the first to suggest surrendering. In the end the others were swayed. We tied a handkerchief to a rifle and waved it and the English came and rounded us up. We were very depressed but we knew that once we had surrendered the English wouldn't shoot us. We could see from their faces they were as pleased as we were that it was all over, but they took all our watches from us. *Unteroffizier* Gustav Lüttgers, 10/R109[11]

At approximately 10 a.m. the British had already advanced as far as the battle headquarters of the III/R109 and had set up a machine gun in close proximity of the dugout. For the next two hours the heavy defensive fire, mainly from machine guns and *Musketen*, had kept the British infantry at bay and fighting raged non-stop.

All this time the III Battalion staff was trapped inside their badly damaged dugout, unable to make their way back to safety. It was dangerous for the staff members to become exposed as they attempted to survey the situation around their position. As a result they were in the dark for most of the fighting and could not direct the defense of the sector.

About 2 p.m. the battalion adjutant went up the dugout stairs and into the adjoining trench in order to determine just what was happening around them. He quickly saw that the dugout and trench was completely cut off by what he considered to be an extremely large enemy force and that under these circumstances there was no chance for escape. The staff of the III Battalion was eventually forced to surrender and was taken to the rear as prisoners.

On the right of the *Carnoy Mulde*. (*An der Somme*)

During this period heavy British artillery fire also lay on the *Gabel Graben* and the western part of the *Staubwasser Graben*. The eastern portion of the latter trench had already been taken by the British.

Despite the setbacks suffered by the men of RIR 109, many were still providing serious resistance to every movement made by the enemy. Every attempt to advance further into the German lines between Mametz and Montauban was met by heavy fire from a machine gun still operating near the *Staubwasser Graben*. Finally, this gun was discovered and placed out of action as a result of a direct hit from an artillery shell.

British forces continued to advance relentlessly. There seemed to be no end to the number of men being thrown into the fighting. As the British moved toward the villages of Mametz and Montauban along the Carnoy-Montauban road the parts of RIR 109 that were still holding out inside the *Staubwasser Graben* were forced to withdraw and retreat toward the *Artillerie Schlucht*. Still, some of the men retreating still had some fight left in them.

By the afternoon we were very low in numbers and were nearly out of ammunition. We took all we could from the dead and wounded but we were not strong enough to hold out for long. The day closed with another English attack which we fought standing up in the open. When our last cartridge had been fired we retreated through the enemy barrage to *Klein Bazentin* [Bazentin le Petit]. When the regiment collected in le Transloy that evening, my company consisted of twenty men. *Unteroffizier* Paul Scheytt, RIR 109[12]

According to RIR 109, the British had successfully installed a mine thrower in the

Staubwasser Graben that resulted in heavy losses for the men who were retreating toward the *Artillerie Schlucht*. The retreating German infantry did have a brief opportunity to return the favor.

> We found a battery of our own guns completely deserted and, out of pure cussedness, we decided to fire them although we were only infantrymen. So we fiddled about with all those little levers and eventually got two guns loaded and fired two rounds. The English immediately replied, so we cleared off as fast as we could. *Unteroffizier* Paul Scheytt, RIR 109[13]

By 10.30 p.m. a new line was being formed inside the *Gabel Graben*. From their new position the men could clearly observe the British digging in at the northern edge of Mametz. The situation was critical as there were far too few men available to offer any serious opposition to any further British attacks. Fortunately the British seemed content with their gains for the day and made no attempt to continue the advance. The men of RIR 109 considered this a great success. While the regiment had lost a large portion of the German front line the much feared 'breakthrough' had not occurred.

The time spent in the new position was short lived. Fresh enemy artillery fire was directed against the *Grabel Stellung* and the men were forced to continue their withdrawal. Some men occupied the battery position of the 2/RFAR 29 and the trench located just in front of this position. Later in the night the withdrawal continued with the men moving into the II Line that ran from Longueval to Mametz Wood. Upon arrival in the new defenses the men came under the command of Major Schmidts.

Schmidts had taken command of this line earlier on 1 July and was in charge of the men who were holding Longueval. The men under his command might not be considered to be of the highest caliber. His force consisted of clerks, orderlies, cyclists, carrying troops, almost anyone that could be rounded together and given a rifle. Most of these soldiers had not actively been involved in any fighting or even trench duty for some time and probably could not be relied upon to provide any serious level of defense.

One of the men who took part in the defense of the second position was Emil Goebelbecker, 9/R109. At the start of the battle Emil was located in the second line in Longueval where he operated a generator. At the end of June he received orders to move into positions in the second line of the German defenses. Upon his arrival he was told to stay in his position by the battalion commander where he was able to watch much of the fighting on 1 July.

> That morning [1 July], we saw them [the British] all coming and we fired from the second line. In that section, they overran the first line but they didn't go farther. When evening came, we went back toward Longueval. There was one man from the artillery with us. We found a battery there and decided to take a rest in a dugout. In a short time, the shells started [falling] nearer and nearer and one blew up in the entry. The guy sitting on the stairs was killed. We dug ourselves out and a short distance away was an artillery officer. He asked, 'Who are you? The 109th? Go back, you have to go back.'

Infantry Group, RIR 109. (Author's collection)

Then we came back to Longueval and the first thing I saw was the company orderly. He saw me and said, 'Are you coming back too?' I said, 'Yeah boy!' We came back with only 7 from the company. We went in with 120.[14]

At the end of the day the quarry near Montauban was still in German hands. The *ad hoc* unit holding this position was formed from the survivors of the left hand regimental sector, now under the command of *Leutnant* Beier. Reinforcements as well as ammunition, water and food were desperately needed by the small group.

During the heavy fighting on 1 July the regimental musicians had earned their pay. The musicians were divided into several detachments and acted as stretcher-bearers during the fighting. It was difficult and dangerous work as the men made their way through the German trenches with their heavy loads. As a result of being exposed to enemy fire the band members lost approximately ten men wounded, captured or missing. The survivors were then consolidated into a single detachment later in the evening.

Some welcome relief for the regiment came during the night when one battalion from Bavarian IR 16 and one battalion from IR 51 arrived and took up positions for a counter attack against the neighboring village of Montauban and the eastern portion of the *Staubwasser Graben*. At the same time the survivors of RIR 109 were ordered to assemble in the village of Le Transloy. The losses suffered by RIR 109 had apparently been so high as to render the regiment unfit for any further fighting.

Emil Goebelbecker, 9/R109. (Richard Baumgartner)

When the rolls were called after the fighting had died down the regimental losses were reported to be 14 officers and medical officers killed, 6 officers wounded, 24 officers missing. 94 Other Ranks were also reported killed, 261 were wounded and the vast majority, 1,749, were simply listed as missing. The relatively few men listed as wounded were among the luckiest in the regiment. They had managed to make their way to the rear for treatment and safety during the fighting on 1 July. For the vast majority of the losses, almost 1,800 officers and men who were missing, there simply was no news of their fate.

I was wounded quite early in the morning and remember lying semi-conscious and seeing British soldiers jumping over our trench but we were not rounded up and several of us took shelter in a dug-out. Once, during the morning, an English grenade came down and exploded with a loud crash. No one was hurt and one of my comrades said 'Pardon me' as if he had made a rude noise. We laughed. A second grenade followed and again no one was hurt. Then an English soldier came down but we all hid in a dark corner and weren't seen. It was many hours later that one of our men went out with a white handkerchief and we were taken prisoner by two soldiers from the Devonshire Regiment. They were very friendly and the doctor who attended me asked where I came from. When I told him 'Freiburg', he told me that was where he had studied and asked me about certain girls that he knew there. *Grenadier* Emil Kury, 1 MG Coy RIR 109.[15]

The problem of clearing dugouts required far greater effort and diligence than the British were using, as can be seen by the account of Emil Kury. Fortunately, for all involved the men with Kury simply wanted to give themselves up and make it safely from the battlefield and not carry on fighting.

By the end of the day the fighting died down. The German lines by Montauban and Mametz had been penetrated but the fear of an enemy breakthrough seemed to be over for the present. The new line was being held by a mixed group of men, many who were physically and mentally exhausted from fighting all day, others who had not fired a rifle in anger for more than a year and whose fighting capabilities was suspect at best.

Still, when the dust settled the British did not continue their advance. Even a small advance into some key features near Mametz and Montauban probably could have avoided much of the fighting and thousands of casualties in the months that followed. Even the common German soldier recognized their precarious position.

What puzzled me most all day was the lack of further forward movement by the British. The whole of our line had collapsed and it would have been a simple matter for them to have advanced much further than they did. *Soldat* Emil Goebelbecker, RIR 109.[16]

The fear of being cut off and surrounded was of great concern to the men of RIR 109. For the last 21 months the men had been involved in trench warfare. The days of open fighting and mass maneuvering was long past. All the men knew was the safety and protection of their extensive network of trenches and that to leave them to cross open ground was tantamount to suicide in most cases. If the men realized their only escape route was being cut off they had little choice at this point in the war. It was either withdraw, if it was still possible, or surrender to the enemy.

The losses suffered by RIR 109 were among the heaviest suffered by any German regiment fighting on 1 July 1916. The official casualty return taken shortly after this day does give an indication of the extent of the fighting. However it does not reflect an accurate picture of the true losses suffered by the men of RIR 109.

The majority of the German losses for RIR 109 were published on three separate *Verlustlisten* in the weeks following the battle – on 28 July, 31 July and 1 August. Subsequent lists published in the months that followed provided corrections and additions as new information on the fate of some men was received and passed along to the public.

The numbers of men lost in total clearly indicate that the regiment suffered heavy losses, but they are deceiving. The largest numbers of officers and men, 1,773, were simply listed as missing. Given the events of that time there could be any number of reasons a man was listed as missing. He could have been killed, separated from the regiment and subsequently returned, a prisoner of war, wounded and unable to identify his name or unit while in a hospital or in a very few instances he could have been missed during the roll call and was actually still with the regiment.

The lists published in the months following the publication of the initial casualty reports provided new details of the status of the men who had been shown as missing or wounded. By reviewing these lists through the end of 1916 it is possible to obtain a clearer picture of the actual losses suffered by RIR 109 during the preliminary bombardment and the fighting on 1 July.

British prisoners captured by RIR 109. (*Das Reserve-Infanterie-Regiment Nr. 109 im Weltkrieg 1914 bis 1918*)

The *Verlustlisten* associated with the fighting on 1 July indicate that RIR 109 suffered casualties of 2,121 officers and men in the reporting period covered by the lists. The regimental account indicates a total of 2,104 casualties between 24 June and 1 July.

By reviewing subsequent *Verlustlisten* as well as the regimental *Ehrentafel* it is possible to determine the true level of casualties suffered by RIR 109 on this momentous day. 59 of the men named in the *Verlustlisten* can be positively identified as being killed or died from wounds between 23 June and 30 June.

Of the remaining 2,062 names; 556 can be positively identified as being killed or died from wounds as a result of the fighting on 1 July 1916. 943 of the officers and men originally listed as missing in action were prisoners of war (14 officers, 929 Other Ranks). The remainder suffered wounds and injuries of varying degrees of severity. It is difficult at present to determine the exact dates of these injuries.

Regardless of the statistical details, the fact is that two-thirds of RIR 109 had become casualties in one day of fighting. 556 officers and men had been killed or fatally wounded in a single day, one man less than the number of men killed in the regiment between the time RIR 109 had arrived on the Somme in September 1914 up until 30 June (557 officers and men). It was truly a dark day for the men of RIR 109.

Notes:
1.   While most accounts indicate that RIR 109 had 15 machine guns divided between two machine gun companies, the description of the sectors and number of guns distributed in each based on the regimental account bring the total to 16.
2.   Middlebrook, op. cit. p. 156.
3.   The two brigades from the 7th Division included the 8th Devonshire, 9th Devonshire, 2nd Border and 2nd Gordons in the 20th Brigade while the 2nd Queen's, 1st South Staffordshire, 21st Manchester and 22nd Manchester formed the 91st Brigade. The two brigades from the 18th Division consisted of the 53rd with the 8th Norfolk, 8th Suffolk, 10th Essex and 6th Royal Berkshire and the 54th with the 11th Royal Fusiliers, 7th Bedfordshire, 6th Northamptonshire and 12th Middlesex.

4. Middlebrook, op. cit., pp. 156-157. The mine explosion heard by *Unteroffizier* Scheytt could have been the 2,000 pound mine detonated under a portion of the German line designated Bulgar Point by the British. Two mines, 500 pounds of explosives each, were detonated just in front of the 11/Royal Fusiliers at 7.27 a.m. Four additional mines, 500 pounds each, were detonated south of the *Kuchenwäldchen* [Hidden Wood] where no attack had been planned.

5. The *Verlustlisten* printed after 1 July indicates 224 members of the 4/23 were listed as casualties from the fighting on or about 1 July. Only one man on the list can positively be identified as having become a casualty some 10 days later. Of the 223 other names 43 were killed on 1 July while another 121 most likely became prisoners of war on this date with two of these succumbing to their wounds at a later date. 49 men were listed as being either severely or slightly wounded, again most probably on 1 July. The 4/23 effectively ceased to exist following the heavy fighting on 1 July.

6. Schmückle, *Schwäbische Kunde aus dem grossen Krieg*, pp. 66-67.

7. Middlebrook, op. cit., p. 203. The man from Pforzheim mentioned by Emil Kury was most likely Eugen Katz, who is shown as the only man killed on 1 July from this town.

8. *Musketen* usually operated in pairs. The guns were air cooled and would fire in turn in order to prevent any one gun from overheating.

9. Schmückle, op. cit., pp. 63-65.

10. Middlebrook, op. cit., pp. 203-204.

11. Middlebrook, op. cit., p. 204.

12. Middlebrook, op. cit., p. 232.

13. Ibid.

14. R. Baumgartner, *Der Angriff*, No. 3, August 1979, p.

15. Middlebrook, op. cit., p. 233.

16. Ibid.

11

Montauban – Hardecourt – Curlu

Part 1: Montauban – Hardecourt

The fighting that occurred between the villages of Montauban, Hardecourt and Curlu involved the southernmost portion of the British attack and the northernmost portion of the French attack on the Somme on 1 July 1916. With the exception of the village of Montauban, little has been published on the fighting on this portion of the front. It would be difficult to omit this aspect of the fighting from the narrative and still provide the reader with the full picture of the fighting on 1 July.

This portion of the battlefield involved two German divisions, the 12th (Prussian) Division and the 10th Bavarian Division. The 12th Division consisted of three regiments – (2. *Oberschlesische*) *Infanterie Regiment* Nr. 23 'von Winterfeld', (3rd *Oberschlesische*) *Infanterie Regiment* Nr. 62 and (4th *Oberschlesische*) *Infanterie Regiment* Nr. 63. The majority of the men from the 12th Division came from Silesia.

This division had occupied the trenches north of the river Somme up through Mametz prior to the Battle of the Somme. It was only when additional troops were available further north that the division boundaries were shifted slightly to the south. Now the right wing of the 12th Division was located at the village of Montauban. The left wing still rested on the banks of the River Somme near the village of Curlu. Normally, two of the three regiments would occupy the front line trenches of the division sector.

The trenches from Montauban to Curlu had seen very little fighting since the end of 1914. As such this portion of the front had not been developed in the same manner as the trenches further north near the villages of La Boisselle, Ovillers, Thiepval and others located along the Somme front. The lack of fighting and the subsequent lack of development of the defenses before 1 July would play a key role in the events that unfolded on this date.

The sector occupied by the men from the 12th Division had other disadvantages when compared to the rest of the Somme front. Unlike areas further to the north, the land near the river was mainly flat with a few low, rolling hills. Much of the terrain was also very swampy in places, especially the closer the trenches came to the river. With such a high water table it was almost impossible to create large, deep mined dugouts along much of the division front line. In many ways the terrain was also like the land along the swampy Ancre ground or parts of Flanders where much of the defensive positions had to be created above ground. While not as bad as Flanders, it did provide a challenge to create effective defensive works.

Many of the early attempts to create deep dugouts close to the river were failures. They soon filled with water and become uninhabitable. In the portions of the line where deeper dugouts could have been created, in areas further north near Montauban and Mametz, there was apparently little effort made to construct them. Both the division and regimental commanders did not see any real benefit to their men in relation to the effort required to construct this type of shelter. Consequently, when the attack began on 1 July there were far too few mined dugouts that could protect the front line garrison from the heavy enemy fire.

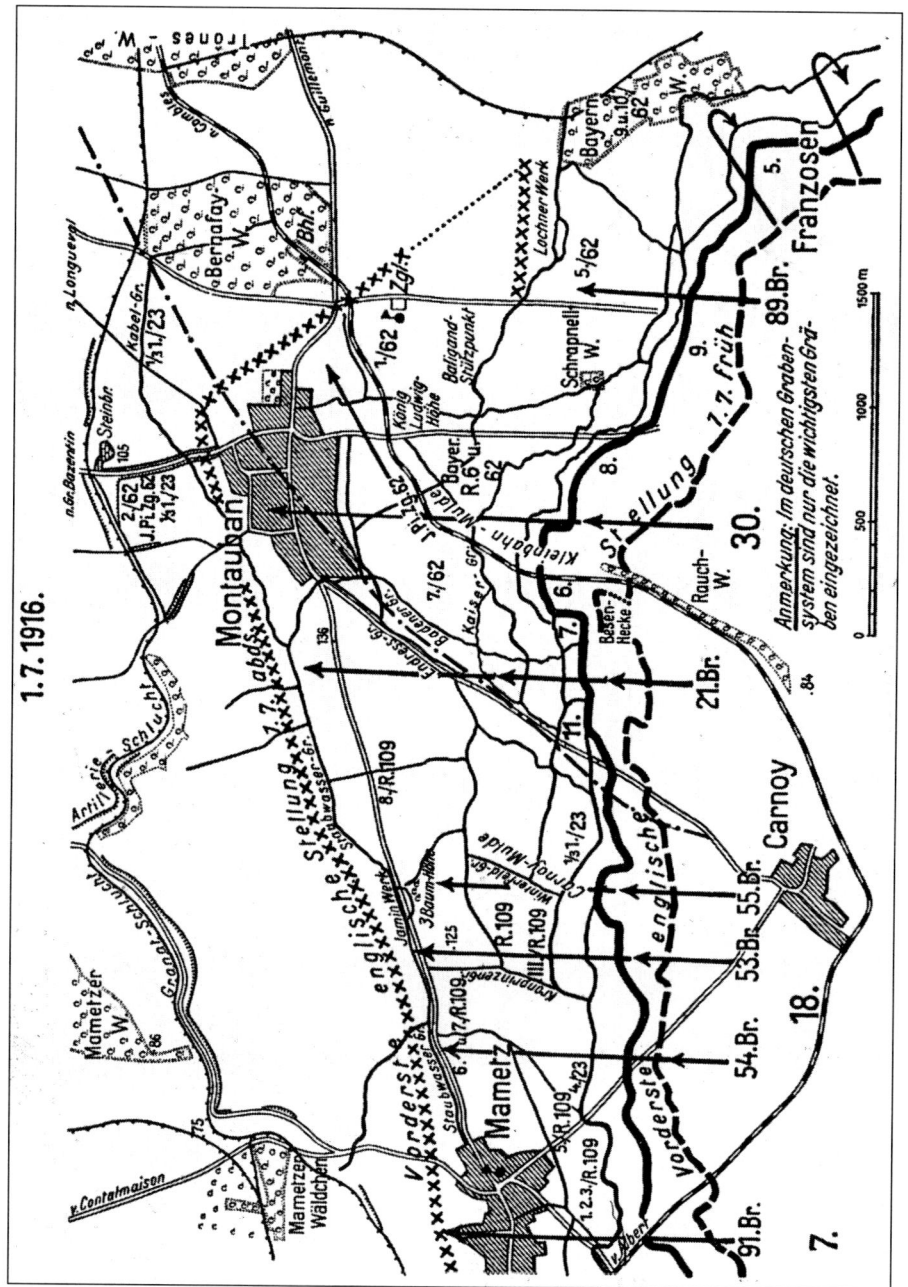

Mametz-Montauban.

Most of the existing dugouts had only a few meters of earth covering them at best and could not withstand the fire from even light and medium caliber guns.

There were too few communication trenches leading up to the front line positions. The wire entanglements protecting the trenches were inadequate. There were insufficient numbers of telephone lines and other methods of communications between the front line and the rear. The telephone lines that were in place were either buried just below the surface of the ground or in some places still strung along the trench walls where they could easily be cut. Overall, the defensive positions occupied by the 12th Division could be considered inferior to those created further north by the other divisions now under General von Soden.

Just prior to 1 July two regiments from the division were holding the front line sector from Montauban to Curlu, IR 62 and IR 63. IR 23 had already been designated to replace the men from RIR 109; however the events just before 1 July prevented this from occurring. The men from IR 23 were then positioned at different locations along the 28th Reserve Division front as reserves and would not be available to support the 12th Division in the upcoming fighting.

The men from IR 62 held the front line from Montauban to the *Bayern Wald* [*Bois Faviere*] while the men of IR 63 held the front line from the *Bayern Wald* to the village of Curlu on the northern bank of the River Somme. These regiments had come under heavy fire during the preliminary bombardment, primarily from French batteries. Unfortunately for the men of the 12th Division the French utilized a far larger number of heavy guns against their positions than the British were capable of at that time.

The powerful bombardment, the reports being circulated with information obtained from prisoners and through the Moritz listening posts all clearly indicated that an enemy attack was imminent. However, for some in the 12th Division it was felt that the enemy would soon run out of ammunition given the immense amounts being fired each day. It was not considered reasonable to think the British and French could keep up this level of fire forever.

There was also a controversy concerning French involvement in the approaching battle. Many senior officers in the 12th Division were of the opinion that the French would not be involved in the fighting because of the numbers of men they were deploying further south at Verdun. The fighting there had been raging since February without signs of letting up. Many felt that the French bombardment was merely a feint used to draw critical reserves away from the main focus of the attack by the British. Others were convinced that despite the obvious problems facing the French they were going to be involved attack but only with weak forces. Only time would tell which group was correct in their assumptions.

An attack was not expected in our sector; still on 29 June an English patrol was captured, who upon questioning denied that an attack was planned here. It was believed that the French had been weakened through the fighting at Verdun and that they were not capable of a new big push. *Hauptmann der Reserve* Klug, 5/6th Bavarian RIR[1]

IR 62 had reported a large number of men killed, wounded or missing during the preliminary bombardment during the last week of June but not in any numbers that would seriously affect the ability of the regiment to properly defend the trenches. Losses had also been considered severe in IR 63 as one position after another had been destroyed in the heavy fire. The sector held by IR 63 was probably the most vulnerable as their trenches came closest to the river and therefore were the shallowest of all.

As early as 25 June numerous dugouts along the front held by IR 62 collapsed under the impact of medium and heavy shells. There was a serious disruption to command and control on this portion of the front on 26 June when two battalion headquarters dugouts collapsed. The dugout containing the battalion staff of the III/62 was crushed in the heavy fire, killing the battalion commander, *Hauptmann* Settegast and a large part of his staff. *Hauptmann* Gubisch, commander of the I/62 was seriously wounded along with many members of his staff when his dugout also collapsed. With the attack only a few days away these losses were keenly felt.

The shallow trench system and dugouts, as much a result of the high water table as well as the lack of firsthand combat experience, magnified the destructive effect of the enemy bombardment. Many of the poorly constructed trenches were slowly leveled and many sections simply collapsed under the ceaseless pounding. The *Kanzel Stellung* and *Curlu Graben* were particularly hard hit. Many of the losses being reported resulted from men being buried in shallow shelters and when trench walls collapsed on top of them.

Narrow trenches were quickly created across the front line in an attempt to connect as many of the surviving shelters as possible. Parts of the 6th Bavarian RIR had been assigned to assist in this work. One platoon of Bavarians was positioned in the *Bayern Wald* and two other platoons worked on the creation of a new approach trench coming from Guillemont to the front. In an attempt to remedy some of the deficiencies of the position a new switch line had been ordered constructed during the height of the bombardment.

This last task had been completed in the sector held by IR 62 in the night of 29/30 June. The new position created would allow the defenders to stand upright inside the trench.

Men of the 12th Division on the Somme. (*An der Somme*)

Portions of the new trench were even provided with rudimentary wire obstacles but nothing even approaching the level that would be required to prevent an enemy breakthrough.

Further attempts were made to expand the existing position on 27 June when parts of the I/6th Bavarian RIR along with the 2/*Pionier* Bn. 6 worked on the switch line along the western edge of the *Bayern Wald* that was supposed to connect the *Lochnerwerk* and the *Franzosen Graben*. While the new trenches would be useful in defending the position there was still a shortage of wire entanglements. Much of the existing wire had already been badly damaged or destroyed. Only a small amount of new wire entanglements could be created due to the incessant shellfire. Any attempt to work in the open only resulted in further losses.

Over the next few days many of the remaining shallow dugouts throughout the line simply could not withstand the weight of enemy fire. One shelter after another was destroyed or badly damaged, killing and injuring their occupants. Many of the surviving shelters were now packed with men trying to find protection against the shells. Others sought refuge in small sections of trenches that had survived the shelling or in the numerous shell craters formed during the bombardment.

A debate was taking place at division headquarters during the week-long bombardment that involved the possibility of relieving the men of the 12th Division from the front line. Perhaps it was the lack of combat experience; perhaps it was the opinion that the French would not be involved in the upcoming attack or perhaps it was simply that the 12th Division found it increasingly difficult in supplying hot food to every portion of the division sector at any one time since 25 June that resulted in the decision to order its relief.

While the losses suffered by the two regiments had been higher than either had experienced in some time, the numbers of men killed and wounded had not reached a level

Trench in the *Bayern Wald*. (*An der Somme*)

that would impair the defensive capabilities of the two regiments. In fact, the lack of warm food and the losses experienced by the men of the 12th Division were no different than those experienced by other regiments along the front, from Gommecourt to Mametz.

In regard to the issue of losses, IR 62 could be considered one of the hardest hit regiments. However, in the period between 25 June and 30 June IR 62 reported losses of 7 officers, 91 Other Ranks killed, 7 officers, 201 Other Ranks wounded and 4 Other Rank missing. These numbers indicate that the regimental strength had been reduced by slightly more than a single company. This left the regiment with the combat strength of almost eleven infantry and two machine gun companies. These losses, while larger than some other regiments, simply did not warrant removing the men most familiar with the conditions and terrain from the front line.

However, apparently one or more of these reasons prompted the commander of the 12th Division to ask General von Soden to approve his request to relieve IR 62 and IR 63. The replacement of the two regiments could not have been at a worse time.

Von Soden agreed to the request and plans were set in place to have the entire front line of the 12th Division relieved. Since IR 23 was no longer available it would fall on the 6th Bavarian RIR from the 10th Bavarian Division to provide the troops needed. It should be noted that since 14 June the men from the Bavarian regiment had been used solely as labor troops. The Bavarians had been creating new trenches and repairing damage caused by the bombardment along large portions of the front line. This regiment also supplied carrying parties that brought food, ammunition and building supplies to the front line. One battalion from the regiment had been assigned to assist the 28th Reserve Division while the remaining two worked on the trenches of the 12th Division. The Bavarian battalion and company commanders all received their orders from the divisions they were assigned to.

Oberst Leibrock, the commander of Bavarian RIR 6, had great reservations about how his regiment was being utilized during this period of time. He had almost no control over the various parts of his regiment. He only had a basic idea of what the men were assigned to do each day and for much of the time between 14 and 30 June he had minimal contact with his subordinate commanders. In his estimation his regiment was scattered across at least 10 kilometers of trenches.

For more than two weeks the men from Bavarian RIR 6 worked every night in exposed locations where many of the men came under enemy fire without having the chance to find adequate protection. The men then returned to their quarters in and around Longueval, but only after a grueling march in the early morning hours. Then, British and French artillery fire prevented the men from getting much sleep during the daylight hours and once darkness fell it was back to the front to perform hard labor.

There were never enough building materials needed to create all of the defensive positions the front line required. The regiment did suffer losses from British and French artillery bombardments but they were fortunately light, only 52 men being reported as killed or wounded from 26 through 30 June. The effectiveness of the regiment was being reduced more from the hard labor and the distance the men needed to travel each day going to and from the front line than by combat losses. By the end of the two weeks many of the Bavarians were simply physically exhausted.

In spite of these circumstances, the men from Bavarian RIR 6 were given orders to relieve IR 62 and IR 63. The exchange would begin in the night from 29/30 June. It proved to be a very difficult task. The men had to move under the cover of darkness and as many

Terrain near Montauban. (An der Somme)

of the approach trenches had been destroyed or badly damaged the columns were often delayed. In order to reduce possible casualties from enemy fire the men also moved forward in small groups.

Further difficulties were encountered when the men were being directed to the front line, as areas of it were no longer recognizable as such, so their guides had difficulty locating the assigned positions. The initial portion of the relief was not completed until the early morning hours of 30 June.

The replacement of the front line troops was not what the men had been accustomed to previously. The decision had been made to replace both IR 62 and IR 63 by the 6th Bavarian RIR alone. Normally one regiment would replace a unit of comparative size. Here, the Bavarians would occupy the entire division sector front line with one regiment instead of two. The reserve and readiness sectors would be occupied by the two regiments that had been relieved and the Silesians would provide support for the Bavarians.

Two of the three battalions of the 6th Bavarian RIR would now face a total of fourteen battalions from the 91st, 54th, 53rd, 55th, 21st, 89th and 90th Brigades from the British army in the northern sector. In addition, the southern sector held by the Bavarians faced Regiments d'Infanterie 146, 153 and 156 from the French 11th and 39th Divisions. Regiment d'Infanterie 160 from the XX Corps (General Balfourier) would support the advance against the position of Major Bezzel, I/6th Bavarian RIR, that was supported by *Hauptmann* Heck, II/IR63.

Northern Sector
Montauban – Hardecourt

The confusing situation the Bavarians found themselves facing in the unfamiliar trenches on 1 July was compounded even further by the decisions made over the command of each sector. This decision was to have a major impact in the upcoming events. The Bavarians in the northern or right hand division sector would not be under a unified command with officers that were familiar to the men. Instead, they were parceled out between three different commanders, only one of which was from the Bavarian regiment.

The right hand sector of IR 62, just to the south of Montauban was relieved by the 11th and 7/6th Bavarian RIR. This portion of the front would fall under the command of the II/62 under *Hauptmann* Baucke. The center sector was relieved by the 6th and 8/6th Bavarian RIR. This portion of the front line would remain under control by officers known to the men, *Hauptmann* Horn, and the staff of the II/6th Bavarian RIR who had relieved the staff of the I/62. The left hand sector of IR 62 was relieved by 9th and 5/6th Bavarian RIR and would be under the command of the III/62 under *Hauptmann* Bruck.

Offizier Stellvertreter Joseph Busl, platoon leader of the 3rd Platoon of the 8/6th Bavarian RIR, provided another account of these eventful days.

> The 8th Company marched with its platoon leaders *Leutnant* Salfner, *Vizefeldwebel* Schlegel and *Offizier Stellvertreter* Busl on Sunday, 22 June 1916 from Rancourt to the hill of Morval, and there to work on the 3rd Position. About 3 o'clock in the morning the company was ordered into the 2nd Line by Maurepas via Combles and here occupied the sector from the Railroad line Peronne – Combles up to in the village of Maurepas. My third platoon lay on the left wing of the company until about the end of the month under especially heavy artillery-fire, presumably because of the battery at Maurepas.
>
> In the night from 28/29 June I sent a patrol through the heaviest enemy artillery fire to the connection in the front. The strength of the company was about 190 men; my platoon consisted of 6 *Unteroffiziers* and 56 men.
>
> At 8 o'clock in the evening on 29 June orders came for the relief of IR 62 in the forward line south of the small railway Montauban-Carnoy and west of Hardecourt. I went in advance to takeover the position, my platoon came after led by *Unteroffizier* Gareis. A quick meal in the quarry at Montauban, the company reached the ordered position about 5.30 o'clock in the morning after an extremely exhausting march through heavy artillery and machine gun fire throughout.
>
> As a result of the daylong shelling the trenches were partially leveled, the fire-positions hardly still usable. The platoon had only 3-4 dugouts. Our men were greatly exhausted through the continued fatigues and deprivations since 22 June, a further dugout became pressed in with the loss of 8 men. As to food only coffee could be obtained because of the constant heavy fire.[2]

Once relieved the 7/62 occupied the 3rd trench behind Sectors G and H. the 1/62 was positioned at the *König Ludwig Höhe* and the *Kaisergraben*. The 5/62 was placed in the *Lochnerwerk* while the 2/62 and the regimental *pionier* platoon were placed in the quarry north of Montauban. The 9th and 10/62 were positioned inside the *Bayern Wald* while the 8th, 6th, 4th, 3rd and 11/62 were spaced along the II Position. Finally, the 12/62 remained in Maurepas as a sector reserve. The staff of the I/62 was moved to a position at the crossroads where the Ginchy-Maurepas road intersected the Guillemont-Combles road.

The regimental headquarters of IR 62 was then relieved by *Oberst* Leibrock and the staff of the 6th Bavarian RIR. When this was completed, the regimental staff of IR 62 was ordered to occupy a dugout by Moislains. This all took place mere hours before the start of the British/French attack on the morning of 1 July.

At approximately 4 o'clock in the morning I reached the dugout with my staff that had we had been assigned, still quite safely. In addition to the regimental staff: the Artillery Liaison Officer *Hauptmann* Ottens from Field Artillery Regiment 22 with his adjutant, a runner detachment that were to bring orders and messages over the open field to the telephone position, and a few infantry pioneers that should repair the dugout as well as 1 machine gun with crew, all from IR 62, were accommodated in the same dugout.

The commander of IR 62, *Oberstleutnant* von Poser, explained the unfavorable situation of the dugout to me, particularly that it had no connection to the front through a communication trench. He also said that the telephone connection to both right battalion sectors had already been interrupted for a long time, likewise the connection with the intermediate position. However a telephone connection existed to the left battalion sector in the *Bayern Wald*, likewise from the intermediate position.in Bernafay wood to the division. The runners for the connection to the intermediate position.were organized and the regimental adjutant from IR 62 has control over their use. Because of the unfavorable situation of the regimental dugout he has had a severe argument with the division commander, however without success. The Artillery Liaison Officers *Hauptmann* Ottens complained that the artillery has already ordered telephone cable very often and very desperately, but so far nothing was received.

Saturday, 1 July 1916. During the ride before and the advance to the dugout the enemy artillery fire generally became active in both wooded areas and between the woods and the dugout. At approximately 4.30 in the morning the delivery of the regimental sector had been carried out, at 5 o'clock new fire activity started. The enemy was apparently not oriented precisely on the dugout so that, in part, the heavy projectile impacts were mostly immediately behind it. The Regimental Sector included the Position Sectors g-h-I-k-l-m.[3]

Once inside his new headquarters *Oberst* Leibrock found he still had almost no control over his regiment and the overall situation was somewhat less than perfect.

I only had connection with the four companies of my regiment that were subordinate to *Hauptmann* Bruck of IR 62 because of the destruction of the telephone lines and the unfavorable situation of the regimental dugouts. Ammunition and food replacement were in the hands of officers who were neither personally well known to me or to my subordinates. The independent and automatic cooperation of all departments, on which rightly so much emphasis and value had been placed during training and in the past year of war, and which had to be considered a main factor of our combat capability, was altogether absent. *Oberst* Leibrock.[4]

In the final hours before the attack all of the men were in their positions. The night from 30 June to 1 July had passed relatively quiet but still numerous shells fell along the entire sector held by the 12th Division. The morning hours of 1 July were not much different than those experienced during the height of the bombardment. Dense fog had settled along the entire front line and visibility was down to a few meters at best.

At 5 a.m. the enemy artillery fire fell on the German positions as it had never before.

The noise was deafening and men standing only a few feet from one another could not hear anything but the constant explosion of the shells falling everywhere. The earth appeared to tremble and roll under their feet while fountains of earth and debris shot up into the air as high as a house. Large timbers from the few existing trench sections were hurled about as if match wood. For many it seemed to be a miracle that anyone was able to survive such intense fire.

To many of the German defenders it was apparent that the enemy must have thought that no one could possibly survive such a bombardment. Who could watch such destruction and believe anyone would be physically capable of resisting an attack? At 7.30 a.m. the artillery fire suddenly lifted from the German front line and was transferred onto the rear and support trenches, wooded areas and suspected battery positions.

The shifting of the artillery fire and the subsequent approach of the British skirmish lines largely went unnoticed by the Bavarians holding the front line trenches. Fog, smoke from the exploding shells, dust and debris filled the air making it impossible to see more than a few feet. The men who were lucky enough to occupy one of the few still intact dugouts or small niche cut into the side of a section of trench did not realize that the heavy fire had moved to the rear at first. The enemy soldiers were able to cross no man's land with minimal delay, least of all from the much-vaunted German artillery that now appeared almost silent.

Along much of the German front line from Montauban to Hardecourt there were attempts to alert the artillery batteries in the rear of the British attack. The telephone lines were all cut during the bombardment. Light signaling stations were almost useless in the heavy mist and smoke and it would take runners too much time to reach the rear and sound the alarm. Flares were the only means left and every attempt was made to alert the batteries. Red flares rose high into the sky across the front line that under normal circumstances

Road near Montauban. (*An der Somme*)

should result in heavy defensive barrage fire falling on no man's land within a few minutes.

However, the air was so filled with dust and debris that even the normally reliable signal flares went unnoticed in the rear and the German guns remained unusually quiet. Only a few random shells fell along the front line. In part this was due to the lack of any messages coming from the front line. In part it was due to the extremely high number of guns that had been placed out of action during the British bombardment. Many more guns were knocked out on 1 July as British planes circled the battlefield and transmitted the individual gun locations back to the British batteries. As each gun position was discovered it came under heavy and accurate fire. It was only a matter of time before one or more shells found their target and more guns were hit and rendered unserviceable.

The guns in *Artillerie Gruppe Nord* under *Oberstleutnant* von der Burg from FAR 57 were already providing as much support to the men of the 12th Division front as they could. The real problem facing the gunners faced was the lack of direct communication with the front line; they did not have any reliable targeting information on where to send their shells. In addition, there were far too few guns still in service to be able to provide an effective wall of barrage fire across such a large area.

The 89th Brigade, the right wing of the British attack, had been waiting for the moment to begin their assault. At 7.22 a.m. there was a hurricane of fire directed at the German front line that included rapid fire from six batteries of Stokes Mortars. The only setback experienced was when a mortar shell grazed the edge of the emplacement and blew up The explosion caused hundreds of mortar rounds stacked nearby, ready for quick use, to detonate in a spectacular series of explosions.

The men of the 89th Brigade had taken up position in front of the British wire before Zero hour in a plan designed to avoid any German defensive fire that would surely fall upon the British trenches. At 7.30 a.m. the men double timed across the open terrain as they headed toward the German lines. It was difficult to determine where the German trench was located as much of the wire had been destroyed and large sections of trench had been leveled by the heavy bombardment.

A wide expanse of the German front line was overrun in the opening minutes of the attack before the Bavarians could offer much resistance. Within a short time after reaching the German trenches the 89th Brigade had managed to round up approximately 300 prisoners and four machine guns. Most of the prisoners were from IR 62, indicating that the front line had been breached and the fighting was now taking place in the reserve positions. The 9/6th Bavarian RIR had almost been completely destroyed in the fighting in the opening minutes of the attack.

The 9th Coy reported 107 casualties from the fighting on 1 July 1916. Of these losses 22 men had been killed, many from artillery fire. The largest portion of the company had been taken prisoner, 72 men, many of whom were also wounded. The only officer that had become a casualty from this company was *Oberleutnant der Reserve* Friedrich Beck. Beck had initially been reported as missing in action. His actual fate became known some weeks later when three men from his company signed an affidavit concerning the facts of his death. From their statements he must have died at the start of the infantry attack as he was struck in the head by a bullet and died according to *Infanterie Rekruit* Johann Simon, *Infanterist* Johann Reuther and *Sanitäts Unteroffizier* Hans Vetter.

French troops advancing on the right flank of the 89th Brigade penetrated into the *Bayern Wald* about 8.30 a.m. The support companies for this portion of the front, the 9th,

Memorial card for *Landsturmmann* Hans Spielbauer, 8/6th Bavarian
RIR. Killed in action 1 July 1916. (Author's collection)

10th and 5/62, were thrown against them and a bloody forest battle quickly developed.
Hauptmann Bruck urgently sent messages to *Oberst* Leibrock requesting support. However,
without any telephone connections to the rear it would take a great deal of time before any
reserve troops could be assembled and sent to this critical sector. Before any action could be
taken by the 12th Division staff, Bruck was able to clear the enemy from the northwestern
part of *Bayern Wald* by mid afternoon. During the heavy fighting inside the wood he had
received critical support from the nearby 2/FAR 57 and the 3/62.

The concept of a solid defensive front, where one sector supported another, was a key
factor in the overall German defensive plan. While this concept provided for a strong
defense at the same time it could also turn into a weakness that both sides experienced in
the war. If the idea of mutual support was eliminated or if the flanks of a position became
exposed, then the threatened position became vulnerable to attack and could eventually be
destroyed.

The 11/6th Bavarian RIR occupied the trenches alongside the left wing of RIR 109 by
Mametz. Shortly after the attack began the positions occupied by RIR 109 were overrun.
When the British pushed deeper into the German lines in the sector formerly held by RIR
109 then the right flank of the 11th Coy became fully exposed and the position became
compromised. The supporting company, the 7/62 also became attacked on the right flank
in the same manner and later also from the rear as the trenches held by the men from RIR
109 fell one after the other in the British advance. The 7/62 was also being pressured on the
left flank as the British pushed deeper into the German trench system.

Survivors from the 7/62 were forced to withdraw under the constant pressure coming from three sides. The men made their way toward Montauban where they hoped to find some protection from the British advance. Any idea that the village of Montauban offered protection to the men was soon destroyed when advancing British troops entered the village about 11 a.m.

The men from the British 30th Division were able to quickly penetrate the position of the 8/6th Bavarian RIR in Sector K where it had been reported that many of the men had been placed out of action from the intense bombardment. Even though the Bavarians were caught off guard by the sudden attack the survivors quickly became organized and put up a fierce resistance against the approaching British troops. 179 men from the 8th Coy ended up as casualties by the end of the day. The vast majority of the men who were captured were also wounded. In total 79 soldiers from the 8/6th Bavarian RIR were taken prisoner while 83 were killed in action on 1 July. Only 17 wounded men made it safely to the German rear for treatment.

Even if a man was fortunate to have been taken to a medical dugout after being wounded, it was not a guarantee that he would be safe from further harm. It was not until 1919 when a returning prisoner of war, *Ersatz Reservist* Paulus Held was able to provide some details on the death of *Gefreiter* Georg Maurer, 7/6th Bavarian RIR.

> Maurer was wounded in the upper arm during the English attack and came into the medical dugout near where Held had been taken prisoner. While there an Englishman bombarded the dugout with a hand grenade. The hand grenade tore off Maurer's foot and as a result of this wound he bled to death.[5]

One of the defenders, *Reservist* Michael Theurlein, 8th Coy, provided an account of the heavy fighting on 1 July.

> I was very badly wounded during a struggle with hand grenades at the beginning of the attack when British troops advanced into our trenches. My right leg was smashed and my arms and head were bleeding from many wounds. I had the misfortune to stay like that for one and a half days without being dressed until I was found by an English Army Medical Officer. I was taken to the field ambulance by some men and still today I give the greatest praise and gratitude to the English people who attended me so well.
>
> I was taken to England on 9th July to a hospital near Dartford and stayed there for twelve months until I was able to walk with two sticks. The treatment in this hospital was also very good, especially a nurse [called] Williams who took care of me for six to eight months without any trouble to her. She dressed my wounds and those of my comrades every day without fatigue.
>
> When I recovered I was sent to Dorchester Camp for five months and then to another camp at Brockton for some weeks. From this place, I was exchanged as an unfit soldier to a wonderful Switzerland.[6]

Like Theurlein, *Infanterist* Josef Weingartner, 6/6th Bavarian RIR had been wounded and taken prisoner on 1 July. He was sent to a hospital in England where his wounds were treated. On 12 July 1916 he was taken to the Royal Victoria Hospital, Netley, Hants with a diagnosis of 'bullet wound in the chest, penetrating wound that opened out into the left pleura, blood and pus was removed, considered serious.'

Medical dugout inside the *Bayern Wald*. (*An der Somme*)

It was a serious wound, and like Theurlein, once Weingartner had recovered sufficiently he was exchanged as an unfit soldier. On 17 December 1916 he was recovering in Weggis, Switzerland, just across the lake from Theurlein, where he was interned for the duration of the war.

With many of the men from the 8th Coy placed out of action from the heavy artillery fire the British had been able to penetrate into the German trenches at several locations. Bombing fights occurred between the opposing sides as the British pushed deeper into the German lines.

Offizier Stellvertreter Joseph Busl, platoon leader of the 3rd Platoon of the 8th Company, provided a personal insight into the fighting on the morning of 1 July.

As of 5 o'clock in the morning heavy artillery fire and mine fire lay upon our position, again a dugout collapsed. About 6 o'clock we also believed that gas was discharged. However the gas masks were soon removed again. Shortly after 7 o'clock the infantry attack began. While the enemy came forward against our flanks somewhat, he was held back a very long time through our frontal fire. After I was wounded at about 8.30 o'clock, *Vizefeldwebel* Dratz took over the platoon and one the few extra remaining *Unteroffiziers*, Löb, took over the left half platoon. It was above all possible to still maintain lively fire until 10.15 in the morning.

At individual positions, where the bombardment had torn large gaps, the enemy was successful in penetrating. However our men soon fell on these Englishmen with hand-grenades and annihilated them after some time. Nevertheless the platoon was at the end of its power to resist because of the Englishman's superior strength. In the

Memorial card for *Landsturmmann* Josef Haslbeck, 1/6th Bavarian
RIR. Killed in action, 10 a.m., 1 July 1916. (Author's collection)

meanwhile, of the 6 *Unteroffiziers* and 56 men of the platoon approximately two-thirds were killed.

Throughout the attack there was no depressed mood among the men anywhere. Quite the opposite, they were visibly relieved when the Englishmen turned to the attack after the days of bombardment. The Other Ranks struck back marvelously, the joy of battle shone out of everyone's eyes. I, severely wounded by an infantry bullet in the head and in the shoulder, ended up in English captivity.

Our men did not surrender easily at all, as an English officer, Captain Horn, later wanted to make us believe, but at the focus of the battle, we bore the initial impact and heroically fought back, until even the infantrymen, like the artillerymen, had to yield to superior strength.[7]

The British continued to advance deeper into the German lines. They were only being held up as they waited for their own artillery barrage to lift off of the next line of defenses and move further to the rear. A small number of Germans located in *Schrapnell Wäldchen* [German Wood] quickly surrendered when approached and the advance continued toward the next main German trench line that contained the *Baligand Stützpunkt* [Glatz Redoubt] and the *Lochnerwerk* [Dublin Redoubt].

At the start of the attack the British had initially been forced to hesitate in front of the 7th and 6/6th Bavarian RIR. However men from the 21st Brigade succeeded in penetrating the German front line at individual saps and small sections of trench occupied by these two companies. After heavy fighting the men from the 7th and 6/6th Bavarian RIR in Sectors

H and J managed to expel most of the British troops who had penetrated their lines. The British were now firmly established close in front of the German trench and a lively firefight began with rifles and hand grenades.

The British were able to penetrate the German trenches in the neighboring sector once occupied by the 11/6th Bavarian RIR. Once inside the German trenches the British then attacked the exposed left flank of the 6th and 7th Coy and soon it appeared that the path leading toward Bernafay Wood was open to the enemy advance. Only a few weak companies from IR 62 stood in their way at this time.

While many of the German defenders had been killed or captured, *Oberleutnant der Reserve* Dauberschmidt was still determined to resist regardless of the situation facing his men. The overall situation was confused as small pockets of Bavarians, some still containing intact machine guns being manned by men from IR 62, put up strong resistance and caused many casualties among the attacking troops for as long as the ammunition supply lasted.

Dauberschmidt personally directed the fire of one machine gun into the flank and rear of the advancing British troops from the 18th Division. It is very likely that Dauberschmidt and his men were also the cause of so many losses in the 18th King's as the machine gun was turned and now fired into the advancing masses from the 89th Brigade, 30th Division from a location described as a small railway hollow, an area known to the British as 'The Warren'. While Dauberschmidt and his men were causing many losses to the 18th King's, other battalions continued to press forward and were slowly making their way toward *König Ludwig Höhe*.

Dauberschmidt continued to defend what was left of his company sector for as long as possible. It has been reported that he knew there were still many artillery pieces in the hollow between Montauban and the 2nd position, the *Artillerie Schlucht*. He also suspected that there were valuable supplies of ammunition, food and water in the quarry 1 kilometer north of Montauban. Even knowing that fresh supplies could be nearby he did not go back into this 2nd position like many of the troops around him. Dauberschmidt was inevitably forced further toward the German rear by the constant British pressure and the shortage of ammunition. He moved his small force back through Montauban and took up positions inside the quarry, where he hoped that his men could halt the English advance.

At the quarry Dauberschmidt linked up with men from the 2/62. The men quickly prepared the quarry for defense and awaited the enemy advance. Every man was needed to defend the position including *Assistenzarzt* Dr. Piazza, who had been attending the slightly wounded men that had been collected at a dressing station located there.

Dauberschmidt and his men were able to repulse two British attacks later in the day with support from a battery located by Bazentin le Grand. While the British were able to penetrate deeper into the German lines near Mametz through the *Staubwasser Graben*, just north of Montauban, they could not make any headway toward the quarry. In recognition for his actions on 1 July Dauberschmidt was awarded the military Max Joseph medal.

The actions of several other men from the 6th Bavarian RIR were recognized with the awarding of medals for bravery following the heavy fighting. *Vizefeldwebel der Reserve* Matthias Schraufstetter of the 7th Company was among them. Shortly after the commencement of the attack at 7.30 a.m. two Group leaders sent back messages that most of their men were already dead and the English had penetrated into the neighboring sector.

Schraufstetter apparently rallied his men with the words: 'Men, remain with me. As long as we still have hand-grenades, we cannot give ourselves up for lost'. Shortly afterward

German soldier inside trench by Montauban. (Lawrence Brown)

Schraufstetter and a few men attacked a distant crater position that was being used as an enemy sentry position. The attack was successful and the British were thrown back from the crater.

Once in the captured position Schraufstetter and his men remained and defended the crater until their last cartridge had been fired and their last hand grenade had been thrown. Only when this occurred did the survivors withdraw and moved toward the rear. Schraufstetter was later awarded the Gold Medal for Bravery.

Vizefeldwebel der Landwehr Hermann Heimann, 7th Coy was to receive the Silver Medal for Bravery. He had remained with his platoon during the defense despite being wounded in the knee and ear. He defended the trench while his men fired at the British. At the same time Schraufstetter was involved in the capture and defense of the crater, Heimann also proceeded to advance with a few men still remaining with him. He spurred on his small group through his example and caused the British heavy losses by the use of hand grenades. When the fighting died down briefly he was convinced to go back to the dressing station to have his wounds dressed. He had been struck by three bullets during the fighting.

Gefreiter der Landwehr Thomas Pühler, 7th Coy also acquired the Silver Medal for Bravery for his actions on 1 July. His commendation stated that that he defended the trench section assigned to him with great bravery and inflicted the heaviest losses to the enemy advancing in masses. Once the ammunition was all fired off, he hurried from shell hole to shell hole in the heaviest fire, from one destroyed piece of trench to another, in order to obtain ammunition. He contributed to the stabilization and extension of the resistance against an extremely powerful opponent and by his boldness and fearlessness gave all men a brilliant example that spurred them to the highest achievements.

Vizefeldwebel der Reserve Paul Blank of the 6th Company also received the Silver

Medal for Bravery. He held his small sector by Montauban for two hours against the attacks by superior English forces that had already broken into the position beside him. Not until after firing off the last of the ammunition and when he with the 16 men remaining with him were almost entirely surrounded, did he withdraw to the 2nd trench. Here he afforded renewed opposition, after he remedied the jam of a machine gun and now directed its fire against the advancing Englishmen proceeding in dense masses. Once his position had been passed by the advancing British troops he then moved under enemy artillery and machine gun fire through the open terrain back to the 3rd trench and offered opposition there, so long as the ammunition held out.

As the British moved deeper into the German lines the speed of the advance caught many of the defenders in the 2nd and 3rd trench line unaware and suddenly the German troops found themselves embroiled in close combat. The staff of the II/62 commanded by *Hauptmann* Baucke was overrun in this manner. The battalion staff did put up some stiff resistance but soon the overwhelming number of British soldiers took the upper hand. Baucke and several other members of the staff had been killed while the remainder were captured, including his adjutant *Leutnant der Reserve* Strauss. Strauss ended up as a prisoner of war with a slight grazing wound to his head.

The British advance also quickly overran the battalion headquarters of *Hauptmann* Horn, II/6th Bavarian RIR. The battalion staff resisted the British advance as best they could, but without any additional support and quickly running short of ammunition, Horn and his companions were forced to surrender. The entire staff of the II Battalion ended up as prisoners of war or had been killed including *Leutnant der Landwehr* Stenz, *Assistenzarzt* Dr. Kirschbaum, the AVO *Leutnant* Schönbrunn, 3/FAR 57 among others. Important maps and documents also fell into British hands that could provide valuable intelligence in the future.

Information regarding the advance of the British deep into the German lines first became known in the support lines when a wounded Bavarian soldier arrived. He had worked his way back to the position held by the 1/62 by *König Ludwig Höhe* at about 8 a.m. The company commander, *Leutnant der Reserve* Siegmund had little time to evaluate the situation as shortly afterward the first British troops started to appear nearby.

The men from the 1/62 opened fire at the advancing enemy columns but they soon realized they did not have enough men to hold their position. Within a short time after the fighting had started the men from the 1/62 started to withdraw toward Montauban. Their predicament had been observed by one of the few intact reserves still located by Montauban, the Infantry *Pionier* platoon from the 1/62 and the platoon from the 1/23 under *Vizefeldwebel* Vollgrabe.

This *ad hoc* unit advanced out of the quarry and made their way toward a small hill southwest of Montauban where the men opened fire upon the advancing British troops. While this small force was effective at slowing down the enemy advance there were too few men to completely stop the British. *Vizefeldwebel* Vollgrabe ordered a withdrawal and the men started to work their way back toward the part of the *Staubwasser Graben* that was located just north of Montauban.

Much of the fighting had broken down into small detachments of German defenders that still held out inside their lines. Often they had one or more machine guns from IR 62 that were still operable. The advancing units from the British 89th and 21st Brigades came up upon these areas of resistance and the advance slowed. Eventually the machine guns

German soldier inside Montauban. (Lawrence Brown)

were either destroyed or forced to withdraw and the accompanying German infantry were finally driven out of their trenches and shell crater positions.

German artillery fire throughout this time continued to be very light. Almost all of the artillery observation officers had been killed, captured or forced to withdraw. The guns further to the rear that were still serviceable still had no target coordinates. They simply did not know where the opposing lines stood and many of the guns were sending shells at coordinates where the fighting had long passed by.

If everything had gone according to expectations it would have been reasonable to expect that *Oberst* Leibrock would have some idea of the events taking place along the front line. Telephone reports, runners and light signal messages should have been constantly arriving at his headquarters dugout located at the *Ziegelei* [*Briqueterie*]. However, with the destruction of most telephone lines Leibrock only had direct contact with *Hauptmann* Bruck who was located nearby in the *Bayern Wald*.

> The Sectors l and m dugouts of *Hauptmann* Bruck with the command post in the *Bayern Wald*, still conversed with me through the telephone connection. At approximately 8 o'clock he reported that the French had penetrated into this wood and that there was no clear picture of the course of fighting here. Later this message became corrected that it was not the French, but Englishmen who had attacked and that swift support was urgently required. The left flank was strongly threatened and curved back.
>
> About 10 o'clock *Hauptmann* Horn reported that the enemy had penetrated into the *Bayern Wald* and likewise into the western part of Montauban.

Since I had no telephone connection with sectors g and K and also received no messages, I believed that Battalion Bruck was dealing with a small raid. I sent the message to the 12th ID with the further appeal about the Division reserve being sent there. The back and forth of the runners between the dugout and the investigation place took a great deal of time because of the enemy artillery fire, also low flying pilots fired on our men, and when I received the consent of the division, my orders were given in the same manner via the switch center to the division reserve in Guillemont. I charged their leaders to immediately send 4 companies to the *Bayern Wald* where they would become subordinate to *Hauptmann* Bruck. Meanwhile enemy planes flew very low (approximately 100 meters and lower) over the dugout, so that I took all of the men out of the *Quergraben* behind the dugout that was only sparsely covered over with branches, because the men could be seen and it was not of any use.

Approximately 10 o'clock a single Englishman was reported behind the dugout, who first of all did not want to surrender, but claimed that the men in the dugout were his prisoners. However he was soon taken prisoner and brought into the dugout. The artillery fire had significantly lessened about this time and mainly lay on the wood. The Englishman stated that the English attack had thrown back the Germans and that the Regiment 109 on the right of R6 had surrendered with hands held high. The Englishmen were long ago behind our dugout. Because of the unfavorable effect on our Other Ranks I professed this to be impossible. The fact however that this Englishman was mistakenly alone behind the dugout and the fact that a connection with the right Battalion Sector could not be established and finally the message from *Hauptmann* Bruck led me to suspect something bad.

Meanwhile *Hauptmann* Bruck reported that the situation in the Bavarian wood seemingly had improved and he hoped that the wood could be held, if support arrived soon. Simultaneously he applied for the relief of his battalion, it was at the end of its effectiveness.

These messages allowed me hope that the attack on the right had probably come to a halt and a German counter attack was to be expected, although the German artillery fire was almost completely silent. From the noise of the shells flying away over the dugout one could infer that they came from the enemy side.[8]

While *Oberst* Leibrock struggled with the lack of firsthand news regarding the events taking place by Montauban, Hardecourt and Curlu the British continued to advance toward Montauban. The British 90th Brigade had been held in reserve during the initial attack and now it was time for the men to advance and capture their objectives. The 90th Brigade advanced across the newly captured terrain under sporadic artillery fire. There were very few shells falling around the men and in many cases the soft ground minimized the effect of the explosion.

During the advance the columns suddenly came under heavy and accurate machine gun fire from 'The Warren', very possibly the machine gun being directed by *Oberleutnant der Reserve* Dauberschmidt, 6/6th Bavarian RIR. The machine gun fire slowed the advance briefly; the real obstacle facing the 90th Brigade was the British barrage fire.

The men of the 90th Brigade were forced to stop their advance briefly in order to allow the barrage fire to lift from its current target and move further to the rear. Once this was accomplished the annoying German machine gun was located and destroyed by a Lewis

Gun team from the 16th Manchesters. According to the Manchesters the enemy machine gun was operated by a 'gallant crew' that had stood by their gun to the very end.

The advance was stopped one further time when it was found that the 55th Brigade on their left flank had not been able to keep up with the advance. Despite having an open left flank the decision was made to continue the advance toward Montauban. Their right flank was covered by an effective smoke screen and in a short time the men reached the village while encountering very little opposition.

One German trench located just outside of the village was in relatively good condition with an excellent field of fire. The only problem was that it was not being defended by any German troops. By 10.50 a.m. the village was occupied and ten minutes later the portion of the *Staubwasser Graben* just north of the village was also occupied. The 30th Division had taken all of the objectives assigned to it for 1 July.

There were obvious signs that the defenders of Montauban had suffered a great deal during the preliminary bombardment. Approximately 100 Germans found inside the village surrendered without putting up much of a fight. A great deal of intelligence material was found in many of the dugouts. Regimental orders, maps of the position and other valuable documents were recovered. At least one dugout was filled with the bodies of Germans killed the week before that could not be buried.

The British inside Montauban could see hundreds of German soldiers running toward the rear on the other side of the *Artillerie Schlucht*. Forward artillery observers were able to relay this information to the British batteries in the rear and the fleeing men came under accurate fire.

With the loss of Montauban and the collapse of the German defenses it was possible for the men of the 30th Division to capture a number of field guns located near the village. While it appeared there was an opportunity to continue the advance deeper into German lines, the men of the 30th Division were compelled to hold their positions. No orders had been given for a further advance into the German position and there were the issues of consolidating the captured village, replacing ammunition, evacuating the wounded and restoring order to the different battalions that had become mixed together in the victorious assault.

There was also another reason. Not every German soldier was fleeing toward the rear and safety. The garrison of the quarry, the 2/62, was still intact and had been joined by men from several different units. The quarry was now being defended by the men of the 2/62 under *Oberleutnant der Reserve* Troch, *Pionier* platoon from the I/62, Platoon Vollgrabe from the 1/23, another platoon from the 1/23 under *Leutnant der Reserve* Chrzaszcz as well as the remnants of the 1st and 7/62, 6/6th Bavarian RIR and a few men from *Minenwerfer* Coy 12. Until the situation inside Montauban could be straightened out, combined with the sporadic fire coming from the quarry any idea of a further advance was out of the question.

There was one last thing that the men of the 30th Division could accomplish, the capture of the first German artillery pieces taken in the battle. Several battery positions were located near Montauban and without any infantry support the guns were completely vulnerable. The closest guns belonged to the 4/FAR 21 and 4/RFAR 29. By this time on 1 July most of the infantry that had been protecting the gun positions had fled their positions and were now behind the batteries, moving toward the rear as quickly as possible.

Under these circumstances the commander of FAR 21, *Oberst* Pietsch, gave the order to abandon the guns. There was no opportunity to bring up the limbers and battery horses in the British fire and there was no possibility of removing the guns by hand using the crews. The men obeyed the order but were very disturbed at the thought of leaving their guns to fall into enemy hands. While the gunners moved toward the rear they came under machine gun fire coming from Montauban. They were also subjected to strafing fire from British aircraft that dove down to within 150 feet of the ground and fired into the mass of retreating men.

Oberst Leibrock and his staff were apparently unaware of the events that were taking place nearby. While he had some telephone communication to *Bayern Wald* he was cut off from the other two parts of the Montauban Sector. In an attempt to remedy some of these issues Leibrock sent a *Radfahrer* to the telephone exchange in Bernafay Wood with four messages at 11.20 p.m.

1. A renewed request for support for *Bayern Wald* and Montauban.
2. Request for a fighter pilot, because an enemy pilot continuously circled 40 meters above the Regimental battle headquarters and fired at every individual man with his machine gun.
3. Request for artillery fire for *Kaisergraben* and *Bayern Wald*.
4. To establish connections within the regiment again.

The runner, who had managed to reach Bernafay Wood with the messages, had wanted to return to the regimental battle headquarters after delivering them. He had managed to travel about 100 meters south of Bernafay Wood when he came under infantry fire from the direction of the Regimental dugout. He quickly determined that in the time since he had left with the four messages the dugout had been surrounded by British troops. He returned to the telephone exchange and sent a message to the rear about the situation. 'According to declarations of a runner the Regimental command post of R6 is surrounded Englishmen.'

One of the runners, *Radfahrer* Hopf provided an account of the situation facing the regimental commander and his staff on 1 July.

In the process of conveying my reports I escaped capture on 1 July 1916 together with Regimental *Radfahrer* Kussinger and a runner from Infantry Regiment 62. We three had been sent from the regimental dugout to the telephone exchange in Bernafay Wood. Because of the artillery fire it was already difficult to come out of the dugout and the return on the road to the wood had to be made at the run.

The urgent message from *Oberst* Leibrock was passed along over the telephone exchange office in Bernafay Wood. It was only partially understood, still it was sent further to the Prussian 12th ID. Shortly before we left the regimental dugout an individual English prisoner was brought into it. When we wanted to return to the Regimental Battle Headquarters after the completion of our duty we received enemy infantry and machine gun fire from this direction. Thereupon we went back to the telephone exchange office and sent a message to the 12th ID. The parts of the different troops sent forward as support were not to move out to attack from the southern edge of Bernafay Wood against command post Leibrock. When I asked an officer to rescue the regimental commander through an attack I received the answer: 'There is nothing more to do, your regimental staff is lost, you can go.'

Now we went back to the Recruit Depot of the 12th ID that should have undertaken a counter attack that, however, did not occur. We then went back to our regimental baggage column and delivered the one message of the disintegration of RIR 6 and the capture of its staff.

The last runner sent to the telephone switching station came back after a long time, stating they could only be wounded, cut-off or made prisoner.[9]

There appeared to be little that could be done to assist *Oberst* Leibrock and the men who remained at the headquarters dugout with him. Leibrock provided a detailed account of the last hours of his staff.

Our observer now reported that our men in front of the *Bayern Wald* were standing, firing out of the 2nd trench and shortly after that the Englishmen were behind the dugout. I now went out, to explore the area. However, I had hardly raised my head above the observation area, when I received infantry and machine gun fire from the rear. Therefore I could not make an accurate determination; however I had seen enough to know that our men were not standing firing out of the 2nd trench, but that they were Englishmen who were entrenching there. Similarly I could perceive an English skirmish line of about 60-70 men behind the dugout in shell holes. The leader of the machine gun, an *Unteroffizier* from IR 62, had already attempted to bring the machine gun into position several times. He, like his replacement, a *Gefreiter*, had been wounded. Since only the stairway of the dugout in the *Quergraben* that was covered over and disguised with planks could be used to exit, it was easy for the Englishmen to prevent every attempt through superior fire. Meanwhile the enemy had worked closer, and was quite near to the dugout so that they could also throw hand-grenades into the *Quergraben*. Officers with revolvers and Other Ranks with rifles stood at the opposite end of the stairway ready for the defense. However the Englishmen succeeded in gobbling up several dugouts. I now burned maps and orders once again.

The losses had increased to 2 dead and 7 wounded; also the captive Englishman was severely wounded by a hand-grenade. The dead and wounded as well as the men occupied with bandaging the men occupied so much room that traffic within the dugout became almost impossible. The Englishmen continuously threw hand-grenades in the stairway entrance; the men looked to avoid these and crowded to the rear. Any overview was lacking and also every attempt to use the rifles in a unified manner was useless. Also the men of IR 62 only reluctantly followed the orders being given. They were apparently in a state of greater physical and mental exhaustion. In addition however the unaccustomed commanders were probably responsible in that they allowed good will to be lacking and that being new and unaccustomed to this doubtful situation, they had let discipline relax.

I called *Hauptmann* Bruck on the telephone again, reporting to him that we had been cut off by English infantry who were attacking with hand-grenades and requested that he send a company to eject the Englishmen. He stated that he was unable to comply because all of his men were employed and that reserves still had not arrived. An extraction of Other Ranks was impossible.

An English breakthrough, such as the one described by the captive Englishman, appeared to me ever more likely. Under these circumstances I considered further sacrifice to be pointless and I also could not expect a counter attack in view of the total silence of the German artillery, therefore I decided after still further discussion with remarks to the officers to surrender.[10]

The situation facing *Oberst* Leibrock and his staff was dire. Any organized resistance along the northern sector of the 12th Division had collapsed. Only small pockets of men still put up any resistance and those who could were making toward the rear as fast as possible. It was difficult to determine where friendly and enemy troops were located and parties from both sides often ran into one another unexpectedly.

Only a small number of men from the six companies of the 6th Bavarian RIR that had been holding the front line had managed to escape death or capture. Many of the support troops from IR 62 were also either dead, captured or forced to retreat further to the rear. The battalion command posts and the battalion staff members from all three sectors had been killed or captured. *Hauptmann* Horn, II/6th Bavarian RIR had tried to escape along with several other members of his staff. They all ended up as prisoners.

There was little time left for the officers and men inside the regimental command post at the brick works. After all of the intense fighting and stress placed upon the men fighting on 1 July the final moments for the regimental staff were almost anti-climatic.

About half an hour after the English prisoner had been brought in the Englishmen surrounded the regimental dugout. The garrison defended it with infantry rifles and hand-grenades. The machine gun from IR 62 broke down. After 6 men were already dead or wounded and the defense proved to be pointless, the English prisoner was employed to start surrender negotiations. Under the influence of an English Medical Officer the surrender proceeded without any further losses. The garrison exited the dugout individually with hands held high. *Radfahrer* Ziehrer[11]

The final push to capture the regimental command post was undertaken by men from the 30th Division. Troops moved into positions close in front of the brickworks while others occupied any avenue of escape. In the afternoon the buildings were rushed, at first there were only dead Germans and no resistance. It was not until the men reached the far side of the structures that they came under fire. A machine gun had been quickly set up near the headquarters dugout and opened fire, but only for a short time before it was silenced.

The final haul of prisoners included numerous officers, two machine guns, documents and other material. *Oberst* Leibrock and his staff were assembled and sent back to the rear under escort:

The English platoon leader, I considered him to be at least that, had only a little influence upon his men. They were very bitter, seemed ready for excesses and wanted one small thing, to shoot a German officer after the surrender. An English doctor that was with the detachment apparently had more influence than the officer, and prevented this and further excesses. Outside the dugout one noticed no battle noise in the immediate proximity. Only Bernafay Wood was bombarded now and then by enemy artillery. The English lines must be further behind us. In front of us the Englishmen were in groups and worked on their new trench and wire obstacles. English and French artillery still fired in a lively manner from more considerable distance. German artillery still fired upon two positions west of Maricourt, however neither troops, nor batteries, or anything else could be observed there. The shots fell too short if they were on the old English position, and many too wide if they were to fall on the new English positions. They always fell on the same spot. On the entire road to Maricourt, whither we were led, I saw only a single dead German. Therefore they were already long buried and the wounded had been taken away, and our front line had been taken much earlier, as we suspected.

The German prisoners were assembled in Maricourt. Field glasses, electric torches, knives, notebook etc. were removed. During this period the English officer who spoke very good German (he had studied philosophy in Berlin) was surprised that the English offensive had succeeded so well, although it could have been presumed otherwise based on the evidence before them. He said that parts of the regiment had offered almost no opposition.

We were now conducted via Bronfay farm, where the journey of the ambulance concluded, and where a wounded collecting point had been established, then to Bray sur Somme. We could see English and French batteries on all of the roads. A string of field batteries had their caissons close behind the guns. The heavy batteries (long-barreled guns, howitzers, mortars and heavy naval guns) were nearby along the road and arranged consecutively, most only slightly covered over. Many French Artillerymen stood around in shirtsleeves, cooking, chatting, and ran up us to in order to scorn us. The entire bowl of the valley gave the impression of a festival. However further firing continued in the background. I was amazed about it that not a single German shell smashed into this throng.

The French ridiculed us everywhere, several times tearing the caps off the heads of our officers in order to retain them as 'souvenirs'. However they were regularly forced to return them by the accompanying English Other Ranks. The Englishmen behaved worthily and properly without exception.

With satisfaction we saw, from the non-stop traffic of the medical ambulances, that not all our regiment had surrendered without opposition, as this English officer had wanted us to believe.[12]

Along other parts of the front by Montauban there were still active pockets of German resistance that needed to be eliminated. Each of these was taken under attack. In many cases active resistance was broken once the avenues of retreat had either been cut or seriously threatened. German holdouts in the 'Loop' and in the 'Warren' had been a serious obstacle to the British troops advancing toward Mametz as well as toward Montauban. Once these positions became outflanked and threatened with capture many of the defenders began to slip back toward the rear while there was still time to do so.

In some instances the Germans put up a strong defense until it became evident that their position was untenable. In these cases the survivors often stopped resisting and surrendered. One such group of Bavarians and a few Silesians from IR 62 near the *Endress Graben* south of Montauban surrendered as a group. Two officers and 150 Other Ranks gave up and were marched back into captivity.

When advancing British troops encountered strong German resistance, every attempt was made to neutralize it. The British found that by using machine guns and close support from Stokes Mortars that the Germans would quickly surrender or withdraw.

The overwhelming firepower directed against them was simply too much for most of the German defenders.

During the fighting on the afternoon of 1 July the commander of the 12th Division considered the possibility of a counter attack that would hopefully restore the original German position. The idea was quickly dismissed when it was realized that there were insufficient reserves at hand to participate in such an attack. Besides the few companies still left in the second position the only other troops available were several untrained companies from the Recruit Depot.

It was then decided that it would be better to hold onto the positions currently held and all resources were utilized to achieve this goal. As part of this plan the 3/62 was ordered to proceed to the *Bayern Wald* and support the troops still fighting there. Later in the afternoon the 8/62 with parts of the 2/*Pionier* Bn 6 were sent to occupy the southern and western edge of Bernafay Wood. The 4/62 joined the defenders in the wood a short time later. Until this time Bernafay Wood had been unoccupied and open to any British advance. Two of the Recruit Companies were assigned to occupy Trônes Wood while an additional company, the 6/62, was sent to the *Bayern Wald* to bolster the defenses.

The few artillery pieces that were still capable of firing continued to send shell after shell into the old British lines or against targets that could be identified, mainly by direct observation. By the early afternoon there were still three guns from the 2/FAR 57 that were able to fire. One gun under the command of *Fähnrich* Glatzel was approximately 100 meters from the edge of Montauban and as British troops entered the village Glatzel directed his fire into the nearby target. Being so close to the enemy the gun quickly came under small arms fire, Glatzel was soon killed while he stood near his gun.

AVO *Leutnant* Schaeffer now took command of the gun. Schaeffer had been driven out of his observation post during the British advance and had managed to make his way to the battery position. Within a short time of taking over the gun he was severely wounded after being struck in the head by infantry fire. *Unteroffizier* Selka was now in charge as he

Infantrymen – IR 62. (Author's collection)

was the senior NCO present with the gun. He continued to fire into the village until all of the ammunition had been fired. There was no more ammunition at hand and no hope of obtaining more from the rear. Selka then disabled the gun and he and his men withdrew to the rear, carrying *Leutnant* Schaeffer with them.

Two other guns from the 2/FAR 57 were located at the western edge of the *Artillerie Schlucht*. The gun positions were covered in smoke and dust as the gunners loaded and fired as rapidly as possible while under heavy British counter battery fire. By late morning both guns became unserviceable and the crews were forced to abandon them. Losses had been heavy among both gun crews from the constant rain of shrapnel and shell splinters.

The battery commander, *Oberleutnant der Reserve* Oelze ordered the breechblocks removed from each gun and buried nearby. Once this was accomplished Oelze and his men withdrew to the rear under intense British machine gun fire. Once safely in the rear two of the men, *Gefreiters* Hoffmann and Michalke located several stretcher-bearers and sent them back to the battery position in order to save the severely wounded men they had been forced to leave behind.

The guns of the 3/FAR 57 also stood in the *Artillerie Schlucht* and they fired at the approaching British troops as fast as the guns could be loaded. The range the guns were firing at continued to grow shorter as the morning passed. Soon the guns were firing at trenches that were only a few hundred meters away, trenches that should have been occupied by German troops. Telephone lines and forward artillery observers were no longer required. The approaching British troops could clearly be seen by each gun crew.

In the course of the morning two of the three guns in the battery received direct hits from British artillery fire and were destroyed. The last gun was pulled out of the emplacement by the crew so that the gun could be directed at targets in Montauban. The gun fired at British infantry and two machine guns at the northern edge of the village and helped to prevent any further advance by the enemy.

The gun continued to fire until the ammunition supply had been exhausted. The battery commander, *Hauptmann* Richter had the men disable the gun by removing the breechblock. He then led his men to a nearby battery that was still able to fire and his men filled in for the members of the gun crews that had been killed or wounded.

Richter remained with the infantry in their positions and continued to observe the British lines and his gun positions. He still had hopes that his guns could be salvaged after darkness fell. It soon became evident that this would be impossible when British infantry could be seen occupying the battery positions.

The 4(F)/FAR 21 under *Oberleutnant der Reserve* Pietsch, and the 4(F)/FAR 39 under *Hauptmann* Wolff were located south and west of the quarry located just north of Montauban. Both batteries fired throughout the fighting in the morning and it soon became evident that the British infantry would reach the batteries if they were not stopped.

Just after 10 a.m. Pietsch observed British troops approaching to within 300-400 meters of his howitzers. Both batteries were under especially heavy fire as they had been discovered by British observation aircraft that circled overhead while directing counter-battery fire on the positions as well as strafing the gun positions from a very low altitude.

Soon one howitzer became buried by enemy fire while the remaining guns became damaged in the heavy shelling. Ammunition supplies ran out and there was no hope of obtaining any more from the rear. It was considered impossible to drive ammunition wagons into the position without suffering heavy losses. Runners were sent to the headquarters dugout of the I/FAR 57 but were unable to reach their goal in the enemy fire.

All communication with the neighboring batteries had been destroyed and there was little that Pietsch and his men could do at this point in the fighting. As a result Pietsch and his men withdrew to the rear under a hail of shells, machine gun and rifle fire. The men in the battery did make an attempt to recover their howitzers on the evening of 2 July and were successful in recovering several of them.

The 6/FAR 57 under *Hauptmann* Uebe was positioned inside Bernafay Wood. The battery had been directing fire against *König Ludwig Höhe* when they received word from *Unteroffizier* Lorenz, one of the few surviving artillery observation officers that British troops had taken the position. They were joined by heavy field howitzers from the 2/*Fuss Artillerie* Regiment 44 that had only recently arrived in position at the eastern edge of Bernafay Wood.

Almost immediately the batteries were spotted by a British aircraft circling over the wood. Within moments 28cm shells came down on their positions. The very first shell destroyed a gun in the 6th Battery. Within an hour two more guns from Battery Uebe had been destroyed by direct hits.

Virtually all communication with the front had been cut and the battery had no information on where the enemy targets were located. All the remaining guns could do was to send shells at targets that they had obtained hours earlier or at targets clearly visible to the gun crews. For all they knew the guns were shelling empty trenches or open ground. Without an observer the effect of the guns would be negligible.

It was finally decided to send a patrol toward Montauban to see if it could be determined where the opposing lines stood. *Leutnant der Reserve* Fritz Hanke and *Unteroffizier* Staroste advanced through the wood until they reached the southern edge. It was approximately 1 p.m. and the two men quickly determined that no German troops stood between the guns and the approaching British troops.

The two observers were spotted by British soldiers and soon came under fire from machine guns located in Montauban as well as from enemy aircraft flying overhead. The men returned to the battery to report their findings that allowed the last serviceable gun to fire at targets that would provide some support to the hard-pressed German infantry. *Fahnenjunker* Müller and *Richtkanonier Gefreiter* Sobotka operated the last gun in the battery still capable of firing until it too gun broke down from heavy use. It did not matter at this time as the remainder of the battery ammunition supply had been destroyed in the British fire. *Hauptmann* Uebe then ordered his men to the rear after disabling the guns and taking the breech blocks back with them. All of the wounded men were also carried back under the watchful eye of *Sanitäts Offizier* Peritz.

The 5(F)/FAR 21 under *Oberleutnant der Reserve* Peppel was positioned inside Trônes Wood and like the rest of the batteries in the 12th Division, they came under heavy British fire that was being controlled by circling observation aircraft. The battery did not have to rely upon observers to locate their targets. Once the morning fog and mist had lifted the lines of advancing British troops could clearly be seen from the battery position.

Leutnant Schölzel quickly directed the fire from his guns at the approaching enemy skirmish line. The battery attempted to remain in contact with the telephone exchange located at the southern edge of Trônes Wood and the line needed to be repaired over and over as British shells cut it in numerous places. One by one the howitzers became unserviceable until finally only one was still operable. The defensive fire from this battery was credited with holding the enemy back and preventing any further advances beyond Montauban. Soon the last gun also fell silent.

Now the battery was vulnerable to being captured as no German infantry were located nearby to offer assistance. *Leutnant* Schölzel remained in his observation post located high in the trees and watched the British infantry moving closer each hour. The enemy finally reached the edge of Trônes Wood by the evening but before the guns could become captured horse teams and limbers were driven up and the guns were withdrawn.

Additional guns were saved after darkness fell when four 9cm cannons from *Fuss Artillerie Batterie* 565B were withdrawn from their position inside the sunken road northeast of Montauban. The front by Montauban, Hardecourt and Curlu now had virtually no artillery support against any further enemy advances that might take place in the following days.

Part 2: Hardecourt – Curlu

On 30 June front line troops from IR 63 were relieved by 6th Bavarian RIR. The sector southwest of *Bayern Wald* to the area south of the Clery-Maricourt road was now occupied by two platoons each from the 12th, 10th and 3/6th Bavarian RIR. The remaining three platoons from these companies were held in reserve at the *Rotes Haus* located at the eastern edge of *Leiber Wald*, along the Hardecourt-Curlu road.

The command structure in the Hardecourt-Curlu sector was very similar to that employed in the northern part of the division front. The right wing battalion sector was under the command of Major Bezzel, I/6th Bavarian RIR. His battle headquarters was located at the eastern edge of *Leiber Wald,* not far from the *Rotes Haus*.

The southern part of the sector from *Neutrales Wald* up to the river was being held by the 1st and 2/3 of the 2/6th Bavarian RIR. Curlu was defended by 1/3 of the 2nd and the 4/6th Bavarian RIR. This sector was under the command of *Hauptmann* Heck, commander of the II/63, whose headquarters dugout was located in Curlu.

The Intermediate position southeast of Hardecourt – *Rotes Haus* – *Rote Farm* – Hem Farm was occupied by weak forces of the 9th, 12th, 1st, 2nd, 3rd and 4/63 with Bavarian Marksman Detachments 41 and 88, both attached to the 6th Bavarian RIR. *Hauptmann* Kupfer, I/63 was in command over the Intermediate position with his headquarters located at Hem Farm. The 7th and 1/3 of the 6/63 were in the intermediate position Maurepas – Hem.

The 10th, 5th, 8th and 11/63 and the Machine Gun Coy/6th Bavarian RIR were under the orders of Major Bender, III/63. These units were located in the II Position Maurepas – Clery and in Maurepas as Division Reserve South. The commander of IR 63, Major von Weller, was the overall Sector commander with his Battle Headquarters located in Maurepas. Major Bezzel provided an account of the events leading up to 1 July.

> Orders arrived from the 12th Prussian ID between 5 and 6 o'clock on 29 June that the regiment was to be used for the relief of IR 63. The division had received orders from the corps for this relief, as the tactical situation allowed. The division seemed to be of the same opinion. Thereupon I gave orders to replace the left wing of IR 63 at Curlu with the 3rd Company of the battalion, to send out the 1st Company to Maurepas, to send back the 7th Company to their battalion at Guillemont and that I would go to

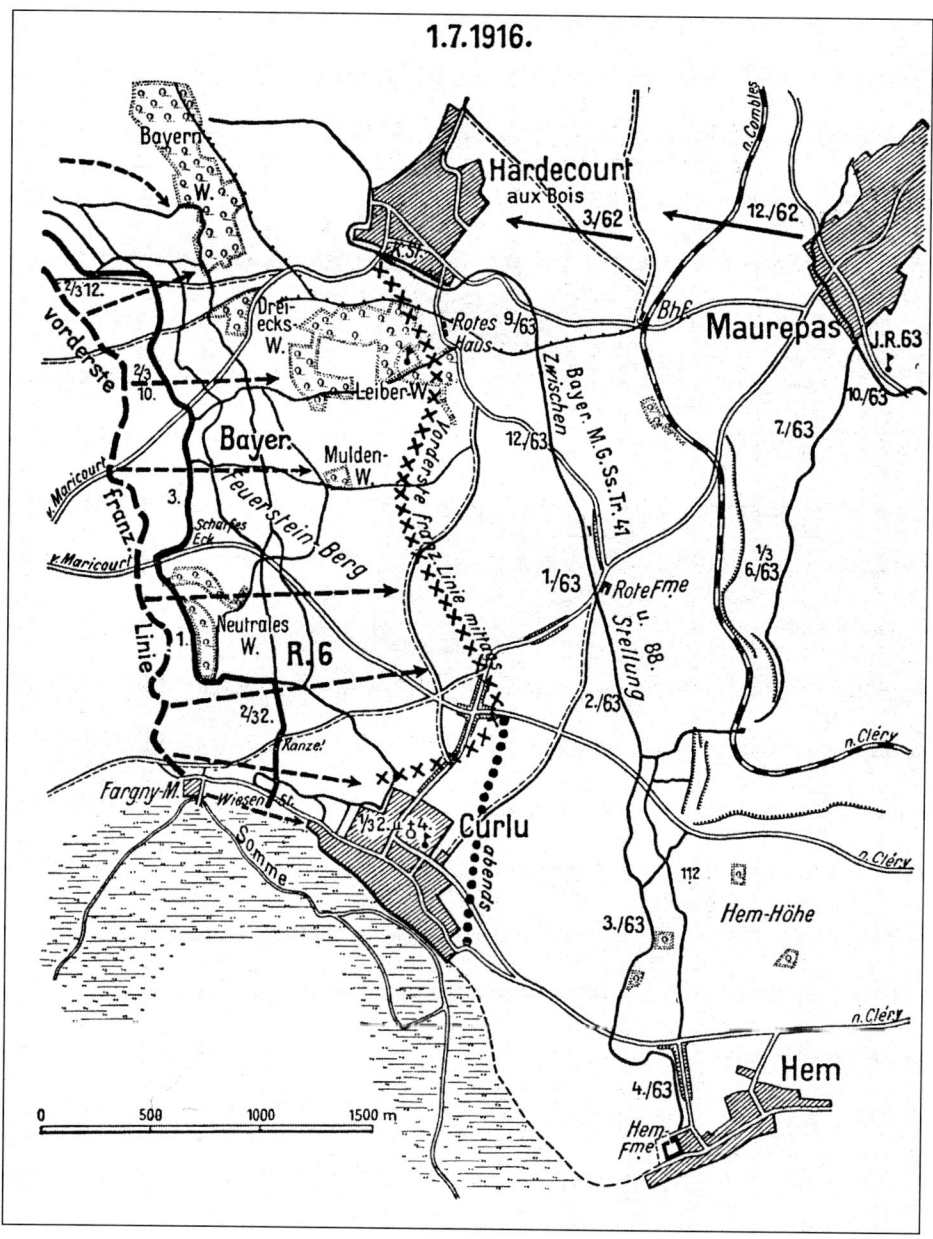

Hardecourt-Curlu.

the command post of IR 63 southeast of Maurepas for the receipt of further orders. The Machine Gun Company remained in Clery.

After the distribution of my orders that placed the 2nd and 4th Companies marching on the route into the meadow ground of the Somme to the 1st Company while avoiding the Clery-Hem road, I hurried before the 3rd Company with my staff through the 2nd Position to Maurepas. At the moment they left this trench at the southeastern exit of this village strong artillery fire was employed. The enemy had probably observed the movement, which took place partly outside the trench, with numerous observation balloons and pilots.

I arrived at the regimental command post with the brigade commander General von der Hende of the 24th Infantry Brigade and the commander of Regiment 63 Major von Weller. I received instructions to relieve his III Battalion forward of the *Rotes Haus* with the 12th, 10th and 3rd Companies, while the remaining companies of my battalion remained subordinate to a *Hauptmann* of his regiment at Curlu. I was already concerned that the largest part of my battalion was snatched away so disagreeably, and particularly regarding the entirely inadequate reports about the situation, condition of the position and the situation of the relieved III/IR63 (Battalion Bender). It turned out that this battalion had suffered greatly under the bombardment and hardly any dugouts still existed. Furthermore I had greater length of service and I was patently older than Major von Weller. Only the threatening situation and the consideration of the companies entrusted to me caused me nevertheless to remain subordinate.

Under unprecedented fierce artillery fire I then went forth into the position between 9 and 10 o'clock and arrived in the battalion dugout *'Tropfsteinhöhle'* at the *Rotes Haus* after midnight. Here I met the relieved Major Bender with his staff and officers, who had had to lead the companies into their sectors, and found out that the wire obstacles and the 1st and 2nd trenches with exception of a few dugouts were shot up and that the Other Ranks were taking refuge in the dugouts of the 3rd trench as well as in the communication routes in order to have some form of protection. I discussed with the leaders of the 3rd and 10th Companies – the 12th Company was already in their sector – consequently I could not speak personally to its officers.

The companies occupied the sectors N, O, P (12th, 10th, 3rd companies) in connection with the II/R6. The 3rd Company had a very strong connection on the left. I took one platoon each back into the intermediate position between Hardecourt and the *Rotes Haus* and made them subordinate to *Hauptmann* Stauder of the 10th Company as my reserve, my oldest *Leutnant* of the companies in the foremost line. During the movement into the position as with the advance the 3rd and 10th Companies had suffered considerable losses through the bombardment.

On the morning of 30 June the adjutant of Major Bender instructed us on the map about who had gone back in the position in the meantime with his greatly thinned battalion into the position known to us until now as the 2nd Position west of Clery.[13]

Some of the positions formerly held by IR 63 had been particularly hard hit during the bombardment, perhaps because of the higher percentage of heavy guns being used by the French during the preliminary bombardment. The *Kanzel Stellung* and *Curlu Graben* were in shambles. Many of the losses reported by the Bavarians following the takeover of

The *Kanzel Stellung* as seen from *Neutrales Wald*. (*Das Königlich Bayerische Reserve-Infanterie-Regiment Nr. 6*)

the position resulted from being buried in shallow shelters and when trench walls collapsed on the men.

> The artillery fire in the course of 30 June was being directed by enemy aircraft flying at the height of a few hundred meters above the position. Hundreds of shells of the heaviest calibers fell upon my dugout that, despite only about 2 metres of earth covering it, proved wonderful with only both entrances and the interior framework suffering any damage. The bombardment became so strong that men from both neighboring companies, particularly the 9th Company lying to the right, were dispersed until they were in my dugout. Therefore in the night to 1 July the connection with the neighboring company was established. All night long we continued to repair the still useful dugouts under the most difficult circumstances using the framework from the old dugouts. About 20 men from my company were in my dugout. The artillery fire continued without interruption. The written orders concerning the distribution of the sentries went out from me during the night to the platoon leaders. *Hauptmann der Reserve* Klug[14]

The early morning fog and mist that lay over the lowland near the river was especially thick on the morning of 1 July. The dense ground cover was made even more impenetrable by the smoke of the exploding shells. The position was in ruins. The bombardment had crushed in almost every dugout, only a few still existed at *Scharfes Eck* just north of *Neutrales Wald*. The disposition of the men was far from adequate to defend the position. Large gaps had been created when the garrison was forced to find protection in the rear trenches or to crowd into the few remaining dugouts.

Because of the intensity of the bombardment on the early morning of 1 July Artillery

Group South, *Oberstleutnant* von Gilsa FAR 21, opened barrage fire on the French lines. He gave the order to fire without waiting for any signal from the infantry as had been directed by General von Stein in his overall instructions in the event of an imminent enemy attack. It was doubtful if von Gilsa or any of his observers could have seen a signal coming from the front because of the dense smoke and fog.

At 7.30 a.m. the French artillery fire lifted from the front line and was directed to the rear positions, the signal for the attack to begin. As the fire shifted strong waves of troops from the French 11th Division advanced.

> The entire position lay under the strongest fire all night, so also this sector. Still in the earliest morning hours a runner from the 2nd Company reported the total destruction of the dugouts and positions as well as heavy losses and in regard to IR63 and *Oberst* Leibrock – Bezzel had not received any further information regarding their employment. Afterwards, there was no connection with the commanders of both regiments, with Battery 3/21 at the *Rotes Haus* and with the reserve company. Shortly before there was an unexpected attack by the French 11th ID that was aided and supported by natural as well as by artificial fog. *Hauptmann der Reserve* Klug.[15]

The garrison of the front line was overwhelmed almost immediately as the enemy troops were not observed until it was too late and the French were on top of the Bavarian defenders. Most of the men had been caught inside their dugouts or improvised shelters scraped into the trench walls, not even aware the French were nearby. Isolated groups put up some resistance but their efforts were of little consequence against the overwhelming numbers of French troops and the small pockets of opposition by the Bavarians were uncoordinated and easily destroyed one by one.

> Every connection to the front was impossible during the day; all other connections had broken down. The connection with the companies could only be established during the night through orderlies and food and water were brought up. Artillery fire of all calibers lay on the position and battalion command post for the entire day.
>
> In the early hours of 1 July runners brought messages that the rest of the dugouts were shattered, the restoration work on the trenches and in the position had been useless and only a few dugouts had been repaired to some extent, and the 3rd and 12th Companies had suffered heavy losses. *Minenwerfer* and machine guns had been inserted during the night again at particularly important points.
>
> These runners returned to IR 63 under the stress of the extremely difficult situation and under the indication of an attack, which could be expected soon. From then on every connection with this regiment – the remaining batteries south of the *Rotes Haus*, the reserves in the intermediate position as well as forward areas that afterward were cut off later in the morning – was severed due to the hurricane-like storm of artillery fire. Major Bezzel, I/6 Bavarian RIR[16]

Shortly after the attack had started Bezzel was wounded and unable to participate in the defense of his position. He was carried down into his dugout that had been named the *Tropfsteinhöhle*.

Trenches near *Scharfes Eck*. (*Das Königlich Bayerische Reserve-Infanterie-Regiment Nr. 6*)

About 9 o'clock in the morning I got a shell splinter in the right thigh by the battalion command post. While my servant, *Gefreiter der Landwehr* Fuchs, bandaged me, I heard shouting in front of the dugout and the terrifying cries of the battalion adjutant *Leutnant der Reserve* Baritsch, "*Herr* Major, the French are here." Under the protection of rolling fire they had overrun those in the 1st Line and had since already penetrated up to the battalion command post which, I later learned in the military hospital, the severely wounded *Leutnant der Reserve* Riegel (12th Company), had in vain ordered barrage fire using a flare pistol.[17]

While being bandaged, Major Bezzel became injured again when a French soldier threw a hand grenade into the dugout. He was wounded several times from the hand grenade fragments, as was his orderly, and both were severely dazed. The French entered the dugout and took everyone prisoner. His adjutant, *Leutnant der Reserve* Baritsch, and AVO *Leutnant der Reserve* Niesar 3/FAR 21 were among the occupants that were also captured.

It was later determined from details provided by the badly wounded *Leutnant der Reserve* Riegel, 12/6th Bavarian RIR, that the enemy had used the protection of the rolling barrage fire as well as the dense smoke and fog to quickly overrun the German front line. The surviving members of the garrison including Riegel had attempted to call for barrage fire using flare pistols but the signals were either missed in the confusion or never seen by the artillery observers because of the poor visibility. The French were therefore able to quickly penetrate the front line and advance up to the battalion command post. *Sanitäts Unteroffizier* Marks was in the battalion dugout when the French arrived:

The night to 1 July proceeded without any special happenings. Towards mornings however the picture changed. The opponent's artillery worked on our positions with bombardment that continuously increased.

A wooded sector, that lay between the position and the Battalion dugout, prevented the view to the front and when the blows of the enemy artillery fire were transferred to the rear (approximately 30-40 meters behind us), the French had already broken through in front and attacked us with hand-grenades and revolvers. The entrance to the Battalion dugout was occupied by the French, Major Bezzel was wounded and ended up as a French prisoner of war. I was not allowed to move from my spot to assist my wounded commander who had asked for me under the reproach of a revolver. One [soldier] removed everything from us and then led us off with our wounded comrades towards Maricourt.[18]

As French troops approached the *Rotes Haus* a lively firefight developed. *Hauptmann der Reserve* Staudinger, leader of the 10/6th Bavarian RIR, instantly recognized the danger with the appearance of the French between the battalion headquarters at the eastern edge of *Leiber Wald* and the *Rotes Haus*. He decided to attempt to rescue the battalion staff using part of the reserve company. He became severely wounded during the attempt and died five days later in Nurlu. When Staudinger became wounded the momentum of the advance fell apart. It quickly became evident that they would be unable to assist the battalion staff under the present circumstances.

The speed of the enemy advance caught many of the Bavarians off guard. The French had managed to penetrate deep inside the German lines where no one had ever expected them to reach.

On the morning the 1 July 1916 about 7 or 8 o'clock hand grenades were suddenly thrown through both entrances of the dugout. This raid came as a complete surprise for us, because the termination of the artillery fire that would indicate an approach by the enemy was not observed, a circumstance that allowed us to conclude the following – that we had become passed by the enemy on the right and on the left while the enemy artillery fired on our position up to this surprise. Half of the Other Ranks found in the company commander's dugout were rendered *hors de combat* by the hand-grenades; I became wounded in the left hand. I rushed out of the dugout with the rest of the Other Ranks – the enemy had fortunately omitted to guard the dugout – and immediately picked up the battle against the French and Englishmen approaching from all sides. For support we still had one machine gun with us that the Prussians had left in the position. I succeeded in holding back the enemy for about an hour with 10 men and this machine gun. This small group was the only fighting German detachment in the surrounding area. The rest of my company was apparently immediately overpowered by the invading enemy, the right platoon by the Englishmen, both other platoons by the French. The right platoon lay north of the road to Montauban, which road apparently formed the border between the English and French battle front. I fired all of the ammunition with my small group, also that from the dead and wounded, and inflicted considerable losses on the enemy, holding them off for a considerable time in order to recognize their intentions. We also especially succeeded in shooting down different French officers, by which *Gefreiter* Heldmann from Hahnbach particularly stood out. I succeeded in informing the artillery observation post Hébuterne of the attack on our position by firing flares so that the onrushing enemy could be taken under fire from there. This was acknowledged by *Unteroffizier* Hans Stelzl from the 10th Bavarian Foot Artillery battery.

After we had fired our ammunition, we attempted to strike through to the rear, because we could no longer hold our position alone against the thousand-fold superior enemy. During the first attempt one man fell from a headshot; we were surrounded on all sides. During the breakthrough attempt we reached a dugout, in which French soldiers had already positioned themselves, which we dealt with before we were overpowered by the French penetrating into the trench. *Hauptmann der Reserve* Klug[19]

The reserve company under *Offizier Stellvertreter* Kelber and a few men from IR 63 under *Offizier Stellvertreter* Zill held the *Rotes Haus*. There was still fighting in *Leiber Wald*, but the largest part of the Bavarians that had been in the front line from the 10th, 12th and 3/6th Bavarian RIR were dead, wounded or prisoners and the situation looked hopeless. The French now began to entrench at the western edge of the *Feuersteinberg*.

There is little known about the events that occurred in the sector held by the men from the 12/6th Bavarian RIR. Few men managed to return to the rear once the attack began. Those not killed had been captured within moments of the attack. Some details of the heavy fighting and destruction of the 12th Coy became known many months or years after the battle as affidavits were collected from the survivors, many of whom were still prisoners of war.

About 8 a.m. on 1 July 1916 near Hardecourt, *Gefreiter* Bühler from my company was in a shell hole and shot by the advancing Frenchmen. Bühler was wounded and had sought protection in the shell hole, I have seen his body. Sworn testimony from *Ersatz Reservist* Johann Hader[20]

Several affidavits were collected regarding the fate of *Landwehrmann I* Karl Rinn. It is very possible that both are true accounts, or at the very least how each man recalled the events that occurred that fateful morning.

The soldier Karl Rinn from my company was bringing back wounded to Hardecourt on 1 July 1916 when he was torn open by a shell. I saw his remains. Sworn testimony from *Ersatz Reservist* Johann Hader[21]

Affidavit in reference to *Landwehrmann I* Karl Rinn. On 1 July 1916, about 7 a.m. while running through the trench I saw him lying on the slope with a severe head wound and he was probably dead. *Ersatz Reservist* Karl Muskat[22]

Ersatz Reservist Karl Muskat provided an affidavit for *Gefreiter der Reserve* Johann Untheim.

I spoke to *Gefreiter* Untheim about 8 a.m. on 1 July 1916. He had received a severe abdominal wound that had torn open the right side of his stomach. He had been taken prisoner and bled to death.[23]

Trenches near Curlu. (*An der Somme*)

Ersatz Reservist Johann Winkler provided some clues to the possible fate of his comrade *Ersatz Reservist* Johann Fuchs.

> It was his belief that in the morning of 1 July 1916 during the attack he was struck in the chest by an infantry round, that in any case he was severely wounded and afterwards he went back to the rear and collapsed and died.[24]

For some of the men simply listed as missing in action the details were quite simple and to the point. *Infanterist* Johann Zauner reported that *Infanterist* Johann Kunzel was killed on 1 July 1916 when he was shot in the head. *Ersatz Reservist* Johann Hader apparently had a great deal of information regarding the men in his company that had been killed. He also confirmed the death of *Infanterist* Max Schreiner but did not add any details on how or where it occurred. *Gefreiter der Landwehr I* Johann Holfelder reported that his comrade *Ersatz Reservist* Johann Baer had been killed at 7.30 a.m. on 1 July in the French attack. He also provided details on *Ersatz Reservist* Karl Frosh, who he observed lying dead inside the trench.

Even with some affidavits there was still a level of uncertainty about the fate of a missing man. *Infanterist* Wolfgang Eibl provided some details about the possible fate of *Landsturmmann I* Franz Lurz.

> It was on 1 July 1916 as the French were entering our trench when the subject Lurz exited the dugout with me at the same time as an enemy hand grenade flew by Lurz and exploded and struck both of his lower thighs. I immediately bandaged him but

Village of Curlu. (*An der Somme*)

then however I had to surrender and I was not allowed to stay with Lurz. I cannot say anything further about his fate.[25]

Once the fog and smoke grew thinner the observers for the Artillery Sub-Group of *Hauptmann* Ulrici, I/FAR 21, could clearly see lively enemy movement on the hill at Maurepas. A short time later they could also see French infantry busily entrenching. Artillery *Gruppe Süd* was now directed to fire on these targets. Despite the heavy bombardment of Hardecourt with heavy caliber guns, the 3/FAR 21 remained in its battery position while the exposed observation position was still manned by *Leutnant der Reserve* Scholz.

Scholz was able to maintain telephone contact with the battery at the Maurepas-*Rotes Haus* railway station. He sent regular reports on the fighting in *Bayern Wald* as well as the enemy advances in *Leiber Wald* and towards *Mulden Wald*. These reports proved very useful in directing what little artillery defensive fire that was still available. They also provided the regimental and brigade headquarters with some idea of what was taking place at the front line, even if it was only a small portion of it.

Scholz's luck was bound to run out and later in the morning his telephone line was destroyed by enemy artillery fire. Since all connections with the batteries had finally been cut, the observation position was then transferred to the western edge of Maurepas. It soon became apparent that the French had placed artillery observers on the *Feuersteinberg* as the batteries in the small railway hollow south of the Maurepas railway station came under heavy and accurate fire.

The French artillery literally blanketed the German battery positions with hundreds of shells. At this time the 3/FAR 21 still had three guns capable of firing; the fourth had been destroyed the previous day due to a direct hit. The 3rd Battery was presented with an

10.5cm Light Field howitzer in position. (*Der Weltkrieg 1914-1918*)

opportunity to inflict damage on the exposed flank of nearby advancing French troops. In order to accomplish this required the guns to be moved. The gun crews manually hauled their field guns out of their emplacements and positioned them in the open and prepared to fire.

The battery opened fire against the French troops and the gunners could clearly observe the effect of their efforts as shell after shell exploded in the enemy positions. At the same time however, the guns were completely exposed and subjected to increased French artillery and machine gun fire. Many of the gunners and officers became wounded or killed by the withering fire. Any attempt to communicate between the guns or to the rear required the use of runners. However, the fire being directed against the battery was so severe that few runners made the journey in safety.

The particularly dependable runner *Gefreiter* Scyrba was among those killed while attempting to deliver a message. Finally, the remaining three guns were placed out of action, one by one. The nearby 1/FAR 21 under *Hauptmann der Reserve* Huch, had already lost two guns from direct hits in the early morning fighting. Both remaining guns in the 1st Battery were destroyed in the afternoon.

Two 10.5cm light field howitzers in the 6/FAR 21 and all of the howitzers in the 5/ FAR 30 had finally broken down as a result of their heavy use. Most of the other batteries in *Gruppe Süd* had also lost a considerable number of guns from enemy fire and mechanical

Church of Curlu. (*Das Königlich Bayerische Reserve-Infanterie-Regiment Nr. 6*)

breakdowns. The overall effectiveness of the German artillery fire reduced with each passing hour.

In addition to the critical loss of guns, the nonstop fire of the batteries had used up all available stocks of shells, fresh supplies were needed urgently. Despite clear skies and the ever-present French observer aircraft the wagons of the Light Ammunition Column for FAR 21 and the II/FAR 30 drove forward up to the batteries. The French pilots were watching every movement in the small railway hollow and within minutes of the wagons being sighted, shells began to fall all around them. Two wagons from the 1/FAR 21 were hit by the French fire and destroyed, accompanied by immense explosions as the cargo of hundreds of shells exploded. Fortunately other wagons did succeed in bringing up the badly needed ammunition.

Further south, in the sector closest to the river, the village of Curlu and its garrison had been under some of the heaviest artillery fire they had experienced in the war. The men from the 4th and 6/6th Bavarian RIR had been cut off from the front line by an impenetrable wall of fire falling on the western edge of the village. The dust and smoke blocked any observation of the front and effectively prevented any communication by light signals or flares.

During the morning, while particularly heavy French artillery fire fell on the village, *Leutnant der Reserve* Buckel, leader of the 2/6th Bavarian RIR left the safety of his cellar dugout with four men and attempted to reach one of his platoons positioned far out in front in the marshy Somme low land. Without any warning, Buckel and his companions ran into the French attack. It was immediately apparent that the French had overrun the front line. The five men quickly looked for cover inside a large shell crater just west of the village.

The situation inside Curlu grew more ominous by the minute. The remnants of the houses were quickly being destroyed under the numerous high explosive shells being fired into it. Dirt, stones and wooden beams were sent whirling through the air. Losses began to mount quickly among the men taking cover inside the village ruins.

Leutnant der Reserve Spaeth assembled the 4th Coy and one platoon from the 2/6th Bavarian RIR under *Leutnant der Reserve* Hoch that was also subordinate to him. The men took cover near the ruined church in the southern part of the village. French artillery fire falling on the village continued to grow in intensity almost by the minute. Finally, the defenders were forced to move to the eastern edge of the village. At 9 a.m. a sentry was running back from the western edge of Curlu and reported that French troops had penetrated into the village. There was no doubt in the minds of Spaeth and his men, the front line must have been overrun.

Spaeth quickly assessed the situation he faced. He formed the remnants of the 4th Coy and Platoon Hoch into three assault groups. *Leutnant der Reserve* Obermeier and his men were positioned at the northern edge of the village. *Leutnant der Reserve* Hoch would take his men and advance through the village, while Spaeth would advance between the southern edge of the village and the river. The three detachments advanced into the heavy fire as planned.

The three assault groups ran into elements of Regiment d'Infanterie 37 that were moving deeper into the village. In the course of the fighting the French troops were forced back. Several French prisoners were captured and Spaeth's men managed to clear the enemy from the village. Losses were high among the three assault groups. *Leutnant* Hoch was among the many casualties suffered during the attack, he had fallen at the head of his men. The staff of *Hauptmann* Heck, including a machine gun from IR 63 and a detachment from *Minenwerfer* Company 12 under *Leutnant* Peter, also participated in the fighting inside Curlu.

Leutnant Haselbach, commander of the 4/63 located at Hem Farm, had observed the Bavarian attack. Within a few moments he attempted to provide additional support and advanced toward Curlu accompanied by several detachments from his company. Haselbach and his men were prevented from reaching the Bavarians by a wall of fire that the French had placed across the middle of the village.

Once the French had been expelled from Curlu, Platoon Obermeier was placed in position in front of the ruined church. The platoon had a machine gun from IR 63 for support. On his left were a few Bavarians from Platoon Hoch and a few men from the 4/63, including orderlies from the III Battalion under *Leutnant* Hans Zinnemann, Adjutant of the II/63, and the AVO *Vizefeldwebel* Weber. Once the French realized that village was still occupied by the Germans, the entire village came under heavy bombardment once again. Curlu would now remain under heavy French fire for the rest of 1st July.

Late in the morning, when the 12th Division headquarters had been able to assess the overall situation, plans were made to restore the German front line. Shortly after 10 a.m. Division Reserve South received orders from *Generalleutnant* Châles de Beaulieu to occupy the *Feuersteinberg*, or, to recapture it if the French had already occupied this strategic position. The nature of the order indicated that the division staff was still unsure of where the new front line was located and the exact situation facing the division.

Orders were sent to the reserve companies to advance toward the front line. However, the exact location of the new front was still uncertain as the men moved toward the sounds of heavy fighting. The men moved slowly, in part because of the heavy French fire falling around the men. It was not until late afternoon that the reserves were able to reach the positions north of Hem Farm, the area where the new front line had formed.

The overall situation was still very unclear. IR 63 had lost all connection with IR 62 in the morning. It was re-established at noon by the 7/63 but the circumstances by Hardecourt were still uncertain. *Offizier Stellvertreter* Probst, 3/FAR 21 and a volunteer from IR 63 set off on a reconnaissance patrol to see what they could learn about the conditions at

Memorial card for *Landsturmmann* Johann Hoffmann, 2/6th Bavarian RIR, killed
in action 1 July 1916, struck in head by a bullet. (Author's collection)

Hardecourt and the surrounding area.

When they returned, Probst reported that Hardecourt was abandoned and was not
occupied by French or by German troops. By traveling further east they were able to
make contact with the 3/62 that had been advancing toward *Bayern Wald* to support the
Bavarians still fighting in the wood. Once it was learned that Hardecourt was unoccupied,
orders were sent immediately to the 12/62 to advance from the II Position north of
Maurepas and to occupy the village.

From all reports being received in the rear it appeared that the French advance had
stopped. The enemy troops were busily entrenching along the new front line while the
German positions remained under strong artillery fire.

The German 121st Division, south of the river Somme, had also been subjected to
strong French attacks. The right wing of the division had been forced back and the French
were already in possession of the wood of Mereaucourt, therefore almost in the rear of the
German garrison of Curlu. In view of these events the protection of the left flank of the
12th Division was assigned to Artillery *Gruppe Süd*. Additional support came from the
121st Division that placed a field gun detachment at the railway station Hem facing south.

In the afternoon the 3/*Pionier* Bn 6 was ordered to prepare the southern edge of Hem
for defense and for the protection of the Somme crossings. In order to ensure the safety of
the left wing of the 12th Division a request was made for infantry and artillery support. The
extremely weakened Artillery *Gruppe Süd* was unable to provide sufficient support for the
anticipated counter attack as well as protecting the sector of the 121st Division south of the
river. Under these circumstances the counter attack ordered by *Generalleutnant* Châles de
Beaulieu had to be called off.

The fighting continued throughout the afternoon and evening hours. The French
finally captured Curlu late in the day. After failing in their first attempt on the morning of
1 July, the French attacked twice more, both attacks following a lengthy period of artillery
preparation fire. Each time they were repulsed by the surviving members of Company
Spaeth and small groups of Upper Silesians from IR 63. At times the fighting had become
hand-to-hand.

Each time the French attack failed the heavy bombardment of the village had resumed.

Any sign of life spotted by French observers immediately brought down heavy fire. Dozens of huge craters formed where houses once stood only a short time before. Each French attack and subsequent bombardment resulted in mounting losses for the few Germans remaining inside the village. By late evening the defenders were finally forced to abandon Curlu or face annihilation.

Communications with the village garrison had broken down hours earlier. Runners were the only means left to maintain contact with the different parts of the new front line. All too often hours would pass before any news reached the headquarters dugouts located in the rear. Just before Curlu fell to the French, *Hauptmann* Kupfer with the staff of the I/63 went out on patrol in order to clarify the situation inside the village.

Shortly before reaching the smoking ruins they ran into *Leutnant* Haselbach with a few of his men. The patrol had been spotted by French observers and the staff came under fire. Several of the men were hit, including *Leutnant der Reserve* Jordan, battalion adjutant and the AVO, *Leutnant der Reserve* Baillant, 6/FAR 21, who were wounded.

Leutnant Obermeier, who still clung to the western edge of the village ruins with parts of the 4/6th Bavarian RIR into the evening, had finally been overwhelmed and captured when Curlu fell. There had been no escape for the men; every route to the rear was blocked by French troops.

Leutnant der Reserve Buckel and his four companions who had remained in their shell crater the entire day, under fire from both sides, had hoped to make their way back to friendly lines when darkness fell. However, they were captured by French troops that were advancing into Curlu in the evening.

In the late evening, *Leutnant* Späth returned to Hem Farm in accordance with orders. He was accompanied by a small handful of men who had evaded capture when Curlu fell. The remnants of the battalion then moved from Hem Farm to Lieramont on 2 July.

By the end of the fighting on 1 July the overall situation was still unclear in many sectors. Fresh reserves had started to arrive and take up position. One unit that was brought up from the rear during 1 July was the Machine Gun Company of the 6th Bavarian RIR.

> While we lay under cover, in the course of the afternoon, an artillery ammunition column came roaring down the same hillside, also actively bombarded by the enemy. However they galloped up, threw their projectile baskets off and were off again, without anyone becoming injured. This was for us a special delight and we admired and exalted the performance of our drivers and their horses above all praise.
>
> About 10 p.m. we received orders through the battalion from the 63rd to move up into the 2nd line approximately 600 meters east of the chapel of Curlu. There we found out that according to an order from the 12th Prussian ID a counter-attack was to be conducted in the direction of the chapel at 2 o'clock the next morning. There the overall infantry garrison of the position numbered only approximately 50 rifles and moreover, through the efforts of the last days, they were absolutely exhausted, in part were utterly apathetic and furthermore our artillery was almost entirely destroyed. Serious misgivings were raised against this attack order. Because of the fatigues of the last few days and finally through the unfeasible attack order the Prussian battalion commander collapsed. Oberleutnant Merkel as the officer with the longest service time took command in the sector and sent four machine guns in the front line, to

advance north of the Clery-Maricourt road via Rote Farm towards Hardecourt. Two machine guns remained as reserve with the battalion.

After repeatedly receiving orders and counter-orders the order from the 12th ID came about 1.45 in the morning: 'The ordered attack is cancelled, the present position is to be held up to the last man.' *Leutnant der Reserve* Gruber[26]

The day had finally ended. The fighting along the Somme front had died down for the most part. There were places where small clashes broke out between the opposing sides but for the majority of the men the night brought a welcome relief to the heat, thirst and strain of the events that had just taken place.

During the course of 1 July literally hundreds of men from the 6th Bavarian RIR were being led off the battlefield as prisoner of war. Many of the men had been wounded, some severely; they were all receiving the best medical attention possible by their captors. It was no different than what was being provided to the British and French wounded. Others, those fortunate enough to be uninjured, were being directed toward one of many prisoner of war holding areas set up behind the front line.

For some men such as *Gefreiter der Landwehr* Johann Kern of the 9th Company, being taken prisoner resulted in a few tense moments because, as he told the story, the saw teeth on his bayonet were considered to be an illegitimate weapon of war. After he was captured he was taken into a dugout in front of an English captain who was reported to have said:

'I already imagined that Bavarians lay over there, because they did not want to come into the trenches at all.' When he understood what the essence of the 6th Bavarian

Bavarian machine gun crew. (Author's collection)

Reserve Regiment was, he still let the characteristic remark remain: he had believed that this regiment had been ordered to Verdun.[27]

In reality, the saw-like teeth on the bayonet were used for chopping and cutting and it was not an illegitimate weapon, as Kern had been led to believe. No further action was taken against him. It is possible it was simply a method being tried to obtain information from the prisoner. Kern remained in a prisoner of war camp until his release after the war was over.

The scenes behind the British and French lines must have been a revelation to the officers and men of the 6th Bavarian RIR, in particular regarding the inequality of the situation facing their opponents. *Hauptmann der Reserve* Klug, 5/6th Bavarian RIR:

> I made the following observations in the rear of the enemy: the fire trenches were virtually completely undamaged – that alluded to the ineffectiveness of our weak artillery. Maricourt, the village that was behind the enemy front, showed no trace of destruction. The enemy moved there completely unmolested. The hills behind the enemy infantry position were covered by an unheard number of guns of all calibers. The ammunition lay as high as a mountain, completely unprotected on both sides of the road.[28]

Once the scope of the Allied attack had been recognized by the German commanders, immediate steps were set in motion to provide the necessary support required by the infantry as well as the artillery. Fresh troops and new batteries were quickly moving toward the threatened front, but it would take time before many of them could reach the areas where they were needed most. Until they did arrive the existing units would have to hold their positions as best they could. By end of the day the British were in the village of Montauban, at the edge of Bernafay Wood and held parts of the *Bayern Wald*. The French had advanced as far as the *Feuersteinberg* and held the village of Curlu. The lines had stabilized to some degree but the situation was considered precarious.

As early as the morning of 1 July *Generalleutnant* von Stein had sent an urgent request for the use of the approaching 11th Reserve Division from AOK 2 [2nd Army Headquarters (Staff)]. This division was being transported from Cambrai by train and had received orders to place itself in readiness in the area Sailly-Rancourt-Bouchavesnes. From this location it was felt that the division could throw back the enemy that had broken through north of Curlu and also prevent any attempt by the enemy to cross the Somme at Feuilleres to the north.

The request was granted but the transport of the division did not begin until late afternoon on 1 July and therefore parts of this division would not be available until the next day at the earliest.

Following the fighting on 1 July there was a strong opinion by many of the officers and men in the 6th Bavarian RIR that they had been sacrificed unnecessarily. *Hauptmann der Reserve* Klug was of the opinion that the regiment could have been used more effectively in the fighting, instead the men had been thrown into battle with almost no support from the artillery and the air service:

Memorial card for *Infanterist* Michael Dirscherl, 5/6th Bavarian RIR.
Died from wounds as a prisoner of war. (Author's collection.)

The Prussian troops replaced by us had lost the greatest part of their existing Other Ranks. As hard as it sounds, we should not have replaced them. Our unimpaired division could have then led a counter-attack with full strength following the attack on 1 July.[29]

When looking at the actual numbers of men lost by IR 62 and IR 63 it was clear that the statement made by Klug that these regiments had lost the greater part of their 'Other Ranks' was not exactly true. Perhaps the most vocal criticism of the events that took place on the Somme involving the 6th Bavarian RIR came from *Oberst* Leibrock. Leibrock provided a report about the use of his regiment in the time from 14 June to 1 July in his detailed battle report. He had time to consider his position and statements in the months spent as a prisoner of the English.

a) Reasons and causes for the tragedy of the R.I.R. 6 on the Somme 1916.
1. R.I.R. 6 first became for a time subordinate to the 28th Prussian Reserve Division and the 12th Prussian Infantry Division as labor troops, because the enemy artillery already started to systematically bombard the village billets and work positions under pilot observation.
2. Dugout and obstacle materials were not available in sufficient quantities. Either circumstance had the consequence that the labor could not become used to its full extent.
3. The battalions and companies very often changed their work places and housing and could finally only work at night. Also this lack of rest decreased their performance.

4. If the tearing apart of the regimental formation with the work was made palpably disagreeable, so it became later during the tactical employment of the regiment a main reason for the catastrophe.

For over a week the battalions from my regiment were almost completely withdrawn from my authority on external duty, while the running of internal matters was connected with great difficulties. During the tactical deployment would 10 companies and 1 Marksman Detachment become subordinate to the Prussian commander previously here? From the last two infantry companies and two machine gun formations from my regiment many would become casualties in the course of the enemy attacks.[30]

Leibrock was of the opinion that the results of the fighting on 1 July could have been different, even with the 10th Bavarian Division having been parceled out across the entire front line, if his regiment had been able to fight as a cohesive unit:

If at least the regiment was employed close together, then the regiments of the 12th I.D. would have fought in their shrinking battle sectors with the same relief and with more feeling of responsibility. If and how much influence this resolution would have at the end of the day, I could not assess. Also reasons were surely present for the arrangement to actually take place, which likewise eludes my knowledge. The individual parts of the regiment had, after all, performed as well as was humanly possible, based on what we learned about them through the statements of the captured officers.

If I prominently described details of distasteful circumstances and of uncommon orders for major movements, the reason is that I am induced to do this. Besides the obligation to report truthfully, the main regret was that despite the amazingly astonishing expenditure of heroic bravery, of tough endurance and despite the quite huge losses mentioned in enemy reports as wearing down the regiment, the enemy attack could not be repulsed.[31]

Leibrock also commented on the statements made to him by British officers that parts of his regiment did not put up any resistance at all in the attack on 1 July. Apparently these comments annoyed him greatly. Other reports concerning the praise of the opposition put up by the Bavarians clearly refuted these earlier comments made to Leibrock, who placed far greater value on the positive comments than the criticisms.

Out of this clear enemy testimony [of the Bavarian opposition] arises thus that the English officer, who reported to our regimental commander of only slight resistance, could not have meant our regiment, if it did not concern a ruse at all, whose aim was to cause the prisoners to talk.[32]

Once the fighting had ended the required casualty reports were created and sent in to headquarters on 10 July in accordance with army regulations. Some regiments later determined what their losses were specifically on 1 July as it was recognized as a momentous day. Others did not and could only provide loss details covering a far longer period of time. During the fighting in and around Montauban, Hardecourt and Curlu the 6th Bavarian

RIR had suffered the heaviest losses reported by the three regiments of infantry involved in the battle. The regiment reported losing a total of 35 officers, 1,774 *Unteroffiziers* and men killed, wounded and missing from the time the regiment arrived at the Somme front until relieved during the night of 1/2 July.

The published *Verlustlisten* for this regiment appeared on four separate days between 11 and 18 August. 1,832 officers and men were named on these lists. Of these names, 52 were shown to have become casualties in the week-long bombardment. Another 19 were shown to have become casualties in the days following 1 July. A total of 1,761 officers and men became casualties in the fighting on 1 July 1916, the regiment with the second highest number of losses suffered by any German regiment fighting on this date, just slightly less men lost than the neighboring RIR 109.

The official losses reported by IR 62 for 1 July were 4 officers, 79 Other Ranks killed; 3 officers, 214 Other Ranks wounded; 6 officers, 431 Other Ranks missing for a total of 13 officers, 724 Other Ranks. This regiment remained in the front line on 2 and 3 July. Some companies were relieved on 2 July while others on 3 July by units from the VI Reserve Corps.

IR 63 suffered the fewest losses of all three regiments. The official loss returns for the three weeks ending on 8 July 1916 show that IR 63 had lost 5 officers, 147 Other Ranks killed; 6 officers, 290 Other Ranks wounded and 61 Other Ranks missing. The total losses were 11 officers, 498 Other Ranks. Given this number of losses spread over a three week period, including the week-long bombardment and the heavy fighting on 1 July, I can see no valid reason why this regiment was relieved from the front line on the eve of battle. From all of the evidence it does appear that the relief of the front line units of the 12th Division hours before the British/French attack could be considered one of the biggest German tactical blunders of the battle.

Notes:

1.   O. Bezzel, *Das Königlich Bayerische Reserve-Infanterie-Regiment Nr. 6*, p. 93.
2.   Bezzel, op. cit., p. 92.
3.   Bezzel, op. cit., pp. 111-112.
4.   Bezzel, op. cit., p. 118
5.   *Stammrolle* records of *Ersatz Reservist* Paulus Held.
6.   Michael Theurlein was born 5 November 1894. He joined the regiment on 11 March 1915 and he had already been wounded once before, on 6 September 1915, when he received a grazing shot to his head. He was sick for several weeks between 14 January and 2 February 1916. Upon being exchanged as an unfit soldier he was sent to Beckenried, a lakeside town near Luzern with views of the snow-capped Alps, where he could recuperate.
7.   Bezzel, op. cit., pp. 91-92.
8.   Bezzel, op. cit., pp. 112-113.
9.   Bezzel, op. cit., p. 114.
10. Bezzel, op. cit., pp. 114-115.
11. Bezzel, op. cit., pp. 115-116.
12. Bezzel, op. cit., pp. 116-117.
13. Bezzel, op. cit., pp. 96-98.
14. Bezzel, op. cit., p. 92.
15. Bezzel, op. cit., p. 94.

16. Bezzel, op. cit., p. 98.

17. Ibid.

18. Bezzel, op. cit., p. 99.

19. Bezzel, op. cit., pp. 92 93. *Gefreiter* Martin Heldmann, 5th Coy, from Hahnbach, Oberpfalz., listed as MIA on Bavarian *Verlustlisten* 289, 15 August 1916. Heldmann had been taken prisoner on 1 July 1916.

20. *Stammrolle* records of *Ersatz Reservist* Johann Hader.

21. Ibid.

22. *Stammrolle* records of *Ersatz Reservist* Karl Muskat.

23. Ibid.

24. *Stammrolle* records of *Ersatz Reservist* Johann Winkler.

25. *Stammrolle* records of *Infanterist* Wolfgang Eibl.

26. Bezzel, op. cit., p. 101.

27. Bezzel, op. cit., pp. 1186-119.

28. Bezzel, op. cit., pp. 93-94.

29. Bezzel, op. cit., p. 93.

30. Bezzel, op. cit., p. 117.

31. Bezzel, op. cit., p. 118.

32. Bezzel, op. cit., p. 119.

Epilogue

The events described in this book primarily deal with one day, 1 July 1916. The Battle of the Somme would continue for almost five more months until it was finally declared to have ended in November 1916. Before the battle concluded the casualty lists on both sides of the wire numbered in the hundreds of thousands. For many of the families from both sides of the fighting all that remained of their loved ones were a few letters, some old photographs and perhaps a personal item or two.

Over time they have faded from memory in many instances – men Like *Vizefeldwebel* Karl Losch, who tragically died on 1 July. Decades after his death his photographs and letters were sold at auction including his memorial scroll. These scrolls were given to each family who lost someone in the war. While the scroll and accompanying letter were designed to convey the sympathies of the state it in no way could make up for the loss of a son as in the case of Karl. It is depressing to see such family history ending up for sale but perhaps the saddest aspect of his life is that the scroll and official letter sent after his death were both still in the original mailing tube some 90 or more years later.

The fighting would last almost two more years following the end of the battle. Much would change in the world during these months. For the regiments in the 26th and 28th Reserve Divisions the war took on a different aspect. No longer were the men stationed in a single sector for months or years. The men were moved around the front where they were

British prisoners under escort. (*An der Somme*)

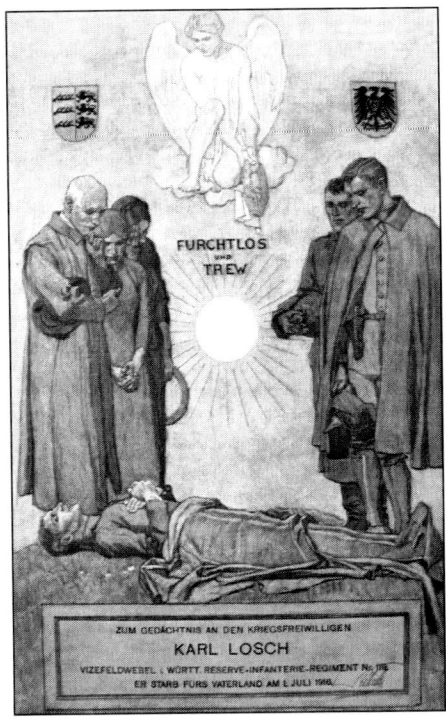

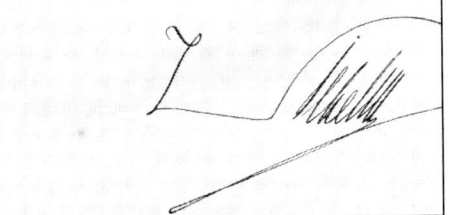

Der ſchwere Kampf für die Verteidigung des Vaterlandes hat auch ein teures Glied Ihrer Familie als Opfer gefordert. Zum Gedächtnis des auf dem Felde der Ehre Gefallenen und in Anerkennung der von dem Verewigten bis zum Tode bewieſenen Pflichttreue, verleihe Ich Ihnen in herzlicher Anteilnahme an Ihrem ſchweren Verluſt das beifolgende

Gedenkblatt.

Möge es als ein Erinnerungszeichen an die große Zeit und an den unauslöſchlichen Dank des Vaterlandes in Ihrer Familie dauernd bewahrt werden.

Stuttgart, den 15. Juni 1917.

Left: Memorial scroll for Karl Losch. (Author's collection)
Right: Official condolence letter for Karl Losch. (Author's collection)

The face of modern warfare, men from IR 55. (Author's collection)

needed most. The makeup of the divisions would change, one regiment would end up being moved to another division and old friends would return to the division after being absent for the three years. Losses continued to grow and more and more men suffered death or were wounded before the Armistice was signed. By the end of the war in November 1918 the regiments that marched back to Germany from these divisions contained very few men who had marched to the Somme in September 1914.

The entire nature of the war had changed. In 1914 the fighting was more reminiscent of the fighting from the 19th Century. By 1918 modern 20th Century warfare had become the norm. The men who served took on a more uniform appearance, a more industrial appearance, both with the weapons being utilized as well as the equipment the men wore.

Following the fighting on the Somme and the end of the war the men of the XIV Reserve Corps would face even greater challenges. They would face an uncertain future of political upheaval, the rise of Fascist governments and communism and the eventual return of global warfare in 1939. Volume 3 of this series will take the reader through the remainder of the Great War and into the decades that followed in order to provide an account of the experiences of the men who went off to war with such high hopes in August 1914 in the XIV Reserve Corps. It is still my hope that these accounts help to bring these forgotten men back into modern memory and to preserve their lives and the events that shaped them for decades to come.

Appendix I

German Order of Battle, 2nd Army, 1 July 1916

Army Commander: *General der Infanterie* Fritz von Below
Chief of Staff: *Generalmajor* Grünert
Chief Quartermaster: *Oberst Frhr.* von Hammerstein-Gesmold
1st General Staff Officer: Major Faupel
General der Fussartillerie: Generalleutnant Limbourg
General der Pioniere: Generalmajor Fremel

XIV Reserve Corps

Commanding General: *Generalleutnant* von Stein
Chief of Staff: Major Kirch
1st General Staff Officer: Major Solger
General der Fussartillerie: *Generalmajor* Stüve

Corps Troops

Staff and II(F)/Württemberg FAR 116
Fussartillerie Battalion 51 (with the 26th Reserve Division)
Fussartillerie Battalion 229 (Batteries 749, 750 and 751) (Staff, Batteries 750 and 751 with the 28th Reserve Division, *Batterie* 749 with the 26th Reserve Division)
Artillerie Messtrupps 1, 2, 3, 4 and 6; *Schall Messtrupps* 1 and 49
Motorisieren Flak Zug 4; K *Flak Gesch.* 36 and 63; K *Flak* Batteries 5 and 7
Reserve *Fernsprecher Abteilung* 14 with *Festungs Signal Trupp* 1, 2 and 133
Artillerie Scheinwerfer Zug 1
Feld Luftschiff Abteilung 2
Feld Flieger Abteilung 32 and Bavarian 1; *Artillerie Flieger Abteilung* 221
1 M.G. on *Kraftwagen*
Staffelstäbe 152, 153, 246, 266, 267 and 268

2nd Guard Reserve Division

Commanding General: *General der Infanterie* Frhr. von Süsskind
General Staff Officer: *Hauptmann* von Stünzner
   26th Reserve *Infanterie* Brigade:
      RIR 15 with one M.G. Coy, M.G. *Ergänzungszug* 662, M.G. Marksman Detachment 73
      RIR 55 with one M.G. Coy and M.G. *Ergänzungszug* 663
   38th Reserve *Infanterie* Brigade:
      RIR 77 with one M.G. Coy, M.G. *Ergänzungszug* 331, M.G. Marksman Detachment 106
      RIR 91 with one M.G. Coy and M.G. *Ergänzungszug* 352
      Reserve *Ulan* Regiment 2 (3rd Squadron)

RFAR 20
Flak Zug 58
4/*Pionier* Bn 10
Scheinwerfer Zug 260
Garde Minenwerfer Coy 2
Fernsprecher Doppel Zug 2 with *Festungs Signal Trupp* 222 and 223
Guard Reserve Division *Brückentrain* 2
Reserve *Sanitäts* Coy 2
Feld Rekruit Depot
Attached units:
I/Bavarian FAR 19 (From 10th Bavarian Division)
2/*Fussartillerie* Battalion 52 (From 52nd Division)
Attached Army units:
3 Belgian 5.7cm guns
Fussartillerie Batterie Apel
Fussartillerie Batterie 692
Staff II and ½ 5/2nd Guard *Fussartillerie* Regiment
Fussartillerie Batterie 706
3/II Bavarian *Landsturm Fussartillerie* Battalion, I Army Corps
½ /*Fussartillerie Batterie* 212
K. *Flak Zug* 38
M. Fr. 55
3/*Armierungs* Battalion 31; 4/*Armierungs* Battalion 69
Reserve *Eisenbahn Bau Kompanie* 22

Notes: Staff 26th Reserve Infanterie Brigade and Reserve *Ulan* Regiment 2 with the Corps Reserve XIV Reserve Corps; RIR 15 (without the I Battalion) with the 52nd Division

52nd Division
Commanding General: *Generalleutnant* von Borries
Staff Officer: Hauptmann Prager
104th Infanterie Brigade:
IR 66 with two M.G. Coy
IR 169 with two M.G. Coy
IR 170 with two M.G. Coy and M.G. Marksman Detachment 74
4/*Ulan* Regiment 16
52nd *Feld Artillerie* Brigade:
FAR 103
FAR 104
Flak Zug 108
Radfahrer Kompanie 52
Pionier Companies 103 and 104
Scheinwerfer Zug 103
Minenwerfer Company 52
Fernsprech Doppel Zug 52 with *Festungs Signal Trupp* 158 and 159
Division *Brückentrain* 52

Sanitäts Company 52
Feld Rekruit Depot
Attached units:
    Regimental Staff and II/Bavarian FAR 19 (From 10th Bavarian Division)
    2/Bavarian *Fussartillerie* Regiment 10 (From 10th Bavarian Division)
    Fussartillerie Battalion 52 (without the 2nd Battery)
Attached Army units:
    3 Belgian 5.7cm guns
    ½ 7/2 *Garde Fussartillerie* Regiment
    2/3 *Fussartillerie* Batterie 471
    ½ *Fussartillerie* Batterie 472
    1st and 2/II Bavarian *Landsturm Fussartillerie* Battalion II Army Corps
    Fussartillerie Batterie 10
    Staff I, 2nd and 3/*Fussartillerie* Regiment 7
    2 *Ersatz/Fussartillerie* Regiment 18
    M.Fr. 137
    1/Bavarian *Pionier* Regiment
    2/*Armierungs Battalion* 31; 3/*Armierungs Battalion* 78

Notes: ½ 5/FAR 103 *Bahnhof Flak Zug* Puisieux; 2/*Fussartillerie* Battalion 52 with the 2nd *Garde* Reserve Division.

26th Reserve Division
Commanding General: *General der Infanterie Frhr.* von Soden
General Staff: *Hauptmann* Fischer
    Württemberg 51st Reserve *Infanterie* Brigade:
        IR 180 with two M.G. Companies
        RIR 121 with one M.G. Coy, M.G. Coy Fassbender and M.G. Marksman Detachment 198
    Württemberg 52nd Reserve *Infanterie* Brigade:
        RIR 119 with two M.G. Coy
        RIR 99 (4 Battalions) with two M.G. Coy
        Württemberg Reserve Dragoon Regiment (3 Squadrons)
    Württemberg 26th Reserve *Feld Artillerie* Brigade:
        RFAR 26
        RFAR 27
    Flak Zug 137
    Württemberg *Radfahrer* Coy 2
    4th and 6/Württemberg *Pionier* Bn 13
    Württemberg *Scheinwerfer Zug* 256
    Württemberg *Minenwerfer* Coy 226
    Württemberg Reserve Division *Brückentrain* 26
    Württemberg Reserve *Sanitäts* Coy 26
    Württemberg *Sanitäts Kraftwagen Kolonne* 5
    Württemberg *Feld Rekruit* Depot
Attached units:
    Bavarian RIR 8 with one M.G. Coy, M.G. Marksman Detachment 45 and M.G. Marksman

Detachment 89 (From 10th Bavarian Division)
Bavarian FAR 20 (From 10th Bavarian Division)
Bavarian *Minenwerfer* Coy 10 (From 10th Bavarian Division)
I/FAR 104 (without ½ of the 2nd Battery) (From 52nd Division)
I/RFAR 12 (From 12th Reserve Division)
Attached Corps units:
Staff, 1st, 2nd and 3/*Fussartillerie* Battalion 51
Fussartillerie Batterie 749 (*Fussartillerie* Battalion 229)
Attached Army units:
4 Belgian 5.7cm guns
Fussartillerie Batterie 471
Fussartillerie Batterie 551
½ 7/2 *Garde Fussartillerie* Regiment
½ *Fussartillerie Batterie* 550
Fussartillerie Batterie 683
Fussartillerie Batterie 709
Fussartillerie Batteries 235 and 236
1/*Fussartillerie* Regiment 20
M.Fr. 43
Festungs Signal Trupp 46 and 47
2 Auto *Scheinwerfer* from A.O.K.
1/*Musketen* Battalion 1
Bavarian *Pionier (Mineur)* Coy 5
5/*Armierungs* Battalion 31

28th Reserve Division
Commanding General: *Generalleutnant* von Hahn
General Staff Officer: Major Buchrucker
56th Reserve Infanterie Brigade
RIR 109 with two M.G. Coy and M.G. Marksman Detachment 131
RIR 110 with two M.G. Coy and M.G. Marksman Detachment 161
RIR 111 with two M.G. Coy
28th Reserve *Feld Artillerie* Brigade:
RFAR 28
RFAR 29 (II *Abteilung* Württemberg)
1st and 2 Reserve/Württemberg *Pionier* Bn 13
Minenwerfer Coy 228
Reserve Division *Brückentrain* 28
Reserve *Sanitäts* Coy 14
Feld Rekruit Depot
Attached units:
IR 23 with M.G. Coy and M.G. Marksman Detachment 132 (From 12th Division)
Staff I, 2nd and 3/FAR 57 (From 12th Division)
4(F)/FAR 21 (From 12th Division)
Staff and 1/Bavarian *Fussartillerie* Battalion 10 (From 10th Bavarian Division)

Attached Corps units:
  Staff, 2nd and 3/*Fussartillerie* Battalion 229 (Batteries 750 and 751)
Attached Army units:
  Landwehr Brigade Ersatz Battalion 55 with M.G. Coy
  2/*Musketen* Battalion 1
  II(F)/FAR 39 with Staff, 5(F) and 6(F)/FAR 39 and 6(F)/FAR 50
  III(F)/RFAR 12 (From 12th Reserve Division)
  2 Belgian 5.7cm guns
  ½ *Fussartillerie Batterie* 550
  2/3 Bavarian *Fussartillerie Batterie* 468
  ½ *Fussartillerie Batterie* 473
  Fussartillerie Batterie 337
  Fussartillerie Batterie 718
  Fussartillerie Batterie 11
  4/*Fussartillerie Batterie* 7
  Fussartillerie Batterie 381
  ½ *Fussartillerie Batterie* 473
  1st and 3/*Fussartillerie Battalion* 44
  7/Reserve *Fussartillerie* Regiment 12
  K. *Flak* 72
  M.Fr. 122
  1st Reserve and 2/Bavarian *Pionier* Regiment
  Saxon *Pionier (Mineur)* Coy 323
  1st, 4/*Armierungs* Battalion 31; 2/*Armierungs* Battalion 64; 2/Bavarian *Armierungs* Battalion 5

Notes: 5/RFAR 29 *Bahnhof Flak Batterie* Grévillers; ½ 6/RFAR 29 *Bahnhof Flak Zug* Flers.

12th Division
Commanding General: *Generalleutnant* Châles de Beaulieu
General Staff Officer: *Hauptmann* von Tempelhoff
  24th *Infanterie* Brigade
    IR 23 with M.G. Coy and M.G. Marksman Detachment 132
    IR 62 with M.G. Coy
    IR 63 with two M.G. Coy
    3rd and 4/Ulan Regiment 2
  12th *Feld Artillerie* Brigade:
    FAR 21
    FAR 57
    Flak Zug 17
    2nd and 3/*Pionier* Bn 6
    Minenwerfer Coy 12
    Fernsprech Doppel Zug 12 with *Festungs Signal Trupp* 116, 117 and 118
    Division *Brückentrain* 12
    Sanitäts Coy 2

Staffelstab 27
Feld Rekruit Depot
Attached units:
  Bavarian RIR 6 with M.G. Coy, M.G. Marksman Detachment 41 and M.G. Marksman Detachment 88 (From 10th Bavarian Division)
  Regimental Staff and II/RFAR 12 (From 12th Reserve Division)
Attached Army units:
  2 Belgian 5.7cm guns
  II(F)/FAR 30, consisting of the 5(F) and 6(F)/FAR 30 and 5(F)/FAR 50
  Fussartillerie Batterie 565
  1/3 Bavarian *Fussartillerie Batterie* 468
  Fussartillerie Batterie 685
  Fussartillerie Batterie 563
  8/*Fussartillerie* Regiment 6
  4/*Fussartillerie* Regiment 20
  Staff and 2/*Fussartillerie* Battalion 44 (From 1 July)
  M.Fr. 70
  Pionier Coy 264
  3/*Armierungs* Battalion 64; 3rd and 4/Bavarian *Armierungs* Battalion 5

Notes: IR 23 with the 28th Reserve Division; 3/*Ulan* Regiment 2 with *Etappen Inspektion* 2; 4(F)/FAR 21 with the 28th Reserve Division; 1/FAR 57 *Bahnhof Flak Züg* Ginchy and Maurepas; Staff I, 2nd and 3/FAR 57 with the 28th Reserve Division

10th Bavarian Division
Commanding General: *Generalmajor* Burkhardt
General Staff Officers: Major Hierl, *Hauptmann* Leeb
  20th Bavarian Infanterie Brigade:
    16th Bavarian IR with M.G. Coy, M.G. Marksman Detachment 44 and M.G. Marksman Detachment 87
    6th Bavarian RIR with M.G. Coy, M.G. Marksman Detachment 41 and M.G. Marksman Detachment 88
    8th Bavarian RIR with two M.G. Coy, M.G. Marksman Detachment 45 and M.G. Marksman Detachment 89
    3/Bavarian 5 *Chevauleger* Regiment
  10th Bavarian *Feld Artillerie* Brigade:
    19th Bavarian FAR
    20th Bavarian FAR
  Bavarian *Flak Zug* 97
  Bavarian *Fussartillerie* Battalion 10
  Bavarian *Radfahrer* Coy 10
  Bavarian *Pionier* Coy 20
  Bavarian *Scheinwerfer Zug* 19
  Bavarian *Minenwerfer* Coy 10
  Bavarian *Fernsprech Doppel Zug* 10 with *Festungs* Signal Trupp 29 and 30
  Bavarian *Sanitäts* Coy 10

Bavarian *Staffelstäbe* 13 and 14

Notes: 16th Bavarian IR with the corps reserve, XIV Reserve Corps; 6th Bavarian RIR with the 12th Division; 8th Bavarian RIR (without the 2nd M.G. Coy) with the 26th Reserve Division; Regimental staff and II/Bavarian FAR 19 with the 52nd Division; I/Bavarian FAR 19 with the 2nd *Garde* Reserve Division; Bavarian FAR 20 with the 26th Reserve Division; Bavarian *Flak Zug* 97 with the 28th Reserve Division; Staff and 1/Bavarian *Fussartillerie* Battalion 10 with the 28th Reserve Division; 2/Bavarian *Fussartillerie* Battalion 10 with the 52nd Division; Bavarian *Radfahrer* Coy 10 with the corps reserve, XIV Reserve Corps; Bavarian *Pionier* Coy 20 with the 28th Reserve Division; Bavarian *Minenwerfer* Coy 10 with the 26th Reserve Division; ½ platoon Bavarian *Sanitäts* Coy 10 with the 28th Reserve Division

Artillery complement of the 26th Reserve Division

At the start of the Battle of the Somme the 26th Reserve Division had 148 artillery pieces attached to the division:

70 Field guns (7.7cm)
24 Light Field howitzers (10.5cm)
16 Heavy Field howitzers (15cm)
17 9cm guns
4 Russian Heavy Field howitzers (15cm)
4 Heavy Ring Cannon (15cm)
4 Russian Ring Cannon (15cm)
3 Belgian 9cm guns
2 10cm guns
2 Russian Mortars (21cm)
2 Belgian 12cm guns

These weapons were divided among the different artillery groups and sub-groups that were established to cover the division during the attack.

At the disposal of the Artillery Commander, *Generalmajor* von Maur:
2 10cm guns
2 Russian 21cm mortars

Sub-Group Adolf:
14 Field guns (7.7cm)
4 Light Field howitzers (10.5cm)
4 9cm guns
4 Heavy Field howitzers (15cm)

Sub-Group Beauregard:
16 Field guns (7.7cm)
12 Light Field howitzers (10.5cm)
2 Russian heavy Field howitzers (15cm)
2 Heavy Ring Cannon (15cm with Chase rings)

Sub-Group Berta:
16 Field guns (7.7cm)
3 Belgian 9cm guns

4 Heavy Field howitzers (15cm)
4 Russian Ring Cannon (15cm)
2 Russian heavy Field howitzers (15cm)

Sub-Group Zollern:

16 Field guns (7.7cm)
4 Light Field howitzers (10.5cm)
2 Belgian 12cm guns
4 Heavy Field howitzers (15cm)
2 Heavy Ring Cannon (15cm)

Sub-Group Cäsar:

8 Field guns (7.7cm)
4 Light Field howitzers (10.5cm)
13 9cm guns
4 Heavy Field howitzers (15cm)

Appendix III

Review of German casualties, 1 July 1916

The charts present on the accompanying disc were created using the *Verlustlisten* that were originally published in Germany from Monday through Saturday of each week from 1914 through 1919. These lists represent the losses reported by each unit in the German army in accordance with the normal 10 day reporting requirements (10 *tägigen Truppenkrankenrapporten*).

There have been many attempts to estimate the actual losses suffered by the German army during the war and for specific battles and dates such as 1 July 1916 without much success. One reason why earlier attempts were abandoned was the issue of the cost required to complete such a review.

At one point in time it might have been possible to assemble and review each 10 *tägigen Truppenkrankenrapporten* that had been submitted, each one providing key details on every casualty reported by each unit. The passage of time and subsequent historic events have made this impossible with the loss of many of these records through bombing raids as well as an unfortunate scrap paper drive during WWII when many documents were recycled and therefore lost.

There are still sources that help researchers compile the casualty data from the war. This includes a massive post-war review of the losses suffered by the German Army that was published in the early 1930's. The official numbers of men lost in this period were reported in the *Sanitätsbericht über das Deutsche Heer (Deutsches Feld und Besatzungsheer) im Weltkrieg 1914/18, III. Band* that was published in 1934. This effort was the result of years of work sifting through the mountains of official reports and casualty returns that still existed at the time the project was being completed.

Part of the findings included a section on the losses suffered in the fighting on the Somme in 1916. In the period from 1 to 10 July the 2nd Army consisted of 21 Divisions with the ration strength of 469,585 officers and men. This number includes the original divisions that fought on 1 July as well as reinforcement divisions that began to arrive almost immediately following the start of the battle.

During this period, 1-10 July, the losses of the 2nd Army consisted of 7,539 officers and men reported sick, 22,095 wounded, and 24,224 killed or missing of whom 18,438 were officially shown as missing. This leaves 5,786 men listed as killed during this period. In the same 10 day period, 5,273 officers and men were returned to duty.

Breaking the numbers down even further to the division level, the 26th Reserve Division of the XIV Reserve Corps reported the following numbers. Ration strength 20,700. Of these 265 officers and men reported sick, 1,691 officers and men were wounded. The number of men listed as killed and missing is unfortunately unavailable in the records provided. The same goes for the 28th Reserve Division.

While the statistics provided for individual divisions do not have all of the data the overall losses for the XIV Reserve Corps for the first 10 days of July were 11,632 officers and men. Of this number 5,934 officers and men were killed or missing. As 3,917 men were reported missing it leaves 2,017 officers and men listed as definitely being killed in action as of the time the reports were filed.

This method of reporting losses does make it harder to establish the exact numbers of men who became a casualty on 1 July 1916. Fortunately, some regiments did provide exact details on the losses they suffered for this one date while others either provided numbers over a longer period, keeping with the reporting time frames. Unfortunately, a few units did not report losses in detail at all. The larger units, the infantry and artillery regiments generally provided more details than the smaller units involved in the fighting.

In my search for each unit I combed through the *Verlustlisten* published at the end of July and continued into September until I was satisfied that I had found all of the initial lists necessary for loss reports that should relate to 1 July 1916.[1]

In addition to the research needed to locate each primary list of casualties there was also a need to review subsequent lists. This can be seen clearly in the loss returns for regiments such as RIR 109, 6th Bavarian RIR, and others that reported large numbers of men as missing. These regiments reported the raw numbers of men lost on this date without taking into account the possible changes in their status over time. The fate of the high numbers of missing men would eventually be determined as additional details were discovered.

Many of the corrections came from reports from the comrades of the missing men who could establish if a particular soldier had been killed or captured. The same goes for reports from enemy sources if the remains of any men belonging to a particular German regiment were discovered. The enemy findings were eventually reported to the Red Cross that in turn would pass along these details to German authorities. In some cases men who had been missing and that had been captured were identified through personal letters sent home from the P.O.W. camps. Other corrections were made as official reports were prepared on the status of the different casualties, an example would be if a man was listed as M.I.A. and it was found that he was actually in a hospital sick or wounded. All of these corrections were published on subsequent *Verlustlisten*, some appearing as late as 1918.

In attempting to locate the subsequent lists indicating the fate of so many missing men it was necessary to review each *Verlustlisten* up through the first months of 1917. The sheer size of the lists and the changes made in how losses were reported made it extremely time consuming to continue beyond this point in time.[2]

The date a man became a casualty is identified whenever possible, regardless if they had become a casualty on 1 July 1916 or any other date. If their status changed over the time period being checked the initial status is listed and any subsequent changes will appear in parenthesis alongside it. The reader may note that some of the men listed became casualties in the bombardment period in the last week of June. Others might be from an earlier period while some became casualties in the days and weeks following 1 July.

By reproducing the lists taken from the published *Verlustlisten*, I have attempted to provide all of the names and details of the men who were killed, wounded or captured on this fateful day. In order to present the lists in a format that is easier to utilize by the reader I have placed the names in alphabetical order by company or battery. The original lists were published with the names presented in a random fashion, most likely in the same manner they were reported on the 10 *tägigen Truppenkrankenrapporten*.

One particularly odd finding was the complete absence of any losses related to the

Musketen Battalions that fought on the Somme on 1 July 1916. In searching the *Verlustlisten* I found several entries that clearly indicated the losses occurred in the time period before 1 July. I also came across several lists many months past this date that contained the names of one or two men. Since the records appear to be an accurate representation of the reported losses and since earlier and subsequent losses were reported it would appear that the *Musketen* detachments were among the luckiest groups to have fought in the battle.

This could be an accurate representation as these weapons were used in small groups, generally two guns placed together as a single operating unit. The weapons were small and portable and did not create a large target or provide a telltale sign of their presence as did the steam from the heavy MG 08 machine guns when in use. The *Musketen* were normally placed in support locations and generally not in the front line so it is possible, as improbable as it seems, that these men escaped any serious injury throughout the heavy fighting in early July.

Hopefully the charts will provide further details on the fate of the men who fought on 1 July 1916 and in particular the eventual fate of the numerous missing of the XIV Reserve Corps. My goal is to provide the most accurate information possible of the true losses suffered by the German Army on 1 July 1916.

While many of the families received word of the fate of their loved ones killed, wounded, missing, it was the latter category that could produce much anguish. At least the others knew the fate of their family member. In the case of men listed as M.I.A. it could be weeks, months or years before there was a determination of their fate. When it became clear that the missing man was not in an enemy P.O.W. camp, was not listed as a prisoner who had died, been found on the battlefield and buried etc. then he could be declared dead. The family would be notified through official channels. I suspect that many families in this situation kept their hopes alive well after they received the news that the missing man was presumed to have been killed.

The lists represent 20,790 names of the men who most likely fought on the Somme in early July. Of these 6,226 can be identified as having been killed, wounded, injured or captured on 1 July 1916. An additional 1,912 can positively identified as having become a casualty before or after this date. Of the remainder, 12,642 names, only time will tell if the details of their fate can be established.

Notes

1. The one exception to this statement concerns the losses suffered by the *Rekruit* Companies such as those from IR 180 that were involved with the counterattacks against *Feste Schwaben*. I did not come across any specific lists showing the losses suffered by these companies. I suspect that the losses were either added to the lists for IR 180 without identifying the men as being in a recruit company, or, the losses were listed without identifying the unit they belonged to at all. In the Württemberg *Verlustlisten* there were often short lists of names of losses where no particular unit was attached.

    I am confident that the men in these companies were shown on the *Verlustlisten* as I have come across the names of the officers who were reported killed or wounded. For example, *Leutnant* Schnürlen, 1st Rekruit Coy, IR 180 who was killed on 1 July 1916 was shown on the Württemberg *Verlustlisten* of 2 October 1916 under the names for the 1st Coy, IR 180.

2. The *Verlustlisten* up until the end of 1916 were printed in a format that provided the individual unit designations, each listing the men who belonged to these units. At the end of 1916 the

format was changed to show all names in alphabetical order with no unit designations. To continue to search for each man would then require a search of each individual name from list to list until everyone was accounted for.

Bibliography

Unpublished sources

Feldpost Letters (1915-1916), *Kriegsfreiwilliger* Karl Losch, 3rd Company, RIR 119
Feldpost Letters (1914-1915), *Unteroffizier der Reserve* Fritz Rohr, 2nd Company, RIR 111
Feldpost Letters (1915-1916), *Gefreiter der Reserve* Rudolf Siegele, 4th Battery, RFAR 29
Feldpost letters (1916) *Leutnant der Reserve* Richard Seeger, 8/R121
Feldpost letters (1916) *Reservist* Gottlob Mauss, 3/R119
Feldpost letter (1916) *Krankenträger* Wilhelm Schaibb, 3/R119
Diary of Ernest Shephard, 1st Dorset Regiment

Regimental Stammrolle books: *Kriegsstammrollen, 1914-1918.* Bavarian State Archives. Department IV, War Archive, Munich.

Bavarian RIR 6
Bavarian RIR 8
Bavarian FAR 19
Bavarian FAR 20
Bavarian *Fuss Artillerie* Regiment Nr. 10
Bavarian *Pionier* Regiment
Bavarian Pionier Coy 20
Bavarian *Chevauleger* Regiment Nr. 5
Bavarian *Mineur* Coy 5
Bavarian *Sanitäts* Coy 10

Newspapers

Birmingham Daily Post
Freiburger Zeitung

Printed sources (books and articles)

Anon, *An der Somme, Erinnerungen der 12. Infanterie Division an die Stellungskämpfe und Schlacht an der Somme Oktober 1915 bis November 1916,* Berlin, 1918.
Anon, *Deutsche Verlustlisten,* (1916-1917), Berlin, 1914-1919
Anon, *Die 26. Reserve Division 1914-1918,* Stuttgart, 1920
Anon, *Illustrierte Geschichte des Weltkrieges 1914/16,* Band 7, Stuttgart, n.d.
Anon, *Kriegstagbuch aus Schwaben,* Stuttgart, 1914-1919
Anon, *The Principles in Trench Warfare as laid down in the XIV Reserve Corps,* Ia/13590, 19th May 1916. Document SS 490
Anon, *Vom westlichsten Teil der Westfront,* Frankfurt a.M., 1917
Atkinson, C.T., *The History of the South Wales Borderers 1914-1918,* London, 1931
Bachelin, Major Eduard, *Das Reserve-Infanterie-Regiment Nr. 111 im Weltkrieg 1914 bis 1918,* Karlsruhe, 1938
Baumgartner, Richard (Ed.), 'An der Somme, An interview with Soldat Emil Geobelbecker',

Der Angriff, A Journal of World War I History, 1979, No. 3

Baumgartner, Richard (Ed.), 'The Somme 1 July 1916', *Der Angriff, A Journal of World War I History,* 1981, No. 13

Baumgartner, Richard (ed.), *This Carnival of Hell,* Huntington, W. Va., 2010

Bayerisches Kriegsarchiv, *Die Bayern im Grossen Krieg 1914-1918,* München, 1923

Bezzel, Oberst a.D. Dr. Oskar, *Das Königlich Bayerische Reserve-Infanterie-Regiment Nr. 6,* München, 1938

Brown, Malcolm, *The Imperial War Museum Book of the Somme,* London, 1996

Cooksey, Jon, *Barnsley Pals,* London, 1996

Delmensingen, General der Artillerie Konrad Kraft von & Feeser, Generalmajor a.D. Friedrichfranz, *Das Bayernbuch vom Weltkriege 1914-1918,* Stuttgart, 1930

Edmonds, Brigadier-General Sir James E., *History of the Great War. Military Operations France and Belgium 1916. Sir Douglas Haig's Command to the 1st July: Battle of the Somme,* London, 1932

Ehrler, Hans Heinrich, *Ehrenbuch der Gefallenen Stuttgarts 1914-1918,* Stuttgart, 1925

Fabeck, Hans von, *Im Orkan der Sommeschlacht. Ein Abschnitt aus der Kriegsgeschichte des Reserve-Infanterie-Regiment Nr. 99,* Berlin, 1930

Falls, Cyril, *History of the Ulster Division,* Belfast, 1991 reprint

Fiedel, Paul, *Geschichte des Infanterie Regiments von Winterfeldt (2, Oberschlesisches) Nr.23, Das Regiment im Weltkriege,* Berlin, 1929

Forstner, Major a.D. Kurt Freiherr von, *Das Königlich-Preussische Reserve-Infanterie-Regiment Nr. 15,* Oldenburg, 1929

Frick, Leutnant der Landwehr Albert, *Erlebnisse in den Ersten Tagen der Somme-Schlacht (24 Juni bis 7 Juli 1916),* 1916

Frisch, Georg, *Das Reserve-Infanterie-Regiment Nr. 109 im Weltkrieg 1914 bis 1918,* Karlsruhe, 1931

General Staff, *Handbook of the German Army in War, January 1917,* Wakefield, 1973

Gerster, Matthäus, *Das Württembergische Reserve-Infanterie-Regiment Nr. 119 im Weltkrieg 1914-1918,* Stuttgart, 1920

Gerster, Matthäus, *Die Schwaben an der Ancre,* Heilbronn a.N., 1918

Gerster, Matthäus, *Treffen der 26.R.D. am 5 Juli 1936,* Stuttgart, 1936

[Greiner & Vulpius], *Reserve-Infanterie-Regiment Nr. 110 im Weltkrieg 1914-1918,* Karlsruhe, 1934

Holtz, Hauptmann Freiherr Georg vom, *Das Württembergische Reserve-Infanterie-Regiment Nr. 121 im Weltkrieg 1914-1918,* Stuttgart, 1921

Horsfall, Jack & Cave, Nigel, *Serre, Somme,* London, 1996

Ihlenfeld, Oberst a.D. v. & Engle, Major a.D., *Das 9. Badische Infanterie-Regiment Nr.170 im Weltkrieg,* Oldenburg, 1926

Jäger, Herbert, *German Artillery of World War One,* Marlborough, 2001

Kaiser, Generalmajor a.D. Franz, *Das Königlich Preussen Infanterie-Regiment Nr. 63 (4.Oberschlesisches),* Berlin, 1940

Kameradschaftsbund, *Ehrentafel Res. Inf. Regt. 119,* n.d.

Klaus, Major a.D. Justizrat Max, *Das Württembergisches Reserve-Feldartillerie-Regiment Nr. 26 im Weltkrieg 1914-1918,* Stuttgart, 1929

Klett, Fritz, *Das Württembergische Reserve-Dragoner-Regiment im Weltkrieg 1914-1918,* Stuttgart, 1935

Knies, Oberstleutnant L., *Das Württembergishe Pionier Bataillon Nr. 13 im Weltkrieg 1914-1918*, Stuttgart, 1937

Kölbig, Kurt Siegfried, Kuhn, Hans-Karl, *Gedanken an der Westfront 1914-1917. Das Tagesbuch des Leutnants der Reserve Karl August Zwiffelhoffer*, Nyon, 2007

Korfes, Hauptmann a.D. Dr. Otto, *Das 3.Magdeburgische Infanterie-Regiment Nr. 66 im Weltkriege*, Berlin, 1930

Korps Buchhandlung, *Der Schützengraben, Feldzeitung des XIV Reservekorps (1915-1917)*, Bapaume, 1915-1917

Korpsverlagsbuchhandlung, *An der Somme*, Bapaume, 1917

Korpsverlagsbuchhandlung, *Zwischen Arras und Péronne*, Bapaume, 1916

Kühl, Hermann von, *Der Weltkrieg 1914-1918*, Berlin 1933

Kümmel, Leutnant d.Res. a.D. Studienrat Dr. Phil., *Reserve-Infanterie-Regiment Nr. 91 im Weltkriege 1914-1918*, Oldenburg, 1926

Lais, Otto, *Die Schlacht an der Somme*, Karlsruhe, 1940

Lehmann, Generalleutnant a.D. August, *Das K.B. Pionier-Regiment*, München, 1927

Lutz, Hauptmann Ernst Freiherr von, *Das Königlich bayerische 16.Infanterie-Regiment im Kriege 1914-1918*, Passau, 1920

Maddocks, Graham, *Montauban, Somme*, Barnsley, 1999

Merkatz, Friedrich von, *Unterrichtsbuch für die Maschinengewehr-Kompagnien Gerät 08*, Berlin 1918

Middlebrook, Martin, *The First Day on the Somme*, New York, 1972

Moos, Leutnant d. R. a.D. Ernst, *Das Württembergische Res.-Feld-Artillerie Regiment Nr.27 im Weltkrieg 1916-1918*, Stuttgart, 1925

Moser, Generalleutnant Otto von, *Die Württemberger im Weltkriege*, Stuttgart, 1938

Mücke, Kgl. Preuss. Rittmeister a.D. Kurt von, *Das Grossherzoglich Badische Infanterie-Regiment Nr. 185*, Oldenburg, 1922

Müller, Major d.R. Paul, Fabeck, Oberst a.D. Hans von & Riesel, Oberstleutnant a.D. Richard, *Geschichte des Reserve-Infanterie-Regiment Nr. 99*, Zeulenroda, 1936

Müller-Loebnitz, Oberstleutnant Wilhelm, *Die Badener im Weltkrieg*, Karlsruhe, 1935.

Neubronn, Leutnant Dr. Carl & Pfeffer, Leutnant d. R. Dr. Georg, *Geschichte des Infanterie-Regiments 186*, Oldenburg, 1926

Offiziersverein des I.R. 180, *Totenbuch des 10.Württembergischen Infanterie-Regiment Nr. 180. Namentliches Verzeichnis der im Weltkrieg 1914-1918 gefallenen Offiziere, Unteroffiziere und Mannschaften*, Stuttgart, 1936

Orr, Philip, *The Road to the Somme, Men of the Ulster Division tell their story*, Belfast, 1992

Reichskriegsministerium, *Der Weltkrieg 1914 bis 1918. Die Militärischen Operationen zu Lande, Zehnter Band*, Berlin, 1936

Reymann, Oberleutnant a.D. H., *3.Oberschlesische Infanterie-Regiment Nr. 62 im Kriege 1914-1918*, Zeulenroda, 1930

Riedel, Frieder, *Zwischen Kriegsgericht und Heldentod, Der Grabenkrieg an der Somme 1914-1916*, Echterdingen, 2008

Anon, 'Report on the Defence of Gommecourt on July 1st, 1916' (*Royal United Services Institution Journal*, August 1917)

Sheldon, Jack, *The Germans at Beaumont Hamel*, Barnsley, 2006

Sheldon, Jack, *The Germans Army on the Somme 1914-1916*, Barnsley, 2005.

Sheldon, Jack, *The Germans at Thiepval*, Barnsley, 2006

Shephard, Ernest, *A Sergeant-Major's War. From Hill 60 to the Somme*, Trowbridge, 1988

Silbereisen, Leutnant der Reserve, Ehrler, Landsturmmann Hans Heinrich, Eisenmann, Landsturmmann Alexander & Schulze-Etzel, Gefreiten Theodor, *Schwäbische Kunde aus den grossen Krieg,* Stuttgart, 1918

Soden, General der Infanterie a.D. Freiherr von, *Die 26.(Württembergische) Reserve-Division im Weltkrieg 1914-1918,* Stuttgart, 1939

Stedman, Michael, *Salford Pals,* London, 1993

Stein, General von, *A War Minister and his work,* London, n.d.

Stosch, Oberstleutnant a.D. Albrecht von, *Somme-Nord I.Teil: Die Brennpunkte der Schlacht im Juli 1916,* Oldenburg, 1927

Taylor, James W., *The 1st Royal Irish Rifles in the Great War,* Dublin, 2002

Turner, William, *Accrington Pals,* London, 1992

Vischer, Oberstleutnant Alfred, *Das 10. Württembergische Infanterie-Regiment Nr. 180 in der Somme-Schlacht 1916,* Stuttgart, 1917

Vischer, Oberstleutnant Alfred, *Das 10. Württembergische Infanterie-Regiment Nr. 180 im Weltkrieg 1914-1918,* Stuttgart, 1921

Volksbund Deutsche Kriegsgräberfürsorge e.V., *Deutsche Kriegsgräber, Am Rande der Strasse, Frankreich, Belgien, Luxemburg und Niederlande,* Kassel, n.d.

Wissmann, Oberst von, *Das Reserve-Infanterie-Regiment Nr. 55 im Weltkrieg,* Berlin, n.d.

Wohlenberg, Oberleutnant d.R. a.D. Rektor Alfred, *Das Reserve-Infanterie-Regiment Nr. 77 im Weltkriege 1914-18,* Hildesheim, 1931

Wurmb, Herbert Ritter von, *Das K. B. Reserve-Infanterie-Regiment Nr. 8,* München, 1929

Related titles published by Helion & Company

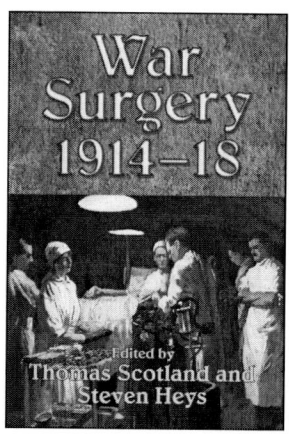

Playing the Game. The British Junior Infantry Officer on the Western Front 1914-18
Christopher Moore-Bick
328 pages Hardback
ISBN 978-1-906033-84-2

War Surgery, 1914-18
Edited by Thomas Scotland & Steven Heys
288 pages Hardback
ISBN 978-1-907677-70-0

A selection of forthcoming titles

A Considerable Achievement. The Tactical Development of the 56th (London) Division on the Western Front 1916-18
Matthew Brosnan   ISBN 978-1-908916-47-1

Muddling Through. The Organisation of British Army Chaplaincy in World War One
Peter Howson   ISBN 978-1-909384-20-0

Three Wings for the Red Baron. Von Richthofen, Strategy, Tactics and Airplanes
Leon Bennett   ISBN 978-1-907677-13-7

HELION & COMPANY
26 Willow Road, Solihull, West Midlands B91 1UE, England
Telephone 0121 705 3393   Fax 0121 711 4075
Website: http://www.helion.co.uk